EAGLES AND EMPIRE

ALSO BY DAVID A. CLARY

EAGLES AND EMPIRE

THE UNITED STATES, MEXICO, AND
THE STRUGGLE FOR A CONTINENT

DAVID A. CLARY

BANTAM BOOKS

Published in the United States by Bantam Books, an imprint of
The Random House Publishing Group, a division of Random House, Inc., New York.

Bantam Books and the rooster colophon are registered trademarks of Random House, Inc.

Library of Congress Cataloging-in-Publication Data
Clary, David A.
Eagles and empire : the United States, Mexico, and the struggle for a continent / David A. Clary.
p. cm.
Includes bibliographical references and index.
ISBN 978-0-553-80652-6 (hardcover) — ISBN 978-0-553-90676-9 (ebook)
1. Mexican War, 1846–1848. I. Title.
E404.C55 2009
973.6'2—dc22
2008055701

Printed in the United States of America on acid-free paper

www.bantamdell.com

9 8 7 6 5 4 3 2 1

First Edition

Text design by Catherine Leonardo
Maps by David Lindroth

To the memory of Thomas D. Clark (1903–2005),
who told me I should become a historian.

Things fall apart; the centre cannot hold;
Mere anarchy is loosed upon the world,
The blood-dimmed tide is loosed, and everywhere
The ceremony of innocence is drowned;
The best lack all conviction, while the worst
Are full of passionate intensity.

—WILLIAM BUTLER YEATS

CONTENTS

CONTENTS xiii

CONTENTS

NOTE ABOUT PLACE NAMES

Places are spelled as they were in the 1840s. Most notably, Vera Cruz has become Veracruz, and Monterey, Nuevo León, Monterrey in the years since; Monterey, California, has always been so spelled. San Juan de Ullúa has had many spellings, but this was the most common at the time. Places whose names have changed entirely in the years since are noted in the text.

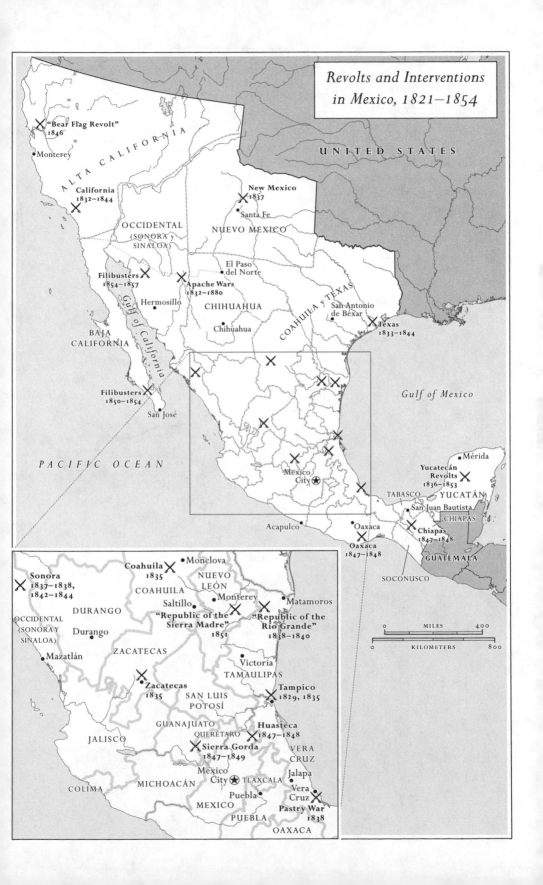

Revolts and Interventions
in Mexico, 1821–1854

UNITED STATES

"Bear Flag Revolt"
1846
Monterey

ALTA CALIFORNIA

California
1832–1844

New Mexico
1837
Santa Fe

OCCIDENTAL
(SONORA y
SINALOA)

NUEVO MEXICO

El Paso
del Norte

Filibusters
1854–1857

Apache Wars
1832–1880

Hermosillo

CHIHUAHUA

COAHUILA y TEXAS

San Antonio
de Béxar

Texas
1833–1844

Chihuahua

BAJA
CALIFORNIA

Filibusters
1850–1854

San José

Gulf of Mexico

PACIFIC OCEAN

Mexico
City

Yucatecán
Revolts
1836–1853

Mérida

TABASCO

YUCATÁN

San Juan Bautista

CHIAPAS

Acapulco

Oaxaca

Chiapas
1847–1848

Oaxaca
1847–1848

SOCONUSCO

GUATEMALA

MILES   400

KILOMETERS   800

Sonora
1837–1838,
1842–1844

Coahuila
1835

Monclova

NUEVO
LEÓN

OCCIDENTAL
(SONORA Y
SINALOA)

COAHUILA

Saltillo

Monterey

Matamoros

DURANGO

"Republic of the
Sierra Madre"
1851

"Republic of the
Rio Grande"
1838–1840

Durango

ZACATECAS

Mazatlán

Victoria

TAMAULIPAS

Zacatecas
1835

SAN LUIS
POTOSÍ

Tampico
1829, 1835

GUANAJUATO

Huasteca
1847–1848

JALISCO

QUERÉTARO

Sierra Gorda
1847–1849

VERA
CRUZ

Mexico
City

TLAXCALA

Jalapa

COLIMA

MICHOACÁN

Puebla

Vera
Cruz

MEXICO

Pastry War
1838

PUEBLA

OAXACA

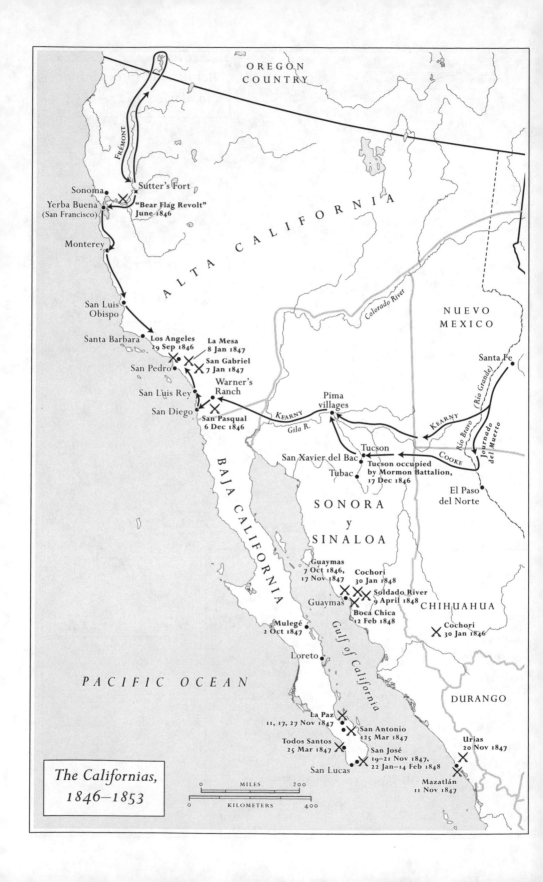

OREGON
COUNTRY

FRÉMONT

Sutter's Fort

Sonoma

Yerba Buena
(San Francisco)

"Bear Flag Revolt"
June 1846

Monterey

ALTA CALIFORNIA

Colorado River

NUEVO
MEXICO

San Luis
Obispo

Santa Barbara

Los Angeles
29 Sep 1846

La Mesa
8 Jan 1847

Santa Fe

San Pedro

San Gabriel
7 Jan 1847

Warner's
Ranch

San Luis Rey

Pima
villages

KEARNY

KEARNY

San Diego

San Pasqual
6 Dec 1846

Gila R.

Rio Bravo

Tucson

BAJA CALIFORNIA

San Xavier del Bac

Tubac

Tucson occupied
by Mormon Battalion,
17 Dec 1846

COOKE

Journado
del Muerto

(Rio Grande)

El Paso
del Norte

SONORA
y
SINALOA

Guaymas
7 Oct 1846,
17 Nov 1847

Cochori
30 Jan 1848

Soldado River
9 April 1848

CHIHUAHUA

Guaymas

Boca Chica
12 Feb 1848

Mulegé
2 Oct 1847

Cochori
30 Jan 1846

Loreto

PACIFIC OCEAN

Gulf of California

DURANGO

La Paz
11, 17, 27 Nov 1847

San Antonio
125 Mar 1847

Urias
20 Nov 1847

Todos Santos
25 Mar 1847

San José
19–21 Nov 1847,
22 Jan–14 Feb 1848

San Lucas

Mazatlán
11 Nov 1847

The Californias,
1846–1853

MILES   200
0

0   KILOMETERS   400

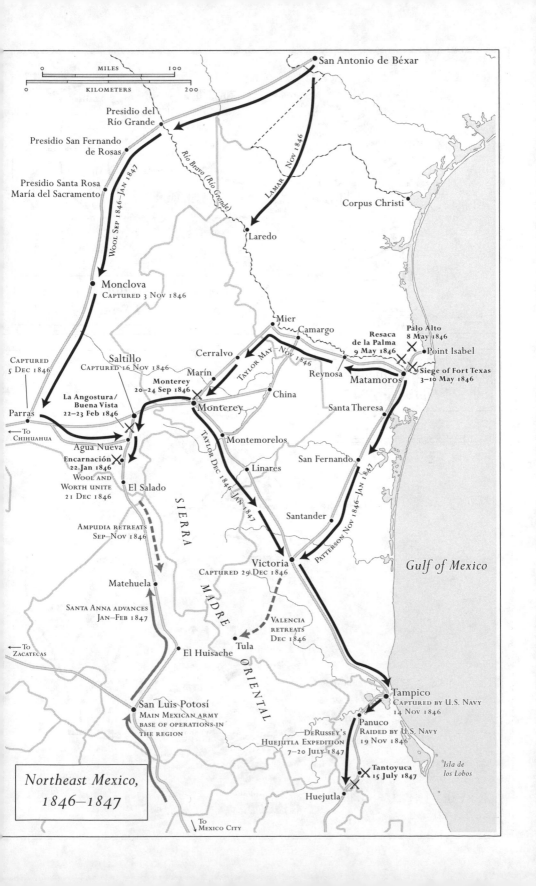

Northeast Mexico,
1846–1847

San Antonio de Béxar

LAMAR NOV 1846

Presidio del
Río Grande

Presidio San Fernando
de Rosas

Río Bravo (Río Grande)

Corpus Christi

Presidio Santa Rosa
María del Sacramento

Laredo

WOOL SEP 1846 – JAN 1847

Monclova
CAPTURED 3 NOV 1846

Mier   Camargo

Palo Alto
8 May 1846

Resaca
de la Palma
9 May 1846

Point Isabel

CAPTURED
5 DEC 1846

Saltillo
CAPTURED 16 NOV 1846

Cerralvo

Marín

TAYLOR MAY – NOV 1846

Reynosa

Siege of Fort Texas
3–10 May 1846

Monterey
20–24 Sep 1846

Matamoros

Parras

La Angostura/
Buena Vista
22–23 Feb 1846

Monterey

China

Santa Theresa

→ To
CHIHUAHUA

Agua Nueva

Encarnación
22 JAN 1846

WOOL AND
WORTH UNITE
21 DEC 1846

El Salado

TAYLOR DEC 1846 – JAN 1847

Montemorelos

Linares

San Fernando

PATTERSON NOV 1846 – JAN 1847

SIERRA

Ampudia retreats
SEP–NOV 1846

Santander

Gulf of Mexico

Matehuela

MADRE

Victoria
CAPTURED 29 DEC 1846

Santa Anna advances
JAN–FEB 1847

VALENCIA
RETREATS
DEC 1846

→ To
ZACATECAS

El Huisache

Tula

ORIENTAL

San Luis Potosí
MAIN MEXICAN ARMY
BASE OF OPERATIONS IN
THE REGION

Tampico
CAPTURED BY U.S. NAVY
14 NOV 1846

Panuco
RAIDED BY U.S. NAVY
19 NOV 1846

DeRussey's
HUEJUTLA EXPEDITION
7–20 JULY 1847

Isla de
los Lobos

Tantoyuca
15 July 1847

Huejutla

↓ To
MEXICO CITY

MILES   100

KILOMETERS   200

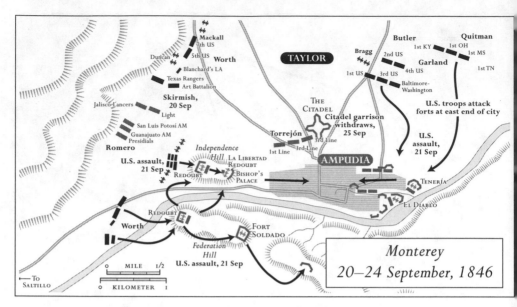

Mackall
7th US
Duncan
5th US   Worth
Blanchard's LA
Texas Rangers
Art Battalion
Skirmish,
20 Sep
Jalisco Lancers
Light
San Luis Potosí AM
Guanajuato AM
Presidials
Romero   Independence
Hill   La Libertad
U.S. assault,   REDOUBT
21 Sep
REDOUBT   Bishop's
PALACE

Worth   REDOUBT

FORT
SOLDADO
Federation
Hill
U.S. assault, 21 Sep

← To
SALTILLO

0   MILE   1/2

0   KILOMETER   1

TAYLOR

THE
CITADEL
Citadel garrison
withdraws, 25 Sep
Torrejón
3rd Line
1st Line   3rd Line

AMPUDIA

Bragg   Butler   Quitman
2nd US   1st KY   1st OH
1st MS
1st US   3rd US   Garland
4th US
1st TN
Baltimore-
Washington
U.S. troops attack
forts at east end of city

U.S.
assault,
21 Sep

TENERÍA

EL DIABLO

Monterey
20–24 September, 1846

La Angostura / Buena Vista
23 February 1847

0   MILE   1/2

0   KILOMETER   1

TAYLOR

To
SALTILLO   Hacienda
Buena Vista

U.S.
camps

Bragg   1st MS
3rd IN

Washington
1st IL

2nd KY
2nd IL   U.S. left
Sherman   gives way
Bragg
2nd IN
Blanco   Main
Mexican   O'Brien
attack   1st KY   1st AR
Ortega   Pacheco

Torrejón
Lombardini   Juvera

SANTA ANNA   Ampudia

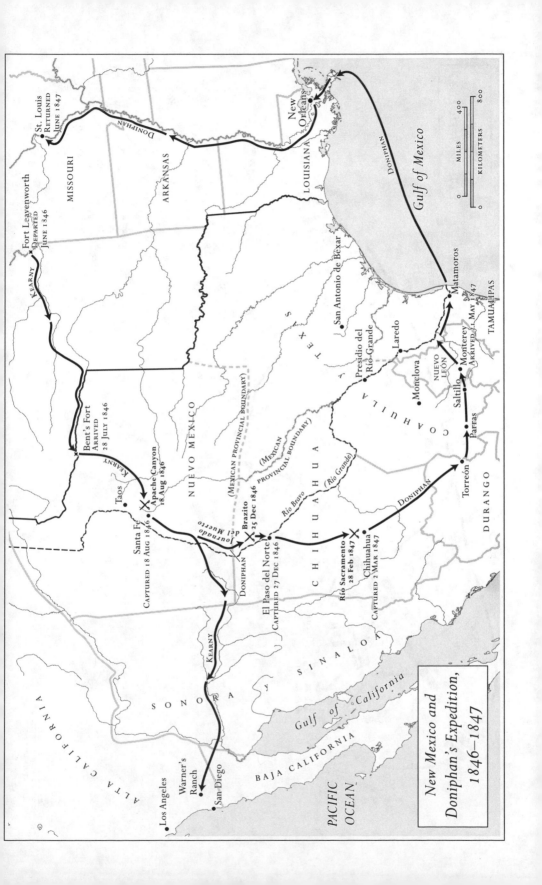

New Mexico and Doniphan's Expedition, 1846–1847

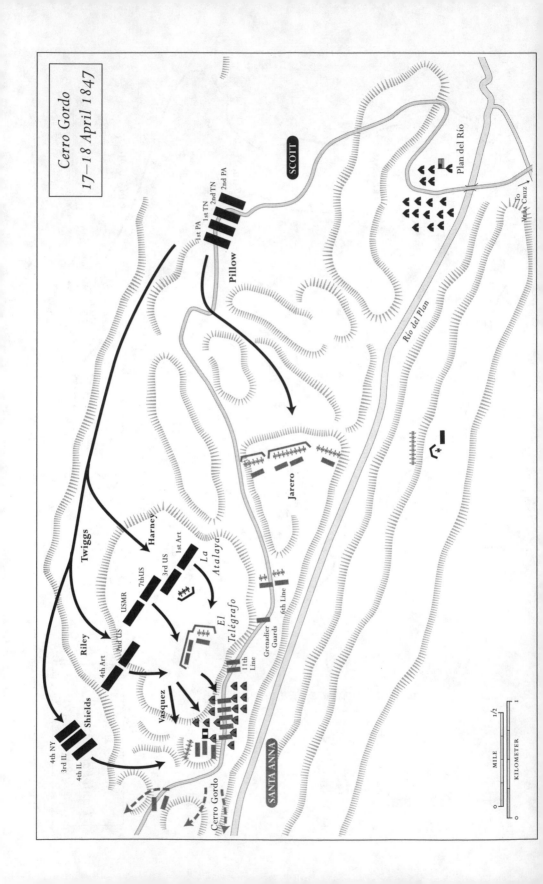

Cerro Gordo
17–18 April 1847

SCOTT

Plan del Río

To Vera Cruz

Río del Plan

Pillow

1st PA
1st TN
2nd TN
2nd PA

Jarero

Harney

Twiggs

1st Art
3rd US
7thUS
USMR
2nd US
4th Art
Riley

La Atalaya

El Telégrafo

6th Line

Grenadier Guards

11th Line

Vásquez

Shields
4th NY
3rd IL
4th IL

SANTA ANNA

Cerro Gordo

0   1/2   MILE
0   1   KILOMETER

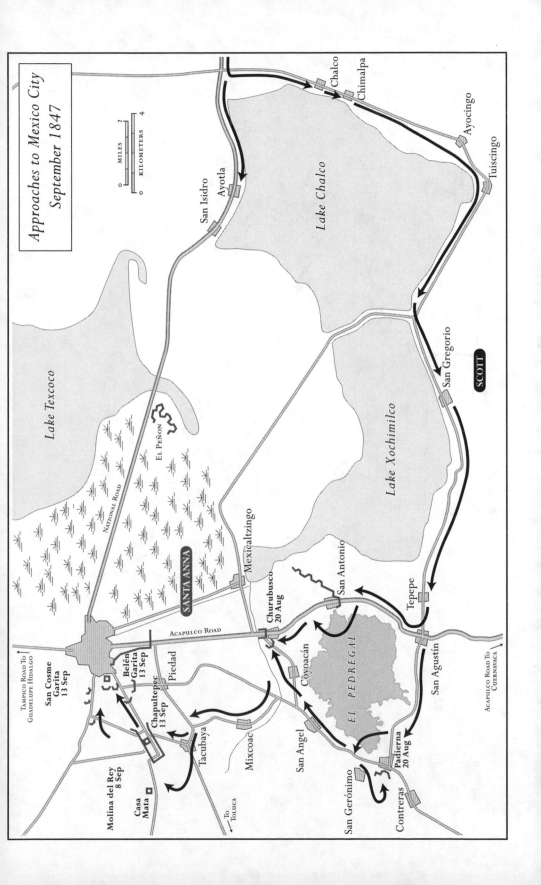

Approaches to Mexico City
September 1847

MILES 0 2
KILOMETERS 0 4

Lake Texcoco

Lake Chalco

Lake Xochimilco

Chalco
Chimalpa
Ayocingo
Tuiscingo
San Isidro
Ayotla
San Gregorio
SCOTT
Tepepe
San Antonio
Mexicaltzingo
EL PEÑON
NATIONAL ROAD
SANTA ANNA
Churubusco
20 Aug
Coyoacán
San Agustín
ACAPULCO ROAD TO CUERNAVACA
EL PEDREGAL
Padierna
20 Aug
Contreras
San Gerónimo
San Angel
Mixcoac
ACAPULCO ROAD
Piedad
Belén Garita
13 Sep
Chapultepec
13 Sep
Tacubaya
To TOLUCA
Molina del Rey
8 Sep
Casa Mata
San Cosme Garita
13 Sep
TAMPICO ROAD TO GUADELUPE HIDALGO

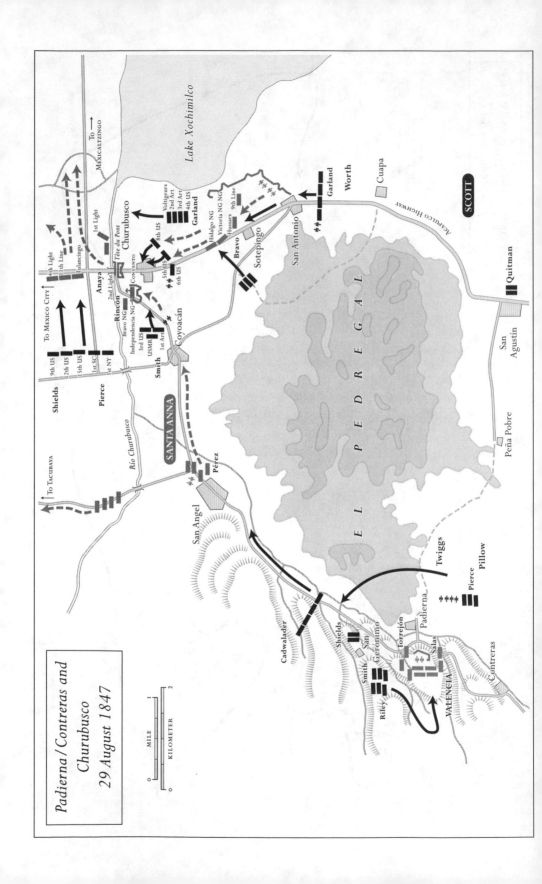

Padierna/Contreras and Churubusco
29 August 1847

MILE
0   1

KILOMETER
0   1   2

Lake Xochimilco

To Mexicaltzingo

To Mexico City

To Tacubaya

Río Churubusco

SANTA ANNA

SCOTT

E L   P E D R E G A L

Worth
Garland
Cuapa

Acapulco Highway

San Antonio

Sotepingo

Bravo

9th Line
Hussars
Victoria NG NG
Hidalgo NG

Garland
4th US
3rd Art
2nd Art
Voltigeurs

8th US
5th US
6th US

Churubusco
Tête du Pont
CONVENTO

1st Light
Tulancingo

4th Line
4th Light

Anaya
2nd Light

Rincón
Bravo NG
Independencia NG

Coyoacán
USMR
3rd US
1st Art

Smith

Shields
9th US
12th US
15th US
1st SC
1st NY

Pierce

San Angel

Pérez

Quitman

San Agustín

Peña Pobre

Twiggs

Pillow
Pierce

Cadwalader

Shields
San Geronimo

Smith
Riley

Torrejón

Padierna

Salas

VALENCIA

Contreras

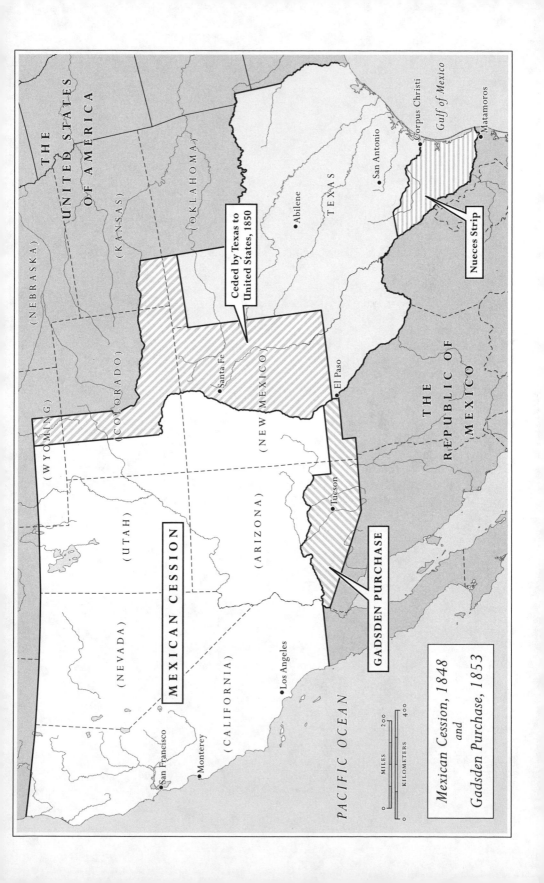

THE
UNITED STATES
OF AMERICA

(NEBRASKA)

(KANSAS)

(OKLAHOMA)

(WYOMING)

(COLORADO)

Ceded by Texas to
United States, 1850

Santa Fe

(NEW MEXICO)

El Paso

TEXAS

Abilene

San Antonio

Corpus Christi

Gulf of Mexico

Matamoros

Nueces Strip

THE
REPUBLIC OF
MEXICO

(UTAH)

(NEVADA)

(ARIZONA)

Tucson

MEXICAN CESSION

GADSDEN PURCHASE

(CALIFORNIA)

Los Angeles

Monterey

San Francisco

PACIFIC OCEAN

MILES
0   200   400
KILOMETERS
0

Mexican Cession, 1848
and
Gadsden Purchase, 1853

EAGLES AND EMPIRE

WAR EAGLE

So in the ancient fable it is told
That once an eagle, stricken with a dart,
Said, when he saw the fashion of the shaft,
"With our own feathers, not by others' hands,
Are we now smitten."

—Aeschylus

THE LAST OF THE MÉXIC INVADERS ENTERED the Great Valley in the thirteenth century, far from their homeland, Aztatlán (Place of Cranes, also rendered Aztlán). They had been told to march south by their chief god, Huitzilipochtli (Hummingbird Wizard). They were a dirty, savage, bloodthirsty people with a bad habit of stealing women and a disgusting one of sacrificing humans wholesale. They introduced into the valley a new weapon—the bow and arrow. As allies on the battlefield, the México were invaluable; as neighbors, they were frightening, dangerous. These México called themselves Tenochca (People of the Sun).[1]

The México were falconers, so their "war eagles" flew over them. Huitzilipochtli had taken on the additional identity of War Eagle, the dominant spirit that had arisen over all other gods in the valley. The old gods remained, but War Eagle ruled the minds of men. War Eagle told the México to look for a lake. In its center would stand an island, and on that island a rock, on which grew a *tenochtl* (sun plant, also today called *nopal* or prickly pear). Atop the cactus they would see a golden eagle, their falcon, marking the spot where they would found an empire.[2]

The México called the island México Tenochtitlán (Place of the México-Tenochca), and proceeded to extend their control over the valley. By the fifteenth century they held sway over an empire extending to the seas both east and west.

Early in the sixteenth century the México faced a new tribe of barbarians, strangers who came over the sea, men with light skin, hairy faces, and peculiar clothing. They did as the México had when they arrived from the north—they wielded new weapons, these spitting balls and fire, with which they invaded the Great Valley. These newcomers also imported terrible diseases, which slaughtered people by the millions. Within a few years, the Mexican empire was no more. What remained were villages of farmers tending their lands in common. *Indios,* the newcomers called them.

The conquerors called themselves Spaniards. The old Mexican empire became Nueva España (New Spain), and the chief memory of the recent past was in a new name for the Great Valley, el Valle de México (Valley of Mexico). In the center of it stood Ciudad México (Mexico City), rising from the ruins of México Tenochtitlán.

The Spaniards expanded their reach south into the jungles and north into the lands of desert wild men, *Indios bárbaros* (barbaric Indians) to the Spaniards. The king of Spain had introduced a new kind of empire, one that tried to dominate the landscape rather than just civilized nations. He did this in competition with kings of France and Britain. The three great kings sent soldiers, priests, and settlers to see how much of America they could claim, asserting power over *Indios bárbaros* who recognized no such authority.

So it went, until the British and French fought their Great War for Empire. The French king lost, and in 1763 his American territories were divided between Britain in the far north and Spain in the west, the latter a land called Louisiana. Then the British Americans rebelled against their king. The idea that people could govern themselves without royal supervision sent a shock wave through Europe and America.

Next France took back Louisiana and sold it to the Anglo-Americans, then invaded Spain. The French king of Spain decided to extend his power to America. The ruling classes of New Spain did not like that idea, so they took up arms. Out of their rebellion was born a new country, *México,* which had a totem, a flag bearing a cactus surmounted by an eagle, which now held a snake in its beak. War Eagle had returned.

Meanwhile, the Anglo-Americans crowded against the borders of Mexico. Their totem also was an eagle—the American bald eagle. Truly, it seemed, they worshiped this bird god. They displayed it everywhere—even on the buttons and belt buckles and cap devices of their soldiers, who carried flags on staffs tipped with eagles.[3]

This time there was not just one War Eagle in the air but two, and they were about to wage their own struggle for empire.

PART ONE

LA GUERRA DE TEJAS

(The Texas War)

(1783—1847)

THIS YOUNG MAN WILL LIVE
TO MAKE HIS COUNTRY WEEP
(1783–1823)

The history of México since 1822 might accurately be
called the history of Santa Anna's revolutions. . . . His name
plays the major role in all the political events of the country,
and its destiny has become intertwined with his.

—Lucas Alamán

LIEUTENANT GENERAL DON JUAN DE O'DONOJÚ landed in Vera
Cruz on July 30, 1821. His job was to implement the Spanish Constitution
of 1812, but he turned out to be the last Spanish viceroy of New Spain.
The city was under siege by a small army of insurgents, led by a former
royalist officer—New Spain had risen up against Old Spain, because the
Criollos (Creoles, native-born descendants of Spaniards) objected to that
liberal constitution. Government might be nominally imposed by the king
back in the Iberian Peninsula—implemented by native-Spanish officers
known as *Peninsulares,* in America more commonly called *Gachupines* (an
insult suggesting foppishness)—but their numbers were small. The real
power was in the hands of greater numbers of *criollo* soldiers, priests, and

landowners. The liberal constitution would deprive them of their privileges, so they rebelled.

The young officer besieging Vera Cruz was famous for unprincipled opportunism. Not long ago he had been a captain in the royal colonial army; a small victory over the rebels earned him the rank of lieutenant colonel, but then he offered to change sides if it gained him another promotion. It did, and he became a colonel among the insurgents. When the whole fray was over he was a brigadier general and right-hand man to the new ruler of independent New Spain, Agustín de Iturbide. The besieging officer arranged a meeting between O'Donojú and Iturbide, and on August 24, 1821, the two signed the Treaty of Córdoba, granting independence to New Spain. The officer next marched against the remaining royalist garrisons inland, obtained their surrenders, and returned to Vera Cruz to finish the insurgent business there. Royalist holdouts, sheltered in the island fortress San Juan de Ullúa in the city's harbor, gave up late in October.

O'Donojú got to know this officer well. He was a handsome fellow, born to wear his uniform, blue and red with plenty of gold trim, lace, and sweeping epaulets. Its high Napoleonic collar seemed to raise his head, making it appear somewhat large for his slender body, and making him seem taller than his already impressive five feet ten inches. He had a high forehead beneath a tousled shock of black hair. Below the brow were a Roman nose, a prim mouth, and a squarish chin. His eyes were deep-set and dark, not overly large, but striking because of the way they were always in motion, side to side, over one shoulder, then the next. They were the eyes of a guest looking for something to steal from his host.

He had a rich voice and a commanding manner for one so young, but he was friendly, polite, and deferential when he should be, and he loved a joke. He was thoroughly likable—and completely untrustworthy. It was apparent to anyone who met him that he had many cards hidden up both sleeves—he was, in fact, also an inveterate gambler. After their last meeting, O'Donojú said of the other: "This young man will live to make his country weep." The young man was Antonio López de Santa Anna.[1]

YOU WILL BE HELD RESPONSIBLE FOR CONSEQUENCES

Santa Anna's country, New Spain, claimed between a third and a half of North America late in the eighteenth century, from Panama in the south far to the northwest, where the British and the Russians claimed Oregon, British Columbia, and Alaska; almost due north to beyond the Great Salt Lake; and, east of the Rocky Mountains, up the Great Plains and along the Mississippi River to British Canada, not to mention the two Floridas along the Gulf Coast. Those far-flung boundaries were colonialist fantasies—over half of New Spain was in the possession of *Indios bárbaros*. If there was a Spanish colonial northern frontier, it started on the lower Río Bravo del Norte (Rio Grande) and tracked roughly westward to the Pacific Coast, with many wild, vacant spaces along the way. Scattered small outposts in Texas, in New Mexico, and in Alta California did not represent real possession. Spain might claim that vast realm, but its presence was too sparse to ward off anyone determined to enter and stake a counterclaim.[2]

The government of New Spain grew increasingly nervous about its hold on its northern territories. The greatest threat came from the United States of America. The Spanish crown had been an ally of the United States' ally France during the war of independence, but it never overcame its nervousness about having a rival on the Mississippi River. Spain dragged its feet on recognizing the new North American power, closing the great river to its commerce until 1795. Then came "the great betrayal." The first consul of revolutionary France, Napoleon Bonaparte, pressured Spain into returning Louisiana to his own country in 1800. Three years later he sold the territory to the United States. Spanish opinion was outraged. A buffer between New Spain and the Yankee republic had been jerked away, and the colonial governors felt threatened. They established new presidios—frontier military outposts—in Texas and New Mexico, but not with enough manpower to prevent an invasion. Dread of the United States festered.[3]

There were many people in the United States who objected to the purchase of Louisiana by President Thomas Jefferson. They worried that the sudden expansion of national territory would disperse the country's people and energies into an area too vast to hold. Jefferson sent a military expedition—a tiny one, but who knew?—to cross northern Louisiana to the Pacific Ocean. The president assured the Spanish ambassador that there was nothing hostile in what he called a scientific exploration. Authorities in Mexico City ordered the governor of New Mexico at Santa Fe to send out troops to capture the expedition and its leaders, Meriwether Lewis and William Clark, but several small parties missed their quarry. From then on Spain and Britain had a mutual interest in containing "expansionism" on the part of the United States.[4]

That expansionist tendency became even more alarming in 1806 when the United States Army commander in southern Louisiana, Brigadier General James Wilkinson, sent Major Zebulon Montgomery Pike out to explore that part of the territory. Wilkinson acted without authority, sending Pike to make peace with the nomadic Indians of the Great Plains, then proceed on to the headwaters of the Rio Grande ("Grand River," Wilkinson called it) in New Mexico—a deliberate invasion of Spanish territory. "Your conduct," Wilkinson wrote, neatly handing the bag to Pike, "must be marked by such circumspection and direction as may prevent alarm or conflict, as you will be held responsible for consequences."[5]

Word of Pike's plans leaked to Spanish agents before he marched out. When Pike held his first parley with Pawnee Indians on the plains he learned that a Spanish column had been prowling for him. In fact, the governor of New Mexico had ordered out several detachments. One of them found Pike and his men nearly starving in what is now southern Colorado in January 1807, and took them prisoner. They were freed and returned to the United States after a few months. Spanish troops made every effort to stop Yankee interlopers over the next few years. They bagged a variety of explorers, fur hunters, and merchants, confiscated their goods, and either sent them home or afforded them the hospitality of Spanish prisons.

Adding to official Spanish anxiety were claims by successive United States presidents that Louisiana included Texas. But what was Texas? It was a vaguely defined region somewhere north and east of the Río Nueces and west of the Sabine River on Louisiana's western border. The French had maintained that Texas was part of Louisiana, but the Spanish never acknowledged that. Yankee efforts to take over the territory ran up against Hispanic pride. Following on the "betrayal" of the Louisiana Purchase, the Anglo habit of infiltrating and squatting on Spanish-Mexican territory made conflict inevitable. There could not be two dominant powers on one continent, especially when their cultures and outlooks were so different. The *hispano* culture, moreover, appeared even to its own leaders to be stagnant or declining, while the United States was growing and dynamic. Honor and self-esteem were at work, so there was no chance that *hispano* leadership would surrender gracefully to "expansionism."[6]

The difficulties were partly of Spain's own doing. The acquisition of Louisiana in 1763 had prompted a need for settlers to colonize the northern provinces, but residents of New Spain were reluctant to pull up stakes and make new homes in the north. The Spanish government invited French Canadians and Irish Catholics, and even some Protestant Prussians, Dutch, and Anglo-American Tories, to settle in Louisiana in 1786; there were few takers. The government closed the borders of New Spain after 1803, but Anglo adventurers and traders were already crossing them freely. Spanish efforts to colonize Texas as a buffer against the invaders failed.

One United States president after another tried to get hold of Texas. The Anglos' reach exceeded their grasp—Jefferson was the first president to seek a western border for Texas on what North Americans today call the Rio Grande. Jefferson did not know what he was talking about, and neither did many other people at the time. The southern and western borders of Texas had never been fixed. If a line had to be drawn, history suggested it would fall along the Río Nueces (the next river north and east of the Rio Grande), because settlements along both sides of the Rio Grande answered to provincial governments farther south. The few along the Nueces were governed out of San Antonio de Béxar, the capital (when there was one) of Texas.

The North Americans, however, developed a fixation on the Rio Grande as the "natural" or even "legal" border of Texas. They did not know what to call it—Bravo, Grande, del Norte, and a few other labels bounced around. Spanish authorities had at least sorted that question out. The stream first showed up in their records as the Río de las Palmas (River of the Palms) in 1519, and over the next century it was also called the Río de Nuestra Señora (River of Our Lady, meaning the Mother of God), Guadalquivir (after another river in Spain), Turbio (Turbid), and several others referring to the lower river. Far upriver, the first explorers of New Mexico encountered the Río Bravo del Norte (Bold River of the North) in the 1540s, sometimes shortened to Río del Norte or expanded to Río del Norte y de Nuevo México. Río Grande (Great or Grand River) and Río Grande del Norte also appeared in the records, as did such localisms as Río de Tiguex (after a New Mexico Indian pueblo). It was clear in New Spain if not in the United States by the eighteenth century that the river that began in New Mexico was the same one that entered the Gulf of Mexico near Matamoros. In New Spain, people usually called it Bravo, sometimes Grande or del Norte. All the Anglo politicians knew was that if they got their hands on Texas, they wanted to float their boats on that stream, whatever it was called.[7]

The sparring between Spain and the United States could not go on forever. General Andrew Jackson invaded Spanish Florida without authority in 1817, to put down marauders raiding across the border. Spain had to face facts—it could not hang on to Florida. In 1819 the Spanish minister to the United States, Luis de Onís, approached Secretary of State John Quincy Adams, who had recently negotiated a treaty fixing his country's boundary with British Canada. Onís proposed a trade—the United States could have Florida if it gave up its claims to Texas. What the Spanish wanted was a defensible buffer against Anglo encroachment. The wily Spaniard countered Adams' demands for a Rio Grande boundary by dangling before him a wider western territory for the United States, perhaps all the way to the Pacific Ocean, in return for setting the border between the countries on the Sabine River. From there it would run west along the Red River, then north along the Rocky Mountains, then west to the

Pacific. Adams swallowed the bait, so enamored of a widened Louisiana that he agreed that his country would assume $5 million worth of U.S. claims against Spain. The Adams-Onís Treaty of 1819 was a deal.[8]

The two diplomats separated much pleased with themselves. Adams had gained his country a much larger Louisiana Territory than it had previously conceived. Onís and his government hoped that this wedge-shaped concession, widest at the north, would divert Anglo-American encroachment that way.

The Spanish government readdressed its failure to colonize Texas, where the sparse population was under fierce attack from Comanches. Moses Austin petitioned to allow him to bring 300 families to colonize Texas, and in 1821 the Spanish Cortes (parliament) in Madrid approved. Santa Fe was opened to trade with United States merchants from Missouri in the same year. Spanish North America had just handed her enemy the means of her own destruction.[9]

HE LEFT A TRAIL OF BLOOD IN HIS WAKE

The bishop of Valladolid described this endangered realm in the twilight of Spanish rule to King Carlos IV. "The population of New Spain is composed of three classes of men: to wit, whites or Spaniards; Indians, and castes," he explained. "All property and wealth are in Spanish hands. The Indians and the castes till the soil; they serve the upper class, and live only by the labor of their arms." Here is where he heard the bell tolling for his country: "This puts, between Spanish and Indians, contrary interests and mutual hate, which easily arises between those who have everything and those who have nothing—between masters and slaves."[10]

When Spanish *conquistadores* invaded the country early in the sixteenth century, they brought no Spanish women with them, so they produced children by native wives. Spanish women did land in America over the following decades, along with more Spanish men, from laborers and convicts to governors; slaves were imported for a few decades from Africa; and the intermingling grew more complex. The colonial government prepared an official classification of races reflecting the many ways boy could meet girl. There were two groups of whites of European stock, *Peninsulares* and *Criòllos.* The children of a white and an Indian were *Mestizos,* those of a white and an African were *Mulatos,* and the various crosses between pure and mixed heritages produced a staggering catalog. All that was aside from the pure descendants of the people who had been there to begin with. By the late colonial period, they were *Indios* (those who could speak some Spanish and were at least nominally Christianized), *Indígenas* (mostly farmers in isolated areas who spoke little or no Spanish, lived on communal lands, and were more dutiful to the Church's festivals than its beliefs), and *Indios bárbaros* (or in the north, *bravos*), the "wild" Indians of frontier areas. To make it more confusing, *Indígenas* sometimes included *Indios*, which sometimes included *Indígenas*.

Society was divided by the late eighteenth century into the two kinds of whites, *Mestizos*, *Indios* and *Indígenas*, and everybody else, lumped as *Castas* ("castes"). The social hierarchy was really one of skin tone—lighter *Mestizos* often stood among the *Criollos*, while darker crosses were *Castas*. Levels of wealth and education paralleled the skin-color hierarchy, and the resulting inequalities were a prescription for upheaval. In the last Spanish census of New Spain in 1810, *Indígenas* made up 60 percent of the population, *Mestizos* 22 percent, and whites 18 percent. The census was incomplete in areas where *Peninsulares, Criollos,* and *Mestizos* were comparatively scarce, and did not account for the majority of the "barbaric" Indians.[11]

The country had two groups (mostly white, with some lighter-skinned *Mestizos*) at the top—the army and the Church. Each enjoyed *fueros*, special privileges or rights. Officers or churchmen were subject to trial not in civil courts but in military or church courts, where conviction was unlikely. The *fuero* was, in other words, a license to steal—or to kill. This produced the political divisions that would characterize Mexico for decades to come, between liberals favoring democratic equality and conservatives who wanted no changes in the existing order.

Spain had missed out on the Enlightenment and the Industrial Revolution, and so had its colonies. The result was a corrupt government and society where the entrenched powers resisted any hint of reform or modernization. Pretensions to aristocracy at the upper end meant that those who could have developed an economy and a government sniffed at getting their hands dirty. Mexico came into being, then, as a nearly medieval society, lacking a class of people who could lead it into the modern industrial world. The dead hand of the past held the whole country back. The Church was the most conservative and corrupt power, controlling over half the wealth in the forms of land and treasure. Its higher prelates, *Gachupines* all, wallowed in luxury, worked the *Indios* to death on their estates, and fathered bastards. Tending to parish flocks was left to darker *Mestizos*, with Indians almost never admitted to the priesthood. The colonial army was an even worse plague. Its generals were all *gachupín*, the lesser officers *criollo*. It numbered about 33,000 men in 1810, mostly on paper because officers stole the money appropriated for their ghost soldiers. About half the army was officers, because the king and viceroys found a rewarding source of income in selling commissions. Getting one bought the protection of the military *fuero*.[12]

The colonial civil service, if it could be graced with such a term, reflected the society's late-medieval corruption. All offices were moneymaking propositions. Down to the lowest clerk or customs collector, the colonial experience gave birth to the venerable Latin American tradition of *la mordida* (the bite), the bribe paid to a functionary either to do his job or to look the other way from something he should crack down on. This system deprived both New Spain and Mexico of the money they needed to function. The idea of the rule of law was so alien as to be unheard of.

It was not that New Spain lacked people who could conceive of a better way of running a country. There was a growing *criollo* intellectual class by the late 1700s, but creative genius was notably lacking. A few thinkers borrowed alien concepts from French, North American, and English liberalism, but those did not mean a lot to them. They were fascinated by the notion of popular sovereignty, but invariably identified "the people" with themselves, the top of a system of unequal classes and castes, which denied the concept of "the people" anyway. There was no such thing as a Mexican.[13]

The mother country decided to "reform" the government of New Spain late in the eighteenth century. It began by replacing virtually all *Criollos* holding high positions in government and the Church with *Gachupines,* who arrived intending to mine their offices for profit. Part of what caused this reformation was that the abuse of the Indians had become scandalous—even the Pope in Rome complained. All over the settled parts of the country *ejidos* (communal farmlands) were confiscated and transferred to white or light *mestizo* overlords, and the original owners were forced to work for their new masters. The viceroys cracked down on these expropriations, backed by new laws enacted in Madrid. *Criollos* were suddenly forced into second-class citizenship—they could not rise in government, nor could they build personal fortunes at the expense of the *Indios.* They fought back, at the same time that resentment among Indians and rural *Castas* grew, rebellions became more frequent, and *hacendados* (proprietors of haciendas assembled from Indian lands) turned up with their throats cut.

A curious thing happened amid this mounting chaos—the construction of a Mexican national identity. It evoked a mythical past arising mostly from romantic notions of the Aztecs (as the México were called); the eagle on the cactus reappeared, now with a snake in his beak. The cult of the lower *Castas,* devotion to the Virgin of Guadalupe, was appropriated to this emerging new nation, replacing Spain's Virgin of the Remedies. The *Criollos* and lighter *Mestizos* were the descendants and heirs of the ancient Aztec tradition, authors of a new society that combined the best of America and Europe. Nothing in this backward-looking glorification of

Indians did any good for the current *Indios*. The whole mythology justified resistance to the Crown's attempts to protect those very same Indians from the rampages of the new Aztecs.[14]

An uprising was bound to happen. The question was who would strike first—the new Aztecs against the Spanish, or the *Indios* and *Castas* against their oppressors. It was the oppressed against the masters first. The spark that set New Spain ablaze was ignited in Spain, which was taken over in 1808 by the French, who imposed their revolutionary ideas about the Rights of Man. All of this inspired a hollow-cheeked, pistol-packing priest in Querétaro, Miguel Hidalgo y Costilla, a combination Enlightenment rationalist, Catholic moralist, social liberal, self-proclaimed nationalist, and fire-breathing demagogue. He raised the *grito* (cry) for revolution in September 1810 and soon had around him other socially liberal priests, a few renegade army officers, and thousands of aggrieved *indio* and *casta* farmers and vagabonds. He claimed to oppose the French enemy who threatened the Church, but what his followers heard was a call for land and liberty. It was infectious, and over the following months the rebellion spread. The *criollo* elite might have exploited the popular rebellion to mount an independence movement. Instead, fearing a threat to their own privileges, they became counterrevolutionists. They conscripted armies, then defeated the rebels outside Guadalajara in January 1811, and soon the popular insurrection was on the run.

One place some of its leaders ran to was Texas, where they had inspired a parallel revolution. It also drew on a minor independence movement that had drawn up a constitution and elected a congress by 1813. Led by Bernardo Gutiérrez de Lara, a *criollo* insurgent from Mexico City, this pretender government sent out calls to the United States for help. Hundreds of Anglos, mostly from Kentucky, responded, invading Texas with muskets in hand. The rebels proclaimed a ruling junta in San Antonio and issued a declaration of independence. A royalist expedition marched into Texas and squashed the rebellion. "A great expense of powder and shot was saved by the cutting of the throats of prisoners," said one of the Spanish generals.[15]

Royalist armies swept over New Spain, slaughtering rebels by the thousands, wreaking bloody havoc wherever they went. The French were tossed out of Spain in 1813, so there was no longer a danger that the home government would threaten the *fueros* of Church or army in New Spain. After independence, Mexican leaders wrapped themselves in the bloody shrouds of the *insurrectos,* boasting of the role they played in the War of Independence. It was nothing of the kind—the *Criollos* were content to stay within the Spanish orbit so long as it supported their privileged positions.

A decade of revolution and counterrevolution left a half million people dead, about a twelfth of the population. Farms, towns, whole regions were burned-over wastes. In big towns and cities the streets filled up with starving widows, orphans, and the blind and crippled. For ten years and more, the most prosperous inhabitants of New Spain were blowflies, coyotes, and *zopilotes* (buzzards). Human population growth stopped for twenty years.[16]

The years of chaos produced new leaders, *caudillos* (military strongmen), who by 1820 realized that the slaughter and destruction must end. The catalyst was a new liberal government in Spain, which revived the Constitution of 1812. Here was the threat to privilege risen anew, and a *caudillo* rose to confront it. He was Agustín de Iturbide, born in 1783 in Valladolid to conservative Spanish parents, a lieutenant in the army by the age of fourteen, who rose fast in rank by virtue of his successes during the wars against insurrectionists. He was a big, burly man with large, wide eyes, a low forehead, muttonchop whiskers, and absolutely no conscience. He was the most dangerous kind of thug—an intelligent and ambitious one. "Over a period of nine years," Lorenzo de Zavala said of Iturbide, "he was known for his brilliant campaigns and for his cruelty toward his fellow countrymen." Lucas Alamán said simply, "He left a trail of blood in his wake." He was the founding archetype of the Mexican *caudillo,* right down to the habit of giving himself vainglorious titles and nicknames.[17]

Iturbide earned promotion to general by the age of thirty. Further success—measured in thousands of throats cut—gained him appointment as guardian of bullion shipments from northern mines to the capital in 1815. He became fabulously wealthy in this position, so far beyond the norm for official corruption that he was sacked the following year. He retreated to a convent, nursed his pride, and developed a plot to overthrow the Spanish government. His chance came in 1820 when the viceroy sent him at the head of an army to put down the last major revolutionary force in the south, under Vicente Guerrero, a skillful *guerrillero* (guerrilla fighter).

Iturbide lost one skirmish with the irregulars, retreated to plunder some bullion trains, and spent nights in his tent drawing up a plan for an independent nation. It had twenty provisions, of which "three guarantees" stood out: independence under a suitable monarch, continuation of Roman Catholicism as the state religion, and citizenship and racial equality for all Mexicans. It nodded to the desires of the true revolutionaries while ensuring that the existing order would continue. He and Guerrero together issued it as the Plan de Iguala on February 24, 1821. Iturbide also adopted the flag of Guerrero's irregular army—a red-white-green tricolor emblazoned with the eagle holding a snake and sitting on a cactus.

The Plan enticed nearly the entire *criollo* part of the officer corps to de-clare for independence—persuaded further by Iturbide's promises of pro-motions to any who went over to his side. It was not so much that the insurrection succeeded as that the royal army evaporated, in the form of opportunistic officers and enlisted deserters who turned by the hundreds to banditry.[18]

Still, Mexico was independent. "Who then failed to foresee days of glory, of liberty, and of prosperous times?" Zavala asked afterward. "Who did not anticipate an auspicious and untroubled future?"[19]

MEXICO WAS BORN WITH ITS BACK TURNED

The Mexican National Congress, composed of delegates from all the for-mer Spanish administrative provinces (renamed "states") assembled in Mexico City early in 1822 to secure that "untroubled" future. Lucas Alamán, Mexico's first scholarly historian, concluded afterwards that Mexico had failed to take advantage of its own history. The colonial period should have been formative, as it was for the United States, and the decade of bloodshed preceding independence should have been unnecessary. Mexico could have gained independence by peaceful means, he believed, retaining its Catholic and Spanish traditions. He contrasted the country's experience to that of the United States, which had continued the forms and customs of the British period. Mexico, instead, had "destroyed all that formerly existed" and set itself onto a path of permanent disorder.[20]

Iturbide was optimistic, or at least he sounded like it. "Mexicans," he proclaimed, "now you have liberty and independence. It is for you to find happiness." That would happen only under his supervision, however. The Treaty of Córdoba had called for a monarchy in Mexico, presumably under a Spanish prince, but in May 1822 Iturbide intimidated Congress into pro-claiming him emperor of Mexico. Joel R. Poinsett, a visitor from the United States, was not impressed. He called the emperor "distinguished for his immorality," not a "man of talent," but "prompt, bold and decisive, and not scrupulous about the means he employs to obtain his ends."[21]

So were established two traditions. One was the government of Mexico by *caudillos* serving their own interests instead of the nation's. The other was a doubtful attitude in the United States toward its neighbor, as expressed by a man regarded as an expert whose words would be con-sulted over the next three decades.[22]

Bad attitudes went both ways. Like the people of other Spanish colonies who gained independence at around the same time, Mexicans at first called themselves *Americanos,* in sharp distinction from the Spanish. Even as they adopted national identifications—Mexican, Peruvian, and so on—they bristled at the idea that the people of the United States claimed the label "American" as wholly their own. Throughout Latin America, those to the north were *Angloamericanos, Norteamericanos, Anglosajónes* (Anglo-Saxons), or, disparagingly, *Yanquis* or *Gringos.* This went to strange lengths, with such twisted neologisms as *Estadounidenses* (Unitedstatesians).

Iturbide wanted to begin his empire on good terms with the United States. He hoped for diplomatic recognition, commercial treaties, settlement of boundary disputes, and above all a loan of $10 million. On the other side, President James Monroe extended recognition to all the new American nations because he wanted to promote republican governments in all of them. Elevation of Iturbide to emperor discouraged the northern president, but he predicted that the Mexican monarchy would not last long. Monroe recognized Mexico's independence in 1822 but did not appoint a minister until January 1825, when he selected Poinsett. In the meantime, Iturbide sent José Manuel Bermúdez Zozaya as his minister to the United States. The Mexican minister was not happy about his reception. "The haughtiness of these Republicans does not permit them to look upon us as equals," he complained to the emperor. He warned: *"They will be our enemies."* [23]

The two countries had to live together. Their border was between Louisiana on one side and Texas and New Mexico on the other. The scarcity of *pobladores* (frontier settlers) gave the appearance of a vacuum waiting to be filled. The presidio garrisons were few and scattered, undermanned (often with convicts), and thoroughly neglected. One reason for that was a pattern emerging in Mexico—generals kept their troops near the capital looking for an opportunity to seize power. Regular troops entered the frontier provinces over the next decade only when there was a threat of rebellion or foreign invasion, as in Texas in the 1830s. [24]

The first wound to the Empire's borders did not come from the United States, however. The Central American provinces assembled a congress late in 1821 to consider what to do about their status. Iturbide sent an army in December to persuade the delegates to hitch their wagons to his star, and they did so. However, Central America seceded from Mexico in March 1823 to form its own republic (which in due course broke up into its constituent parts). Nervous nationalists in Mexico City thought: *First Louisiana, then Florida, now this. What other territories is Mexico in danger of losing?* [25]

Iturbide was out of the picture by that point. He had only one signal accomplishment during his reign—his government abolished racial categories, making everybody in Mexico a citizen. This was not good news for the *Indios* because it removed Spain's feeble protection of their *ejidos.* If everyone was an individual citizen, then landownership also should be individual. The assault on communal lands resumed, the government over the next decades parceling out huge estates to rich *hacendados*. The *Indios* and *Castas* were either driven off or trapped on their former lands by the heritable debt slavery called peonage.[26]

Lucas Alamán later said that Iturbide reigned over not an empire but rather "a theatrical performance, or a dream." The emperor established himself in the palace of the viceroys and spent most of his time dreaming up honors and awards for himself, adorning his uniform with gaudy decorations. He held eleborate receptions and festivals, paid for by selling commissions in the army and other beneficences such as haciendas. If he left a legacy, it was the Congress he had emasculated as soon as it proclaimed him emperor. Thence forward Mexican politics would be dominated by a succession of *caudillos*. Instead of equality between executive and legislature, the executive would dominate. "Mexico was born with its back turned," said the national poet Octavio Paz, seeking inspiration from a mostly inglorious past of bloodthirsty Aztec emperors and rapacious Spanish *conquistadores*.[27]

Iturbide's empire lasted about ten months. His ally Santa Anna brought him down. Iturbide accused him of conniving with the Spaniards and sent two armies to take him out of the picture. Santa Anna put his finger to the political winds, observed that several states had declared independence, decided that the country now wanted power dispersed in a federal system, declared himself a republican opposed to "absolutism," and got the generals marching against him to join in proclaiming the Plan de Casa Mata, calling for a constitution founded on federalist principles. The whole country—or at least the whole army—turned against the emperor. Iturbide abdicated on March 19, 1823, and a call went out for a constitutional convention.[28]

THE AGE OF SANTA ANNA

So began what Mexicans called "the Age of Santa Anna," a turbulent period covering the first three decades and more of the country's independence. Who was Santa Anna? Supporters named him "Defender of the Homeland," "Illustrious Hero against the Spaniards," and "Intrepid Son of Mars." Detractors called him "Traitor to the Homeland," and such adjectives as "devious," "overambitious," "vulgar," and "corrupt." When he was a royalist officer his superiors said he was "active, gallant, zealous, indefatigable in the royal service, and of a fairly good level of education," papering over his atrocities. The South American liberator Simón Bolívar called him "the most perverse of mortals." Iturbide called him a "volcanic genius."[29]

He was born Antonio López de Santa Anna Pérez de Lebron, February

21, 1794, in Jalapa, Vera Cruz, the son of a discharged Spanish army officer, who was always in debt because of gambling, and a *criolla* mother.
Theatrical talent and a weakness for gambling ran in the family. He always
wanted to be a soldier, and became a cadet in the royal colonial army in
1810. "I cannot deny that when I was young the idea of glorifying my name
passed through my mind," he said in his memoirs. As he got older, he said,
"the love of liberty and the desire to glorify the name of my country" replaced his earlier self-centeredness.[30]

By engineering the overthrow of Iturbide, Santa Anna posed himself
as a republican. He was really conniving his way to power, as he would
many times through the 1850s. Sometimes a *pronunciamiento* from him
would be enough to bring down a government. Other times he incited rebellion in secrecy, and if the government had more troops than his party,
he would switch sides or become a peacemaker. After every political adventure he retired to his great hacienda Manga de Clavo (Sleeve of a Clove)
in Vera Cruz. He fancied himself a Mexican Cincinnatus or George
Washington, waiting for history's next call—and another chance to line
his pockets.[31]

Santa Anna wanted to be a leader, or at least be acclaimed as one, but
he lacked the patience, tenacity, purpose, even the will to rule that leadership requires. His energies went into gambling, womanizing, cockfighting,
making speeches, and even forging commercial documents. He was a
steady consumer of opium and, rumors held, of other substances as well.
When he was in power—he was president eleven times—often Santa
Anna retreated from the responsibilities of the capital to Manga de Clavo
to spend his ill-gotten gains expanding his *finca* (estate). By the 1840s his
holdings extended thirty-five miles, almost from Jalapa to Vera Cruz, and
covered 483,000 acres supporting 40,000 cattle and thousands of horses.
There also he raised, trained, and babied his prize fighting cocks, which he
entered in matches whenever and wherever he could. Santa Anna had a
more or less human side, if it served his ambitions. He courted Iturbide's
sister—thirty years older than he was—until he turned on the emperor.
He married fourteen-year-old Doña Inés García, a *Gachupina* who bore
him several children, in 1825. When she died in 1844, he married another
teenager before the formal mourning period expired. Neither slowed him
down with other ladies, who called him "gentlemanly" and "good-looking."
Naturally charming, he treated them to his talents as a gourmet.

Antonio López de Santa Anna was the greatest scalawag in the history
of the Western Hemisphere, and the most frenetic. "He is a man who has
within him some force always driving him to take action," said the liberal
intellectual Lorenzo de Zavala, "but since he has no fixed principles nor

any organized code of public behavior, through his lack of understanding he always moves to extremes and comes to contradict himself. He does not measure his actions or calculate the results."[32]

Historian Justo Sierra thought Santa Anna had "just enough intelligence to develop in himself . . . the faculty called astuteness." He believed God had chosen him to be the "Republic's savior," his ambition sustained "by figments of Catholic superstitions." He was vain, easily flattered, had no principles "save his own ambition." A "hero to his soldiers, he never hesitated to take charge of any military campaign though he had no qualifications except the ability to infuse the troops with his own ardor."[33]

Zavala again: "The soul of the general cannot be contained by his body," he observed. "He lives in perpetual agitation, he gets carried away by an irresistible desire to acquire glory." Defeat "maddens him . . . then he abandons himself to a feeling of weakness though not cowardice. He pays no attention at all to strategy."[34]

It is little wonder that this agitated bundle of contradictions has fascinated his fellow Mexicans for nearly two centuries, nor that in the United States Santa Anna's image has been reduced to that of a colorless cartoon in a colorful uniform in movies about the fall of the Alamo in 1836. He was an inveterate gambler and a consummate showman. Besieged in Oaxaca during an uprising in 1823, he took one risk after another and played one role after another, sometimes in costume. He raided businesses and church properties at night for supplies. He dressed up as a woman to spy on the enemy. He climbed the walls of a convent and single-handedly disarmed its defenders. Disguising himself and some of his troops as friars, he entered a church, summoned the people to mass, then extorted loans from the congregation to finance his operations. It was hard not to admire this flamboyant national actor.[35]

For all his boyish charm and flair for the dramatic, Santa Anna harbored a vicious, downright murderous streak. José Fuentes Mares accompanied him to Texas to put down the rebellion there in 1836, and said of the "Napoleon of the West" (yet another title), "Blind to all values, physically resolute in the face of risks, he almost always, at the critical moment, lost his moral bearings. A hybrid-like specimen, he roared like a lion and fled like a gazelle."[36]

Santa Anna was loved and hated, sometimes by the same people at the same time, welcomed back into Mexico as often as he was exiled. He cast a shadow over his country's history that still darkens the landscape. He was alternately a liberal and a conservative, a federalist and a centralist, a liberator and a dictator—switches that ought to have alienated everyone. Yet Santa Anna dominated Mexico for more than a generation, because one side or another found his energy useful. That he endured for so long was owing to a persistent band of *Santanistas* (his loyalists) led by José María Tornel y Mendevil, soldier, politician, diplomat, and schemer, who brought out both the best and the worst in the man. Tornel's sole political principle was to keep Santa Anna in power or return him there. He adapted political ideas to changing circumstances, from radical federalism in the 1820s to reactionary dictatorship in the 1850s. Without Tornel there might never have been a Santa Anna. Others, most notably Lucas Alamán, deluded themselves that they could control this human dynamo, but Tornel came closer than anyone else.[37]

With or without Tornel, the "Age of Santa Anna" was at hand in 1823. Mexico was cursed to put up with him for years to come. So was the United States.

TO FEDERALIZE OURSELVES, NOW UNITED, IS TO DIVIDE OURSELVES

(1823–1835)

There is no good faith in America, not among nations.
The treaties are papers; the constitutions are books;
the elections are combats; freedom is anarchy; and life a torment.

—Simón Bolívar

DURING SPAIN'S LONG STRUGGLE against the Moors there appeared *el bandido en el héroe*, the bandit in the hero, who took from the rich, gave to the poor, and all that. The bandit rallied to his country's cause when the chips were down; otherwise he was a criminal and a rebel. The tradition of *el bandido en el héroe* took root early in Mexico, and banditry became an economic and social outlet for dispossessed *Castas* and *Indios* and a permanent fixture on the Mexican scene.[1]

The Spanish people took up arms after 1808 to defend king, country, and religion against the French. Thus was born the original *guerrilla* (little war)—original not in tactics but in name. Bands of *guerrilleros* harassed the invaders with hit-and-run raids, bombs thrown over fort walls, small parties waylaid, throats cut in the night, all methods of the weak fighting the strong. This tradition spread quickly to the Spanish colonies. The *criollo* generals who dominated Mexico after independence glorified the *insurrectos* whom they had spent a decade slaughtering before the *Criollos* discovered the attractions of independence. Out in the countryside, the bandit remained a hero. In the palace vacated by the viceroys, the *guerrillero* became a figure of public mythology.[2]

Mythology collided with reality from the outset. Regular armies were raised by press gangs, and about half the manpower of the armies during the independence wars were Indians and another quarter *Castas*. Troublemakers, vagabonds, and criminal prisoners were drafted first, but the continuing need for cannon fodder pressed tens of thousands of illiterate men into years of service. These conscripts deserted whenever they could, in droves when the royal army fell apart after 1820. They had learned from their *criollo* generals that violence was the way to solve all problems, to preserve their communities and traditions, and to gain an income.[3]

The cities of Mexico were overrun by violent criminal gangs and the countryside by bandits. Travelers from Vera Cruz to Mexico City typically were robbed two or three times. The country suffered, a foreigner said in the 1840s, a "pestilence of robbers" everywhere, and respectable citizens always went out of their houses armed to the teeth.[4]

Bandit gangs assumed respectability by calling themselves insurgents, *insurrectos*. Mexico harbored hundreds of little guerrilla armies that, in the event of a foreign invasion, could make that switch from banditry to heroism.

WE ARE LIKE CHILDREN BARELY OUT OF DIAPERS

Mexican historian Justo Sierra, observing the widespread disorder, described his country's condition after independence as "anarchy." Mexico suffered at least fifty changes in the presidency from 1821 to 1857. Governing political principles swung wildly back and forth between centralism, the conservative belief that power should be concentrated for the sake of order and stability, and federalism, the liberal belief that power should be dispersed to the states. These ideas were held by self-righteous and mutually hostile factions who assembled five constitutional conventions that produced three constitutions, a governing charter, and an "act of reform." The Mexican government was not a means of governance but something to be seized.[5]

A tradition of peaceful transfer of political power was established in the United States by presidents George Washington and John Adams. The transfer of power in Mexico came through a *golpe de estado* (coup d'état), usually a *cuartelazo* (barracks revolt) announced with a *pronunciamiento* (a declaration of the coup), sometimes presenting a "plan" for the new government. There was a saying common when one of these started: "*¡Ay! ¡Viene la bala!*" ("Here comes the musket ball!").[6]

The North Americans led by Washington had fought against government, but Mexican revolutionaries—mostly disaffected lower *criollo* and *mestizo* lawyers, teachers, petty bureaucrats, and others lined up behind a *caudillo*—fought to seize government and exploit it. A successful revolution was therefore no more than a successful coup d'état. Born out of misery and humiliation, an unsuccessful one deteriorated into a bloody class struggle on the local level.[7]

Two general political tendencies emerged in Mexico, each trying to develop a national identity based on myth. The conservatives wanted a nation based on rational conservatism mixed with material progress. Hence this faction often looked to monarchy to continue the traditions of the Spanish period. On the other side were the liberals, who wanted to build a Mexican identity out of romantic evocation of an idealized Aztec past. This depended on the construction of a mythical history—all Mexicans were heir to an ancient grandeur. Restoring this ideal world made no place for the majority of its people—the real *Indios* and other *Castas*. The founders of the United States had debated political theories and principles in 1787 but devised a practical form of government intended to work far into the future. The counterpart founders in Mexico after 1821 fell into a battle between myths and forgot about building a nation with a workable government.[8]

Delegates assembled in Mexico City to produce what would become the Constitution of 1824, and the centralist-federalist split broke open at once. The clergy, the rich, and the generals favored a strong central government. Declarations of independence by several provinces meant that the liberals rode a federalist tide, however. Moreover, except for Alamán, they seemed to have a monopoly on serious political thought—many of them had been poring over the documents that came out of the United States and French revolutions.[9]

The United States Constitution impressed the liberals the most. Their newspaper *El Sol* called it "one of the most perfect creations of the spirit . . . the foundation for the most uncomplicated, most liberal, and most fortunate government in history."[10]

A conservative delegate, Fray Servanda, warned against modeling Mexico's government on that of the United States, because the northern states "were already separate and independent one from another. They federalized themselves in union against the oppression of England." It was too late for that in Mexico, he believed, because "to federalize ourselves, now united, is to divide ourselves." Mexico, he said, "buckled for three hundred years under the weight of an absolute monarch, scarcely moving a step toward the study of freedom. We are like children barely out of diapers." Mexicans were not ready for democratic self-government, so Servanda wanted a centralist system to replace the Spanish king.[11]

Servanda did not carry the day. The Constitution of 1824 dispersed power to prevent any *caudillo* from controlling the whole country—the president was elected by the states, not the Congress as the centralists wanted. There was a fatal flaw—it gave the president extraordinary powers in case of national emergency. Still, the framers paid great heed to the charter of the United States, down to calling their nation "los Estados Unidos Mexicanos" (the United Mexican States). The country was a federal republic of nineteen states and four territories with the *Distrito Federal* (Federal District) surrounding Mexico City. Besides the presidency there were an independent judiciary and a national legislature. The Congress was bicameral, the upper house called the Senate, with members chosen by the states, and the lower house the Chamber of Deputies, its membership apportioned according to state populations. In contrast to the North American model, this Constitution forbade slavery (a case of theory divorced from practice). The conservatives scored some points, however—Roman Catholicism remained the official religion, and the clergy and military retained *fueros*.[12]

The Constitution of 1824 meant that Mexico, on paper at least, formed its government in admiration of that of the United States. But the two countries started out on different footings. Mexico's chances of keeping its republic did not look good.

I AM NOT A POLITICIAN, NOR DO I LIKE THAT CAREER

Keeping a republic was impossible, because Mexico had too few politicians interested in building a nation and too many generals who lusted for glory. The *caudillos* wanted governmental power, but they shunned the hard work that went with it. "I am not a politician," one general said, "nor do I like that career, which brings only worries and enmities; I am a soldier by profession."[13]

Mexico was a wreck following the independence wars; even the chief source of the country's wealth, its silver mines, was ruined. Spain continually tried to reconquer the country, which kept the nation on a war footing. Soldiers served as cabinet ministers, governors, regional military commandants, regular army generals, and diplomats. There were chronic separatist movements in outlying states, and centrally nobody was able to solve the country's economic and social crises. Mexico was governed by plots and counterplots, punctuated by coups. With the execution of ousted president Vicente Guerrero in 1831, four of the five main leaders of the independence war had fallen in front of firing squads.[14]

Most of the population lived in grinding poverty without hope. Of an estimated 7 million Mexicans in the early 1830s, the vast majority were Indians living in isolated villages where they were tyrannized by local *caciques* (rural chiefs). These were mostly *mestizo,* although there were a few *indio* or *casta* chieftains. The *caudillos,* mostly *criollo,* could spread their destruction over wide swaths of the country. They were characterized by their utter ignorance of economics or anything else to do with government or diplomacy.[15]

The national army nominally numbered 80,000 soldiers when Iturbide took power, but half of them were officers and noncoms. The emperor worsened this imbalance by selling commissions wholesale, and his successors followed suit. The army had been brutalized by eleven years of civil war and was used to terrorizing civilians, looting towns, and massacring prisoners. One government after another tried to figure out how to get rid of troublesome generals even as it appointed more. There were 160 generals of the line for a nominal 30,000 troops by 1838. Military appropriations continually increased, bribes to keep the generals in line. The ranks were filled by Indian conscripts with no appetite for waging war. The few efficient officers were a handful of foreign mercenary battalion leaders. When generals contended with each other, officers changed sides and privates deserted. Overriding all was the tendency of the national politicians to cosset the army and then fail to pay its costs, sparking *cuartelazos.*[16]

The army budget was usually more than twice the national income through the 1820s. Nobody who gained power had any background in economics, or even an understanding of what money was. The Mexican government had unwisely assumed responsibility for a national debt left by the Spanish government, but essentially had only customs duties for income—along with burdensome excises on the very poor. Little national income made it to the government because of graft.[17]

Mexico remained intensely factional, burdened by mistrust, self-righteousness, rancor, and despair. The conflicts embedded themselves in an unusual place—the lodges of *los Masones* (the Freemasons). The conservative centralists established themselves in the Scottish Rite, left over from the colonial period. These *Escoseses* were opposed to the *Yorquinos,* who preferred the York Rite, introduced to Mexico City by Joel Poinsett in the early 1820s. It was the headquarters of federalist defenders of the Constitution of 1824 and opponents to Spanish designs for reconquest.

Poinsett got himself thrown out of the country for this kind of political meddling, but he left behind a network of contentious Masonic lodges across Mexico. They housed plots and counterplots on local and national stages.[18]

Federalists saw centralism as an attempt to restore authoritarianism on the Spanish model, but some also recognized that too much centrifugal force could cause outlying states and territories to break away. The push and pull never was resolved, because in the background were continuing agrarian revolts—the main constant of Mexican life for more than a century. When federalist constitutions were replaced by centralist ones, as in 1836 and 1843, the threats to state power caused more regional uprisings against the national government. Banditry and guerrilla warfare flourished.[19]

THE INDIAN LABORERS UPON THOSE FARMS RARELY HAVE ENOUGH MEAT

Mexico did not have to be that way. "The vast kingdom of New Spain," suggested German explorer Alexander von Humboldt, "could by itself produce everything that commerce goes searching after throughout the rest of the world." Mexico was rich in natural resources, in particular silver and gold, and its agricultural production was potentially enormous, especially in sugar, cotton, wool, and tobacco. Yet there was little industry and no economic system to develop one, and farming and grazing lands were swallowed by great but mostly fallow estates.[20]

At the center of it all stood Mexico City, with a population of about 170,000. It was a bustling place, centered on the great cathedral facing the *Zócalo* (the main plaza), with lesser churches on lesser plazas scattered around the city's heart. There were schools for the rich, a university, and many public parks. Neighborhoods ranged from those made up of private palaces to outlying *colonias*—the slums of the very poor. The city attracted the richest and the poorest from all over the country.[21]

The poorest drew the most attention from foreign visitors—the *léperos* (literally "lepers," often translated primly as "vagabonds"), outcasts even from the miserable *colonias* inhabited by displaced Indians from the countryside. They were a permanent, homeless underclass who belonged nowhere, starving, sick, often drunk. They were the wretched refuse of a country torn by perpetual war and disruption, and their counterparts existed in every city in Mexico.[22]

There was little employment for them beyond begging or stealing, and little more for the Indians eking out an existence in the *colonias*. They could work as domestics and gardeners or as stoop laborers, but little else. There was one notable line of work, however, and it explained why the city's streets were so clean. Instead of horses and mules, human beasts of burden, *cargadores,* moved nearly all goods. Poinsett's secretary Edward Thornton Tayloe observed that "everything is carried upon the backs of these poor creatures, who are enabled to carry a load of 300 lbs. by means of a leather band or strap. . . . With so heavy a load they travel great distances, moving in a brisk walk or trot." This labor developed in tens of thousands of Mexican men (and not a few women) the amazing endurance they would demonstrate in later military campaigns.[23]

Relief from oppressive poverty for the majority of Mexicans was found only in weekly or biweekly markets, in the frequent festivals sponsored by the Church, and, every day they could afford it, in *pulque* (known regionally in the north as *mescal*), fermented from the succulent plant maguey (called regionally agave or mescal). Available from street peddlers or at grog shops known as *pulquerías,* it tasted like rotten meat, but it provided alcoholic relief from the misery of life. It was the national drink of Mexico.[24]

Mexico City was not the only urban center. Provincial cities ranged from populations of a few thousand to the largest, Puebla, at about 71,000 inhabitants. They were commercial centers for their regions, laid out in the Spanish Baroque fashion in grids around a *zócalo,* the streets usually paved and lighted. They were the lowest level of settlement retaining any connection to the national center, with more entertainment and business than in the rural towns. The proportion of *Criollos* to *Mestizos* was lower in the lesser cities than in the capital. There were schools, but just for the rich. Neighborhoods ranged from fancy in the centers to squalid on the outskirts.

There were also hundreds of towns with populations ranging from about a thousand to 3,500 people, mostly *Mestizos* and hispanicized *Indios.* The gridded streets were dirt, schools were few, and housing was typically one story and of adobe or stone, or, in the south, cane and thatch—*jacales* (shacks), mostly. Life centered around the weekly markets and the *pulquerías* and street vendors. Poinsett complained that buildings in these places hosted every species of insect that feasted on human blood.[25]

Mexico was neither an urban nor a town-dwelling country, but a rural one. The *Indígenas* lived in thousands of tiny villages, where Spanish was seldom heard and the old languages were still in use. These *pueblos* were self-governing and inward-looking, concerned with daily survival on communal lands. There were scarcely any whites or even *Mestizos* to be found in these places, and the bug-infested housing was *jacales* with regional variations in materials. Here, too, *pulque* granted relief from the pains of life, along with the dried leaves and flowers of hemp smoked in *cigarrillos* (cigarettes) with corn shucks as the wrappers—*marijuana* (Mary Jane).[26]

"It is a very great mistake to suppose they enjoy anything like a social equality," said diplomat Waddy Thompson, "even with the Indian population; and although there are no political distinctions, the aristocracy of color is quite as great in México as it is in [the United States]." He also complained, "The lands of the country belong to a few large proprietors, some of whom own tracts of eighty and one hundred leagues square, with herds of sixty and eighty thousand head of cattle grazing upon them, whilst the Indian laborers upon those farms rarely have enough meat to eat."[27]

Aristocrats waxed fat on fancy foods while the majority of Mexico's people led lives of poverty and hard labor, feeling blessed if they could put together a meal of corn tortillas wrapped around beans and peppers, with *pulque* to dull the pain. Poinsett thought things ought to change, and he had a typically Anglo-Saxon solution. "All these evils, if not cured entirely, would be greatly mitigated by education," he said. Few statements better reflect the inability of United States officials to understand the vast differences between their own society and that of their neighbor to the south. Getting Mexicans to think like North Americans would not solve their problems anyway.[28]

Most territory claimed by Mexico was not inhabited by Mexicans, although there were pockets of settlement in the northern territories. In Texas and New Mexico and in most of Sonora and Chihuahua, the country really belonged to *los Indios bárbaros*. California was exceptional, because local Indian populations were small and unthreatening, and further reduced by disease. Termination of the missions in 1833 removed any protection the Indians had had, and the few Mexican *Californios* amassed vast estates covered with livestock.

Spaniards moving north in the sixteenth and seventeenth centuries had collided with other warlike peoples migrating southward—especially the Athapaskans in New Mexico. These clans and tribes, speaking a common tongue, had left northwest Canada and Alaska centuries earlier and had divided into two camps—Navajos and Apaches. The Navajos established themselves in a vast area of canyonlands west of Santa Fe and proceeded to borrow from Spanish culture, including horses, muskets and lances, agriculture and sheepherding, and orchards. They also began centuries of warfare with the New Mexicans and Pueblo Indians in the Rio Grande Valley. The various Apache bands were less settled or unified but no less adaptive and no less ferocious. To the north, the Utes also acquired horses and used them to carry on a continuing warfare against New Mexicans, Pueblos, and Navajos. To the east, early in the eighteenth century there appeared another and especially fearsome nation of raiders—the Comanches, who when they acquired horses left their Shoshone kin in lands west of the Ute territories, migrated to the Great Plains, and took aim at the settlements and Indians of both New Mexico and Texas. Kiowas and others soon joined them. Farther south, Mexico inherited Spanish wars of mutual extermination with the Yaquis and Mayos of Sonora and the Tarahumaras of Chihuahua.

Mexico's northern territories were lands of round-robin wars and raiding among all the parties on the scene—the stealing of horses, sheep, and other plunder, and especially of people, captives enslaved by the winner of a given fight or sold into slavery elsewhere. It was not all one-sided—Mexicans and settled Indians raided the "bold" Indians as much as they were raided themselves. And it was not all constant—occasionally two or three of the parties would stop to trade with each other. Still, blood soaked the ground over incredibly vast territories, causing bitter resentments and vendettas not easily put to rest. The Apaches and Comanches widened their range in the 1820s, raiding as far south as the outskirts of Mexico City. Also during the 1820s, in California and New Mexico and Texas, new bands of pugnacious people established their own presence in these bloody landscapes—*Norteamericanos.*[29]

THE FIRST SPENDS AS LITTLE AS HE CAN, THE SECOND SPENDS WHAT HE DOES NOT HAVE

It appeared that the two great powers on the continent would get along after Mexico became independent in 1821. Opening the Santa Fe Trail and letting Anglos colonize Texas were seen as neighborly gestures. The proclamation of the Monroe Doctrine in 1823, warning Europe to keep its hands off the Western Hemisphere, was viewed in the United States as a blessing for the new republics of Latin America. They took it as a patronizing move by a dominant power to look after its lesser sisters, out of a belief that the new nations could not defend themselves. As a Mexican historian put it, the northern neighbor was cloaked in self-awarded superiority that grew out of its Calvinist Protestant heritage, its anti-Catholic traditions, and its smug assumption that its form of government was superior to all others.[30]

A rankling issue between the two republics was the fixation northern leaders had on acquiring Texas. John Quincy Adams regretted not making a stronger case for that in the treaty of 1819. When he became president in 1825, he appointed Joel R. Poinsett as the first minister to Mexico and ordered him to buy as much of Texas as he could, all the way to the Rio Grande if possible. The instructions were arrogant and presumptuous, and so was the man carrying them. Relations between Mexico and the United States were bound to be difficult, but Poinsett made them insufferable.[31]

He looked like an ideal choice as ambassador. He spoke Spanish fluently and had considerable experience as a consul and commercial agent in several South American posts from 1810 to 1816. By the time he retired to enter politics in his home state of South Carolina in 1816, he was regarded as the outstanding authority on Latin America in the United States. His record of interfering in the politics of his host countries should have made the president think twice before sending him to Mexico.[32]

Born in 1779, educated in the United States and England, Poinsett was a veteran of a long tour of Europe and western Asia before becoming a diplomat. He was a tall, slender man, with a long face divided by a long nose, crowned by a mass of dark curls and framed by sideburns. His stern eyes under a high brow gave off an air of disapproval, the attitude of a judgmental missionary among the benighted. That was the problem— Poinsett was a missionary, not a diplomat. He passionately believed that the democratic-republican system of the United States was perfection on earth. Poinsett made no secret of his contempt for other forms of government, in particular the conservative or monarchist. The man he would have to deal with in Mexico was the foreign minister, Lucas Alamán, who was both conservative and monarchist.

Lucas Alamán y Escalada, born in 1792 and a veteran of several governmental posts, was a scholar, and he looked it. He had a professor's high forehead crowned by a mass of curly hair, with jowly cheeks, a Roman nose, and thoughtful eyes magnified by strong spectacles. An introspective, soft-spoken man, he wrote with a pen dipped in fire. He believed that monarchy was the natural form of government for humankind and he spent his life trying to restore it to Mexico. Always he was disappointed that others could not see the wisdom of his theories. Alamán was a brilliant man, who saw in the United States nothing but a crude threat to his country.[33]

The Anglo missionary and the Mexican nationalist were bound not to get along. When Poinsett proposed buying Texas, Alamán ironically suggested that the United States sell Mexico the land between the Mississippi and Sabine rivers. Poinsett extended his offer to include New Mexico, Sonora, and California, but Alamán declared that his country expected the United States to stand by the treaty of 1819. Poinsett countered with an offer of a new boundary treaty that would transfer Texas to the United States. He finally got a new treaty in 1828, without Texas, and Mexico dragged its feet on ratification until 1832.[34]

Poinsett and Alamán met often during most of 1825, argued constantly, and got nowhere diplomatically. Introducing the York Rite as a platform, Poinsett allied himself publicly with the federalists, publishing tirades in Mexico City newspapers and generally doing his best to stir up trouble. Mexico's minister in Washington formally protested this undiplomatic behavior, yet the Adams administration kept Poinsett at his post until Mexico flatly demanded his recall late in 1828. Why the United States would send and then retain such an undiplomatic diplomat in Mexico City was a mystery. Mexican politicians concluded that the United States feared competition from its neighbor, and so had sent a troublemaker to Mexico to spread dissension. Never, after Poinsett went home—carrying samples of the plant that would bear his name, poinsettia—would Mexican officials expect anything but the worst from the United States. The British minister in Mexico City told his government that the prevailing sentiments there toward the Yankees were "jealousy, suspicion, and dislike." Poinsett's sour reports on the Mexican character produced a countervailing contempt in Washington toward Mexico.[35]

Poinsett did make some friends before he packed up his houseplants and left. Among them was Lorenzo de Zavala, a highly educated and well traveled liberal, social reformer, defender of the rights of Indians, *Yorquino*, and staunch federalist who would later sign the Texas Declaration of Independence. Zavala toured the United States in the early 1830s and returned with some comparisons between the two cultures. "The North American works," he observed, "the Mexican entertains himself; the first spends as little as he can, the second spends what he does not have." The solution to Mexico's problems, he believed, was to adopt North American habits of thrift and hard work, general education for the masses, and wider economic opportunity.[36]

Texas more than any other issue divided Mexico and the United States, exciting fears and resentment in the former, a growing obsession in the latter. Texas petitioned for statehood in 1824. Its population was too small and isolated for that, however, so rather than accept territorial status its representatives agreed to become part of the new state of Coahuila y Tejas. The state constitution forbade slavery and made Catholicism the sole religion. Anglo settlers ignored both provisions. The national Constitution of 1824 was ambiguous, especially on whether abolition of slavery would supersede the property rights of one major settler with over a hundred slaves in Texas. Congress granted authority over colonization to the state government in August 1824, to enlarge Texas' population to where it could withstand ferocious Comanche raids. Coahuila encouraged settlement by making large blocks of land available to *empresarios* at nominal cost. There were over 1,800 Anglos in Texas by 1825, most there illegally. As Stephen F. Austin lobbied for even more concessions, the colonists united against the Indian attacks, but their refusal to become Catholics or cast off slavery became an increasing source of friction with higher Mexican authorities. One *empresario* near Nacodoches, on the border with the United States, rebelled, declaring an independent republic. Mexican troops and Austin's militia together put that down.[37]

Trouble was brewing in Texas by the late 1820s. Anti-slavery sentiment was strong in Mexican officialdom, while the Anglo colonists rejected Catholic traditions that supported manumission and allowed slaves to buy their freedom. Texas slaves developed a habit of jumping the border to gain freedom in Mexico, and Mexico established a customs house in Texas, ending years of tax-free imports. A new state constitution for Coahuila in 1827 declared that no one could be born a slave in the state after the charter's adoption. The colonists wrote phony contracts with their slaves, pretending they were hired labor. Before that dodge could play itself out, on September 15, 1829, President Vicente Guerrero decreed emancipation throughout Mexico, although he rather unclearly exempted Texas.[38]

As tensions between colonists and the Mexican government seethed, United States presidents could not get Texas off their minds. Perhaps the best explanation for this obsession was the expanding population of frontiersmen in the Mississippi Valley, who provided most emigrants to Texas. They were descendants of those Anglo-Americans who had defied the British Proclamation of 1763. They were also Andrew Jackson's kind of people, and he took their sentiments into office with him when he became president in 1829. They wanted Texas to become part of the United States. Jackson believed with Jefferson that Texas was part of Louisiana, and had objected to leaving Texas out of the Adams-Onís Treaty in 1819. He viewed Texas as similar to what Florida had been before he invaded it—a vacuum that could draw in foreign interests. There were also Indian raids across the border into Louisiana, and slaves escaping in the other direction. Jackson expanded the range of lands that he thought more properly belonged in the United States than in Mexico, casting his eye beyond Texas to the whole of northeastern Mexico and even farther, to the Pacific Ocean. He feared that France or Britain would get Texas or California as payment for financial claims against Mexico.[39]

Jackson was a worse judge of diplomatic talent than Adams had been, appointing his old friend Anthony Wayne Butler to be his minister to Mexico. Born in 1787, like Poinsett a South Carolinian, Butler had served under Jackson during the War of 1812 and then became a land speculator in Mississippi and Texas. Butler was possibly the worst diplomat in the history of the United States, with a talent for doing the wrong thing at the wrong time. He was brash, utterly lacking in decency, and a bully who thought the way to deal with Mexico was not to negotiate but to cajole, threaten, or bribe. Veteran of several personal bankruptcies, he was a teetotaling blowhard, ignorant of both the Spanish language and diplomatic niceties, and a sloppy administrator of his diplomatic station. Butler gained a commercial treaty by dropping a demand for the return of fugitive slaves, but he got nowhere on Texas. As he continued to wear out his welcome in Mexico City over a period of six years, he indiscriminately gathered up North American claims against the Mexican government—something that would blossom into a cause of war.[40]

Jackson's motives for wanting Texas were more complicated than just serving his constituents in the Mississippi Valley. He had a vague idea of the geography, and proposed a border midway between the Nueces and the Rio Grande to serve as a buffer between United States and Mexican settlements. "The grand prairie," he said of a landscape that was anything but grand, "would be a boundary that would give permanent peace to the two republics." Above all, he did not want Texas to become an independent nation that would cause trouble for both countries. But the very suggestion that the United States might acquire Texas stirred up trouble in his own backyard—the beginnings of debate over extending slavery into western territories.[41]

Trouble was also brewing in Mexico over Texas. The sporadic revolts in the province that began in 1827 were interpreted in Mexico City as reflecting United States territorial ambition. The Mexican government sent General Manuel de Mier y Terán, a talented engineer and soldier, to inspect Texas in 1828. He advised changing the colonization laws to forbid future immigrants from the United States and finding ways to encourage Mexicans to move to Texas. Some of his proposals became law, but he remained pessimistic.[42]

As Butler continued to annoy the Mexican government over Texas, the claims issue rose to the fore because he diligently gathered reports with dubious cost figures from any Anglos who claimed to have suffered loss at the hands of the Mexican government. There was a long list of United States claims going back to 1821. The chaotic state of Mexican affairs resulted in frequently arbitrary and often brutal actions by state and local officials against foreign nationals, each with its diplomatic claim for redress. Most of these turned out to be exaggerated, many downright phony, but they were a growing annoyance to diplomats from other countries, France and Britain in particular. According to the British chargé d'affaires in

Mexico City, "There is scarcely one foreign power with whom they have had any relation, which has not had more or less cause to complain of the iniquity and persecution to which its subjects here have been exposed." Dubious as many of the claims turned out to be, the United States government accepted all of them at face value and lobbed them at Mexico as if they were cannonballs.[43]

"The influence of the United States over Mexico will over time become a force of opinion, of teaching, of instruction, the much stronger because it is purely moral, founded on its doctrines and lessons," said Lorenzo de Zavala. "Ten thousand citizens of the United States settle annually in territory of the Mexican Republic," bringing with them "habits of liberty, of economy, of hard work; their stern customs and religions, their individual independence and their republicanism." The North American way would in the end gain a "victory complete and at the same time bloody," because its bearers would not submit to the military and ecclesiastical powers that dominated Mexico. He could see that happening already in Texas, so he moved to Texas and took the side of the "Texians" in their war for independence.[44]

The obnoxious Butler had his own idea how to get Texas when a new *caudillo* seized power in Mexico in 1832. In an unenciphered letter he advised Jackson to bribe the new leader into selling Texas. Jackson was appalled, because if it had been intercepted, the letter would have made it appear that the president of the United States was trying to buy the president of Mexico. He responded that he would purchase Texas openly, for no more than $5 million. Butler shot back that *la mordida* was a way of life in Mexico and should be pursued. "Resort must be had to bribery—or by *presents,* if the term is more appropriate," Butler told Jackson. The president rejected the idea flatly, out of his sense of honor and because it would not work anyway.[45]

The incoming *presidente* was Antonio López de Santa Anna.

WHAT MEN OR WHAT DEMONS THEY ARE!

Detractors called him "Fifteen Claws," owing to his habit of reaching out like a double-rigged octopus to grab whatever treasure he could. Santa Anna was clever, but he was not wise. His loyalties were always up for sale, and he inspired others to behave the same way. He could raise an army to seize an opportunity, but he could never retain lasting political support, so his every success turned into a setback.[46]

Santa Anna came into his own during the 1820s, when two factors created a national environment in which he swam as menacingly as a shark. One was Spain's refusal to accept the loss of New Spain. The Spanish launched repeated attempts to reconquer the country, fanning the flames of hostility toward the *Gachupines* still in Mexico. They were driven out by act of Congress combined with mob action in 1827.[47]

Santa Anna was an early plotter against the Spanish. From Yucatán late in 1824 he cooked up a plan to invade Spanish Cuba. Foreign Minister Manuel Gómez Pedraza thought it was a good idea. "If it succeeds," he said, "it ought to be a great honor to Mexico; if it fails at least it will rid us of Santa Anna." Word of the plan leaked, and the United States government objected. The government recalled Santa Anna to Mexico City.[48]

The Spaniards made him a hero, however, when they invaded in one of the worst-planned campaigns in history, landing a small army at Tampico in 1829. Once the army was ashore the ships sailed away, depriving the ground force of support and supplies. The campaign occurred at the opening of the plague season in Mexico's coastal lowlands, the *vómito negro* (literally "black vomit," yellow fever). Santa Anna happened to be marching in that direction with troops mostly from the fever belt in Vera Cruz and Jalapa, so they were resistant. The surviving Spaniards were in no condition to fight, and surrendered and went home on October 28. Santa Anna was instantly a great national hero, although he had not done much, because his victory was achieved by the combination of Spanish incompetence and the *vómito*.[49]

That ended the last Spanish attempt to retake a country determined to remain independent. Tributes piled up on Santa Anna's vain shoulders— his uniforms became steadily more gaudy, and always in step with fashion, he replaced the tousle on his head with a wavy pompadour and sideburns. Congress struck a medal in his honor inscribed "At Tampico he defeated Spanish arrogance," and formally named him *Benemérito de la Patria* (an honor to the fatherland). That sort of thing suited the "Savior of His Country," as he was also called, and from then on Santa Anna habitually bestowed honors and titles on himself. He signed a routine document in 1853 as "Santa Anna, Savior of the Fatherland, General of Division, Knight of the Great Cross of the Royal and Distinguished Spanish Order of Charles III, President of the Mexican Republic, Grand Master of the National and Distinguished Order of Guadalupe."[50]

The other factor that fostered Santa Anna's rise to the top was the continuing factionalism between conservatives (mostly centralists) and liberals (mostly federalists). They were not parties in the North American sense, and it is easy to oversimplify what the factional labels meant. Conservatives favored a society based on hierarchy, tradition, and authority, and opposed political ideas that threatened to weaken differences between social classes or the privileges of the Church and the military. The liberals

were a more complicated bunch, although in general they favored constitutional government with freedoms of press, speech, and association,
along with a variety of social reforms to reduce or eliminate the *fueros* of
the Church and army. They divided into two groups, *moderados* (moderates) and *puros* (purists). The *moderados* favored a gradual reduction in the
power and wealth of the Church. The *puros* wanted to transform Mexican
society top to bottom, with a wide suffrage and various other social reforms.

Santa Anna was an opportunist, all things to all people. He earned his
credentials as a *puro* in 1828, when *moderado* Manuel Gómez Pedraza was
elected president by a small margin over former guerrilla master Vicente
Guerrero, a *puro*—really an illiterate peasant dressed up in a dazzling uniform. He was an old ally, so Santa Anna gave his friend a hand. He organized several riots to protest the electoral outcome, then started a bloody
military coup. Gómez Pedraza, to make the story short, was out, and
Guerrero became minister of war until named president in January
1829.[51]

This blatant trampling of republican principles sent waves of disgust
throughout the Western Hemisphere. Simón Bolívar, liberator of northern South America, declared his outrage. "The casual right to usurpation
and pillage has enthroned itself as King in the capital of México," he
roared, "and in the provinces of the Federation. A barbarian from the
southern coast [Guerrero] . . . has climbed over two thousand corpses, at
the cost of twenty million pesos seized from private ownership." He
blamed it all on "Santa Anna, the most perverse of mortals," and wailed,
"What men or what demons they are!"[52]

Santa Anna had become an international symbol of the sorriest legacy
of Spanish colonialism—a passel of new countries unable to govern
themselves in a civilized manner. He backed the wrong horse in another
coup soon after his victory at Tampico, and earned himself an official exile
at Manga de Clavo. He shed no tears when Guerrero was overthrown and
put in front of a firing squad in early 1831.[53]

Guerrero had been betrayed and replaced by his vice president,
General Anastasio Bustamante, a rock-hard conservative who imposed a
military dictatorship. Santa Anna struck up a partnership with Valentín
Gómez Farías, an extreme *puro* locked in a vicious feud with *moderado*
Gómez Pedraza. Gómez Farías had the solemn face and demeanor of an
undertaker, with the eyes of an injured deer. A small man with a meek appearance, he harbored a fierce hatred of the Church and a strong urge to
remove the army from political power. Where Santa Anna's principles
were adaptable, Gómez Farías' were unbending. Santa Anna wanted power

for his own sake, but Gómez Farías saw it as a tool to turn his country into a democratic republic.[54]

Santa Anna ran for president and Gómez Farías for vice president on one of Mexico's first political tickets, that of the Liberal Party. Having overthrown Bustamante in late 1832, they won early in 1833 by a whopping majority of state legislatures, who still elected the president. Having become president, however, Santa Anna lost interest. He retired to his hacienda and did not even attend his inauguration. Gómez Farías, as interim president, implemented his radical program, including a wholesale assault on the *fueros* of the army and the Church.

The army, the clergy, and the aristocrats rose up in outrage. One general raised a rebellion under the banner *Religión y Fueros*, another general marched against him, and the two united in common cause against the government. They then did something that could happen only in Mexico—they proclaimed Santa Anna the "supreme dictator" of the country, meaning that President Santa Anna was part of a *cuartelazo* against President Santa Anna. In June 1833 he issued a "manifesto" supporting Gómez Farías' reform program. "I detest military dictatorship," he declared, so he would be a peacemaker "between the belligerent parties, to listen to their complaints and to establish myself as the peaceful arbitrator of their disagreements." Santa Anna the actor was always playing a role, striking a pose.[55]

The uproar over Gómez Farías' attempts to reform the country could not be ignored. José María Tornel talked Santa Anna into riding the wave of conservative outrage. It took nearly a year, until in April 1834 Santa Anna assumed his office and shoved Gómez Farías aside. They had been elected as liberal federalists, but now Santa Anna instituted authoritarian rule, and with Tornel doing the engineering arranged for the installation of a centralist Congress in January 1835. The Constitution of 1824 soon went out the door and the former liberal Santa Anna was dictator.[56]

He was not really interested in all that. Instead, he catered to his own vanity, surrounded himself with large bodyguards, rode around in gold-plated carriages, chased women, and above all conducted cockfights. He tired of the presidency and left it in 1835. From May 1833 to August 1855 the presidency changed hands thirty-six times.[57]

The centralism Santa Anna installed caused rebellion, especially among state governments. His successor as president gave him what he wanted most—command of a national army with orders to put down the uprisings. Two were of the greatest concern. First Santa Anna would stomp out the one in Zacatecas, then he would settle accounts with those impudent *Gringos* who had raised their own revolution in Texas.

THERE CAN BE NO CONCESSION OR COMPROMISE

(1835–1845)

As [Santa Anna's] men had fought and conquered,
they had a right to be called soldiers; but certainly heroes exhibiting
so unmilitary and extraordinary an appearance, I have never witnessed
before. They were attired in shreds and patches formed of
every color in the rainbow. Some had no uniforms at all.

—Henry Tudor

THE UNITED STATES NAVY'S PACIFIC SQUADRON hove to in the sparkling waters off Monterey, California, on October 19, 1842. Towns-people gathered to wonder at this visitation. Commodore Thomas ap Catesby Jones surveyed the scattering of adobe houses strung along dirt streets radiating from the waterfront, framed by green-and-brown hills and mountains rising in a protective arc inland. Jones was about to make history, the first conquest of a foreign port by United States forces in wartime. The commodore was fifty-two years old, a spare man with a leathery face reflecting a life at sea. He had commanded a gunboat during the Battle of New Orleans in 1815 and since then had commanded ships and flotillas wherever his navy sailed. Jones had seen copies of diplomatic exchanges between Mexico and the United States suggesting that war was imminent. He also knew that his government feared that France or Britain had designs on California. A clipping from a Mexican newspaper said that a war really had started. Jones planned to take California.

Jones ordered his guns to fire a few rounds. The crowd on shore cheered, because the governor, General Manuel Micheltorena, told the people that the *yanqui* sailors were saluting. A ship's boat flying the Stars and Stripes headed ashore, and the portly governor drew his sword in order to salute in return. A young officer stepped out of the boat and read a statement declaring that a state of war existed between his country and Mexico. The United States Navy was taking possession of the port of Monterey and demanded its surrender. The governor said that there was no war that he had heard of, and he must confer with his council before answering the summons. A party of sailors and marines landed the next morning, the demand was renewed, and the governor surrendered to the overwhelming naval power. The Mexican flag came down, the United States flag rose, and the marines began patrolling a very friendly place. Jones received a dispatch that night informing him there was no war. The next morning he apologized and returned Monterey to its own leaders in a ceremony oiled by many toasts of brandy. Jones' ship fired a real salute, this time to the Mexican flag, the happy people of Monterey waved good-bye, and the Pacific Squadron weighed anchor and headed out.[1]

MY CANNON WILL ESTABLISH THE BOUNDARY BETWEEN MEXICO AND THE UNITED STATES

Santa Anna had Mexico's government in hand by January 1835, with a compliant Congress carrying out Tornel's plans. The main project was to replace the Constitution of 1824 with the Bases of the Reorganization of the Mexican Nation, also called the Seven Laws. This put Mexico under a military dictator; states became military departments, and the president picked their commanders.[2]

Santa Anna reached out for absolute power. He had a new national army under him, and he all but abolished the state militias. The governor of Zacatecas rose up and mustered about 5,000 poorly armed and untrained militia in defiance. Other states and territories followed suit, including Yucatán and Texas. One of Santa Anna's defenders claimed that the Texas troublemakers used his actions as "a pretext for their insurrection, to which they were already disposed."[3]

Santa Anna marched out of Mexico City in April 1835 with an army of about 3,400, assisted by Generals Martín Perfecto de Cos and Juan José Andrade. Andrade marched into the city of Zacatecas and told the governor, Francisco García, that he had abandoned Santa Anna and would fight alongside his federalist allies. The governor believed him. Santa Anna and the main body arrived in front of the city on May 10 and demanded its surrender. Rebuffed, he attacked García's army the next morning, Andrade striking in the rear. Santa Anna's forces slaughtered 2,000 rebels and captured another 2,700, losing just 100 men in the bargain. The Savior of His Country told his men to pillage the rich mining city. Dispatching Cos to Texas to put things right there, he cut a swath of terror through Querétaro, Jalisco, and Michoacán. Yucatán quieted down and only Texas defended the 1824 Constitution.[4]

After Santa Anna's bloody suppression of the other state rebellions, the people of Texas raised the Mexican flag with "1824" emblazoned across it, called up their militia, rose up in San Antonio and sent Cos packing, and in late 1835 prepared to meet an invasion from the south.[5]

The "Texians," as the rebels called themselves (others called them Texicans, Texans, or *Tejanos*), were mostly Anglos from the United States, with substantial Mexican and German minorities. "If the North Americans do not behave themselves," Santa Anna told the French ambassador, "I will march across their country and plant the Mexican flag in Washington."[6]

Santa Anna later described himself as furious at the "usurpation" of Mexican territory by the United States. As "chief executive of the government," he declared that he would "maintain the territorial integrity whatever the cost. . . . I took pride in being the first to strike in defense of the independence, honor, and rights of my nation." This vainglorious *caudillo* all but guaranteed that a provincial rebellion would turn into a war of independence and his country into an implacable enemy of the United States.[7]

Forcing loans from several states and taking out a mortgage on Manga de Clavo, Santa Anna moved to San Luis Potosí late in 1835 and built a 6,000-man army from scratch. "The government of the United States," he told an audience of foreign and Mexican dignitaries in San Luis, "is responsible for the disturbances" in Texas. "I personally will march forth to subdue the rebels, and, once this is done, my cannon will establish the boundary between Mexico and the United States."[8]

Santa Anna treated the rebels in Texas as filibusters rather than Mexican citizens—and he had not been any too kind to the latter when they rebelled. His government issued the "Tornel Decree," named for its author, then minister of war, on December 30, 1835. Alleging that money, men, and arms from the United States were pouring into Mexico, it declared: "Foreigners landing on the coast of the republic or invading its territory by land, armed with the intention of attacking our country, will be deemed pirates and dealt with as such." It was a license to murder prisoners.[9]

President Andrew Jackson was taken by surprise at the growth of the violence in Texas. Santa Anna's outbursts and diplomatic protests against North American interference in Mexican affairs startled him. He told the Mexican minister that his government had no control over its citizens outside the country's borders. He formally declared neutrality toward the Texas revolt, which he called a purely internal Mexican dispute. Jackson was as good as his word, ordering the navy not to help the Texians.[10]

Santa Anna set off for Texas at the end of 1835 leading his poorly clad, ill-shod, worse-fed, and mostly untrained army through snow and sleet over very rough country. Those few soldiers who had actually fired their muskets flinched when they did so, because Mexican ordnance officers charged the cartridges with double the usual measure of powder. The recoil was punishing, so aim was bad. This hungry, thirsty, exhausted, strung-out mob of bad shots straggled into San Antonio de Béxar in February 1836. They found about 180 Texians forted up in an old mission outside town called the Alamo. Commanded by Colonel William Barrett Travis, they were under orders from General Sam Houston to demolish the place and get out. Travis, a young lawyer, defied the order. Also with him were Colonel James Bowie, inventor of the bowie knife and a Mexican *hacendado* with well-connected in-laws, and (the place was thick with colonels) Colonel David Crockett, former congressman from Tennessee. The risk of offending world opinion if celebrities were killed should have given Santa Anna pause. It did not. After besieging the Alamo for the better part of two weeks, he announced by bugle call that the coming battle would be to the death; the Texians did not recognize the music. The Mexican troops stormed the place before dawn on March 6, killing most of the defenders and capturing about a half dozen, including Crockett. They were put to the sword.[11]

Ending the action without prisoners caused the word "massacre" to pop up in newspapers across North America. Colonel James W. Fannin— who also had disobeyed an order to evacuate his post—found himself later in March surrounded near Goliad by troops under General José Urrea. Assured that he and his men would be treated as prisoners of war, Fannin surrendered. Urrea wrote to Santa Anna urging clemency, then marched off and left Lieutenant Colonel Nicolás de la Portilla in charge of the 365 prisoners. Santa Anna reminded Portilla on March 23 about the Tornel Decree and flatly ordered the colonel to slaughter the Texians. The young officer anguished over this order when he got it on the twenty-sixth, and that night got another message from Urrea telling him to treat the Texians well. "What a cruel contrast in these opposite instructions!" he wailed. But at dawn on the twenty-seventh he ordered his men to "carry out the orders of the supreme government and the general-in-chief." It became known as the Goliad Massacre.[12]

This atrocity inflamed the men marching under Sam Houston. He led his enemy on a chase armchair generals called "the Great Skedaddle," tiring Santa Anna's men, scattering them in detachments while their supply line stretched thin. Houston with 910 men caught Santa Anna and more than 1,300 soldiers literally napping at San Jacinto (near present Houston) on April 21. His troops overran the Mexican camp, with great loss (630 killed, 730 captured) on the Mexican side, very little (9 dead, 30 wounded) on the Texian. Santa Anna hid out in the brush until the Texians found him the next day. Texas had declared independence on March 3 and had a government. Vice President Lorenzo de Zavala negotiated two treaties between Santa Anna and the Republic of Texas. One was public, ending hostilities, providing for prisoner exchanges, and ordering the Mexican army back across the Río Bravo. The other treaty was secret, but not for long. In return for safe passage to Vera Cruz, Santa Anna promised to talk the Mexican government into recognizing the independence of Texas. Both treaties were disavowed by the Mexican Congress.[13]

Houston kept Santa Anna prisoner in Texas until Jackson invited the Mexican general to Washington. Jackson had wanted to gain Texas for the United States, not to see another independent state on the continent. He gave Santa Anna a courteous reception in the fall of 1836 and suggested that Mexico could settle the Texas question in a deal that included $3.5 million and the United States' acquisition of California.[14]

Most Mexican politicians believed that their country was under attack from the north. The Texas rebellion was a *yanqui* plot, and such events in Mexico as the scrapping of the Constitution or Santa Anna's beastly behavior had nothing to do with it. The man himself was back at Manga de Clavo by the end of the year. "I was disillusioned and resentful," he said later. "It seemed that my country had abandoned me to my enemies." Santa Anna refused to accept responsibility for the loss of Texas, claiming his soldiers were inexperienced, tired, hungry, worn out by the march. He even blamed the venerable custom of siesta (the midday nap) as the reason Houston caught him asleep. "I never thought that a moment of rest . . . could be so disastrous."[15]

YET THE FORMER GRIEVANCE WAS UNREDRESSED

Jackson continued to treat Texas as an internal Mexican affair and delayed recognizing the Republic of Texas until March 1837. European powers were even slower to follow suit—nobody but the Texians wanted a third independent nation in North America. In April 1836 Jackson replaced

Butler in Mexico City with Powhatan Ellis, a federal judge no more qualified to be a diplomat than Butler. Ellis had only one instruction—step up
the demands that Mexico settle the claims against it for damages to United
States citizens. This was interpreted on the Mexican side as a cynical attempt to weaken the country's position just as it prepared to take another
stab at Texas. Minister of Foreign Relations Luis Gonzaga Cuevas tried to
mollify Ellis, but the North American envoy belligerently provoked him.[16]

The claims issue, not Texas, became the chief source of friction between the two nations. The diplomatic principle was that if a citizen of
one country suffered damages at the hands of another, he asked his
government to press his case against the other. The administration of
Jackson's successor, Martin Van Buren, assembled a package of fifty-seven
damage claims totaling over $6 million in 1837, which Mexico took as a
diplomatic insult. When Van Buren told the United States Congress that he
saw "little reason to hope" that the issues between the countries would be
resolved, the Mexican minister, Francisco Pizarro Martínez, declared that
his continued presence in Washington had "no practical utility." He went
home "to the bosom of my family."[17]

Any hope of settling the issue was squashed by Mexican intransigence
and by the United States' refusal to recognize any claims against it on the
part of Mexico. Mexico City was incapable of controlling its lower and
state officials, and power at the top changed hands often. United States
leaders persisted in badgering nominal heads of state who felt no duty to
assume blame for what had happened during previous governments. If
Anglo officials had considered the realities, they could have advised their
citizens that they traded in Mexico at their own risk. Instead, the claims
continued to pile up.[18]

"The conduct of the Mexican government towards the American
claimants . . . has been the most infamously perfidious ever practiced by
one country and submitted to by another," groused the *New Orleans
Picayune* in 1842. It was not North Americans alone who were affected. "In
Mexico British Subjects have been oppressed, harassed, and maltreated
without redress except that which has been extorted by unceasing remon-
strance," reported Her Majesty's Foreign Office in 1844. Other nations
agreed.[19]

Economic depression in the United States after 1837 caused the Van
Buren administration to moderate its harsh tone toward Mexico. Other
developments also pushed the two countries into compromise. One was
the establishment of the International Claims Convention. Another was
the appointment of a Whig politician from South Carolina, Waddy
Thompson, as minister to Mexico City—the first diplomatic diplomat the

United States had sent there. He supported the Mexican government's desire, under an arbitration agreement the two countries reached in 1838, to
submit the claims to international arbitration. Many of the claims were
phony. A tribunal of Latin American governments pored through the $6
million worth of claims until 1842, when it awarded just over $2 million
to North American claimants. In 1843 Mexico agreed to pay the full award
in quarterly installments over five years. After just four payments, Mexico
defaulted in 1844 because its treasury was empty. United States politicians
suggested that Mexico could solve its financial problems by selling part of
its territory, and were answered with outrage.[20]

Other nations had claims against Mexico. One of them was France,
and thanks to its way of enforcing its demands Santa Anna returned to the
bosom of his fatherland.

THE HEART AND SOUL OF THIS EMPORIUM OF CONFUSION AND LICENTIOUSNESS

A bunch of Mexican soldiers went on a drunken spree in 1833 and destroyed a French-owned bakery, damages estimated at 800 pesos. The
French government protested, then combined the pastry chef's figure
with other claims and interest, and presented a bill for 60,000 pesos. In
March 1838 a French fleet and army showed up off Vera Cruz and bombarded San Juan de Ullúa. The garrison bailed out of the place and French
troops moved in. So began "the Pastry War."[21]

The war stalled until late in the fall when French troops began operating against Vera Cruz. Mexico City called on the Savior of His Country,
who arrived with a party of troops on December 5. Santa Anna waved his
sword and the French answered with a cannonball, smashing his left leg
below the knee; it was amputated soon afterward. In the national dog-
house since San Jacinto, Santa Anna was a hero again. The Pastry War was
over, and French troops left in March 1839 after the Mexican government
agreed to settle the French claims. The bill was never paid.[22]

Santa Anna became president for the fifth time and was in and out of that
office over the next six years. He was up to his old tricks all the while. To
the wife of the Spanish ambassador, "it seemed like a game of chess, in which
the kings, castles, knights, and bishops are making different moves, while the
pawns look on without taking part in the game." Everything was stage-
managed, said another awed observer, so that Santa Anna would be begged
to do "whatever he considered to be best for the happiness of the nation."[23]

Enormous balls and banquets were staged in Santa Anna's honor. He
built a glorious new theater called the Gran Teatro Santa Anna. His busts

and statues appeared on every street. According to journalist Guillermo Prieto, "The most remarkable thing was the way those who believed themselves to be men of principle would change their colors at a whim. Although this was due in large part to their ignorance, it was also due to Santa Anna, who was a Proteus, assuming all shapes and enlisting under all banners." Historian Justo Sierra said that the rich, by "their selfishness and cowardice, were almost wholly withdrawn from public affairs." Beneath them, the "bureaucrats served those who paid them, and . . . plotted with deadly, unrelenting solidarity against those who failed to pay them." Together, the army—Santa Anna sold 12,000 officer commissions in the early 1840s—and the Church dominated everything.[24]

While Santa Anna was temporarily out of the presidency, several regional uprisings spilled into Mexico City during the summer of 1841, in revolt against Anastasio Bustamante, a hawk-faced, weak-willed *caudillo* whose vacillations created a vacuum at the top. Musketry and artillery smashed up the city for twelve days while criminal gangs looted everything they could grab. Inevitably Santa Anna was called back into office. Besides political uprisings, Mexico faced repeated agrarian revolts by aggrieved *Indios,* each one put down by slaughter. National income never matched outgoes; industry and commerce were stagnant or declining. Santa Anna changed the value of the peso, exacted forced loans, voluntary loans, foreign loans, seized properties, and laid new luxury taxes. He sold many of the country's silver mines to British investors and instituted a poll tax. Expenditures still ran double the government's income.[25]

Exploiting the chaos, *Indios bárbaros* from the north raided into the "civilized" parts of the country, bandits and militias stormed back and forth between Mexico and Texas, and illegal Anglo immigrants increased their stake in New Mexico and California. Merchant caravans on the Santa Fe and Chihuahua trails turned themselves into rolling forts to stave off marauders. Travel between Mexico City and Vera Cruz became nearly impossible, the road lined with bodies, blood, and burned carriages.[26]

Santa Anna was no longer the dashing young officer of earlier days, and he grew a noticeable paunch. His face was puffy and sagging, reflecting his intake of opium and alcohol. The sideburns were gone and his thinning locks were combed back from a receding hairline. Yet he remained attractive to women. The wife of the Spanish ambassador called him "gentlemanly, good-looking, quietly-dressed, rather melancholy-looking." Another foreigner said, "There is no ferocity, vindictiveness or ill-temper in his expression." This dissipated cutthroat could still fool those who wanted to be fooled.[27]

Santa Anna had abandoned the last decency left in his character. As the "Napoleon of the West," he traded his fancy uniforms for Napoleonic simplicity and made the other generals wear scarlet to exaggerate the effect. Six colonels attended his chair when he dined. He robbed the treasury to put on parades, fiestas, and cannonades. Santa Anna's most wretched excess came in 1842, when he ordered his lost leg dug up from its grave at Manga de Clavo. It was paraded through Mexico City in a fancy coffin and installed in a great urn atop a huge stone pillar in the cemetery of Santa Fe. The daylong festival praised Santa Anna for giving his leg to the fatherland. He followed this with the erection of a gigantic statue of himself, arm raised and pointing toward Texas.[28]

Santa Anna's consuming passion was cockfighting, and the real seat of government was in the cockpits of San Agustin de las Cuevas. Prieto called him "the heart and soul of this emporium of confusion and licentiousness. He was something to see at the fights, surrounded by the leading loan sharks of the city, taking the money of others, mingling with employees and even junior officers. He borrowed money but did not repay it, was praised for contemptible tricks as if they were charming manners."[29]

A little affair brought Santa Anna down. His wife, Doña Inés García de Santa Anna, died in Puebla on August 13, 1844, age thirty-three. She had given him four children, alongside at least five bastards he acknowledged by other women. Forty-one days after his wife's death Santa Anna, age fifty, married fifteen-year-old Señorita María Dolores Tosta. He sent a proxy to stand in for him at the wedding in Mexico City, while he lazed at Manga de Clavo. The country was outraged.[30]

Mobs smashed all the statues of Santa Anna they could find in December 1844, then stormed the cemetery and, according to Prieto, "with savage ferocity exhumed Santa Anna's leg, playing games with it and making it an object of ridicule." Congress condemned the Savior of His Country, and one general after another came out against him. It was all over by the end of the year. Rather than take the opportunity to shoot him, however, temporary president General José Joaquín de Herrera exiled Santa Anna in the spring of 1845, "for life." Supposed to go to Venezuela, instead he went to Cuba.[31]

ETERNAL WAR AGAINST *TEJANOS* AND THE
BARBAROUS COMANCHES!

John Louis O'Sullivan was a man with a gift for a phrase. In the July–August 1845 edition of his *United States Magazine and Democratic Review,* with Santa Anna in Cuba, Sullivan declared of the United States, "Our manifest destiny is to overspread the continent allotted by Providence for the free development of our yearly multiplying millions." He echoed this in the December 27 edition of the *New York Morning News,* justifying the United States' claim to Oregon "by the right of our *manifest destiny* to over-spread and to possess the whole of the continent." [32]

Sullivan did not declare a holy war to put the continent under the United States flag. Instead, he predicted that that would happen by the logic of history. The remarks reflected blossoming nationalism combined with missionary zeal. The North American way of life, this view held, was so obviously superior that all others must sooner or later adopt it. Manifest destiny was not an official policy of the government, just a popular sentiment. [33]

Mexicans never saw it that way. They believed that the United States had a plan to take over all of North America. The *Yanquis,* so it was said, justified this by a self-assumed superiority over others with different ways of life. A plot to conquer Mexico began with the Louisiana Purchase in 1803—or even, some believed, with the settlement of Jamestown in 1607. [34]

Foreigners could not understand why Mexico refused to accept the loss of Texas. Mexico had declared its own independence from Spain and maintained it through years of attempted reconquest, so it made no sense to deny that Texas was gone. Mexicans, however, did not accept the idea that Texians had rebelled for reasons of their own. "The Mexican Republic," said Ramón Alcaraz in 1848, "offered an easy prey for whoever could exert a respectable force against it." The United States simply took Texas. [35]

Mexicans had grounds to believe that the North American government was behind the loss of Texas. Southern politicians said that Texas offered an opportunity to add slaveholding states to the United States, while their opponents charged that the "slave power" wanted to do just that. The independent Texians were good propagandists, reminding the world about the Alamo and Goliad. Presidents Jackson and Van Buren rejected any calls to annex Texas, but Mexicans doubted their honesty. Van Buren recognized the Republic of Texas in 1837 and Mexicans saw that, according to the British minister to Mexico, "as the consummation of a design long since entertained" to rob her of Texas, igniting a "bitter animosity" that no reason could mitigate. [36]

If there was Anglo expansionism involved in what happened next, it was on the part of Texas, not the United States, although the Mexicans did not see the distinction. The Texas Congress declared in December 1836 that the country's border was along the Rio Grande all the way to its source (in present Colorado), then north to the forty-second parallel,

then east to the border of Louisiana Territory. The sole justification for this
was Santa Anna's agreement after San Jacinto to withdraw troops across
the Río Bravo. The British consul in Texas warned the foreign secretary
that the boundary claim "would embrace a large extent of territory *not before belonging to Texas.*"[37]

After France (1839) and Britain (1840) recognized the Republic of
Texas, British diplomacy in both Texas and Mexico aroused fears in the
United States that Britain aimed to acquire territory in both countries. In
reality, the Britons desired trade positions rather than territory, and
wanted to keep the peace. They tried to talk Mexico into recognizing
Texian independence, and Texas into abolishing the slave trade.[38]

Considering that Texas was under increasing attack from Comanche
and Kiowa raiders, it seems remarkable that the Texians would court trouble with their neighbor. That they did, both sides fighting on land and sea
for years. They raided each other's coasts and commerce, and when their
warships collided the Mexicans usually won.[39]

The hatred between the two countries was tribal and accordingly
bloody. The conflict focused on the land between the Rio Grande and the
Nueces River, a wilderness later called the "Nueces Strip." It was dominated by bandit gangs that raided across the area and beyond both rivers.
The forces were small, a few hundred on each side, and their impact was
more psychological than physical. When raiding *Indios bárbaros* added
themselves to the mix, Mexicans complained that the tribes were urged on
by Texas, and Texians made the reverse claim against Mexico.[40]

Both countries accomplished nothing more than spilling blood, and
British efforts to mediate appeared likely to pay off by 1840. Mexican
leaders generally concluded that recognizing Texian independence might
avoid more serious dangers posed by the United States. Prompted by British
diplomats, Texas sent an envoy to Mexico City to negotiate. Given the
general unpopularity of catering to the "ungrateful" Texians, everything
had to be kept quiet if there was to be any hope of a settlement.

A commission headed by Lucas Alamán assembled to formulate a new
policy toward Texas. His group admitted that it could not "hide all the difficulties" that accompanied recognizing Texas, which would "open the
door increasingly to the undertakings of the insatiable Anglosaxon invaders." The panel concluded that a war with the United States would happen sooner or later, so it advised the Council of Government to consider
opening negotiations with Texas. Terms should include keeping Texas
within its "established boundaries," meaning the Río Nueces. Texas would
guarantee not to annex itself to another country; it would indemnify
Mexican citizens for their losses, in particular lands expropriated by Texas

authorities; and it would stop Indian attacks on Mexico mounted from Texas. The council declined to act, and punted the matter to Congress. Word leaked to the press, and the Texas question became untouchable again.[41]

"Peace! Peace! Eternal peace among Mexicans! War! War! Eternal war against *Tejanos* and the barbarous Comanches!" So roared General Mariano Arista, who expressed his country's sentiments perfectly early in 1841. As it happened, however, the Texians mounted the first major campaign.[42]

Texas troops scored a significant victory over the Comanches in 1841. This emboldened the president of Texas, Mirabeau Buonaparte Lamar, who set out to create a Texian empire on the Rio Grande. The republic was broke, and Lamar saw riches in diverting the Santa Fe trade from Missouri to Galveston. The "Texan–Santa Fe Expedition" of 1841 was a hare-brained project. A trading caravan of fifty-one wagoneers, 270 volunteer soldiers, and three commissioners set out on a beeline for Santa Fe in blistering weather over difficult country. Heat and thirst took a heavy toll. Mexican troops found the survivors east of Santa Fe and herded them into the capital. The prisoners appealed to the United States consul, Manuel Álvarez, but he could do nothing for them because they were not citizens of the United States. He watched the Texians trudge out in chains through a jeering mob and onto the road south.

The Texas party included George Wilkins Kendall, editor of the *New Orleans Picayune*. He claimed to be a neutral observer, but the authorities shackled him with the rest. The first stretch of travel, downriver to El Paso del Norte (present-day Juárez, Chihuahua), was horrible, made worse by a sadistic Mexican army officer and a lack of food, water, or rest. Those who fell behind were bayoneted, their ears cut off and strung on a cord. The prisoners ended up at Perote Castle, a prison fortress east of Mexico City. Santa Anna, hoping to improve relations with the United States, released all but one of the captives in the spring of 1842. The exception was José Antonio Navarro, a signer of the Texas declaration of independence, who got loose in 1844.[43]

North American newspapers were full of lurid complaints about Mexican "abuses" and "atrocities." Santa Anna decided that the Texas government was unsettled enough that the time had come for an all-out war. The Napoleon of the West began with a reconnaissance in force in March 1842. Mexican troops had formerly been content to show the flag on the south bank of the Nueces with small patrols. This time about 700 men penetrated all the way to San Antonio. Most Anglos fled at his approach, which sparked panic all over central Texas. The Mexicans bagged a few prisoners, plundered San Antonio, and retired to the Río Bravo.[44]

If the intent was to intimidate Texians and their North American supporters, it backfired, as money, arms, and volunteers poured into Texas. Santa Anna countered with a diplomatic offensive—against the United States. Foreign Minister José María Bocanegra asked Secretary of State Daniel Webster in May 1842 whether the United States could injure Mexico more than it already had, short of declaring war, and then answered his own question: "Certainly not." The foreign minister charged the United States, in a circular to all the diplomatic corps in Mexico City, with aggressions against Mexican territory. Mexico would do whatever was "imperatively required for her honor and dignity." Bocanegra fired another protest at Webster, accusing the United States government of "conduct openly at variance with the most sacred principles of the law of nations." A continuation of that, he threatened, would be regarded by Mexico as "a positive act of hostility."[45]

Webster answered Bocanegra's first letter by denying the charges leveled against his government. The United States would remain neutral in the war between Mexico and Texas, "but the continuance of amity with Mexico cannot be purchased at any higher rate." He answered the second letter by saying that the United States regarded its tone as "highly offensive." President John Tyler had declared that the policy of neutrality would "not be changed or altered in any respect or in any degree."[46]

Bocanegra accepted this "frank declaration." Waddy Thompson, U.S. minister in Mexico City, advised Webster that feelings in Mexico toward the North Americans were "most bitter." The British and Prussian envoys in Mexico told their governments that Bocanegra's notes had driven the two countries to the brink, with the Mexican press thumping the war drums. The British consul in Texas warned, "The most strenuous endeavors have been made . . . to create and fix the impression that Mexico was secretly prompted by England in her persevering hostility to Texas."[47]

Webster tried to defuse the situation in the summer of 1842, asking Thompson to relay his opinion that the continuing war across the Nueces Strip was "not only useless, but hopeless, without attainable object, injurious to both parties." He repeated this advice the following January, but he did not take sufficient notice that the raiding went both ways; his cautions to Texas were guarded. Mexicans saw this as further evidence that the United States was behind it all. "Who is not aware of that criminal connivance, that stubborn and insolent project," howled a Mexico City newspaper, "which—in violation of righteous law and in violation of the treaties with Mexico—is given by the Policy of North America to a Department [Texas] filled with rebels from every land?"[48]

The diplomats of Britain and France were alarmed by the bloodshed on the border. They wanted to check North American "expansionism," but they ran up against Mexico's refusal to accept the loss of Texas. Britain offered to guarantee Mexico's northern border, while advising that that nation's stubbornness could endanger other regions, especially California. The Texian attempt to take New Mexico, followed by naval raids on the Mexican Gulf coast, undercut any attempts at peacemaking.[49]

Aggravating the diplomatic mess was the continued insistence of Texas that its border was the Rio Grande. A British agent in Texas warned his foreign minister that Texian intransigence on that issue killed any hope of peace. "It does not seem possible," he said, "that the Mexicans will be brought to admit the actual Texian demarcation of the western frontier and I *certainly have never discovered upon what former territory the pretention to the line of the río Grande is founded.*"[50]

While the diplomats jawed, the Mexicans and Texians warred. Santa Anna sent another force against San Antonio in September 1842, a thousand men who captured the town and along with it many prominent citizens. This time the Texians were galvanized, and several volunteer battalions flocked to counterattack. There were several sharp skirmishes aggravated by clumsy leadership and murder of prisoners on both sides. The bloodshed and atrocities were horrendous until the Mexicans withdrew after about three weeks. They took along not only the surviving prisoners but also about 200 Mexican-born *Tejanos* who went into uncertain exile in northeast Mexico, while the Texian prisoners ended up in Perote. They were not alone there for long. The Texian volunteers increased in number, and before long there was a sizable army howling for blood. They wanted to invade Mexico, but the Texas government said it could not afford to finance an expedition. Many of the volunteers went home, but diehards decided to march on. They crossed the Rio Grande in December and attacked the town of Mier. Most were captured and marched off toward Perote. They tried a mass escape but were rounded up by Mexican cavalry. Santa Anna ordered that the captives be decimated, meaning one in ten executed. The others enjoyed the hospitality of Perote until released in September 1844, another goodwill gesture from Santa Anna.[51]

This mutually assured bloodshed could not go on forever. British chargé P. W. Doyle reminded Foreign Minister Bocanegra on April 20, 1843, that Texas had been "recognized as an independent nation by the Government of Her Majesty." French minister Alleye de Cyprey echoed him: "The Mexican Cabinet has doubtless overlooked the fact that with respect to France and most of the states of Europe Texas is absolutely in the same position as that in which Mexico was before her independence had been recognized by Spain."[52]

In June 1843 Santa Anna announced a renewed campaign to reannex Texas and defend California, warning that all foreigners taken under arms in Texas would be executed. An exasperated secretary of state declared that United States citizens could not be prevented from serving abroad. If any were captured in Texas, he warned, they must be treated as prisoners of war under international law. "On this point," he concluded, "there can be no concession or compromise."[53]

John Quincy Adams gave a widely reported speech accusing the Tyler administration of plotting to annex Texas in order to enlarge the influence of the "slave power" in Congress. Mexican newspapers took notice, and the theme of *yanqui* depredations against Mexico was on the front pages again. Santa Anna thought he had all the support he needed to continue the fight when Anglo newspapers reported that negotiations had begun to annex Texas. Bocanegra declared on August 23, 1843, that Mexico would consider the conclusion of an accord to annex Texas as "a declaration of war against the Mexican Republic." He left it "to the civilized world to judge the cause of the Mexican people in a struggle they have been far from provoking." His nation was ready to "court the disasters of war to defend her unassailable rights."[54]

For any politician or *caudillo* to even think of giving up Mexico's claims to Texas was impossible. Yet annexation talks between the United States and Texas proceeded, and by its stubbornness Mexico gave up any chance of influencing the outcome—in particular where the border of the disputed province was. Helpless to control events, all the *caudillos* had left in their arsenal was threats. The minister to the United States, Juan Nepomuceno Almonte, told the secretary of state in November 1843 that, should a decision be made to go forward with annexation, he must consider his mission in Washington finished. "My country," he declared, "is resolved to declare war as soon as it receives information of such an act." The North American answered sharply that the United States recognized Texas as an independent nation, with whom it could do what business it chose.[55]

MEXICO HAS NEVER BEEN ABLE TO PROTECT US

Mexico was on the minds of many North Americans by the early 1840s, and not just on account of Texas. Reports of explorers and tales of mountain men pictured what used to be called "the Great American Desert," the western half of the continent, as a spectacular, rich, adventuresome landscape. Anglo emigrants had already staked places for themselves in New Mexico and California, and others were moving to Oregon. It was a vast wonderland, ripe for the taking. Shimmering above all was a new Garden of Eden, California, which leaped suddenly into public consciousness in 1840 when Richard Henry Dana published his *Two Years Before the Mast*. His adventures as a merchant seaman were thrilling enough, but his detailed account of California seized the imagination. Here was a world of forests and furs and limitless room for agriculture.[56]

Alongside the California dreaming that Dana inspired were the five volumes of the *Narrative of the United States Exploring Expedition,* published by Lieutenant Charles Wilkes in 1845, documenting the round-the-world explorations of a United States Navy flotilla from 1838 to 1842. Wilkes described such formerly hidden wonders as Antarctica, but again the west coast of North America tickled the national fancy. The great bays and harbors gripped the attention of sailors, investors, politicians, merchants, and others who saw a gateway to the Orient.[57]

Merchant ships from New England had traded on the California coast since late in the eighteenth century and greatly increased their visits since the 1820s. The first North Americans to arrive overland were a party of fur trappers who entered the territory in 1826. Other parties of bearded Anglo and French Canadian wild men followed through the 1830s. In their wake came a substantial population of United States expatriates in California by the 1840s. Some arrived by sea, others by land, spinning off the migrations to Oregon that began in 1843.[58]

Interest in the west coast exceeded that in Texas. New England shippers monopolized the hide-and-tallow trade, supporting large leather and candle industries at home. In the Democratic Party's Mississippi Valley power base, others looked for overland approaches to the Pacific. For politicians, there was that old enemy England, presumably trying to grab California, although it was not.[59]

The United States Navy established a Pacific squadron in 1839 to protect merchantmen and whalers using California's ports. The U.S. consul reported in 1846 that California's annual exports included 85,000 hides, 1.5 million pounds of tallow, 16,000 bushels of wheat, 1 million board-feet of timber, 20,000 beaver and otter skins, 1,000 barrels of brandy and wine, and 100 ounces of gold. Nearly all of it was shipped out in U.S. bottoms.[60]

The *Californios* were in a constant state of rebellion. They had driven out the Mexican governor in 1836, only to render sullen submission when Micheltorena showed up in 1842 with 300 rowdy troops. He maintained good relations with California's foreigners but not with its Mexicans, because his army was a riotous, drunken pack of thieves. The locals tossed him and his troops out in February 1845, and an expedition to reestablish central control was canceled after the anti-Santanista coup in December 1845. The government recognized the *insurrectos* under Pío Pico as its power in California.[61]

California was filling up with foreigners, most from the United States but others from England, Canada, and mainland Europe. The Mexican government tried to drive them out in 1840, but failed for want of support among *Californios*. The minister of war tried again in July 1843, ordering the governors of all northern provinces to expel U.S. citizens. This earned a protest from Washington, but it had little effect on the scene. President John Tyler wanted to add Texas to the Union, but he was also a California dreamer.[62]

Between the United States and California stood New Mexico. It was closer to Mexico City, but the national government's grip was no stronger. The chaos of Mexican politics prevented any effective administration or defense of the frontier territories, and rebellions against the centralist power were frequent after 1835. "Hopes and promises are only what it [New Mexico] has received . . . from its mother country," complained Mariano Chávez, president of the New Mexico assembly, in 1844. Observed another *Nuevomexicano*: "Mexico has never been able to protect us because, unfortunately, of continuous revolts." Northern Mexicans from Texas to California were thoroughly disgusted with their national government.[63]

How many Anglos had squatted in the northern territories is not known. There were probably several score in New Mexico by 1840, a few hundred in California. Some became Mexican citizens, most did not. The Mexican authorities were on guard against a repetition of what happened in Texas, but the old problem of building a human barrier remained—few Mexicans wanted to be frontier *pobladores*.[64]

The most visible and growing Anglo influence in the north was the expanding commerce over the Santa Fe Trail. More and more ox-drawn caravans made their way to Santa Fe every year, then down the Camino Real to Ciudad Chihuahua. There the merchants sold their cargoes of manufactured goods, and even their cartage and livestock, and headed back to Missouri with Mexican mules loaded with silver. Authorities in Mexico City had never been happy about this trade, partly because it was too distant to rake any graft off it. Santa Anna ordered an end to the commerce out of Missouri in 1843, sparking yet another outcry in the United States. He followed that decree with another prohibiting the import of a wide range of articles, and requiring forfeitures of those already in Mexico if they were not sold within a year. The aim was to drive out the warehouses and trading posts maintained by Anglo merchants. Many of them had well-cultivated friends in Washington, so the secretary of state called these measures "a manifest violation of the liberty of trade" secured by treaty between the two countries. Santa Anna's answer to that was to ban aliens from retail business altogether.[65]

Santa Anna could not have been pleased by the reading tastes of North Americans during the early 1840s. William H. Prescott's *History of the Conquest of Mexico,* published in 1843, ignited fantasies about the adventures of Cortés and the fall of the Aztecs in the early sixteenth century, and inspired the catchphrase "Halls of the Montezumas." Hundreds of copies of it later followed Cortés' route from Vera Cruz to Mexico City, in the knapsacks of officers who saw it as a point of reference for their own adventures in conquest.[66]

WE HAVE NO CHOICE BUT TO GO TO WAR

John Tyler, who read Prescott, personified manifest destiny. The white people of his country, he believed, had a divine mission to carry the blessings of Protestant Christianity and liberty to the lesser peoples of the planet. "I have seen her," he once said of his country, "overturning the strong places of despotism, and restoring to man his long-lost rights." He described himself as the "instrument of Providence," but he was also a Virginia slaveholder who advocated the extension of the southern states' "peculiar institution" across the North American continent.[67]

He was a tall, thin man with an angular face, an aquiline nose, deep-set and thoughtful eyes, jug ears, and a wild shock of hair circling a high brow. Tyler looked stern in his portraits but in person he was a friendly, affectionate—he fathered fifteen children—and humorous man who enjoyed jokes, dancing, champagne, music, and lively parties. He had one of the largest private libraries in the country, knew more than most people did, and behaved accordingly. Tyler became president a month after the inauguration in 1841 when his predecessor, William Henry Harrison, died, making him the first vice president to gain the presidency that way. The Constitution was not clear about succession, but Tyler had himself sworn in immediately, defying everyone to question his legitimacy. Rivals called him "His Accidency." The newly minted president was fifty-one and a founder of the Whig Party.

Tyler surrounded himself with able people, most notably his secretary of state, Daniel Webster. A New England abolitionist, Webster carried out Tyler's expansionist aims so far as they challenged the British Lion in North America. The Webster-Ashburton Treaty of 1842 established the boundary with Canada, and resolved a number of other disputes except for Oregon, which was accorded "joint occupation" until competing claims could be resolved. Webster also concluded a trade pact with China. When Tyler made it clear that he wanted to take Texas into the Union, Webster resigned on principle. Tyler replaced him with his attorney general, Hugh Legare, an old friend from Virginia, who promptly dropped dead at the age of forty-six. The job next went to the secretary of the navy, Abel Upshur, a Virginia judge who agreed with Tyler about everything. He became secretary of state in 1843 and died in a freak accident in 1844. Tyler was therefore his own chief diplomat, and the architect of Texas annexation—to the great alarm of other southerners, in particular John C. Calhoun. That South Carolinian feared that any attempt to extend slavery to the west would irreparably divide the country north from south. He nevertheless agreed to succeed Upshur as secretary of state.

Tyler sent out "confidential agents" to see what was going on in England, Texas, Mexico, and other places, and to make things happen. By the spring of 1844 his spooks in Texas had done their work well, and a treaty of annexation was signed on April 12. Tyler called it a move to confound the designs of the British in Texas. Now was the time to ramp up the pressure on annexation opponents at home, on the British, on any waverers in Texas, and on Mexico. The Mexican minister to Washington, Almonte, went to see Calhoun at about that time, and suggested that his government realized that Texas was lost, and would be willing to accept payment for its claims to the territory to "minimize the misfortune." In the middle of April a package of instructions went out to the United States chargé d'affaires in Mexico City, Benjamin S. Green, telling him to notify Mexican officials that, while feeling an "anxious desire" to continue friendly relations, the United States was compelled for its own security to conclude an annexation treaty with Texas. The Tyler administration, the message said, was aware of Mexican attitudes and was ready to negotiate all difficulties "on the most liberal and satisfactory terms."[68]

Tyler next made sure the Mexicans understood that he was serious. The United States chargé d'affaires in Texas, William J. Murphy, informed Calhoun that the Texas government had asked for troops and ships to protect it pending ratification. Brevet Brigadier General Zachary Taylor was assigned to Fort Jesup, Louisiana, on the Texas border. Commodore David Conner took the Home Squadron to the coast of Mexico and Texas. The ships were off Vera Cruz and Galveston by May. Taylor's orders were slow to arrive, and he began moving troops in June.[69]

The Mexicans were not yet impressed. Green notified the Mexican government on May 30 that Tyler had signed the annexation treaty and sent it to the Senate. Foreign Minister Bocanegra immediately shot back that "Mexico has not renounced, nor ought it to renounce, and it follows that it will not renounce nor in any way cede all or parts of its rights" to Texas. He referred the North American envoy to the ultimatum of August 23, 1843, and repeated that Mexico would consider annexation of Texas to be a declaration of war.[70]

A similar scene played out in Washington when Calhoun notified Minister Almonte about the treaty. Almonte protested, but privately told his foreign minister that he doubted that the Senate would ratify it. Bocanegra told the minister to advise the secretary of state, as he had advised Green, that annexation would be an act of war. Meanwhile, Santa Anna resumed the presidency on June 4 and asked for funds to mount another campaign to retake Texas. He got the money over strong federalist opposition, but word arrived that the Senate had refused to ratify, so the expedition was postponed.[71]

The Senate rejected the annexation treaty on June 8 by a vote of 35–16. Tyler's administration had cast a foul odor with what many people thought were shady maneuvers to bring the treaty about. Northern abolitionists opposed it as an attempt to expand slavery to the west. Tyler had lost a lot of friends in a short space of time—he had failed to gain his party's nomination for reelection in May, the nod going to Henry Clay, no friend of annexation. Not even his own cabinet was of one mind on the issue.[72]

In his reports to Mexico City, Almonte oversimplified what had happened, saying annexation had been discredited as a power grab by the pro-slavery interests, while the forces wanting to restrict slavery were in the ascendance. This fanned a belief in Mexico that the United States would not fight a war with its neighbor. Green warned Bocanegra that the "aggression" Mexico had threatened against Texas would be considered an attack on the United States. One commentator said the *gringo* envoy talked that way either because he truly believed that war was about to begin, "or because he sought an excuse to oblige Mexico to declare war on the United States, making us appear the aggressors."[73]

As always where Texas was concerned, Mexico and the United States talked past each other, like two tribes pounding their spears against their shields. The chief United States spear-carrier, Zachary Taylor, arrived at Fort Jesup on June 17 and notified President Sam Houston that the United States would honor its commitment to protect Texas. Houston also heard from General Adrián Woll, Mexican commander on the Río Bravo, who warned him that he had received orders to resume hostilities against Texas.[74]

Tyler had a powerful ego and a strong sense of his power as president, and he was clever and determined to boot. He sent the annexation treaty to the House of Representatives on June 10, 1844, saying that it could be implemented by joint resolution of the Congress, provided its counterpart in Texas followed suit. That required only a simple majority of both houses.[75]

Santa Anna had never really understood the dimensions of the Texas problem. He had accepted Texas' proposal for an armistice, but nothing came of that after annexation talks began. In November 1844, he accepted conditions offered by the British minister to Mexico, Charles Bankhead, for Mexico to recognize Texas independence, and the country blew up again. General Mariano Paredes y Arrillaga rose against Santa Anna in November, and by December Santa Anna was on his way out. General José Joaquín de Herrera—an unassuming man, for a Mexican *caudillo*—became provisional president. Bankhead went to work on Herrera over the Texas issue, but it remained explosive. Whenever a hint came to light that the power of the moment considered abandoning Texas or dealing with the United States, the streets of Mexico City erupted in fury.[76]

Tyler sent his last annual message to Congress on December 3, 1844, charging that "Mexico has threatened to renew the war, and has either made or proposes to make formidable preparations for invading Texas." Tyler knew that Mexico was in no condition to threaten Texas, let alone the United States, but his tirade fell on willing ears. His political opponents outnumbered his supporters in Congress, but a majority of his opponents also favored acquiring Texas. The president signed the joint resolution on March 1, 1845. It was too bad, he said, that Texas had taken so much time, or he might have gained California also. Now all that was needed was for the Texas Congress to extinguish its own independence and join the Union.[77]

The British government had worked hard to bring things to a happier conclusion. Foreign Minister Lord Aberdeen tried to enlist French help in guaranteeing Mexico's territorial integrity and the independence of Texas. The French were not interested, so he told his minister in Mexico City, Bankhead, to see what he could work out. Bankhead obtained a Mexican acceptance in principle of Texas' independence in January 1845. The British chargé d'affaires in Texas, Charles Elliott, achieved a corresponding response, and late in March the last president of Texas, Anson Jones, agreed to delay annexation. The two countries initialed an agreement in Mexico City on May 17, but time had run out. Tyler's signature on the joint resolution had set the process in motion, Texas went over to the United States in June, and Mexico was mad as hell.[78]

The United States had acquired Texas, but the new state was no prize. The republic was torn by partisan wrangling and the treasury was always empty. Liberal land laws had boosted the population to 100,000 freemen and about 38,000 slaves, but the cashless economy operated on barter. Texians paid no taxes, so no foreign government would offer loans to the republic. The territory was sprawling, its borders were undefined, its people were unkempt and unruly, and all around it were mobs of bandits and Indians who looked on Texians as prey.[79]

The Massachusetts essayist Ralph Waldo Emerson tried to be optimistic when he gazed into the future. "The annexation of Texas looks like one of those events which retard or retrograde the civilization of ages," he wrote in his diary. "But the World Spirit is a good swimmer, and storms and waves cannot easily drown him." In Mexico at the same time, one general told another, "We have no choice but to go to war."[80]

NO DOUBT SHE WILL MAKE SOME NOISE

(March 1845–March 1846)

In War, the first casualty is Truth.

—Thucydides

MARCH 4, 1845, WAS INAUGURATION DAY, and an unrelenting downpour confounded those who wanted spring sunshine for the occasion. Dignitaries and their ladies slogged onto the Capitol grounds mud-splattered and dripping. At the other end of Pennsylvania Avenue the outgoing president, John Tyler, greeted his successor, and the two politicians rode to the Capitol in an open carriage. The new president, of middle height and build, was not an impressive specimen, especially with his gray hair, thrown back from his squarish forehead, plastered to his scalp. He was comparatively young, only fifty, but he had a hard-bitten look. Wrinkles over his whole face surrounded deep creases between his eyes, and canyons ran from his nose to the corners of his mouth, turned down in a permanent frown. His ears were big and his nose was bulbous, but his face was dominated by large, deep-set gray eyes locked into a penetrating stare.

The frown opened and the new president exalted the Union and condemned north-south sectionalism. He promised to lower the tariff and establish an independent treasury. One of his campaign slogans had been "Fifty-four Forty or Fight!"—meaning that all of Oregon belonged to the United States, none to Britain—so his country's title was "clear and unquestionable." The president also celebrated the "reunion" between the United States and Texas. The pending annexation was a purely internal matter, "belonging exclusively to the United States."

When he was through, President James Knox Polk's scowl defied anyone to disagree with him. He and his wife climbed into their carriage and rode down Pennsylvania Avenue to the presidential mansion and a set of dry clothes.[1]

WHO IS JAMES K. POLK?

Polk was born in North Carolina in 1795, the son of a prosperous planter who moved the family to Tennessee in 1803. His grandfather had fought in the American Revolution, and established a family tradition of hostility to everything British. Polk was denied baptism because of a doctrinal dispute between his father and the local preacher, and he became a lifelong foe of religious intolerance. James was not a healthy boy, underweight, weak, and wracked by stomach pains. He was diagnosed with urinary bladder stones when he was seventeen, and surgery was advised. Strapped naked to a table with his legs stretched over his head, the pain numbed only by brandy, Polk endured excruciating torture. The surgeon cut through the peritoneum with a knife, then punctured through the prostate and into the bladder with a pointed instrument; the stones were removed with a scoop. The operation tore ducts, tissues, nerves, and blood vessels, and left Polk sterile and probably impotent.[2]

Polk graduated first in his class at the University of North Carolina in 1818. He read law and passed the bar in 1820, and entered politics. He was elected to the Tennessee House of Representatives in 1823 and two years later began the first of seven terms in Congress. He was an early booster of Andrew Jackson and the Democratic Party. "Old Hickory" took him under his wing, so Polk became known as "Young Hickory." He was a partisan bigot instead of a religious one—Democrats were the only real Americans, he claimed, while the Whigs were stooges for the British.

Polk became Speaker of the House in 1835 and resigned in 1839 to run for governor of Tennessee. He served one term and was twice defeated for reelection. He was nominated for vice president at his party's convention in 1844, but the delegates could not agree on the head of the ticket. Polk emerged after several ballots as the dark horse. Polk's opponents were the Whig Henry Clay, a foe of annexation, and the former Whig John Tyler, nominee of a third party. One of the Whig campaign slogans was "Who is James K. Polk?" They found out when he won 170 electoral votes to Clay's 105. He intended "to be *myself* the president," not the tool of any faction, and he would serve only one term. That was one of the annoying things about him—Polk was as good as his word. He was also pompous, suspicious, secretive, humorless, pedantic, and vindictive, a man who saw enemies under every bed, and whose mind was rigid, narrow, and blinded by partisanship. On the other hand, he was honest, hardworking, and as stubborn as a rock. He knew what he wanted to get done, and labored day and night to do it. George Bancroft recalled that at the start of his presidency Polk told him, "There are four great measures which are to be the measures of my administration: one, a reduction of the tariff; another, the independent treasury; a third, the settlement of the Oregon boundary question; and, lastly, the acquisition of California."[3]

Polk was a frumpy man who wore baggy frock coats with papers stuffed into every pocket. His speech was stiff. "He has no wit," John Quincy Adams said of him, "no literature, no point of argument, no gracefulness of delivery, no elegance of language, no philosophy, no pathos, no felicitous impromptus; nothing that can constitute an orator, but confidence, fluency, and labor."[4]

Polk set out to enlarge his country to the limits, and once his mind was set on that there was no diverting him. His territorial ambitions were naked and unashamed and there was never any hesitation on ethical grounds. Texas was not among his "four great measures," because as far as he was concerned, the Texas question had been settled.

VICTORY WILL PERCH UPON OUR BANNERS

Daniel Webster told his son after annexation that he had "no doubt" that the new president and his cabinet would try to keep peace with Mexico. "The responsibility of having provoked war by their scheme of annexation is what they would greatly dread." Webster did not know Polk.[5]

Polk never established an intelligence operation. He decided that Mexico must see the wisdom of his proposals. His consul at Tampico warned that all of Mexico harbored "the most stubborn and malignant feeling" against the United States, but he ignored the warning. Wishful thinking, however, found a receptive ear. The consul at Mexico City said he could not predict the country's reaction to annexation, although "no doubt she will make some noise." He did not think that any Mexican leaders had "any serious idea of carrying on any kind of war against us." All communications between the Polk administration and the Mexican government were one-way. Polk talked *at* the other side and had no interest in what it had to say.[6]

Polk's counterpart in Mexico was a man who could be dealt with, but his position was vulnerable. The interim president, General José Joaquín de Herrera, a former druggist turned soldier, was a barrel-chested man with slicked-back hair, a low brow, sad eyes, and a firm jaw. He had the look of honesty and reason written all over him, but he had little education. Herrera thought that Texas was lost and that the United States was using it to provoke his country into a war it could not win. To mollify those on his right, he repeated his country's claims to Texas and threatened war. To avoid war, he followed British advice and quietly offered conditions for negotiations.[7]

Herrera's government did not make it easy to conduct peaceful relations. The minister in Washington, Almonte, called annexation "an act of aggression, the most unjust which can be found in the annals of modern history." Mexico, he vowed, would maintain its claim to Texas "at all times, by every means." Secretary of State James Buchanan tried to pacify him, but Almonte demanded his passports and went home.[8]

Polk still had to get annexation completed in Texas, while British agents tried to get Mexico to accept Texian independence and Texas to back out of annexation. Texas' secretary of state offered preliminary terms for a treaty with Mexico on March 29, 1845. The government of Mexico agreed to the terms in mid-May, unless Texas joined the United States.[9]

This gave rise to a false belief in Washington that Mexico took orders from Britain. It also threatened to unhorse annexation. A show of force seemed in order, so in late March Commodore David Conner of the navy's Home Squadron was ordered to take station off Vera Cruz. Another flotilla under Commodore Robert F. Stockton was sent to Galveston early in April.[10]

Conner, a fifty-three-year-old Pennsylvanian, was a thorough professional in a service dominated by hacks. He had earned two congressional medals for bravery during the War of 1812 and had held various overseas and stateside commands. He was a handsome man with a long face and nose, a high brow, penetrating eyes, and glorious muttonchop whiskers. He was very slender, even frail, owing to long service in the tropics. Secretary of the Navy George Bancroft wanted to replace him on grounds of health, but Conner did not want to step down while affairs with Mexico were unsettled.[11]

Stockton, fifty years old, was from a rich New Jersey family. He had been in the navy since 1811. He went to England in 1837 to learn from nautical engineer John Ericsson about screw propulsion for steam warships and about new kinds of big guns. Stockton stole Ericsson's ideas, made some ill-conceived modifications, and talked Congress into authorizing USS *Princeton* and its new gun, which he called "Peacemaker." The big gun blew up on a demonstration voyage in 1844 and killed a number of high government officials and their wives. Stockton was a small man with a helmet of dark hair, a receding chin, and an attitude of smug superiority. He was vain, thin-skinned, tactless, and a glory hound who hated all foreigners.[12]

Polk sent Andrew Jackson's adopted son, Andrew Jackson Donelson, to Texas to lay the joint resolution on annexation before President Anson Jones. He also hoped that the family connection would win the support of Jackson's old friend Sam Houston. Jones grumbled about the terms of the United States plan, but called his Congress into session for mid-June and a convention in Austin on July 4 to settle the business.[13]

Then Stockton put his oar into the diplomatic waters. He arrived at Galveston on May 12 and linked up with a United States agent trying to cut the British diplomats off at the knees. They cooked up a plan to raise troops in Texas and start a war with Mexico by attacking Matamoros under the guns of Stockton's ships. President Jones put his foot down. "*One word settled Com. Stockton's business,*" he said later, "and I assured him I never had the least idea of *manufacturing a war for the United States.*" Stockton claimed that he acted on Polk's authority, but nothing in the record supports that.[14]

Polk offered Texians protection against threats from south of the border. The secretary of state told Donelson on May 23 to advise the Texas government that 3,000 United States troops would march as soon as annexation was accepted. Zachary Taylor was ordered to get ready on May 26. Polk personally told Donelson that he could call on Taylor to repel a Mexican advance into Texas.[15]

The Texas Congress met in June, with few members still interested in British security guarantees. Mexico did its part by refusing to cooperate when Jones issued a unilateral armistice. The Texas Congress voted unanimously for annexation, and the Austin convention on July 4 rubberstamped the decision.[16]

Polk backed the claim that Texas extended all the way to and up the Rio Grande. The case for that was incredibly weak, and the Texian congressional declaration of 1836 was so much wind. The Polk government justified its Rio Grande assertion by citing an order from the Mexican minister of war to General Woll on July 7, 1843. Woll was to withdraw to "the line under your command," meaning the Río Bravo. Mexicans said correctly that the United States' claim to the Rio Grande was groundless.[17]

The North American attitude toward Mexico was "of the most conciliatory character," said Bancroft in May 1845. "I hope war . . . is not to intrude itself into the relations of American republics with each other." That repeated Polk's line—he wanted peace, not war. The Texas boundary was wrapped up with United States claims against Mexico, that country's national debt, and the future of California. It seemed perfectly logical to offer the sister republic money in return for real estate. Polk believed that Mexico's leaders would see the reason in all this, but Mexico's contending factions agreed only in their hostility to the United States. Polk never tried to understand the complexities of the Mexican situation.[18]

Polk grabbed at rumors that the Herrera government would negotiate if it did not look like it was bowing to northern pressure. The president sent Dr. William S. Parrott to Mexico City at the end of March 1845. Yet another undiplomatic diplomat, Parrott was a failed dentist who had lived in Mexico for several years and spoke Spanish. He was well known in the Mexican capital, where he had a reputation for shady dealings. Officials there despised him. Buchanan told Parrott to persuade the Mexican government that it was in its interest to restore friendly relations; the United States would send a minister plenipotentiary if he would be received properly. The annexation of Texas could not be reversed, but Parrott was "at liberty to state your confident belief that in regard to all unsettled questions, we are prepared to meet Mexico in a most liberal and friendly spirit." Parrott advised the secretary of state late in April that the only thing all factions in Mexico agreed on was that they would fight a war rather than accept the loss of Texas.[19]

Herrera honestly wanted to avoid war, but he was always in danger of overthrow. He condemned the annexation of Texas on June 4 as a "monstrous novelty . . . in insidious preparation for a long time." Herrera warned the world that Mexico would mobilize its entire army and reserves to reclaim Texas. Next he had to put down a Santanista uprising among the Mexico City garrison, after which he called Congress into session to decide what actions to take regarding Texas.[20]

Mexican leaders did not think their country weak. They believed themselves invulnerable on account of geography, tropical diseases, and other obstacles to invasion. Mexicans also doubted North American willingness to go to war, and counted on intervention from Europe or Central and South America. There was a general feeling that Mexico was superior militarily to the North Americans. The latter's army was small and would have to be expanded with volunteers. The British ambassador in Texas dismissed volunteers, saying, "They could not resist artillery and cavalry in a Country suited to their arms; they are not amenable to discipline, they plunder the peasantry, they are without steadiness under reverses, they cannot march on foot." Soldiers and diplomats in Europe also believed that the Mexican army was superior to the North American one.[21]

Belief in Mexican military superiority was widespread. "We have numerous and veteran forces burning with a desire to gain immortal renown," boasted the *Boletín Oficial* of San Luis Potosí. "We have more than enough strength to make war," shouted *La Voz del Pueblo*. "Let us make it, then, and victory will perch upon our banners." The United States was at a disadvantage because Texas was far away from its supply centers, nearer to those of Mexico. If the *gringo* army invaded Mexico, it would bog down in the rough landscape and be ground to pieces by defensive action. Some newspapers predicted that the Mexican army could break the North American one on the border, then march into the United States and free the slaves with the support of vengeful Indians.[22]

That was not the voice of a nation likely to give in to Polk's demands. Mexico had another advantage—its troops had been in the area between the Bravo and the Nueces since 1836, although their condition was doubtful. Those "valiant soldiers," one Mexican complained, were "in a state of near abandonment . . . due to the negligence of our government." They felt themselves "truly forgotten." Posted at towns along the Bravo, patrolling toward the Nueces, this demoralized corps upheld Mexico's claims to Texas.[23]

WE ARE LITERALLY A HUGE BODY WITHOUT A HEAD

"The occupation of the country between the Nueces and the Rio Grande," Donelson told Taylor at the end of June 1845, "is a disputed question." The Polk administration had decided to ramp up the dispute. Taylor had been on leave and had no idea what had gone on in his absence or what he was expected to do next. That was not unusual for the man who was about to become the tip of his country's lance.[24]

Taylor was sixty-one years old, a son of the Kentucky frontier and an infantry officer since 1807. He had performed ably during the War of 1812 and the Black Hawk War and in 1837 had led 1,100 soldiers to victory over the Seminoles. He had been stationed on the Louisiana frontier since 1840. Taylor carried a potgut on his blocky body supported by remarkably short legs. His face was weather-beaten, crisscrossed with lines on his wide brow under a tangle of gray hair. Deep furrows ran from his potato nose to a thick mouth, always on the verge of a smile. The gray eyes seemed to twinkle. His soldiers called him "Old Zach." Newspapers later dubbed him "Old Rough and Ready."[25]

Only twice during the campaign did anyone ever see Taylor in uniform, and this gave rise to folklore about how he was often mistaken for a common soldier. Far from being indifferent to his appearance, Taylor gave it a lot of attention. Letter writers in his army described him at different times wearing a blue-checked gingham coat, a "dusty green coat," a linen roundabout, a linen waistcoat, linen trousers, "Atakapa pantaloons" in the style of a Louisiana Indian tribe, a "common soldier's light blue overalls," blue trousers without officer's stripes, even a "frightful pair of trousers." He covered his head with a "broad-brimmed straw hat," a Panama hat, a "big Mexican straw hat," and an "old oil cloth cap." Old Zach earnestly cultivated his image as an uncultivated old soldier.[26]

The general in chief of the army, Winfield Scott, assigned Lieutenant William Wallace Smith Bliss to be Taylor's adjutant. Forty years old, "Perfect" Bliss was the son of a West Point graduate and himself a product of the academy in 1829, returning there as a mathematics instructor. He looked like a scholar, with a high forehead, a chubby face, and an inquisitive manner. He could speak six languages and read thirteen more, and he was curious about everything. He and his future father-in-law, Taylor, became close, and Bliss wrote the barely literate general's paperwork.[27]

The War Department ordered Taylor to move into Texas on June 15, 1845; he received the message on the twenty-ninth. The commander of the "Army of Observation" sent his infantry by sea from New Orleans and his cavalry overland to Corpus Christi, at the mouth of the Nueces. He knew too little of the country to go farther. He had also heard reports that a large Mexican army was en route to Matamoros on the lower Rio Grande. Corpus Christi suited the secretary of war's orders not to molest Mexican posts beyond the Nueces. Only if Mexico declared war should United States forces drive Mexican troops beyond the Rio Grande. Polk believed that he could get what he wanted out of Mexico by upping the pressure, now with armed force.[28]

The president continued to be deluded by rosy reports from the consul in Mexico City, John Black, who predicted that friendship, firmness, and readiness to deal would bring positive results. He claimed in mid-July that the Herrera government would do nothing about Texas. However, Herrera asked Congress to declare war as soon as word of annexation arrived or Anglo troops entered Texas. Black reported on July 24 that Congress had postponed any action until after presidential elections in August.[29]

Black was the sort of envoy who told his masters what he thought they wanted to hear. Polk believed that his policy would work, therefore it must be working—and that was what he wanted to hear. In reality, Mexico City exploded in outrage when news of annexation arrived. "The hour of danger for the country has sounded and she has a right to look to you [Congress] for salvation," screamed *La Voz del Pueblo* on July 17. "War and only war can save us!" had been echoing through the streets since March.[30]

It appeared by the end of July that war would come to Mexico, despite Congress' failure to declare it. Herrera asked the states and departments to fill their quotas of troops, and the cabinet scrounged for loans. The foreign minister told his diplomats in London and Paris, "Mexico has been left no choice except to fight the United States," reporting that 14,000 troops were on the march and 6,000 more would be raised. Those figures were exaggerated, but the Polk government was shocked, especially after Mexico closed its New Orleans consulate early in August. The United States consul in Havana reported that his Mexican colleague had told him that a state of war existed.[31]

If any of this was true, the Polk administration had just bought itself a major headache. The United States Army was authorized about 8,600 officers and men, but its actual count was around 5,500 in 1845. They were dispersed in small detachments west of the Mississippi or at posts on the seacoast and the Canadian border. The War Department ordered the scattered army to move to Texas in midsummer. "The residue of the army," reported the secretary of war in December, "consisting of one regiment of dragoons, sixteen companies of artillery, and five regiments of infantry, constituting more than half the whole military force of the United States, is now serving in Texas."[32]

Getting them there was not easy, owing to lack of preparation. The first regiment left New Orleans on July 14 aboard a steamer, while others were told to follow whenever they found a ride. The first ship reached Aransas Pass at noon on the twenty-fifth, but there was only three feet of water over the bar. The captain tried to land the men at St. Joseph's Island, but winds and high seas prevented that until the twenty-sixth. The ship's boats hit bottom about seventy-five yards offshore, so the men waded to the low island of white sand dotted with live oak trees. They were stuck there because Taylor had never ordered a reconnaissance and a steam-powered lighter he had counted on could not operate in the shallow bay. Local fishermen came to the rescue.[33]

Secretary of War Randolph B. Marcy told Taylor, "It is expected, that in selecting the establishment of your troops, you will approach as near the boundary line—the Rio Grande—as prudence will dictate." Taylor should station a few detachments beyond the Nueces, putting United States troops in the disputed territory before negotiations began. Polk hoped this would encourage the other side to deal.[34]

Most of the "Army of Occupation," as Taylor restyled his corps, had reached Aransas Pass. Taylor arrived from New Orleans on the fifteenth, crossed over to the little village of Corpus Christi on the south bank of the Nueces, picked a nearby area for a campground, and ordered his officers to begin training. The town, a collection of driftwood *jacales*, was scattered down a shelf of land overlooking the beach, and at one end there was a bluff about a hundred feet high, covered with grass and scrub. This, Taylor claimed, was defensible.[35]

He was in no hurry to move closer to Mexico, but the location was far from ideal. The village of Corpus Christi was a smuggler's outpost, and the arrival of the soldiers attracted every species of human parasite—liquor peddlers, gamblers, whores, pimps, cutpurses, and murderers. Some of them robbed, attacked, even murdered his men, but Taylor believed that he lacked the authority to do much about it.[36]

Colonel Ethan Allen Hitchcock complained that Taylor knew nothing about moving an army on the parade ground, let alone a battlefield. Without drill or discipline the army was not much more than a mob, distracted by the vice in Corpus Christi. Sanitary conditions in the camp went downhill fast, men fell sick or deserted, morale evaporated. Hitchcock groused that no officers—himself excepted—could maneuver battalions, let alone regiments. Those who were not West Pointers were beneath his contempt, but even former cadets had forgotten what they had been taught of tactics. The men hacked out 150 acres of brush not far from camp, and the younger officers tried to drill them. One soldier complained that his days were "nothing but drill and parades, and your ears are filled all day with drumming and fifeing."[37]

Taylor had with him nearly 4,000 officers and men, all of them regulars, by the end of September. The sillier problems of an army grown bored by a long stretch of peace emerged. Taylor ordered a review of the whole corps and designated Colonel David Twiggs of the 2nd Dragoons as "commander of the troops," because he ranked highest on the army list. Colonel William J. Worth protested on the grounds that he had a brevet (honorary) rank of brigadier general and therefore outranked Twiggs. The other officers divided into factions. Disgusted, Taylor canceled the review and asked Washington for a ruling. Scott, as commanding general, declared that a brevet rank took precedent. Twiggs' supporters then got up a petition to the United States Senate. Polk blew his stack over Scott's "interception" of Taylor's message, calling it "highly exceptional." He said further that Scott's action "amounted to insubordination," and reversed the decision in favor of Twiggs. In fact, Scott had been ordered to take care of the matter by the secretary of war. Nearly all officers in Texas lost confidence in Taylor. Worth grumbled, "Whether an idea, strategic or of any other description, has had the rudeness to invade the mind or imagination of our chief is a matter of doubt. We are literally a huge body without a head."[38]

Taylor's services of supply were a mess. The quartermaster general, Thomas Jesup, had asked for funds so he could have 300 to 400 wagons ready if war threatened. He was turned down until Taylor marched into Texas, so his agents had to order wagons in haste. Wagons began to arrive at Corpus Christi by early August, but not enough. The shortage was compounded by a scarcity of good drivers. The quartermaster department hired scores in New Orleans who proved to be incompetent or worse. Jesup asked permission to build a corps of trained soldier-drivers, but was refused. Taylor roared throughout his campaign that he never had enough transport, yet not once did he submit an estimate of his requirements. The quartermasters also had trouble finding regulation heavy canvas for tents, and substituted lighter material.[39]

Taylor lost interest in both training and intelligence and sent few scouting parties toward the Rio Grande. He never knew what the Mexican side was up to, but told the War Department that he thought he should advance some troops to the Rio Grande and asked for a change of orders. Taylor was confused, because he kept receiving uninvited information from the other side. A "spy" rode in from Matamoros in September, saying that the garrison had not been reinforced, but rumor held that 3,000 additional troops were on the way. Another such agent reported that General Mariano Arista had arrived on the Río Bravo saying that Mexico was willing to negotiate. Taylor wanted to occupy one or two places near the river to press Mexico into a settlement but he did not feel ready to march out in force, while Polk and his cabinet thought Taylor was about to move his entire command to the river. Marcy told him on October 16 to establish winter quarters on the Rio Grande, but Taylor changed his mind and decided to stay at Corpus Christi.[40]

Texas and the Gulf of Mexico were subject to fierce "northers," masses of cold air that raced down the plains and out into the ocean. Dry weather in the early fall of 1845 was followed by a wet winter, one norther after another. The tents leaked and the men slept in puddles. Training stopped, the men grew sullen, and many deserted. There was not enough wood for cooking, let alone warmth, and the only water supplies were brackish. About a fifth of the men were on sick call at any one time. The human varmint population in Corpus Christi grew to over a thousand by November and lured Taylor's men into trouble. The officers, instead of exerting control, entertained themselves by organizing regimental messes, horse races, and theatrical performances. The Army of Occupation dissolved in brawls and debauchery. Thus sat the Polk administration's attempt to intimidate Mexico into selling a third of its territory. There was soon another alarming development—an increase in Yankee atrocities against Mexican civilians, "outrages of aggravated character," Taylor called them. He ordered the camp closed at tattoo and established patrols around the place, while Polk entertained fantasies that Mexicans would welcome United States troops as liberators.[41]

SETTLE OVER BREAKFAST, THE MOST IMPORTANT NATIONAL QUESTION

Polk and Marcy were astoundingly ignorant of what was going on in Taylor's army. The secretary had diverted the only two inspectors general to mustering duties. An inspectorate was essential to a commander's understanding of troop readiness, but Taylor never saw the need. Marcy did not understand such principles because he had spent his life as a politician in New York. He was a large man with a square face and the frank look of a good listener. He kept the paranoid Polk and the vain Scott off each other's throat, but he was not up to managing the War Department and its tangle of semi-independent bureaus. The general-in-chief, also called the commanding general, did not command staff departments, but Scott devoted himself to the administrative as well as the strategic, planning, and command roles of the army.[42]

On August 23, 1845, Marcy authorized Taylor to call on the governors of five southern states to provide volunteers. Marcy also told the general that ten companies of heavy artillery serving as infantry ("red-legged infantry") were on their way to him. In case this did not intimidate Mexico enough, Polk and his cabinet devised their first wartime strategy on August 29. If the Mexicans declared war or invaded Texas, Taylor should drive them back and take Matamoros, but not advance farther. The navy should blockade or seize all ports except for those in Yucatán and Tabasco, then in rebellion against the Mexican government.[43]

Polk told a visitor in early September that the land and naval forces on the border and in the Gulf "would probably deter and prevent Mexico from either declaring war or invading Texas." He also reacted to words from his yes-man in Mexico City, Parrott, who reported in August that Herrera had declared that a minister from the United States "would be well received." Parrott assured Washington that an envoy "might with comparative ease, settle over breakfast, the most important national question."

Consuls at Mexico City and Vera Cruz were equally chipper. Another influence was Polk's hatred of Britain, with which the dispute over Oregon was catching fire and which he believed was behind anything happening in Mexico. This belief leaked into North American newspapers, unleashing hysterical calls for war in a toxically racist tone. The Mexican "barbarians" were asking for it, so it was said. If Polk still intended to grab Mexican territory without going to war, he was running out of time before public opinion demanded that he take up the sword.[44]

While the president tried to sort through these confusions, the commander of the western division, Major General Edmund P. Gaines, threw a wrench into the works. He was Taylor's superior, but he had not been assigned to the Texas campaign because, at sixty-eight years old, he was too frail to take the field. Age showed on him, his face nearly skeletal and his remaining hair snowy white. He had been in the army since 1799 and wanted to reassert his authority. Gaines received copies of correspondence between Taylor and the War Department and he also read the New Orleans papers. When the advance of a huge Mexican army toward the Rio Grande hit the news (the story was not true) in August, Gaines called on the governor of Louisiana to raise four regiments of volunteers and two artillery companies. He also advised the adjutant general that he could assemble 250 battalions of mounted troops on the Rio Grande by November. On September 2 he asked for authority to call out fifty mounted battalions in case war broke out, with himself in command. This widely publicized gambit left Taylor, Scott, Marcy, and Polk sputtering, and the call-up was canceled. Marcy reminded Gaines that only the president had authority to call for volunteers, and the general turned this near reprimand into a public claim of praise.[45]

Polk faced the possibility of two wars, one with Britain and the other with Mexico. The *New York Herald* expressed a common sentiment: "It is not for a moment to be supposed that Mexico would dream of war, if she were not urged to it by our foreign rivals." This belief added to fears that Britain had traded its designs on Texas for ambitions in California. Even as it pressed the Oregon claims, the Polk administration wanted to avoid trouble in London over Mexico. The president, Buchanan advised the minister to England, "is ready to present the olive branch to Mexico at the moment he knows it will be accepted."[46]

Britain not only had no ambitions in California but was earnestly trying to prevent war. The Mexican minister in London told the foreign minister, Lord Aberdeen, that war was inevitable. Aberdeen suggested that Mexico "merely suspend relations with the U.S." to avoid the loss of California, the bombardment of Vera Cruz, and a blockade. Buchanan warned Polk as late as December 1845, however, that war with Britain might come in the "next two weeks" and urged him to begin "vigorous preparations for defense." The president, however, did nothing to put the country on a war footing.[47]

Mexican opinion was generally that war with the United States already existed, the ultimatum of August 1843 making a declaration unnecessary—the Anglos had started the war. Mexico had a right to tame its rebellious province of Texas, so that afforded no excuse to the *Yanquis* to blockade Mexican ports or grab California.[48]

Mexico and the United States continued to talk past each other, except that newspapers on one side would bristle when those on the other called them "barbarians." Polk told his cabinet on September 16, 1845, about the latest happy news from Consul Black, that the Mexican cabinet had agreed to reopen discussions. Polk seized on this to predict that he could get Mexico to agree not only to the Rio Grande boundary of Texas but also to sell Upper California and New Mexico. The two countries would also settle the outstanding claims. The president estimated that Mexico would surrender all that for $15 to $20 million, although he was willing to go as high as $40 million. He heard on the seventeenth that Mexico was still talking war, so he asked Black to get an official statement that the Mexican government would receive a minister.[49]

While Black cleared the way in Mexico City, Polk selected his minister to that capital. He was John Slidell, fifty-four, a pudgy politician from New Orleans with sloped shoulders, a sagging face, hair that was thinning and too long, and the posture of a lawyer hanging around a county courthouse trolling for clients.[50]

Polk received disturbing news from California on October 11. Thomas O. Larkin, a Monterey businessman who served as United States consul, warned the secretary of state that the Hudson's Bay Company had offered to equip and pay an army to reassert the Mexican government's authority over Alta California. This dovetailed with other rumors that there were plans to settle 10,000 Irish Catholics in the province. These yarns were false, but Polk believed them.[51]

Polk told Larkin to oppose the transfer of California to Great Britain "or any other Power." Buchanan declared that the United States "has no ambitious aspirations to gratify and no desire to extend our federal system over more territory than we already possess, unless by the free and spontaneous wish of the independent people of adjoining territories." This was an invitation to start or support an uprising. The United States would welcome California into the Union "whenever this can be done without affording Mexico just cause of complaint." Polk talked to his old political ally, Senator Thomas Hart Benton of Missouri, whose son-in-law, army topographical engineer John Charles Frémont, might just be in California. Frémont had last been seen heading west with a party of mountain men guided by Kit Carson.

Benton may have suggested the messenger to send to Larkin. He was a thirty-two-year-old lieutenant in the marine corps, Archibald H. Gillespie, who spoke Spanish. He would travel to California by crossing Mexico disguised as a merchant, then by ship to Monterey. Gillespie was a vainglorious officer consumed by dreams of adventure, with inflated notions of his own talents and importance and a bigot's hatred of all foreigners. He memorized the message to Larkin, then destroyed it to prevent interception. Gillespie had a private meeting with Polk. The president called it "a confidential conversation" about "the secret mission on which he was about to go to California. His secret instructions and the letter to Mr. Larkin . . . will explain the object of his mission." Gillespie left Washington in November, taking along a packet of letters to Frémont from his wife and father-in-law. Whatever he and Polk agreed on, war with Mexico could begin in California, not on the Texas border.[52]

Black meanwhile met with the Mexican foreign minister, Manuel de la Peña y Peña, on October 13; the Mexican asked for a proposal in writing. Black gave it to him on the thirteenth, offering to send a minister to settle all questions between the two countries. The foreign minister replied that Mexico would receive a *comisionado* (commissioner) empowered to settle the "present dispute," meaning Texas. It would not receive a *ministro* (minister), which would imply a resumption of diplomatic relations. The United States fleet would have to withdraw from waters off Vera Cruz, and the proposed envoy must be acceptable to Mexico—meaning anybody but Parrott.[53]

Black, the consul at Vera Cruz, F. M. Dimond, and the rest of the government up to Polk himself believed that they would get their way on everything. Dimond told Commodore Conner what Peña had said, and he withdrew his squadron. The consul told Buchanan, "I am rejoiced to have the honor to inform you that God has opened the eyes of these people, and they have consented to negotiate rather than fight." Parrott met with Polk and, according to the president, "he confirmed the opinion I had entertained that Mexico was anxious to settle the pending difficulties between the two countries, including those of boundary."[54]

Peña had made it clear that his government would accept a commissioner but not a minister, but a minister plenipotentiary was what Slidell became. Even allowing for sloppy translation, there was no excuse for Polk and his cabinet's failure to heed these diplomatic niceties—the distinction between commissioners and ministers had been around for centuries. Slidell's instructions were completed on November 10. The first one was to institute a graduated set of payments for boundary concessions, from the Rio Grande to northern California. Buchanan heard from Larkin in December that California was ready to secede and fly any flag but the Mexican one, and told Slidell to soft-pedal any mention of California. Polk nevertheless told Slidell that Parrott had said Mexico would sell California and New Mexico for $15 million. It galled the Mexicans that the United States inserted the claims issue into these negotiations because, although they were in arrears, they had made payments under the earlier arbitration. To this insult was added the assignment of the obnoxious Parrott as Slidell's secretary. Polk nevertheless told Slidell that if his mission failed, the United States would redress its grievances by more drastic means.[55]

Claims that Herrera's government would receive a minister plenipotentiary from the United States exploded on the streets of Mexico City. The newspapers were aflame. "It is hardly possible to believe such perfidy, such baseness and such audacity," cried *El Amigo del Pueblo* on November 1. "To listen to talk of peace from these men [*los Gringos*] is to take the road to perdition, death, ignominy," roared *Patriota Mexicano* on November 18. "The treason has been discovered," proclaimed *La Voz del Pueblo* on December 3. "We no longer own the very ground on which we walk!"[56]

Slidell landed at Vera Cruz on November 30, 1845. The Herrera government had not expected to see Slidell before January at the earliest. Peña told Black, "You know that the opposition are calling us traitors, for entering into this agreement with you." He wanted Slidell to stay out of the capital until invited. Black hit the road, caught Slidell at Puebla, and asked him to return to Vera Cruz. The minister-designate insisted on going to Mexico City, on the ground that not to do so would be to admit that his mission was invalid.[57]

Slidell reached Mexico City on December 8 and asked for an appointment with Peña. The minister said that he was reluctant to see the envoy before Congress met in January, but he would accept Slidell's credentials. He pointed out on the sixteenth that the credentials contradicted the agreement of October, so he would have to take the matter to the Council of Government. The council decided against receiving Slidell. Peña softened that by saying he would be received if his commission was revised. Slidell responded arrogantly that the October agreement had not limited discussions to Texas. The North American retreated to Jalapa to await revised instructions, asking for them in a letter charging bad faith on the part of the Mexican government.[58]

The Mexicans believed that the Polk administration had behaved arrogantly and obtusely. Their refusal to receive Slidell was treated in the United States as not only arrogant but belligerent. Buchanan sent Slidell a revised commission on January 20, 1846, saying that if the government still refused to receive him, "the cup of forbearance will then have been exhausted." A wiser man would have tried to learn what the situation really was and worked something out.[59]

It was too late anyway. The clumsy Slidell mission had destroyed Herrera's government and with it any chance for peace. Slidell himself hung around Mexico for several more weeks but accomplished nothing.[60]

NOW I, IN HER NAME, SOLEMNLY PROTEST

The annexation of Texas and Slidell's arrival opened a vigorous debate in Mexico on the country's future. Conservatives favored a constitutional monarchy to protect the Church and the upper classes, while liberals favored a federal republic under the constitution of 1824. That document was replaced by a centralist model in 1835, but the ouster of Santa Anna a decade later trended the government back toward federalism. Herrera was a federalist, so the centralists spent all of 1845 looking for a chance to strike.[61]

The Spanish minister to Mexico, Salvador Bermúdez de Castro, received a secret money chest from his government, with instructions to engineer a plot to create a Mexican monarchy with a Spanish prince on the throne. Bermúdez chose as his instrument General Mariano Paredes y Arrillaga, commanding the reserve division at San Luis Potosí, where Herrera had sent him to keep him from stirring up trouble. Paredes had been ordered to reinforce troops on the Río Bravo in August 1845. Instead, he had stayed where he was. Warned by Bermúdez's agents that federalists would hold a majority in the new Congress, on December 14 Paredes declared against Herrera for receiving Slidell "to arrange for the loss of the integrity of the republic." Paredes marched on the capital with his division, and the Mexico City garrison defected to him on December 29. Herrera left town, leaving behind Major General Gabriel Valencia, commandant of the capital district, as his legal successor. Valencia claimed the presidency, but Paredes declared that anybody opposing him, "whether the archbishop, general, magistrate, or anybody else," would be shot. Paredes became acting president of Mexico.[62]

Paredes was a slight man, forty-eight years old, with wide, fierce eyes separated by a great Roman nose and capped by heavy eyebrows, a lush mouth over an unimposing chin, his face surrounded by luxurious, curly hair and sideburns. He favored extremely gaudy uniforms. The barely literate Paredes was a veteran of several coups, including the one that replaced Santa Anna with Herrera. He was brave, and not quite as corrupt as Santa Anna. His latest treachery, however, earned him a place in Mexican history similar to that of Benedict Arnold farther north, because he had overthrown the government instead of advancing against the enemy.[63]

The ham-handedness of the Polk administration that had discredited Herrera dogged Paredes as well. Polk and his cabinet failed to see that Paredes' defiance of the United States reflected a desire to salvage Mexico's national honor. Nor could North American officials believe that Mexican leaders acted without prompting from the British. Paredes, in fact, rejected British pleas to negotiate his way out of the dispute.[64]

Britain was always on Polk's mind. The president expanded the Monroe Doctrine in his annual message of December 1845. He asserted "that the people of this continent alone have the right to decide their own destiny. Should any portion of them, constituting an independent state, propose to unite themselves with our Confederacy, this will be a question for them and us to determine without any foreign interposition."[65]

That meant California, if it petitioned for annexation, but it also meant Oregon, since 1843 filling up with immigrants from the United States. Britain had rejected the "whole Oregon" position of the North Americans in July 1845, but was not inclined to go to war with the United States, not over Oregon, not over any part of Mexico. It was just the president's favorite whipping boy for all his foreign interests.[66]

As for Mexico, its condition after Paredes' triumph was described by a Mexico City newspaper as "genuine chaos." When the new president was accused of upsetting public order, he declared, "None existed." His coup was to blame for that. He used the fear of invasion by the United States to pave the way for a monarchy, but federalist outrage in the provinces scotched that. Former vice president Valentín Gómez Farías, reemerging on the political stage, prompted troops in Guadalajara to rise against Paredes and in favor of Santa Anna. Soon the new president had uprisings in México state, Mazatlán, and others to contend with.[67]

Polk had his eye on territories that Mexico owned, and would not let anything stand in his way. When he thought he had found a way to exploit the divisions in Mexico, he did so. "Colonel" Alexander Atocha visited Polk on February 13, 1846, claiming that he was both a citizen of the United States and an agent for Santa Anna; he was both, but much else about him remains unknown. He said that Santa Anna would settle all disputes with the North Americans if he returned to power. Polk suspected at first that the man was just angling for money, but when Atocha returned on the sixteenth for two more private chats he persuaded the president that he did speak for Santa Anna. The deposed dictator suggested establishing a new boundary between the countries by following the Rio Grande and then the "Colorado of the West down through the Bay of San Francisco," whatever that meant; geographical ignorance plagued both sides. This would cost the United States $30 million. To make it appear that the *caudillo* was forced into making such concessions, he proposed that Taylor be ordered to invade northern Mexico, the fleet to blockade Vera Cruz, and Slidell to make a peremptory demand for payment of delinquent claims.

Then came the dodge. If Polk provided $500,000 at once, Santa Anna could return to power by April or May. Polk and his cabinet agreed that the plan was interesting and decided they would like to take it up with Santa Anna directly and in secret. Was this scheme real? It seems likely that Santa Anna really did send Atocha to Washington, because he wanted to return to power no matter how he got there. He also had agents in Mexico dickering with the *puro* federalists led by Gómez Farías, telling them that he wanted to return to his homeland as a soldier. He had no higher ambitions.[68]

Paredes was a fire breather, his inaugural address blistering the United States for its "aggressions." He followed that with a manifesto on March 21, 1846, when he declared war to be "one of the most grievous and serious evils" in human affairs. But peace, he said, must be compatible with the "prerogatives and independence of nations." Having been robbed of Texas by "the highest authorities of our neighboring republic," Mexico "had to protest, did protest, and now I, in her name, solemnly protest" that Mexico would not accept a United States flag in Texas. The president asked Congress to declare war. Congress never did that, however. The closest it came was a decree in July authorizing the government to repel attacks and inform friendly nations why Mexico was forced to defend her rights.[69]

That was too late, because even as Paredes issued his manifesto, Slidell was packing his bags and Taylor's army was closing on the Río Bravo.

WE HAVE NOT ONE PARTICLE OF RIGHT TO BE HERE

When Paredes marched on the capital late in 1845, he took the better part of Mexico's northern manpower with him. After the coup, his troops were distracted putting down countercoups, so instead of fighting the North Americans Mexican armies fought each other. There were too few men available to contest Taylor's advance. Strategically, Mexico retired behind the Río Bravo. In the early months of 1846 Paredes scraped up a small army—about 3,000 men—concentrated on Matamoros with about twenty guns of various sizes. Before Taylor reached the river, a marine regiment and a coast-defense battalion marched into town from Tampico.[70]

Matamoros, about sixty years old, was an important port on the south side of the river, well fortified owing to a history of conflict with Indian raiders, the legacy of the Texas Revolution, and its strategic importance. About 16,000 people lived there in 1846, occupying houses of stone and adobe laid out on a grid of streets in the Spanish Baroque pattern common in Mexican towns.[71]

The garrison commander late in 1845, General Francisco Mejía, had already told his superior at Monterey, General Mariano Arista, that Matamoros was indefensible. He advised meeting the North American army north of the Río Bravo. Opinion in Mexico City, however, held that the town was impregnable. Mejía, about fifty years old, was experienced and humane (he had refused to massacre Texian prisoners in 1842), and knew the country. Arista, about forty-two, also an experienced and humane soldier, was called out of medical retirement by Paredes early in 1846 to command the Division of the North. He agreed that a forward defense of northeast Mexico would have been best, but Paredes' shenanigans had closed that option.[72]

Paredes further weakened Mexico's position early in 1846 by assigning the Cuban-born General Pedro de Ampudia, age forty, to command over Arista. He was a stone-faced soldier with dull eyes, a guardsman's mustache, and a Spanish goatee, always meticulous about his appearance and his prerogatives. He was widely despised as a cutthroat. He had executed the Texian Mier prisoners in 1842 and in the same year conquered a rebellious town in Yucatán, beheaded the captured insurgents, and decorated the place with their heads. When Ampudia's appointment was announced the citizens of the northern states protested. Paredes had no choice but to restore Arista and demote Ampudia; Mejía resumed command in Matamoros. The Mexican army facing Taylor, therefore, was divided between rival chiefs.[73]

Polk learned of the rejection of Slidell's mission on January 12, 1846, and put his army in motion. Marcy ordered Taylor to advance to the Rio Grande as soon as he could, but not treat Mexico as an enemy until war was declared or Mexican forces attacked him. Secretary of the Navy Bancroft said that Polk believed that this would intimidate Mexico into seeing things Polk's way. If a war started, Taylor would at least be closer to Mexico if he was on the Rio Grande. The justification for this was that the United States owned the territory and must enforce its claim by occupation.[74]

Taylor got his own introduction to the complexities of Mexican politics before he received his order. A group in northern Mexico plotted a declaration of independence as the República del Río Grande early in

1846. One of the group, a Camargo lawyer and bandit named General Antonio Canales, sent a message to Taylor late in January asking if the United States would support the rebels if there was no other way to return Herrera to the presidency. Canales' messenger promised that Canales would side with the United States in return for a pile of weapons, ammunition, and money. This kind of thing was beyond Taylor's authority or ability to sort out, so he referred the matter to Washington. The equivocal Marcy told Taylor to use whatever Mexican defectors became available if war broke out. That was the end of the Republic of the Rio Grande, but not of Canales—he raided Taylor's supply lines for the rest of the war.[75]

Taylor received the order to advance on February 3, and three days later sent Captain Ebenezer S. Sibley to scout the road to Matamoros. Sibley reported that the way was muddy but passable. Taylor sent most supplies and heavy artillery by ship, the rest overland. Quartermasters bought every horse and mule they could find, but rounded up only enough to give each company one wagon for every 1,500 pounds of baggage. About 1,900 horses and mules and 500 oxen dragged a train of 307 wagons carrying twenty days' rations and sixteen days' grain for the livestock. Taylor established an advance supply depot on Santa Gertrudis Creek (near present Kingville) to spread the burden.[76]

Taylor left 900 sick behind when he marched out of Corpus Christi. He tried to rid his army of its horde of camp followers, but his order was ignored. He issued another order to curb atrocities and win the favor of the Mexicans in his path. Translated into Spanish and forwarded to communities on the Rio Grande, it told everyone "to observe, with the most scrupulous regard, the rights of all persons who may be found in the peaceful pursuit of their respective avocations." In particular, "no person, under any pretence whatsoever, will interfere in any manner with the civil rights or religious privileges of the people." Looting, Taylor concluded, would not be tolerated. The troops were fairly disciplined regulars, but this order had limited effect. The men supplemented their dreary rations by buying vegetables, bread, eggs, cheese, fruit, and other niceties from villagers. When they had no money, they bartered. When the prices were too high, "some of the boys were compelled to adopt the old mode of mustering into service," as one veteran called stealing.[77]

The army trooped out of camp on the morning of March 8, dragoons and an artillery battery in the lead. The three infantry brigades followed, each a day behind the other, with Taylor and his staff bringing up the rear. The weather was dry and not too hot at first, but very humid. Most of the route of march—up the Nueces, across Hogwallow Prairie, over the Agua Dulce and San Fernando rivers to Santa Gertrudis—was on a flat prairie.

Before long, the heat became blistering. "The sun streamed upon us like a living fire," one soldier wrote home. The farther the men advanced, the more the land became a place where everything either stuck, stabbed, stalked, or stung them. The semi-arid, almost treeless plain was covered by tough grasses and chapparal, mesquite, and other thorny shrubs, inter-rupted by prickly pear, cholla, and succulents with names such as "dagger" and "bayonet." Herds of mustang horses roamed at a distance.[78]

A week into the march, the men's feet hardening, the country became more agreeable. "The flowers during today's march were gloriously rich," said one soldier. "I do not think I have ever felt a sweeter or fresher morn-ing," wrote another. "The air from the sea was delightful, and everything in nature appeared so happy that it was perfectly exhilarating." The air was filled with the sound of birds.[79]

Mejía reacted to Taylor's advance by stepping up his patrols. He had not been allowed to march his army out, but at least he could send scouts to see what the *Yanquis* were up to. Twiggs' advance saw a small party of Mexicans who set the prairie afire and took off on March 14. Lieutenant Ramón Falcon and a small detachment waylaid a six-man advance under Lieutenant Fowler Hamilton the next day. Falcon demanded an explana-tion for Hamilton's presence. The Yankee said that his army was going to occupy the left bank of the Rio Grande. Falcon warned that Mexico would fight if the United States troops advanced farther. Twiggs ordered a halt.[80]

Taylor decided to concentrate at Arroyo Colorado, a brackish slough about a hundred yards across, with timbered banks too steep for wagons to cross. On March 19 his scouts reported that Mexican pickets had con-fronted them, saying that Mejía would contest the crossing. They also heard bugle calls from the direction of what they believed was a Mexican camp, invisible behind brush and timber. Taylor planned to force a crossing of the arroyo the next day. Captain José Barragan of Mejía's staff rode into his camp with a proclamation issued on the eighteenth, calling on all citi-zens to take arms against the "degenerate sons of Washington." Barragan promised Taylor that the Mexican army would fight the crossing, to which Old Zach answered that he would cross the arroyo immediately. Barragan had been bluffing, because Worth and four companies waded over the wide ditch without opposition. Taylor took position on the far side, his soldiers cutting the banks so the supply train could cross.

This gave him a chance to read Mejía's purple prose. His long proc-lamation to the people of Coahuila and to his troops excoriated the low character of the United States and its people and raved about the ille-gal crossing of the Nueces and other foul deeds. "Fellow countrymen!" he cried near the end. "With an enemy which respects not its own laws, which shamelessly derides the very principles invoked by it previously, in order to excuse its ambitious views, we have no other recourse than arms." After more in that vein, Mejía hit his stride. "The flames of patriotism which burn in our hearts," he roared, "will receive new fuel . . . when we take up our march to oppose our naked breasts to the rifles of the hunters of the Mississippi."[81]

Taylor resumed marching on March 23 with his infantry in four parallel columns and flankers keeping an eye out for the enemy while hacking their way through the brush. Taylor received a messenger from the prefect of the northern district of Tamaulipas at Santa Rita, telling the general that his people would never consent to being dragged under foreign control, so Taylor should turn back or suffer the consequences. The army kept going. It reached the junction of roads to Point Isabel, near the mouth of the Rio Grande, and to Matamoros upriver on the twenty-fourth. Taylor and some dragoons went ahead to Point Isabel, which would be his main supply base. Transports with goods and artillery arrived from Corpus Christi and Taylor assigned two artillery companies as a garrison and put other men to work digging field fortifications.[82]

Old Zach and the dragoons returned to the main army about ten miles from the Rio Grande on March 27, and the next day resumed the advance. The troops saw Matamoros by midmorning, and that afternoon they camped across river from the town. "The roofs of the houses and the tallest buildings were crowned by the entire population, curiously awaiting the arrival of the enemy," one citizen recalled. Taylor set up a parley flag, and Mejía sent Brigadier General Rómulo Díaz de la Vega across the river to see what the *Yanqui* had to say. As soon as his boat hit the bank, the Stars and Stripes rose over the North American camp, and Mexicans on the other side took that as a deliberate insult.[83]

Mejía sent a subordinate to deal with him, so Taylor did the same, sending Worth. The two generals sat down under a tree and tried to communicate, but the *Yanqui* knew no Spanish and the *Mexicano* knew no English. Members of their staffs who spoke French stepped forward, and Worth's words went through French into Spanish, and Díaz's into English the other way. Worth avowed that Taylor's intentions were peaceful. Díaz assured the northern general that so far as General Mejía knew, there was no war between the two countries.[84]

It was not a war, but a joint campout around Matamoros. Taylor's army set up its tents and began to build an earthen fort. The men went to sleep spooked by strange sounds in the night. Howls of wolves and the yip-yowl of coyotes were often mistaken for Mexican bugles, rousing the camp to meet attacks that never came. One toad was so loud that it sparked arguments about whether its noise came from an Indian or a bear.[85]

There were diversions, however, and for young men that meant above all women—in particular, women bathing in the river. This was a great curiosity to North Americans throughout the war. The weekly bath had not yet come into fashion, and for most Anglos cleanliness was keeping outer clothes brushed and "linens" (underwear) washed every few days. Winfield Scott had fought hard to get a change in the regulations in 1841 requiring soldiers to bathe once a week, "where conveniences for it are to be had." Where "conveniences" were not to be had, the men stank. Mexican *Indios* and *Castas* followed traditions of personal hygiene that went back to ancient times, while the upper classes had adopted the love of bathing made fashionable by the French nobility. Most Mexican towns and cities had public bathhouses.[86]

The sight of Mexican women trooping down to the river, stripping, and bathing was so remarkable that almost every literate Yankee in Taylor's army wrote home about it. It was also too much for some of the young officers, who did likewise on the opposite bank. Their Victorian prudery caused them to misjudge high Mexican standards of female chastity. When the *Gringos* got to the middle of the stream, sentries on the bank leveled their muskets and ordered them back. Frustrated, "they returned after kissing their hands to the tawny damsels," said one officer, "which was laughingly returned."[87]

Giggling girls just out of reach, yipping coyotes, and barking frogs did not keep camp life from descending into a boring routine. More than 200 men had other uses for the river besides bathing—they swam across and disappeared into Mexico, fourteen in one night. Many were foreigners who had not adjusted to army life, but not all—desertion was the United States Army's biggest headache throughout the nineteenth century. Taylor ordered sentries to shoot, and desertion dropped after two escapees were killed.[88]

Taylor had obeyed his orders and marched his army to the Rio Grande. What he was supposed to do next was not clear. Polk had thought once again that a little more intimidation would drive Mexico to the bargaining table, and once again he had been proven wrong. Doubts about the purpose of the whole business spread through the army. "We have not one particle of right to be here," Colonel Hitchcock groused to his diary. "It looks as if the government sent a small force on purpose to bring on a war, so as to have a pretext for taking California and as much of this country as it chooses."[89]

HOSTILITIES MAY NOW BE CONSIDERED AS COMMENCED

(April–June 1846)

I am not at all for battles, especially at the start of a war,
and I am convinced that a skillful general can go all his life
without being forced to fight one.

—Maurice of Saxony

IF THERE HAD NEVER BEEN A JOHN CHARLES FRÉMONT, James
Knox Polk would have had to invent him. Intelligent and highly determined, wrapped up in his own ego, a man of boundless energy and terrible judgment, Frémont was happily free of doubt. Born in Savannah,
Georgia, in 1813, Frémont was the bastard son of a wandering French actor, from whom he inherited a theatrical manner. He was not well educated, but he became a lieutenant in the army's corps of topographical
engineers in 1838, demonstrating a sharp eye for landscape and botany.
Frémont was a slender, strikingly handsome man with a fashionable half-
starved look. His long face with its great, straight nose was surrounded by
a mass of curly, dark hair and a full beard. A wild look in his eyes combined
with his mane to give him the aura of an Old Testament prophet. His west-

ern adventures made him one of the most famous people in North America in the 1840s because he had the good sense to marry Jessie Benton, daughter of Thomas Hart Benton, who became Frémont's patron. The senator dictated the explorer's orders, the chief of the topographical bureau wrote them down, and Benton secured appropriations. Jessie wrote up the reports.

Frémont's first famous exploration was in 1842, when he surveyed the Oregon Trail up to South Pass (in present-day Wyoming). Jessie turned his notes into a thrilling best-seller. Frémont took off again in 1843, completed mapping the trail into Oregon, then made an unauthorized detour down the length of California and back east over the southern desert. The journey produced another best-selling report. It was apparent by 1845 that Frémont and Senator Benton were in cahoots and that the officer obeyed his father-in-law rather than his military superiors. He was ordered to take a party to explore the upper Arkansas and Canadian rivers that summer, but let his military detail do that while he led a party of mountain men, Indian scouts, and roughnecks to the Pacific shore.[1]

Jessie Frémont made her husband a hero of the frontier; newspapers called him "Pathfinder," but he lacked woodcraft and common sense and had a talent for stumbling into danger. His success was owing to his guide, protector, and savior, Christopher "Kit" Carson—someone else Jessie turned into a celebrity.

Carson was born on the Missouri frontier in 1809 and left home at sixteen in a merchant caravan headed for Santa Fe. There he began a career as a trapper and mountain man, an Indian trader, a sometime merchant, but mostly a man of the wilderness. He lived with Indians, fought Indians, killed Indians, and married two Indians whom he outlived. He based himself by the 1840s in Taos, New Mexico, and married Josefa Jaramillo, from a prominent nuevomexicano family. Jessie Frémont did not exaggerate his skills, his instinct for spotting and avoiding danger, or his willingness to kill if he had to. William T. Sherman met him in 1848, expecting to see a giant, finding instead "a small, stoop-shouldered man, with reddish hair, freckled face, soft blue eyes, and nothing to indicate extraordinary courage and daring." Army officer George Brewerton called him a "plain, simple, unostentatious man; rather below the medium height, with soft, brown curling hair, little or no beard, and a voice as soft and gentle as a woman's."[2]

Carson was about five foot five, stocky, with bowed legs and the shoulders of a trapeze artist. He had an oval face in which no single feature stood out. He was loyal to a fault to whoever led him. His bashful, awshucks manners and cornball Missouri accent were downright charming.

Frémont and Carson together rekindled the California dreaming first fired by Dana and Wilkes. Polk entered office determined to add California to the Union. The flamboyant Frémont, with the sober Carson watching out for him, set out to do just that.

A GRAND OPPORTUNITY NOW PRESENTED ITSELF

In March and again in May 1845, his eye also on California, the secretary of the navy ordered Commodore John D. Sloat of the Pacific Squadron to concentrate his ships in Mexican coastal waters. He told the commodore on June 24 that if he learned "beyond a doubt" that Mexico had declared war, he should occupy or blockade the California ports. This instruction was clear enough, but it fell on the wrong ears.[3]

Sloat was sixty-four years old, a veteran of the War of 1812. He was a hypochondriac, always complaining about his ill health (he lived to be eighty-six years old), and in 1845 asked to be rotated home after a year on station. Sloat was paralyzed by two fears—one that the Royal Navy's Pacific Squadron threatened his operations, and the other a mortal dread of repeating Thomas ap Catesby Jones' blunder at Monterey in 1842.[4]

Sloat sailed into Mazatlán in the frigate USS *Savannah* in mid-November 1845. This was the major Mexican port on the Pacific, with fairly direct communications to Mexico City. When he heard that Slidell had been sent to negotiate with the Mexicans and that Conner's Home Squadron had left its station off Vera Cruz, Sloat scattered his squadron to smaller ports.[5]

The presence of a British squadron kept Sloat nervous. There was a threat of war with Britain over Oregon, and Sloat's orders had stressed that. Then Lieutenant Gillespie showed up in Mazatlán with papers saying he should receive transportation to Alta California, but he refused to tell Sloat what his mission was. The commodore sent him off in a sloop-of-war on February 22.[6]

Sloat dithered at Mazatlán. Navy surgeon Dr. William Maxwell Wood left on May 1, 1846, to go home on leave by crossing Mexico. He met John Parrott—on his way to become consul at Mazatlán—at Guadalajara on the tenth and heard an unverified tale about shooting near Matamoros. Wood sent a note to Sloat, who notified Consul Larkin at Monterey that because hostilities might have broken out, "it is my intention to visit your place immediately." He sent this off in a sloop-of-war on May 19, ordering its captain to seize any Mexican vessels he came across—an act of piracy if there was not yet a war.[7]

The flagship of the British Pacific Squadron left Mazatlán and disappeared on the twentieth, and naval and diplomatic officers there agreed that it was probably headed for Alta California. Still Sloat sat. He heard more definite news of fighting on the Rio Grande on May 26 and wrote the secretary of the navy that he had been preparing to go north but had changed his mind after "more mature reflection." He would not do anything hostile until he learned officially that there had been a declaration of war. He received another note from Wood in Mexico City on June 7, confirming his earlier report. Sloat bravely decided "upon my own responsibility" to undertake offensive operations. *Savannah* sailed for Monterey, Sloat dreading the coming battle with the Royal Navy. However, Larkin had told the secretary of state on June 1 that a British agent assured him that Britain had no designs on California.[8]

Frémont started a war with Mexico while Sloat vacillated. When Frémont abandoned the upper Arkansas survey during the summer of 1845, he and Carson headed west to the Salt Lake country. Mountain men flocked to them from every direction. By the time they entered California near the end of the year there were about five dozen of them. They were a frightful sight, according to one observer: "Their rifles, revolving pistols, and long knives, glittered over the dusky buckskin which enveloped their sinewy limbs, while their untrimmed locks, flowing out under their foraging caps, and their black beards, with white teeth glittering through, gave them a wild savage aspect."[9]

This bunch might be civilians, but they followed Frémont, and he was a serving officer of the United States Army. But he answered to a higher power, at least in his view. That was his father-in-law, Benton, who wanted to know if there was a route from Missouri to California as passable as that to Oregon. The California adventure became known in some circles as a "Benton family plot."[10]

Frémont and his party arrived at Sutter's Fort in northern California late in 1845 in the aftermath of the uprising that had driven out Governor Micheltorena. The province had divided mountain-and-forest north against prairie-and-desert south under factions headed by the nominal governor, Pío Pico, based at Los Angeles, and the military commander, General José Castro, at Monterey. Their struggle with each other was in the face of threats by Mexico City to reassert control, of war with the United States, and of unrest among illegal Anglo immigrants in the north. Those aliens lived in several settlements among the towering forests along the Sacramento and Napa river valleys, and were in a state of alarm over tavern rumors that the Mexican government would run them out of the province.[11]

Frémont and his band left Sutter's Fort in January, reaching Monterey near the end of the month. He presented himself to Larkin, who introduced him to Castro. They assured the general that Frémont and his crew were peaceful explorers who would leave soon. Frémont decided in February to do some exploring in California, and on the way abused Mexican citizens. Castro ordered the *Norteamericanos* to leave his province on March 5. Frémont was near present-day Salinas, about thirty miles from Monterey. He claimed that he was astonished at General Castro's "breach of good faith," so he "peremptorily refused compliance to an order insulting to my Government and myself." This meant that he saw himself as acting in an official capacity. Things got worse fast.

Frémont trooped his men up a ridge overlooking Monterey on the night of March 5, built a crude log fort, and ran up the Stars and Stripes. "If we are unjustly attacked," the Pathfinder wrote Larkin on the ninth, "we will fight to extremity and refuse quarter." Castro organized several hundred militia and demonstrated against the fort, but did not attack it. Frémont suddenly realized that he had gone too far in hoisting the U.S. flag over foreign territory without orders. His men wanted to attack the *Californios,* but he stopped them, because that would have made him a common freebooter. On the night of March 9 a wind blew his flag down. Taking that as an omen, Frémont abandoned the fort.[12]

The band of mountain men, Carson in the lead, went north. Frémont visited settlements of foreigners, looking for a route to Oregon and, at the request of the settlers attacked neighboring Indians, slaughtering many natives who had no hostile designs on the aliens. The party reached Oregon by early May, passes farther north snowbound.

Gillespie landed at Monterey on April 17, met Larkin, and recited the memorized instructions. These said the two of them should cooperate against British efforts to take California, and support any local independence movements. Larkin had written to Mazatlán requesting a United States warship to be stationed at Monterey; USS *Portsmouth* arrived on April 23. Gillespie asked permission to take a packet of correspondence to Frémont, and Larkin agreed. Still in civilian clothing, the marine scampered northward. Guided by an Anglo settler, he found Frémont camped in the snow at Klamath Lake on May 9. Frémont later testified that Gillespie delivered information from Benton emphasizing the importance of countering British moves in California. Gillespie most certainly related the rumors of war between the United States and Mexico. "I saw the way opening clear before me," Frémont recalled later. "War with Mexico was inevitable; and a grand opportunity now presented itself to realize in the fullest extent the far-sighted views of Senator Benton, and make the Pacific Ocean the western boundary of the United States." The Pathfinder decided to march to the Sacramento Valley to see what he could stir up. His departure was delayed, however, by a four-day battle with Klamath

Indians wanting to avenge his earlier atrocities. The band of mountain men headed south on May 13.[13]

They returned to find the province in chaos, *Californios* divided among themselves—Castro versus Pico, north versus south, civil versus military. United States warships were parked in the bays of Monterey and San Francisco. Gillespie was unmasked as a *yanqui* agent. The illegal aliens threatened to take California over. Larkin urged the *Californios* to secede from Mexico and join the United States. There was a general feeling that Frémont and his hairy riflemen represented the start of an Anglo invasion. Frémont and Gillespie decided to rally the immigrants. These settlers were a mixed lot: farmers from Oregon, sailors who had jumped ship, retired fur trappers, criminal fugitives, and every other manner of social outcast. Manifest destiny wore a long beard and buckskin breeches.[14]

One of the retired mountain men was Ezekiel "Stuttering" Merritt. Frémont called him "fearless and simple, and not given to asking questions when there was something he was required to do." Merritt set out with about a dozen men to challenge Castro. They attacked soldiers driving horses to Santa Clara on June 10, rustled the animals, and defied Castro to take back the livestock. Frémont sent Merritt and thirty men to attack Sonoma four days later. They surrounded the home of Colonel Mariano Guadalupe Valléjo, Mexican commandant in the area. He was a friend to the settlers and openly favored annexation to the United States. That did not stop Merritt's hooligans from drinking all his brandy and looting his property, seizing his arms and horses. They returned to Frémont's camp near Sutter's, bringing Valléjo and three others along. Frémont told Valléjo he was not to blame for what had happened, but he ordered the prisoners confined for the next two months.[15]

Castro was outraged, and on June 17 issued two proclamations rousing his fellow *Californios*. He denounced the "contemptible policy of the agents of the United States" who had "induced a portion of adventurers, who . . . have daringly commenced an invasion. The defence of our liberty, the true religion which our fathers possessed, and our independence, calls upon us to sacrifice ourselves." He aroused pity for "these innocent little ones, which have unfortunately fallen into the hands of our enemies, dragged from the bosoms of their fathers, who are prisoners among foreigners, and are calling upon us to succor them," although there were no children in chains. He summoned all citizens to rise against the invaders and declared that "he who first will sacrifice himself will be your friend and fellow citizen, José Castro." He next promised that all foreigners in California would be protected "whilst they refrain entirely from all revolutionary movements."[16]

When Governor Pico, in Los Angeles, heard about the Valléjo incident, he was Castro's equal. "Fly, Mexicans," he roared, "in all haste in pursuit of the treacherous foe; follow him to the farthest wilderness; punish his audacity; and in case we fail, let us form a cemetery where posterity may remember to the glory of Mexican history the heroism of her sons."[17]

Another rebellion broke out in Sonoma after Merritt and his gang returned to Sutter's. William B. Ide, an Anglo newcomer, issued his own bombastic proclamation on June 18, vowing to establish a republican government and overthrow the oppressive Mexican regime. This declaration was followed by a flag raising, when Ide's men hoisted a hastily made banner with the crude outline of an animal. His adherents said it was a bear. Local people said it was a pig. Nevertheless, the Bear Flag Republic was born. Frémont heard of it, and took ninety men into Sonoma on the excuse of protecting the people there. He hijacked the Bear Flag revolt, calling himself *Oso Numero Uno* (Number One Bear). Anglo and Mexican militias marched hither and yon for the next week until the Mexicans retired under a threat from the United States Navy. Sailors raised flags at Monterey and other towns, saving Frémont from charges of being a filibuster, because his actions were legitimized by a real invasion by the navy.[18]

Or was it? Sloat arrived at Monterey on July 1 and met with Larkin. He made no effort to secure the port and gave his sailors shore leave on the third. He still had no official word that there was a war on, so he was not about to take any hasty actions. Sooner or later, however, he was going to have to deal with Frémont, whose campaign had not been all comedy. Right after Sloat's appearance at Monterey, Frémont ordered Carson to execute an old man and his two teenage nephews on the false charge that they were spies. "I have no use for prisoners—do your duty," he said.[19]

THE DANGER WAS IMMINENT

The Paredes government was under political pressure to bring California back into the national orbit. Paredes sent Lieutenant Colonel Rafael Téllez to Mazatlán in March 1846, officially with instructions to raise an army and reconquer California. Privately, Téllez's orders told him to sit tight in Mazatlán, because the real purpose of his expedition was to mollify critics in Mexico City. Even colonels were freelancers in the Mexican army, however. Téllez seized power in Mazatlán and raised a federalist rebellion in favor of Santa Anna.[20]

The approach of war aggravated the tensions between the factions in Mexico. Paredes concentrated on domestic issues, promoting new elections, a possible new constitution, and the monarchist campaign. The country's financial situation continued to worsen. The president thought that Taylor's advance to the Río Bravo would come to nothing because the North Americans faced a threat of war with Britain over Oregon. The monarchist plot fizzled, so Paredes declared himself a republican. Federalist uprisings in the western states that began in April 1846 forced the president to weaken the northern defenses in an unsuccessful effort to put the rebels down. Several contradictory changes in army leadership produced divisions among leading generals.[21]

Hanging over everything was the specter of Santa Anna. The *London Times* correspondent in Mexico City reported in February that his return to power "would be regarded by all classes as the greatest affliction that could befall the nation." That changed as dissatisfaction with Paredes blossomed, and Santa Anna adeptly played the various factions against each other. The liberals led by Gómez Farías were the most seriously interested in him, hoping he would be their best weapon against the monarchists. "I detest no man more than I do pegleg Santa Anna," snorted one of them, "but in spite of that I would gladly throw myself in his arms if he wanted to come back and fight the dangerous faction that dominates us."[22]

Paredes had overthrown Herrera for being insufficiently belligerent toward the United States, but the identical charge rained down on his head. "*¡A las armas, Mexicanos!* [To arms, Mexicans!]," howled a broadside circulating in Mexico City during the spring of 1846. "People, a horrible treason, an infamous treason threatens our independence, our adored independence, for which our fathers gave their lives!"[23]

Mexico was chaotic, and not just at the top. It appeared that a national race war might become reality in the spring of 1846. Village Indians rose up in great numbers in the Chilapa district of México state at the end of March, attacking several state and federal targets. One cabinet official called it "a war of the most barbarous nature." Paredes sent an army of occupation to Chilapa. It failed. Uprisings spread into other states by May. A force of 200 rebels attacked and sacked San Luis de Azoya, and a few weeks later a similar force led by *guerrillero* Faustino Vallalua occupied Acutumpa, then mauled a corps of about eighty government soldiers. Uprisings in Puebla state cut the road between Mexico City and Vera Cruz by June. Chaos spread all over Mexico.[24]

Polk remained oblivious to the fact that Mexico's government was paralyzed. Instead, the North American had decided by late February 1846 that Mexico was the aggressor, threatening the United States. Ordering Taylor into the disputed region and Conner into the Gulf caused the two service secretaries to recommend asking Congress for more appropriations. Congress, however, would have to be "roused by a special message." Polk did not want to appear to be preparing for war and could not figure out how to ask Congress for more funds without producing "a panic in the country."[25]

Polk received a warning from Dimond at Vera Cruz on April 6 that Slidell would probably not be received. The president suggested to his cabinet that he recommend to Congress that the United States "take the remedy for the injuries and injustices we have suffered into our own hands." Just what those "injuries and injustices" were was debatable. Word arrived from Slidell on the seventh that Mexico City's rejection of his mission was final. Polk bowed to the wishes of his cabinet that he not send a message to Congress until Slidell reported in person. He next talked to his staunchest allies in the Senate, Calhoun and Benton, and received a shock. Calhoun wanted to delay a crisis with Mexico until the Oregon dispute was resolved, and Benton echoed Calhoun, saying that territorial gains could be had from Mexico without war. Polk told him there was "ample cause of war, but that I was anxious to avoid it if it could be done honourably and consistently with the interests of our injured citizens," meaning the claims issue.

Slidell arrived on May 8 and said that "but one course towards Mexico was left to the United States," and that was war. Polk promised to ask Congress for a declaration. His cabinet concurred the next day, stipulating that a hostile act by Mexico on the Rio Grande should be the cause. Polk regretted that so far there had been no word of Mexican aggression, but the "danger was imminent," so he decided to ask for a declaration anyway. Secretary of the Navy Bancroft—a tweedy scholar unhappy in his job, angling for a diplomatic appointment to Britain so he could resume work on his history of the United States—alone among the cabinet objected. Without a hostile act on the other side, he held that a declaration of war by the United States would be naked aggression. That question was resolved later on the ninth, when Adjutant General Roger Jones rushed over a message from Taylor, written on April 26. It said that Mexican troops had attacked a party of his dragoons north of the Rio Grande. Polk summoned the cabinet into session that evening and they all agreed to send a war message to Congress. Polk spent the weekend briefing Democratic congressmen and revising drafts of the message. Newspapers on the streets thumped the drums for war.[26]

The United States might have to wage one war with Mexico and another with Britain. Polk had said all along that he did not think Britain would fight over Oregon. After Her Majesty's government rejected his "whole Oregon" demand in July 1845, he quietly dropped it. The British government wanted to quiet the war talk. The chief interest in Oregon had been the fur trade, and the country was trapped out by the 1840s. The territory was filling up with settlers. The British did not want Mexico as an ally, and their trading interests with the United States were more valuable than those with Mexico or than Oregon itself. The logical solution was simply to extend the existing line between the United States and Canada on the forty-ninth parallel to the Pacific. Polk urged Congress to "terminate" the joint occupation of Oregon, which happened April 23, 1846. The British government sent a draft treaty over the water. Polk liked it and passed it to the Senate, which ratified on June 12. Now Mexico stood alone.[27]

I HAD THE PLEASURE OF BEING THE FIRST TO START THE WAR

The War Department's best information on Mexico was Zebulon Pike's report from thirty years before. It did not say much about northeast Mexico. Taylor's ideas of tactical intelligence did not extend much beyond what he could see with his own eyes. He rejected instructions from Marcy to hire native scouts, saying they could not be trusted. Scott advised him to hire bandits, but he waved that off also. Taylor expected a fight at first and asked the adjutant general to hurry along recruits to bring his regiments to full strength; that got him 300 green enlistees and four companies of the 1st Infantry. However, he told Governor J. Pinckney Henderson of Texas on April 3 that, owing to his good relations with Mejía, he did not expect the Mexicans to "attempt any offensive operations." Three days later he predicted to the adjutant general that that would change when Ampudia showed up.[28]

The standoff between Taylor and Mejía was polite but tense. Repeated alarms that Mexican troops had crossed the river kept the Anglos awake and dragoons out on patrol, but a party sent to Point Isabel saw no Mexican soldiers north of the river. Mexicans were patrolling, however, and when they nabbed two dragoons Taylor asked for their return and Mejía sent them across.[29]

The two armies entertained each other. The *Norteamericanos* appeared to the Mexicans to be a dreary mass of blue-clad plodders. United States officers thought the Mexican officers looked splendid in their colorful uniforms, but the enlisted soldiers were "half-starved-looking devils." The bands of both armies played often, and here the Mexican army was superior—to one Yankee soldier, Mexican music was "exquisite." Taylor ordered his engineers to locate a permanent camp and build batteries to command Matamoros. The main position was a star-shaped earthwork, Fort Texas, designed to house 800 men.[30]

Mejía had no orders to fight Taylor, and was too weak anyway until reinforcements arrived in April. His heaviest gun was a 12-pounder. He had earlier scorned the need for fortifications, but by early April Mejía had his men digging away. Upstream from Matamoros and commanding the Las Anacuitas ferry he started a large earthwork. Two redoubts about 800 yards from the United States camp put it under a cross fire. His engineers were excellent at siting and laying out these positions, but they lacked enough artillery.[31]

The shuffles in command over his head did Mejía no good either. Ampudia was on his way to take command of the Division of the North when the protests from northeast Mexico hit the desk of the minister of war. Tornel ordered Arista to resume command and attack the *yanqui* invaders. Arista might be minimally competent, but the people trusted him not to cut their throats. Ampudia surprised everyone by staying in the division as second in command.[32]

Arista was a redhead, but Ampudia was the fiery one. He rode into Matamoros on April 11, 1846, with a 200-man cavalry escort after riding nearly 200 miles from Monterey in four days. Behind him came 2,200 men under Brigadier General Anastasio Torrejón. When Ampudia passed through Reynosa upriver, he gave United States citizens there twenty-four hours to evacuate, and did the same at Matamoros.[33]

Ampudia aggravated Taylor's main headache when on April 2 he sent an open letter to foreign soldiers in the United States command asking them to desert. Aiming specifically at English and Irish men but including Germans, French, Poles, and others, he urged, "Do not contribute to defend a robbery and usurpation." When Arista succeeded him, on April 20 the new commander sent another message telling Taylor's men that they were being forced to wage an unjust war. If they became "peaceful Mexican citizens" they would receive grants of land.[34]

Yankees disdained the harsh discipline and hard work of being a soldier, so almost half of Taylor's army were immigrants chiefly looking for a way to learn English. They went over the hill as soon as they got the chance. Matamoros offered a peaceful haven with its own attractions. Topping the discontents was anti-Catholic bigotry in the army, and the Mexican propagandists played on that. "The evil of desertion . . . increased to an alarming extent" after Ampudia's proclamation, Taylor complained. He gave oral orders to shoot any who would not stop for a sentry. He felt himself justified when some of the deserters fought against him in the Mexican army, and this ended a congressional investigation into his shoot-to-kill order.[35]

Desertion on the Rio Grande gave rise to the legendary Irish soldiers of the Mexican army. Only about 200 or so deserted despite harassment in the army and abuse of their Catholic relatives back home, but the thirty to forty-eight (depending on who was counting) who were Irish and did join the other side gave rise to the legend. They were recruited into the Legión Extranjera (Foreign Legion), later renamed the Batallón de San Patricio (Battalion of Saint Patrick), its green flag bearing an Irish harp. It was not a mass Irish exodus from Taylor's command, however, and more than 5,000 native Irish continued to serve in the United States Army during the war. The battalion included many other Europeans already resident in Mexico, but the flag, name, idealism, and esprit de corps of the "San Pats" reflected Irish Catholic values. They were comfortable with Mexico's Catholicism and were willing to fight to the death for a losing cause. Nothing could be more Irish than that, but their commander was a native of Mexican Florida, Major Francisco Rosendo Moreno. The highest-ranking deserter was Acting Major John Reilly (also rendered Riley and O'Reilly), a former British soldier from Canada.[36]

Ampudia sent Taylor an ultimatum on April 12—withdraw beyond the Nueces or face a fight. Taylor took that as a signal that war had started and asked the United States Navy to blockade the mouth of the Rio Grande, cutting Mexican forces off from their source of supply at New Orleans. An improvised blockade turned away two civilian schooners carrying flour to Matamoros on the seventeenth. Ampudia protested, and Taylor answered that he was "surprised" that the Mexican commander would complain about an event "which is no other than a natural result of the state of war so much insisted upon by the Mexican authorities." The pugnacious Ampudia therefore ordered Torrejón to cross the river, but canceled the order when Ampudia's recall came.[37]

Taylor's quartermaster, Colonel Trueman Cross, disappeared on April 10. Taylor asked Ampudia if he had any information on the colonel's whereabouts, but he did not. A patrol found his stripped body on the twenty-first, and a board of officers concluded that Cross had been waylaid by bandits. The suspect was Ramón Falcón, a notorious local *bandido*. Lieutenants Theodoric H. Porter and Stephen D. Dobbins went out on separate patrols to look for the culprit. Dobbins came back without result. Porter rode into an ambush and he and one man were killed.[38]

Arista rode into Matamoros on April 24, 1846, and his escort brought the force there to about 5,000 men. Arista told Taylor that Mexico was a victim of North American aggression and the time had come to fight. "The Mexicans have been calumniated as barbarous, in the most caustic and unjust manner," but his troops would display "the feelings of humanity and generosity which are genial to them." The term "barbarian" had become a national sore point in Mexico, but Taylor did not use it. The Yankee general said that he had tried to keep the peace but Mexican provocation had forced him to blockade the river mouth.[39]

Meanwhile, in Mexico City Paredes proclaimed a state of defensive war because hostilities had "been begun by the United States of America" in the northeast and in California. Consul Black told the secretary of state that the manifesto was "nothing but a piece of humbug." War, he continued to believe, was not in the works.[40]

He was wrong, as usual. Arista had sent Torrejón's brigade across the river on a reconnaissance in force. Taylor received a report on April 24 that a Mexican corps was crossing the river downstream and sent some dragoons out to take a look. They found nothing. Another report that evening said the enemy was upriver, so Taylor sent a squadron under Captain Seth B. Thornton in that direction. On the morning of the twenty-fifth, near Rancho de Carricitos, about twenty miles out, Thornton blundered into a well-laid ambush, losing eleven killed and six wounded in a sharp fight. Most of his seventy men were captured, including himself and his second, Captain William J. Hardee. The first Taylor heard about this was on the twenty-seventh. About noon a Mexican cart rolled in carrying a badly wounded dragoon and a note from Torrejón saying that he did not have medical facilities to care for the man. He assured Taylor that the rest of the detail were prisoners, well cared for. The injured soldier confirmed that Thornton's outfit had been attacked by soldiers, not bandits.

Thornton, Hardee, and the rest were safe at Matamoros, where Hardee was permitted to send a report to Taylor. He took pleasure, he said, "in stating that since our surrender I and my brave companions in misfortune have been treated with uniform kindness and attention." Hardee and another officer were living with Arista at his hotel, sharing his meals. "General Arista received us in the most gracious manner; said that his nation had been regarded as barbarous, and that he wished to prove to us the contrary." Thornton joined the party that evening and also sent a report to Taylor.[41]

News of this victory over the *Gringos* spread joy in Mexico. In Tampico a broadside offered "honor and glory a thousand and one times" to the Mexican army. Arista congratulated Torrejón, saying that his action had caused "rejoicing to all the Division of the North." Arista later bragged, "I had the pleasure of being the first to start the war."[42]

There was no joy on the North American side, where United States regulars had been thoroughly whipped. Taylor called on the governors of Texas and Louisiana to raise volunteers, then limply told the adjutant general that "hostilities may now be considered as commenced." Elsewhere in

Taylor's camp a gloomy Lieutenant Ulysses S. Grant complained, "We were sent to provoke a fight, but it was essential that Mexico should commence it. It was very doubtful whether Congress would declare war, but if Mexico should attack our troops." Now Polk could stampede a declaration. "Once initiated there were but few public men who would have the courage to oppose it."[43]

WHAT HAS THIS UNFORTUNATE COUNTRY DONE TO YOU?

Polk spent May 10, a Sunday, drafting his war message. That evening he called in congressional leaders to ask their advice about authorizing war and paying for it. Before reaching the White House, John C. Calhoun assembled his own allies to head it all off. He would postpone war with Mexico and instead appropriate money to make sure that Taylor's troops were supplied. Calhoun also retained his objection to expansion westward out of fears of a debate over slavery.[44]

The rudest shock for the president came from an old ally, Thomas Hart Benton. Sixty-four years old, he had been a senator from Missouri since 1821. No one was a stronger advocate for national expansion, but he had been a colonel in the War of 1812, an experience that made him believe that negotiation was always better than war. Benton was at heart a fighter—he spent his life battling tuberculosis with a Spartan regimen of cold baths and exercise—and a veteran of several duels, including one in which he shot Andrew Jackson. He was deaf in one ear, but that did not slow him down. Neither did anything else when he had an object in view. Benton was a book collector, his libraries in St. Louis and Washington each claiming the title of largest private holding in the country. He was especially devoted to the Greek and Roman classics, but he consumed everything as ammunition for his politics. The senator was a mountain of a man, with a great mountain of a head. He had a lantern jaw, a large, noble nose, and wide, knowledgeable eyes, all crowned with a thatch of white hair. His voice was Olympian—his colleagues called him "Thunderer." Some of his speeches lasted twelve hours, and he orated like a volcano, erupting great fountains of fiery prose that rained down on his audience the way ash and cinders had descended on Pompeii. Benton was a man to reckon with.[45]

After he read Polk's war message, Benton "was willing to vote men and money for defence of our territory," Polk recorded, "but was not prepared to make aggressive war on Mexico." The senator told the president for the first time that he had all along opposed the order for Taylor to advance to the Rio Grande. Polk was positively shocked, because he could not count on Benton's support for his war measure. Their alliance remained intact, but it had suffered its first strain.[46]

Polk sent his proposed legislation to Congress on the morning of May 11 under the title "An Act for the Prosecution of the Existing War between the United States and the Republic of Mexico." The president did not want to declare war, in other words, just to declare that one had already begun. He explained that he had sent Taylor to Corpus Christi to "meet a threatened invasion of Texas by Mexican forces, for which extensive military preparations had been made." He offered no evidence to support that charge. Sending Taylor on to the Rio Grande was an "urgent necessity" to defend "that portion of our country" against Mexican aggression. He did not acknowledge that title to the Nueces Strip was in dispute. The United States, Polk averred, had tried everything to resolve the differences between the two countries, but to no avail. Then came the clincher: "Mexico has passed the boundary of the United States, has invaded our territory and shed American blood upon the American soil."

Neither Mexico nor the United States ever declared war. Each announced that the other had invaded, and therefore that a war existed. Polk knew he could not get away with that alone. Accordingly, his proposed resolution was "for the prosecution of the existing war." The legislation authorized calling up 50,000 volunteers to serve at their own choice for a year or the duration of the conflict. Together with authority to complete warships under construction, the legislation ensured that the troops under Taylor would be supplied. The total bill would be $10 million—far too little if the war went on more than a few months.[47]

By combining the war resolution with an appropriation for the soldiers, Polk boxed in the opposition—no one could vote against the war without being accused of not supporting the troops. Opponents were furious, as were some of Polk's Democratic supporters. John Quincy Adams led Whigs in the House against this "most unrighteous war," but the Democratic leadership cut debate off at two hours. The vote was 174 in favor, 14 anti-slavery Whigs opposed, and 20 abstentions, on May 11.

The Senate was trickier, because even members of Polk's party did not like being bulldozed and debate could not be cut short. Calhoun demanded an examination of the facts before a declaration of war. On Benton's recommendation the war parts of the resolution went to the foreign relations committee, the military appropriations to the military affairs committee. Calhoun failed to delete the bill's preamble blaming Mexico for the war. Benton opposed "aggressive war" but favored money for the troops. Polk's allies dominated the committees, which both reported favorably. Debate continued through the twelfth, the chief issues being that the ownership of the Nueces Strip was debatable, not grounds for war, and that Polk had sent Taylor's army into the danger he now de-

manded it be protected from. The "support the troops" argument prevailed, rolling over almost all the Whigs. The final vote was forty yea, two
(both Whigs) nay, and three abstentions—Calhoun and two Whigs.[48]

The lawmakers rubber-stamped every other war measure Polk sent up
over the next month. Those included further expansions of the navy, increasing the number of privates in the regular army from sixty-four to one
hundred per company, authorizing a company of sappers and miners and a
regiment of mounted riflemen, and empowering the president to appoint
general officers (a license to appoint Democrats). Polk signed the first
measure on May 13 and issued a war proclamation modeled on that of
1812. He did not understand that he had just repeated the most serious
blunder of the War of 1812, relying too much on short-term volunteers.[49]

Polk had gained a victory, but he gave no thought to the consequences
of how he did it. He had made partisanship venomous; instead of trying to
gain support among Whigs he had alienated them on the strength of his
own party's majority, ramming through Congress authorization for a war
against a country that posed no threat to the United States. Polk's justification, that Mexico had invaded the United States, was even more dubious.
Once the first flush of war fever wore off, the questions squelched in
Congress would arise again. The Whigs in particular resented the way they
had been log-rolled. Joshua Giddings predicted disaster for his party because it had caved in to the president. Congressman John McHenry
lamented, "It is useless to disguise the fact that we have been brought into
this war by the weakness or wickedness of our prest. and his cabinet,
and . . . it is grevious [sic] to know that when we pray 'God defend the
right' our prayers are not for our own country." Elections were approaching, however. If the Whig Party could overcome its complicity in what it
saw as an immoral act, the political landscape would change.[50]

Polk and his minions celebrated their triumph on the evening of May
13. Secretary of State Buchanan—a pudding-faced temporizer whose
presidential ambitions had ceased to be a secret—had drafted a message to
all United States embassies. To Polk's annoyance it renounced any territorial ambitions, specifically California. "I told him," Polk wrote in his diary,
"that though we had not gone to war for conquest, yet it was clear that in
making peace we would if practicable obtain California and such other
portion of the Mexican territory as would be sufficient to indemnify our
claimants on Mexico, and to defray the expenses of the war which that
power by her long continued wrongs had forced us to wage. I told him it
was well known that the Mexican Government had no other means of in-
demnifying us."

That was as clear a statement of his motivations as Polk ever gave. He had wanted California and the other territories, had kept pressuring Mexico, and had blundered into a war if that was what it took to achieve his goal. The claims issue justified all of that. Buchanan replied that the British and French would want to know if the United States aimed to take California; if they did not get a straight answer, they just might join Mexico's side. Polk declared that he would not let foreigners dictate United States policy. The rest of the compliant crowd nodded, isolating the secretary of state. Buchanan agreed to amend his message. "I was much astonished," Polk wrote later that night, "by the views expressed by Mr. Buchanan." He would tolerate nothing but absolute agreement in his government.[51]

Benton was disgusted. Polk had got his war, but in the Thunderer's opinion he had no idea what to do with it. The president and his allies clung to the notion that just by increasing the pressure they could get Mexico to cave in. They failed to take account of the Mexican view, and so they assumed the war would be short and sweet. Benton thought he knew better than men who knew little of geography, less of military principles, and still less of their Mexican opponents. He called them "men of peace, with the object to be accomplished by means of war . . . but they wanted no more of it than would answer their purposes. . . . Never were men at the head of a government less imbued with military spirit, or more addicted to intrigue." Benton feared that Polk had set a pattern that would be repeated far into the future, leading the country into calamity after calamity.[52]

When word of Polk's triumph reached Mexico City, Paredes prepared his own message to the Mexican Congress, which assembled on June 6. He also asked for a declaration of war against the invader. Instead, the lawmakers gave him authority to repel the invasion. Paredes formally proclaimed defensive war on July 9 and hit the Church up for a hefty loan. The president was deathly afraid that raising taxes or rousing the masses would cause a backlash against him. Paredes still hoped that the British would intervene and believed that monarchists in Mexico and their friends in Europe would come to his aid, but they no longer had much following. In fact, there was little support in Mexico for the war, whatever its cause. So Paredes let word slip to Consul Black that he might be willing to negotiate.[53]

Yet the war had to be faced. Foreign Minister Peña sent a circular to all state governors saying, "Realistically, our only hope would not be for victory, but simply the avoidance of certain defeat." Paredes' cabinet adopted a strategy for the war in three phases. First, the army should try to confine the fighting to the north. Failing that, the country should fortify the mountain passes to the east, confining the invader to the *vómito* country. If both of these failed, the country would turn to guerrilla warfare.[54]

"It is enough to say that the war was caused by the insatiable ambition of the United States," Ramón Alcaraz said when it was over, "aided by our weakness." That was fair enough. Mexico had been in chaos since before 1821. Polk took advantage of that weakness to waltz into war. War could have been avoided, except that there were not enough strong voices on either side willing to stop the march into it.[55]

In the legislature of Chihuahua, Roque J. Morón rose to ask of the United States, "What has this unfortunate country done to you? . . . Oh! Is a benign and hospitable state, afflicted and desolated for fifty years by savages and inundated by the blood of its men and by the tears of its widows and orphans—is this a fitting theatre for displaying the power of the United States, drowning out in the clamor of an unjustifiable war the indignant voices raised from the tombs of Franklin and Washington?"[56]

It was already too late to ask that question. Even as Polk scored his triumph in Congress, more blood had been shed near the Río Bravo. And as Señor Morón spoke, armies were marching in his direction.

CHAPTER

6

EVERYTHING ANNOUNCED
A GRIEVOUS DISASTER
(May–June 1846)

The corpses stripped naked, the enemies dying in agony,
the awful scenes, the wounds steaming in the air. . . . Triumph is the most
beautiful thing in the world . . . but its foundation is
human blood, and shreds of human flesh.

—Marquis d'Argenson

GENERAL WINFIELD SCOTT WAS A MAGNIFICENT statue of a man,
six feet four inches tall with an iron frame. He was sixty years old in 1846,
a soldier since 1808. Age and comfortable living had added bulk to his
body, but he still cut a commanding figure. Scott's square jaw had an extra
chin or two under it, his small mouth was almost prim, and his hawkish
nose and large, fierce eyes gave him the look of a giant bird of prey. He was
going gray, and his receding hairline bared a magnificent brow. His face
was carved by deep furrows on his forehead, downward from his mouth to
his chin, and from his nose to his emerging jowls.

Scott was a Virginian, but he really had no home save the army. During
the War of 1812 he distinguished himself at Queenston Heights in 1812
and Fort George the next year. At the "camp of instruction" in New York

he turned raw recruits into regulars. His men stunned the redcoats at Chippewa and Lundy's Lane in July 1814, making Scott a national hero, earning him a severe wound, a brevet promotion to major general, and a congressional gold medal. In 1815 the War Department published *Scott's Exercise,* the first new tactical manual since independence. Six years later he produced the army's first set of general regulations, and he prepared a wholly new book of infantry tactics in 1835. Scott was a voracious reader of military literature and a master of planning, logistics, training, strategy, and tactics. His stress on hygiene, discipline, and soldierly appearance earned him the nickname "Old Fuss and Feathers." In person he was charming, an expert cook, a brilliant conversationalist, and a sharp hand at whist. He was also vain and thin-skinned. Literate in several languages, Scott had absorbed all the lessons of eighteenth-century regular warfare. Every campaign should be preceded by logistical planning and conducted with troops disciplined and trained by professional officers. Scott was a strong supporter of West Point.[1]

He had been commanding general since 1841, so Polk had to deal with him. Polk wanted to raise a mass of volunteers and send them out to victory. Scott knew that war was not as simple as that. Polk invited Scott and Marcy to the White House on May 13, 1846, and when the general presented his plan for a long mobilization before invading Mexico, the president told him to revise it. Then he offered Scott command of the field army, and the general accepted. Scott and Marcy returned the next day, and again the general explained all that was involved in raising, training, equipping, feeding, and moving a large army; again the president objected. Polk thought it was a simple matter of calling up volunteers and—just like that—conquering Mexico. "General Scott did not impress me favourably as a military man," Polk groused that evening. "He has had experience in his profession, but I thought was rather scientific and visionary in his views."[2]

This did not, as the saying went, look like the beginning of a beautiful friendship.

THE SONS OF TWO DISTINCT RACES WERE
TO MEASURE THEIR STRENGTH

Far from Polk and Scott, after bagging the hapless Thornton, Torrejón continued on a wide loop around Taylor's army, aiming downstream to cover the crossing of Arista's main force. On the Matamoros–Point Isabel road on April 28 his advance under Major Rafael Quintero jumped a Texas Rangers company commanded by Captain Samuel H. Walker, killing five and capturing four; the rest scattered. Quintero continued on to the

Longoreño Ford on the river about thirteen miles below Matamoros and waited for both Torrejón and Arista. Once they arrived, Taylor would be cut off from Point Isabel.[3]

News of the attack on the rangers caused an uproar at Point Isabel. Walker, who had not been with his company, set off early on the twenty-ninth to take the alarm to Taylor. Walker was a strapping thirty-year-old with striking blue eyes beneath a royal pompadour, a veteran since 1842 of wars against Comanches and Mexicans, who took him prisoner at Mier. "War was his element," said a fellow ranger, "the bivouac his delight, and the battlefield his playground."[4]

Walker reported to Taylor on the night of the twenty-ninth and said that he had seen no enemy troops on the road from Point Isabel. He rounded up men at loose ends and went back for a better look. On the lower river on April 30, Walker observed Ampudia's brigade with four guns crossing at Longoreño. The troops had only three small barges, so the crossing was slow. Arista and the remainder of his striking force got across the next day. Walker galloped back to Taylor, but the Yankee commander was not inclined to contest the crossing. Instead, he ordered work redoubled on Fort Texas. He judged it ready on May 1 and put about 500 men under Major Jacob Brown into the place, armed with two field batteries and four 18-pounders. Taylor took 2,000 men to relieve Point Isabel, setting out at midday on May 1. Arista wanted to cut Taylor off, but the crossing had delayed him too much and Taylor covered eighteen miles before camping at midnight. The next morning he marched into Point Isabel and set men to digging fieldworks.[5]

Arista faced a choice. He could drive on Point Isabel, aiming to destroy Taylor's base and its stores and the enemy army as well. He thought Taylor's position was too strong for that, however, so he picked his second option—take Fort Texas. Arista sent Ampudia's brigade and another 1,600 men from the Matamoros garrison under Mejía to surround Fort Texas and start bombarding it the morning of May 3. If he could knock the place out before Taylor relieved it, the entire Mexican army could concentrate on Point Isabel. However, Arista's guns were few and small and his army was mostly inexperienced conscripts led by green officers, not up to assaulting a fortified place.[6]

The first rounds from the Matamoros works at daylight on the third were answered with the heavier United States 18-pounders, which dismounted two Mexican guns. Mejía ceased fire, then ordered artillery downstream to join the party. Those pieces were more effective against the North American field batteries, which shut down. The 18-pounders tried to set Matamoros on fire with hot shot, but failed. The Mexican guns went quiet around sundown, the United States batteries continuing without effect until midnight. Mexican troops muscled several guns and a mortar across the river during the night and set them up behind the fort. Ampudia showed up with four more guns and 1,230 men to complete the investment on the fifth. Bombardment and counterfire continued, but Ampudia did not attempt an infantry assault because his artillery was too light to break up the fort's earthen walls. He sent Brigadier General Antonio Canales' irregular cavalry toward Point Isabel while he surrounded the works with infantry. Arista had dug himself into a dilemma. Besieging the fort was a waste of effort, and an assault would be disastrous. The only possibility of a decisive engagement was between the two main armies, but he had already given up that option. Arista might be able to starve the fort out, but he had divided his army, leaving it open to destruction piecemeal if Taylor headed back toward Matamoros. Arista therefore ordered Ampudia to speed things up at Fort Texas.

Taylor heard the thump of guns at dawn on May 3, but believed that he had to fortify Point Isabel before he did anything else—his thinking was as muddled as Arista's. He sent Walker to Fort Texas with a vainglorious order to Brown to defend the fort to the last man. Walker got into the place before dawn on the fourth but could not get out until the afternoon of the fifth. He got back to Point Isabel late on the sixth.[7]

A cannonball mangled Brown's leg the morning of May 6; he later died after an amputation. Captain Edgar S. Hawkins assumed command. Arista, meanwhile, had ridden up to supervise the siege. He sent a letter under a flag of truce, demanding a surrender. Hawkins politely apologized for being "unskilled in Spanish" but he must "respectfully decline." He was in no real danger as long as his supplies held out. The deadlock continued until the eighth, when Arista recalled Ampudia's men and lifted the siege, owing to movements in Taylor's direction. Besides Brown, one United States soldier had been killed and nine wounded. Mexican casualties were minimal.[8]

The bombardment of Fort Texas gave rise to a legend about a remarkable woman, Sarah Borginnis (or Bourdette), laundress wife of a sergeant. Called "the Great Western" because she was a raw-boned six feet tall, she had been "inducted" into the 7th Infantry in 1840. Other army women had gone by sea to Point Isabel, but she had insisted on going overland, driving her burro cart, feeding the soldiers. At Fort Texas she set up a tent in the middle of the parade and gave food and coffee to the men as Mexican shot smashed her crockery. Her specialty was bean soup, which inspired another legend among *Indios* in the Mexican army—that bean soup gave the

Yanquis superhuman powers. Sarah continued serving food and drinks, tending the wounded, making musket cartridges, and inspiring the soldiers, without receiving a scratch.[9]

Taylor could have used some of that soup. He finally decided on May 5 that he should ride to the sound of the guns, but he delayed to await the arrival of recruits expected from New Orleans. His column set out at midday on the seventh, no doubt spurred on by a grandiloquent order from its commander advising the infantry that "their main dependence must be in the bayonet."[10]

Taylor attached 200 wagons to his column. His train was vulnerable to cavalry raids, while a pair of 18-pounders hauled by oxen dragged at the tail end. Most of the route was over a flat to gently rolling, treeless prairie, but the expedition plodded only seven miles the first day. Taylor rode in a "Jersey wagon of ponderous materials and questionable shape," according to a disgusted officer. The caravan made eleven miles on the eighth before scouts spotted the enemy ahead.[11]

Arista's patrols reported Taylor's movements as soon as the North American left Point Isabel. After summoning Ampudia, he led his troops out of camp at Tanques del Ramireño. Taylor's scouts spotted his army just before noon, as Ampudia's men were coming up. The Yankees stopped at a pond to fill canteens while the rear units closed up. Arista's force was deployed east-west, facing north, blocking Taylor's movement down the road. His cavalry under Torrejón was on the road to the left, against an expanse of chaparral across the highway. Trees rising above the thorny brush gave the area its name, Palo Alto (Tall Timber). Arista stretched his infantry rightward for about a mile, his guns dispersed along the line in pairs, to a 4-pounder anchoring the far right. Canales' irregular horsemen were beyond that. Taylor deployed his army facing south across a nearly flat field broken by small depressions filled with water from recent rains. The space between the two forces was covered by shoulder-high grass, which made it difficult for men on foot to move. The sky was clear and bright, the afternoon hot. Taylor put two infantry regiments in front, two others to his right across the road, covering the supply train to his rear. He had some cavalry along the road and his main line was punctuated with artillery. "For the first time," said a Mexican witness, "the sons of two distinct races were to measure their strength."[12]

The armies finished deploying around two in the afternoon. Arista had 3,300 men under him and estimated that Taylor led about the same; actually, the Anglo strength was around 2,200. The Mexican general surveyed the opposition carefully and noted that his foes "were superior in artillery, since they had twenty pieces of the caliber of sixteen and eighteen pounds. The battle commenced so ardently, that the fire of cannon did not cease a single moment," he reported afterward.[13]

That was both exaggeration and understatement. The Mexican artillery was of poor quality and low caliber (4- and 8-pounders), the shot and gunpowder both substandard, the crews not well trained. Taylor had his two 18-pounder siege guns, not very mobile but packing a wallop, four 12-pounder howitzers, and several 6-pounder howitzers mounted on large-wheel carriages, known as "flying artillery." While the Mexican gunners had only solid shot, the Anglos also had grape and canister, and for the 12-pounder howitzers exploding shell. The infantry on both sides were armed with smoothbore muskets, mostly flintlocks, firing "buck and ball"—paper cartridges each holding two or three buckshot along with the musket ball and powder; as always, Mexican cartridges were overcharged. Arista's troops were footsore from fast marches; Taylor's had made a leisurely stroll from Point Isabel. The Mexican cavalry outnumbered the United States' horse, but the mounts had been in the field for several days, so they lacked stamina for a major battle owing to fatigue and inadequate feeding.

The North Americans approached to within 800 yards, and the Mexican guns opened fire—too early, because the enemy was out of range. The Mexican cannonballs, mostly copper instead of iron, fell short and then ricocheted toward the *Yanquis,* who jumped aside to let them pass. Arista ordered Torrejón to charge the enemy right, not knowing that Taylor had put his stoutest infantry regiments there, planning a bayonet assault on the Mexican left. Twice Torrejón's lancers thundered through the mesquite thicket, only to bog down in a wet slough and be driven back by volleys fired by doughboys in square formation. This did, however, check Taylor's plan to advance on his right. Then the Anglo guns opened, concentrating on the infantry on Arista's left. Solid shot, canister, and exploding shell smashed into the Mexican ranks, tearing men to pieces. The enemy guns, a Mexican reported, "wreaked horrendous damage. . . . The soldiers died, not like victims in combat where they could kill as well as be killed . . . but in a fatal situation where they were helpless." Some of the officers "raised a cry to attack the enemy with the bayonet, because they wanted to get in close and sacrifice themselves as brave men should." That was civilian glorifying, but the terror in the ranks was real and the *soldados* (soldiers) were helpless. A bayonet charge into that gunnery would be suicide, so Arista tried to maneuver his way to victory.[14]

He threw his infantry on the right at Taylor's left, and because the North American also had strengthened his right at the expense of his left, the two armies began a slow wheel until they faced each other on a northeast–southwest axis. The Mexican infantry made little headway against the devastating artillery until the grass caught fire in front of the North American right and drove across the grass between the armies, the smoke so dense and the flames so hot that the battle stopped for an hour. Arista took advantage of the break to pull his cavalry back on the left and advance his infantry and guns on the right and center. When the smoke cleared the firing resumed, spraying blood and bone on both sides. The Anglo artillery tore bloody holes in the Mexican ranks, which the sturdy *soldados* filled in with more bodies. A United States infantry regiment, supporting both the 18-pounders (now on the road) and Major Samuel Ringgold's flying battery, also was mauled by Mexican gunnery and fell back in disorder. Mexican counterbattery fire killed Ringgold and forced his guns back.

The battlefield was choked by stinking gunsmoke and the blasts of musketry and cannons were deafening. Lieutenant Ulysses S. Grant described a common event in gunpowder warfare. "One cannon ball passed through our ranks," he said. "It took off the head of an enlisted man, and the under jaw of Captain [John] Page of my regiment, while the splinters from the musket of the killed soldier, and his brains and bones, knocked down two or three others."[15]

Arista's attack on Taylor's left was repulsed by the deadly artillery. He ordered another infantry charge on the right, supported by the irregular cavalry. The horsemen did not join in, the charge was poorly planned, and the foot soldiers were enfiladed by an enemy battery. The infantry broke and ran away across the Mexican front, carrying other soldiers along in their panic, leaving the army in disorder. It was growing dark then, about six in the evening, and both sides were exhausted, so Taylor and Arista called a truce. The landscape was a grisly scene: dead men and animals, shattered equipment, earth gouged by cannonballs, fire-blackened grass. The moans and cries of the injured, the screams of horses, and the whine of blowflies filled the air. It was too dark for buzzards, but the coyotes spent the night feasting on the carnage. Men prowled on both sides to plunder the dead and bring in the wounded. Taylor's casualties went to Point Isabel by wagon the next morning. The Mexican injuries were mostly from cannon fire, so the men were "mutilated horribly," reported a witness. There was nobody to tend them because the medical officer had disappeared at the first shot and nobody knew where he had left the surgical stores. Some men went to Matamoros on supply wagons, while others were simply abandoned as the army moved out the next morning.[16]

Arista reported his loss as 102 men killed, 129 wounded, and 26 missing. He thought the other side had about 200 killed and wounded, but

Taylor reported 5 killed, 48 wounded, and 2 missing. The lopsided butcher's bills reflected the role played by North American gunnery—the bayonet got no use. Arista had tried to manage his part of the battle according to his limited abilities. On the other side the battle just happened—Old Zach's chief contribution was to strengthen his right to protect the supply train he should have left behind. Both commanders claimed victory and both were wrong. Fort Texas had not been relieved, the Mexican army was still intact, and Arista had not destroyed Taylor's army. The gruesome business would have to be conducted all over again.

THE MOST HORRIBLE CONFUSION REIGNED ON THE FIELD

The sun dawned over a ground fog on the morning of May 9, 1846, and burned away the mist to reveal the aftermath of the Battle of Palo Alto. The day quickly grew hot and steamy. The North American soldiers ate breakfast, then sat on their haunches. Old Zach could not decide what to do next, and dithered until a patrol reported that the enemy was in the direction of Matamoros. Taylor sent a light infantry battalion to probe the Mexican position while the rest of his men dug fieldworks to guard the wagon train.[17]

Arista was more embarrassed than dismayed by the battle on the eighth, but he also knew that his army had been badly shaken. He had to find a place that would hinder the enemy artillery and provide his men cover to steady their nerves. It was right in front of him as he left Palo Alto. About a half mile ahead the open prairie dotted with brush thickets gave way to a dense snarl of chaparral and other brush under a canopy of trees, hardwoods with a few palms. It extended almost seven miles to the Río Bravo, a gently rolling terrain cut by a series of old riverbeds called *resacas,* many with pools of stagnant water at their bottoms, home to leeches, mosquitoes, and wondrous dragonflies. Arista picked the most forbidding, Resaca del Guerrero (Warrior Slough), which the North Americans would call Resaca de la Palma (Palm Slough). It was about three miles from the river and extended west to east several miles, turning northward at the east end. The *resaca* was 10 to 12 feet deep and about 200 feet wide where the Matamoros road crossed it. Both sides of the trough were thick with forest and brush. Taylor later grumped that Arista had thrown away his advantage in cavalry, but terrain favorable to horses was also favorable to Anglo artillery. The forest would channel the Yankee infantry within the range of Arista's guns when it entered the *resaca.*

Arista called in the remaining troops from around Fort Texas and put two line and two light infantry regiments east of the road, along with a battalion of sappers. To the west of the road he placed two more line infantry regiments and a battalion of militia. To the rear and on his flanks sat his cavalry. He put a three-gun battery on the south bank to sweep the road as it crossed the trough, and a single gun on the west, near the middle of his left wing. The other four guns would bear on any force breaking through along the road. A swarm of skirmishers covered the whole front, out ahead in the brush and trees. The nervous *soldados,* about 3,600 strong, felt safer behind all this natural cover, despite the mosquitoes. Arista had made excellent use of the terrain and resources available to him and his position was as strong as he could manage. His biggest worries were the steadiness of his enlisted men and the political machinations of Ampudia, who was plotting to resume command of the Division of the North. Not believing that Taylor would challenge this stronghold, Arista gave General Rómulo Díaz de la Vega "the honor of leading the action" while he stayed in his command tent.

Taylor left a battalion of artillerymen, the 18-pounders, and two 12-pounders behind to guard the supply train. About two in the afternoon of May 9 he received reports that his advance was in contact with the Mexicans north of the *resaca.* Thousands of brightly colored birds streamed into the sky above the forest, shrieking with terror at the first shots. Old Zach galloped forward and conferred with infantry officers who had scouted the position. After some men drew fire to reveal the location of the enemy artillery, Taylor devised a simple plan of attack. Ringgold's flying battery, now commanded by Lieutenant Randolph Ridgely, would move straight down the road at the enemy. Two infantry regiments were dispersed to each side of the road to serve as skirmishers protecting Ridgely's guns. The plan was too simple, because the brush was too thick, and regiments dissolved into small bands. Fire from the Mexican skirmishers was fierce, but overwhelming Anglo numbers pushed them back to the bank of the *resaca.* Clothing and skin on both sides were shredded by the thorny underbrush, and no soldier had any idea what was in front of him. The dank air became a cloud of stinking gunsmoke and ear-ringing noise. Ridgely, meanwhile, went forward without support and got into trouble. His guns beat off a charge by lancers, but musket fire from the other side was too heavy for him to silence the Mexican artillery.

Ridgely called for help. Taylor told Captain Charles May to take his dragoon squadron and charge the Mexican guns on the opposite side of the *resaca.* May rode up to Ridgely's position and shouted, "Hello, Ridgely, where is that battery? I am ordered to charge it." Ridgely answered, "Hold on, Charley, till I draw their fire and you will see where they are." The two batteries exchanged fire, and before the Mexicans could reload and level May thundered over them in a column of fours. The dragoons cleared the battery with few casualties, but May had charged so hard that he was a quarter-mile down the road before the horses pulled up. Under heavy fire from both sides of the road, the horsemen scattered and left May with only six men around him. The dragoons abandoned the Mexican guns and retreated across the *resaca* with a few prisoners. One was General Díaz de la Vega, nabbed by May's bugler.

Taylor ordered the colonels of two infantry regiments, "Take those guns and by God, keep them!" The advance across the *resaca* and through the brush turned into a bloodbath, but the doughboys took the guns. It was now about four-thirty and Arista remained in his tent, sure that what was happening was just a skirmish. Ridgely's guns began to devastate his ranks, and at about the time the Mexican battery in the center was lost, Yankee infantry found a way around Arista's left. He tumbled to the seriousness of the situation and rushed reinforcements to meet the threat. A detachment of Anglos behind the protection of the *resaca*'s south bank beat off two counterattacks and took the solitary Mexican gun on the left wing. This turned Arista's left flank, which collapsed to the rear, throwing the whole army into panic. Troops ran for their lives, leaving behind all the army's baggage and a trail of dropped muskets and accoutrements. "The most horrible confusion reigned on the field, and everything announced a grievous disaster to our arms," said a Mexican with a gift for understatement. Anglo troops ransacked Arista's tent, seizing his records and personal property—and, most important, a map of northeast Mexico, prepared in 1840 by José Sánchez. It gave Taylor and his staff their first look at the landscape they were invading.[18]

Taylor ordered some of his units to pursue the fugitive Mexicans, but they were too worn out. They picked up a few stragglers, then camped on the bank of the Rio Grande while other refugees streamed over the river through the night, many drowning. The colorful birds settled back into the trees to roost. Arista, utterly dazed, staggered into Matamoros about ten that night. His defeat had been total. Of 1,700 North Americans engaged, Taylor lost 33 killed and 89 wounded. The official toll on the Mexican side was 154 killed, 205 wounded, and 156 missing, although Taylor later reported burying more than 200 *soldados*. The defeat was also humiliating. The Anglos acquired 8 pieces of artillery, 474 muskets and musketoons, and the colors of the Tampico Battalion. Arista and his officers had not shown enough attention to the morale of their conscript army and were overconfident about the strength of their position. "If I had had with me yesterday $100,000 in silver," Díaz de la Vega told his captors, "I would have bet the whole of it that no 10,000 men on earth could drive us from our position."[19]

Taylor's army trooped on to its former camp opposite Matamoros. Across the river, Arista and a council of war agreed that it would take about 7,000 men to defend Matamoros but could not decide whether to stay or leave. Arista sent a flag to Taylor proposing a prisoner exchange, and Old Zach agreed. Thornton and his men were traded for prisoners taken at the *resaca,* except for General Díaz de la Vega and his staff—there were no Yankees of equal rank in Mexican hands to trade them for.[20]

North American troops and Mexican prisoners spent the next two days burying the dead of both sides, on both battlefields. "Already, the vultures were at their widespread feast," Lieutenant E. Kirby Smith reported home, "the wolves howling and fighting over their dreadful meal." The stench was tremendous in the heat and humidity and the flies swarmed in great, black clouds. The river began to drop, revealing more bodies, a feast for gar and catfish. Conditions for the burial details were so horrible that they did a hasty job, putting bodies—many already torn apart by scavengers—into shallow graves, and leaving everything else. A party of Texas Rangers passed over the battlefields two weeks later, finding the landscape littered with human bones, hats, belts, cartridge boxes, broken bayonets, and the torn and bloody clothing of Mexican troops. As one of them described the ghastly scene, "The free fresh air of heaven was tainted by the horrible effluvia arising from the dead bodies of horses, mules, and oxen which lay on every side." They spurred their mounts, "leaving the wolves and carrion birds to gorge and fatten undisturbed upon the dainty feasts prepared for their revolting appetites by man."[21]

Some United States officers drew comparisons between their army and the one it had mauled. One area was practicality—Anglo troops had shed excess clothing during the battle because of the brutal heat. Mexican soldiers had kept their heavy quilted overcoats buttoned tight, a habit from a lifetime of poverty. Mexican officers were elegantly dressed, stylish in behavior, and thoroughly incompetent. Mexican foot soldiers marched thirty miles a day, sometimes fifty, while United States troops seldom covered more than fifteen miles. The Anglos thought that the illiterate *indio* conscripts on the other side were courageous and, according to U. S. Grant, "with an able general would make a good fight."[22]

Other officers were not so sympathetic. Kirby Smith called Mexicans savages. "Our men, however, knew that if conquered they would receive no quarter and there was no possibility of retreat, and though surrounded by vastly superior numbers fought with determination." This was a gross exaggeration of the situation at the *resaca,* but not unreasonable when Santa Anna's atrocities in Texas came to mind. Anglo officers throughout the war repeatedly accused Mexicans of murdering the wounded and mutilating the dead on the battlefield. The Mexican side usually lost the ground it fought over, so that was pure bigotry.[23]

Taylor was not sure what he should do next. He had provoked the Mexicans into firing the first shots, as Polk expected him to do, but without a declaration of war he hesitated to cross the river. He needed information about the landscape, and sent an officer on a small steamer upriver to gather intelligence for possible future operations. The boat went as far as the rapids above Laredo, then the officer ventured overland to Presidio del Río Grande. He saw no Mexican troops.[24]

Of more immediate concern were reports that Mexicans were massing at Barita, near the mouth of the Rio Grande. Taylor rode to Point Isabel—soon renamed Fort Polk—on May 11 to confer with Commodore Conner. Knowing that sailors respected fancy uniforms, Taylor donned his, one of the few times he did so. Knowing that Taylor disdained uniforms, Conner met him in mufti. They apologized to each other while their aides snickered. Volunteers had begun to arrive at Point Isabel, and Taylor assigned a mixed force of regulars and Louisiana volunteers to take Barita, which they did on May 17 without naval support because heavy seas kept the ships away. The operation was a waste of time—there were no Mexican troops in the area.[25]

Taylor decided he might as well take Matamoros. Arista observed his preparations, and sent Taylor a message saying that he had received news of negotiations between their governments in Mexico City, so he proposed an armistice. Old Zach decided that his foe was stalling and demanded the capitulation of the city and surrender of all public property, and "then and only then may the Mexican army march out and retire." Arista evacuated on the sly. Taylor started troops across the river about two miles above Matamoros on the morning of May 18, and sent mounted units into the city. They were met by city officials who reported that the Mexican army had left. Taylor promised them that property and nonmilitary persons would be safe, women would be protected, and the civil laws would continue in effect. Ordering the ferries to resume service, he hauled the rest of his army over the river and sent a force of dragoons to chase Arista. They returned on the twenty-second with two dozen prisoners, following a skirmish with the Mexican rear guard twenty-seven miles south of town.[26]

Arista left over 400 wounded *soldados* in the town, but so terrified were they of *yanqui* barbarity that many left the hospitals to follow the retreating army, most dying on the way south. Also left behind were stores for the soldiers and the personal effects of officers. Five cannons and all ammunition for which there was no cartage went into the river. For eleven days the defeated corps slogged southward to Linares, Nuevo León. The weather was hideous, alternately hot and cold; water, food, and medical care were all scarce. Heavy rains turned the road into a long mudhole, and the army was further burdened by about a thousand camp followers, mostly families of the *soldados*. Joining this dismal parade was the Foreign Legion, including deserters from the United States Army. They were among the just 2,638 men still present for duty when the sad procession trudged into Linares on May 28. The ordeal was the end of Arista's military career. Early in June he transferred his command to Mejía, who continued the march on to Monterey. Arista was hauled before a board of inquiry, which absolved him, saying *"perdío peleando"* ("he went down fighting").[27]

THINK OF ONE OF THEM SHOOTING
A WOMAN WHILE WASHING

Old Zach did not come off as well, at least in the eyes of the West Pointers in his command. They grumbled that he had been a slow plodder, had not protected his rear, had burdened his column with the supply train, should have kept Arista from crossing the river, and so on. One said Taylor had a "perfect inability to make any use of the information" given to him. Another called him "*utterly, absurdly* incompetent to wield a large army." One of his own staff groused that Taylor had had "no conception" beforehand of Arista's preparations before the battles. But he had won, and that made him a national hero.[28]

Other officers attributed Taylor's victory to the weaknesses of the other side. "The war is pretty much over," Kirby Smith told his wife, "two thousand men were it our policy could with ease march to the City of Mexico." He called the Mexican people "completely cut up—so panic-stricken," because they had "staked their all upon the turn of a die, and at one fell swoop they have been laid perfectly helpless." This would not be the last time that Smith would predict that Mexico was about to give up.[29]

Some of his fellow officers warned folks back home that the Mexican soldier remained formidable. Newspapers in the United States, however, exaggerated Taylor's victories and predicted an early end. There was also a lot of markedly racial commentary about the inferiority of Mexican troops. The most idiotic tale held that wolves preferred Anglo to Mexican corpses, although some explained this by pointing to the spicy Mexican diet. George Wilkins Kendall of the *New Orleans Picayune* thought it was Mexican society that was inferior. He blamed the rulers for that, with the people oppressed by despots and the Church, kept ignorant, manipulated and deceived by "meaningless manifestoes and proclamations." The army existed mostly to suppress *indio* uprisings or carry out coups. One United

States diplomat chimed in, saying that the *soldados* were "political engines, designed for the domestic police of cities" rather than real military service. The soldier's life was "a mere strife for bread under military despotism." Running down the Mexican character, however, minimized the North American victories. Some newspapers realized that. "In praise of our own soldiers, let us not forget the foe," said one editor. The Mexicans had fought bravely, their courage "worthy of the days of chivalry." Another declared that the conduct of the Mexican army on the Rio Grande had "redeemed the reputation of the whole nation."[30]

News of the battles and the fall of Matamoros was received with stunned shock in Mexico City, according to the British minister. The public had been assured "in the most inflated tone that Victory would follow the steps of the Mexican Army and that annihilation and dishonour would be the portion of their enemies." Now, "profound and bitter sorrow" had settled over the government.[31]

Mexico seemed demoralized, to the extent there ever was a valid generalization about that country. Common people and *soldados* spread tales about the extraordinary strength of the "barbarians from the North," which did not help to recruit an army to fight the invasion. One Mexican soldier told a newspaper correspondent that the *yanqui* troops swallowed gunpowder and whiskey before battle.[32]

North Americans put too much stock in such reports. Paredes had lost public confidence, and the lower classes had no connection to the nation, yet Mexico had been attacked and could be expected to react accordingly. "All Mexicans have felt the pain and outrage," admitted the governor of Nuevo León. "One loss does not lose the war. Mexico should fight to the end."[33]

That was a civic leader. Generals knew how to deliver real bombast. "Soldiers!" General Anastasio Parrodi at Tampico bellowed when he announced the news from the Río Bravo. "Another time we shall conquer. Such is the fate of war, a defeat today and glory tomorrow; that glory which shall be ours at the end of this holy struggle." In true Mexican tradition, Parrodi went on and on, until he ended with a verbal cannonade: "Soldiers! Vengeance for our brothers! Glory for our children! Honour for our country!"[34]

Even in Mexico's stepchild, the neglected northern frontier, the country rallied in anger at the news of Taylor's campaign on the Río Bravo. The prefect of El Paso del Norte told the secretary of state of Chihuahua that all the people in his district "with the greatest enthusiasm" had offered "their persons and every variety of sacrifice to repel the unjust aggression of the North Americans."[35]

No matter how many North Americans—Polk foremost among them—predicted that Mexico would give up, Mexicans would fight an invasion. What they saw as naked aggression against their homeland was incentive enough. If resistance needed more encouragement, the soldiers of the United States provided it.

When Taylor's regulars entered Matamoros, they found it a delightful place. Lemon and other citrus trees were "hanging full of fruit." One officer reported a "delicious evening climate" with *fandangos* (dance parties) every night. Wandering the clean streets, he saw through the windows of the houses a "great deal of beauty—some most strikingly beautiful faces." And there were the *puros* (cigars), seized as public property because the Mexican government held the tobacco monopoly. They were distributed to the troops, giving every man "enough to keep him smoking two months."[36]

The men loved the food served at hotels and market stalls or prepared by street vendors. Tortillas and beans, the Mexican staples, caught on with most Anglos, although a taste for hot chile peppers took some developing. Soldiers bought such comestibles as rabbit, eggs, kidney, coffee, wild game, beefsteak, fried bananas, and fruits. The biggest hit was hot chocolate, which Anglo troops developed a great craving for, complaining that no one back home knew how to make it right.[37]

Taylor distributed proclamations in Spanish and English declaring that the United States was at war with the government of Mexico, "usurpers and tyrants," not its people. The liberators should be welcomed by the Mexican people because the newcomers would overthrow their oppressors while safeguarding their lives, liberties, and religion. Mexicans, however, had generations of experience with empty promises from generals.[38]

And the promises were empty. Most of a long general order renaming Fort Texas as Fort Brown was given over to this sort of thing: "The commanding general is pained to find himself under the necessity of issuing orders on the subject of plundering private property. . . . Such conduct will not be tolerated." Taylor went on at length condemning theft, threatening to court-martial any officer or enlisted man who committed such crimes. "The commanding general is determined that the army under his command shall not be disgraced by scenes of plunder."[39]

The behavior of his troops was worse than he admitted. Most of the problems were caused by the volunteers arriving in his camp, especially from Louisiana and Texas. They were short of supplies, which encouraged stealing, and many had been promised plunder by recruiting officers. According to a regular officer, the volunteers were "the living embodiment of a moral pestilence. Crime followed in their footsteps, and wherever they trod, they left indelible traces of infamy." The streets of Matamoros were overrun with drunken, brawling, insolent armed men, who murdered many civilians.[40]

Mexican civilians quickly made the distinction between *regulares* and *volontarios*. They could abide the former, but they ran from the latter. The failure of volunteer officers (many of them politicians back home) to discipline their men (many of them voters back home) caused no end of conflict with officers in regular units. Taylor, whose political ambitions were surfacing, was ineffective. "The Volunteers have murdered about twenty persons in Matamoros, have committed rape, robbery etc., etc.," complained Lieutenant D. H. Hill early in June. The Louisiana volunteers who occupied Barita downriver destroyed the village, pulling houses down and burning the wreckage, tearing up fences, and obliterating cornfields and gardens. A regular officer told Taylor that the citizens grabbed whatever they could save and ran away.[41]

Murder, rape, robbery, and other atrocities fell hardest on the poorest people. "They lived for the most part in small thatched-roof cottages," barely scratching a living from the earth, one volunteer admitted, yet they were the first victims of plunder. "The majority of the Volunteers sent here," a regular private wrote his father, "are a disgrace to the nation; think of one of them shooting a woman while washing on the bank of the river—merely to *test* his rifle; another tore forcibly from a Mexican woman the rings from her ears. Their officers take no notice of these outrages, and the offenders escape." Owning up to atrocities committed by United States troops was not something either the government or the press wanted to do. A few crimes were reported as exceptional, committed by a few bad eggs who were rooted out and punished. More commonly the papers claimed that North Americans and Mexicans were having a lovely time together. "Intercourse with our soldiers," crowed one correspondent, "inspires the descendants of Montezuma with a profound respect and warm affection for the American people."

Taylor sent a few offenders to the local courts for criminal prosecution, but the Mexican authorities were afraid to act. He sent some of the worst criminals to New Orleans for discharge. He even went so far as to prohibit liquor, but that was shouting into the wind. Robberies and murders became routine. The problems multiplied as discharged soldiers, deserters, and blacklegs multiplied along the Rio Grande, and Taylor complained, "There is scarcely a form of crime that has not been reported to me as committed by them." The most persistent problem was looting of foodstuffs. The injury was only partly redressed when officers compensated the victims. Taylor never found a way to punish crimes against civilians, let alone prevent them.[42]

Stationing an army inside Mexico, Polk believed, would "conquer the peace," a phrase that became common in administration and army circles. There had been a strong secession movement in northeast Mexico and Taylor was under orders to encourage it, but the litany of drunken brawls, fights, gang rapes, stabbings, shootings, arson, robberies, theft, livestock rustling, looting and desecration of churches, and other crimes ended any hope for cooperation before the Army of Occupation had been in the area a month. Matamoros had been turned into a hellhole. "About the principal corners loiter groups of men of all colours and countries who are collected cursing, swearing, fighting, gambling, and presenting a most barbarous sight," complained an officer. "Murder, rapine and vice of all manner prevails and predominates here. . . . As it now stands, it is a disgrace to our country; for our own citizens are much worse than the Mexicans who are mixed up with them. Oh vice! How hideous thy features!"[43]

The *comandante-general* of Nuevo León issued a broadside later in the summer declaring that "people near Matamoros, previously inclined to favor the North Americans, have written these weighty words: 'The domination of the Grand Turk is kinder than that of the North Americans. Their motto is deceit. Their love is like the robber's. Their goodness is usurpation; and their boasted liberty is the grossest despotism, iniquity and insolence, disguised under the most consummate hypocrisy.'"[44]

EL BANDIDO EN EL HÉROE

Kirby Smith could not have been more wrong when he told his wife that the fight had gone out of the Mexicans. He did not know that there was a great, dark army out there. He did not know about *el bandido en el héroe,* the bandit in the hero, although this legendary figure had already introduced himself. A troop of irregulars commanded by Rafael Quintero, serving under General Antonio Canales, "the Chaparral Fox," in the van of Torrejón's column, had attacked Walker's Texas Rangers before the siege of Fort Texas. Canales remained active throughout the war, fought at Palo Alto and the *resaca,* then devoted himself to raiding Taylor's supply trains. That was a continuation of a *guerrilla* he had waged in northeast Mexico for years, and it persisted years more as a combination of insurgency and banditry. He was not alone in defying all flags because there were many other *guerrilleros* in the territory, notably Ramón Falcón, whose band had skirmished with Taylor's scouts since they marched out of Corpus Christi.

United States leaders never appreciated the combined military and social forces represented by the guerrillas. "War made systematically by guerrillas would in the long run have ruined the enemy and given success to the Republic," lamented a Mexican after the war. He thought his government had not fully exploited Mexico's bandit tradition. According to one Yankee officer, however, "The truth is . . . the Americans could positively claim only so much of the soil as they occupied with an army."[45]

Mexico had a large livestock industry, which produced skilled horsemen practiced with every manner of weapon, in particular the lasso. It also had a great outlaw tradition, outcasts from society practiced in hit-and-run tactics, who had often put their irregular talents to military use when one *caudillo* or another gave them a chance. There were others who joined in the persistent agrarian revolts, flying their black flags against the armies and the *hacendados* who oppressed them. When the oppressors were *Gringos,* their energies were easily placed in service to the nation. The hero-bandit was a remarkable combination of social forces and military power. He was the hero of the oppressed. He was the rebel, the *insurrecto,* the *insurgente,* who had driven the *Gachupines* out of the country, then fought against centralist dictators, then reverted to banditry. In 1846 he turned his deadly talents against the *Yanquis.* United States and Mexican authorities alike dismissed the hero-bandit at their peril.

North Americans typically called irregulars "banditti," an Italian word, not a Spanish one. In Mexico bandits were *bandidos* or *bandoleros,* the latter meaning outlaws in large bands. In war these criminals became *irregulares,* irregulars, meaning soldiers who did not follow the tactics of uniformed armies. They were also called *guerrilleros,* guerrilla fighters. United States commanders refused to recognize the legitimacy of irregulars and their tactics, even when a *guerrillero* corps had been patented by the Mexican government. They were "cowards" because they would not stand and fight against a stronger enemy. They hit and ran, plundered supplies, and attacked soldiers caught alone or in small parties.

Anglo officers often called them *rancheros* (farmers or ranchers). This promoted a tendency to view all rural Mexicans as insurgents. Despise Mexican guerrillas though they might, fascinated Yankee soldiers developed a stereotype of their shadowy foes. They called them "hawks of the chaparral," comparing them to Cossacks, "ever on the alert, never to be surprised, and untiring in the pursuit of the foe when plunder . . . is to be obtained." In the North American eye the *guerrillero* was a half-Indian, half-Spanish figure, lean, dark, swarthy, with ferocious brows and a great mustache. These irregulars were the "Arabs of the American continent," feared by citizens and soldiers alike, "but little advanced in civilization." They were expert horsemen who lived in the saddle. They dressed in leather leggings, embroidered shirts, serapes, straw sombreros, and colorful sashes, and they carried pennanted lances and wore belts full of pistols and knives, with swords dangling. The bandit's horse was "as savage and unmanageable as himself."[46]

The Mexican hero-bandit made an indelible impression on the North American mind. He might be an enemy of the *yanqui* invaders, and sometimes he wanted to be an ally. He could be just a resident of the neighborhood aggrieved at a particular atrocity. He might be more concerned with a peasant rebellion or a state struggle for power than with the national war. Sometimes he was just a bandit.

The conquest of Mexico, which had seemed so certain after Palo and the *resaca,* suddenly acquired a new and frightening dimension.

CHAPTER

7

NOTHING IS WANTING TO MAKE THEM GOOD SOLDIERS

(May–June 1846)

There be triple ways to take, of the eagle or the snake,
Or the way of a man with a maid;
But the sweetest way to me is a ship's upon the sea.

—Rudyard Kipling

THE WAR BEGAN ON WATER WHEN THE Home Squadron under Conner took station off Mexico and Texas. As soon as Congress declared war, Secretary of the Navy Bancroft ordered Conner to seize all Mexican war vessels. There were not many. The pride of the Mexican fleet in 1846 were the steam-powered frigates *Guadalupe* and *Moctezuma,* which matched anything in the North American fleet. Six smaller but still formidable gunboats were under construction in the United States. The Mexican navy on the Gulf coast included seven old schooners, three brigantines, and a dozen gunboats. The North Americans seized the gunboats abuilding in their shipyards. The two steam frigates took refuge in Havana. The rest of the fleet scattered to various Mexican ports. The brigs and schooners took refuge at Alvarado, where three were scuttled to block the harbor entrance. The sailors mostly served coastal artillery during the war, while their warcraft were scuttled or captured along with the ports where they were hiding.[1]

Mexico threatened to license privateers to raid United States commerce, and on June 15, 1846, the Mexican Congress authorized letters of marque and reprisal, as this ancient art of legitimizing pirates was called. The United States had used privateers in the Revolution, the Quasi War with France during the 1790s, and the War of 1812, but this time announced that it would treat privateers as pirates (meaning hang them on capture). There was no real threat, however. Two privateer commissions were issued in Spain, and vessels outfitted, but they never operated.[2]

In the absence of a Mexican Navy or privateers, there were no bluewater engagements between Mexico and the United States. There was, nevertheless, a naval war along with the one on land.[3]

NOT A SOLITARY TRACE IS LEFT TO MARK THE SPOT

The United States Navy numbered thirty-three fighting ships early in 1846, mounting 1,155 guns in all. There were also a variety of support and messenger vessels. Two ships were on the Asia station, others on the Brazil station, and five were in African waters. The Pacific Squadron under Sloat included seven warships of various types, soon raised to nine. Most of the fleet was assigned to the Home Squadron under Conner, in the West Indies and the Gulf of Mexico.

The war bill of May 13 funded completion of warships already authorized and raised the enlisted force to 10,000. The navy competed with the better-paid merchant marine, so enlisted strength stayed around 8,000. Conner did not need more big ships, because the waters on the Mexican coast were too shallow. Only two nearing completion, both sloops-of-war, were commissioned under the May 13 law. Conner eventually put together a "mosquito flotilla" of small vessels for near-shore service, and the big-ship appropriation mostly bought small steamers, schooners, brigs, and storeships. The first two small craft were sidewheelers sitting at a shipyard in New York, built for the Mexican Navy. The Navy Department also bought three schooners originally intended for Mexico. The schooners did not reach Conner until mid-July, the sidewheelers until fall, so he lacked the resources to attack Mexican ports during the good weather season.

The United States Marine Corps began the war with 42 officers and 986 enlisted men and expanded to 75 officers and 1,757 enlisted men at its peak in 1847. Total navy casualties during the war were eleven killed and twenty-eight wounded, most of them marines.

The Navy Department was organized into staff bureaus similar to those of the War Department, but considerably less efficient. The United States Navy had assumed a world lead in technology—screw propulsion and modern guns especially—but it was dominated by graybeards who had last seen action in the War of 1812. Like the army, the navy had no retirement plan for officers. Secretary Bancroft tried to reform the service but ran up against furious opposition. He became minister to England in September 1846 and Polk replaced him with John Y. Mason, a fat, easygoing, accommodating Democrat not interested in offending anyone.[4]

Bancroft promised Conner he would raise his squadron to two frigates, three sloops-of-war, two steamers, five brigantines, and one schooner. The secretary advised the commodore to "make such a use of this force as will most effectually blockade the principal Mexican ports, protect our commerce from the depredations of privateers, assist the operations of our army, and lead to the earliest adjustment of our difficulties with Mexico." Conner should let neutral warships and British mail packets through the blockade, but none others. Neutral merchantmen in port should be ordered to leave.[5]

There was not much the navy could do to help the ground force, and Conner was discouraged. "The Navy in this war will I fear have few opportunities for distinction," he told his wife. Lieutenant Raphael Semmes recalled, "There was no town on the whole Gulf Coast of Mexico, within effective cannon range of which, a sloop-of-war could approach. The maritime towns of the enemy were more effectually defended by reefs, sand-bars and shallows, than were his inland towns by redoubts and intrenchments." Coast and harbor defenses were mostly nonexistent.[6]

The Polk administration looked for yet another way to intimidate Mexico. Vera Cruz was the country's main port. Bancroft asked Conner what it would take to overcome San Juan de Ullúa and seize Vera Cruz. Conner doubted that the place could be taken from the sea. He suggested instead landing and besieging the fort. Conner also told his superiors to beware of the *vómito* season and the threat of storms. There would be no point in seizing Vera Cruz except as a base for a campaign against Mexico City, and he thought Tampico would be better for that anyway. For the moment, the Polk administration gave up on taking Vera Cruz.[7]

The commodore had more immediate problems. His ships were all low on drinking water and had to rotate through Pensacola before taking station. New Orleans became the main point of supply, but the Navy Department had not the slightest idea how to provision ships on foreign stations. The navy's experience had been peaceful, commanders resupplying at any convenient seaport. That was not possible on a hostile coast.

Conner sent a party to draw water from the Antigua River in June, but his men were driven off by Mexican irregulars. Frustrated, in December 1846 Conner contracted with a Texian firm to supply his ships with drinking water.[8]

Conner sent an officer to Campeche to see whether supporting the uprising in Yucatán would increase pressure on the Mexican government. The delegate was told to "conciliate" the rebellious state in order to keep it separate from the national government—in other words, out of the war. Rebel leaders assured him that they would not fight the North Americans, but they would not help them either.[9]

An attempt to win friends in northeast Mexico was even less successful. Conner ordered his captains to remain open to the possibility of an alliance with the people ashore. Commander John L. Saunders of the sloop-of-war *St. Mary's* was assigned to Tampico. He proclaimed his blockade on May 20 and threatened to bombard the place unless port authorities released a United States brigantine caught there by the outbreak of war. Saunders' success at that encouraged him to believe that the port could be taken with his one small ship, and he declared that defensive digging going on at the river mouth justified an attack. *St. Mary's* blasted away at the uncompleted fort and three gunboats anchored near it on June 8, but shoal water kept her out of effective range. Saunders sent his ship's boats upriver to cut the gunboats loose on the night of June 14–15, but sentries drove them back. North American invaders would not find a welcome in Tampico.[10]

Conner's main order of business was the blockade. Mexico had eight significant ports on the gulf. Matamoros had already fallen to the United States and Carmen was in the hands of the *insurrectos* in Yucatán. The next five—Tampico, Soto la Marina, Tuxpan, Alvarado, and San Juan Bautista (which Anglos called Tabasco, and Mexicans now call Villahermosa)—were up rivers with shallow bars at their mouths. Each could be blockaded by stationing a warship near the bar, but the coast was open and provided no protection against storms. The major port, Vera Cruz, had no harbor to speak of, and was protected only by Gallega Reef and the fortress of San Juan de Ullúa perched on it. The North American squadron could control Vera Cruz's anchorages, which stretched behind low islands and reefs for about twenty miles to the south. When the blockaders were forced offshore by storms, blockade runners easily ran past inshore. Moreover, the *vómito* season ran from April to October. October to April was normally the dry season, but the ferocious northers (*norteños*) could strike at any time.

Conner proclaimed a blockade of Vera Cruz, Alvarado, Tampico, and Matamoros on May 14. When his ships returned from their water calls he extended the blockade to the whole coast. International law required that a blockade must be "effective" (physical, not just on paper) to be legal, and that a neutral flag protected all cargoes except contraband. The Home Squadron was so obedient to international law that all its prize captures were sustained by admiralty courts, and aroused few diplomatic complaints. In June Conner let neutral mail packets carry gold and silver bars outward and quicksilver (used in refining precious metals) inbound. Mexican mines were almost all owned by foreigners, as was their product, and neutral goods were not subject to seizure. The same applied to the mercury.[11]

Conner established his command post about twelve miles south of Vera Cruz in Antón Lizardo, the best anchorage on the coast. His blockade was hampered by an absence of good coastal charts, shortages of vessels, the scarcity of pilots, and haphazard supplies. Navy Department ineptitude was compounded by the commodore's failure to provide notice of expected requirements in time for supplies to be shipped.

Blockade duty was incredibly monotonous, ships cruising back and forth or riding at anchor outside a port. The vessels were usually alone and the only break in the routine was the occasional sighting of a sail. "During the parching heats of summer, and the long boisterous nights of winter," one of Conner's officers remembered, "our vigilance was expected to be, and was, unremitting." Still, it was a grueling ordeal. Scurvy was prevalent by early summer 1846, owing to a shortage of fruits and vegetables, and much of the squadron would have been useless for offensive action. The Navy Department stepped up its shuttles of supply ships from New Orleans and Pensacola, and on his own authority the commodore bought fruit at Carmen.[12]

The duty could be hazardous as well as stifling. The heat was exhausting during the first summer and more than one sailor became careless. In a typical case, a fifteen-year-old seaman apprentice ordered aloft "left the deck and was seen to gain the top," wrote a witness. "A moment after, was heard one piercing shriek—a crash—and the mangled and bloody corpse of our young and beloved shipmate was stretched upon the deck—his brains literally besprinkling his fond associates." The boy "had broken his back in two different places, his neck was broken, and his skull shattered to atoms."[13]

Such incidents accented the tedium of a stark blue world whose only sounds were the creaking of the hull, the groaning of masts, the wind in the rigging. Officers kept the men busy making everything shipshape. Sailors became so restive that the captains increased the number of whippings as punishments. The culprit would be spread-eagled and lashed while the ship's company watched. Inevitably one man or another snapped. Seaman Samuel Jackson exploded in September 1846 when he was reprimanded for leaving his shoes on deck after an inspection. He punched the officer of the deck twice, and uttered "mutinous and seditious words." Tried and convicted, Jackson was sentenced to hang. Several officers believed that was going too far, but Conner thought the time had come to make an example to deter others. Jackson swung on September 17. Morale did not improve, but at least there were no more incidents as serious as his.[14]

The Home Squadron's sailors had their own war, and they wrote their own epitaph. "There is something peculiarly melancholy and impressive in a burial at sea," said Daniel Noble Johnson. "The body is . . . dropped into the waves, the deep waters close over it, the vessel passes quickly on, and not a solitary trace is left to mark the spot." The blockade was a lonely life, and it led to a lonely death. "There is nothing that can point to the deep, unvisited resting place of the departed Mariner," Johnson concluded his haunted eulogy.[15]

IT WOULD NOT BE A BATTLE BUT A MASSACRE

The war would be decided on land by the differences between the two nations. Their geographic area was roughly the same, but Mexico's population was about 7 million, North America's nearly 22 million. People in both countries lived mostly in rural areas. Those in Mexico were illiterate and downtrodden. Those in the United States were literate and politically aware. Hunting provided part of their diets, so many young men in the north were familiar with firearms, while those in Mexico handled guns only when they were drafted into the army. The United States economy was a burgeoning industrial one, Mexico's nearly medieval and bankrupt. One could supply the matériel of war; the other would have to make do. One country was united under a stable government; in the other the next *caudillo* always waited in the wings and many states and departments were in a constant state of revolt. One nation had a mystical sense of its own mission; the other was demoralized at the top and beaten down at the bottom.

The president of the United States, Polk, was legitimately elected. He also exerted a greater control over both his civil government and the military than any president before him. He micromanaged everything, down to drafting orders to officers in the field. Polk was the first president to supervise a major war (given that Madison had practically abandoned his role during 1812 to 1815), and asserted the primacy of the civil power over the military. On the other hand, Polk was so pigheaded a partisan that he never trusted his two main generals, Scott and Taylor, because they were Whigs. Polk's political influence was pervasive. When a congressman tried to get a commission, Marcy told him, "It is proper to say what I presume you are not ignorant of, that the selections are not made by the War Department, but by the President himself." Polk imposed on the army a set of sorry political generals at the brigade and division levels, his law partner Gideon J. Pillow being the worst. And Polk deserves the greatest blame for the short-term enlistments that hampered both Taylor and Scott.[16]

The president of Mexico, Paredes, had shot his way into office and had been in cahoots with the Spanish ambassador ever since. His government was ineffective in every respect and he exercised no real control over anything, civil or military. He surrounded himself with effete intellectuals, outright thieves, and not a few others looking for a chance to stab him in the back. The bright spots in his administration were his war minister, Tornel, and his foreign minister, Peña, but there was only so much they could do in a country full of defiant governors and independent generals. Paredes was comparatively honest and patriotic, but he was stupid and a drunkard. Just offstage, Santa Anna undercut any chance Paredes had to rally the country.[17]

The War Department of the United States was divided into a number of nearly independent staff bureaus, answerable more to their friends in Congress than to any other authority. These supply agencies were thoroughly professional, however. This was in spite of the fact that Congress had gutted the army budget since the end of the Seminole War in 1842, and forbade stockpiling of supplies even when it was obvious that a campaign loomed on the Mexican border. The first appropriations for wartime supply came in May 1846, and the mobilization was often chaotic. Scott's position as commanding general was made dubious by the regulations. The staff bureaus reported to the secretary of war, not the commanding general, yet he was held accountable for fiscal efficiency. Marcy was unenergetic, so Scott made himself a sort of one-man general staff, preparing war plans and advising the president, estimating requirements, working out operational details, and supervising execution. But he lacked intelligence on Mexican capabilities or even geography and climate. There were no good maps, and Polk and his underlings were indifferent to the need for such things. Communications were poor over long distances, so later in 1846 Scott abandoned Washington to go forward with his own campaign. The one-man general staff became none at all. Because of the professionalism in the supply bureaus, things worked out amazingly well. Quartermaster General Thomas Jesup bragged at the end of 1847, "We accomplished more in the first six months of our operations in Mexico, than, France, the first military power in Europe, has accomplished in [North] Africa in seventeen years."[18]

Mexico had a general staff, but mostly on paper. The Estado Mayor (General Staff) had been created in 1823 and after the Pastry War was expanded into the Plana Mayor del Ejército (General Staff of the Army). It was a small organization, devoted mostly to political infighting, with engineers the only ones who did any work. There were garrison staffs (*mayores de plaza*) headed by officers known as town majors at all cities and most large towns. Armies in the field had a variety of administrative officers roughly equivalent to the Anglo supply bureaus. It all might have worked well, except staff officers shared the weaknesses of the army at large—competition, corruption, and incompetence. The army had become unpopular by the 1840s as a profession among the upper classes, who except for engineers—the one bright spot in this army—were not inclined to educate themselves for technical work. Line and staff officers alike had only one general talent—rebellion.[19]

The United States Army enjoyed increasing professionalism because of the military academy at West Point, which since 1805 had been filling the officer corps with young leaders educated in every sense. Mexico also had a *colegio militar* (military college), established in 1823 as the Academy of Cadets, temporarily housed in the former palace of the Inquisition, then moved to the fortress of Perote. It returned to Mexico City in 1835, housed in Chapultepec "castle," an old viceroy's palace. The school taught officers of both the army and the navy, its seven-year course covering general and military subjects at the high school and college levels. There were usually no more than fifty cadets at any one time, and their career prospects were limited. A young officer wanting advancement had to attach himself to a *caudillo* on the rise.[20]

The United States Army entered war in 1846 with eight regiments of infantry in the regular army, two of dragoons, and four of artillery. Desertion was a constant drain on the enlisted force, but isolation in frontier posts gave the younger officers self-reliance. They had just over 5,000 soldiers under them. The May 13 legislation raised the size of an infantry company from sixty-four privates to one hundred and authorized a one-hundred-man company of sappers and miners and a ten-company regiment of mounted riflemen. Enlistment terms were five years. Congress authorized nine more regular infantry regiments and one of dragoons in February 1847, enlisted for the duration rather than a set period. In March the lawmakers added two more companies to each infantry and artillery regiment. In all, 30,476 men served in the regular army during the war. This was enlarged by volunteer recruitments. A total of 73,352 men served in units other than regulars during the war, including those called up for three or six months at the start of the conflict. The total strength of all United States Army forces probably never exceeded 50,000 at any one time. Regulars and long-term volunteers, despite Polk's insistence on the short-term volunteer, made up 90 percent of the fighting force. About 15,000 of the enlistments into the regular regiments happened in Mexico as transfers from volunteer units. Dedicated soldiers waged the campaigns and battles, and for the most part volunteers consumed supplies and caused trouble.[21]

They also died. United States casualties during the war included 1,548 killed in action or dead of wounds, 10,970 who died of sickness, and more than 10,000 others discharged by surgeons as unfit for duty. Volunteers made up most of the last two groups. Causes of death were diseases above all, sunstroke, bad water, poor medical care, and Mexican irregulars way-laying stragglers. Proportionately the war with Mexico was the deadliest the United States ever fought, with a death rate of 110 per thousand, compared to the Civil War's 65 per thousand.[22]

This was the first United States army to be organized into post-Napoleonic divisions (combinations of brigades) and the first to march under the Stars and Stripes as well as regimental banners. Regulations had adopted the national banner for the army in 1834. This army carried along slaves owned by southern officers. Some died of disease, some ran away to freedom in Mexico, and some died in battle. Their presence reinforced Mexican beliefs that the United States had started the war to spread slavery.[23]

Officers were both the strength and the weakness of the United States Army. The regular subalterns were mostly West Pointers and good at what they did. Regimental officers of volunteers, with some notable exceptions, were inept. Higher leaders, including veterans, were a sorry lot, and the Democrats Polk inflicted on the high command ranged from mediocre to miserable failures. Scott himself thought success in the war was owing to West Pointers, including the more competent volunteer leaders. "I give it as my fixed opinion that but for our graduated cadets the war between Mexico and the United States might, and probably would, have lasted some four or five years, with, in its first half, more defeats than victories falling to our share," he said.[24]

Some North American observers thought that Mexico had an advantage, with a larger army facing a smaller, inexperienced one. The war ministry reported 24,550 enlisted men enrolled in May 1846, although the figure included "ghost soldiers" put on the roster by officers who were stealing pay and subsistence money. The government announced in August

that "all Mexicans from the age of fifteen to sixty" could be drafted and deserters would receive pardons if they returned to their units. For all his
talents at creating armies from scratch, Santa Anna never put together
more than 25,000 men.[25]

The army suffered from repeated reorganizations since 1821. There
were three types of troops in 1846—the permanent troops of the line, the
milicia activa (active militia), and the *milicia civica* (civic militia), the last reorganized and renamed the *guardia nacional* (national guard) in 1845. The
permanent troops comprised the regular army, but many of the active
units, descendants of Spanish provincial troops, were in service for many
years. The national guard was the country's basic reserve, and all Mexican
males between the ages of eighteen and forty-nine were subject to call-up.
They were volunteers or conscripts who were unpaid and supposed to be
armed and clothed at their own expense, which few of them could afford.
Theoretically the federal government could summon them, but they were
really at the call of the state governors and their stooges and provided
manpower for military coups. A national artillery militia existed only
on paper. The overhead for all of this confusion was also reorganized
repeatedly. There were six territorial divisions, under four general com-
mandancies, in the 1840s. Most cities and large towns also had military
commandants. Auditors, treasurers, clerks, and other ink splashers provided staff for each division and commandancy.[26]

The Mexican officer corps was unschooled, corrupt, incompetent,
and heavy with generals. The enlisted men were nearly all conscripts,
dragged from their rural *pueblos* and subject to unbelievable abuse. Their
first introduction to the barracks was to be beaten by a corporal with a rod
and issued a cotton smock and little else. The army was supposed to feed
them, but in practice the troops were given a small amount of what they
were due and told to scrounge. There was seldom any training to speak of,
and few of the troops got to wear the colorful uniforms the regulations
called for. Yet throughout the war the Mexican *soldado* earned high praise
from United States officers for his endurance and gallantry. Commodore
Matthew Calbraith Perry declared, "The Mexicans are not deficient in
personal courage, nothing is wanting to make them good soldiers, other
than military discipline and national ardor which cannot be expected of
men impressed as they are into service, in the most cruel and ruthless
manner."[27]

Indios and *Castas* lived lives of deprivation and hard labor in rural *pueblos* or city slums. This unfortunate background prepared them to make
long, forced marches over bad terrain, doing without food, water, shoes,
medical care, and other necessities. It also engendered a fatalistic accep-

tance of their lot in life. "If the Mexican soldier has something to eat, he eats it," one of them explained to a *gringo* reporter; "if not, he goes without. That is all." When they got the chance the *soldados* deserted, running away from appalling conditions to become fugitives or guerrillas.[28]

The North American soldier was a volunteer. The *soldado* was a conscript. This circumstance produced an element of the Mexican army that persisted well into the twentieth century—*soldaderas,* female soldiers. United States regiments were allowed a small number of camp followers, mostly as laundresses and mostly the wives of noncoms. When a Mexican was dragged away from his *pueblo,* along with him went the main source of support for his family. The families followed their men into service as their only chance for survival. "At this time," one general said, " 'soldaderas' were active in Mexico. They traveled along with the soldiers, fed them, cooked for them, made their uniforms. They even cared for them when they were sick or wounded. These women traveled on foot, often carrying babies on their backs, carrying small grills for cooking, accompanying the soldiers. And many times they died, too—hungry, sick, and abandoned." Anglo soldiers were appalled to find large numbers of women among the Mexican dead after battles. (Mexican casualties in general are discussed below.)[29]

The *soldaderas* presented a tactical burden that the army could have avoided if the national leadership had provided decent quartermaster and medical services. But then, Mexican military experience was mostly coups and countercoups, chess games rather than real battles—which made the ferocity of some of the troops all the more amazing to North Americans.[30]

Mexican officers lived in a fantasy world when it came to the realities of war. Waddy Thompson, United States minister in the early 1840s, saw disaster ahead if shooting started. "They have more than two hundred generals, most of them without commands," he grumped. "Every officer who commands a regiment has the title of general, and is distinguished from generals who have no commands by the addition of 'general effectivo.' " They did not have the slightest idea how to conduct a battle, Thompson thought. He once told a colonel that he had noticed that Mexican units never attempted a tactical evolution in the face of the enemy. They resorted instead to "mere melées" that ended with a cavalry charge, "which is, therefore, the favorite corps with all Mexican officers." In his opinion, both Mexican horses and their riders were inefficient against infantry. The colonel answered that there were no infantry squares impregnable against Mexican horse soldiers because "the cavalry *armed* with lassos rode up and threw them over the men forming the squares, and pulled them out, and thus made the breach." Thompson opined that Mexican troops might fight each other well enough, "but in any conflict with our own or European troops, it would not be a battle but a massacre."[31]

North Americans nevertheless admired Mexican proficiency with the rope. "The Mexicans have always been justly celebrated for their dexterity with the lasso," one Yankee recalled, "and while crossing the prairies I had several opportunities of seeing a man use it. He, having a very well-trained pony, boasted that he could hold anything, even a buffalo, with his nicely plaited lasso of deerskin." The man proved his boast.[32]

That talent did not make up for the lack of food, clothing, good weapons, or medical care. The United States soldier was in comparison well supplied. Rations were as they had been for decades, salt meat and flour mostly, along with hardtack, beans, and the occasional fresh meat from a herd driven along with the army. North American commissaries had funds to purchase rations locally, and so did the soldiers because they were usually paid every other month as the regulations required.[33]

Clothing for North American troops was less dependable, owing to transportation and manufacturing shortages. Volunteers were required to clothe themselves in return for a monetary stipend. They did so in wondrous variety, many of them trying hard not to look like regulars. Red flannel shirts were uniform in some regiments. Regulars packed away their parade-ground shakoes, pompons, and trim in favor of a fatigue uniform of a navy-blue blouse over sky-blue trousers with a forage cap on top. Troops wore their clothing out and replaced it with whatever they could get. Straw hats were especially popular, and at one point a quartermaster issued captured stocks of Mexican army uniforms. Long hair and beards, violating the regulations, became popular during the war; Taylor did not care, but Scott did.[34]

The North Americans benefited from competent technical services. All West Point graduates were trained as engineers, and those assigned as military engineers were the tops in their classes. The army also had a corps of topographical engineers who mapped everything everywhere they went. Medical services, on the other hand, were a mixed story. The medical corps suffered shortages of supplies and facilities, not to mention surgeons, but it was a field that was improving rapidly. The first battlefield use of anesthetics occurred in both armies during this war. The tendency of volunteers on the northern side to violate basic sanitary principles, however, caused the high mortality from disease. One soldier called his division's hospital "the soldier's grave-yard."[35]

Uncle Sam wanted his army to be musical, so every regiment, regular or volunteer, had a band. Besides the marches of the day, the most popular number was "Yankee Doodle," with "Hail Columbia" next in favor. "The Star-Spangled Banner" first caught on during the war, and in camp song-fests troops chorused such old favorites as "The Girl I Left Behind Me" and "She Wore a Yellow Ribbon" and sentimental hits including "Home Sweet Home" and "Oh! No, I'll Never Mention Him." Minstrel music, called "Ethiopian," played with banjos and bones, was also popular. Between numbers, the soldiers could tell their stories to newspapermen. The war between the United States and Mexico was on both sides the first to be covered on the scene by journalists.[36]

NOT ONE SHOT IN A THOUSAND COULD HIT ITS TARGET

The essential supply for an army was its weaponry, and there the Mexicans were at a disadvantage. The war ministry counted 635 cannons, 15,789 muskets, 8,155 swords, 100,000 artillery rounds, and more than 400,000 musket balls on hand at the end of 1845. Tornel imported 104 new cannons early in 1846, before the blockade cut off supplies. As in the United States forces, most small arms were flintlocks and all were smoothbores except for a few *carabinas* (rifles) imported from France in the 1820s but never put to much use. The chief infantry weapon was the *fusil* (flintlock musket), loaded from the muzzle with a small powder charge in the pan under the flint, and mounting a socket bayonet about a foot and a half long. Cavalry firearms were mostly *escopetas* (musketoons, short muskets), also muzzle loaders. Experience facing North American *rifleros* (or *carabineros*, riflemen) led to the distribution of a few rifles. Most firearms were Napoleonic War surplus bought from Britain in the 1820s.

The cavalry was the darling of the Mexican army, the one branch where the men were fairly well treated and valued for their skills. North American officers thought Mexican horses were too small and frisky to be effective in the charge, but often they were proven wrong. At the beginning of the war there were nine permanent cavalry regiments, each supposed to have 782 officers and men, although most were on a peacetime footing of 300 to 400. Each heavy squadron also had twelve lancers, in principle providing ninety-six lancers per regiment, grouped together when needed. There were also several light cavalry regiments—cuirassiers, chasseurs, and all lancers. They wore brightly colored uniforms with shakoes or plumed helmets. Mexican lances had shafts about six feet long with iron tips of about one foot. Infantrymen fired muskets in the .70-caliber range (supply was complicated by a variety of calibers in use) firing a one-ounce ball. The *escopeta,* when not used as a shotgun, fired a heavier round. The weapons suffered from all the limitations of smoothbores—

limited range and accuracy, compounded by the flinching produced by the overloaded cartridges. The Mexican army's tactics, such as they were, like its uniforms, owed much to emulating those of the Napoleonic Wars. The absence of training and fire discipline made musket volleys typically ragged.[37]

Fascinated as Mexican generals were with horsemanship, they neglected what the Napoleonic campaigns had taught was the pivotal arm in that day, field artillery. The government planned a school of application for artillery and engineers in 1843, but never funded it. Paredes reorganized the artillery and assigned 250 officers and 5,000 enlisted men, along with 200 clerks and laborers to run it. Mexico had a notable bronze-founding industry because of the demand for church bells, which themselves could be recast as cannons. But the metallurgy of the two products is different, so Mexican bronze guns cast during the war were notorious for poor performance. There were a good arsenal at Mexico City and old-fashioned powder mills at nearby Santa Fe and in Zacatecas, but their product was of variable and generally low quality, with low propellant efficiency. Many of the guns in service were very old, including Spanish pieces from the eighteenth century, and their carriages were often rotted copies of an outdated French pattern. Ammunition was carried on campaign in carts hired when the need arose, and for the guns oxen, mules, and drivers also were hired. Once guns were emplaced they seldom moved during a battle.

Field guns were mostly antique Spanish bronze 4-, 6-, 8-, and 12-pounders. Only about 150 of them were fit for service in 1846. A small iron industry limited the supply of iron cannonballs, so the army often used copper balls, a poor substitute because of lower weight. Domestically made grapeshot was so badly put together that gunners would not use it unless there was nothing else on hand. Heavy artillery was an even sadder story. There were some old bronze Spanish 16- and 24-pounders for garrisons and siege, mounted on carriages without traversing platforms. Guns in forts tended to be very old, such as some at Puebla that had been around for 150 years. The best stuff was at Vera Cruz, where there were about seventy British heavy iron guns, many of them 32- and 24-pounders. Waddy Thompson said of Mexican gunnery that "not one shot in a thousand could hit its target."[38]

United States troops were better equipped, owing to professional interest at the top and the establishment of government arsenals, along with a growing manufacturing sector. Uncle Sam issued 38,000 muskets, 20,000 rifles, 400,000 flints, and 950,000 percussion caps during the war, on top of substantial supplies available in federal and state armories.

Dragoons carried musketoons, sabers, and horse pistols. The mounted rifles organized in 1846 received percussion rifles and Colt revolvers but no sabers. Volunteer cavalry were armed with sabers, rifled carbines, and Colt revolvers. Compared to the Mexicans, however, the North Americans weighted their armies more toward infantry, less toward mounted troops.

The perfection of the percussion cap—mercury fulminate in a small copper pill, placed on a nipple at the weapon's breech where the flintlock had been—allowed United States arsenals to stop producing flintlock muskets in 1842, and the percussion Model 1841 musket became the standard. Scott, however, distrusted the newfangled form of ignition, so the majority of muskets at the start of the war were flintlocks. Rifles—more accurate than smoothbores, but slow to load—remained a minor part of the army's arsenal, although the adoption of the Model 1841 rifle by a volunteer regiment commanded by Jefferson Davis gave the "Mississippi rifle" its nickname. Most muskets issued at the beginning of the war were .69-caliber, weighing about ten pounds, fifty-eight inches long with a long socket bayonet—comparable to Mexican models. They were sighted for 120 yards, with adjustment in sighting possible, but smoothbores were not accurate or lethal at more than 200 yards. The Model 1841 percussion musket came into greater production as the war went on, its smaller .54-caliber ball proving good enough.[39]

The North Americans showed real superiority in field artillery. The reason was devotion to study and improvement following the army's dismal record in the War of 1812. Congress authorized improvements in the artillery in 1821, but except for academic work nothing happened until 1838, when the secretary of war ordered the mounting of four batteries of light artillery, each with six guns. "Camps of instruction" began the following year with artillery batteries maneuvering along with infantry and dragoons. The first public demonstration was so impressive that Congress increased appropriations for field artillery. More exercises and improvements in carriages and other equipment followed, along with experiments to perfect powder mixtures, cartridge design, and solid, canister, and grape projectiles. Exploding shot, case or shell, remained mostly the province of heavy artillery, and was not very effective anyway. The gunnery star by the start of the war was the "flying battery." The chief field guns in those units were bronze 6- and 12-pounders introduced in 1841, each mounted on a two-wheel carriage behind a horse-drawn limber. The 6-pounder threw solid shot 1,700 yards, the 12-pounder 1,800 yards, so Anglo gunners could devastate enemy ranks while standing out of musket range. In 1841 and 1844, the United States adopted several howitzers—guns with shorter range but able to fire at a higher angle over, for instance, hilltops. The bronze field tubes came in 12-, 24-, and 32-pounder calibers, while two iron siege howitzers had calibers of 24-pounder and 8-inch. These heavier items, like other siege equipment including mortars, were not really usable in the field because they were hard to drag over bad roads. On the other end of the scale, there were small mountain howitzers that could be dismantled and carried on mules.

The North American field batteries hit the ground running in 1846, typically as four-gun or six-gun groups of bronze pieces, including two or more 6-pounders and one or two 12-pounders. The mixing of calibers and the speed with which a battery could move around the battlefield devastated the Mexican army at Palo Alto. Two batteries there got off 3,000 rounds against about 750 by the Mexican gunners. United States guns broke up every infantry charge before it could exert any effect.[40]

The army's ordnance bureau had experimented with many things over the years, among them rockets. It produced about a hundred a year on the pattern designed by William Congreve for the British service in the late 1700s—the model that provided "the rockets' red glare" at Fort McHenry, Maryland, in 1814. Their flight was stabilized by dragging a long stick behind, but they were wildly inaccurate. United States ordnance experts received samples of an improvement designed by William Hale, also of the Royal Arsenal, in 1846. He replaced the stick with three small vanes in the rocket exhaust, slotted so as to induce spin and thereby increase accuracy—the same principle as rifling in a gun barrel. In December 1846 the ordnance bureau bought the specifications from Hale; they had a few models ready for trial in January 1847, then went into full production. A 100-man battalion of rocketeers joined Scott at Vera Cruz in March 1847.[41]

NO PUEDE CAMBIAR

The Mexican army was outgunned by the North American army but was clearly superior in one art. That was music, as Anglos had discovered at Matamoros. Every regiment had a first-class band, playing a wide range of music. But the *soldados* had many other musical traditions of their own, brought along from their *pueblos*. There was a great variety of ballads (*corridos*) and laments, and especially a tradition of satire to skewer those who made their lives so miserable. *Patrón* or *hacendado* or *general* or even *el presidente* himself appeared disguised as something else. For instance, there was *la cucaracha*, the cockroach, a comical bungler that never learned, that messed up everything it touched, that could not improve itself. A typical song began, *"La cucaracha, la cucaracha, ya no puede cambiar"*—the cockroach, it can never change.

The secretary of the navy sent the following message to Conner on May 13, 1846: "Commodore:——If Santa Anna endeavors to enter the Mexican ports, you will allow him to pass freely." *La cucaracha, Don Antonio, ya no puede cambiar.*[42]

I DECLARED MY PURPOSE TO BE TO ACQUIRE, FOR THE UNITED STATES, CALIFORNIA

(May–June 1846)

The drums, the drums, the busy, busy drums,
The drums, the drums, the rattling, battling drums,
The drums, the drums, the merry, merry drums!

—W. R. Benjamin

PRESIDENT POLK AND GENERAL SCOTT AGREED on very little, but they shared absolute disgust for religious bigotry. There were two chief targets of this in the United States of the 1840s—Catholics and Mormons. Scott's daughter had converted to Catholicism and entered a convent in 1843, dying there in 1845. Polk had felt the sting of religious intolerance as a boy and was often beaten over the head by bigots for not abusing one or the other religion. He told one "that if I could interfere with the Mormons, I could with the Baptists, or any other religious sect; and that by the Constitution any citizen had a right to adopt his own religious faith."[1]

Polk was president of a mostly Protestant country, where anti-Catholic bigotry was linked to nativist prejudice against immigrants. He was at war with a country where the Catholic Church was the official religion. Catholics and Protestants both supported his war at the start, but on different grounds. Catholics thought taking parts of Mexico into the United States would add Mexican Catholics to their ranks. Protestants wanted to make Mexico a happy hunting ground for their missionaries.[2]

Polk wanted to relieve Mexican fears about threats to their religion, and asked Archbishop John Hughes to persuade Mexicans that there were no "hostile designs of this country on their religion." Hughes agreed to prepare messages to the Mexican people, and the president of Georgetown College recruited two Jesuit priests as chaplains. They served with Taylor's army into 1847.[3]

Fear of a holy war against Taylor ran high in the Polk administration. With the archbishop's help Scott drafted a proclamation and translated it into Spanish, and Marcy sent it to Taylor with orders to disseminate it. "Your religion, your altars, and churches, the property of your churches and citizens, the emblems of your faith and its ministers shall be protected and remain inviolate," it declared. The Mexican people could trust this promise because "hundreds of our army, and hundreds of thousands of our people are members of the Catholic Church."[4]

Catholics may have made up a majority of enlisted men in the regular army because of heavy recruiting of immigrants. They faced bigotry from Protestant officers. One Catholic soldier warned a diocesan paper in Cincinnati about the "mutinous spirit" of the "two thirds" of the army he said were Catholic. Their officers forced them "to attend the sermons of a Presbyterian minister, whose words are mainly directed to insulting, calumniating and abusing the Catholic Church." He was not alone in his complaints.[5]

In contrast to the regular army, the volunteers were nearly all Protestant. Their atrocities devoted special attention to the Mexican Church, robbing and killing priests, raping nuns, looting altars, and desecrating holy buildings. Taylor issued orders against this behavior but did little to stop it. When an officer tried to enforce respect for the Church, it ignited nativist outrage in the United States. Polk's volunteer army inspired lingering hatred in Mexico toward *los Gringos malditos* (damned Gringos).[6]

DISPOSE THE ENEMY TO DESIRE AN END TO THE WAR

Taylor had taken Matamoros, but what would come next was up in the air in May 1846. He wanted to move his regulars upriver to Camargo and use that as a base for an advance inland, leaving behind the volunteers to guard his supply lines. Taylor told the secretary of war on May 21 that he planned to move on Monterey and asked what he should do after he got there. Before that message reached Washington he received his orders: Taylor should prosecute the war "with vigor, in the manner you deem most effective." Marcy told Taylor on June 8 that 20,000 reinforcements were on the way to him. The secretary also approved an attack on Monterey and offered the Polk administration's first hint of a strategy. The Army of Occupation should structure its operations with a view to "dispose the enemy to desire an end to the war" as quickly as it could be done. Everything else was open, so Taylor essentially received no guidance other than to figure it all out on his own. The government did grant him authority to conclude an armistice if the Mexicans asked for it in a manner "sufficiently formal and sincere."[7]

Old Zach had called on the governors of Texas and Louisiana in April each to raise four regiments of volunteers. General Edmund P. Gaines extended the summons to four other states. By May 11 Gaines had called for over 11,000 men in fifteen regiments, their enlistments for six months, in some cases just three. The War Department had made no provision for equipping, feeding, or moving such a force. Taylor envisioned a horde of volunteers descending on him to eat his supplies and then go home. The War Department sent officers out to intercept the six-month units and give them a chance to sign up for a year or go home. They did not catch up with all of them.[8]

Many of the six-month volunteers went home. Others proceeded on to the old 1815 battlefield near New Orleans, where they pillaged the neighborhood and died from swamp diseases. Gaines chartered steamers, so thousands of men were headed for Texas by May. Taylor ordered most of them camped at Brazos Santiago, near Corpus Christi, or at Point Isabel. There they continued to die. "I am growing sick & tired at hearing so often the dead march," Captain Sydenham Moore lamented. Taylor warned Washington that "this force will embarrass rather than facilitate our operations."[9]

Hundreds of the six-month men made it to Matamoros by late May, showing up with no equipment, no supplies, and no willingness to be trained. They added to the crime and other disorder in the town. Private George Ballentine called them "strange, wild-looking, hairy-faced savages of the half-horse and half-alligator breed . . . armed with sabres, bowies, and revolvers, and in every uncouth variety of costume peculiar to the American backwoodsman." A member of a traveling theatrical troupe called his audience "the most motley that ever filled a theater."[10]

Texas volunteers led by Governor J. Pinckney Henderson also arrived in May. Henderson's call for volunteers brought in enough horsemen to make two regiments and enough on foot for a regiment of infantry. The governor decided that was enough for a division, to be commanded by a major general, so he showed up at Taylor's tent to be mustered in. He became a general in the federal service in July.[11]

The most useful Texians were the Gonzales Rangers, commanded by Captain Ben McCulloch. He had become a highly talented scout fighting Indians and Mexicans, so Old Zach attached his company to his own headquarters. The unit was accompanied by two New Orleans journalists, George Wilkins Kendall and Samuel Reid. Because of their reporting the Texas Rangers became nationally famous, and all Texian volunteers were called rangers, although most of them were not.[12]

The Texians proved themselves able fighters, but as soldiers they were disgraceful. Even other volunteers condemned them. They looked different from everyone else, wearing buckskins caked with grease and blood, skin caps, bright red flannels, and filthy trousers tucked into their boots. Their bearded faces, lean, muscled figures, wild eyes, and swaggering ways caused others to call them "savage." The Texians were armed with rifles, pistols, and big knives, and some carried swords. They were veterans of a generation of warfare against Comanches and Mexicans, and deadly marksmen. The Mexicans called them *los diablos tejanos* (Texian devils). One non-Texian complained that the chaparral was "strewed with the skeletons of Mexicans sacrificed by these desperadoes."[13]

These long-haired savages carried on a tribal war against Mexicans. A regular soldier told his diary, "The Mexicans dread the Texians more than they do the devil, and they have good reason for it." Taylor had wanted them at first, but soon realized that they were too much trouble to be worth it. "If they could be made subordinate," he told a friend, "they would be the best, at any rate as good as any volunteer corps in the service, but I fear they are and will continue too licentious to do much good." He later blamed Texian atrocities for the guerrilla warfare that broke out in his backyard.[14]

The undisciplined behavior of Taylor's volunteers was not improved by the alcohol flowing in and around Matamoros. Old Zach again outlawed the sale or barter of liquor, without success. Soldiers found one way or another to fill themselves with *pulque, aguardiente,* or anything else with alcohol in it. Some troopers made money buying the stuff from Mexicans and selling it to comrades. "With a canteen on their sides, and a little cup in their pockets," according to one volunteer, these "traveling groceries" were always ready.[15]

Taylor's quartermaster, Major Charles Thomas, based at Point Isabel, might have taken a clue from the bootleggers. Getting transportation for military supplies was his biggest challenge. He asked Washington on May 15 for one or two river steamers, and nine days later Taylor raised that to four. The quartermaster at New Orleans asked the quartermaster general for permission to buy eight. Some showed up on the Texas coast in June, and by July 23 at least a dozen were working the Rio Grande. That did not make up for the persistent shortage of wagons. Jesup had ordered 700 at the outbreak of war, but there was not enough production capacity to fill the order, so only a handful reached Point Isabel by August. Poor logistical support was the army's biggest complaint throughout the war. Nevertheless, by midsummer Taylor's became the best-supplied field army in United States history up to that time, and the same was true in the navy.[16]

Taylor's strategic objective, if any, never was clear, other than going in the direction of Monterey. As Old Zach eventually would realize, an advance to Mexico City was all but impossible. Polk simply hoped that having Taylor occupy some Mexican territory would force the opposition to make peace, but Taylor's logistical incompetence and the atrocities against citizens guaranteed that his campaign would not achieve much.[17]

NO MAN CAN SEE THE END OF THE BUSINESS

If Taylor was in over his head, so was Polk. The president was the "Napoleon of the backwoods," as a London newspaper called him, "the unscrupulous ruler of a democratic state confidently appealing to the passions of the populace." He remained stubbornly sure that the Mexicans were about to give up. Polk thought he would gain victory within four months, and proposed that the first war bill authorize volunteers for six months. Wiser heads—for once he listened to Scott, and for once Marcy backed the general up—prevailed, and the terms were set for one year. That was still too short a time to train, equip, transport, and feed the new levies and get useful service out of them. Leaving officer appointments to the states, as Polk insisted, guaranteed a corps of vainglorious hacks.[18]

Polk assumed that marching an army into northern Mexico would impel its leaders to surrender. He failed to consider that they had a sizable army in the central part of the country. He also failed to consider why Mexico should be expected to surrender territory when for a decade it had fought against the loss of Texas. Polk nevertheless remained fixed on the idea that the war would be short. He also faced a monumental economic problem. The nation's credit was almost nil, the economy was in the mud, and passage of the war declaration had caused the stock market to fall. Yet it was a pillar of Democratic Party ideology that the tariff of 1842 was too high, so Polk and his allies in Congress cut the tariff, the government's chief source of income. Democratic ideology also railed against the idea of a central national bank, although previously destroying the Bank of the United States had left the government unable to finance the War of 1812. Polk came up with a dodge, the "independent treasury." Established along with the tariff reduction in August 1846, the revised treasury department in effect became a new national bank. "Our administration seems enamoured of ruin," wailed a Whig newspaper, predicting budget deficits far into the future. But the aftermath of the Irish famine and the repeal of the British corn laws increased United States grain exports. Polk paid for his war.[19]

There was another reason Polk needed to press his war aims quickly, and that was because enthusiasm was at a high pitch. News of fighting on the Rio Grande "swept like a tornado through the land," said a Tennessee volunteer. "To arms! to arms! came from the mouth and heart of every American freeman." Recruiters promised "roast beef, two dollars a day, plenty of whiskey, golden Jesuses, and pretty Mexican girls" to those who signed up. Jingoist editors thumped the drums for manifest destiny, and "To the Halls of the Montezumas!" was the cry on every side. Enrolling 20,000 volunteers was no challenge, although what came next was.[20]

Polk knew that the national ardor would fade as Taylor continued to sit tight, and even faster when casualty returns came in. He was not worried about the pacifists, led by the American Peace Society, as ineffective at cooling war fever as such groups always have been. They did enjoy support among New England intellectuals, who dominated national publications. One of them, Charles Sumner, had asked in 1845, "Can there be in our age any peace that is not honorable, any war that is not dishonorable?" Such notable writers as Herman Melville and Henry David Thoreau agreed with him. James Russell Lowell lampooned Polk mercilessly in his satirical essays.[21]

Political opposition to the war had more effective voices. A combination of Whigs and anti-Polk Democrats publicly doubted its morality. The Whig Party was divided between conservatives ("Cotton Whigs"), a combination of southerners and some northerners, and radicals ("Conscience Whigs"), mostly abolitionists from the north and northeast. The Cottons, who included Daniel Webster, thought the war was based on fraud and abuse of a helpless neighbor. The Consciences, led by John Quincy Adams, charged that the war was naked aggression in service to the slave power. Most Whigs, the moderates, had voted for war in Congress out of fear of being branded unpatriotic, and so were compromised into funding it.[22]

Polk also faced opposition within his own Democratic Party, which was dominated by expansionist "doughfaces" who believed in manifest destiny and cared not a fig for the slavery issue. Yet it was just that subject that widened the sectional fissures in the country, cutting across party lines. Many northern Democrats opposed the war out of constitutional doubts about how it started and opposition to spreading slavery. Most distressing to Polk loyalists was the growing resistance of South Carolina's Senator John C. Calhoun, a fire-eater with the mane of a lion and the roar to go with it. He had opposed the war because he feared it would aggravate sectional tensions, threatening his region's commanding position in Congress.[23]

Many ordinary Americans harbored doubts about Polk's enterprise, even as the flags waved and the politicians speechified. G. Mott Williams warned his father, "No man can see the end of the business in which we are now embarked. Under these circumstances I would dissuade all movements at Volunteering."[24]

I CAN HAVE NO CONFIDENCE IN
GENERAL SCOTT'S DISPOSITION

Polk therefore had to work fast to achieve his aims, or find himself waging war alone. He was an extremely hard worker, but he was not alone, because Scott toiled around the clock, trying to put the army on a war footing. But he did not keep Marcy or the president sufficiently informed about what he was doing.[25]

The president invited the general and the secretary of war to visit him again on May 14, 1846. He told them that he thought "the first movement should be to march a competent force into the Northern Provinces" of Mexico. They agreed. They also bowed to his desire to send a 2,000-man army to Santa Fe and another of 4,000 against Chihuahua. Scott, superseding Taylor, would occupy the lower Rio Grande and extend United States power into northeast Mexico. This would require 20,000 men to be drawn from eleven southern states, Illinois, and Indiana. Scott advised that volunteers could not reach the Rio Grande in substantial numbers until early August, during the rainy season, and even then the horses' hooves would not yet be hard enough for heavy service. He recommended training the troops in the United States before marching them off in September. These practical military considerations took no notice of Polk's political interests. Polk grumbled to his diary that night that Scott was not the man for the job.[26]

The president was wrong. Scott was a good soldier, but duty-bound to offer his best professional advice. He also performed heroic labors beyond the talents of Marcy or even the energies of Polk. He issued a stack of orders on May 15 for arms, supplies, and transports for the volunteer army. He also prepared the secretary of war's requisitions to the state governors to raise troops. These were complicated, especially because of the militia

tradition. Governors were to ask militia officers or county sheriffs to assemble the local militias and call for volunteers. These would go to rendezvous designated by the governors, where they would be organized and
enrolled. Once a regiment had been assembled, a federal officer would
muster it into federal service. In the general absence of standing militias,
the states must figure out on their own how to provide officers. Regiments
followed the regular organization, except that companies were limited to
eighty privates in the infantry and sixty-four in mounted units. In practice,
the sizes of volunteer regiments varied from 691 men in one Tennessee
outfit to 1,182 in another from Virginia. Over Scott's objections, Marcy
told the governors that their volunteers could choose between serving for
the duration or for one year. All took the latter.[27]

Polk remained blithely unaware of the mountain of paperwork that
Scott had just produced. The president told the cabinet on May 16 that he
would go ahead with the campaigns against Santa Fe and Chihuahua, "leaving General Scott to occupy the country on the lower Del Norte and in the
interior." He secured Senator Benton's blessing for this, but things became
increasingly tense when Polk, Marcy, and Scott were in the same room.
Marcy backed Polk, who thought Scott was "embarrassing" them "by his
schemes," meaning his devotion to careful planning and assembly of resources.[28]

There was an explosion building between president and general. Once
Polk had decided on an objective he was deaf to any contrary facts. Scott
was thin-skinned and almost as bullheaded as Polk. The president wanted
Scott to rush his 20,000 green soldiers into Mexico and end the war fast,
and resented the general's refusal to understand his political concerns.
Scott was annoyed by Polk's refusal to recognize that it was not possible to
turn volunteers into good soldiers overnight. Untrained soldiers, the general knew, were dead soldiers in camp or in battle. When Scott said that it
would take until September to have a competent army on the border, Polk
concluded that the general was just stalling.[29]

Western and southern Democratic senators had already objected to
Scott's appointment to command the field army. Polk searched for a way
to sidestep the general. Marcy asked Congress on May 19 for authority to
appoint a major general from civilian life to command the volunteer force.
His measure would also let the government retire Scott at the end of the
fighting, putting the new general in his place. Scott got wind of this the
next day, and "smelt the rat." He told Marcy he "saw the double trick."
Marcy then jumped all over the commanding general for being slow to
leave for the front. This infuriated Old Fuss and Feathers, who had not
been getting enough sleep. He sent an intemperate letter to the secretary

of war complaining about the ceaseless nagging to rush the mobilization. He roared "that I do not desire to place myself in the most perilous of all positions; *a fire upon my rear, from Washington, and the fire, in front, from the Mexicans.*"

Polk saw a copy of a letter Scott had written refusing to reinstate an officer who had been dismissed for cause, a Democrat. "I can have no confidence in General Scott's disposition to carry out the views of the administration as commander-in-chief of the army on the Del Norte," the president grumbled to his diary. If Polk was "compelled" to continue Scott in command, "it will be with the full conviction of his hostility to my administration," and to Polk's "plans and views in the campaign." He saw a political enemy where there was just an honest but short-tempered soldier.

Then Marcy handed Polk another unfortunate Scott letter, from the previous February. "The proposed [regiment of mounted] riflemen," the general had snorted, "are intended by western men to give commissions or rather *pay* to western democrats. Not an eastern man, not a graduate of the Military Academy and certainly not a *Whig* would obtain a place." Polk felt confirmed in his belief that a nefarious Whig was plotting behind his back. On May 23 Marcy handed the president Scott's letter about "a fire upon my rear," giving Polk an excuse to rave to his cabinet about all the generals in the army being Whigs hostile to his person. The cabinet dutifully agreed that Scott should not receive command on the Rio Grande, because he persisted in delaying his move there. Polk and Marcy drafted an order to the commanding general, and on the twenty-fifth the cabinet rubber-stamped it. The long, stiff letter went to Scott that day, telling him that he would not be sent to the front. A messenger handed it to the general just as he sat down to "a hasty plate of soup" in his office. He was stunned. He meekly told Marcy that he had no quarrel with the president or the secretary. It was no use. Scott was out of the war.[30]

With Scott shoved aside, Polk charged ahead. He hit the cabinet up on May 26 with a new idea—send an expedition to California if it could be done before winter. They also agreed to order the third-ranking officer in the army, Brigadier General John E. Wool, to San Antonio to command the expedition against Chihuahua. Polk and Marcy would have preferred giving a Democratic politician that position, but Wool—an experienced veteran and ramrod straight despite his sixty-two years—was the obvious choice because of his record. Troops were ordered to meet him at San Antonio.[31]

Senator Benton hustled an expanded generals bill through the Senate at the end of May, and the House took it up. The bill provided for not one but two new regular major generals and four regular brigadiers, and authorized appointing militia generals to command the volunteers. Whigs were suspicious that one of the major general slots would go to Benton and cut the plan to one new major general, keeping the two brigadiers. The regular commissions went to Taylor and to colonels Stephen Watts Kearny and David E. Twiggs. Militia generals, all Democrats selected by the administration, were to command volunteer brigades and divisions.[32]

There was also the new regiment of mounted riflemen to staff. Polk said he "determined to select the officers from civil life, for the reason that if any of the officers of the present army are promoted, it will produce heartburning with all officers of the same grade." That was a lame excuse for loading the regiment with Democrats. The only exception was Benton's son-in-law Frémont, who Polk said had earned an appointment with his experience on the Oregon Trail.[33]

Polk got his cabinet's final agreement on May 30 to his plan to send a mounted expedition to California that year. "I declared my purpose," he told his diary, "to be to acquire, for the United States, California, New Mexico, and perhaps some others of the Northern Provinces of Mexico whenever a peace was made." Ignorant of the geography, he worried whether California could be conquered before winter. The cabinet agreed that he should order the commander of the Santa Fe expedition to speed up his preparations. The only disagreement was between Polk and Buchanan, who objected to seizing too much of Mexico and opening a north-south rift in the United States. That issue was postponed. The secretary of the navy was told to order the Pacific Squadron to take possession of the California ports, win over the people of that province, and encourage them to secede from Mexico and join the United States.[34]

Polk had made it clear since he took office that he aimed to get California into the United States. With war a fact, the president could openly go after what he wanted all along. He would take California, and he would not give it back.

THE EAGLE OF LIBERTY WOULD SPREAD
HIS BROAD PINIONS OVER THE PLAINS

If Frémont's escapades in California early in 1846 were a Benton "family plot," the conquest of New Mexico was the Thunderer's personal project. Trade between Santa Fe and Missouri was valued at over a million dollars a year. Benton naturally wanted to protect that commerce, and like Polk he wanted to add California to the Union. New Mexico stood in the way. Under Polk's prodding, the War Department had been quizzing officers for information about New Mexico since 1845. One of the more knowledgeable officers, Kearny of the 1st Dragoons, advised the War

Department in March 1846 on how to conduct a war that had not yet started, because he communicated with Benton, who communicated with Polk, who wanted New Mexico.[35]

Kearny was fifty-two years old, a New Jersey native who had been in the army since 1812. He had been on both Yellowstone exploring expeditions, had built Jefferson Barracks near St. Louis, and had established several other army posts. When the new dragoon regiment was authorized in 1833, he became second in command, and succeeded to its command as colonel in 1836. He had spent his life in the saddle and was a splendid horseman. Nobody, not even Frémont, knew the western trails and Indian peoples better. Kearny was a short, slope-shouldered man with a long, clean-shaven face surmounted by a thinning helmet of light brown hair. He had a lantern jaw, a thin mouth, and large, wide-open eyes with a look of innocent wonder. His was the face of someone who educated himself constantly, a gentleman and born diplomat. It was a boyish and also a kindly face, which masked a character that could be hard when necessary. Kearny's intellect made him a natural friend to the heavy-reading Benton. Ulysses S. Grant called Kearny "one of the ablest officers of the day." Susan Shelby Magoffin, wife of a Santa Fe trader, saw a man "small of stature, very agreeable in conversation and manners, conducts himself with ease, can receive and return compliments." She gushed, "How candid and plain spoken the general is; he speaks to me more as my father would do than any one else."

Kearny was a man of decency and humor as well as regulations. An army newspaper recounted a yarn that he had once rebuked a lesser officer for calling his troops "gentlemen." There were colonels, captains, lieutenants, and soldiers in his command, Kearny advised the man, "but no such persons as 'gentlemen.' " Kearny had a reputation as a disciplinarian who knew when to relax as well as when to crack down. His Army of the West did not commit the atrocities that Taylor's army did. His volunteers were homogeneous and mostly from Missouri, and he knew he could discipline them on the march and need not break heads from the outset. In return for obedience, Kearny allowed his men a degree of familiarity other regular officers would not tolerate. A newspaper writer saw a volunteer private slap the general on the back at Fort Leavenworth. "You don't git off from us, old hoss!" the man told Kearny. "For by Ingin corn we'll go plum through fire and thunder with you. What'll you drink, General? Don't be back'ard! Sing out!" Kearny laughed and offered the man some wine, but the backwoodsman thought wine was fit only for women. "Why in thunder don't you go for the corn juice, General?" another Missourian piped in. "It's the only stuff for a military feller to travel on." The general

did not drink the moonshine, but he made friends of men who would willingly follow his orders.[36]

Benton told Polk that if he wanted to take New Mexico, Kearny was
the man for the job, even if he was a Whig. Polk and Marcy were beginning
to understand that while politicizing the army in favor of the Democratic
Party was in their personal interest, detached commands were best
handed to professionals who knew what they were doing. Benton certainly
reinforced this thinking, and he trusted Kearny. During Polk's meeting
with Marcy and Scott on May 13, they agreed that the United States
should send Kearny and his dragoons out to protect trade on the Santa Fe
Trail. They also agreed to send an expedition to conquer New Mexico,
without naming its commander. Polk called on Governor John C. Edwards
of Missouri to supply a thousand mounted volunteers to support Kearny's
regulars. In the meantime, on Benton's advice Polk sent Santa Fe trader
George T. Howard down the trail to warn merchants that a war had
started. There were fears that the Mexicans would confiscate any North
American goods on the trail.[37]

Howard left Washington immediately, reaching St. Louis on May 21.
He rode on to Independence, Missouri, the trailhead, but many of the caravans had already left for Santa Fe. Riding hard to get ahead of them, he
galloped into Bent's Fort and put out word to halt all wagon trains coming
up behind him. He sent messengers to Santa Fe and Taos, but news of the
war had already reached New Mexico.[38]

Taking New Mexico became Polk's first priority as the days passed, because it was on the way to California. He also responded to reports that
the *Nuevomexicanos* were disaffected from the government in Mexico City
and increasingly attached to the United States by the trade over the trail.
As with his daydreams about California, he pictured a New Mexico eager
to declare independence and join the United States. The die was cast during Polk's cabinet meeting on May 30. Kearny would command the Santa
Fe expedition, then march on to California. The cabinet agreed a few days
later to send a heavy artillery company and its guns by ship to the Pacific
Coast, and to authorize Marcy's ally John D. Stevenson to raise a regiment
of New York volunteers and send them to California by water.[39]

"The only doubt which remained," Polk worried in his diary, "was
whether the season was not too far advanced" to reach California before
winter. Everyone he talked to said the expedition was impossible, with
one exception. "Col Benton had given me his opinion" that if the expedition left Leavenworth at once, it should make it. Under the president's
orders, on May 31 Scott instructed Kearny to get ready to move. Another
thousand volunteers from Missouri would follow him as soon as they were

ready. Once Kearny had New Mexico in hand he should march by "the most southern practicable route" to California. He must hurry, Scott emphasized, both for tactical effect and to beat the snows to the mountains.[40]

The additional Missourians were a mounted regiment created to give a command to Democrat Sterling Price, a Benton supporter. Then an extra source of manpower presented itself in the person of Elder Jesse C. Little of the eastern branch of the Church of Jesus Christ of Latter-day Saints, the Mormons. That sect had been unbelievably persecuted, its founder Joseph Smith dragged from an Illinois jail and lynched, its members driven first out of Missouri and then out of Illinois by military and mob action. The larger congregation was camped on the Missouri River, planning to migrate to California (they actually stopped at Salt Lake). The leader, Brigham Young, had asked Little to see about getting government aid for the migration, and Little called at the White House. Polk's eyes lit up at the possibilities—he could increase the Army of the West, as Kearny's command had been named, and raise the number of Anglos in California. Polk invited 500 to 1,000 Mormon men to follow Kearny to New Mexico and California. He did this, he said, "with a view to conciliate them, attach them to our country, and prevent them from taking part against us." But his decision kicked up a national storm of bigotry. The Mormons were especially despised in Missouri, where Governor Edwards lodged a strong protest. Polk brushed that aside.[41]

Marcy sent Kearny his final orders early in June. They called for establishing temporary governments in the conquered areas, retaining "all such of the existing officers as are known to be friendly to the United States, and will take the oath of allegiance." The secretary also forwarded a copy of Taylor's proclamation to the Mexican people for Kearny to use as a guide for his own statements. The order reconfirmed Kearny in command of the Army of the West, and promised him a brevet as brigadier general as soon as he left Santa Fe for California. Kearny received a permanent brigadier's rank under the generals bill ushered through the Senate by Benton.[42]

Benton had one more card to play. He had summoned James W. Magoffin, a trader with extensive dealings in Mexico, to Washington, and when he arrived took him to meet Polk and Marcy on June 15. The president, with Benton doing the thinking, asked Magoffin to go to Santa Fe and Chihuahua ahead of the Army of the West, to smooth the way for conquest and occupation. Magoffin later claimed credit for undermining the defense of Santa Fe and opening the way to Chihuahua. After the war he submitted a bill to the War Department for expenses exceeding $37,000. Rumors circulated that he had bribed the governor of New Mexico to abandon his province's defense, but these were never confirmed. The government concluded that he had a legitimate charge of $17,670, and the War Department recommended paying him $30,000 for both expenses and salary. In the short run, Marcy simply commended Magoffin to Kearny, saying the trader "will give important information and make arrangements to furnish your troops with abundant supplies in New Mexico."[43]

James Magoffin, secret agent, with his brother Samuel had been a merchant in Mexico for decades and United States consul at Saltillo in the 1820s. The Magoffins had stores and warehouses all over the country, and were heavily penalized by the Mexican government's efforts to drive foreign merchants out. They had a large caravan getting ready to leave Independence when the war started, commanded by Samuel, age forty-five, who brought along his bride of eight months, eighteen-year-old Kentucky belle Susan Shelby Magoffin, a winsome brunette.[44]

Susan Magoffin left behind the most delightful original document of the whole war—a diary that she kept for the benefit of her family back home. As she rode creaking wagons across eastern Kansas in June, she was alternately appalled at the mosquitoes and heavy rains and enchanted by the many beautiful wild roses lining her route. She could not, however, understand the ancient style of communion between mules and their drivers. "It is disagreeable to hear so much swearing," she complained; "the animals are unruly tis true and worries the patience of their drivers, but I scarcely think they need be so profane." As time went on she would get used to that, and to much more.[45]

While Susan Magoffin began her journey, Kearny organized his expedition. He ordered his scattered dragoons to assemble at Fort Leavenworth and sent an aide to Jefferson City to speed up the recruitment of volunteers. He hoped to assemble a mounted regiment, two companies of horse artillery, and a small infantry battalion.[46]

Kearny's war almost began before he was ready. Early in June he received reports, which turned out to be erroneous, that Manuel Armijo, governor of New Mexico, had a train headed to Santa Fe carrying arms and ammunition along with trade goods, and had sent two companies of Mexican dragoons to escort the shipment. Kearny ordered two companies of his own dragoons to head off the Mexican troops, which did not exist. The dragoons left on June 5, ordered to seize Armijo's goods, Kearny advising that "if we can secure that property, we hold the governor as our friend & ally." The governor's property proved to be as elusive as the Mexican dragoons.[47]

The first of Colonel Alexander Doniphan's 1st Missouri Mounted

Volunteers arrived at Fort Leavenworth on June 6, and the rest of the regiment dribbled in over the next two weeks. Kearny had them mustered in,
organized and outfitted, and given the most basic training. Then he sent
them off toward Santa Fe, because the Army of the West had to string itself out to conserve grass and water en route. There was little danger of
meeting Mexican troops north of the Arkansas River, so Kearny's real
challenges were distance and logistics. The regular dragoons led off,
followed by Doniphan's regiment on June 25–28, with Kearny and his
staff and artillery bringing up the rear. The Army of the West counted
1,458 men, with Price's thousand to follow. The guns included twelve
6-pounders and four 12-pounders in the Missouri Volunteer Artillery.
Before he left Leavenworth, Kearny sent Captain James Allen to raise four
or five companies of Mormons and take temporary command of them.

The army on the march included 1,556 wagons, 459 horses, 3,658
mules, and 14,904 cattle and oxen. Kearny enjoyed the support of an energetic quartermaster staff in St. Louis, not to mention his own energies
and abilities. He never had a regular quartermaster assigned to him during
the war. His men were equally resourceful, many of them carrying Indian
trade goods to barter on the way, hoping to supplement the army's taste-
less rations. And they griped, one complaining that the army "was not well
provisioned; nor was it furnished, in all its parts, with stout, able, and efficient teams." The divisions strung out impossibly during the day because
of the variable quality of wagons and teams.[48]

This was an adventure for country boys from Missouri, most of whom
had not left their home counties before. Regular officers thought they
would never be disciplined enough to be good soldiers, but predicted they
would be good fighters when the need arose. That might happen sooner
rather than later, as Kearny received reports that a Mexican army of 3,000
to 5,000 men was marching out of Chihuahua to confront him. Indians
were a more immediate danger to the enlisted men, however. "Numerous
stories of Indian massacres and cases of starvation on the prairies were
told to us by our friends," one of them remembered, "in the hope to deter
us from going."[49]

Kearny's expedition was headed across hot, dusty, dry country 537
miles to a rendezvous at Bent's Fort, in present-day southeastern Colorado.
"The boundless plains," remembered Private John Taylor Hughes, "lying in
wavy green not unlike the ocean, seemed to unite with the heavens in the
distant horizon. As far as vision could penetrate, the long files of cavalry,
the gay fluttering of banners, and the canvas-covered wagons of the merchant train glistening like banks of snow in the distance might be seen
winding their tortuous way over the undulating surface of the prairies."

He changed his tune within a few days, complaining about the heat and the tall, rank grass. Wagons broke down, and the mules were "refractory and balky" because they were not used to the harness or the work. The horses were "wild, fiery, and ungovernable."[50]

As these sons of the woodlands trudged across what was long known as the Great American Desert, they looked for omens of what was ahead of them. One was relayed to them from a merchant train headed from Santa Fe to Independence, whose traders "beheld, just after a storm and a little while before sunset," according to Hughes, "a perfectly distinct image of the 'bird of liberty,' the American eagle, on the disc of the sun. When they beheld the interesting sight they simultaneously and almost involuntarily exclaimed that in less than 12 months the eagle of liberty would spread his broad pinions over the plains of the West."[51]

CHAPTER

9

OPERATING ON THE MINDS AND FEELINGS

(July–August 1846)

It is time for the age of Knight-Errantry and mad-heroism to be
at an end. Your young military men, who want to reap the harvest of
laurels, don't care (I suppose) how many seeds of war are sown;
but for the sake of humanity it is devoutly to be wished,
that the manly employment of agriculture and the humanizing benefits
of commerce, would supersede the waste of war.

—George Washington

NORTH AMERICAN SUPPORT FOR THE WAR fell off by the end of
June, as the initial enthusiasm gave way to dismay over casualties. Editors
asked whether the country could afford the men and money it would take
to end the mess. Polk had an even greater fear—that his party could lose
control of Congress and the presidency. Palo Alto and the battle at the *resaca*
had made Taylor an instant hero, likely to leap over all other potential
Whig nominees. It looked as if Taylor had been shoved into danger by the
administration, had tried to avoid bloodshed, and had been attacked by the
other side. Military experts such as Henry Wager Halleck claimed that
the war could have been avoided. To march against Mexico with a small
force "was holding out to them the strongest inducements to attack us."

Already the conflict was called "Mr. Polk's War," the way the inept struggle of 1812–15 had been "Mr. Madison's War." What was needed, people believed, was a competent soldier to save the country from Polk's blunders. Immediately after news of Taylor's victory at the *resaca,* Thurlow Weed, the Whig genius behind the election of William Henry Harrison (also a war hero) in 1840, started a campaign to get Old Rough and Ready the Whig nomination. Taylor reacted with apparent indifference at first, but he could be counted on to give in to flattery.[1]

HE WILL ONLY ADD TO THE DISTRACTIONS OF THE COUNTRY

Polk needed a rescuer, and he thought he had one in the unlikely person of Santa Anna. After talking to Colonel Atocha, Polk sent Commander Alexander Slidell Mackenzie to Cuba. Mackenzie met with the *caudillo* twice, on July 6 and 7, 1846. The naval officer advised Santa Anna of the orders issued in May to let him pass through the blockade. He also gave the Mexican the North American peace terms—settlement of all claims against Mexico if it sold the Nueces Strip and the western territories to the United States. Santa Anna handed Mackenzie a paper affirming his willingness to negotiate. He promised to govern in the interest of the people, reduce the power of the clergy, and pursue free trade with the United States. In other words, he said what he knew Polk wanted to hear.[2]

Polk remained beguiled by his Pollyannaish consul in Mexico City, John Black, who still promised that the Mexican government would receive a proposal to resume negotiations. Polk told the secretary of state on July 17 to prepare such a proposal. After hearing Mackenzie's report on August 2, he told Buchanan to forward this "peace overture" to Mexico City, proposing to pay a fair price for the desired lands. So confident was Polk that he asked Congress for an advance appropriation of $2 million as earnest money for a treaty. Buchanan delivered the request to a secret meeting of the Senate Foreign Relations Committee, which liked the idea. The whole Senate agreed on August 6, also in secret, to grant the funds and bless the negotiations. The price of winning the Whigs over was for Polk to send a similar confidential message to the House of Representatives. The president dodged the request by sending memoranda to the chairmen of the Finance Committee and the Ways and Means Committee. The Whigs were greatly annoyed at this double-dealing.[3]

Santa Anna wasted no time making the trip to Mexico. He hired a British merchantman and set sail for Vera Cruz with his teenage wife and a load of *Santanistas.* Conner told his captains not to challenge her, making it appear that Santa Anna had entered Mexico without the concurrence of the United States. The commodore reported, "It is now quite certain the whole country—that is, the garrison of every town and fortress—have declared in his favor. But," he snorted, "unless he has learned something useful in his adversity, and become another man, he will only add to the distractions of the country, and be hurled from power in less than three months."[4]

The reunification of Mexico and Santa Anna was a triumph of hope over experience. Conspirators as varied as Tornel and Gómez Farías had wanted to get him back, and even the skeptical said that the *caudillo* had turned into "a real democrat." There was no basis for such a belief. "We will say to Santa Anna," declared a federalist newspaper, that if he had changed his ways, Mexico would "forget the past."[5]

Don Antonio was certain that his country would see him as the man to solve all her problems. Cannons boomed, an infantry regiment marched to the docks and formed a double line, and just after noon on August 16 the Savior of His Country marched up from the wharf wearing a splendid uniform. Exile had done him good, because he had shed some (but not all) of his paunch and looked fit in every way. He was preceded by his wife, "the Flower of Mexico," on the arm of an officer, with his retinue following. The reception, however, was stiff from the sullen crowd herded to the waterfront. There were audible snickers about the dictator's child bride. The only sound of celebration came from boys shooting off firecrackers. The procession continued on to the mayor's palace, where a common laborer lectured Santa Anna about his past misdeeds. The *caudillo* answered with a pep talk declaring against monarchy and the Church. Peace, democracy, and "the concert of the army and the people" would be Santa Anna's political principles, and he would be "the slave of public opinion."

"Mexicans," he declared, "there was a day, and my heart expands with the recollection, when . . . I was hailed by you with the enviable title, Soldier of the People. Allow me again to take it, nevermore to be given up, and to devote myself, until death, to the defence of the liberty and independence of the Republic." He vowed to restore the constitution of 1824 and give Congress control over the executive. The Soldier of the People concluded by issuing a ten-page *pronunciamiento* blistering the exiled Herrera for wanting to deal with the United States and Paredes for his royalist tendencies."[6]

Santa Anna knew that Mexican politics would not permit dealing with the United States as he had led Polk to believe. When a North American merchant advised him of the need to make peace, Santa Anna said that he agreed but he would not propose negotiations. He would call for a new Congress and follow its wishes. In the meantime, as a soldier he had a duty to fight the northern invasion. With Santa Anna's blessing, the new minister of foreign relations denounced Polk's peace overture on August 31 because it did not admit that the United States was the aggressor.[7]

The United States government should have known that neither Santa Anna nor anybody else could treat with the *Yanquis* in Mexico's explosive political climate. Polk again was cocksure that his aims simply must be realized, facts be hanged. He had tried to use Santa Anna to get his way, but the *caudillo* had used him instead. Polk came out of the business looking like a fool.

THEY HAVE FORFEITED THE PUBLIC CONFIDENCE

Polk wanted to control every aspect of the war, so he led his cabinet in further discussions of strategy. If Mexico continued to resist, new campaigns would force it to the peace table. Polk proposed taking Vera Cruz. The cabinet liked that idea, having not the slightest idea what it would involve. Bancroft gave the president Conner's reconnaissance report on the port's defenses. Polk asked for information on what it would take to invade at either Vera Cruz or Tampico and march inland.[8]

Polk also had to hold the political line at home. Late in July his party controlled Congress with a majority of 30 to 25 in the Senate and 142 over 74 Whigs in the House. Elections for the Thirtieth Congress would extend over seventeen months, from July 1846 to November 1847. Polk used the Democratic majorities to pass the tariff reduction and the independent treasury, measures that alienated manufacturing and banking industries, especially in the northeast. He announced that he would veto a pork barrel measure whose funds he would rather spend on the war. The attempt to gain a secret appropriation for $2 million stalled, so on August 8 Polk asked for the funds openly. Whigs and northern Democrats concluded that he wanted even more Mexican territory than before, hence more slave states and greater southern domination of the Congress. A group of northern Democrats got together, worried about the impact of the $2 million legislation, the slavery extension issue, and what it all meant. David Wilmot of Pennsylvania offered a solution. The House adopted an amendment to the $2 million bill, providing that "neither slavery nor involuntarily servitude shall ever exist in any part of said territory, except for crime whereof the party shall first be duly convicted." This passed the House by 83 to 64 votes but bogged down in the Senate. Polk's devious ways had brought him the death of his appropriation.[9]

The 1846 election returns looked progressively worse for the Democrats, better for the Whigs, who in the end controlled the House 115 to 108, although they lost 5 seats in the Senate. "We presume that our

President and his Cabinet are by this time convinced," crowed a Whig newspaper, "that they have forfeited the public confidence—the confidence, that is, of their own party; that of the other they never possessed."[10]

The political situation was even messier in Mexico, where coups and countercoups continued. As for foreign affairs, Mexico denied reality, especially where Texas was concerned. As late as August 6, 1846, Texas was called on to elect members of the Mexican Congress. The struggle with the United States remained the "Texas War."[11]

The Mexican Congress reconvened on July 6, 1846, and there was a temporary revival of national morale, owing to Taylor's inaction and a tendency to discount Arista's defeats. The lawmakers ratified Paredes as provisional president again and ordered him to "repel the aggression which the United States has initiated and sustained against the Mexican Republic, having invaded it." Paredes assumed command of the army, but his stock was falling while that of Santa Anna was on the rise. Paredes left for the front, and on August 4 learned that General José Mariano Salas, commander of the Mexico City garrison, had gone over to the federalists. Paredes was clapped into prison, and Salas and Gómez Farías formed an interim government. In the ensuing months a struggle between moderate and radical federalists paralyzed Mexico. The national government had full responsibility for conducting the war, but its only sources of income were state quotas and customs duties. The states were broke, and the United States Navy had cut off customs receipts.[12]

Officials in Mexico City were more concerned with divisions in their country than with the North American invasion. Political disputes entirely disrupted the state governments of Sonora, Coahuila, and Chihuahua. Mexico was torn by agrarian rebellions by *Indios* and *Castas* in México state, Puebla, present-day Colima, Michoacán, Oaxaca, Tabasco, and Yucatán. Each uprising required federal or state troops to suppress it, as did separatist movements in other states. Federal troops usually won their battles but could never claim that they had defeated an insurgency. Besides the armies of the two countries fighting each other, the Anglos faced federally patented guerrillas, spontaneous local guerrilla groups fighting Anglo troops or state or federal Mexican troops, and peasants rebelling against the state or federal government or the *hacendados* who oppressed them or the *Gringos* who abused them.[13]

WE HAVE CUSTOMS WHICH NEITHER THE OFFICERS NOR THE SOLDIERS WILL FOREGO

"Nothing can exceed the beauty of that portion of the Mexican coast in the vicinity of Vera Cruz," sang Raphael Semmes, Conner's flag lieutenant.

There was nothing the Mexican government could do to drive the enemy ships away. Paredes tried to circumvent the blockade on July 21 by naming Tecaluco, Tuxpan, and Soto la Marina as extra ports of entry. His successor Salas exempted blockade runners from port dues, but the United States Navy still intercepted many smugglers.[14]

The biggest hole in Conner's blockade was the Alvarado River, about twenty miles southeast of Antón Lizardo. It had become an alternate port for munitions imports since Vera Cruz was closed off. If Conner took Alvarado, he could close the port, but he would have to do that before the northers started blowing in October. The water over the bar ran eight to ten feet deep, so only the smaller gunboats could make the attempt. The defenses of the town just upriver were weak, commanded by Commander Pédro Díaz Mirón of the Mexican Navy. All he had were a brigantine, three gunboats, and a small fort mounting four guns.

Conner started his first attack on July 28, but his flagship, USS *Cumberland*, ran aground leaving Antón Lizardo; she was freed the next day. A spell of nice weather early in August inspired the commodore to try again. Two steamers, two frigates, and three gunboats joined the sloop *Falmouth* standing off the Alvarado bar on the seventh. The current across the bar kept the steamers from getting close enough to damage the fort. The gunboats and steamers exchanged fire with the Mexican gunboats early in the evening, and the steamers shot at Mexican infantry on the riverbanks. Conner sent a flotilla of ships' boats to take the fort that night, but again the current was too strong. The Mexican commander strengthened his defenses, called in militia from surrounding villages, and built a new fort on the north point of the river mouth. Conner decided not to try again until the river fell, the weather improved, and the new small vessels he had been promised showed up. He was also told to stay his hand because the Polk administration believed that Mexico would soon agree to negotiate.[15]

Conner was convinced that he could not assault any location until his mosquito flotilla arrived, so he tried to tighten the blockade with what he had. He ordered the brig USS *Truxtun* to relieve another off Tampico on August 12. She headed north into a strong gale and at Tuxpan, halfway to Tampico, Commander Edward W. Carpender headed inshore to get fresh provisions on the fourteenth. The wind drove his ship onto reefs and she stuck fast. Carpender sent a ship's boat to Antón Lizardo for help, but before anybody could reach him he surrendered to the Mexican troops pelting his ship with musketry and field guns. Conner sent a steamer, which reached *Truxtun* on the twentieth, by which time she was a wreck. A party from the rescue ship took off some spars and burned the rest. At last the

Mexican army had prisoners high enough in rank to exchange for General Díaz de la Vega and his staff, captured at the *resaca*.[16]

Conner was stuck off the Mexican coast, and Taylor was stuck on the lower Rio Grande, where he received letters and newspaper editorials urging him to run for president in 1848. He coyly turned them aside, saying, "For that office I have no aspirations whatever. Although no politician, having always held myself aloof from the clamors of party politics, I am a Whig." Party leaders did not miss his subtext—when the time came, Taylor would accept a nomination.[17]

There remained a war to fight. Responding to requests for his advice, on July 2 Taylor sent off two letters to Washington. An attack on Mexico City, he said, was not practical from where he was, but taking Monterey and Chihuahua could separate the northern states from Mexico. The United States should not try to conquer the entire country, especially not by a march on Mexico City. Cutting off the northern provinces, he thought, should be enough to "conquer the peace." Planting Taylor's army in the north would give him a strong position, and the enemy must attack to drive him out. Taylor did not believe the Mexicans would fight for either Monterey or Chihuahua, let alone dare to attack him.[18]

Taylor received a long statement of the United States' strategy before his letters reached the capital. It was the joint work of Polk, Marcy, and Benton. They advised Taylor to send agents into the Mexican armies to talk the leaders into negotiating. Polk personally added a section emphasizing that it was desirable to promote secessionist or independence movements. The president also wanted Taylor to declare whether Tampico or Vera Cruz would make the better base for an invasion of the Mexican interior. Polk had decided to conquer the peace by conquering the heart of Mexico.[19]

Taylor answered this on August 1. He was not taken with the idea of subverting Mexican generals, and thought it was too early to talk about secessionist movements in the northeast. Taylor repeated his earlier advice, adding that if the War Department gave him 10,000 men competently trained and equipped, he could march on San Luis Potosí. He thought that would "speedily bring proposals for peace." If Taylor could not advance beyond Monterey, he advised simply occupying the northern conquests and landing another force at Vera Cruz. Tampico would not be a good place to begin a march on Mexico City because of poor roads, long supply lines, and rough terrain.[20]

Taylor needed to sort out his supply and transportation problems. Volunteers were descending on him, most inadequately supplied, so he had a growing army to feed and equip. Quartermaster General Jesup sent Brevet Brigadier General Henry Whiting to Matamoros to be Taylor's chief quartermaster. He was appalled at the general's negligence in arranging for transportation, and especially his clamor for wagons. Pack trains would give better service in a country with terrible roads, he said, "provided we could bring ourselves to make war as the enemy makes it." Whiting doubted that would happen because "we have customs which neither the officers nor the soldiers will forego [sic], excepting in cases of extremity. Our camp equipage, so comfortable and yet so cumbrous, our rations, so full and bulky, all must be transported." These luxurious tastes required wagons; moreover, supplies were not shipped from the United States in units for packing on mules. The demands of the war exhausted stocks of many basic items, and Taylor had been remiss in arranging for local purchases. Then there was the shortage of river transport. Taylor began moving to Camargo in July, when there were seven steamers working the upper river for him. This was still the rainy season upstream, however, so high flows and shifting currents made the river unpredictable, and it overflowed its banks. Troops could go upstream by terrifying steamer rides, but wagons and artillery must slog over muddy roads. Taylor's answer was to ship his regulars and leave the volunteers to follow later.[21]

Camargo formerly had a population of about 2,000 people living in adobe houses surrounded by beautiful orchards, on the right bank of the San Juan River about three miles above its mouth on the Rio Grande. Taylor had selected it because it was supposed to be the head of navigation on the Rio Grande, about 120 land miles or 300 river miles above Matamoros. He never bothered to check it out before he moved his army there. A flood had wrecked the town in June. The water left behind a sea of mud that turned into a fine, gritty yellow dust. The place was too far inland to get a sea breeze, and the river was flanked by bare limestone hills so there was no other breeze, either. Temperatures hit as high as 112 degrees, turning the area into an unbearable furnace during the day.

The first regulars arrived by boat on July 14 and over the next month the rest of them and most volunteers, more than 7,000 men in all, trickled into camps strung for three miles along the river. It was hell on earth. The flood had spawned a biblical plague of frogs, along with scorpions, tarantulas, mosquitoes, centipedes, flies, fleas, biting ants, chiggers, rattlesnakes, and every other varmint imaginable. The place was deadly, especially for volunteers with sloppy camp sanitation. It soon became known as the "Yawning Grave Yard," and the dead march was played so often that the mockingbirds imitated it. Dysentery, measles, and various fevers slaughtered men by the hundreds. When Taylor marched out in August, about a thousand men lay buried there.[22]

Taylor decided that Camargo might not be the best base of operations against Monterey. He had picked it on the advice of McCulloch's rangers, who had scouted the region and said Camargo had the best roads to the capital of Nuevo León. It turned out that the *diablos tejanos* had spent much of their scouting time looting liquor and food from farmers and villagers. Taylor sent McCulloch out again in August to check out the road to the village of China and while he was at it to hunt down a band of guerrillas. The rangers missed the Mexican irregulars but scouted out three alternate routes to Monterey, preferring the one through Cerralvo.[23]

Taylor shifted his base to Cerralvo, about sixty miles in the direction of Monterey. Worth's division left Camargo on August 19. The road was so wretched that the troops had to rebuild it on the way; they entered Cerralvo at noon on the twenty-fifth. It was a lovely highland town of about 1,800 people, the houses mostly stone, surrounded by the fruit orchards that North Americans were beginning to expect in Mexican communities. Taylor and his staff arrived behind most of the troops on September 9, and the last of the volunteers he had ordered up plodded into camp on the thirteenth. Logistics were a nightmare. About 1,500 mules and 180 wagons went back and forth from Camargo to Cerralvo, carrying up 160,000 rations for the 6,640 soldiers Taylor had with him. The whole operation suffered repeated guerrilla raids. Taylor, meanwhile, sent scouts forward. He had thought that he would be able to walk into Monterey without a fight. His spies told him that the Mexicans were digging in there.[24]

Taylor's advance out of Matamoros raised alarms in Mexico City, where leaders saw Monterey as a gateway to the country's interior. General Tomás Requeña, second in command of the Division of the North, left Linares on July 9 with 1,800 survivors of Arista's army, to garrison Monterey. He rounded up other stragglers from the aftermath of the *resaca* and his commander—Ampudia had gotten that post again—was on the way from Mexico City with more troops, arriving with the lead elements on August 29. If Taylor wanted Monterey, he would have to fight for it.[25]

While Taylor pondered this challenge, General Wool organized the Chihuahua expedition at San Antonio, Texas. He was a slender, erect man with a thatch of gray hair and a habit of looking at people with a sideways, almost skeptical expression. He was rigorous about discipline and details, oversaw everything, and earned complaints as well as respect from the men, who called him "Old Fussy." Nobody was better prepared to take a mob of volunteers and turn them into an army, despite the fact that in May Polk told him to "see that the volunteers were speedily raised and marched to the Rio Grande with the least possible delay." Wool's orders reached him at Louisville in June while he was mustering troops in the Ohio Valley.

He collected two regiments of Illinois infantry and took them by riverboat to New Orleans for shipment to Port Lavaca. His cavalry rode overland to San Antonio, where parts of both regular dragoon regiments waited. Wool found no logistical arrangements for his expedition at Lavaca, rode on to San Antonio, and found things no better there.[26]

Wool galloped back to Lavaca, then led the Illini and about 500 wagons through mud—Scott had been correct, this was the rainy time—to San Antonio, which he reached on August 14. The town of about 2,000 people could not provide the supplies his army needed. Worse, Lieutenant Colonel William S. Harney, a dragoon officer commanding in Wool's absence, had taken twenty wagons to the Rio Grande, and rain that went on for twenty days nonstop bogged everything down. Harney had also taken most of the supplies previously stocked at San Antonio on his pointless dash to the Rio Grande.[27]

Harney was slow in returning to San Antonio, so Wool ordered him arrested and recalled, then released him when he reached the army's camp three miles from the Alamo. He was not happy that some of his volunteers also took their sweet time, the last of his 3,400 men walking in on September 4. Only 600 of his troops were regulars, the rest volunteers from Illinois and Arkansas, a battery of regular light artillery, and some Texas Rangers serving as a "spy company." Wool instituted a training program and applied it to the volunteers as they arrived. The Illinois infantry complained but obeyed, and later performed well in action. The Arkansas cavalry, however, resisted all efforts to turn them into competent soldiers. Wool complained that the Arkansawyers were "wholly without instruction, and Colonel [Archibald] Yell is determined to leave them in that condition." He charged that Yell displayed "total ignorance of his duties as Colonel." Cracking his whip, Wool expected to head out for Chihuahua by September 25, and he did.[28]

Wool did not know what regular forces Mexico would send against him, but he shared Taylor's belief that the enemy would not challenge him. What he did not know was that they did not have to. The landscape would fight him.

THEY EMPHATICALLY "MADE WAR ON THEIR OWN HOOK"

Taylor, like Wool, had expected volunteers to reinforce his army. The mobs that descended on him in the summer of 1846 were wildly undisciplined, and not many of them looked like soldiers. Kentucky volunteers sported full beards, tricorner hats, and hip boots faced with red morocco. Various "Guards," "Rifles," "Killers," "Gunmen," "Blues," "Grays," and so on wore gray, green, blue, or white, trimmed with red, yellow, or pink. They were ordered to wear army uniforms, but many objected. "I'll be blowed if they make a regular out of me," roared a Hoosier.[29]

There were a few West Pointers in volunteer regiments, most notably Colonel Jefferson Davis of the Mississippi Rifles, but they were few. Civilians could not become military men merely by hanging swords on their belts. The company officers were elected and so were beholden to their men. They could neither train their units nor keep them in order, so the troops ran wild. Some disorders involved whole regiments, as when a Georgia outfit rioted at the end of August. When the colonel of an Illinois regiment took a detachment to quell the uproar it turned into a free-for-all that killed one man and wounded several. Not even the threat of arrest and court-martial made these men behave; when one was arrested, his friends broke him loose.[30]

Volunteer regiments also were rent by political disputes among officers. Democrats squabbled with Whigs, and members of the same party feuded. Officers even dueled each other. Not surprisingly, volunteer officers also quarreled with regulars, who uniformly looked down their noses at untrained mobs led by people given military rank without qualifications. George B. McClellan railed against the "cursed volunteers" and complained that "from the general down to the dirtiest rascal of the filthy crew" they were always "scared out of their wits (if they had any)." At any given time at least a third of them were sick.

Scott explained the problem to Marcy late in 1846. "A regiment of regulars, in 15 minutes from the evening halt, will have tents pitched & trenched around, besides, straw, leaves or bushes for dry sleeping," he said; "arms & ammunition well secured & in order for any night attack; fires made, kettles boiling, in order to [have] wholesome cooking; all the men dried, or warmed, & at their comfortable supper, merry as crickets, before the end of the first hour." Volunteers, on the other hand, "neglect all these points . . . lose or waste their clothing; lie down wet, or on wet ground—fatal to health, &, in a short time to life; leave arms & ammunition exposed to rain, mud & dews . . . In a short time the ranks are thinned, the baggage wagons & hospitals filled with the sick, & acres of ground with the graves of the dead!"[31]

These were the realities that Scott had failed to explain to Polk, who never understood the need for training or the folly of short enlistments. The vague promises of recruiting officers aggravated the situation, because many men had enlisted for just three or six months. Taylor tried to get short-timers to re-up for the full year, but in early August the Texas infantry regiment rebelled and went home. Taylor was short of shipping, the volunteers were ineffective and drained his supplies, and their behavior ruined his attempts to win over the civilian population, so Old Zach discharged any volunteers who would not extend their enlistments. Most either went home or hung around the Rio Grande causing more trouble.[32]

Those who stayed continued to cause disorder because their chief occupation was drinking, brawling, whoring, and plundering. The "entertainers" they attracted to the area added to the uproar, and Protestant preachers who flocked to Mexico to condemn the Catholic religion did nothing to win favor in the community. There were some efforts to get along, however. North Americans and Mexicans discovered a common love of card playing. The former introduced faro to the latter, who returned the favor by teaching the Anglos monte. The card suits were different but the rules were simple and the game was an effective way to lose money and start a fight. There was other socializing as well. The Yankees generally had a low opinion of Mexican men, but they admired the women of all classes. They danced at fandangos where the mothers sold food and drink, but Mexican propriety held—the girls had to be chaperoned. There were romances and marriages, and some women who thought they were married until their husbands went back to the United States. Like all conquering armies, the North American one left a trail of bastards in its wake.[33]

Some Anglos tried to learn Spanish in order to communicate with the people; others refused to. Private William Henry remembered an officer looking for a lost horse and a Mexican he came across. "Look here, my man," the officer started, "have you seen anything of a d———d *caballo* a *barnosing* about here, with a *cabrista* on his neck?" The citizen spoke no English and had no idea what the *Gringo* was saying; the "Spanish" was gibberish except for *caballo* (horse). The officer snorted, "Why the d———d fool *don't know his own language!*[34]

Regular officers sometimes understood why a few Mexicans accepted the North Americans with "cold civility." Many Mexicans opposed their own government, but that did not make them welcome the U.S. invaders. One wealthy citizen of Matamoros, in a gesture of Latin hospitality, entertained some Anglo officers in his home, but he did so aloofly. As a devout Catholic, he explained, he was opposed to the corrupt priests in his country, "as a republican opposed to all the recent military Governments, and as a patriot opposed to the North Americans." The Mexican press called *yanqui* soldiers "half savages" and "infidels who worship the devil." The papers relayed yarns about barbarity, told of Mexican citizens sold into slavery in the United States, and broadcast that old propaganda staple about invading troops spearing babies with their bayonets. One Anglo soldier thought that people believed such stories because that was the kind of treatment they expected from their own troops. More likely, they believed them because too many of them were true, except for the spitted babies.[35]

Scott and a few other high officers knew that an invading army must tread carefully to minimize resistance. Scott realized, as Polk never did, that pressure on the Mexican government alone was not going to drive Mexico to the peace table, unless influential people decided that was the best course. Those people would not come around if the United States treated them and their country barbarically. Scott drafted a letter that Marcy sent to Taylor early in July. "In a country so divided into races, classes," he said of Mexico, "there must be great room for operating on the minds and feelings of a large portion of the inhabitants, and including them to wish success to an invasion which has no desire to injure their country." Winning "minds and feelings," unfortunately, required more subtlety than Taylor possessed, and more willingness to discipline his troops.[36]

The volunteers "have killed five or six innocent people walking in the streets, for no other object than their own amusement," regular George Gordon Meade complained. "They rob and steal the cattle and corn of the poor farmers, and in fact act more like a body of hostile Indians than of civilized whites."[37]

As usual, *los diablos tejanos* were the worst. A regular army surgeon wrote home about eight Texians who rode up to a Mexican ranch and started stealing pigs and chickens. The owner came out of his house with his small son to protest, and the Texians shot them both, then killed two servants. They were not punished. The surgeon complained, "Genl. Taylor has much to answer for." But Taylor had already given up, feeling that the volunteers were no good and he had no power to curb them.[38]

"But, my dear Sir," Scott told the secretary of war when he learned about what was going on, "our militia & volunteers, if a tenth of what is said to be true, have committed atrocities—horrors—in Mexico, sufficient to make Heaven weep, & every American, of Christian morals, *blush* for his country. Murder, robbery & rape of mothers & daughters, in the presence of the tied up males of the families, have been common all along the Rio Grande. . . . Truly it would seem unchristian & cruel to let loose upon any people—even savages—such unbridled persons—free-booters, &c. &c." This, he knew, was no way to win "minds and feelings."[39]

What explains this savage behavior? The lack of discipline in the volunteer regiments provides a large part of the answer, with the caution that many of the reports came from regular officers. Another element of the story was the hostility toward Mexicans among those who had lost relatives or friends in Texas. Then there was the boredom of camp life, compounded by drunkenness. Studies of other wars suggest that atrocities tend to be committed by troops on occupation duty who do not see combat, which drains bloodlust. Such was the case with most of Taylor's volunteers.

Not all the atrocities in northeast Mexico were committed by soldiers, however. Taylor complained that too many discharged volunteers hung around the occupation zone. They were joined by other lowlifes who extended their misbehavior at Corpus Christi to the Mexican mainland. Some of these malefactors formed criminal gangs, preying on United States soldiers as well as civilians. To their numbers were added teamsters, laborers, and others drawn to the area by the promise of jobs, only to be disappointed because not all of them could be hired. A regular officer blamed most atrocities on "some of the quartermaster's men, who . . . did not consider themselves as being amenable to martial or any other law; and by desperate adventurers, called by the army 'outsiders,' who followed the army for plunder, and frequently organized themselves into bands to carry on their depredations, not being very particular as to whether they robbed Mexicans or their own countrymen. They emphatically 'made war on their own hook.'"[40]

Superior officers could lead obedient troops into atrocious behavior. United States supply lines were raided from the outset. Regular officers, from Taylor on down, decided that that kind of resistance—or criminality, as they viewed it—must be countered by military means. But regulars always have been brutally clumsy when dealing with irregulars. The raiders were elusive, so it was easier to go after their alleged supporters, meaning civilians. Indiscriminate attacks on civilians on the assumption they were all enemies merely increased the numbers of enemies.

The mostly unplanned invasion of Mexico led to two years of chaos in the northeastern part of that country. That could have been prevented. Taylor could have established a military government to lay down the law on everyone. A strong military police force could have prevented disorder and caught and punished malefactors. Instead, Taylor threw up his hands in frustration.

By the end of Taylor's campaign nearly all the small towns from Matamoros to Mier to Saltillo were destroyed. Among those doing the damage were United States volunteers, discharged volunteers, Mexican and North American gangsters, civilians seeking revenge for crimes against themselves or their families, irregulars waging a guerrilla war, and regulars waging a counterguerrilla war. They left a wasteland of ashes and dust, and uncountable individual and family tragedies.

MY WORD IS AT PRESENT
THE LAW OF THE LAND

(July–August 1846)

The most extravagant idea that can arise in a politician's head is
to believe that it is enough for a people to invade a foreign country
to make it adopt their laws and their constitution.
No one loves armed missionaries.

—Maximilien-François-Marie-Isidore de Robespierre

MANUEL ARMIJO, EVERYONE KNEW, would steal a red-hot stove.
He started out poor, taught himself to read by campfires while he tended
sheep, and raised himself in the world by rustling livestock. He would
gamble on anything from a cockfight to the next day's weather. Armijo's
personal motto was "It is better to be thought a brave man than to really be
one." Don Manuel told these stories on himself, to disarm competitors.
He was really the son of two of New Mexico's oldest and most prominent
families. He was well educated, had expanded an inherited fortune by being a sharp businessman, owned most of Albuquerque, had trading interests from Missouri to Chihuahua, and was prudently generous to the
Church. Don Manuel could be charming, but when the occasion called for
it he erupted with threats, bluster, and bragging.

Armijo was forty-five years old in 1846 and had been governor of New Mexico on and off since 1837. He was a big man, about six feet tall, who had picked up a lot of weight. His Anglo rivals in the Santa Fe–Missouri trade called him "His Obesity." He rode around in a Dearborn cart because he was too fat to mount a horse. The governor had a large head, dark deep eyes, a long nose, and a thin upper lip above a full lower one. His jaw was heavy and clean-shaven, and he wore his dark hair short. He favored lavish uniforms, and was a grand and colorful sight in a territory mired in poverty. In other words, he was just another provincial *caudillo*.[1]

Don Manuel faced two great worries in July 1846. One was that he had learned on June 17 that an Anglo-American army was marching in his direction. The other was that he had a caravan of goods on the same trail. The United States consul had advised Armijo that it would "be better for himself and the people under his government to capitulate." Consul Álvarez reported that the governor's advisers "were rather easily won over," but Armijo planned to resist. Anglo merchant Charles Bent asked the governor about the rumors of a war between Mexico and the United States. Armijo replied that he had heard the same rumors. In any event, there was a Mexican army marching north from Chihuahua to defend New Mexico. Bent passed this information to Kearny, as Armijo expected him to.

Don Manuel was more worried about his heavy investment in imported goods—which included no munitions—on the Santa Fe Trail. If the North Americans captured it, he could go bankrupt. Fortunately, the caravan pulled into Santa Fe ahead of the *yanqui* invasion and Armijo sent it on to Chihuahua. His fortune safe, now the governor could address the other problem: What could he do to keep the *Angloamericanos* from conquering New Mexico?[2]

AN UNCERTAIN DESTINY AWAITED US

Kearny's dragoons and Missourians struggled toward New Mexico through tall-grass prairie. "We found it sprinkled with flowers which, although neither so beautiful nor so abundant as I had anticipated, gave it a pleasing appearance," said Private Frank Edwards. The tall grass gave way to the drier, short-grass prairie and the landscape became overwhelming. "How discouraging the first sight of these immense plains is."[3]

The Great Plains were as alien as the moon. Cooking over dried buffalo chips because of the lack of wood was a novel experience. Prairie dog villages were more entertaining, but nothing beat the sight of a grassy sea "thick with buffaloes, extending as far back as the eye could reach," according to one of the men. He called hunting buffalo "exciting and ani-mating," and like their predecessors on the trail, "no one was satisfied with killing a number sufficient to supply all his wants." The country was "like a slaughter pen, covered with bones, skulls and carcasses of animals in every state of decay." After crossing Pawnee Fork men started falling sick. They were carried on the freight wagons, "a miserable arrangement."[4]

The farther the Army of the West went, the hotter the weather. "The earth was literally parched to a crust and the grass in many cases crisped by the heat of the sun," a private named John Hughes marveled. "In the dis-tant horizon upon the green plains might be seen ephemeral rivers and lakes...all, however, a tantalizing illusion, for as you approach the en-chanting spot the waters recede."[5]

The ordeal seemed endless, the men and animals trudging onward in a timeless daze, the sun a fire in the sky. There was no time to celebrate July 4, "the hottest day that ever shone," according to a soldier. The infantry "had no spirits and could not observe the day in the usual manner." Instead, they tramped thirty-two miles, twenty without water. The regular dra-goons had a sutler and bought liquor "to celebrate as best they might the national anniversary." The mounted Missourians also had a booze supply. That night, "the greatest good humor prevailed in camp." As another man put it, "It seems we have as much of the spirit of '76 as the spirit of John Barleycorn."[6]

Along the Cimarron, "this part of the country abounds in serpents, cameleons [sic], prairie lizards, horned frogs, dry-land turtles, and the whole tribe of the entomologist," Hughes noticed. "Grasshoppers are as numerous as were the locusts...upon the land of Egypt." It was not all ominous, because "in many places a rich variety of flowers blossom and 'waste their sweetness on the desert air.'" The farther the army went the tougher the going, with wind and driven sand grinding away at man and beast. Progress slowed as wagon wheels sank into sandy patches and the animals could find nothing to graze on. "The water was scarce, muddy, bit-ter, filthy," Hughes complained. "Dreary, sultry, desolate, boundless soli-tude reigned as far as the eye could reach and seemed to bound the distant horizon."[7]

While the army struggled across this hellish waste, rumors erupted in Jefferson City and in Washington that Armijo would challenge the invasion with a large force. Kearny met trader George Howard returning from his mission and learned that there was no fact behind these tales. Howard said that the Nuevomexicanos would accept Anglo occupation, but their leaders would not and were gathering 2,300 soldiers to defend Santa Fe.[8]

Captain Philip St. George Cooke told his diary on July 21 that he "took a singular pleasure" from the nightly howls of wolves. The night breeze helped also, after a "very hot and still day with swarms of horse flies." He had stopped several times to brush the pests from his suffering horse, which next endured a dust storm, then thunder, hail, and a downpour. One of the army's herds of horses and mules got so excited that they stampeded off.[9]

The ordeal came to an end on July 28 when Kearny and his dragoon escort reached Bent's Fort on the Arkansas River. The rest of the army trailed in over the next two days. The fort was a great adobe square with high, blank walls and a higher watchtower. Two bald eagles gazed over everything from cages in the tower's belfry. The compound enclosed living quarters, storerooms, and other rooms for drinking, gambling, and even one with a billiards table. There were Indian encampments all around. The fort had been headquarters for the fur-trading business of the brothers William and Charles Bent for over fifteen years. When the furs were trapped out the Bents expanded their enterprises into merchandising, freighting, and the Indian trade. William usually presided over the fort while Charles based himself at Taos.[10]

Kearny talked William into rounding up some mountain men and going into New Mexico as a "spy company." The general ordered his men to camp along both sides of the Arkansas, dragoons separated from infantry, and instituted training. The Missourians did not much care for that, but still the halt was a welcome relief. The most notable event came when about a thousand of the army's horses stampeded after being turned out to graze, taking off in "wildest and most terrible confusion." While the infantry howled in glee, dragoons grabbed whatever mounts were left and went after the fugitive livestock. Sixty-five of the horses were never seen again.[11]

Kearny wrote a proclamation to the people of New Mexico and sent it off to Santa Fe on July 31. He declared that he was entering the province with a large military force "for the purpose of seeking union with and ameliorating the condition of its inhabitants." He ordered the citizens "to remain quietly at their homes, and to pursue their peaceful avocations." So long as they did this, "they will not be interfered with by the American army, but will be respected and protected in their rights, both civil and religious." All who resisted "will be regarded as enemies, and will be treated accordingly."[12]

Kearny then ordered his army to march out. "The future was pregnant with consequences of the greatest moment," remembered Private Hughes.

"An uncertain destiny awaited us. . . . Were we to be defeated and completely overthrown, or were we to enter triumphantly into the capital and plant the flag of our country on its adobe walls?"[13]

CALIFORNIA WILL BE A PORTION OF THE UNITED STATES

Kearny was under orders to conquer California as soon as he took New Mexico. He did not know that a conquest, after a fashion, was already under way. Frémont and his rebels had been sowing chaos in the northern part of the territory, while at Monterey Sloat had been sitting in the harbor since July 2, 1846, trying to decide what to do. He received a note on July 5 from Commander John B. Montgomery, stationed in San Francisco Bay, reporting that Frémont—an officer of the United States Army—was supporting the Bear Flag rebels in the north. That news gave Sloat grounds to take action. If Frémont was in the fight, then there was a war on. If Frémont had acted prematurely, Sloat could blame him for whatever went wrong. The commodore announced on July 6 that he would occupy Monterey and ordered Montgomery to do the same at San Francisco. "I am very anxious to know if Captain Frémont will cooperate with us," he said. Captain William Mervine and a small party rowed ashore from USS *Savannah* to demand Monterey's surrender early on the morning of the seventh. Captain Mariano Silva, the commandant, answered that he had no orders to surrender. He suggested that the commodore make arrangements with the *comandante-general,* José Castro. Sloat announced to his sailors the landings to come, the rules of conduct ashore, and the importance of gaining the goodwill of the people. A gun from *Savannah* signaled, and soon about 225 sailors and marines stood in front of the customs house. Two midshipmen raised the Stars and Stripes and the Anglos cheered three times.

Sloat proclaimed that Mexico had "commenced hostilities against the United States of America" but that Arista's army had been destroyed. He came among the people of California not as an enemy but as "their best friend—as henceforward California will be a portion of the United States," replacing Mexican tyranny with prosperity for all. Anyone who did not want to enjoy those benefits was free to leave. Those who stayed would find their land titles and their religion protected. Sloat invited all civil officers to remain in office under military supervision. He had no authority to annex California, which was something for the diplomats and politicians to work out. It would not be the last time a North American officer would reach too far.[14]

The first reaction to the announcement was the resignation of all civil officials, including judges. Sloat appointed a purser and a surgeon as jus-

tices of the peace but did little else to organize a government. Captain
Mervine took charge of the marine garrison and more or less became military governor. Mervine closed all *tiendas* (shops) in town for two days and
forbade the sale of liquor indefinitely. Purser Daingerfield Fauntleroy organized a company of sailors to round up horses, and started patrols of
the surrounding area.[15]

Montgomery received Sloat's order on July 8 and had the United
States vice consul at Yerba Buena translate the commodore's proclamation
into Spanish. He sent a lieutenant to find Frémont and tell him about the
seizure of Monterey, and to hand him two national flags to raise at Sutter's
Fort and Sonoma. Montgomery and seventy sailors landed at Yerba Buena
at about eight in the morning on the ninth and marched to the customs
house, watched by a few curious citizens. Montgomery read his own
proclamation announcing the replacement of the Bear Flag by that of his
country. A lieutenant read Sloat's proclamation, and the United States flag
was hoisted to a twenty-one-gun salute from USS *Portsmouth*. The lieutenant looking for Frémont landed with a handful of men at Sonoma,
north of San Francisco, raised the flag, read Sloat's proclamation, and sent
it and the flags to Sutter's Fort with orders to raise the United States banner in place of the Bear Flag. Another detail inspected the presidio of San
Francisco. The old fort was a wreck, armed with three Spanish bronze
guns, all more than 200 years old, three iron 42-pounders, and four small
iron guns. All had been spiked by the Bear Flaggers. The party saw nobody
but "a few inoffensive Indians."[16]

Sloat's worst nightmare sailed into San Francisco Bay on July 11 in the
form of the British sloop HMS *Juno*. North Americans assumed she was
there to interfere with the conquest, and Montgomery posted marines to
defend Yerba Buena. The sloop's captain, however, was there only to observe. His commander, Rear Admiral Sir George F. Seymour, had explicit
orders to observe and report but definitely not to take a hand.[17]

Sloat was happy to see USS *Congress* sail into Monterey on July 15, carrying his new second in command, Robert F. Stockton, transferred to the
Pacific after trying to stir up trouble in Texas. Sloat greeted his junior with
relief and told him that he would transfer command to him soon and go
home on sick leave. First, however, he wanted to see Frémont.[18]

The Pathfinder had set out from Sutter's Fort with his "army" on the
twelfth. The party reached San Juan Bautista on the sixteenth and ran into
Fauntleroy and his scouts, who turned around to join the march. Frémont
led about 170 men, including a company of "Fremonters," as the men who
followed him over the mountains were called, and two companies of im-
migrant settlers from the north. Frémont and Carson with their Delaware

Indian scouts led the parade into Monterey on the nineteenth, creating quite a spectacle. "They defiled, two abreast, through the principal street of the town," a navy chaplain reported. "The ground seemed to tremble under their heavy tramp." They were a dirty, hairy, smelly mob, armed to the teeth. "The individuality of each man was very remarkable," said a navy purser. "Frémont was the conspicuous figure. Kit Carson and the Indians accompanying him were the objects of much attention." [19]

Sloat asked to see the army officer's orders to join the Bear Flag rebels. Frémont wanted approval from Sloat, as senior United States officer, for his actions, along with an agreement to continue operations on land. Sloat was horrified that the explorer had acted without orders or even information of a state of war. Frémont was offended that he would get no backing from the navy. Sloat was so undone by Frémont's lack of authority that he ended the meeting and went to his cabin. The hypochondriac sailor had had enough. He decided to go home, to escape what consequences might follow on his own actions and whatever new messes Frémont or others might create. Among those others was Stockton, who, instead of being a help, was a domineering blowhard. Sloat transferred command of forces ashore to his subordinate on July 23. Six days later he transferred the whole squadron. [20]

Stockton enrolled Frémont's mob of mountain men and Bear Flaggers as the "California Battalion of United States Troops," with Frémont as major and commander and Archibald Gillespie as captain and second. This mobilized a land force under naval authority, subordinating an army officer to a naval superior. The battalion accorded with no law governing volunteer troops; in the end it took a special act of Congress to pay its expenses. Stockton established garrisons, equally unsanctioned, at Sonoma, San Juan Bautista, Santa Clara, and Sutter's Fort. [21]

Stockton and Frémont shared a gift for melodramatic vainglory and a disdain for any limits on their self-assumed greatness. Frémont had set out to conquer California, and now he had the backing of a man who wanted not only to conquer but also to rule. Either man alone could cause enough trouble in a delicate situation. Together they were a disaster. Stockton began by issuing a howling proclamation to the people of California, smashing any hope of winning them over. His screed included vicious personal attacks on Mexican officials combined with brutish threats against them. In particular, Stockton targeted Castro, accusing him of "lawless violence" and a plan "with the aid of hostile Indians [to] keep this beautiful country in a constant state of revolution and blood." This was a silly lie. The commodore called Castro "a usurper, [who] has been guilty of great offenses, has impoverished and drained the country of almost its last dollar, and has deserted his post now when most needed." Stockton had been moved, he said, by "reports from the scenes of rapine, blood and murder" and because people had "invoked his protection." There had been no such crimes, and nobody had asked for protection. Stockton ended by vowing to drive the criminals out of California. Consul Larkin was horrified when he saw Stockton's text and tried to get it softened, to no avail.[22]

Castro was not a usurper but a lawful officer of the Mexican government. He was not a deserter but a California patriot. He was not a criminal but a respected member of the community. He had tried to win his province's independence as a republic and did not want to trade a master in Mexico City for another in Washington. *Californios* had resisted Frémont's hooligans, but so far they had not raised a hand against the armed forces of the United States. Stockton's behavior changed that.

Castro went to Los Angeles to meet with his old rival Governor Pío Pico, and they agreed to cooperate. Stockton set about driving Castro and Pico out of the territory. He sent a ship to drop a small garrison at Santa Barbara, then to land in force at San Pedro. About 360 men armed with an odd collection of muskets, musketoons, pistols, cutlasses, and boarding pikes waded ashore on August 6. Alone, this party stood no chance against the nimble *californio* lancers, so the sailors landed a few 6-pounders.

Stockton had sent Frémont's men by ship to San Diego with orders to acquire horses and provisions, then ride inland to block any move by Castro south from Los Angeles. The Fremonters met no resistance when they landed at San Diego on July 29, but their hunt for horses was mostly futile. Thomas Larkin, meanwhile, had been trying to negotiate a settlement. The consul's efforts seemed to pay off on August 7 when Castro, trapped between two North American forces, proposed a truce and conference between the two commanders. Stockton snorted that he would agree on the condition that California accepted United States occupation.

When Castro read Stockton's insulting message, he called a council of war, which advised leaving California for Sonora. Castro had only about a hundred armed men, no money, and not much support. Nevertheless, he wrote to Stockton on August 10 denouncing his "insidious" letter and declaring that the Californians were ready to fight. Stockton, who had landed at San Pedro, set out with his motley crew for Los Angeles on the eleventh, dragging the cannons along. When word of that reached Castro and Pico, they disbanded their little army and left for Sonora with a few supporters. Most of what remained of the California Army moved to Rancho San Pasqual (in present-day South Pasadena). The Mexican government of California, independent as it had been, was no more. Stockton's column, marching behind a ship's band, trooped into Los Angeles on August 13, roundly ignored by the town's 1,500 people. Frémont's troops arrived soon after, having accomplished exactly nothing. The remaining California troops surrendered and were turned loose on parole, meaning they promised to stop fighting until "exchanged" for prisoners on the other side.[23]

Stockton planted himself at Los Angeles and proceeded to become the ruler of California, establishing customs duties on August 15. Two days later he promised early elections and the establishment of a territorial government. He declared on the twenty-second that elections would take place on September 15. Once again, he was out of line. In international law, civil governments in conquered territories were expected to continue to function under military occupation. In the absence of such governments military government could be imposed, respecting the previous civil codes. There was no tolerance for the formation of a civil government by military diktat. In the United States, only the Congress had power to provide territorial governments. Stockton later justified himself on the grounds that a functioning civil government would be proof of United States possession, make opposition to Anglo forces a civil rather than a military crime, and protect the rights of the people better than military rule. Stockton told President Polk privately that he feared an influx of Mormons in California, so he acted. The commodore was a bigot, but mostly he was arrogant. He had the right because he had the might.[24]

Stockton proclaimed a blockade of the entire west coast of Mexico on August 19. He did not have enough ships, so his "paper" blockade violated international law. As soon as Secretary of the Navy Mason heard about it he ordered Stockton to replace his proclamation with something enforceable. He never bothered to do that.[25]

The commodore sent a sloop-of-war against San Blas in September. The sloop landed a shore party that spiked the thirty-four guns at San Blas, then went on to the fishing village of La Paz, the capital of Baja California. The captain negotiated a neutralization of the whole peninsula with Governor Francisco Palacio Miranda. The Anglo sloop then went to the Sonora port of Guaymas, which it reached on October 6, and the commander demanded the surrender of all shipping there. The commandant refused, so the next day a party burned two gunboats and the wreck of an old brig. Another sloop tried and failed to conquer Mazatlán by bluff.[26]

Stockton issued a circular to United States merchantmen in the Pacific warning about Mexican privateers based at Acapulco. There were no privateers. He had cooked up a scheme to attack and capture Acapulco using privateers as an excuse, then march his sailors and marines inland to take Mexico City from the rear. The commodore had no authority for that, but he wanted to become the hero who won the war. He would take all his naval resources with him, so he ordered Frémont to increase the California Battalion to 300 men, to garrison several California towns, and to raise a mobile force. Stockton also promised the Pathfinder that he would become governor and Gillespie secretary of the Territory of California when he sailed away. In the meantime, Frémont became military commandant.[27]

Stockton proclaimed victory in California in a personal letter to the president, written from Los Angeles on August 26. "My word is at present the law of the land," he crowed. "My person is more than regal." As for Frémont and Gillespie, "they both understand the people and their language and I think are eminently qualified to perform the duties." Frémont would "send this letter with my despatches to the Secretary of the Navy, by Express over the mountains," as if such a thing existed.[28]

Frémont sent Kit Carson and fifteen men to carry the letters to Washington by way of Taos early in September. As Carson struggled across the wilderness of Sonora and southern New Mexico, California exploded behind him. *Californios* did not take kindly to being conquered.

WHAT CHILD WILL NOT SHED ABUNDANT TEARS AT THE TOMB OF HIS PARENTS?

East of California, Kearny's Army of the West advanced on Santa Fe, and the reinforcements organized themselves in Missouri. About 500 men of the Mormon Battalion filed into Fort Leavenworth in early August. There they received clothing, equipment, supplies, muskets, and basic drill before marching out in the middle of the month. The Mormon Battalion would offer Kearny two complications when it reached Santa Fe in mid-October. One was a horde of wives, children, laundresses, and other camp followers. The other was that the commander, Captain Allen, died on the trail. The battalion reached the New Mexico capital needing a leader.[29]

The 2nd Missouri Mounted Riflemen left Leavenworth about two weeks after the Mormons and passed them on the trail. Both outfits endured all the trials the main army had faced on the march across the plains, saving only that the later season meant somewhat less heat, and they got to New Mexico after most of the annual rains. The Mormons, despite the family-outing appearance of their unit, were self-disciplined. The Missourians were not. Their commander, Colonel Sterling Price, was a slithery politician who wanted his men's votes for governor after the war.[30]

The Army of the West prepared to leave Bent's Fort on August 1 when two more troops of dragoons rode into camp escorting James Magoffin, confidential agent for Polk and Benton. Kearny sent Magoffin with a message to Armijo, escorted by twelve dragoons under Captain Philip St. George Cooke, who actually carried the letter, protecting the party from attack by making it a communication between generals. Kearny's letter repeated his earlier message to the people, ending with a warning that resistance would only cause suffering for civilians. "A negotiation is being carried on between the two Generals through brother James," Susan Magoffin chirped, "who has the confidence of the Mexican Gen. so completely, we may look for pleasant results."[31]

The army crossed the Arkansas River on the second and climbed out of the prairie with its sunflowers and yuccas toward Raton Pass, which it reached on August 7. The Missourians passed through a windswept wilderness of "dreary, sultry, desolate, boundless solitude . . . heat, thirst, and driven sand." By the time they reached the pass over very rough trails, the troops were on short rations, horses were giving out, and wolves and buzzards were in constant attendance. "Col. Doniphan's Regiment to a man is sick and tired of the business," complained an officer. The junipers and piñon pines dotting the slopes gave way to Ponderosa pines; off in sheltered canyons aspen groves whispered at the slightest breeze. "Lowlanders never see such pure blue skies," Captain Cooke marveled, "and now snow-white clouds drifting over, intensified the blue above, and by their shadowings, added life and beauty to the landscape pictures below." A gentle breeze gave "that spirit-like music of the leaves, and in harmony with the purl of the mountain brook."[32]

Before Magoffin and Cooke reached Santa Fe, Armijo heard from the *comandante-general* of Chihuahua, Colonel Mauricio Ugarte, that he would send troops to New Mexico. Don Manuel issued a proclamation to his people on August 8, calling on them to show the "highest and best devotion to home and country." Each man should be ready to sacrifice "life and interests" for the homeland. The windy declaration was mostly a string of allusions to Mexican history that few *Nuevomexicanos* would understand. This appeal to nationalism rather than localism, in a province long disaffected from the national government, had its moments, however. "The eagle that made us equal under our national standard, making of us one family," Armijo sang, "calls upon you today, in the name of the supreme government and under the Chief of the Department, to defend the strongest and most sacred of all causes." The governor ended with a grand rhetorical flourish. "The God of Armies is also the protector of the justice of nations," he declaimed, "and, with his powerful help, we will add another brilliant page to the history of Mexico." To defend New Mexico, "your governor depends entirely upon your own pecuniary resources, your determination, your convictions, all founded in reason, justice, equity and

public convenience. Rest assured that your governor is willing and ready
to sacrifice his life and all his interests in the defense of his country."[33]

The remarkable thing about this bombast was that it worked, or appeared to. New Mexico was one of the nation's poorest stepchildren, overrun by *Indios bravos,* neglected by the central government. Many of the
inhabitants were Pueblo Indians who had never regarded themselves as
Mexicans. The province's wealth was concentrated in the hands of a few,
while most inhabitants were *peones,* locked into hereditary debt slavery.
Even they called themselves *Hispanos* rather than *Mexicanos.* Yet somewhere
between 2,000 and 4,000 of them—mostly Pueblos and *peones*—gathered
under the command of Colonel Manuel Pino near Cañoncito at the mouth
of Apache Canyon to fight the invaders. The Santa Fe Trail ran through
the canyon between steep cliffs only forty feet apart. The volunteers
blocked that with an abatis, a bristly arrangement of sharpened tree
trunks. A one-gun battery on a hill commanded the entire pass.

Magoffin and Cooke rode into Santa Fe on August 12 and handed
Armijo the letter from Kearny. The governor declared that the people of
New Mexico had arisen against the invaders and he must lead them. Then
he proposed direct negotiations between himself and Kearny and sent a
letter to that effect, delivered to Kearny north of Las Vegas on August 14.
"Say to General Armijo," Kearny sent a message back, "I shall soon meet
him, and I hope it will be as friends." Armijo, Cooke told his journal, "is
said to be in painful doubt and irresolution." The governor was torn between his military duty "and a desire to escape the dangers of war upon
terms of personal advantage."[34]

Armijo was indeed nervous. Just what he talked about with Cooke and
Magoffin may never be known. Whether *la mordida* played a role in his behavior the next few days has been a subject of debate for a century and a
half, and Magoffin's postwar claim remains suggestive. Kearny had no official cash supply for such activities, but Magoffin could have advanced such
a sum out of his own pocket.[35]

The Army of the West passed the first hamlet, Moro on the Río Moro,
on August 13. "Nothing could be more discouraging" complained one soldier, "than the first view of this town." It was a collection of half-
subterranean *jacales* roofed with logs. "The few Mexicans who came
around the camp certainly did not inspire us with fear," he snorted,
"swarthy, lean and dirty . . . pictures of misery." Not all the men had his
jaundiced eye, however. "The first object I saw," said another, "was a pretty
Mexican woman, with clean white stockings, who very cordially shook
hands with us and asked for tobacco."[36]

Just before Kearny reached Moro, a large party of Navajos thundered into Las Vegas on horseback on the night of August 12. Before the villagers could react, the raiders drove off hundreds, perhaps thousands, of sheep and goats, with all the horses they could round up, and disappeared to the west after killing one shepherd boy and kidnapping another. The Anglo army was to the north, Pino's was to the west, yet the Navajos made it safely home, a hundred miles west of Santa Fe, with all their plunder.[37]

Kearny entered Las Vegas on August 15. Armijo was not there. Kearny had his troops round up about 150 nervous citizens and read a new proclamation. "For some time the United States has considered your country a part of our territory," he claimed, "and we have come to take possession of it. We are among you as friends—not as enemies; as protectors—not as conquerors; for your benefit—not your injury." He absolved the people of all allegiance to the Mexican government.

Since Mexico and the United States both were vague abstractions to these villagers, what effect Kearny's words had on them can only be imagined. They could see the invaders' guns, however, so when the general ordered the local officials to swear allegiance to the United States, they did. Kearny added, "From the Mexican Government you have never received protection. The Apaches and Navajos come down from the mountains and carry off your sheep, and even your women, whenever they please. My government . . . will keep off the Indians." Kearny repeated this expanded proclamation at Tecolote, San Miguel, and finally Santa Fe. The *alcalde* (mayor) at San Miguel objected to taking the oath to the United States and asked for the reason behind that. "It is enough for you to know, Sir," Kearny replied, "that I have captured your town."[38]

Cooke rode into Las Vegas later on the fifteenth and could not explain Armijo's whereabouts. Magoffin had remained in Santa Fe to persuade Anglo and *hispano* merchants, the real powers in local politics, that United States rule would increase their trade. Magoffin told Lieutenant Governor Diego Archuleta that Kearny would install him as the governor of New Mexico west of the Rio Grande. Armijo, increasingly nervous, withdrew his ninety dragoons—all the regular troops he had—from Cañoncito and posted them as a personal bodyguard. On August 16 Armijo called a council of war, including the principal militia officers and leading citizens. They were all opposed to making a stand at Apache Canyon because nobody expected Mexican troops to march up from the south. Armijo sent another letter to Kearny. "We would defend our country," he claimed, "we desire to defend it, but we cannot do so, our general government being hundreds of leagues distant, it is impossible for me to receive the necessary aid to make such a defense."[39]

Armijo climbed into his Dearborn on the seventeenth and with his dragoons lit out for Albuquerque, his ultimate destination Ciudad Chihuahua. He left Juan Bautista Vigil y Alarid as acting governor and the city in a state of panic. Vigil handed the department secretary, Nicolás Quintaro, a letter to Kearny. Quintaro rode into the army's camp on the eighteenth and shouted from atop a sweat-flecked mule, "Armijo and his troops have gone to Hell and the canyon is clear!" The militia had evaporated from Apache Canyon, which Kearny's troops passed through on the eighteenth. "The prospect now is that we shall march into Santa Fe without firing a gun," groused one soldier. "This news throws rather a gloom over the spirits of the army. They are sadly disappointed at learning that we shall have no fighting." Not many of the footsore troops thought that way, however. "We all felt well satisfied to pass without being attacked," said another; "we now saw how difficult it would have been to have forced the pass."[40]

After a march of 856 miles in under two months, Kearny's advance trudged into New Mexico's capital early in the afternoon of August 18. Kearny entered the plaza, where Vigil greeted him. The general gave a short reply echoing his proclamations. He next paraded his army through town and raised the United States flag over the adobe palace of the governors; the troops fired a salute. The Army of the West encamped on high ground to the north, overlooking the collection of adobe and stone structures along the Santa Fe River about a dozen miles east of the Rio Grande.

Kearny offered a more formal address on the nineteenth, annexing the province and emphasizing how much better off New Mexicans would be as United States citizens. Vigil formally accepted New Mexico's annexation but he was clearly not happy about it. The chiefs of the nearest *pueblos* came into town to submit to Washington's power on the twentieth. Kearny issued his final proclamation on August 22, mostly repeating what had gone before. On the twenty-third the general attended Mass in the cathedral, and on the twenty-seventh he threw a ball that attracted a few hundred Anglo and *hispano* dignitaries. His declaration of annexation exceeded his authority, however.[41]

"Our first view of this place was very discouraging," Frank Edwards complained. "Although much larger than any we had seen yet, still there were the same mud walls and roofs and the accompaniments of dirt, pigs, and naked children. The city was, in a measure, deserted, the inhabitants having been persuaded that we should rob and ill-treat everybody and destroy everything; sobbing and crying were heard from the houses." Edwards observed that the Anglo army had brought measles to the community, starting an epidemic that killed many children.[42]

Kearny did not seem to notice that many Santa Feans were hiding from his troops. Nor did he hear the cries of grief for the dead and dying children. He did not understand that when his soldiers looked down on the people of New Mexico, those people noticed. It escaped him that the *Nuevomexicanos* did not in fact welcome the North American invasion or celebrate their change in nationality. Kearny reported to the War Department on August 24 that he had conquered and annexed New Mexico without bloodshed. He planned to go down the Rio Grande to visit the towns, then return to Santa Fe to set up a government. Kearny would proceed to California, he hoped, by the end of September. However, he had not yet heard from either Price or the Mormons. He planned to take the Mormon Battalion with him to California and send any surplus troops to join Wool at Chihuahua. He believed that his conquest had been welcomed by the people of New Mexico, and that there was no reason to expect trouble ahead.[43]

Kearny should have paid more attention when Acting Governor Vigil told him, "Do not find it strange if there has been no manifestation of joy and enthusiasm in seeing this city occupied by your military forces. The power of the Mexican Republic is dead. No matter what her condition, she was our mother. What child will not shed abundant tears at the tomb of his parents?"[44]

Whatever Kearny thought, New Mexico had not been conquered.

THE DUTY OF THE GOVERNMENT IS TO AFFORD PROTECTION

New Mexico composed the vast majority of the real estate added to the United States by the war. At various times historically the territory included all the modern states of New Mexico and Arizona, parts of Sonora, Chihuahua, Texas, Oklahoma, Kansas, Nebraska, Colorado, and Wyoming, and almost all of Utah and Nevada. In principle, this vast landscape was governed out of Santa Fe. In practice, that government noticed only the settlements along the Rio Grande and to the east up to the edge of the plains. On July 6, 1824, the Congress separated New Mexico from Chihuahua, of which it had been a subordinate territory. New Mexico became a separate federal territory, transformed into a department during the centralist regimes of the 1830s. The 1824 measure made El Paso, historically part of New Mexico, a city in Chihuahua.[45]

The Santa Fe Convention of October 1848 estimated the province's people at "from 75,000 to 100,000 souls," but "souls" meant principally Spanish-speaking Catholics and Pueblos. Other people lived in New Mexico. There was a sizable minority of Anglos concentrated around Taos. These economic imperialists caused persistent bad blood between Anglos and *Hispanos.* The latter called Kearny's campaign the "conquest by merchants," while Charles Bent spoke for the *Gringos* when he said, "The

Mexican character is made up of stupidity, obstinacy, ignorance, duplicity, and vanity." The other side returned the favor. Territorial governor William Carr Lane told his wife in 1853 that "the opposition, to every thing American," was "uncompromising."[46]

The antipathy between *Angloamericanos* and *Nuevomexicanos* was aggravated by the corruption that infected Mexican governments at all levels. Anglos assumed that Armijo had sold out his province for Magoffin's gold and declared that the territory had never had a real government, just a despotism based on bribery, greed, and corruption. Charles Bent snorted in 1845 that all officials and justices in the territory were "equally ignorant, insolent, and avaricious" and that delay and bribery were invariably the court procedure. He was especially riled at the capricious manner in which justices extracted fees from parties before their courts.[47]

Anglos and New Mexicans were not going to get along in any circumstances, so when Kearny established an Anglo-American form of government and tilted it to the Taos merchants in September he lit the fuse on a bomb. New Mexico had a history of rebellions among *peones* and Pueblo Indians going back to the seventeenth century. Sometimes the rich and government officials rose against Mexico City. There was no sentiment among either rich or poor for joining the United States.[48]

The economy of New Mexico was not promising. The majority of "souls" barely scratched out a living in their villages. The rich masters of the *peones* grew richer through the sheep business, supplemented by other trading with Missouri. There was a small but growing cattle industry and deposits of valuable minerals, although these were mostly undiscovered. New Mexico wine, especially from the El Paso area, was world-famous, as was *aguardiente* (brandy) distilled from it. When Anglos settled in northern New Mexico, several of them set up stills to produce whiskey—"Taos Lightning"—from corn or wheat, thus encouraging a cash crop for a few farmers. This tanglefoot became notorious all over the West.[49]

It was not likely that Anglo-Americans were going to fit into this world easily. Even the landscape was too alien for most of them. "The bible says that it tuck God almighty six days to make the world," one of Kearny's men wrote home in 1846, "and that on the seventh day he rested. Now *I* never believed a d——d word of this before, but now I do:—and all this region . . . was made late Saturday evening—when he was d——d tired *and in a bad humor at that!*"[50]

Kearny's topographer, William H. Emory, thought that the environment would prevent the kind of agriculture North Americans were used to. "In no part of this vast tract can the rains from Heaven be relied upon, to any extent for the cultivation of the soil," he reported. "The cultivation of the earth is therefore confined to the narrow strips of land which are within the level of the waters of the streams and wherever practiced in a community, or to any extent, involves a degree of subordination and ab-solute obedience to a chief, repugnant to the habits of our people." As for extending the southern slave economy into the region, Emory, a Maryland slave owner, thought there was no chance. "No one who has ever visited this country and who is acquainted with the character and value of slave la-bor in the United States would ever think of bringing his slaves here with any view to profit," he said, "much less would he purchase slaves for such a purpose."[51]

Nor would it be wise to risk slaves in a land where they could be killed or kidnapped by Utes, Navajos, Apaches, Comanches, or others. Indian raiders, in fact, provided the first substantial contact the Anglo conquerors had with New Mexico. They attacked supply trains and made penetration of the country or removal of troops to other regions almost impossible. Kearny sent expeditions to deal with various tribes, negotiated peace treaties with others, and thought the Indian problem was solved, but it was not. When Kearny promised New Mexicans that he would guarantee pro-tection against Indian attacks, they must have rolled their eyes. They had heard that from Spanish and Mexican authorities for decades. Kearny's promise was impossible, with the "souls" scattered in little adobe villages for 400 miles along the Rio Grande from Taos to El Paso, and others in outposts such as Las Vegas and Cebolleta east or west of the river.[52]

Except for the Pueblos, and the Pimas and Papagos in northern Sonora (now southern Arizona), the rest of the Indian peoples in the region—the Navajos, Apaches, Comanches, Jicarillas, Mojaves, Yavapais, Yumas, Utes, and several smaller tribes or small bands from distant tribes—were hostile to whites, Anglos and Mexicans alike. Some offered to ally themselves with the United States in making war against the common enemy, the Mexicans, but Kearny would have none of that. Soon all whites were the same to the warlike tribes. "One territory, New Mexico, is almost surrounded by numerous tribes of predatory Indians," the secretary of war complained in 1849, "and open at all points to their incursions." Pioneering was hard enough without the constant threat of attack, he ob-served. "The duty of the government is to afford protection."[53]

Polk and his minions had assumed that taking land from Mexico would be easy. They did not imagine the possibility of extended warfare with na-tives who had lived there for centuries. Throughout the nineteenth cen-tury United States officials viewed Indians as if they were alien invaders from another world. This prevented them from understanding the com-plexities of the ancient interactions among New Mexicans and the several tribes. Raiding went both ways, for slaves and for profit. For the Navajos in particular the acquisition of sheep in the hundreds of thousands created prosperity, so their economy by the 1840s stood on the twin foundations of herding and raiding, supplemented by their farms and orchards.[54]

Even more difficult for outsiders to appreciate was the mutual dance of blood and money between New Mexicans and Comanches. The "Lords of the Plains" had been raiding into New Mexico since at least 1705, but in 1786 they and the Spanish government entered a long truce. The two sides sent traders into each other's camps and settlements without fighting—those on the *hispano* side were called *Comancheros*. This peace between New Mexico and the Comanches did not extend to other whites or other regions. The arrangement saved New Mexico (which had its hands full with Apaches, Navajos, Jicarillas, and Utes) from the destruction that rained down on settlements in Texas and from raids like those that went deep into Mexico. The *Comancheros,* in fact, did a fine business buying horses and other stolen property from their trading partners, then selling them back to their countrymen farther south.[55]

Raiding was as mutual an activity between *Nuevomexicanos* and other Indian tribes as was the trade relationship with the Comanches. New Mexicans raided Indians, especially Navajos and Apaches, with the same ferocity as was directed against themselves. The objectives were also the same—take livestock and other valuables and kill or capture as many of the target people as could be done. New Mexicans and Indians robbed, terrorized, slaughtered, and enslaved each other. There were several overlapping slave trades going on when Kearny entered the territory, along with intervals of trade among the various enemy groups, all developed over centuries. The presence of a new armed force in the region just added further strain to a terrible situation. The Indian slave trade was common throughout the Mexican north from Texas to California. Raiding Navajos or Apaches was for New Mexicans a common way to get household servants and farmhands. Slavery was nominally illegal in Mexico, but the profits in the trade were so enormous that the range of participants expanded during the 1830s and 1840s. Bands of Shawnees and Delawares from northeast Texas, for instance, raided for slaves as far off as California and traders fed slave markets as distant as Mexico City. In New Mexico, the money to be made from this horrible racket drew the Anglo traders into it, providing guns and markets to Indians and putting the New Mexicans at a disadvantage.[56]

It could become very complicated. Nearly every Mexican settlement had its share of slave labor, all Indians. Nearly every Indian band had its slaves, either Mexicans or members of other tribes. New Mexicans raided various tribes, and tribes raided each other or the New Mexicans, took captives, and either kept them in slavery, ransomed them back, or sold them to distant buyers. This grisly situation produced a secondary trade in scalps. The Chihuahua and Sonora governments offered bounties on Apache scalps and hired Apaches, Comanches, and Seminoles to raid each other. Not to be outdone, a Mescalero chief offered matching rewards for the hair of Anglos or Mexicans. Bands of professional scalp hunters, Anglos and Mexicans alike, worked out of El Paso and Ciudad Chihuahua by 1849, selling their trophies to whoever would pay for them.[57]

New Mexico—northern Mexico in general—was a complicated and explosive mixture of peoples, each with its grievances and bloodlust. Adding the power of the United States government to this lethal stew created dangers that nobody could foresee. Kearny had opened the gates of hell and turned loose the demons.

CHAPTER

11

OH GOD, AND THIS IS WAR!

(September 1846)

We are mad, not only individually but nationally.
We check manslaughter and isolated murders; but what of war and the
much vaunted crime of slaughtering whole peoples?

—Seneca

SANTA ANNA ENTERED MEXICO CITY on September 14, 1846, greeted by a small, quiet crowd. "Every day that passes without fighting at the north is a century of disgrace for Mexico," he declared. Acting President Salas appointed him commander of the Division of the North, superseding Ampudia, on the seventeenth and encouraged him to march north against Taylor. He based himself at San Luis Potosí, about 300 miles south of Monterey on the southern reach of the dry highlands. Santa Anna rode into San Luis in his fine carriage on October 8. He thought he needed about 25,000 men to take on Taylor's force, whose numbers he overestimated. The country was broke. The restored constitution transferred much power back to the states, Durango, Jalisco, and Zacatecas refused to send men, and some states rebelled outright. A federal law pardoning desertion from the army merely encouraged it. Santa Anna got some money from the federal government and a few state governments, forced loans on the Church, seized whatever he could, and mortgaged his own estate to raise and equip an army. All along, he heard charges that he would use it to take over the country.[1]

The detail manager on the Anglo-American side, President Polk, also had burdens to bear. Public opposition to the war became ever louder. Besides the cost in blood and treasure, the administration's promise that the campaign would be short had proven hollow. Taylor proposed holding part of northeast Mexico as bond against Mexican reparations, and both Calhoun and Buchanan agreed with him. That would limit expenses and manpower, but it would not bring the conflict to a close. Polk did not like Taylor's idea of holding the line until Mexico gave up, however. In fact, the president did not like Taylor. He dismissed the general as "unwilling to express any opinion or take any responsibility on himself." Taylor was "unfit," but Polk could think of no one to replace him. Scott offered himself again, but at Polk's bidding Marcy brushed him off.[2]

The note from Mexican foreign minister Manuel Crescencio Rejón rejecting the peace overture arrived on September 19. Polk assembled his cabinet to consider how to deal with yet another frustrating response. The group decided to take Tampico. Bancroft drafted a letter to Rejón saying that the United States would expect an indemnity for additional costs incurred while Mexico refused to negotiate. Polk deleted that, but the final letter clearly implied this would be one of the terms if talks were delayed further.

Conner and Taylor would have to cooperate to seize Tampico. Polk bypassed Taylor and told the secretary of war to put Major General Robert Patterson in command of the land force, mostly because he was a prominent Pennsylvania Democrat. Conner advised that there was no road from Tampico to San Luis Potosí. He did not like the idea of any amphibious invasion, but said there were landing areas near Vera Cruz preferable to Tampico. He could not estimate what land force would be required, and except for beef there were not many supplies available in the area. That left a Tampico campaign up in the air except that Polk had raised Patterson's prominence in the army. Any force he led would be mostly volunteers, who would need regulars to steady them, so the War Department converted the last heavy artillery batteries still in coastal forts to infantry and sent them to Patterson. These transfers concluded a nearly permanent realignment of the army. Coastal fortifications sat virtually unmanned for decades and most heavy artillery served as infantry until near the end of the century.[3]

One of Polk's worst partisan blunders was to introduce his old law partner Gideon Pillow into Taylor's army. Pillow thought that the United States faced two enemies, the lesser one Mexico, the greater the Whig Party. As soon as he reached the Rio Grande he wore out his welcome among regular officers, who called him "Polk's spy." Taylor transferred one of his regiments to another command, and Pillow wrote to Polk and others undermining Old Zach. Pillow portrayed himself as a military genius, but he was incompetent. He put his men to work digging fortifications at Camargo, then summoned news correspondents to show off his creation. Unfortunately, he had put the ditch inside rather than outside the parapet, protecting attackers rather than the defenders. Lieutenant James Stuart mounted a mustang and leaped parapet and ditch in one bound.[4]

A CITY AWAITING A BATTLE IS BEYOND ALL DESCRIPTION

Pillow did not go along when Taylor marched toward Monterey in September 1846. Taylor did not like him and did not think he needed Pillow's troops. Nuevo León, the state Taylor's army marched into, did not look like a formidable prospect. Paredes and Gómez Farías had imposed a succession of military commanders in the area, along with at least four governors during the four months ending in September. The state had few arms and no transport, the militia was untrained, and people did not identify with the nation. Monterey had planned to celebrate its 250th anniversary on September 20. Instead, the local *caudillo* allowed the men of the city to evacuate their families on the understanding that they would return to fight the *Yanquis*. Most did not come back. The state was mostly rural, its people illiterate farmers ignorant of the Texas issue. When one of the governors called on the *alcalde* of a village to send eighty men to Monterey, the mayor answered that he could round up only thirty-three. The farmers were reluctant to go off to the army, he said, because "the fields, planted with grain and beans, will be left unattended and the families reduced to indigence."[5]

Ampudia thought Monterey was the key to the defense of Mexico. It guarded the mouth of a pass called Arroyo Santa Catarina, the principal route through the rugged Sierra Madre Oriental, a towering mountain range that loomed over the city like a great fortress wall. At the other end of the arroyo stood Saltillo. Santa Anna believed Monterey could not be held. Ampudia warned that if the invaders gained hold of the pass, "it will be almost impossible to dislodge them." General Mejía, commanding the city garrison under Ampudia, said that it would be dishonorable to surrender the place without a fight. Ampudia issued a series of bombastic proclamations threatening anybody who aided the enemy. Still, most citizens fled

Monterey. "The lonesome aspect of a city awaiting a battle," said one, "is beyond all description."[6]

Monterey had been a city of about 10,000, inhabiting a dense collection of houses along the left (north) bank of the Santa Catarina River, a tributary of the San Juan. The city was about a mile long and half that wide. The houses were well built, mostly one story, with flat parapeted roofs, each potentially a small fort. The streets were straight and easily barricaded. There was a beautiful old cathedral fronting the *Zócalo,* stocked with ammunition. Ampudia had about 7,300 men and forty-two guns to defend against an attack by about 6,000 Anglos lacking heavy guns. Besides the Sierra Madre to the west, looming over town to the west and east were sharp detached peaks that the North Americans called Bishop's Mitre and Saddle Mountain. The Saltillo road ran out of town to the west, just south of a lumpy hill called Cerro Independencia, with two prominences each about 800 feet high. The western one was called Fortaleza Libertad (Fort Liberty), a small redoubt of earth and rock manned by fifty or sixty men with two light guns. Halfway down the slope of the eastern prominence stood the ruins of the Obispado (Bishop's Palace), fortified and manned by 200 men and four guns under Lieutenant Colonel Francisco de Berra. Across the river to the south stood a hill called Cerro Federación, about 400 feet high, with a one-gun redan at the west and little Fortaleza Soldado (Soldier Fort) at the east. Staring North American attackers in the face was the Citadel, the ruins of an unfinished cathedral fortified by bastioned walls. It stood about a thousand yards north of the city, covering the main roads to the north and east, and was surrounded by farm fields that gave it a clear field of fire. The work mounted thirty guns served by 400 men, including the San Patricios, under Colonel José López Uraga.

Ampudia's engineers had laid out a defense in depth. The Ojo de Agua Canal skirted the northern side of town, crossed by the road to Marín on a bridge called la Purísima, which was guarded by a *tête-de-pont* (fortified bridgehead); Mejía established his headquarters there. Around him were 300 infantrymen commanded by Lieutenant Patricio Gutierrez and protecting an artillery battery. A three-gun earthwork called la Tenería (for the tannery next to it) covered the northeast corner of the city, manned by 200 light infantrymen and another battalion under Colonel José María Carrasco. About 500 yards to the southwest on a long, low ridge stood a smaller fort, el Fortín del Rincón del Diablo (the Little Fort at Devil's Corner), commanded by Colonel Igancio Joaquín del Arenal.[7]

Taylor ordered his army to march the sixty or so miles from Cerralvo to Monterey on September 11. Each man set off with eight days' rations and forty rounds of ammunition. The army was divided into three divisions, two of regulars under Generals David Twiggs and William Worth and one of volunteers under Major General William O. Butler. His division included two mounted regiments from Texas under Governor Henderson. Ben McCulloch's rangers were out in front with instructions to scout the way and if possible drive off General Canales and his guerrillas. The scouts and pioneers, who prepared the road, left Cerralvo on the twelfth, followed at one-day intervals by the divisions. All commands were on alert, because Mexican cavalry was expected to contest the advance. Ampudia did send a cavalry force out to meet the invaders at the halfway point, Marín, but canceled the order when his officers objected that their men could not reach Marín in time. Instead, he sent Torrejón's thousand horse soldiers, tired after a forced march from Saltillo, to harass Taylor's columns, but they failed to engage. Taylor halted to close up his columns on the fifteenth and ordered Henderson, who had diverted to China, to join him. Everybody was ready to go take a look at Monterey by early morning on the nineteenth. Taylor, accompanied by Henderson's Texians and some Texas mounted troops under Jack Hays, led the way.[8]

All along the march the country had become ever more pleasant, the air perfumed by citrus orchards. Taylor and his escort emerged from farms and woodlots onto a wide plain about three miles northeast of Monterey, a spread of cornfields, cattle, and a few farmers' *jacales*. Morning mist obscured the town and the surrounding heights, but as the sun climbed, the bishop's palace and the walls of the Citadel emerged. When the party got to within three miles of the Citadel, Mexican guns started firing and balls bounced all around the riders.

Taylor backed up to Bosque de San Domingo, a beautiful grove of pecans and oaks watered by many springs; for some reason the Anglos dubbed the place Walnut Springs. Old Zach ordered the army to camp and sent an engineer, J. K. F. Mansfield, out to survey the objective, accompanied by mounted Texas Rangers. The Texians taunted the Citadel by riding in circles around the plain, skirting the enemy works. "Their proximity occasionally provoked the enemy's fire," an Ohioan said, "but the Mexicans might as well have attempted to bring down skimming swallows as those racing dare-devils." What *los diablos tejanos* accomplished with their antics was to persuade Ampudia to give in to the Mexican army's tendency to turn all battles into cavalry engagements. Mansfield reported that the west end of Monterey would be easier to attack than the east, and Old Zach made his dispositions for the next day. Worth's division and Hays' rangers would sweep to the north and west, cutting Ampudia's communications to Saltillo. The rest of the army would advance from the northeast, pinning the Mexicans down. This double envelopment divided the army into two units, each vulnerable to attack. Worth's corps would be out of touch, so coordinating the separate movements would be well nigh impossible even if nothing went wrong.[9]

THIS LITTLE ONE IS LIKE YOU—DO NOT KILL IT

With Worth in charge, something was bound to go wrong on the right. A square-built man with a square head and square face, fifty-two years old, he had been in the military since 1813, more concerned with the dignities of rank than with scouting the terrain ahead. His sweep around the Mexican positions was over cane and grain fields, he did not start out until midafternoon on September 20, and the soft ground let him advance only six miles before nightfall. As a diversion, Taylor trooped the rest of the army out onto the plain and halted until dark. Ampudia had figured out what was going on. He ordered a bombardment from two 24-pounders and a 10-inch mortar in a nearby quarry. That noise masked a shift of Mexican troops to Independencia to meet Worth's advance. Ampudia also sent a large cavalry force under Torrejón to cover the road to Saltillo. Worth had gotten at least that far, and he bedded his men down in the fields without shelter, fires, or food. "A cold, chilly rain now set in," D. H. Hill remembered. "We had nothing to eat, no overcoats, no blankets, no tents and scarcely any fire."[10]

Worth roused his sodden, freezing, hungry men about six in the morning on September 21 and they plodded forward with the Texians still in the advance. They ran into about 200 lancers in two squadrons supported by infantry and the cannons on Independencia. The squadrons formed up to charge, so Worth dismounted the Texians and deployed them with two infantry companies behind a fence and hedge along the Saltillo road. Two batteries of flying artillery bolstered the defense. A squadron led by Lieutenant Colonel Juan Nájera foolishly but gallantly thundered into a storm of lead, which killed the colonel and about thirty other horsemen and scattered the rest. Then Lieutenant Colonel Mariano Moret's squadron charged in. Again the North Americans poured volleys and cannon fire into the oncoming horsemen and, according to a Mexican observer, "fifty dragoons following him [Moret] lay suddenly dead; alone and wounded, his lance broken, he attacked boldly, waving his sword and chasing the North Americans right back to their artillery, then he calmly retreated." That was too melodramatic. The reality was a tooth-and-claw brawl that left one Texian dead and seven wounded and about a hundred Mexicans killed or wounded. The lancers retreated to the Obispado, leaving behind a smoke-shrouded field covered in dead and dying men and animals, horses screaming in pain. It had been a foolish waste of brave man-power. Worth overoptimistically sent a note to Taylor claiming, "The town is ours."[11]

This bloody skirmish introduced another remarkable woman into ac-tion in northeast Mexico. A gallant lady known only as Dos Amades (Two Sweethearts) put on the uniform of a lancer captain, exhorted the men to fight, and led a party of horse soldiers on what was called a "devastating charge" against United States troops. One North American officer was filled with admiration. "There's an example of heroism worthy of the days of old!" he told a newspaperman. "It has remained for Mexico to produce a second Joan d'Arc!" Dos Amades survived and returned to her family.[12]

As Worth started moving early in the morning, Taylor sent Henderson with a squadron of dragoons and a Texian regiment to reinforce Worth, but then recalled them. Instead of fighting that day, they trooped back and forth. Twiggs' and Butler's divisions assembled on the plain and sat while Mansfield scouted the eastern and northern sides of the city. Twiggs, how-ever, was not on the scene. He was incapacitated by medicine he had taken to "loosen the bowels," as he explained it, "for a bullet striking the belly when the bowels were loose might pass through the intestines without cutting them." Colonel John Garland was temporarily in command of Twiggs' division. "Colonel," Taylor told him, "lead the head of your col-umn off to the left, keeping out of reach of the enemy's shot, and if you think (or if you find) you can take any of them little forts down there with the bay'net you better do it—but consult with Major Mansfield. You'll find him down there." Garland set off with about 800 men, aiming for the east-ern end of Monterey.[13]

Worth hesitated after cutting the Saltillo road. About a half hour after noon, he ordered Captain Charles F. Smith to lead 300 red-legged infantry and the dismounted Texians against the western knob of Federación. The men waded the waist-deep, cold waters of the Santa Catarina as shot poured down on them, then started clambering up the steep, boulder-bedecked hillside. Worth decided that he had not sent enough men, so he ordered Lieutenant Colonel Dixon F. Miles in support. As soon as Miles and his infantry regiment marched off, Worth told Colonel Persifor Smith to join the party with the rest of the brigade's infantry.

The Mexican conscripts on Federación had never been trained to withstand what was coming at them. Miles found a fairly easy route to the top and got there in time to support Charles Smith's assault on the redan. The Yankees stormed into the defenders, who ran to the rear. The Mexicans abandoned a 9-pounder, which infantry muscled around and turned on Soldado, dismounting its one gun with the first shot. Soldado's garrison bailed out of its post as well. Anglo troops were right behind, remounting the gun and firing at Independencia. Worth had enough force on hand by this time to fight off brave but futile charges by Torrejón's cavalry aimed at isolating the *Yanquis* on the hill. That was the end of the day for Worth's part of the army. The night again was freezing, and a tremendous rainstorm drenched his hungry men along with wounded scattered over the battlefield while wagons wandered around looking for them.

Ampudia faced assaults from opposite ends of the town. Keeping enough men to the west to hold Worth in position, he rushed others to the east to blast away at Garland's force struggling over rough ground. The Anglos drew fire from the Citadel on their right flank and rear and from the Tenería and lower works in front of them, pinning the troops down. Garland had misinterpreted Taylor's orders, thinking he was to mount an assault rather than a distraction. He found Mansfield and ordered his men to resume the advance. Mansfield dodged musket balls to take a closer look at the northeast corner of town and waved to Garland to follow. Garland diverted his line to the right, a mistake that was promptly detected by the Mexicans in the Tenería, who poured fire into his ranks, smashing bodies, severing limbs, spraying blood and brains. Two battalions broke and ran, leaving only Lieutenant Colonel William H. Watson and about seventy men to continue the advance. Trudging bent over as if walking into a hailstorm, they pushed into the town and lost cohesion in the streets, scattered by deadly fire from inside and on top of houses. On Mansfield's advice, Garland withdrew his surviving soldiers.

While Garland was getting his nose smashed, a company of the 1st Infantry took the tannery, where it was reinforced by parts of two other companies. Together they cleared the Mexicans from the rear of the Tenería, opening its gorge to fire from Anglo artillery. Mejía rushed about 140 men and one gun to support Carrasco in holding the Tenería. Meanwhile, two volunteer regiments and Brigadier General John A. Quitman's brigade showed up after Garland had withdrawn. The three lead companies charged into murderous fire from the Tenería, costing them a third of their officers and men before they were driven back in disorder. Carrasco ably kept his men at their grisly work, but he was about to be overwhelmed. Quitman, a Tennessee regiment, and the Mississippi Rifles under Colonel Jefferson Davis went to their objective far enough east of Garland's route that they dodged much of the fire from the Citadel. Davis had no clear instructions and he was tired of waiting for orders. "Now is the time!" he shouted. "Great God, if I had fifty men with knives I could take the fort!" The mixed force assaulted the Tenería head-on and took it and about thirty Mexican prisoners just after noon, but with heavy casualties. Twiggs had recovered from his laxative and arrived to direct the defense of the position, turning the captured guns around.[14]

Twiggs' men came under heavy fire from fortified rooftops. The Mexicans had used cotton sandbags to armor the parapets and accidentally set the bags on fire with sparks from their muskets, which drove them back from their own breastworks. This gave the attackers a break, and Davis himself led one of several parties going house to house to flush the snipers off the rooftops. He entered one house where several Mexican women and children cowered in fear. A mother held her blue-eyed baby up to Davis and begged, "This little one is like you—do not kill it, but take it for your own." The Mississippians went on with their bloody work. In another house they found a Mexican landlady who sold them hot meals of beef and tortillas.[15]

It was the bloodiest kind of street fighting, the two sides shooting at each other across streets or back and forth from streets and rooftops. A Mexican soldier remembered that they often traded shots at "burn-clothes distance," so close that uniforms were singed or set afire by muzzle blasts. The streets filled with stinking smoke and the noise was deafening. As the fight continued the 1st Ohio volunteers crossed the river near la Purísima and dodged through the city to attack Fort Diablo. The leading officers were wounded and the unit withdrew, only to be attacked by two cavalry regiments under Brigadier General José María Conde, charging where cavalry did not belong, the streets of a city. The Buckeyes beat them off with musketry. They reappeared around sunset, but the heavy fire from Anglo artillery was too much.[16]

As dark settled down on the smoke-blurred sight of bodies in the streets, holes blasted into houses, civilians dead or terrified, horses screaming, dogs tearing at the corpses, Taylor had little to be proud of. His orders had been ambiguous; he had committed troops piecemeal, sent unsupported infantry against artillery, and exposed parts of his army to fire from the forts. Old Zach did not even know what was going on in Worth's part of the field. Ampudia had taken advantage of his interior position to respond to the enemy's every move.[17]

SHE, WHO FOUND A MARTYR'S GRAVE, ON THAT RED FIELD OF MONTEREY

Nobody could sleep that night with the rain starting to freeze. Worth got some food and ammunition up to his men and roused them around two in the morning. He had decided to send a mixed force of rangers, artillerymen, and two infantry regiments under Lieutenant Colonel Thomas Childs to take the western post on Independencia. The corps set out in the sleet at about three and groped its way up the hill in the dark. Mexican sentries spotted the Anglos as they got to within sixty feet of Libertad. The North Americans charged and drove off the outnumbered garrison of about fifty men in a melee of bayonets and clubbed muskets. The conquerors of Libertad paused to catch their breath, the rain stopped, the sun came out, and Yankees in and around the city could see the Stars and Stripes flying from Libertad's pole. Ampudia tried to retake the fort, but two more regular infantry regiments moved into positions where they could enfilade any force coming up from the Obispado. One of the Anglo engineers found a suitable path, so soldiers dismantled a 12-pounder howitzer and lugged it up the hill, reassembled it in the fort, and silenced several of the Mexican guns at the Obispado. Colonel Berra, commanding the bishop's palace, was under orders to remain on the defensive. His situation was critical by late afternoon, however, so he ordered his *soldados* to attack Libertad. That they did with stunning ferocity until they were cut to pieces in a crossfire. The exhausted and bleeding Mexicans withdrew to the Obispado with Anglos so close behind that the two corps cleared the walls at the same time. The outnumbered defenders abandoned the place. Worth now held secure control over the western approaches to Monterey.

Taylor continued to fumble at the east end of town. He made no moves on the twenty-second other than to have Quitman's brigade replace Garland's troops in the Tenería. Mejía might have retaken the place, but Ampudia began to have doubts. He abandoned all his outer defenses around midnight except the Citadel, and concentrated his troops around the *Zócalo*. His *soldados* had stoutly beaten off the enemy attacks on the twenty-first and believed they could do more of the same, but the withdrawal demoralized them. Quitman advanced into the city cautiously and by late morning held the eastern districts. Taylor and his staff joined Quitman, "perfectly regardless of danger," according to his political boosters. To everyone's surprise, at two in the afternoon Old Zach ordered the troops, who were within two blocks of the *Zócalo*, to withdraw to the edge of town. He never explained this decision.[18]

Worth had been advancing house to house from the west, Texas Rangers leading each of two columns. When Taylor pulled Quitman's men out of the east, Ampudia shifted his muscle to the west. The street fighting had been severe enough, but now the western side of town exploded. "Cannons and small arms flashed, crashed and roared like one mighty storm of wind, rain, hail, thunder and lightning," a soldier remembered.[19]

"At that moment," recorded a Mexican chronicler, "sublime as the heroines of Sparta and Rome, and as beautiful as the protective goddesses sculpted by the Greeks, a young woman, Doña María Josefa Zozaya, appeared among the soldiers" fighting on the roof of a house. She passed out ammunition, "gave the men courage, and showed them how to face down the dangers. . . . She was a beautiful personification of the fatherland; she was the gorgeous personification of heroism with all its charms, with all its tender seduction."[20]

Despite that flowery romanticism, there really was an "Angel of Monterey," as she was called, and probably two of them, mixed together in accounts from both sides. A North American soldier saw "a Mexican female carrying water and food to the wounded men of both armies. I saw her lift the head of one poor fellow, give him water, and then take her handkerchief from her own head and bind up his wounds; attending one or two others in the same way, she went back for more food and water." As the lady returned to the wounded, "I heard the crack of one or two guns, and she, poor good creature, fell; after a few struggles all was still—she was dead! I turned my eyes to heaven and thought, 'Oh God, and this is war!'" The next day he passed her dead body. "It was lying on its back, with the bread and broken gourd containing a few drops of water. We buried her amid showers of grape and round shot."[21]

Whether this was Doña María Josefa or another heroic lady, she or they became celebrated in two countries, called among other things the "Heroine Martyr of Monterey." James Gilmore Lyns honored her in an epic poem:

> Far greater than the wise or brave,
> Far happier than the fair and gay,
> Was she, who found a martyr's grave,
> On that red field of Monterey.[22]

Despite these brave women, Monterey was lost. Taylor's guns had begun shelling the cathedral and sooner or later a shot would touch off the ammunition there. Ampudia also realized that he had demoralized his men by pulling them back from the outskirts. The governor of Nuevo León, Francisco de Paula y Morales, sent a note to Taylor asking permission to evacuate civilians from the city. Ampudia sent his own note offering to surrender the city and withdraw his troops with their weapons.

Ampudia was entitled to the "honors of war" under time-honored rules of sieges, owing to his gallant defense until his situation was hopeless. That meant that his men could march out under arms, colors flying.

Taylor, however, was not a student of military protocol. He answered by simply demanding the surrender of both the city and the army. Ampudia asked for a personal meeting, which took place the afternoon of the twenty-fourth. The two generals each appointed three commissioners to draw up the terms of capitulation. The Mexicans would surrender the town together with all arms and public property. Officers would keep their personal arms and take one six-gun field battery with them when they left. The Citadel was surrendered immediately and Ampudia would evacuate the city within a week. Mexican forces were to retire behind a line drawn on Rinconada Pass, Linares, and San Fernando de Parras. Taylor would not advance for eight weeks or until either government disavowed the armistice.[23]

Taylor's reasons for agreeing to the armistice aroused debate. His army was beat up, Worth's division especially, and ammunition was short. He believed that the Polk government wanted him only to press the Mexicans to negotiate. Mauling their army unnecessarily would not do that. "These terms are liberal," he told his son-in-law, "but not considered too much so by all reflecting men . . . considering our situation: besides it was thought it would be judicious to act with magnanimity towards a prostrate foe."[24]

Taking Monterey had come at a price. The North Americans lost 120 killed, 368 wounded, many mortally, and 43 missing, out of 6,220 on the scene. Ampudia lost 367 killed and wounded of his 7,303. When the Mexicans marched out they left behind twenty-three serviceable and two unserviceable artillery pieces, along with a few muskets, carbines, lances, and about 60,000 musket cartridges. There remained, however, a Mexican army in the northeast, defeated but still able to fight.[25]

MONTEREY HAD BECOME AN ENORMOUS CEMETERY

The capitulation was sealed on September 25 and Ampudia led his troops out. Ulysses Grant said that his pity was aroused by the sight. The cavalry was "mounted on miserable little half-starved horses that did not look as if they could carry their riders," while the soldiers "looked in but little better condition." His fellow North Americans also were ragged. One of them said they were "about as dirty as they could be without becoming real estate."[26]

When the remaining residents of the city saw the Mexican troops leave, a large crowd of men and women abandoned the place and followed, carrying their children. "Monterey had become an enormous cemetery," a Mexican reporter said. "The unburied bodies, the dead and rotting animals, the empty streets, everything gave the city a frightful appearance."[27]

Recriminations over the armistice broke out on both sides. Governor Paula had wanted to evacuate his citizens, but he also wanted to continue the fight. He accused Ampudia of incompetence and cowardice. Both charges were unfair. Ampudia had planned and performed well, ably moving troops around in battle despite a weak officer corps and lack of maneuver training in the Mexican army. His chief errors were relying too much on cavalry in the open instead of in protected works and his decision to withdraw to the city center.[28]

On the North American side, "Gen. Taylor could not do otherwise than he did, though some say it was treacherous," Private Stephen F. Nunnalee said. "I can't think so, for he never had ammunition, men or provisions to have delayed the [Mexican] attack." The uncharitable Texians were "maddened with disappointment," said one of McCulloch's rangers. Luther Giddings of Ohio said the Texians were "unsated with slaughter, but they waited for morning to avenge signally the hoarded wrongs suffered during their long war for independence. The capitulation of the 24th, of course, disappointed all their sweet and long cherished hopes of vengeance."[29]

Monterey was occupied for almost two years, until June 1848, the longest of any major Mexican city. Taylor's soldiers were dispirited by the shock the Mexicans had given them during the battle, and the army needed time to lick its wounds, replace lost officers, and replenish its supplies and ammunition. News that Ampudia had continued his march past Saltillo to San Luis Potosí restored spirits somewhat.[30]

The occupation started off as sheer hell for the citizens who remained. Worth canceled all security patrols, and the Texians moved into the vacuum. "As a matter of course, all restraint being thrown off," complained D. H. Hill, "the foul spirit of mischief and depravity was not long in developing itself. Murder, rape and robbery were committed by the [Texas] Volunteers in the broad light of day." They would have burned the city to the ground except that most buildings were fireproof, so they "burnt the thatched huts of the miserable peasants." The Texians murdered at least a hundred innocent people. One Mexican soldier was shot dead in the street before hundreds of witnesses. He had Worth's passport in his pocket, so he was buried with military honors by a detail of regulars. Worth was finally offended enough to post guards in the city.[31]

It was the old catalog of atrocities all over again. Fortunately, the Texians went home early in October. "With their departure we may look for a restoration of quiet and good order in Monterey," Taylor advised the adjutant general, "for I regret to report that some disgraceful atrocities have been perpetrated by them." Watching *los diablos tejanos* march off,

Giddings hoped "that honest Mexicans were at a safe distance from their path." They were not safe. Manuel Ramírez of Camargo complained that soldiers there murdered Mexican civilians with impunity.[32]

Taylor exerted no real control over his volunteers, on the excuse that courts-martial could not try soldiers for crimes that in the United States would be handled by civil courts. Scott had proposed a law to cover that situation in May 1846, but Congress did not act. Scott drafted a letter for the secretary of war's signature on October 8, establishing a code to let military courts try offenses against civilians in Mexico. Marcy did not sign. Taylor was especially incensed by the daylight murder of the Mexican soldier in Monterey and asked the War Department for instructions on what to do about the matter. Marcy answered that there was no way to try the murderers because a conviction would not be sustained by appeals courts in the United States. All he could advise Taylor was to send the criminals away.[33]

The departure of the savages from Texas helped the situation some, and relations between North American troops and the citizens of Monterey improved. The stories about the hard-riding Señorita Dos Amades made the rounds, arousing the carnal appetites of young Anglos. Private William Henry visited a girls' school, seeing "some beautiful creatures among them, and with one bright-eyed little one I should most certainly have had a frolic had I been master of her language." He flattered himself, because the virtue of Mexican girls and women was guarded as fiercely as that of those in Victorian North America. Still, "the women are very kind," wrote another private.[34]

The United States had invaded Mexico, and the reaction was predictable: people resisted. Henry was annoyed by the story of a priest caught spreading propaganda encouraging North American soldiers to desert, saying the man "should be hung, in spite of his sanctity." He did not like the Catholic Church in general, declaring that the poorest Mexicans were held "in utter ignorance, and under blind obedience to their priests." This bigotry justified, to Anglos, retaliatory assaults and murders in answer to violence against occupying troops. Who offended first was immaterial once the cycle was established.[35]

The *Norteamericanos* had initially been welcomed in the northeastern states of Mexico because citizens expected protection from Indian raids. Generally the *hacendados* stayed during the invasion to protect their property and sell goods to the northern army. It was amazing, given the situation, that any government persisted in the conquered areas. Governor Paula set up a state government in Linares, but the occupying army made it nearly impossible for him to govern, so he resigned his post in March

1847. The *municipios* (municipalities) of Nuevo León were left without superior authority, but many of them survived. This was an impressive case of local rule in a country dominated by centralism. There was one element of society the local governments could not control, however, and that was the *bandidos* who had long plagued the country. Guerrilla leaders such as Antonio Canales might be heroes when they attacked *yanqui* supply trains and patrols, but they had long since worn out their welcome among the Mexican civilians they had spent decades robbing. The hero-bandit was as perplexing a problem for the Mexican people as he became for the North Americans.[36]

WE WILL NOT PERMIT OURSELVES TO BE OPPRESSED

In contrast to the bloodshed in Nuevo León, President Polk told Congress that the conquest of New Mexico had gone off without a shot fired. Kearny was under orders, Polk assured the lawmakers, to retain the form and personalities of New Mexico's government so far as possible. Polk delivered this message more than a year after Kearny had entered Santa Fe, and the president had no idea what really had been going on there.[37]

He was not the only public official out of touch with New Mexico. Rumors of Kearny's approach reached Ciudad Chihuahua in mid-August, and the *comandante-general* of Chihuahua ordered a reconnaissance to the north. Colonel Mauricio Ugarte led 380 lancers through El Paso and on to Socorro, where he ran into Manuel Armijo. The fat fugitive told the colonel that Kearny was coming with 6,000 soldiers, so he should lead his troopers back south. He did.

Chihuahua and El Paso were so far from sources of news that the people were thoroughly confused. There was a lack of leadership from the Chihuahua state government and none at all from that of New Mexico. The Chihuahua governor's office changed hands eleven times from the summer of 1846 to the spring of 1848, each incumbent issuing orders contradicting those of his predecessor. Sometimes these called for an all-out, scorched-earth defense, sometimes not. "The hour has come," the prefect of El Paso told his people late in September 1846, "when with much ardor and firmness we must as good Mexicans give to the world . . . a testimony that while we exist we will not permit ourselves to be oppressed." No sooner had El Paso's militia officers begun to prepare to fight than the prefect received yet another set of instructions from the state capital, in the form of one extremely long sentence. It was "impossible for the forces of the state to risk a complete and decisive battle on account of the chances of its complete ruin with small probability of favorable outcome," owing to a lack of arms and ammunition, "and since a war of extermination must be waged against the North Americans until they or the state succumb." When the enemy approached El Paso the people should "disperse through the interior all livestock and all supplies of all classes." All troops, national guards, and volunteers should go south, "retreating in such a manner as to give constant annoyance to the enemy." Did this mean that El Pasoans should fight a guerrilla war? ¿Quién sabe? (Who knows?) El Paso just waited for whatever would come. A decision could always be made mañana (tomorrow).[38]

Father north, Kearny toured down the Rio Grande to the village of Tomé below Albuquerque from September 2 to 11. The greetings seemed friendly enough. He was ostensibly showing the flag, but Kearny also wanted to check out rumors that there was an uprising being planned, to be supported by Ugarte's troops from Chihuahua. Learning that Ugarte had gone home, the Yankee general returned to Santa Fe.[39]

Nuevomexicanos did not worry General Kearny, but los Indios bravos did. He sent out calls for delegations from all the tribes to meet him in Santa Fe and ultimately sent troops out to make appeals in person, or offer threats if need be. "General Kearny has taken the treacherous population of New Mexico under his fatherly care and protection," said a naive Missourian, "and looking with an eye of pity upon the bold aggressions of those adventurous savages, he has concluded to send parties out for the purpose of bringing the aggressors to justice or make a treaty of peace with them."[40]

Delegations from several tribes visited Santa Fe to hear what the general had to say. In a typical meeting with Apache leaders on September 23 Kearny told them that they should quit raiding and take up farming, or else. The United States Army would protect them. The chief of one band explained that the Apaches were poor people who had to raid to survive. If the white generals wanted them to be peaceful, he should force the Comanches, Utes, Navajos, and Arapahos to make peace first so that the Apaches could hunt buffalo in their territories. Like the Navajos, the Apaches had welcomed the invaders from the United States because they fought the common enemy, the Mexicans. The demand that the Apaches stop raids on Mexican settlements was astounding, because if they did as the general wanted, they would starve. Besides, one tribal leader pointed out, the people of New Mexico were perfectly happy to buy the cattle, horses, and mules the Apaches brought up from Chihuahua and Sonora. Why should they stop? The conference was a waste of time all around.[41]

Kearny detached garrisons to Abiquiu and Cebolleta north of Santa Fe and sent mounted patrols into Navajo, Apache, and Ute territories with orders to retrieve stolen New Mexican property and bring the "principal men" of the tribes to Santa Fe. The most successful of these forays paraded about five dozen Ute leaders into Santa Fe in mid-October. Kearny's efforts to contain Indian raids by garrisons, patrols, or stern speeches accomplished nothing. He ordered Colonel Alexander Doniphan on October 3 to delay marching on Chihuahua until the Indian problem was solved. He issued a proclamation on October 18 permitting aggrieved settlers to mount retaliatory raids. New Mexico had come full circle, from round-robin warfare to a promise that all that would stop and then back to conditions that had always existed.[42]

Kearny's reach often exceeded his grasp. His orders required him to maintain the existing civil government in New Mexico, but the general believed that something more was in order. He appointed Captain David Waldo, Doniphan, and Private Willard P. Hall—all capable lawyers—to a commission to develop a plan of government. They prepared a document that generally followed the design of the Northwest Ordinance of 1787, which prescribed the standards for territorial governments in the United States. They also borrowed from the laws and constitutions of Missouri, Louisiana, Texas, and Coahuila, and federal laws of the Republic of Mexico, along with some elements of New Mexico's existing law code. Known as the "Kearny Code" after the general promulgated—imposed—it on September 22, 1846, the "Organic Law of the Territory of New Mexico" and "Laws for the Government of the Territory of New Mexico" created a roster of territorial officers roughly analogous to the ones the New Mexicans were used to, but with Anglicized rather than Mexican functions. There was an elected assembly that was legislative rather than advisory, as the old departmental assembly had been. The code established judicial and county systems, both innovations to *Nuevomexicanos*. Finally, almost as an aside, the code made every Indian *pueblo* in New Mexico a corporation, a decidedly alien idea to those peoples.[43]

Kearny had established a territory, drafted a constitution and code of laws, and staffed it all with officers. It was a monumental achievement. It was also illegal. When the news reached Washington, Congress exploded in outrage. The secretary of war informed Kearny's successor, Sterling Price, that the Kearny Code had no standing. "The temporary civil government in New Mexico results from the conquest of the country," he pointed out. "It does not derive its existence directly from the laws of Congress, or the Constitution of the United States." The Kearny Code was abrogated, and with the local civil government long gone, New Mexico endured a military dictatorship until 1850.[44]

Kearny guaranteed trouble by the way he staffed the new government, appointing Anglos to seven of the nine positions. Charles Bent, whose hostility to *Hispanos* was no secret, became governor. Of the *nuevomexicano* appointments, one became territorial secretary and another one of three judges of the superior court. New Mexican merchants, Pueblo Indians, and even *peones* were not happy. Handing the government to Anglo merchants who could be expected to use their positions to corner the military market in goods and transportation caused the people to seethe in frustration and anger. They saw themselves not as citizens of the United States but as *Nuevomexicanos* oppressed by ruthless *gringo* invaders.[45]

Kearny told the adjutant general on September 16 that he planned to leave for California by the twenty-fifth, although the Mormons and Price's 2nd Missouri had not reached Santa Fe. Doniphan would leave for Chihuahua when Price arrived (this was later delayed by the Indian troubles), and the Mormons would follow Kearny. This would leave Price's regiment, a battalion of Missouri infantry, and an artillery battery—enough, Kearny thought, to control the Indians; the New Mexicans were viewed as docile. A smaller garrison would reduce the burden of supply over the Santa Fe Trail. If he needed more troops on his campaign, Kearny would recruit them in California.[46]

Kearny left Santa Fe on the afternoon of September 25 with 300 dragoons on mules, a party of topographical engineers, and a small wagon train. They trooped down the east bank of the Rio Grande to Albuquerque, then crossed to the west bank. The Army of the West proceeded west, Kearny not bothered by reports of a Navajo raid on a village twelve miles to his left. Ahead of him was Kit Carson, riding east with big news from the dreamland on the Pacific.[47]

HAD THEY NOT RESISTED, THEY WOULD HAVE BEEN UNWORTHY OF THE NAMES OF MEN

In California, Stockton spent the first half of September 1846 organizing his campaign to invade Acapulco and march on Mexico City. This diverted him from enforcing his empty blockade proclamation, but he was really bothered when California distracted him from becoming the new Cortés. He took most of the sailors at San Pedro aboard USS *Congress* and sailed for Monterey. When he got there he heard reports that a thousand Walla Walla Indians were mobilizing to attack the settlements around Sutter's Fort, so he sailed north. If that was true, then he would have to marshal his whole force to meet the Indian threat. There was no threat to the settlements, however. The Indians had come in to trade and to ask for justice for one of their chiefs who had been murdered by an Anglo settler the year before.[48]

The commodore resumed planning the conquest of Mexico. A march inland would require more manpower than he could make up from his marines and ships' crews, so Stockton asked Frémont to raise an additional

700 volunteers to join the expedition, but nobody would sign on to his adventure. The *conquistador yanqui* postponed his dreams of glory in late
September because California distracted him again.[49]

The province exploded in rebellion. Mexican accounts said the
Californios acted out of patriotism and against the "despotic" conduct of
United States officers. Kearny agreed, saying the Californians rose up because they had been "most cruelly and shamefully abused by our own people. . . . [H]ad they not resisted, they would have been unworthy of the
names of men."[50]

Stockton had guaranteed a rebellion with his arrogant and overbearing
ways. Moreover, when he left southern California he appointed Gillespie
governor of that part of the territory, based at Los Angeles with a garrison
of forty-eight unruly men. Gillespie spoke Spanish, affected a pointy beard
in the Spanish fashion, and fancied himself some kind of Spanish *hidalgo*
(nobleman). He despised the Californians and made no secret of it. He imposed a military dictatorship in a district where California patriotism was
strong, issuing silly and small-minded decrees, threatening anyone who
grumbled, and insulting prominent citizens. His "soldiers" made it all
worse. They were unkempt, undisciplined, rowdy, and drunken. People in
and around Los Angeles became increasingly resentful, and when Gillespie
heard rumors that there were fugitive Mexican army officers roaming the
streets inciting an uprising, on September 20 he sent a message to
Stockton asking for help. The Californians intercepted the letter. The dictator weakened his position by sending ten of his men to an outpost near
present-day Chino on the road to Sonora. At three in the morning of
September 23, about twenty Californians led by Cérbulo Varela shot at
Gillespie's headquarters in the old Mexican government house, and the
North Americans fired back, rousing the town. Angelenos surrounded
the government house, and Gillespie and his crew were sealed in. "The
women were models of bravery and patriotism," claimed a Mexican account. "Some of them brought their sons, even the little ones, to take up
arms; others spied on the enemy; still others carried arms and ammunition . . . across enemy checkpoints to the camp of the patriots."[51]

Mobs of angry Californians grew and coalesced into true insurgent
forces. About 150 of them gathered at Castro's former camp at La Mesa,
about a mile from Gillespie's headquarters, on September 24. Varela surrendered leadership to Captain José María "Ma" Flores, a capable officer
who, like many others, broke parole to join the revolt, making himself liable to a firing squad if he was captured. Gillespie assembled what ammunition he could find and ordered his men to repair four old spiked guns.
Juan "Flaco" ("Skinny") Brown slipped through the siege on the night of

September 24–25 and rode five days to San Francisco to alert Stockton. The standoff in Los Angeles continued until the night of the twenty-eighth, when Gillespie and his men crept through the blockade to a new position on Fort Hill, about a quarter mile away. The place had no water. The Californians surrounded the *Gringos* again, and on the twenty-ninth Gillespie surrendered. The terms were generous. The North Americans could keep their small arms and cannons and leave Los Angeles. The losers trooped to the coast on the thirteenth, and on October 4 boarded a merchant ship.

Flores fanned out mounted parties to drive the United States from southern California. The garrison on the road to Sonora was captured, along with others. The one at Santa Barbara escaped by ship to Monterey. The San Diego force scrambled onto a ship in the harbor. Stockton had lost all of southern California to Flores and his 400 splendidly mounted but poorly equipped lancers by the end of September. Gillespie may have ignited the spark, but Stockton had nobody to blame but himself. His contempt for the local population made it impossible for the *Californios* to welcome the United States government.

Flores issued a proclamation on October 1. It had been a month and a half, he said, "that, by lamentable fatality, fruit of the cowardice and inability of the first authorities of the department, we behold ourselves subjugated and oppressed by an insignificant force of adventurers of the United States of America." He accused the invaders of "dictating to us despotic and arbitrary laws, and loading us with contributions and onerous burdens, which have for an object the ruin of our industry and agriculture, and to force us to abandon our property." He asked his fellow *Californios*, "And shall we be capable to allow ourselves to be subjugated, and to accept, by our silence, the weighty chains of slavery?" All acts of the United States were null and void. Flores called on Californians to take up arms against the invader, and any who would not were declared traitors "under pain of death." He invited residents of other districts to join the uprising, and by the time he was through he had 300 signatures on his document.[52]

Stockton postponed indefinitely his plans to march into the Halls of the Montezumas. This must have been a terrible disappointment.

WHERE NOW ARE THOSE GREAT GENERALS OF OURS?

(October–December 1846)

It is easy to go down into Hell;
Night and day, the gates of dark Death stand wide;
But to climb back again, to retrace one's steps to the upper air—
There's the rub, the task.

—Virgil

MATTHEW CALBRAITH PERRY CARRIED THE BURDEN of having a famous older brother. Oliver Hazard Perry had defeated the British fleet on Lake Erie in 1813 and announced, "We have met the enemy and they are ours." That ringing pronouncement made the younger Perry the butt of jokes and puns until he was high enough in rank that nobody dared. Matthew was born in Rhode Island in 1794 and entered the United States Navy as a midshipman in 1809. He fought Barbary pirates, aided the settlement of Liberia, helped negotiate a treaty with Turkey, commanded the NewYork NavyYard, supported improved education for naval officers, and campaigned for modernization of propulsion and ordnance. Perry was a big bear of a man whose nickname was "Old Bruin." Broad-shouldered, thick-chested, he had a thrusting jaw, a drooping lower lip, a substantial nose, and deep-set dark eyes. He had a thoughtful look about him.

The Navy Department assigned Perry to succeed Conner in command of the Home Squadron in the fall of 1845, but Conner delayed stepping down. Bancroft assigned Perry in August 1846 to command one of the Home Squadron's frigates, USS *Mississippi,* putting two flag officers into the same squadron. Perry hoisted the red pennant of a vice commodore and contented himself with being second in command. He soon heard complaints about Conner from disgruntled officers, who were really just unhappy with blockade duty. Perry refused to undercut Conner. "I do not choose to share the odium of a mismanagement which every one talks about in the squadron," Perry told his son, "when I have not the power to prevent or avert it." Harmony prevailed in the Home Squadron.[1]

Harmony prevailed in the Navy Department as well. Bancroft became ambassador in London in September 1846 and the president shifted his attorney general, John Y. Mason, to the Navy Department. A Virginia lawyer, politician, and judge, Mason was an old supporter of Polk and the only holdover from the cabinet of President Tyler, whom he had served as navy secretary. Mason had the contented look of someone who liked to eat, with multiple chins, plump cheeks, half-smiling mouth, wide eyes, and vanishing gray hair. He was not as brilliant as Bancroft but he ruffled fewer feathers.[2]

BYGONES SHOULD BE BYGONES

Polk could use some harmony. Mounting costs and casualties with no end in sight gave the Whigs ever more power as congressional elections proceeded. Polk decided that more volunteers must be raised, this time for the duration, and Marcy called for nine new regiments but the response was slow. David Campbell of Virginia wrote to his brother already in the army, "They now say that the war has been badly conducted—agree that the Executive is incompetent to conduct it." He thought that "all who do not want any how to volunteer, will adopt it as their reason for refusing."[3]

There were anti-war rallies in New England, but efforts to block recruitment failed, as did attempts to get state legislatures to declare that the war was immoral or illegal. The New England Non-Resistance Society condemned the hero Taylor as a mass murderer. John Quincy Adams declared that Mexico had done nothing to justify the United States making war against her. Since 1830, he charged, certain parties had plotted to "dismember Mexico, and to annex to the United States" her northern territories.[4]

Polk began working on his annual message in early October, now accepting Taylor's previous advice to sit still in the northern territories until Mexico sued for peace—what Senator Calhoun called "masterly inactivity." Senator Benton objected to that. The only way to end the war, he predicted, would be to march on Mexico City. No other course, the Thunderer claimed, could save the Democratic Party from voter outrage over an endless war.[5]

Taylor's report on Monterey and the armistice arrived in Washington on October 11. "In agreeing to this armistice General Taylor violated his express orders and I regret that I cannot approve his course," the president told his diary. There were no such "express orders" and Taylor did have the authority. Polk asserted that Taylor should have taken the Mexicans prisoners, disarmed them, "and preserved the advantage which he had obtained by pushing on without delay into the country." The cabinet agreed, and Marcy ordered the armistice rescinded on the thirteenth.[6]

When Taylor received the order to cancel his armistice, it reinforced his belief that Polk and his minions were hostile to him, which made Old Zach more receptive to political flattery. He was telling his son-in-law and others by December that he would accept the Whig nomination for president if it was offered.[7]

One complication of Taylor's armistice was that it halted all North American military movements in northeast Mexico, blocking a campaign against Tampico. The secretary of war told Patterson separately that Taylor had been ordered to rescind the armistice. The administration, he said, hoped that Tampico could be taken before the Mexican Congress met in December, thus increasing the pressure on the Mexican government. Polk privately told Patterson that this was the administration's strategy.[8]

Tampico had been selected because Polk and his cabinet were ignorant of the geography and ignored the judgment of Taylor, Conner, and Scott that Tampico had no strategic value. An army stuck there could do little more than feed mosquitoes. Scott again advised that Vera Cruz was the place to start a campaign to force the Mexicans to the peace table. He handed in his plan, called "Vera Cruz and Its Castle," on October 7. Describing the objective physically and strategically, Scott asserted that it would be pointless to invade the Mexican coast unless that was followed by a march into the country's interior. The invader would need 10,000 men and 600 cannons to take the city and the fortress of San Juan. The operation would also need enough landing craft to put 2,500 men and two field batteries ashore in the first wave. Scott believed that the necessary force could be assembled in time to land early in 1847, take Vera Cruz, and march inland before the *vómito* season. Polk summoned the former consul at Vera Cruz, Francis M. Dimond. When the cabinet reviewed all the documentation and heard what Dimond had to say, by November 7 the decision had been made, in a preliminary way—the target would be Vera Cruz.[9]

Polk finally realized that his goal of encouraging Mexican secession movements had been torpedoed when Santa Anna declared for the Constitution of 1824, mollifying federalists in the northeast. The point of both the Taylor and Wool expeditions had therefore been lost, so on October 22 Polk suggested ordering Taylor to stand pat at Monterey and ordering Wool to join him. The whole cabinet went over Marcy's draft of an order informing Taylor of all this, hoping to keep the temperamental general from flying off the handle. Polk himself briefed Major Robert M. McLane and sent him to Taylor to deliver the letter in person.[10]

Picking the Vera Cruz operation's commander was a thorny political problem. Polk and his allies assumed that whoever got the job would become a hero and possibly the next president. They wanted to choose a Democrat, but the only ones worth considering were Patterson, who was foreign-born and not eligible to be president, and Butler, who did not have much of a military record. As far as Polk was concerned, Taylor was both incompetent and his greatest rival. Gaines had made himself unacceptable. Nobody, it appears, considered Wool, a Democrat. Benton proposed himself as commander with the rank of lieutenant general. Congress would have to establish the rank and position, and Polk told Benton that he did not think Congress would go along with either the position or the Thunderer in it. The only suitable candidate was Scott, whose hard work had made a fan of Marcy.[11]

Marcy had asked Old Zach's advice on strategy and his response arrived early in November. Assuming that the Polk administration wanted him to advance farther into Mexico, the obvious next target after Saltillo would be San Luis Potosí. Taking San Luis, Taylor said, would require 20,000 men, at least half of them regulars, and another 5,000 regulars to protect the supply line—volunteers had proven useless at guarding his rear. Taylor suggested that the government decide between advancing on San Luis "or whether the country already gained shall be held and a defensive attitude assumed." Old Zach preferred to sit tight at Saltillo, but if the administration wanted to conduct new operations, he advised taking Vera Cruz from the sea. The general ended with a complaint about the War Department detaching troops from his command, Patterson's Tampico expedition, without consulting him first.[12]

A landing at Vera Cruz was guaranteed by November 14, but Polk declined to tell many important Democrats, among them Calhoun, who was shocked when he learned about it in December. As for Taylor, Polk decided that he had become a partisan enemy. "I had never suffered politics to mingle with the conduct of the war," he told his cabinet with a straight face. "I had promoted General Taylor and treated him very kindly and given him my confidence as chief in command of the army, but that I was compelled to believe that he had been weak enough to suffer himself to be controlled by political partisans."[13]

Scott gave the cabinet an update on his plans for Vera Cruz on the fourteenth. Not much had changed except that he advised transferring 4,000 regulars and 5,000 volunteers from Taylor's army, along with 1,200 sailors and marines from the Home Squadron. Such a force could get to work faster than one of green volunteers. Scott revised his force estimates on the sixteenth to 4,000 regulars, 10,000 volunteers, 1,000 marines and sailors, 50 transport ships in the 500- to 750-ton range, and 140 landing barges.[14]

Polk and the cabinet adopted Scott's latest plans on the seventeenth. It was obvious that Old Fuss and Feathers was the man for the Vera Cruz job. "I have strong objections to General Scott," Polk grumbled. The two strong wills met in Polk's office on November 19, and after consulting with Marcy and Benton one last time the president decided to give Vera Cruz to Scott. The next day, the two of them agreed to get along. Polk told the general that "bygones should be bygones and that he should take the command." Scott was "deeply grateful," and "would show me his gratitude by his conduct when he got to the field."[15]

Scott exploded into activity over the next four days, giving Marcy a further revised and more detailed outline of requirements and adding an item for $30,000 for "secret" services. He drafted a cover story for the *Washington Union,* a Democratic paper, which presented Scott as going to Mexico as an observer, not to relieve Taylor, and hinting that he might invade Tampico.[16]

Having decided to widen the violence in Mexico, Polk challenged his critics directly in his annual message to Congress, read to the members on December 8, 1846. "A more effectual means could not have been devised," he declared, "to encourage the enemy and protract the war than to advocate and adhere to their cause, and thus give them 'aid and comfort.'" This quotation of the Constitution's definition of treason caused both houses to explode in outrage. Claiming that a majority of the people were behind him and the war, Polk digressed into a windy recapitulation of how the conflict had been forced on the United States by Mexican actions and inactions, why he had sent Taylor's army into the disputed area, and how the other side fired the first shots. The president defiantly vowed that the United States would maintain its "possession and authority" over New

Mexico and California. There were voices in Congress talking about cutting off funding, so Polk renewed his call for $2 million to have on hand when Mexico agreed to negotiate, a sop to the peace party.[17]

Polk's strong words set off a debate that went on for years. Whigs from the north and the upper south denied vehemently the president's claim that the Rio Grande was the historic boundary of Texas. Whig Representative Meredith Gentry of Tennessee called Polk's argument "an artful perversion of the truth." Others introduced resolutions calling for United States troops to leave Mexico. The establishment of governments in New Mexico and California before they were acquired by treaty raised their own furies. Whigs rebuked the president and his agents for trampling on the powers of Congress. Polk admitted that the establishment of civil governments had been beyond his authority.

Polk grumbled that Taylor and Scott were both plotting against him and feeding ammunition to his opponents. News of Scott's plan for an invasion leaked to the newspapers, confirming his paranoid fantasies. The president had his allies in the House call for publication of all administration correspondence with Taylor. That backfired when Democrats had to fight off efforts to publish correspondence between Polk's agents and Santa Anna. Polk was outraged when the Calhoun Democrats held up a bill authorizing ten new regular regiments in February. Polk's abandoned idea to create a lieutenant general's rank for Benton surfaced and Whigs claimed that the president played partisan games with the lives of soldiers, simply to place a Democrat over Whigs Taylor and Scott.

Polk meanwhile raised his request for a special treaty fund to $3 million and early in February 1847 both houses of Congress took it up. The loud and acrimonious debates soon sidetracked into a quarrel over how much Mexican territory would be acquired. The chief result of this in the House was readoption of the Wilmot Proviso, 115 to 106. Polk received more support in the Senate, his allies denying that he wanted a "deplorable amalgamation" of large numbers of Mexican Catholics into the country. Northerners led by Daniel Webster countered by introducing resolutions calling for no territorial acquisitions from the war. This ran into trouble with slave-state senators led by Calhoun, not otherwise a Polk fan. He complained that the only place pro-slavery people had a majority in the country was in the United States Senate, so new territories should be allowed to choose for themselves whether to permit slavery. This, however, would repeal the Missouri Compromise, and nobody else had the stomach for that. Pro-slavery and anti-slavery resolutions all withered away and Polk finally got his $3 million in March.[18]

Polk was unhappy about the conflict he had stirred up, but he had nobody to blame except himself. There was a growing feeling in both parties and among the public that the president had exceeded his authority by engineering his way into a war without a declaration. He had also promised that the war would be as easy as a waltz, but seven months later costs and casualties continued to pile up. Suggesting that any complaint equaled treason was just asking for trouble.

WHAT HAS SANTA ANNA DONE?

Santa Anna, like Polk, also faced political problems. His return had inflamed all the old factional struggles. "We must finish with our enemies or die ourselves," roared one partisan rag, "the scaffold must be raised; we must drink their hearts' blood." The British minister in Mexico described conditions there as "universal terror and distrust." This went on in a country invaded by two enemy armies, with another invasion on the way. This was Mexico, a country Polk believed he could persuade into seeing things his way, as if there was a unified decision-making body in the nation.[19]

Santa Anna reached San Luis Potosí on October 8, 1846, leading 3,000 men. He ordered the 4,000 remaining in Ampudia's army to join him. Santa Anna was determined to build this start into an "invincible" army of 25,000. He was welcomed at San Luis. Drafting most of the men in the city and surrounding territory did not win much favor, yet town leaders seemed honored by the *caudillo*'s presence. He stripped garrisons and militias from all over northern Mexico. He ordered Tampico abandoned over violent protests, because he needed the men and guns there. Recruiting became an exercise in frustration. The states of Durango and Michoacán refused to send men, saying they needed their troops to defend against Indian raids. The governor of Zacatecas plotted an uprising against Santa Anna. But Guanajuato sent 5,000 men, Jalisco 2,000. Slowly, an army took shape.[20]

Everything was in short supply, including winter clothing and enough ammunition to train men to shoot. Santa Anna lived in luxury in town, indifferent to the suffering of his troops. He ordered his officers to train their units but did not inspect progress. Infantry drilled by brigades but never tried to maneuver by divisions. The cavalry kept to its individual regiments, and the artillery got practically no maneuver training and none in firing. Additional troops came into camp during the fall, armed indifferently or not at all. Many lacked bayonets, and one reporter saw "many guns held together with leather straps or with cords instead of braces."[21]

Santa Anna's army would require about a million pesos a month to stay together. He squeezed the Church for 15 million pesos, to be raised by loans secured against church property. He never got more than 10 million from the clerics, whom he thoroughly annoyed. Red Comet, a secret society under church sponsorship, arose in San Luis to undermine him. A ceaseless exchange with the government in Mexico City usually earned excuses about the country's bankruptcy, to which the Soldier of the People typically snorted, "Do not reply that the government cannot obtain funds. This would be saying that the nation has ceased to exist."[22]

Stories swept through Mexico City claiming that the Savior of His Country had struck a deal with Polk to abandon half the country's territory. The whole nation was ready to believe the worst about Santa Anna. "Where now are those great generals of ours, who . . . insulted with their luxuriant splendor the misery of the people?" asked one newspaper. The satirical sheet *Don Simplicio* offered "Predictions for 1847: The officers of our army will be divided into fugacious and permanent." A pamphlet asked, "We are invaded, time presses, and what has Santa Anna done?" Public opinion in Mexico had become as impatient with an endless war and immovable armies as that in the north.[23]

Just as Scott feared that he would be fired on from the rear in Washington, Santa Anna had the same problem in Mexico City. Scott was a better general, but the *caudillo* was a tougher street fighter. He had allies in the capital, most notably the odd combination of Tornel and Gómez Farías. Congressional elections brought to Mexico City a large number of idealistic but poorly educated radicals who could not center around a candidate for president to replace Salas, discredited as ineffective. Gómez Farías and the smarter *puros* herded them toward making Santa Anna president and Gómez Farías vice president. Under the Constitution Santa Anna could not be chief of state and chief soldier at the same time. On the understanding that the Soldier of the People would stay in the field and leave the vice president as interim president, they were both elected on December 24. Gómez Farías blundered into a heavy-handed attempt to extort more from the Church early in January and backed down in the face of furious opposition. Still, he was honest, known to support the war, and wanted to keep the corrupt officer corps too busy to meddle in politics. His failure to provide money meant that Santa Anna's army depended on the government of San Luis Potosí for its rations through the end of 1846.[24]

Santa Anna heard from Taylor in November that the armistice had been terminated. Assuming that Taylor would march on San Luis, Santa Anna ordered all water storage tanks and basins between San Luis and Saltillo destroyed. Meanwhile, his order to abandon Tampico ignited outrage across northeast Mexico and in Mexico City. Santa Anna reminded Gómez Farías who was in charge of military affairs. "I do not consider myself, nor should I be considered," he bellowed, "as a mere General commanding a corps of the army, but as the *sole caudillo* of the nation to whom direction of its destinies has been entrusted."[25]

Santa Anna was perhaps the only general in the world who could create an army out of nothing and do it more than once. Distracted by the politics of raising men and money, by political fence tending in Mexico City, by accusations of corruption, by charges that he planned to revive his dictatorship or sell the country to the *Gringos* or worse, the Savior of His Country could claim success. He had assembled an army—inadequately trained, equipped, or fed, but still an army—of 20,000 men, larger than any other army of Mexico during the war. It included three infantry divisions, four cavalry brigades, a regiment of hussars, a "division of observation," and artillery, engineers, and logistical troops. In all, there were 19,996 enlisted men, 1,379 officers, and 162 "chiefs," meaning useless supernumeraries. It was a magnificent achievement.[26]

THERE IT IS—THE SAME FLAG, THE SAME PEOPLE

There was not much Santa Anna could do about the naval blockade. One ship established trading relations in September with the rebels in Yucatán, giving the squadron a source of vegetables and firewood. That venture also seized a merchant schooner, which Conner armed and put into North American service. It was bigger than the three schooners bought in New York, so it was better able to keep to the sea in bad weather.[27]

The promised small craft began reaching the Home Squadron by October, and the arrival of the revenue service steamer *McLane* gave Conner two shallow-draft steamers. He decided to go after Alvarado again, to meet Polk's demand that "the Navy should do something which will answer to make newspaper noise." The steamers, however, faced defenses greatly strengthened by Commodore Tomás Marín since the last attack. He had built five batteries with thirty-six guns commanding the entrance to the river and moored the three largest Mexican warships in a crescent between the batteries and the town. Marín hoped to catch any invading North American craft in a crossfire beyond the range of the heavy guns on the bigger United States ships.

Conner led a steam frigate and his smaller vessels out of Antón Lizardo just after midnight on October 15, reaching the Alvarado mouth just after daylight. The commodore in USS *Vixen* towed a column of small boats toward the bar early in the afternoon. The nearer they got the more the current out of the river slowed them, but they got across and opened fire on the shore batteries. A second column towed by *McLane* reached the bar but grounded, scrambling the tow. Conner abandoned the attack.

Instead of "newspaper noise," the navy suffered the jeers of the Mexicans ashore.[28]

It was time to let Perry earn his keep. Old Bruin proposed sweeping the coast from the Coatzacoalcos River to Carmen, if possible seizing Tabasco and other towns along the Río Tabasco (now Grijalva). Perry left Antón Lizardo on October 16 in *Mississippi,* accompanied by *Vixen* and *McLane,* four schooners, and a 253-man marine landing force. The flotilla sailed right into a heavy storm, scattering it until it reassembled off the mouth of the Tabasco on October 23, missing one of the schooners. The two steamers towed strings of boats in a repetition of the action at Alvarado, and again *McLane* stuck in the mud. *Vixen* and her tow made it over the bar and took the town of Frontera, seizing two steamers at the wharf. Perry left behind a small garrison and a crew for one of the steamers and continued upriver to Tabasco.

The lookouts in *Vixen* spotted the defenses below the town at midmorning on the twenty-fourth. Lieutenant Colonel Juan B. Traconis, the department commander, who had only 300 militia, withdrew from what looked like an overwhelming force. Perry's landing party occupied the place, but as darkness fell Perry recalled his shore parties, afraid that the Mexican troops would infiltrate the streets and attack his troops. They did sneak back in. Perry did not have enough men to maintain a permanent occupation, so he retired downriver. The United States vessels came under fire from Mexican militia at daylight on the twenty-sixth, and the warcraft replied. Foreign merchants in Tabasco frantically asked for a cease-fire. Perry hoisted a white pennant atop *Vixen* and again ordered his flotilla downriver. When one of the prize steamers grounded in front of town at midmorning, however, Mexicans ashore began shooting her up. She was freed, but only after a rescue party was fired on and its officer fatally wounded. Perry returned fire, and the flotilla resumed floating downstream to Frontera. Perry had not taken Tabasco, but he had closed it off from the sea. The adventure had cost him two killed by enemy fire, two drowned, and two wounded. Mexican casualties were five soldiers and four civilians dead.[29]

Perry was back at Antón Lizardo by October 31, leaving the two small steamers behind to close the river and protect neutral merchants. The little steamer *Petrita* and schooner *Laura Virginia* (renamed USS *Morris*), both seized in the operation, joined the mosquito flotilla. This success boosted morale in the squadron and broke the boredom of those who took part. Sailors cheered in every vessel on the blockade.[30]

The obvious next target was Tampico, and orders had already gone out from Washington for Conner to take the port and for Patterson to support him, but the armistice after Monterey stopped all troop movements. Under orders from Santa Anna, the garrison pulled out on October 17 and 18 after demolishing the defenses and shipping the guns upriver.[31]

Tampico was the second most important Mexican port on the Gulf coast, but the bar over the mouth of the Río Pánuco was very shallow, usually less than eight feet, forcing blockaders to stand out in unprotected waters. A carriageway ran through the town, which Polk and his Washington experts somehow assumed was a highway to San Luis Potosí; no such road existed. The Sierra Madre Oriental separated the coastal region from the Mexican highlands, and there were only two possible ways for an army to get into the interior. One was the pass from Monterey to Saltillo. The other was from Vera Cruz to Mexico City. Otherwise, the only routes were goat tracks through the mountains.

Conner could not wait for the army, because the stormy season was approaching. He sailed out of Antón Lizardo on November 11 and 12, aiming to rendezvous off Isla de los Lobos (Isle of Wolves). Two steam frigates and six smaller craft crossed to the mouth of the Pánuco at dawn on the fourteenth. Conner adopted an old pattern—entering the river with the small vessels in two divisions towing ships' boats carrying about 300 men. Conner boarded one of the lead steamers and entered the muddy river late in the morning. The port was defenseless and the local authorities sent a truce party to arrange a capitulation. The Mexican officials persisted in haggling over terms until Conner canceled the talks and sent his men to occupy the town. They seized three former Mexican navy gunboats and two merchant schooners; all five joined the United States Navy. Conner and the local leaders finally came to terms, and he guaranteed the people that they would continue to live under local government.[32]

An old man approached an officer and pointed at the Stars and Stripes. "That flag has been my ruin," he said. "I came from Spain, and I was then young, and was sent into Louisiana; that flag came and I then went into Florida; in a few years the same flag came, and I then came to this place expecting never to be disturbed by it again. But there it is—the same flag, the same people."[33]

Tampico turned out not to be the prize Polk had hoped for. Conner's seizures on the Río Pánuco, however, gave him more gunboats than he had received from the Navy Department in six months. They were not enough to offset losses to bad weather over the next two months. Moreover, a boat from USS *Somers* rowed into Vera Cruz harbor and burned a blockade runner tied up near the fort on November 26. Unknown to the officers who dreamed up that stunt, the burned ship had been Conner's spy.[34]

Conner could not spare enough men to garrison Tampico, so he borrowed some troops from Point Isabel. Conner sent a small detachment of sailors in ships' boats up the Pánuco, but they found none of the munitions evacuated from Tampico. Learning that these were stored at the town of Pánuco, on the seventeenth he sent two small steamers and a landing party, which returned with forty bales of "excellent imported tent pins." [35]

The Home Squadron had only a few more adventures before Conner restricted operations for the winter. Two officers from *Somers* tried to burn a powder magazine in Vera Cruz on the night of December 5–6, and Midshipman R. C. Rogers was captured by a Mexican patrol. The boy was in full uniform but the authorities threatened to try him as a spy. This set off a flurry of efforts by United States and neutral officers, diplomats, and politicians to get him released on parole. Lieutenant Raphael Semmes of the Home Squadron followed Scott's army all the way to Mexico City solely to gain Rogers' release, but the midshipman escaped on his own. [36]

Somers was a hard-luck ship, which years earlier had seen the midshipman son of the secretary of war hanged for mutiny. Shortly after Rogers disappeared she was overtaken by a squall off Vera Cruz, overturned, and sank. Nearby British, French, and Spanish warships tried to rescue the crew, but thirty-two of them drowned. The Home Squadron's blockade capacity was reduced in advance of the invasion. [37]

The blockade still had holes in it. Conner sent Perry in *Mississippi* and three small gunboats to cut the contraband trade out of Yucatán by seizing Carmen. The flotilla anchored off the bar at the mouth of Laguna del Carmen on December 20. Perry took the three small craft into the anchorage off town and gained its surrender the morning of the twenty-first. After taking or burning what munitions they found, the ships departed, leaving behind two gunboats to enforce the blockade. Perry sailed to Frontera below Tabasco and left the other gunboat there. *Mississippi* was back at Antón Lizardo by the twenty-seventh with two prizes she had seized off Alvarado. [38]

Mississippi's boilers were wheezing by that time, her hull was leaking, and the copper on her bottom was ragged. Conner ordered Perry to sail her to Norfolk, Virginia, for repairs, although that left him short an important ship for the Vera Cruz campaign. Perry did not want to miss the landings, however, and used his political pull in Washington to get the repairs done in short order. Meanwhile, he supervised the fitting out of additional small craft for Gulf service, and when he left Norfolk he carried in his pocket firm orders to relieve Conner as commander of the Home Squadron. [39]

The navy was through with Tampico by that time, but Taylor was not. Old Zach ordered Patterson on November 14 to march his division overland from Matamoros. He also told the War Department that he planned to lead a reconnaissance as far as Victoria, capital of Tamaulipas. The two expeditions entered Victoria together on December 29, 1846. "Victoria is taken," announced the *New York Herald*. "It was a bloodless victory. But where is Victoria?"[40]

Taylor led his detail back to Monterey while Patterson's troops continued on to Tampico. "I find Tampico a delightful place & the climate is unsurpassed at this season of the year," one of them sang to his journal. "And such a market I have seldom if ever seen before!" The troops enjoyed every variety of fruit and vegetable, domestic birds and wild game, oranges, bananas—an endless list of eatables available at a good price.[41]

THE MARCH OF ATTILA WAS NOT MORE WITHERING AND DESTRUCTIVE

Good eating notwithstanding, the atrocities committed by Taylor's volunteers continued at a high level. These generated retaliation. Guerrilla raids stepped up all along the supply lines. No *Gringo* could go anywhere alone by the end of December, while no Mexican was safe from the northern barbarians. Taylor made it all worse by ordering that any armed Mexican between the Rio Grande and Saltillo should be regarded as an outlaw. That was a license to murder, and every dead Mexican became a dead bandit.[42]

One regular officer reported that widespread accounts in the northern press of "extreme cruelty" perpetrated by Mexicans ignored the fact that those acts were provoked by Anglo atrocities. "From Saltillo to Mier," he said, "all is a desert, and there is scarcely a solitary house (if there be one) inhabited. The smiling villages which welcomed our troops on their upward march are now black and smouldering ruins, the gardens and orange groves destroyed, and the inhabitants . . . have sought refuge in the mountains. The march of Attila was not more withering and destructive." He believed that United States troops brought everlasting shame onto their nation.[43]

There was one North American, a Texian no less, who deserved his country's pride. That was former ranger Samuel Walker, a captain in the regiment of mounted riflemen. Taylor sent him east to recruit men for his company in October, and ranger Captain Jack Hays went with him. From the time they landed in New Orleans they were national celebrities. Hays returned to Texas and Walker went east. Samuel Colt approached him and they collaborated on a wholly new weapon, the .44-caliber dragoon revolver, commonly called the Walker Colt. The United States Army entered the age of repeating firearms before the war was over.[44]

Taylor advised the secretary of war in October that he objected to his orders to march on San Luis Potosí. If the government insisted on an invasion he advised making it at Vera Cruz. If the invasion happened, he expected to lead it.[45]

Old Zach was being set up for a series of shocks. The order to cancel the armistice reached his headquarters on November 2. Many of Taylor's soldiers were thrilled that they could move again. Lieutenant D. H. Hill, however, thought Polk had made a big mistake. "Oh the folly of our Government," he told his diary. "The Mexicans regarded the armistice as a generous concession of our Government, now they will look upon it as having been extorted by their valor."[46]

Taylor had made it clear that he was "decidedly opposed" to marching farther than Saltillo. Now it looked as if the Polk administration wanted him to slog through 300 miles of barren land to San Luis. Then Major McLane rode into camp on November 12 with the orders for Taylor to stop his movements forward. Old Zach took that as advisory and continued planning to occupy Saltillo. He next received a typically tentative order from Marcy saying there were "serious doubts" in the Polk administration about advancing beyond Monterey. The secretary advised Taylor to hold his present position, but only if he should "concur in this view."[47]

Even paranoids can have enemies, and Taylor had picked up quite a bagful. His intemperate letters to people who circulated them infuriated Polk and Marcy. Scott privately told Old Zach there were plots afoot to replace him with Patterson. "There is, I hear from high authority," Taylor complained to his son-in-law, "an intrigue going on against me, the object of which is to deprive me of the command; my only sin for this is the want of discretion on the part of certain politicians, in connecting my name as a proper candidate for the next presidential election, which I very much regretted." The general protested too much.[48]

Disregarding Marcy's unclear orders, Taylor sent Worth, about a thousand men, and a battery of field artillery toward Saltillo on November 13. Old Zach followed with a dragoon escort. The route of march was about thirty miles up the Santa Catarina River, then south through the narrow Rinconada Pass to its opening on the wide valley that led to Saltillo. In the course of seventy-five miles or so the corps climbed out of the subtropics into a temperate zone, where wheat fields and cherry and apple orchards replaced citrus groves. Taylor entered Saltillo on November 16. If Santa Anna marched north, Taylor had the passes through the Sierra behind him for good defensive positions. The city of Saltillo struck the troops as similar to Monterey. The streets were paved, the stone houses were handsome, and there were four plazas and an imposing cathedral. Flour was abundant but firewood had to be hauled several miles.[49]

Taylor sent dragoons down the road to San Luis to see whether it could carry an army in either direction. The troopers reported that the Mexicans had demolished all water tanks on the way, so Old Zach concluded that Santa Anna could not attack him over that road. His decision to park his advance at Saltillo, while sound strategically, condemned Worth's troops to the boredom of garrison duty, and the people knew full well what abuse to expect from *los Yanquis bárbaros.* Taylor returned to Monterey after ten days and found chaos. A volunteer regiment had sent a detachment up the road to Marín to take revenge on civilians for the killing of two of its men by Mexican irregulars. A Mexican was shot to death in the doorway of his house while a United States officer watched. These deeds inspired an ever growing guerrilla response, and soon virtually every train from the Rio Grande was attacked, inspiring even worse behavior from the volunteers. General José Urrea and his *guerrilleros* owned the road to Camargo by the end of 1846.

Lieutenant D. H. Hill was appalled at the scale of the carnage. "Murders are daily committed" in Monterey, Hill said. "The parents of a murdered boy brought the corpse to General Taylor's tent, which aroused him from his apathy on the subject of the enormities of the Volunteers and upon investigation that the murderer was a Kentuckian he demanded his delivery. More than forty persons of the Kentucky Regiment saw the fiendish act committed but refused to tell who the fiendish perpetrator was." Taylor ordered the regiment to the Rio Grande, but rescinded that when the officers promised to find and punish the culprit; they did not. Hill passed through Monterey again in early January and scarcely recognized the city, "so deserted and mutilated it was." [50]

Even some of the volunteers were horrified at the behavior of their fellows, the men from Arkansas being the worst offenders. A farm boy from Illinois wrote home that he was sickened to see random shooting of farm animals in the fields. "Plundering is getting pretty common and often with bad results," he said; "recently an old gray headed sheep herder was shot because he objected to the shooting of his sheep." [51]

That was at Saltillo, where Worth established strict police regulations, among them banning liquor and declaring curfews. Nevertheless, Mexican dealers sold liquor to the *Yanquis,* and there was a regular round of crime and retribution. Worth told his daughter, "The innocent blood that has been basely, cowardly and barbarously shed in cold blood, aside from other and deeper crimes," by which he meant rapes, "will appeal to Heaven for, and, I trust, receive, just retribution." [52]

While Taylor's army was losing "minds and feelings" in northeast Mexico, the Polk administration knew that Taylor had dodged the vague order to go no farther than Monterey. Marcy wrote him on November 25, telling him why he must stop his advance, and worse—that he was about to lose his best troops to the Vera Cruz operation. From New York Scott wrote Taylor to let him know that he would travel to Mexico, and repeated the bad news—Scott would take most of Taylor's army away from him, relying on Old Zach's "patriotism to submit to the temporary sacrifice with cheerfulness."[53]

THE PANIC WAS PRODUCED BY A SMALL PARTY

Taylor wanted to close his dwindling army up, getting Wool off the pointless campaign to Chihuahua. Wool was the chief cause of Taylor's transportation shortage because he had diverted nearly 300 wagons to his corps at San Antonio. Still Wool did not think he had enough and when he began his campaign left part of his corps behind to catch up later with more wagons. Quartermaster General Jesup fumed that Wool would lose himself "with an unwieldy train of several hundred wagons among the mountains of Mexico." The train, he predicted, would be lost.[54]

Wool sent a party out to scout a route to the Rio Grande on September 23. The main body of 1,400 men and the wagons marched out of San Antonio two days later under Lieutenant Colonel Harney, still chafing from his conflicts with Wool. Wool and a dragoon escort left on the twenty-ninth, leaving behind two Illinois regiments to follow later under Colonel Sylvester Churchill. The advance covered 164 miles to the river, which it reached at Presidio del Río Grande (near present-day Eagle Pass, Texas) on October 8. The small garrison of about 200 retired to Monclova. Engineers assembled a pontoon bridge specially built in San Antonio, and Wool's army was over the river by the twelfth.[55]

Wool was an iron disciplinarian and his volunteers resented it, but except for the Arkansas troops they behaved slightly better than those under Taylor. There was open hostility between the regulars and volunteers, especially the officers, and Wool's hard rule had done little to ease the tensions. He tried another tack after crossing the river, holding a party for all officers. He oiled it liberally with port and champagne he had brought in his wagons, along with some lightning picked up in Presidio. The regulars and volunteers stood in separate groups glaring at each other, much to the amusement of their men.[56]

The hostility between the officers continued to worsen. Regulars and volunteers came from different worlds. "Our officers were all graduates of West Point, and at the worst, were gentlemen of intelligence and education," remembered a regular dragoon private, "often harsh and tyrannical, yet they took pride in having their men well clothed, and fed, in making them contented and reconciled to their lot." The volunteer officers, on the other hand, "would tie up a man one day, drink and play cards with him the next, and excuse their favorites from drill and guard duty; in short, most of them were totally incompetent, and a disgrace to their profession."[57]

A Mexican officer rode into camp with a letter from the governor of Coahuila, protesting the advance as violating the armistice. Wool declared that that did not apply north of Monterey. Churchill showed up on October 12 with the Illinois regiments and more wagons carrying more stores, and on the thirteenth Brigadier General James Shields arrived from Camargo with an escort. He became a diplomatic go-between for Wool and the rambunctious volunteers. Wool gave command of all infantry to Shields.[58]

The Chihuahua campaign had been conceived out of geographical ig- norance in the president's house and the War Department, and Wool knew little more about how to get to Chihuahua than the people who ordered him there. His corps marched away from the river on October 16, past abandoned farms twenty-two miles to the little village of San Juan de Nava, then a short distance to the beautiful town of San Fernando de Rosa, beside the sparkling Río Escandido. The sorry excuse for a road wound through the staggering terrain of the Sierra Madre, climbing into wild country with sharp stone peaks standing against white clouds and blue sky. On the men trudged, wheezing as the air thinned, through a canyon and out onto a great plain, the Llano de San José, and across that thirty miles to Santa Rosa, with its neat layout and fine architecture. The army had come 150 miles from the Rio Grande and fortunately walked into a hotbed of Mexican federalists who welcomed the Anglos as liberators from the cen- tralists. These people were out of touch with events in the capital.[59]

Wool and Harney butted heads again on the march. Harney thought disciplining volunteers was beneath his dignity and demanded to be re- turned to his own regiment, the 2nd Dragoons. Wool bucked the decision to Taylor. There was also a notion spreading among officers and men alike that their commander did not know how to find Chihuahua. The best route there was a mule trail that would not pass wagons or guns. Wool reverted to an earlier plan to go through Monclova to the Saltillo-Chihuahua road at Parras. The army trooped down into the Monclova Valley and on October 29 camped outside Monclova, another neat town of about 8,000 people.[60]

Touring some of the most rugged scenery in North America was not what the volunteers had signed up for. They were welcomed at first in Monclova by more federalists, but it was not long before they caused trou- ble. Wool formally occupied the town on November 3, seized five tons of flour from a government store, and established a supply base. Orders from

Taylor not to move on until the armistice expired caught up with him, but Monclova did not look like a good place for Wool's restless troops to spend the next month. He aggravated his situation by trying to save on rations. He substituted corn for flour and ordered the troops to grind it; the volunteers flatly refused and he retracted the order. Sickness spread through the ranks because of the volunteers' poor camp sanitation and Wool was blamed for that also. He got into a public fuss with an Illinois colonel and heaped abuse on all volunteer officers. Monclova was not a happy camp.[61]

Wool was a hard-core martinet, but the volunteers could try the patience of a saint. Private Samuel Chamberlain of the 1st Dragoons filled his diary with stories of how the soldiers baited the general. He was on Wool's guard detail when the general approached a guard post and found the sentry sitting on the ground eating beans and tortillas with a pretty *señorita* beside him. The man did not stand up or salute, just called out, "Good day, General, hot riding out I reckon." Wool roared at the sentry to call the officer of the guard. Still he did not get up, but shouted, "Lieutenant Woodson, come here right quick, post nine, for the old General wants you!" The man then turned his attention to his *bonita*. The officer of the guard showed up without the required belt and sword, his coat unbuttoned, a Mexican straw hat on his head. Wool fairly thundered in rage, blasting the officer for his appearance and for the slovenly conduct of his sentry. The lieutenant shouted, "Jake Strout, yer ain't worth shucks. If you don't git right up and salute the General, I'll drive your gal away, doggone if I don't." The sentry stayed sprawled on the ground and answered that "if the General wanted saluting the lieutenant might do it, he wasn't going to do anything of the kind."[62]

Chamberlain blamed the troubles at Monclova, where the army stayed four weeks, on the "disgraceful armistice granted by General Taylor." The corps was poorly fed and surrounded by "a hostile population and the most demoralizing influences." The grumbling increased until the Illinois regiments "broke out in open mutiny, and started on their way back to the Rio Grande." Wool's regulars put that down at gunpoint, after which the volunteers "confined themselves to muttered threats." There followed weeks of drunkenness, brawls, murders, and atrocities.[63]

Taylor learned on November 8 that Wool was at Monclova, recommending that the Chihuahua expedition divert to Parras 180 miles southeast, cutting one of the roads to San Luis. Wool said that reaching Chihuahua was impossible. Taylor declared that Wool's campaign was a misbegotten failure. A joke going through the Monterey garrison that Wool was lost produced a common greeting, "When did you hear from

General Wool?" The men thought he was "marching somewhere in the wilderness, hunting for the army of occupation."[64]

Wool had been begging Taylor for relief. He sent scouts out to the south and west, one of them jumping a Mexican supply train, bagging seventy prisoners and 360 mules loaded with food and ammunition. Other patrols reported that there was not enough water en route to march to Chihuahua. Wool got his worst volunteers, the Arkansawyers, out of his hair by sending them toward Chihuahua, but they returned. Not hearing back from Taylor after sending three messages, Wool wrote the adjutant general on November 16 that he would march to Parras, "the key to Chihuahua," on the twentieth if he did not hear otherwise from Taylor.[65]

Wool filled time drilling and failing to discipline his volunteers. Griping increased, morale plummeted, the sick list grew longer, and a makeshift cemetery expanded. At last, Wool heard from Taylor on November 18, with good news and bad news. The good news told him to abandon the Chihuahua expedition. The bad news was that he should sit tight at Monclova. Wool replied to Taylor's adjutant, "Perfect" Bliss, in a model of understatement. "I hope the general will not permit me to remain in my present position one moment longer than it is absolutely necessary," he pleaded. "Inaction is exceedingly injurious to volunteers." On November 26 he received Taylor's permission to march on Parras.[66]

That relief came none too soon. Forty-nine officers had signed a letter complaining that Wool had insulted and threatened them. He retaliated on November 23 with a futile order prohibiting gambling in camp, a pointless provocation of rebellious men. As soon as Wool received permission, he marched out of Monclova. Ahead lay a trackless wilderness of deserts and mountains, with no inhabitants and little water. The troops slogged into Parras on December 5 too worn out and footsore to cause any immediate trouble. They had covered 181 miles.[67]

Parras sat in the middle of a fertile valley growing a wide variety of produce. Private Josiah Gregg thought it was more a collection of vineyards and orchards than a real town, and it was famous for its wines and *aguardiente*. There were about 5,000 people, and as federalists, they were downright welcoming once Wool told them he would pay for supplies. This was a good idea, because Taylor had told him to buy all available flour, bread, and other foodstuffs, to be ready to march on. One soldier said the "camp was constantly crowded with the beauty and fashion of the town, who visited the tents of the officers without hesitation or restraint, and the most cordial feelings and intercourse were established between us."[68]

The idyll did not last long, because on December 17 Wool received an alarm from Worth at Saltillo, saying that Santa Anna was headed his way. Wool had his column moving within two hours; his hard-nosed training had had some effect. The troops reached Agua Nueva on the twenty-first and met new orders directing them to Encantada, but it all turned out to be a false alarm. It was not the first or last of those, which the men called "stampedes." Butler at Monterey was in a continual flutter and Wool and Worth were pulled in several directions. Santa Anna, in fact, had started a probe of Taylor's positions, but pulled it back.[69]

Quartermaster General Thomas Jesup thought that all the North American generals were just too jumpy. "The panic," he told the secretary of war, "was produced by a small party that approached Saltillo, perhaps composed of marauders, or more probably of ranchers who had deserted the standard of Santa Anna and were on their return to their homes." The various garrison commanders, however, thought they had grounds for alarm and increased their cavalry patrols at the end of the year. The *guerrilleros* were having a major effect, psychological more than physical, on the campaign in northeast Mexico.[70]

Polk had spent the last quarter of 1846 trying to save his war, Santa Anna creating an army to save his country, Conner and Perry seizing ports and tightening the blockade, Scott becoming a field commander, Taylor losing "minds and feelings" and ultimately his hold on his army, and Wool getting lost on the way to Chihuahua. None of them had any idea that, at the same time, United States forces were winning, and losing, and trying again to win the West.

HISTORY MAY BE SEARCHED IN VAIN FOR AN EQUAL MARCH

(October–December 1846)

Include in your calculations the fact that within a fortnight,
more or less, you will have an insurrection.
It is an event that constantly occurs in occupied countries.

—Napoleon Bonaparte

ALEXANDER DONIPHAN, colonel of the 1st Missouri Mounted Volunteers, was not a man to trifle with. A lawyer, fire-breathing orator, and militia leader, in 1837 he received orders to exterminate the Mormons of Missouri. He replied flatly that the order was illegal. The Mormons surrendered after a skirmish and his superior ordered him to shoot the prisoners. "I will not obey your order," Doniphan warned. "If you execute these men, I will hold you responsible before an earthly tribunal, so help me God." Doniphan seldom lost a case in court, so the order was withdrawn.[1]

Doniphan was fifty-four years old in 1846, the product of a hardscrabble Kentucky background who passed the state bar in 1829. He moved to western Missouri the next year and earned a reputation as a public speaker and trial attorney. Unlike most volunteer colonels, Doniphan had regular officers drill his men. He became second in command of the Army of the West and chief framer of the Kearny Code. Doniphan was destined to lead one of history's most epic marches, earning wide respect among regular officers. At the end of the war he was appointed to the Board of Visitors of the Military Academy at West Point and addressed the Class of 1848.

Doniphan was a big man, over six feet tall, "well proportioned, altogether dignified in his appearance and gentlemanly in his manners," one of his soldiers said. "His features are bold, his bright hazel eyes dazzlingly keen and expressive, and his massive forehead is of the finest and most classic mold." He was friendly, affable, and a booming speaker. "He is the very fullness of physical and intellectual vigor and possesses in an eminent degree the original elements of greatness," said the admiring trooper. Doniphan was a fount of horse sense, an informal man who spoke in the same huckleberry accent as his soldiers and enjoyed drinking and playing cards with them. His men never forgot that he was their colonel, and would storm hell if he told them to.[2]

THIS IS THE SOLDIER'S FARE BUT I AM SICK OF IT

Kearny marched south along the Rio Grande, then turned west below Socorro and headed for the Gila River, keeping in touch with Santa Fe by couriers. He heard from Price, announcing his arrival and the fact that the commander of the Mormon Battalion had died. Kearny ordered Captain Philip St. George Cooke back to Santa Fe to take command of the Mormons. Cooke was thirty-seven years old, son of an aristocratic Virginia family but orphaned young into poverty, who graduated from West Point at age eighteen. He served first in the infantry and then the dragoons, fought Indians and explored western trails. He was sturdy, somewhat romantic, thoughtful, and entirely dependable. Kearny would have trusted no one else with the Magoffin-Armijo negotiations.[3]

Kearny met Kit Carson and his Fremonters about ten miles out of Socorro on October 6. They were a ragged, sorry-looking bunch. Carson showed Kearny the dispatches from Stockton proclaiming the conquest of California. Kearny sent 200 dragoons back to Santa Fe, leaving him 100 troopers and two mountain howitzers to press on to the Pacific. Carson told him how difficult the trail ahead was, so Kearny sent his wagons back to the Rio Grande to swap for pack frames and more mules. The general asked the mountain man to hand his dispatches to someone else and lead the rump army to California. Carson was crestfallen, because he had looked forward to seeing his wife after two years. The scout considered sneaking away in the night but did not. "He turned his face to the west again," wrote one of Kearny's officers. "It requires a brave man to give up his private feelings thus for the public good; but Carson is one such!"[4]

Kearny's column resumed marching on October 14. The presence of the famous frontiersman raised the confidence of the officers and men, at the same time they were depressed that the honor of conquering California had been snatched from them. Captain Henry Turner complained, "This is the soldier's fare but I am sick of it and have no longer to endure it willingly, particularly when we get no credit for it."[5]

The party had left behind the willows and cottonwoods of the Rio Grande for an arid, dusty country of saltbrush, prickly pear, and cholla, carpeted in fall wildflowers. Kearny met Mangas Coloradas, war leader of the Mimbres Apaches, and traded army goods for some mules. One officer reported, "An old Apache chief came in and harangued the General thus: 'You have taken Santa Fe, let us go on and take Chihuahua and Sonora; we will go with you. You fight for the soil, we fight for plunder; so we will agree perfectly.'" Kearny answered with his usual warning to quit raiding, start farming, or else.[6]

The tiny Army of the West trudged through hell over the next month and a half, roasting in the daytime, freezing at night. The bushes grew thornier, the cactus bigger. Lizards, scorpions, and tarantulas ruled the country along the Gila River, the landscape jagged rocks or sand or alkali hardpan called *caliche*. Mules dropped among the decaying carcasses of those lost by Carson going the other way. "The trials and fatigue that we undergo each hour in the day," recorded Captain Turner, "wading streams, clambering over rocks and precipitous mounts or laboring through the valleys of streams where the loose earth or sand causes our animals to sink up to their knees at about every step. Then our frugal meals, hard bed and perhaps wet blankets."[7]

The ordeal got worse, the country drier, the vegetation stranger— century plants, ocotillos, highland yuccas. This was what the United States wanted to seize from Mexico, "a rough and barren country," Kearny called it. "It surprised me to see so much land that can never be of any use to man or beast. We traveled many days without seeing a spear of grass," and nothing else but thorns tearing at men and mules. That was all the mules had to eat, thorns and branches, so they weakened and died.[8]

At least there was water along the Gila, and on the lower part of the river the country was not entirely uninhabited. Kearny and Carson dickered with a band of Coyotero Apaches and bought some fresh mules early in November. The corps stumbled into the Pima Villages, about ninety miles north of Tucson, on the tenth. The Pimas were bountiful farmers and friendly traders. The expedition rested for two days, then trudged on. Kearny bought some mustangs on November 22 from a party of Mexican herders who told him that there had been a revolt in southern California. The next day the Anglos intercepted a Mexican courier headed for Sonora, carrying messages saying that the *Californios* had thrown off "the detestable Anglo-Yankee yoke."[9]

The Army of the West crossed the Colorado River near the mouth of the Gila on November 25. Ahead the country was flatter, but also drier and hotter. Ahead was California, and Kearny's men would fight for it after all.

WE FEEL HUNGRY ALL THE TIME, WE NEVER GET ENOUGH

Far to Kearny's rear, the Mormons reached Santa Fe on October 9, 1846, and Doniphan greeted them with a 100-gun salute and sent them rations. They were delighted, especially because the colonel had kept his guns silent when Price's regiment arrived a few days earlier. Doniphan knew Price from Missouri and despised him. The disorderly behavior of Price's 2nd Missouri also was annoying.[10]

The Mormons remembered Doniphan as their defender in trials past. They did not know Cooke, given the rank of lieutenant colonel to lead them to the Promised Land. Cooke was dismayed by his new command, which he said "was enlisted too much by families; some were too old, some feeble, and some too young." There were many women and children, the men were worn out, their clothing "was very scant," and he had no money to pay them or buy clothing. The mules "were utterly broken down" and there were not enough of them. "I have bought road tools and have *determined* to take through my wagons; but the experiment is not a fair one."[11]

Kearny was sure Cooke could build a road to California with men who were unknown quantities as soldiers or as laborers. He took command on October 13 and sent eighty-six defectives and all the women and children to a camp near what is now Pueblo, Colorado. Cooke also released married men who wanted to follow their families north. Five women and one small boy remained with the battalion, these belonging to officers.[12]

As the Mormons trudged into Santa Fe, Susan Magoffin went south with her husband's freight caravan, headed for Chihuahua. Cooke and his crew left town just ten days behind her. About 400 men marched out with fifty-five wagons pulled by mules and six equipment wagons drawn by oxen. Cooke had had the vehicles strengthened for the ordeal ahead and carried pack saddles in case the wagons broke down. As this train labored down the Rio Grande, animals broke down or ran away, the men groused constantly, and supplies ran short. The sandy road was too hard on the draft animals, he lost several oxen, and the men ended up pulling some of the wagons. Mexicans refused to sell replacement livestock. The days were hot and dusty and the nights freezing as the Mormons trekked past irrigated farms and flocks of sheep tended by *peones* making obscene gestures at *los Gringos malditos.*

At Albuquerque Cooke bought replacement mules, and south of there he found the hostility reduced. The *rancheros* sold food and other supplies, but the roads were no better. Cooke butted heads with his men over their neglect of the mules. Sometimes the expedition found abundant grass, other times there was nothing but "green and beautiful" but "very thorny" shrubbery. One member of the party was unhappy that he was not familiar with the names of these plants but said, "The familiarity and annoying acquaintance they make with my legs every day keeps my clothes in rags and often penetrate the skin."[13]

The trip worsened once the battalion turned west. Cooke knew from Carson's report that he could not cut a wagon road over the route Kearny took, so he angled south from the Gila to where he expected the going to be easier. It was, but not by much. Parties went ahead of the train clearing brush, cutting hills, filling holes, and rolling stones, making a road. The route was dustier than what Kearny faced, water scarce, rations short, and the only firewood scrub oak, a ground hugger. "We have severe frosts at night, and hot days," Cooke recorded. "I have reduced the ration to nine ounces of flour, and ten of pork." This was not much food for the heavy labor the men did and the shortfall was only partly made up by game. The battalion packed goods ahead to lighten the wagons, returning to bring up the vehicles, leapfrogging across the continent. By November Cooke had entered a land where "the cactus here is ten feet high."[14]

This was not a military expedition but a construction project. Day after day men made a road inch by inch. Cooke was a hard driver and the workdays grew longer. Even this ordeal had its rewards, however. One day at sunrise, "all admired the singular and unusual beauty which followed its rising," Cooke exclaimed about a mirage. "A distant mountain ridge became the shore of a luminous lake, in which nearer mountains or hills showed as a vast city—castles, churches' spires! even masts and sails of shipping could be seen by some."[15]

South of the Gila the land was truly arid, the thorny brush thick, with occasional patches of grass. The country was overrun by wild cattle, with bulls in greater than normal proportion. The battalion camped near the abandoned town of San Bernardino, in present-day Arizona on the Mexican border, on December 2. "This place has been vacated 15 years," one of them wrote in his diary. "The Apache Indians drove them away and scattered their cattle." The whole country had been depopulated and only the feral cattle remained.[16]

Even stringy bulls were meat on the hoof, so Cooke decided to stay at San Bernardino to jerk beef. He had counted his remaining rations, and there were not enough to get to California. "We feel hungry all the time, we never get enough," complained Private Henry G. Boyle. Abruptly on December 4, however, the colonel gave orders to move out, because scout reports said that there were more cattle to the west. He stopped again on the seventh to rest the men and teams and to take more wild beef. The stoop labor continued through country devoid of people, only the ruins of ranches.

The Mormon Battalion's only battle took place on December 11. Some wild bulls got in with the livestock and the drovers shot them. The command stopped for water on the San Pedro River and a battalion of bulls charged. There was confusion and fear all around, the attacking bulls raising so much dust that nobody could see anything. One man was butted, his ribs broken. Another was gored and tossed into the air. Yet another threw himself on the ground as a bull charged him, and it leaped over him. The paymaster's pack mule was gored to death, screaming in agony. A lieutenant overcharged his musket and lost his thumb when it blew up. "I saw an immense coal black bull charge on Corporal Frost," Cooke recalled. "He stood his ground while the animal rushed right on for one hundred yards. . . . He aimed his musket very deliberately and only fired when the beast was within ten paces; and it fell headlong, almost at his feet." The rampaging animals finally passed and Cooke discovered three men wounded, three mules gored to death, several wagons tipped over, and others damaged. There were nine dead bulls on the battlefield. The battalion's animals were in a panic, so Cooke ordered them hitched up and the march resumed. The return to routine calmed them down when the corps left the scene of "the Battle of the Bulls," as they called it.[17]

This frightening ordeal drew Cooke and his men close together, and the struggle between them ceased. As they trudged toward Tucson, the road getting ever harder to build, Cooke decided that he could drill the troops and they decided to put up with it. Still on the San Pedro River on December 13, he put them through their paces, then raised a ruckus over their shortcomings. The colonel told the troops that they would go through Tucson in peace, but he also gave them target practice with twenty rounds each. The battalion made an early start as usual on the fourteenth and came upon a *mescal* (*pulque*) distillery run by a party of Indians and Mexicans on the Santa Cruz River. The Mormons sampled the "whiskey" (tequila) but did not like it much. They camped next to the only other humans the battalion had seen for many days. Seven Mexican dragoons rode up and asked the colonel's intentions. Cooke replied that he was just cutting a road. He could demand a surrender of Tucson but would rather trade for provisions and mules. The Mexicans advised him that the people were running away in fear. Cooke told them to assure the settlers of his peaceful intent.[18]

The battalion was in the land of the upright cactus known as saguaro. Cook described it as "a straight column thirty feet high . . . some throw out one or more branches, gracefully curved and then vertical, like the branches of a candelabrum." The country was also populated with giant prickly pears, chollas, and other things with thorns. "We traveled this day through the most prickly, prongly, thorny country I ever saw," Private William Coray wrote on December 15. "And though the mules were nearly worn out with fatigue, when they came to these prickleys, many of them acted very badly indeed and threw their riders."[19]

Some of the mules scattered that night. After rounding them up, the Mormon Battalion trudged into Tucson. The garrison and most citizens had fled. The place reminded the Mormons of Santa Fe, owing to the flat-roofed adobe houses, and they were too worn out to molest anybody or anything. Cooke camped them on the edge of town, and after a while some citizens returned and sold provisions. Nobody disturbed private property, although Cooke seized a public store of wheat and salt and bought some fruit for the men. The battalion left on December 17 and built a road over seventy miles of sandy desert.[20]

This backbreaking labor in a hellish wilderness must have seemed like it would never end. But it did, at last. The battalion rested at the Pima Villages on December 21 and traded for food, but by this time the men were nearly all shoeless, their clothes rags. The corps worked down the Gila to present-day Yuma, California, crossed the Colorado into California on January 11, and continued making a road across the Mojave Desert. In makeshift sandals and nearly naked, the Mormon Battalion straggled into San Diego on January 29 and 30, its long journey over. The men had gotten the wagons through, leaving a passable road in their wake, after walking 2,000 miles from Missouri. "History may be searched in vain for an equal march of infantry," a proud Cooke told his beaming, weary men. That was an understatement.[21]

CHARGE AND BE DAMNED!

While Kearny and Cooke struggled westward, Doniphan tried to end the ancient war between Navajos and New Mexicans. He sent three columns through the snowy highlands to visit every part of the Navajo country, leading one of the corps himself. He estimated later that his officers met nearly three-quarters of the whole nation. They invited the Diné (People), as they called themselves, to a grand conference at Ojo del Oso (Bear Spring, now Gallup, New Mexico), where about 500 Navajos and 300 Anglo soldiers gathered from November 20 to 22, 1846. In his lawyerly style, Doniphan did not lay down the law, nor did he treat the Indians as alien invaders. He proposed instead to make a three-way treaty among the Anglo-Americans, the New Mexicans, and the Navajos. New Mexico was now part of his country, he declared, so any attacks on New Mexicans would be treated as attacks on the United States. The Missouri lawyer got his treaty, which fourteen Navajo elders signed, each by making an X beside his name. The whole idea was foreign to them but it was a happy enough ceremony. The United States and the Navajo nation were now friends, so the Navajos resumed raiding the New Mexicans, who raided them in return. Doniphan believed he had things in order and could go on to Chihuahua.[22]

The colonel ordered his scattered units to gather at Valverde, downriver from Socorro, in early December. In the process, United States troops met another New Mexico tribe for the first time when Mescalero Apache raiders ran off a herd of army horses and oxen. Soldiers went in pursuit and after seventy miles found the oxen speared to death. The horses and Mescaleros just vanished.[23]

Valverde was a large island flanked by two channels of the Rio Grande, which had many subsidiary channels and marshes in that area. Millions of *grullas* (sandhill cranes) wintered there. They were awkward-looking birds when their long legs were on the ground or in the water, but they were shy and surprisingly hard to shoot. When the hunters were lucky, said Susan Magoffin, "they are tender and nice after being boiled nearly all night—the meat is black as pea fowls."[24]

The Rio Grande began a great sweep to the west at Valverde, then bent back east to Doña Ana north of El Paso. The *camino real* (royal highway) from Chihuahua to Santa Fe officially followed the river, but for centuries travelers had braved a shortcut across the river's arc—a ninety-mile dry march straight north-south known as *la Jornada del Muerto* (the Journey of the Dead). It was a fairly level avenue from twenty to forty miles wide between blue mountain ranges to the east and west. It had some sparse grass, creosote bush, saltbrush, and scattered yuccas, and dust devils danced through the valley. There was no water, and the road was lined with dried bones and derelict wagons. Doniphan advised the Magoffins to camp at Valverde until he sent word back that the way ahead was safe. Doniphan's companies proceeded individually down the *Jornada* to Doña Ana (near present-day Las Cruces) as they arrived at Valverde. The dehydrated and exhausted Missourians gathered at the pretty little farming and trading town in late December. The Magoffin party followed cautiously.[25]

El Paso had been swimming in bloodthirsty rumors all through the fall: the enemy was coming to take everything, rape the women, and brand the people like livestock. Ángel Trías Álvarez, governor of Chihuahua, forwarded what supplies and troops he could to El Paso. He told authorities there to "chastise the enemy if he should have the audacity to set foot upon the sacred soil of this state." He sent a separate warning to Doniphan, telling him to stay out of Chihuahua. About 1,200 men and four small guns were assembled at El Paso by the time Doniphan reached Doña Ana. About 400 were useless presidials, a few hundred were national guards, and the rest had experience fighting Indians. They camped north of the city, digging fieldworks.[26]

Word of Doniphan's approach threw El Paso into an uproar, with disputes between those who wanted to fight and those who did not. The garrison commander, Colonel Gavino Cuylti, fell ill on December 23, his surgeon diagnosed a "brain fever," and both hightailed it for Ciudad Chihuahua. Lieutenant Colonel Luis Vidal ordered Major Antonio Ponce de León to take half the troops at El Paso to face the *Yanquis.* Vidal's orders said that the approaching North Americans were no more than 300 ragged volunteers whom Mexican lancers could spear "like rabbits," but he wanted Ponce to make a reconnaissance, not fight a pitched battle. "The enemy shall be engaged until put to flight," he said, provided they numbered no more than 300 or 400. "In case the enemy should . . . be superior in numbers, you will take precautions, according to your military knowledge, to fall back, with the object of holding the line of defense established at this camp."[27]

Doniphan set out with his loosely organized 856 men in front of a merchant caravan headed south, its teamsters heavily armed, on December 23. Two days later the procession entered a level camping ground on the east side of the river, called by merchants Brazito (Little Arm, meaning the eastern arm of the Rio Grande) and by local Mexicans Temascalitos, for three round hills to the east that resembled sweat houses used by the Mescaleros. The dusty, manure-spotted site was about thirty miles north of El Paso. Doniphan wanted to relax with a card game. His advance let the horses loose to graze as the rest of the command idled into the camping ground. Troops and animals were scattered all over when a dust plume appeared to the south. A soldier told Doniphan it looked like there was a Mexican army approaching, so the colonel threw his cards down and said,

"Boys, I held an invincible hand, but I'll be d——d if I don't have to play it out in steel now." Word went out for the men to grab their muskets and prepare to meet an attack, but there was not much time. Ponce, however, gave the Missourians just that—time.[28]

The Mexicans made a great impression. "They exhibited a most gallant and imposing appearance," said John Taylor Hughes, "for the dragoons were dressed in a uniform of blue pantaloons, green coats trimmed with scarlet, and tall caps plated in front with brass, on the tops of which fantastically waved a plume of horse hair or buffalo's tail. Their bright lances and swords glittered in the sheen of the sun."[29]

Hughes thought there were at least 1,300 Mexicans, but actually there were about 500, mostly the lancers, a party of El Paso militia with a small howitzer in the middle, and a battalion of Chihuahua militia on their left. Major Ponce de León carried a famous name—a distant ancestor had explored Florida—but that did not make him a soldier. He was, even allowing for his youth, a *presumido,* a pompous ass. Ponce sent a rider forward carrying a black flag bearing two death's heads and the motto *"Libertad o Muerte"* ("Liberty or Death"). Doniphan and an interpreter stepped forward to see what the man had to say, while the Missourians filtered onto the scene behind them. The messenger halted about sixty yards off. "Our general summons your general to come before him," he shouted. "Tell him our commander will meet him half way," replied the interpreter. "No, he must come into our camp," was the response to that. "If your general wants peace, tell him to come here," the North American answered. "Then we will break your ranks and take him," the Mexican threatened. "Come, then, and take him," challenged the interpreter. "Curses be upon you; prepare, then, for a charge; we neither ask nor give quarter," shouted the messenger. "Charge and be damned!" roared Doniphan.[30]

Doniphan had most of his men deployed in a crescent facing east across the dusty field, the ends of the line on the riverbank. The merchant train was approaching his left rear. By Ponce's own account, he shouted, "Victory to the glorious General Santa Anna and to my country!" His troops "responded with enthusiasm," so he was "led to predict certain victory." He gave the order to advance, but the militia conscripts on his left did not move and the lancers on the right strayed off the field.

Doniphan ordered his men to hold their fire until he gave the command. About eighteen of his men were mounted, so he sent them against the Mexican right. Only Ponce and those around him were moving. He later claimed that he ordered his bugler to blow the charge but the man blew retreat instead. Whatever really happened, Ponce and his lancers trotted straight into a thunderous volley from the Missourians, lead tearing into men and horses, leaving them screaming on the ground. That, he said, "disorganized the cavalry which turned tail with incredible haste." Doniphan's horsemen charged and scattered the lancers on the Mexican right, and a company sprinted out from the Yankee center and seized the howitzer. Teamsters rushing up from the wagon train drove off a solitary squad of lancers trying to turn Doniphan's left. The action lasted no more than twenty minutes. Ponce was wounded three times by the volley and so was his adjutant. They decided that they could not halt the flight of their men, and joined it all the way to El Paso. The whipped men wandered through El Paso in small groups, stealing supplies and horses and heading south. The militia who had been in the fortified camp to the north either followed them or went home. The city had no defense left.[31]

The Missourians spent the evening wandering over the blood-soaked battlefield, bringing in wounded and burying about forty Mexican dead, against seven Anglos wounded, none killed. "The field was strewed with bodies of men and horses," one of Doniphan's soldiers said, "lances, swords, helmets, trumpets, carbines and other war emblems." The dead men were buried in one big hole, while the animals were left to scavengers. The Missourians discovered the next day that coyotes had dug into the human grave. How many wounded Mexicans died in the desert, nobody ever knew.[32]

Doniphan entered El Paso with his advance on December 27, 1846. The colonel came to terms with the local authorities, continuing the local government but ensuring that they agreed that El Paso was under United States occupation. He fanned his men out to search the town, which they did peacefully for the most part, seizing five tons of gunpowder, 500 stand of arms, 400 lances, four small artillery pieces, and other munitions. Mother Nature celebrated with a four-day dust storm that drove everyone to cover. When the air cleared, the Missourians saw a pleasant city of about 12,000 people living in adobe houses along streets shaded in summer by cottonwoods, bare in the winter. El Paso was actually a string of settlements down the Rio Grande, surrounded by rich farm fields watered from a dam upstream. Doniphan paraded his men to impress the people, but according to Private Edwards they made "a ludicrous sight." No one was in uniform; rather, there was a combination of many colors and buckskins bought from the Indians. Their hats were either gone or silly.

Doniphan halted at El Paso until he heard from Wool and to give time for supplies to be shipped down from Santa Fe. His Missourians made themselves at home, "visiting and conversing with the fair señoritas of the place," said John Hughes, "whose charms and unpurchased kindness almost induced some of the men to wish not to return home." El Paso was the center of a major wine and *aguardiente* region, and as time went on the Missourians became increasingly drunken. They fell sick and fought brawls, and some of them abused citizens. Also contributing to the disorder were the nightly fandangos, cockfights, and card games. There was so much gambling on the streets that Doniphan outlawed it. He wanted to move on to Chihuahua before his regiment disintegrated into a mob.[33]

WE MAY STILL BE, FOR SOME TIME,
ANNOYED BY THOSE DAILY SKIRMISHES

Far to the west, Stockton had no idea that the Army of the West was trudging in his direction, let alone that Kearny had reduced it to a gang sufficient to rob a post office but not to put down an insurgency. Stockton also did not know about the rebellion until it had taken southern California away from him. Flaco Brown rode into Yerba Buena with the bad news atop a sweat-foamed horse on October 1, 1846, and Stockton ordered Frémont to take his men by sea to Santa Barbara, round up some horses, and ride down the coast to Los Angeles. Captain William Mervine would sail directly to San Pedro in USS *Savannah* to relieve Gillespie, while the commodore followed in *Congress.* Unfortunately, the *Californios* had already forced Gillespie's surrender.[34]

Savannah was harbor-bound by fog until October 4 and did not reach San Pedro until the sixth. Mervine found Gillespie and his men sitting dejectedly on a merchantman in the roadstead. The captain decided to march on Los Angeles. On the morning of the seventh, 285 sailors, marines, and Bear Flaggers set off with no supplies, ambulances, or artillery. A mixed gang of men, mostly untrained for fighting on land, was about to take on the agile *californio* cavalry. Mervine halted late in the afternoon at Rancho Domínguez (present-day North Long Beach) and that night the Californians brought up a 4-pounder and rained shot onto the *gringo* camp, inflicting several casualties.

Mervine set off again in the morning and ran into insurgents blockading the road with their gun. He had a vague idea that infantry formed squares to beat off cavalry charges and so deployed his troops, who had no idea how to maintain such a formation. This awkward body advanced down the road, and three times the Anglos charged the gun and the Mexicans pulled it away with their lassos, yee-hahing in glee. The rebels were mounted and Mervine's men were not, so the outcome of the race was predictable. The Yankees would never get that cannon, and as long as the insurgents had it, retaking Los Angeles was impossible. The whole bunch turned around at nine in the morning and plodded back to San

Pedro; they were back aboard ship by early afternoon. The excursion cost the United States forces ten men wounded by cannon shot, four mortally.[35]

While the navy blundered around San Pedro, Frémont and his men boarded a merchantman and left San Francisco on October 12, accompanied by Stockton in *Congress*. The commodore diverted to Monterey when he received a false alarm from the garrison. He landed reinforcements there, then continued on to San Pedro, missing Frémont's ship on the way. *Congress* dropped anchor off San Pedro on October 25, Stockton conferred with Mervine, and they agreed to tackle Los Angeles again. Another motley assembly went ashore on the twenty-sixth, meeting no resistance. After a few days Stockton decided to move everybody and everything to San Diego. He believed that he needed Frémont's corps to hold San Pedro, let alone reconquer Los Angeles. Stockton began preparing for a campaign out of San Diego, marines drilling his sailors in infantry tactics. Frémont, meanwhile, had decided to base himself at Monterey rather than go forward to Santa Barbara. He was closer to his northern garrisons there, and called on them to join him. He also browbeat newly arrived Anglo immigrants into becoming soldiers. He trooped south with about 300 men on November 17.[36]

Stockton's move to San Diego took the pressure off the insurgent leader, Ma Flores. He had only about 400 men available to him, and his ammunition was down to forty artillery rounds and about a thousand *escopeto* cartridges. The scrappy Flores began a guerrilla campaign, claiming the interior and confining the *Norteamericanos* to the seaports. He sent about a hundred men to San Luis Obispo to harass Frémont and another detachment to watch Stockton at San Diego. A *californio* detachment captured Consul Larkin near Salinas on November 15, removing from play the one Anglo who might have worked out a peaceful settlement, if Stockton would listen to him. The next day the same band decimated a party of volunteers on their way to join Frémont.[37]

Stockton fired off a report to the secretary of the navy on November 23. He focused on his successes in taking prizes at sea and said that he had been about to lead his squadron to Acapulco, "when I was informed by express that the Mexican officers had violated their oaths, and commenced anew the war by a midnight attack on the party of fifty men left at Ciudad los Angeles." In other words, he, Gillespie, and Frémont had no responsibility for the revolt in southern California, which was raised by "depraved men." It is doubtful that it occurred to him that the truth—that he had made a hash of his assignment—would come out. Instead, he offered a glorious account of imaginary victories over the rebels, claiming that all that could be done "to suppress this rebellion, has been done." Stockton concluded, "Although we may still be, for some time, annoyed by those daily skirmishes, yet the rebels cannot, in all probability, much longer avert the doom that awaits them."[38]

Despite that bombast, Flores and his horsemen had outfoxed the United States power on the Pacific coast, although his rebellion was small and lacked staying power. California was up for grabs, its future depending on which side, Mexico or the United States, could reinforce its side first. The United States, in the person of Kearny, won the race because the Mexican government really did not enter it. The bedraggled Army of the West, after struggling across the sand and thorns of waterless southern California, staggered into Warner's Ranch, about halfway across the wilderness from the Colorado River, on December 2. Kearny heard that Stockton was at San Diego and sent a messenger to ask for news, supplies, and an escort. Stockton received that late on the third and sent Gillespie with thirty-nine men and a 4-pounder, along with a suggestion that Kearny take a swipe at the guerrillas investing San Diego.[39]

The Army of the West was in sorry condition, but Kearny thought he must continue on to San Diego. He stayed at Warner's Ranch through December 3 while his men slept and his acting quartermaster bought about a hundred mustangs, so wild that they were useless. The corps marched out in the direction of San Diego on the fourth and met Gillespie on the afternoon of the fifth. A scout came into camp that night with the news that Captain Andrés Pico and a party of *Californios* were guarding the road from high ground at the nearby village of San Pasqual. Pico, a flamboyant *caballero,* did not know about Kearny, but he had spotted Gillespie leaving San Diego. He assumed that the *Yanquis* were just a foraging party, relaxed his watch, and let his horses out to graze. A patrol of Kearny's dragoons went forward to take a look at Pico's camp, killing any chance for surprise. Pico's men rounded up their horses. Kearny then made the worst decision of his career, to attack Pico at sunrise on December 6. His men were in no shape for a fight and the mounts were either thoroughly jaded or not yet saddle-broken. Nor had United States dragoons ever trained to fight lancers. Moreover, Kearny's and Gillespie's combined forces were big enough to bull their way past the *guerrilleros* without a fight. Still, Kearny had Stockton's request to engage the rebels, and Carson and Gillespie both urged the general to attack.

The general rousted his bone-weary men at two in the morning and they mounted their sorry horses and mules. The night was very cold for men so tired, and dampness had ruined the powder in the dragoons' firearms. Captain Abraham R. Johnston led off with an advance of twelve men. He was within three-quarters of a mile of Pico's camp when Kearny ordered the whole outfit to advance at a trot. Johnston misunderstood that and ordered his men into a gallop, separating them from Kearny's main body, and they entered the enemy camp without support. The *Californios* were still saddling up when Johnston's detail rode in, but they recovered in time to drive the dragoons back. Kearny's main corps, meanwhile, had lost all coherence because of the varied conditions of the horses and mules. Pico withdrew to level ground behind his camp and steadied his men. Captain Benjamin D. Moore, commanding the larger part of Kearny's dragoons, ordered a charge, which scattered the Army of the West yet further. Pico counterattacked, and the Anglo troopers were no match for the nimble lancers. After a quarter-hour brawl, Gillespie showed up with his men and two guns. Pico withdrew again, but not before a North American howitzer's mules bolted into the Californian lines, where they and the gun were captured.

The engagement was a credit to Pico and a bloody embarrassment to Kearny. The Anglo force numbered about 150 men at the start and lost eighteen killed including two captains and a lieutenant; the thirteen wounded included Kearny and Gillespie. Pico started with about seventy-five lancers and lost twelve wounded and one prisoner. The Californians backed off the scene, and the Army of the West was too whipped to do anything about it. Its men had no food, their mounts were either collapsing or crazy with fear, and they were simply too exhausted. There were no wagons for the wounded, so the Yankees were stuck on a hill near San Pasqual, unable even to go to San Diego. Kearny handed command to Captain Henry S. Turner, who sent a message to Stockton. There was nothing left to do but wait, bury the bodies, and tend the injured.[40]

That morning, according to Kearny's topographer, William H. Emory, "day dawned on the most tattered and ill-fed detachment of men that ever the United States mustered under her colors." Pico had surrounded the Anglos with more than 200 men after word of the battle got out and volunteers rode into his camp. Pico proposed a prisoner exchange on December 8—he had four, Kearny had one—and the Army of the West grew by one man. He had been captured carrying a message from Stockton to Kearny, saying that he lacked the animals to go to Kearny's relief.

That night Lieutenant Edward F. Beale of the navy volunteered to slip through the *californio* lines to San Diego. Carson and a local Diegueño Indian scout named Chemuctah also went along. They crept to the foot of the hill and discovered that there were three circles of mounted pickets all around the camp. The Anglos removed their boots to reduce noise; Chemuctah kept his soft moccasins on. Beale and Carson tucked their footgear into their belts and the three messengers crept for two miles through rocks, brush, and prickly pear until they were beyond the sentries. The boots disappeared during the crawl, so the lieutenant and the mountain man went forward barefoot; Chemuctah's moccasins soon were shredded. The three men kept going twenty-seven miles to San Diego. They ran into heavy patrols outside the town and split up. Beale and Chemuctah entered Stockton's camp separately early on the morning of December 10. Carson took a twenty-mile roundabout and arrived several hours later. All three left puddles of blood every time they put a foot down. This ordeal left Beale so disabled that he was bedridden aboard ship for a month and did not fully recover for nearly a year. Carson got over it faster, although he could not walk for many days. Chemuctah was in bed for a week or so, then disappeared.[41]

This harrowing journey turned out to be unnecessary. Stockton had heard about the skirmish at San Pasqual late on December 6, and Turner's message arrived early on the seventh. He declined, by way of the message intercepted by Pico's men, to send relief. The commodore realized suddenly that he would catch the blame if he made no effort to prevent disaster. He sent a relief column out on the eighth and it reached Kearny's hilltop on the night of December 10. The combined force, too much for Pico's horsemen to challenge, limped into San Diego on the twelfth. Emory remembered, "One of the mountain men who had never seen the ocean before, opened his arms and exclaimed: 'Lord! There is a great prairie without a tree.' "[42]

While Stockton was failing to retake southern California, a separate, unconnected revolt broke out among *Californios* in the north, caused by atrocities against Mexican settlers. Rebels seized the acting *alcalde* of Yerba Buena and a small shore party of sailors on December 8, and tried without success to exchange the *alcalde* for their worst abuser. A company of 100 marines landed, attracted some Anglo mounted volunteers, and chased the *Californios* out of town and on to Mission Santa Clara, where there was a bloodless skirmish on January 2, 1847. A truce followed. The Mexicans agreed to call off their revolt in return for a guarantee that the abuses would stop.[43]

Frémont, meanwhile, had marched south from Monterey expecting to meet opposition at San Luis Obispo. His men surrounded the town on the night of December 14–15 and captured Pío de Jesús Pico, brother of Andrés Pico, and thirty-five others. Frémont ordered a court-martial for Pico on the grounds that he had broken his parole. The court sentenced him to death, but the Pathfinder gave in to the pleas of Pico's wife and several navy officers and pardoned the man. Pico then volunteered to join Frémont's expedition. The party crossed a mountain range in a storm, reached Santa Barbara on December 17, and continued through Rincon Pass. Fighting a short skirmish with rebels near Mission San Buenaventura just after the first of the year, Frémont received separate orders from Stockton and Kearny to break off action.[44]

Kearny got together with Stockton as soon as he arrived at San Diego and they more or less agreed to retake Los Angeles. Stockton had the majority of troops and supplies and thought himself governor of California, so he claimed command of all military operations. Kearny, however, showed him his orders to take command in the territory and establish a government, which he claimed made him governor. Stockton countered that Kearny's orders might have been legitimate, but they did not apply to a vastly changed situation. They butted heads from the day they met, and the reconquest of California remained incomplete.[45]

ALL ARE DISSATISFIED—THE RICH, THE POOR, THE HIGH AND THE LOW

After Kearny and Doniphan left New Mexico, the territory was commanded by Sterling Price and his 2nd Missouri Mounted Volunteers. There were a few outposts at settlements, but most men and some artillery units were concentrated at Fort Marcy, north of Santa Fe. They lacked adult supervision. "The dirtiest, rowdiest crew I have ever seen collected together," a British traveler called the volunteers. Even an Anglo soldier confided to his diary, "A more drunken and depraved set, I am sure, can never be found." While the boozy louts ran riot, their colonel feathered his nest.[46]

What the Missourians did was no secret back home. The *St. Louis New Era* called the New Mexico city "a perfect bedlam; no order in the streets and public places—no discipline among the troops." The *St. Louis Missouri Republican* charged that "all military discipline, all regard for propriety was lost. . . . It was a common occurrence, not restricted by any order of the Colonel, to see *officers* of his regiment dealing *Monte* at the gambling hells of Santa Fe." The same paper called the troops "a disgrace to the name of American soldiers," who would return to Missouri hardened criminals.[47]

An English tourist passing through Santa Fe was disgusted. "Crowds of drunken volunteers filled the streets, brawling and boasting," he complained. Every other house was "a grocery, as they call a gin or whiskey shop, continually disgorging reeling, drunken men, and every where filth—the dirt reigned triumphant."[48]

It was not that Price and his men had nothing better to do than turn Santa Fe into a cesspool. The multisided wars among Indian tribes and *Nuevomexicanos* continued unabated. The problem was so impossible that

William Bent, agent for the Commissioner of Indian Affairs, suggested paying the Apaches to stop raiding. The Navajos and Apaches, it was estimated, made off with over 450,000 New Mexican sheep from 1846 to 1850. When James S. Calhoun became Indian agent in 1849 he reported, "The wild Indians of this country have been so much more successful in their robberies since General Kearny took possession of the country, that they do not believe we have the power to chastise them." He also recommended buying them off, because "the thought of annihilating these Indians cannot be entertained by an American public—nor can the Indians abandon their predatory incursions . . . unless the hungry wants of these people are provided for." The "wild" Indians, not the United States, owned the territory.[49]

Army officers began exploring New Mexico in 1846, at least fifteen major surveys going forward before the Civil War to explore and map the country, find routes across it, and locate sites for military posts. These explorers compiled a wealth of knowledge but the government made little use of it. No effort went into improving roads in New Mexico until 1853, and precious little was done then or later.[50]

The *Nuevomexicanos* felt abused and betrayed—none more so than the former lieutenant governor, Diego Archuleta, who had been promised the governor's role in western New Mexico. Instead, Kearny had annexed the whole province and left him in the cold. *Hispanos* high and low seethed with resentment toward the United States and the Charles Bent government. Bent and Price were told of a plan to raise a rebellion in northern New Mexico on December 15. The snitch's information led to the arrest of two men implicated in the plot, but the ringleaders, Archuleta and others known and unknown, escaped. The prisoners, Manuel Chávez and Nicolás Pino, were tried for treason under the Kearny Code. They were acquitted because, as Mexican citizens, they could not commit treason against the United States.

Bent condemned those who had raised "this blind opposition; who, notorious for their vices, and full of ambition, aspired to the first offices— and those who thought to bind the people slaves to their caprices." The governor asserted that the new government protected the people, taxed imports instead of the common folk, and safeguarded New Mexican land titles. Doniphan's victory at Brazito, he said, demonstrated "the futility and artifices with which these turbulent spirits would delude you!" The governor went on: "Listen not, I beseech you, to their false and poisonous doctrines—remain quiet in your domestic occupations, that under the protection of the laws, you may enjoy the unspeakable blessings offered . . . and thus enjoy, individually, all the happiness which your best friend wishes you."[51]

New Mexico's military commander, Price, and its "best friend," Bent, concluded that the arrests and the governor's wind had headed off trouble. Price returned to his malfeasance while Bent went home to Taos early in 1847. They did not realize that the original passivity of the *Nuevomexicanos* was a result of shock at Armijo's defection and the abandonment of Apache Canyon. Resistance grew throughout the last quarter of 1846, first passively, then increasingly hostile. Stragglers from the Anglo army turned up dead, collaborators with the occupation government received threats, secret meetings took place, weapons were collected, and the Pueblo Indians were brought into the picture. They knew that their ancestors had driven the Spanish invaders out of their country in 1680 and kept them out for twelve years.[52]

"It is clear that the Mexicans here are very much discontented," a Missouri soldier wrote home in December 1846. "The clergy are our enemies . . . the wealthier classes dislike our government . . . the patriotic must needs feel mortification and pain, at seeing our people domineering in their homes; and the lower classes lived too long in a state of abject slavery, dependence, and ignorance, to be at once capable of appreciating the benefits conferred on them by the change of government." He could not believe that anyone would object to the blessings of occupation by the United States. Nevertheless, as he could see for himself, "all are dissatisfied—the rich, the poor, the high and the low." He thought only the Pueblos were "content indeed." That the people of New Mexico might rise up against their liberators remained unthinkable. "I cannot be made to believe, that these people are either so hardy or so foolish, to attempt any thing in the shape of revolt." He blamed all talk to the contrary—and he heard a lot of it—on "Mexican braggadocio." He and Price and Bent and many other North Americans were about to receive a great shock.[53]

CHAPTER
14

WE DO NOT WANT FOR ANY OF YOU GRINGOS TO GOVERN US

(January–February 1847)

Imagine that the earth takes up arms to defend itself against invasion, that the hills, the streams, the gorges, the grottos are death-dealing machines which come out to meet the regular troops.

—Beníto Pérez Galdós

THE TURN OF 1847 SAW AN EXPLOSION OF ATTACKS by *Indios bravos* against Mexicans and Anglos and other Indians, settled and *bárbaros*. Comanches and Apaches raided deep into Mexico; Comanches and Kiowas scorched Texas; Utes and Navajos and Apaches attacked each other and the settlements of New Mexico; Pawnees, Arapahos, Comanches, Kiowas, and others raided over the Santa Fe Trail; and normally peaceful tribes of southern California skirmished with *Californios*. Mexican, North American, New Mexican, and Californian whites and Indians retaliated. Warfare erupted with a scale, ferocity, and geographical extent never seen before. The bellicose Indians made themselves party to a war that Mexico and the United States thought they had to themselves. "Events, which are our best teachers," said a Mexico City newspaper, "awakened the realiza-

tion in the Indians of their true value . . . What they needed was an opportunity. The war against the United States gave them that opportunity."[1]

Mexico's disorganized national army was in no position to respond to
the Indian raids. Local and state militias lacked the military skills and often
the dependable horses required to challenge the raiders. Any response was
bloody retribution when an Indian band was discovered, whether or not it
had committed the raid that called out the militia. The United States tried
formal military measures. When Colonel Price received a report of a raid
he sent out a punitive expedition, which typically missed its quarry. The
War Department reinforced patrols on the Santa Fe Trail but could not
guard all traffic, given the Indians' talent for guerrilla warfare. In a typical
case in June 1847, a party of eighty dragoons escorting a paymaster was
notified of an attack on a nearby supply train. Half the dragoons rode to
the rescue and the Comanches bushwhacked them, killing five and wounding six. Another train in the same area lost two men killed and eighty yoke
of oxen run off.

The War Department established a special military district to guard
the trail. A scattering of regular dragoon patrols rode back and forth between Missouri and New Mexico. Secretary Marcy created a five-company
legion called the "Indian Battalion," which spent the next winter on the
plains to discourage the Indians from resuming their attacks in the spring.
It did not. The United States government had blundered into ancient
multitribal warfare and found itself treated as just another invading tribe.[2]

THE DEVIL IS RUNNING AWAY WITH US

Mexico had another sort of Indian uprising that continued on and off into
the 1920s. It was an old problem—the poorer *campesinos* (farmers), *Indios*
and lower *Castas* mostly, had since colonial times risen up locally against
the government and the *hacendados* who stole their land and enslaved them
in peonage. The North American invasion diverted Mexican military attention and drained the state militias. Yucatán was in a perpetual state of
revolt. Another broke out in January 1847 in the Tabasco region, where
the Chiapas state governor said he hoped at best to contain the "revolution" to the Tabasco vicinity, reestablishing federal control later, "if possible." Attacks on troops in Querétaro became so bloody in January that
Mexico City diverted troops intended to fight the North Americans.
Another rebellion in the Eula district of Oaxaca in February caused the
posting of 500 national guards there. The Sierra Gorda region of north-
central Mexico exploded in an agrarian revolt that went on for more than
three years, and as time passed the violence spread all over the country.[3]

Santa Anna and other leaders underestimated Mexican resistance to war measures even when the call was for help fighting agrarian rebels. Every attempt to raise money for the war met refusals to cooperate from state governors and legislatures. Gómez Farías as interim president talked Congress on January 10 into authorizing the government to seize clerical properties to the tune of $15 million; Santa Anna backed him up. The Church counterattacked and priests organized riots in all major cities. "If the Yankee triumphs," shouted a member of Congress, "what ecclesiastical property or what religion will be left us?" Church-led rioting broke out in Mexico City, and nearly the whole cabinet resigned. Some politicians, the capital garrison, and national guards counterattacked, joined by mobs of *puros* hostile to the Church. One politician called the situation "furious anarchy . . . the Devil is running away with us."[4]

Santa Anna softened his support for the anti-church law and it was repealed in late January. Gómez Farías, however, was as interested in demolishing clerical power as he was in fighting the United States. Congress granted him dictatorial powers to raise money for the war on February 4 and Church authorities fought back again. They enlisted a plot-prone general, Matías de la Peña y Barragán, who was soon approached by Moses Y. Beach, publisher of the *New York Sun,* who handed him a bag of money. Beach was an agent of the secretary of state who decided on his own to see what he could do to win the war. Peña y Barragán commanded Mexico City's five national guard battalions, known as *los Polkos* because they held grand balls at which the polka was a favorite dance. Gómez Farías ordered the *Polkos* on February 24 to march toward Vera Cruz; they refused to go, and on the twenty-eighth they openly rebelled. This turned into a conservative revolt against the liberal government, and the two sides barricaded the streets and shot up the city. Most casualties were civilian bystanders, and many buildings were thoroughly holed. Santa Anna finally ended it with his regiment of hussars, becoming the Savior of His Country yet again.[5]

While Santa Anna saved his country, in Washington Polk tried to hang on to his territorial ambitions. Opposition to the war was growing, and pacifists increasingly made themselves heard. The American Peace Society offered a prize of $500 for the best review of the conflict with Mexico "on the principles of Christianity and on enlightened statesmanship." The winner was *The War with Mexico Reviewed,* claiming that the war was really about expansion of slavery.[6]

The alleged nefarious purpose of "Mr. Polk's War"—the spread of slavery—was combined with growing belief that it had started illegally. Even army officers grumbled. Ethan Allen Hitchcock, Scott's chief of staff, confided to a friend, "I coincide with you in your views of this abominable war." He did not wish "to fall victim to this war without entering my protest against the war itself as unjust on our part & needlessly & wickedly brought about." As a soldier, he would obey orders, but as "an individual, I condemn, I abominate this war."[7]

The slavery issue bothered the president the most, as resolutions piled up in Congress forbidding slavery in conquered territories. Slavery, Polk told his diary on January 4, had no legitimate connection with the war. The issue would do nothing but divide the country, so "such an agitation is not only unwise but wicked." The next day he declared, "There is no probability that any territory will ever be acquired from Mexico in which slavery could ever exist."[8]

Polk was also losing control over his cabinet. At an especially heated meeting on January 2 Secretary of State Buchanan stood firm in his belief that there was no hope of winning the war by marching on Mexico City. If the campaign succeeded in taking the Mexican capital, it "would but excite a feeling against us of races and religions." Buchanan wanted to hold and defend New Mexico and California, but objected to taking any more territory. Almost all the other cabinet members, including Marcy and Mason, agreed with him. Polk responded that the decision had already been made to take Vera Cruz. What came next, he declared, was left to the general's judgment.[9]

Polk grasped at any straw that might drive Mexico to the peace table. Colonel Alexander Atocha showed up again in mid-January bearing, he said, another message from Santa Anna. He would accept the Rio Grande as the border between the two countries provided that the land between there and the Nueces became a buffer zone. He also offered to sell California for $15 to $20 million. The cabinet agreed to a counteroffer that accepted the alleged proposal from Santa Anna, except that New Mexico was added to the territory Mexico must hand over. The president told Buchanan to write it up as a formal proposal, and Atocha took the offer back to Mexico. Meanwhile, planning for the invasion at Vera Cruz went forward under Scott's direction.[10]

A GROSSER ABUSE OF HUMAN CONFIDENCE IS NOWHERE RECORDED

Scott was his usual energetic self throughout the fall of 1846 and into 1847, ably assisted by Secretary Marcy, unusually hardworking. The first challenge was the landing barges. Designed by a navy architect, 140 of them were built by a quartermaster contractor in Philadelphia. Called "surf boats" by soldiers, they were flat-bottomed craft in three sizes ranging from 35 to 40 feet long, so they could be nested aboard transports.

Double-ended, broad-beamed, they were manned by crews of eight and carried forty armed soldiers. Bad weather scattered about half their transports, so only sixty-five surf boats were available for the landing.[11]

The quartermaster department planned to hire transport ships, but bureaucratic snarls plagued the program. Some hires were canceled by mistake; others were delayed because their cargoes had not reached their ports. The weather was especially foul that winter and captains had trouble finding enough crewmen. Eventually 53 ships sailed from Atlantic ports and 163 from Gulf ports.[12]

In contrast to the War Department, the Navy Department did not do so well. The secretary sent Conner a ship-of-the-line and three sloops-of-war and bought four shallow-draft brigs or schooners outfitted as bomb vessels, but none showed up until after the landings. Navy bureaucrats blamed the delays on "inclemency of the weather and other causes." Army-navy departmental cooperation was so poor that Secretary Mason never knew the planned landing date.[13]

Scott left Washington for New York on November 23, 1846, and on the thirtieth sailed to New Orleans. His orders reminded him that the president had given him his assignment personally. He was to go to Mexico, take command "of the forces there assembled," and organize and lead "an expedition to operate on the gulf coast." There was a generous expression of confidence from the president. "It is not proposed to control your operations by definite and positive instructions," the order read, "but you are left to prosecute them as your judgment, under a full view of all the circumstances, shall dictate." This handed Scott the blame for any disaster.[14]

Scott surrounded himself with a good staff. He recruited the former consul at Vera Cruz, Dimond, to manage the "secret services" and sent him to Havana to hire a couple of agents to operate in Mexico. Quartermaster General Jesup became Scott's personal quartermaster. Chief Engineer Joseph G. Totten did the same with engineering. The most important appointment was Ethan Allen Hitchcock as inspector general. A sturdy West Pointer, forty-eight years old, he was a strong-willed, thoughtful soldier, a veteran of just about everything, a man who loved to write on scientific subjects. He received power to do "whatever I thought proper as an Inspector-General and use his name as authority." Hitchcock ensured that the whole command was always ready for battle; that sufficient arms, equipment, and animals were on hand; that camp sanitation was maintained. He, as much as Scott, got the job done.[15]

Scott wrote to Taylor from New York, saying that he would not supersede Taylor because his scene of action would be elsewhere. Unfortunately, he must deprive Old Zach of most of his veteran troops.

He wrote to Taylor again from New Orleans to ask that they meet on the lower Rio Grande. As he wrote, a local paper reported that he was headed for Vera Cruz. This blew a cover story that his target was San Luis Potosí and made Polk and Marcy believe that Scott was conniving against them.[16]

Paranoia could run both ways. Scott heard from friends in Congress about the plan to appoint Benton as lieutenant general, and sent an angry letter to Marcy protesting this "vile intrigue," claiming, "A grosser abuse of human confidence is nowhere recorded." Then Scott heard that Benton had attacked him on the Senate floor, and he fired off another tirade to Marcy, sniffing repetitiously that he had again drawn "a fire upon my rear, even before I have been able to draw the fire of the enemy upon my front." Polk and Marcy took that as an attack on them. Polk had already alienated Taylor. Now he grumbled about Scott where he knew the general would hear about it.[17]

The paranoid club was growing. Scott reached Texas at the end of December to find a letter from Taylor waiting for him. It assured Scott that he was "happy to receive your orders and to hold myself and troops at your disposition," although at Victoria he was beyond the commanding general's control. Taylor complained that the Polk administration had lost confidence in him, and he felt especially abused by having troops taken away from him without his prior knowledge. Old Zach had only a thousand regulars to hold the northern front until some "raw recruits" were sent to him. Taylor told his brother that Scott, Marcy, and Worth were conspiring to drive him from the army. He wrote a nasty letter to the adjutant general on January 27 complaining that Polk had denied him "that assurance of confidence and support so indispensable to success." The break between Taylor and the president was out in the open.[18]

Polk accused Taylor and Scott of plotting against Democratic generals. "General Taylor's camp," he charged, "has been converted into a political arena, and great and palpable injustice has been done to many officers of high merit who happen to be Democrats." Scott had "commenced the same proscriptive and tyrannical course," Polk raved to the cabinet, vowing "at any hazard to check it."[19]

While the president foamed at the mouth, the top two dogs in the army had their own parting of the ways. Taylor's failure to meet Scott on the Rio Grande was insulting enough. Delaying Patterson's transfer to the Vera Cruz campaign by sending him to Victoria and Tampico was downright defiant. Scott violated army protocol by directly ordering Major General William O. Butler to send Worth and his regulars from Saltillo to the Rio Grande. Taylor again complained that he had been run around, Scott sent him an explanation, and that and the order to Butler fell into

Mexican hands. Scott ordered Taylor to fall back on Monterey. Old Zach ignored him.[20]

The Vera Cruz campaign assembled while the generals squabbled. Worth arrived at the Texas coast on January 18 and Patterson's and Twiggs' divisions reached Tampico a week later. The first of the new volunteer regiments sailed from the United States on January 28. Except for those at Tampico, the destination for all was Isla de los Lobos. Scott had selected it as his assembly point because the island was big enough to let the troops go ashore for training and recreation, and there were no gambling dens, saloons, or whorehouses.[21]

Scott was ready to head off to Vera Cruz by late January 1847, but he faced a transportation shortage. He told the secretary of war on January 26 that he expected to start loading men in three or four days and believed he would have enough guns, ammunition, supplies, and landing barges at Lobos by February 10. Then the quartermaster at Brazos Santiago reported on February 2 that at least a dozen ships due from New Orleans had not arrived. Scott told him to charter vessels on the Texas coast, still hoping to board troops there by February 10 and those at Tampico by the fifteenth. At New Orleans the difficulties were maddening. Jesup chartered ships as they came into port, but bad weather slowed the unloading of their cargoes and the loading of the government's.[22]

Scott hung around Brazos until February 15, when he sailed to Tampico and then on to Lobos. Troops from Taylor's army were annoyingly slow to arrive, and a ship carrying volunteers ran aground. Transports continued to be missing, and those that did show up were slow to load. Scott fumed through the month that the *vómito* time was drawing near. He fired off another letter to Marcy on February 28. He had sent some supply ships ahead to Antón Lizardo and would not wait "more than forty-eight hours for anybody," except the tardy regulars. Two-thirds of his ordnance and ordnance stores and half his landing barges were "yet unheard of."[23]

The invasion was about to begin. Those men who had been stuck on the Texas coast were eager to go. "An officer, the other day," one wrote home, said "that he would give Texas back to Mexico and if she would not take it he would be willing to enter into a ten years war to make her do so." On Isla de los Lobos another said, "I have been in sight of their shores so long that I am getting very impatient for a nearer peep. I should like to go over if I could claim the promise made to Abraham that my seed should possess the land," meaning he dreamed about all the pretty women waiting for him.[24]

WHO THE DEVIL IS GOVERNOR OF CALIFORNIA?

As the Vera Cruz campaign took shape, the insurgency in California continued, and so did the comedy. Ma Flores, the rebel leader in the south, was trapped between Frémont's crew in the north and Stockton and Kearny at San Diego. Flores sent Stockton a proposal for a truce on January 1. His people would fight to the end, he boasted, but that should not be necessary because the differences between the United States and Mexico might soon be resolved. Stockton refused to accept the message. Flores, the commodore sneered, "had violated his honor" by breaking parole. Stockton threatened to shoot Flores but offered amnesty to all other rebels who surrendered.[25]

Stockton marched cautiously out of San Diego at the end of December. There were 607 men, armed with a mixture of muskets, musketoons, boarding pikes, and cutlasses, hauling six guns. The horses and oxen were too weak to pull the artillery and supply wagons, so the men helped the animals. A few cattle marched with the troops. Flores planned to ambush Stockton and Kearny at La Jaboneria Ford on the San Gabriel River. Anglo scouts spotted the rebels during the night of January 7–8, so Stockton shifted toward Bartolo Ford upstream. Flores beat the North Americans there and blocked the crossing.[26]

Flores' troops were amateur, a few presidials and *vaquero* (cowboy) militia, most mounted. The ford was about fifty yards wide, knee deep, the bottom sandy in spots. The land on the south side was level, but on the north there was a range of low hills about 50 feet high, 600 yards beyond the stream. Flores posted about 200 men and two small guns on the hills, and 300 yards off each flank he stationed 100 to 150 cavalry. Stockton formed a square enclosing his wagons and cattle and advanced until he saw the *Californios* early in the afternoon of the eighth. He halted about a quarter mile south of the river, reinforced his left, sent some mounted men ahead, and resumed the advance. Flores' men drove a herd of horses against the square but failed to break it. His little guns popped steadily, but bad powder and homemade projectiles made them ineffective.

Kearny ordered his artillery to unlimber and fire across the stream, but the commodore countermanded him and ordered a charge across the river without cover fire. The bottom turned out to be softer than expected, tugging at men trying to pull guns across. When they made it, the artillery set up on the far side while the infantry took cover below the riverbank. Stockton personally laid the guns on the north bank and silenced both rebel pieces. Mounted troopers drove Flores' left off its hill while Flores counterattacked against the Anglo left, but the *vaqueros* were driven off by blasts of artillery and musketry. Stockton's men took the hills as the *Californios* retired in good order. Flores sent his cavalry around to the right to attack the enemy rear, but heavy North American fire scotched that. The Mexican commander resumed his retreat toward Los Angeles. Flores' stalwart little army halted to block the road. The Anglos did not have enough good horses for a real pursuit, so the battle ended late in the afternoon. The engagement lasted about an hour and a half, costing each side two killed and nine wounded. The sailors performed well as infantry, and Stockton bungled the river crossing but otherwise was a solid ground-force commander. The Californians put in a gallant performance for amateurs under inexperienced leadership.[27]

The column resumed its march toward Los Angeles at dawn on January 9, crossing La Mesa, the plain between the San Gabriel and Los Angeles rivers. The corps ran into about 300 *Californios* deployed between the road and a dry arroyo to their left, where Flores' cannons stood. The Anglos formed another square and marched obliquely to their own left to stay out of range of the rebel guns. Flores extended his line to cut the Anglo route of march and brought up two more little guns. Stockton stopped, combined his guns into a battery, and drove the Mexican artillery out of range. The rebel gunners were almost out of ammunition anyway, but Flores and his men were still game. They charged the North American left on horseback, but withering musketry drove them back. Flores resumed retiring on the city, and Stockton stopped about three miles short of town. The commodore did not want to enter Los Angeles at nightfall. The skirmish on La Mesa had cost him one killed and five wounded, while Flores had lost one killed and an unknown number injured. Gallant as the *Californios* might be, they were outgunned, outnumbered, and low on ammunition. The rebellion, as Stockton saw it, was smashed. He led his troops into Los Angeles at midday on January 10, a ship's band blaring. There were some insurgent diehards visible in the distance but no resistance in town. Gillespie raised his flag above the government house, and Los Angeles returned to United States control.[28]

Frémont and his battalion, meanwhile, approached from the north, looking for a fight but finding only a minor skirmish near Mission San Buenaventura on January 5. The Pathfinder received a letter from Stockton on the ninth, advising him to avoid battle. He received another from Kearny on the eleventh notifying him of the capture of Los Angeles and ordering him to march that way. Late in the afternoon Frémont's scouts found Flores and about a hundred men camped near Cahuenga. Frémont

sent his prisoner Jesús Pico into the camp to talk the Californians into surrendering. Flores transferred his command to Andrés Pico and took off for
Sonora. The Pathfinder declared a truce, both sides appointed commissioners, and they drew up what the Anglos called the "Articles of
Capitulation" and the *Californios* called the "Treaty of Cahuenga." The
Californians agreed to surrender their arms and go home. The United
States guaranteed protection of life and property. No Mexican would be
required to take an oath of allegiance to the United States until a peace
treaty was signed. Every citizen of California was granted the rights of citizens of the United States. Frémont and Andrés Pico signed these terms on
January 13. An additional article appended on the sixteenth canceled
paroles and released all prisoners.[29]

Frémont probably was so generous because he expected to become
governor of California and grace in victory would make his rule more acceptable to the natives. He had exceeded his authority, however, because
he was close enough to Stockton and Kearny to consult them but did not.
News of the treaty hit them both like thunderbolts. Stockton was annoyed
because he had no choice but to accept the terms. After Frémont and his
men trudged into Los Angeles during a heavy rainstorm on January 14,
Stockton sent a report to the secretary of the navy. Some insurgents had
escaped to Sonora while the rest surrendered, he declared, and he was
highly incensed that the rebel commander got away, but "still I have
thought it best to approve" the treaty. Miffed about releasing all prisoners
and ending paroles, he grudgingly admitted that California was now
peaceful. Stockton would have preferred to wreak bloody vengeance for
the rebellion.[30]

Frémont stuck his head into a conflict between Kearny and Stockton.
Kearny blazed away first on January 16. He had followed Stockton's orders
during the Los Angeles campaign because his was the smaller part of the
force, but that was as far as he would go. The general sent a note saying that
he had heard that Stockton had organized a civil government and reminding him that that duty had been handed to Kearny. "If you have such authority, and will show it to me or furnish me with a certified copy of it,"
the general said, "I will cheerfully acquiesce in what you are doing. If you
have not such authority, then I demand that you cease all further proceedings relating to the formation of a civil government." He would not "recognize in you any right in assuming to perform duties confided to me by
the President."[31]

Kearny ordered Frémont to cease carrying out orders from Stockton.
The Pathfinder offered a meandering alibi saying that he had found the
commodore in command in California as early as July, that Stockton had

commissioned him as military commandant in the province, and that it appeared to him as though Kearny had deferred to Stockton. "I feel, therefore," he concluded, "with great deference to your professional and personal character, constrained to say that, until you and Commodore Stockton adjust between yourselves, the question of rank, where I respectfully think the difficulty belongs, I shall have to report and receive orders, as heretofore, from the commodore." Signing off as "lieutenant colonel United States Army and military commandant of the Territory of California," Frémont had bought himself a ticket to a court-martial.[32]

Stockton presented the Pathfinder with a commission as governor of California and sent Kearny a nasty letter refusing to recognize any authority the general claimed to have. He added "that I cannot do anything or desist from doing anything on your demand, which I will submit to the President and ask for your recall. In the meantime you will consider yourself suspended from the command of the United States forces in this place." Kearny told Stockton, "I must, for the purpose of preventing a collision between us and possibly a civil war in consequence of it, remain silent for the present, leaving you with the great responsibility of doing that for which you have no authority, and preventing me from complying with the President's orders."[33]

Kearny led his dragoons back to San Diego on January 23. There he was soon joined by Cooke with the Mormon Battalion. The extra force gave him a bigger bargaining chip, but still Kearny refused to make an open issue of the command in the province, let alone start a shooting war over it. He showed real statesmanship, something notably lacking in the other two principals.[34]

Regular troops began arriving in California, among them William Tecumseh Sherman. The officers were appalled to find North Americans fighting each other and asked, "Who the devil is governor of California?" Sherman hoped it was Kearny, who was "a perfect model of the courtly officer and perfect gentleman." None of them thought much of Frémont. "I only wish I could marry a Senator's daughter," another sneered. "I might then set at defiance the orders of my superiors and do as I pleased. Genl Kearny has been most outrageously used by both Frémont and Stockton."[35]

Just after Kearny reached San Diego he learned that Commodore W. Branford Shubrick had arrived at Monterey with orders to take command on the Pacific coast; he outranked every North American officer already there. He had met Commodore James Biddle, his own superior, at Valparaiso, Chile, and Biddle sent Shubrick to California to hold command until he arrived. Kearny met with Shubrick early in February. The two of them agreed on a division of United States authority in the province, with

Monterey the temporary capital. Kearny went on to Yerba Buena, where he met Colonel Richard B. Mason, just arrived from the east. Mason was sent to California to make sure that a senior army officer was present there ahead of Colonel John D. Stevenson, a Democratic hack, and his New York volunteers. Stevenson was diverted to San Diego, where he could do no harm. Mason carried new orders repeating the army's responsibility in California, ratifying everything that Kearny had told Stockton.[36]

Shubrick and Kearny jointly issued a declaration "setting forth responsibility for military and civil authority in California" on March 1, 1847. The navy commander would administer regulations for harbors, imports and exports, and other things properly nautical. The army commander would exercise the authority granted him by the president over operations on land and administrative functions over the territory. Shubrick ordered Stockton to resume operations against Baja California and mainland Mexico. Kearny would deal with Frémont in due course. The comedy was not over.[37]

Kearny exceeded his authority in California as he had in New Mexico, establishing a civil government. "The Americans and Californians are now but one people," he told his new subjects; "let us cherish one wish, one hope, and let that be for the peace and quiet of our country. Let us as a band of brothers unite and emulate each other in our efforts to benefit and improve this our beautiful, and which soon must be our happy and prosperous home."[38]

California was at peace, but Kearny's attempt at Shakespearean eloquence fell flat with Californios, who felt only a great sense of loss. "The language now spoken in our country," Mariano Guadalupe Valléjo reflected sadly, "the laws that govern us, the faces that we encounter daily, are those of the masters of the land and, of course, antagonistic to our interests and rights, but what does that matter to the conqueror?"[39]

I'M FOR GOING HOME TO SARAH AND THE CHILDREN

While Stockton, Kearny, and Frémont threatened to shoot at each other, Doniphan and his Missourians were stuck in El Paso. Doniphan learned that Wool had abandoned his expedition to Ciudad Chihuahua, and also that the Mexicans were preparing to defend the state capital. He decided to finish Wool's work on his own. His artillery arrived on February 1, 1847, and on the fifth a train came in with ammunition and supplies. Doniphan marched south on the eighth, leading 924 soldiers and about 300 civilian traders and teamsters. There were six field guns and 312 wagons, both civilian and military.[40]

The governor of Chihuahua, Ángel Trías Álvarez, a wealthy *hacendado,* prepared to defend his capital. General Pedro García Conde supervised construction of a strong position where the *camino real* crossed the Río Sacramento about fifteen miles north of Ciudad Chihuahua. Trías, an old Indian fighter, put the state's national guard commander, General José Heredia, in command of the troops. As in El Paso, there were people who were either pro–United States or too lazy to help out. Trías, however, was a determined man with deep pockets. He established a foundry on his hacienda and supervised the casting of artillery at his own expense. He assembled a defensive force of 1,200 mostly mediocre cavalry, 1,500 mostly amateur infantry, and 199 gunners with twelve guns, ranging from 4-pounders to 9-pounders, and nine lighter pieces. About a thousand *rancheros* and *vaqueros* showed up with machetes and homemade lances.[41]

The country the Missourians marched through south of El Paso was as dry and dreary as the *Jornada del Muerto,* 200 miles of desert and arid prairie dotted with a few evergreen oaks. Somebody carelessly started a prairie fire early on February 25. A small, brackish lake presented itself, and to save the wagons and supplies the soldiers and civilians drove them all into the water, then set backfires. The corps camped in that blackened waste until the twenty-seventh, when a scout rode in to report that the Mexicans were making a stand at the Sacramento. "Cheer up, Boys," Doniphan announced. "Tomorrow evening I intend to have supper with the Mexicans on the banks of a beautiful spring."[42]

Doniphan woke his men early on February 28 and deployed into a novel arrangement. The wagons moved down the road in four columns, with the artillery and most of the mounted troops between them. The front was screened by three infantry companies. As this odd procession advanced steadily south down a wide valley, "an eagle, sometimes soaring aloft and sometimes swooping down amongst the fluttering banners," one Missourian recalled, "followed along the lines all day and seemed to herald the news of victory." The troops "regarded the omen as good."[43]

About two miles north of the Sacramento, Doniphan halted early in the afternoon and rode forward with his senior officers to take a look. The *camino real* ran straight south to the river, where it was covered by the thick-walled Hacienda de Sacramento on the south side, backed against a steep hill on which García had built a strong redoubt. Most of the defense was forward on the north side of the river, twenty-three earthworks laid out in an inverted L along the east side of the road and beyond to the edge of a deep arroyo. That *arroyo seco* (dry ditch) looked like an impregnable defense of the Mexican left. A western spur of the road ran through it between steep banks and came out at a secondary river crossing about two miles from the main road, the crossing covered by guns at another stout hacienda, El Torreón. Most of the Mexican guns and troops were on a rough mesa to the right. García had thought the North Americans would advance along the main road into his trap because the arroyo led to the guns at Torreón. It was an orthodox defense by an orthodox soldier. Doniphan, however, was neither orthodox nor really a soldier.

Sending his cavalry forward to screen his movements, Doniphan angled his main body to the right, marched parallel to the arroyo about two miles, and stopped. He sent troops into the ditch with tools and orders to ramp the banks. This kept his corps out of range of Mexican artillery and bypassed the main positions, but once his column crossed the arroyo it was vulnerable to attack while dragging the wagons and guns up the far bank. Heredia sent García and about a thousand horse soldiers to stop the *Yanquis* in the arroyo until he could move up artillery and infantry. He had guessed wrong, however, because Doniphan was not going down the ditch to Torreón but was flanking the other force closer on. The Anglos hauled their wagons, teams, pack mules, and guns up the side of the arroyo before the Mexican cavalry got there. Doniphan formed the wagons into a fort and sent his artillery forward. Twice the lancers charged in, and twice they were devastated by canister. The Mexican troopers had never heard cannon fire before, and the ear-ringing blasts stunned them. They began to give way, and the gunners turned on the Mexican artillery, which they outranged. The Mexican copper cannonballs left strange blue streaks in the high desert air, making them easy to dodge. The cavalry, disorganized and shocked, panicked and scattered to the rear. Heredia withdrew the rest of his troops into the fieldworks on the mesa, but his original plan was a shambles and the panic was infecting the infantry.

The Mexican general sent two guns to the left to occupy a redoubt commanding the Sacramento crossing, and several others went along without orders, further weakening the main line. Meanwhile, part of Doniphan's corps pursued the retreating lancers and some infantry, angling to the right to stay out of artillery range. They ran into the southernmost two earthworks on a projection of the mesa overlooking the river, and Heredia parried by sending troops there. Doniphan ordered three cavalry companies and two howitzers to rush the works, but only one of the mounted squads got the order, and it stumbled into an undetected arroyo. A few horsemen got across, but their major went down at the front of the earthworks. Other troops formed a skirmish line and worked their way down the ditch while the howitzers went around its head and opened fire on the Mexicans from about fifty yards off. The troops there drove the Anglos back.

The disorganized Missouri cavalry shifted its aim to the northern redoubt while engineer Garcia attempted a counterattack with a few lancers. They were blasted by Anglo artillery, canister tearing flesh and bone to shreds, men and horses screaming. Then the North American horsemen stormed the northern fort and with the support of the howitzers took the works in a bloody hand-to-hand fight. One more Mexican cavalry charge, this one against the wagons, was broken up by Anglo guns. Guns on the hill behind the Hacienda de Sacramento still fired, and Doniphan could see fugitive Mexican soldiers rallying there. While one battery threw solid shot at the place, more than a thousand yards off, the howitzer battery crossed the river and put the redoubt under a crossfire. This punishment, and the appearance of some Missouri cavalry who had got behind the position, drove the defenders out of the works.

Doniphan's men were too exhausted to pursue. They had lost one dead and eight wounded. Mexican losses were 169 dead, 300 wounded, and 79 taken prisoner, along with surviving livestock, wagons, rations, the army's money, and the equipment that littered the battlefield along with the dead and dying. The Missourians, their faces blackened from gunpowder and smoke, ate and drank well thanks to the captured stores. When the men had rested after bringing in the wounded and shooting injured horses, Doniphan ordered parties out to bury the dead. They did so, but again found many graves torn open by coyotes during the night and had to repeat the ordeal in the morning.[44]

When word of the disaster on the Sacramento reached Ciudad Chihuahua, the people were overcome by terror. For months they had heard nothing about *los Gringos bárbaros* but tales of murder, rape, looting, and desecration of churches. Many families fled down the road to the south, risking the chance of attacks by Apaches. Most of them filtered back into the city over the next several days as the occupation turned out not to be that bad, just uncouth. Governor Trías moved his state government to Parras.

Doniphan's advance approached Chihuahua on March 1, and the next day the whole corps trooped into the city with the regimental band playing "Yankee Doodle." They were received with frosty politeness. The city perched on a high mesa surrounded by low detached mountains and housed about 10,000 people. The houses were one-story stone or adobe, some truly handsome, and there was a grand cathedral and a lively market selling produce from the surrounding irrigated farms. One local product was *el perro de Chihuahua,* the Chihuahua dog, a small animal that brought a big price in Mexico City. Doniphan's men were fascinated more by the many public bathhouses, "one of the choicest luxuries of fashionable life," a soldier called them. "These are constantly filled by the young and gay of both sexes, promiscuously splashing and swimming about with their long black hair spread out on the water without one thought of modesty." This was more than a young Anglo, raised in Victorian prudery without a tradition of bathing, could bear.[45]

Doniphan was stuck in another captured city with less than a thousand men surrounded by hostile people. His men had been in service since the previous June and had not received a cent of pay. Their enlistments would expire the coming June and they wanted to go home after hard campaigns of more than 2,000 miles. The colonel poured all this out in a long letter to Wool on March 20. His men, he said, "are literally without horses, clothes, or money, having nothing but arms and a disposition to use them. They are all volunteers, officers and men, and, although ready for any hardships or danger, are wholly unfit to garrison a town or city. It is confusion worse confounded." Doniphan asked for permission to join Wool at Saltillo.[46]

Doniphan was right to fear that he would lose control of his volunteers. Susan Magoffin arrived on April 4 and was dismayed to find that the Missourians were trashing the town. "The good citizens of Chi. had never dreamed I dare say," she suggested, "that their loved homes would be turned into quarters for common soldiers, their fine houses many of them turned into stables, the rooves made kitchens of, their public *pila* [drinking fountain] used as a bathing trough, the fine trees of their beautiful *alamador* [*alameda,* a promenade lined with cottonwood trees (*alamos*)] barked forever and spoiled, and a hundred other deprivations equal to any of these."[47]

While awaiting a reply from Wool, Doniphan took 600 men and set out toward Ciudad Durango. He turned back about fifty miles out because of a false rumor that a Mexian army was marching on Chihuahua. It was the strangest trek of the campaign, because the country south of the city "swarmed with small black and yellow lizards," according to one of the soldiers. They scattered in all directions, so fast it was impossible to catch them. "Their number was so great at times, as to give a seeming living motion to the ground."[48]

Back in Chihuahua Doniphan called a council of war, Wool still not heard from. The corps faced three choices: stay and wait for word from Wool, go back to Santa Fe, or head for Monterey and home. Doniphan said there might be good reasons to stay, "but gentlemen, *I'm for going home to Sarah and the children.*" This remark spread through the ranks and the rest of the campaign—Wool's permission to join him at Saltillo arrived on April 23—became known as "going home to Sarah and the children."[49]

Because the United States was about to abandon its hold on Chihuahua, the ordeal of Doniphan and his Missourians, and the two battles they fought, had no strategic significance. Yet the adventure continued. Doniphan led his regiment out of Chihuahua on a trek through rough mountains and dry lands across the states of Chihuahua, Durango, and Coahuila, aiming for Encantada, near Saltillo. Outside Parras, the advance helped local settlers beat off an attack by Lipan Apaches, defeating the raiders and freeing thirteen captive women and children. Wool was delighted to receive the Missouri volunteers when they trooped into Encantada on May 21. The next day the proud but ragged bunch passed before him in review, then the Missourians started for home. They got there, greeted by tumultuous crowds, in June. They had marched 5,000 miles.[50]

WE WANT YOUR HEAD, GRINGO

While Doniphan was still at El Paso, far to the north at Santa Fe and Taos, where people hibernated when the snow was deep and the cold was arctic, trouble was brewing. Colonel Price and Governor Bent believed they had decapitated a threatened revolt in December 1846. Without leadership, the Anglos believed, the *Indios* and *peones* would do what they had always done—what they were told. Unfortunately for Price and Bent, these downtrodden people seethed with resentment at the obnoxious behavior of the occupation troops and at the loss of the society they had always known.[51]

The hostility boiled over at Taos, on the Rio Grande about seventy miles north of Santa Fe. Santa Fe had been the Spanish and Mexican capital of New Mexico, but since the early days of the fur trade and the commerce with Missouri Taos had been the capital of Anglo New Mexico. Nowhere in the territory was the contrast between the lives of the rich and those of the poor more evident. Anglos lived very well and warm in fine stone or adobe houses, while the *peones* barely survived in rude *jacales,* working at the beck and call of their rich overlords. It had been bad enough for centuries under those who spoke Spanish. Under those who spoke English it became insufferable.

Charles Bent lived in Taos. He had married into a prominent *hispano* family, the Jaramillos, his wife sister to Josefa Carson, Kit's wife. Like Carson, Bent thought he had become a part of New Mexico. He found out at the very end of his life, however, that to the poor *Hispanos* and the Taoseño *Indios* living in the nearby *pueblo* he was just another *Gringo maldito.* Bent headed home to Taos from Santa Fe on January 14, 1847, slogging through the snow and cold. When he reached his hometown on the eighteenth he confronted a mob of drunken Taoseños demanding the release of friends being held in the Taos jail on trumped-up charges. Bent ordered the rioters to go home and shoved his way through the crowd to his thick-walled house. After midnight the mob, which had continued to grow, confronted the prefect and again demanded the release of the prisoners. When he refused, the rioters killed him and tore the jail open, then went on a rampage through the streets looking for Anglos and their New Mexican sympathizers to kill. They claimed six victims that morning.

Led by Taoseños Pablo Montoyo and Tomás Romera, the *Indios* and *Castas* pounded on Bent's door around six o'clock. The depth of the native resentment was reflected in the exchange between the governor and his killers, as recorded by his daughter Teresina. Bent got out of bed and shouted through the door, asking what the people wanted. "We want your head, gringo," a voice answered, "we do not want for any of you gringos to govern us, as we have come to kill you." Bent asked, "What wrong have I done you? I have always helped you, I have cured you when you were sick and I have never charged you." Another voice answered, "Yes, but you have to die now so that no North American is going to govern us." Then the shooting started, arrows and bullets, and the door fell in. Bent took several arrows, and after he was on the floor someone decapitated him. The mob suddenly calmed down, its bloodlust satisfied. The women and children had been trying to dig their way through a back wall, but the rioters set them free because they were New Mexicans, although they had married Anglos.[52]

That was not the end of the uprising but the beginning. The Taos mob resumed its rampage through town and then outward. The leaders sent runners to other villages and towns, including Santa Fe, urging the Indians and *Hispanos* to kill all Anglos and all Mexicans who cooperated with them. The result was savage violence, put down by even worse savagery. It spread fast. On January 20 and 21, twelve miles north of Taos, several hundred Pueblos and *peones* surrounded a flour mill and distillery at Arroyo Hondo, setting the compound afire and killing seven of its ten defenders. At Mora, a village over the mountains to the east, another group led by Manuel Cortez, one of the runners from Taos, killed seven Anglos and a Frenchman. Another party killed two more on the Río Colorado. At the same time, led by Pablo Chavez, Jesús Tafoya, a Taos Indian named Tomasito (also known as Tomás Baca), and Pablo Montoyo, who dubbed himself "Santa Anna del Norte," the main body of Taos rebels marched toward Santa Fe, driven on by a proclamation issued by Tafoya and Antonio María Trujillo calling for a general insurrection to begin on the twenty-second. Price sent word to his detachments in Albuquerque and elsewhere to close on Santa Fe or join him on the march north. Anglos in Santa Fe had some idea of the scale of the danger. Ceran St. Vrain, Bent's business partner, raised a volunteer company of Anglo laborers, merchants, and mountain men, called them the "Avengers," and offered to join Price.

As the Taos rebels had known from the beginning, it was a *guerra de las Castas,* a race war, Anglos on one side, *Hispanos* and *Indios* on the other. Price led 353 men, including St. Vrain's scurvy crew, out of Santa Fe on January 23, taking along four mountain howitzers, aiming to drive the rebels up the Rio Grande. Two more companies of Missouri volunteers joined him on the march with a 6-pounder. About 1,500 insurgents led by Tafoya assembled on a hilltop near the village of Santa Cruz de la Cañada, but a cannonade drove them off. They left behind thirty-six dead, including Tafoya. Meanwhile, a company of Missourians cornered about 150 rebels at Mora, killing fifteen, capturing another fifteen, with a loss of five on the Anglo side, but the Anglos retreated. Another detachment took the place and burned it down on February 1. Rebels retreating from Mora under Manuel Cortez vanished into the mountains.

The rebels believed they had justice on their side. What they really needed was firepower. They blocked the road to Taos in a narrow canyon near Embudo on January 29; again the Anglo guns drove them off. Four days later Price's corps entered the town of Taos and marched on to the Indian Pueblo de Taos. The insurgents had forted up in the *pueblo*'s church. Price bombarded the place, but his guns were not heavy enough to penetrate thick adobe masonry. He tried again on February 4, his guns opening fire at nine in the morning, his men ordered to charge the church two hours later. A small party dodged through rebel fire to the church's wall, chopped a hole through it, lit the fuses on some artillery shells, and tossed them inside. Another crew ran the 6-pounder up and fired through the hole, after which the church was taken. Many inside escaped into the Taos *pueblo,* while others took to the hills, where the Avengers ran them down and butchered them.

The insurgents surrendered on February 5 after losing at least 150 killed, including Pablo Chavez. Price had lost seven killed and forty-five wounded. As he had done in December, Price summoned a court-martial. Montoyo was convicted of treason and hanged on February 7. Tomasito was shot by a guard while being held for trial. Other defendants were arrested and confined at both Taos and Santa Fe, charged with treason and murder. They were set free when word of the trials reached Washington. Marcy formally reprimanded Price for exceeding his authority, saying the insurgents could not be charged with treason because they owed no allegiance to the United States.[53]

Price declared himself "certain that the New Mexicans entertain deadly hatred against the Americans," and he was not about to let another rebellion occur. The colonel ruled the territory alone through most of 1847. When the legislature met for the first time in December, he ignored it, and by February 1848 he had abolished most territorial offices and ruled as military dictator. His successors continued the practice.[54]

There was never again such an uprising against *gringo* rule in New Mexico. *Nuevomexicano* resistance went underground instead. Banditry plagued the territory into the twentieth century, reflecting hostility to alien occupation reaching back to the Pueblo Rebellion of 1680. Manuel Cortez was the only major leader of the Taos Rebellion who escaped. He organized his men into a guerrilla band and raided outposts in eastern New Mexico and traffic along the Santa Fe Trail until the end of the war and beyond. The *bandido en el héroe,* the hero-bandit, lived on in Cortez, Joaquín Murieta in California, Juan Cortina and Gregorio Cortez in Texas, and Heraclio Bernal, Jesús Malverde, and many others in Mexico and the United States.

CHAPTER

15

THEY WERE REALLY TRYING TO SHOOT US!

(January–February 1847)

War begun without good provision of money beforehand for
going through with it is but as a breathing of strength and blast
that will quickly pass away. Coin is the sinews of war.

—François Rabelais

AYLOR ADVANCED PART OF HIS ARMY to Agua Nueva, seventeen
miles south of Saltillo, in December 1846. Archibald Yell's Arkansas
Volunteers, the "Rackensackers," were on outpost duty around the village.
They celebrated Christmas with an orgy of rape, murder, and destruction.
In retaliation, on February 9 one of them was killed and mutilated just outside the Arkansas camp. About a hundred volunteers went looking for revenge the next morning and entered a nearby *pueblo,* Catana. The
Rackensackers opened fire and chased the civilians into a nearby cave,
where they killed and scalped the victims, men, women, and children. The
official report said there were four Mexicans killed, but Anglo eyewitnesses put the toll at twenty-five to thirty. Troops from other regiments
rushed to the scene, where they found what Private Samuel Chamberlain

called "a horrid sight." The cave "was full of our volunteers yelling like fiends, while on the rocky floor lay over twenty Mexicans, dead and dying in pools of blood. Women and children were clinging to the knees of the murderers and shrieking for mercy." An Illinois company drove the Arkansawyers off at bayonet point. Taylor ordered Yell to produce the murderers, but he did not. "Such deeds," Taylor declared to his whole army, "cast indelible disgrace upon our arms and the reputation of our country."[1]

I'LL BE D——D IF I RUN AWAY!

Taylor's army evaporated around him through January 1847. The heaviest loss came when Scott ordered Worth's division to the Vera Cruz expedition. Scott advised Taylor to pull back to Monterey, but Old Zach ignored him. Taylor was not worried about anything Santa Anna might do. He was more upset about Polk's intentions, calling Worth's transfer an attempt to drive him from his command.[2]

Taylor thought he had good reasons to maintain station beyond Saltillo. Thanks to the atrocious behavior of his troops, the country between Monterey and the Rio Grande was in an uproar. Old Zach preferred facing Santa Anna's army over forting up at Monterey. If he was besieged there, he said later, "it would have been the signal for the rising of the whole country; every depot on the Rio Grande would have been at once abandoned, taken, or destroyed."[3]

Taylor's army gained one important addition in January when Captain Ben McCulloch rode into camp at the head of a company of rangers. Old Zach had been just as happy to see the Texians leave after Monterey, but McCulloch had been a competent scout. The rangers skirmished with irregulars at a fortified hacienda called Encarnación, a lonely spot about fifty miles south of Saltillo. When he heard about that, Wool sent another party, fifty Arkansas cavalry under Major Solon Borland, in that direction. Wool warned the major to "be careful not to let the enemy get the advantage" of him. The patrol got to Encarnación on January 19 but found no Mexicans. Instead of returning to Saltillo Borland stayed in the hacienda and called for more men.[4]

Butler sent some Kentucky cavalry on a three-day trip east and south of Agua Nueva. They found no enemy troops and continued west to Encarnación. The two parties united under Borland's command, probed the country southward, and returned to Encarnación late on January 22. Borland posted no pickets. The Anglos got up the next morning to find themselves surrounded by about 500 Mexican lancers who bagged the five officers and sixty-six men and marched them south.[5]

When Wool heard from an escapee about the capture he sent five companies of Arkansawyers under Yell himself, who disobeyed his orders to be careful by riding his horses into the ground all the way to Encarnación. There he heard that General José Vicente Miñón was in front of him with 3,000 lancers, so Yell limped back to Saltillo. Another patrol of Kentucky cavalry, drunk on stolen *pulque,* got itself captured on the morning of January 27 about thirty miles from Encarnación.[6]

The capture of three patrols in such a sorry fashion persuaded Wool that the Mexican army was coming at him in strength. Taylor assigned Wool undivided command of troops around Saltillo and sent Butler back to Monterey. Butler went home February 9 because the wounds he received at Monterey had not healed. Old Zach left Monterey for Saltillo on January 31 with the last of his reserves.[7]

Taylor did not think it possible that a big army could come up from San Luis Potosí during the winter without water, so he concentrated his army south of the narrow Angostura Pass around the crossroads at Agua Nueva. There were 4,650 men camped there by February 14, spread over a wide plain. There were forbidding heights all around, but scouts warned Taylor that the camp could be bypassed on trails through the mountains. Nevertheless, Agua Nueva went from being a forward outpost to the army's base.[8]

Taylor was leading with his chin. Near Encarnación on February 16 McCulloch's Texians skirmished with Mexican cavalry, the advance screen of the army from San Luis. Old Zach remained cool, his major concern on the twentieth being a fistfight between a brigadier general and a colonel. A large cavalry patrol went out that day, saw some Mexican signals, and captured a lancer, who told them that Santa Anna was nearby. McCulloch's rangers spotted a Mexican encampment near Encarnación and reported that Santa Anna was in the area with a very large army.[9]

According to Samuel Chamberlain, Wool insisted that the army pull back from Agua Nueva to the pass called la Angostura (the Narrows), moving the supply depot behind that to Hacienda San Juan de Buena Vista. Old Zach flatly refused. "I'll be d——d if I run away!" he roared. Wool said he would take responsibility, so Taylor told him to "go to h——l in his own way," and stormed off in a huff. The army pulled back.[10]

Taylor ordered Yell's Arkansas cavalry to provide a rear guard at Agua Nueva to cover the evacuation of supplies. Yell's pickets were driven in by Mexican cavalry about midnight on February 20, and the Arkansawyers panicked and burned the stores. Santa Anna mistook Yell's troops for the whole Anglo army. As for the defense at Angostura, Taylor told Wool to "make such disposition of the troops on the arrival of the enemy as you may deem necessary." Old Zach then rode off with two regiments and two batteries, going the five miles to Saltillo to meet any cavalry raids.[11]

Taylor, not forgetting his presidential ambitions, made sure that he put the best face on the situation. He told a correspondent from the *New York Tribune,* "Let them come; damned if they don't go back a good deal faster than they came."[12]

ALL YOUR WANTS WILL BE SUPERABUNDANTLY SUPPLIED

Santa Anna was indeed coming. He thought to the end of his life that his work that winter was his finest achievement. "By my efforts," he claimed in his memoirs, "in January of 1847, the inhabitants of San Luis Potosí could survey a well-equipped, thoroughly instructed army of some eighteen thousand men, marching in four divisions."[13]

The army was not as magnificent as the Soldier of the People remembered. The illiterate conscripts and jailbirds were scarcely trained and poorly armed with a variety of muskets, many broken, many lacking bayonets. The cavalry carried sabers and flintlock pistols, and most had lances. The artillery could not compete with that of the Anglos in either punch or mobility. Most soldiers had never fired a weapon before. They dreaded the march ahead, and not on their own account alone—thousands of women and children went along. A few men had shabby frock coats, but generally they lacked blankets and hats, except for homemade shakoes of palm leaves lined with calico. The troops started out with some raw meat, a few tortillas, and in some cases a handful of corn.[14]

A Mexican patrol intercepted an Anglo messenger on January 13 and got a copy of Scott's order to Butler listing the troops withdrawn from Taylor's army. Taylor was weakened enough that Santa Anna could do some real damage to the *gringo* cause before the enemy took the logical next step and landed at Vera Cruz. He ordered General José Urrea to take 6,700 cavalry and cooperate with the *guerrilleros* under Canales to cut the Anglo communications between Monterey and the Rio Grande. Miñón with more cavalry would harass Taylor's army, pinning it down until the main corps reached the scene. Santa Anna hoped his army's numbers would offset the superior artillery and musketry on the North American side. In addition, Urrea could block Taylor's retreat. If everything worked out, Santa Anna could entirely eliminate the enemy in the northeast.[15]

The Soldier of the People ordered the Division of the North to march out on January 27, baggage reduced to what the men could carry. "The Mexican soldier is well known for his frugality and capability of sufferance," he told the *soldados.* "Today you commence your march, through a thinly settled country, without supplies and without provisions; but you may be assured that very quickly you will be in possession of those of your enemy, and of his riches; and with them, all your wants will be superabundantly supplied."[16]

Miñón and the vanguard rode out of San Luis on January 27, followed by brigades at one-day intervals under Brigadier Generals Francisco Pacheco, José García Conde, and Francisco Pérez, with the last two brigades under Major General Luis Guzmán leaving on the thirty-first. Santa Anna left on February 2 in a fancy carriage pulled by eight handsome mules, escorted by the Regiment of Hussars. The total manpower on the rolls was 21,553 men with twenty-one artillery pieces of mostly low quality. On the road the army passed the Anglo Encarnación prisoners, who were greatly impressed by the *caudillo* and his staff and by the five mules carrying Santa Anna's gamecocks.[17]

The route was over high, rugged desert, due north more than 300 miles to Saltillo, through passes at Agua Nueva, Piñones, and el Carnero, then down the center of a valley between two ranges of the Sierra Madre. The poor clothing, brutally cold weather, and lack of water told early: three men died of the cold on the first day. A freezing rain fell most of the first week, but on February 5 a few hours of good weather set in, after which the heat rose to furnace levels. The men made their situation worse by throwing away rations and other necessities to lighten their loads. Their leaders were mostly incompetent and ignorant of the rules of the march. The lead division reached Encarnación on February 17, after covering almost 300 miles in three weeks. This amazing performance was all the more remarkable for the burdens this army bore. Still, the road behind was lined with thousands of dead men and women feasted on by coyotes, along with broken wagons, dead livestock, and deserters scattered in the brush.[18]

The horror of the march had one positive effect—it weeded out the weak and the timid. The roll call at Encarnación counted 15,142 troops on September 20, meaning Santa Anna had killed off almost a quarter of his army on the march. Ordering an advance for the next day, the Soldier of the People told the women not to go along, but most did anyway.[19]

Santa Anna, knowing that the Anglos had no idea just how fast a Mexican army could cover ground, force-marched his men across the bone-dry rough land between Encarnación and Agua Nueva. There they camped, the night so cold they could not sleep. Santa Anna sent a note to Taylor the next morning advising him that he was surrounded "and cannot, in any human probability, avoid suffering a rout, and being cut to pieces with your troops." Because the Mexican general held the Anglo one in "consideration and particular esteem," he offered to save him from a "catastrophe." He gave Taylor an hour to "surrender at discretion." Old Zach answered stiffly, "I beg leave to say that I decline acceding to your request."[20]

Santa Anna had been confident of victory because the sight of the burning camp at Agua Nueva had persuaded him that the *Gringos* had panicked. He knew the narrow pass up ahead would not be as favorable a battlefield for his larger force as the broad plains Wool had withdrawn from. Grousing about the refusal of the women and children to stay at Encarnación, he ordered his tired, hungry, and thirsty troops on to Angostura, not letting them fill their canteens or the cavalry to water its horses.

February 22 began as a clear, frosty morning with a breeze as Santa Anna's army closed up on the pass. To an Anglo officer, "Nature was there in her grandeur and her power, and as far as the eye could reach, the peaks of the Sierra Madre were towering in the skies." General Julián Juvera formed a line in front with 3,000 horse soldiers. The shafts of their lances pierced the sky, banners floating on the wind, steel armor and sabers glittering in the sun. The North American position looked to one of the officers "like a gigantic octopus, with the arms or tentacles the hills and ravines reaching out from one or the other line of the mountains, perpendicular to the road and cutting it in a few places." The enemy soldiers, in their dark, dusty uniforms, were not so clearly seen, except for the artillery moving around on the mesa.

The view from the opposite direction was more interesting. Partly offsetting the men lost on the march, Santa Anna had gained a light infantry brigade under Ampudia and a reinforced regiment of engineers under General Santiago Blanco. The infantry deployed behind the cavalry and an Illinois volunteer watched them "in their long tall hats, bedecked with tinsel, & their Blue over coats streaming in the wind:——& what was more *interesting* to us just then, their long glittering muskets pointing directly at us as if they were really trying to *shoot us*!" A Kentuckian focused on the black flag, meaning no quarter, flying behind the Mexican troops. "All with whom I have spoken on the subject told me they expected to die there, and then," he wrote home.[21]

The landscape favored the defense. The road from San Luis ran through Angostura Pass, only forty feet wide and easily blocked. It was guarded on the east by abrupt cliffs and on the west by a small river and a tangle of steep arroyos impossible for artillery to cross. The road proceeded north hugging the steep west side of a mesa that varied from two to three miles wide, cut by a series of arroyos at roughly right angles to the road. Some of these ditches ran almost a mile and half toward the sharp slopes of the Sierra Madre. There was a high ridge beyond the mesa, going around the Yankee position about four miles to Buena Vista, but it did not look inviting to an attacker.

FINISH THE BATTLE AT ONE BLOW

Wool had 4,750 men, including the sick, to confront Santa Anna's 14,000 or so. The North Americans were mostly green volunteers; only 700 had ever seen combat. The artillery serving eighteen guns and the dragoons, however, were well-trained regulars. Wool had scouted the uneven mesa just north of Angostura, extending up the road a mile and a quarter to Buena Vista, in December, and sketched out a defense to bottle the enemy up in the pass.[22]

Wool set up on the "octopus" mesa that dominated the scene. There were only three possible approaches to his position: the main road on the front and two routes around his left. The road from San Luis was easily blocked, hemmed in by the cliffs on the east and the stream and arroyos on the west. Wool stationed a five-gun field battery on the road, covered by the 1st Illinois Infantry divided between two rises on the left and right, where the men set up breastworks. The mesa was an irregular plain flanking the road on the east, wide and flat, elevated about fifty feet. It was accessible to artillery and cavalry via an arroyo about a mile and a half east of the narrows, making the second possible approach to the Anglo position. There Wool posted the 2nd Kentucky on the rise above guns that he planted in two batteries on the south edge of the mesa. On the Kentuckians' left and about a half mile behind stood the 2nd Illinois, with General Joseph Lane's two-regiment Indiana Brigade along the ridge to the left. The troops from Kentucky, Illinois, and Indiana formed a line roughly northwest to southeast, facing southwest. The dismounted Kentucky and Arkansas cavalry regiments were posted to the left of the Hoosiers, covering the area between them and the mountains. The high ridge that reached behind the North Americans to Buena Vista, Wool believed, needed no defense. He kept two squadrons of regular dragoons and the company of Texians in reserve near Buena Vista, to be joined by Jefferson Davis' Mississippi Rifles, on the road from Saltillo.

Santa Anna made the most of the confined space where his army stood. Two infantry divisions under Major Generals Manuel María Lombardini and Francisco Pacheco held the center with fourteen guns backing them up. Santa Anna put his best troops, Blanco's engineers, on his left with three 16-pounders on high ground behind them. Ampudia's light infantry and Brigadier General Julián Juvera's heavy cavalry brigade, with two batteries, guarded the Mexican right. Mexican artillery was relatively

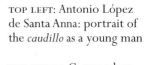

TOP LEFT: Antonio López de Santa Anna: portrait of the *caudillo* as a young man

TOP RIGHT: Commodore Robert F. Stockton of the Pacific Squadron
(Department of the Navy)

MIDDLE LEFT: Lucas Alamán y Escalada, Mexico's conservative conscience

MIDDLE RIGHT: General Mariano Arista, 1847

BOTTOM LEFT: President James K. Polk
(National Archives)

BOTTOM RIGHT: Commodore David Conner of the Home Squadron
(Department of the Navy)

TOP LEFT: Kit Carson and John Charles Frémont
(Department of the Army)

TOP RIGHT: General Zachary Taylor, "Old Zach,"
all gussied up for his presidential campaign
(Department of the Army)

MIDDLE RIGHT: Senator Thomas Hart Benton,
the "Thunderer" *(Library of Congress)*

BOTTOM: Pacific Dreamland: Monterey,
California, 1826, by William Smyth

TOP LEFT: General Winfield Scott, "Old Fuss and Feathers"
(Department of the Army)

TOP RIGHT: a Texas Ranger, as seen by a regular officer
(National Park Service)

MIDDLE RIGHT: *El Bandido en el Héroe* (the hero-bandit),
as stereotyped in Mexico by the late 19th century

BELOW: Flying battery in action,
Battle of Palo Alto *(Department of the Army)*

TOP LEFT:
United States volunteer, as
drawn by a Missourian
*(from Hughes, Doniphan's
Expedition, 1847)*

TOP RIGHT:
General Stephen
Watts Kearny
(Department of the Army)

MIDDLE RIGHT: Manuel Armijo,
by A. Waugh, 1840, on his way to becoming
a "mountain of fat," six years before
losing New Mexico to Kearny

BELOW: Santa Fe, New Mexico, 1846
(Department of the Army)

TOP LEFT: General Pedro de Ampudia, whose gallant defense of Monterey ended in surrender

TOP RIGHT: Commodore Matthew Calbraith Perry of the Home Squadron
(Department of the Navy)

MIDDLE LEFT: Colonel Alexander Doniphan
(Department of the Army)

BELOW: Street fighting, Monterey, contemporary print

TOP LEFT: Manuel de la Peña y Peña, interim president during the peace talks

TOP RIGHT: Nicholas Trist
(National Archives)

MIDDLE RIGHT: Andrés Pico, victor at San Pasqual, signer of Treaty of Cahuenga

BELOW: The Mormon Battalion preparing to march out, contemporary painting
(Utah State Historical Society)

ABOVE: Battle of Angostura/Buena Vista, by Carl Nebel
(from The War Between the United States and Mexico Illustrated, 1851)

BELOW: Battle of Chapultepec, by Carl Nebel
(from The War Between the United States and Mexico Illustrated, 1851)

The Disturnell Map, attached to the United States' copy of the Treaty of Guadalupe Hidalgo (*National Archives*)

immobile, so the Soldier of the People personally emplaced two batteries on high ground behind his center. His chief engineer, General Ignacio Mora y Villamil, and chief of artillery, General Antonio Carona, located the three heavy guns of the Foreign Legion (Batallón de San Patricio) overlooking Blanco on the left. All guns were set up on high ground to enfilade the North American lines.

Santa Anna intended Lombardini and Pacheco to carry his main assault against the mesa, and spent most of the morning getting the troops into position. After noon, however, he discovered that Wool had left his eastern flank open, covered only by the dismounted cavalry in the space between the mesa and the tall ridge to the east. He therefore ordered Ampudia and Juvera to take the high ground that gave access to Wool's rear at Buena Vista. As a diversion, Santa Anna ordered Brigadier General Francisco Mejía's cavalry brigade against the enemy right. As he had done at Palo Alto, Taylor had insisted that Wool reinforce his right, but the ground was impassable, Mejía's movements were a feint, and the Anglo troops were wasted there.

Ampudia and Juvera jumped off a little after three in the afternoon, but their advance bogged down in inconclusive skirmishing. Wool transferred several companies to the area, and toward sundown the North Americans withdrew up the base of the ridge. Darkness put an end to the shooting, and both sides settled down for the night where they were. The night turned bitter cold with a heavy rain, and neither army could light fires. Relief parties brought food and blankets to the North Americans huddled on the slopes. The Mexican *soldados* got neither and suffered all through the dark hours.

Santa Anna proved himself better at planning an action than executing one. His decision to mount a great assault against the *yanqui* center-left with Pacheco and Lombardini's men was a sound one, but he was too easily diverted by the temptation that the enemy's far left could be turned. Ampudia and Juvera already commanded the Anglo left, keeping it immobile, from where they stood at the beginning. Taylor was not much better a tactician. While the skirmishing went on at the east end of the line, Old Zach suddenly developed a fear that Saltillo was vulnerable to Miñón's cavalry. He took Davis' Mississippians and the dragoons and headed north. Satisfied that Saltillo was safe, Taylor returned to Buena Vista with the dragoons early on the morning of February 23. The Mississippians were not far behind him, but they had spent a day and a night marching south, then north, then south again.

Wool was in trouble. He had about 3,000 men spread over too large a position. Santa Anna seemed determined to turn the Yankee left, as the men there could hear reinforcements moving up to Ampudia's position. Also during the night, the Mexican commander moved five 8-pounders to high ground overlooking the United States lines about 800 yards off, close enough for the faulty Mexican guns to be effective. Wool sent reinforcements to his left and shuffled the troops strung along his main front. The dragoons and McCulloch's Texians covered gaps between infantry regiments, while one Indiana regiment was held in reserve. Not much was left to protect Buena Vista.

Santa Anna tried psychological warfare on the twenty-third, putting on a grand sunrise display to awe the *Gringos*. Buglers blew reveille for different units at different times, making the army sound bigger than it was. The bands filled the air with music as the infantry and cavalry deployed in a long line. The North Americans were impressed by what they saw, not knowing that the Mexican uniforms looked better from a distance than close up. "The Cavalry was magnificent!" exclaimed Chamberlain of the dragoons. He counted six thousand "cavaliers" who were "richly caparisoned in uniforms of blue faced with red, with waving plumes and glittering weapons." They slowly advanced and he was sure they would "ride down our little band and finish the battle at one blow." The infantry came forward and the two arms formed a great, colorful line, regimental bands in front. Next, "a procession of ecclesiastical dignitaries with all the gorgeous paraphernalia of the Catholic Church advanced along the lines" while the bands played a solemn anthem. "The air was so clear we could see every movement: The Infantry knelt down, the Cavalry lowered their lances and uncovered, and their colors dropped as the benedictions were bestowed."[23]

The real show was about to begin. Ampudia pressed slowly northward, driving the Anglos back, aiming to open a way for Juvera's cavalry to sweep down the eastern ridge into the enemy rear. On Santa Anna's left Blanco's engineers and some pickup companies, supported by cavalry, jabbed up the road until devastated by blasts from the guns there. Heavy, stinking smoke spread over the battlefield from both ends as Santa Anna put his original plan into motion. Ampudia's steady advance against withering musketry opened a gap toward the North American left. Lombardini's division charged out of an arroyo onto the mesa, faced to the left, and in a startling parade-ground maneuver formed a column of brigades. Pacheco's division came up from behind and performed the same movements on Lombardini's right, while Ortega's division and Juvera's cavalry brigade moved up in support. About 7,000 *soldados* stormed into the 2nd Indiana, which was backed up by three guns. Wool ordered the Indiana Brigade's General Lane to hold the line "at all cost." Lane ordered

one regiment forward with another following in support. Combined musketry and artillery fire tore bloody gaps in the Mexican flank but did not
stop the advance. Pacheco's division took the brunt of this damage, two of
its battalions scattering in disorder—"dispersed," as one Mexican officer
put it. He believed that if Wool had counterattacked then, it would have
produced a disaster on the Mexican side.[24]

Santa Anna rode close behind Lombardini and Pacheco until his horse
was shot from under him. Lombardini was wounded, and the mobile
Anglo artillery wreaked havoc on the stationary 16-pounders toward the
Mexican left. Yet they and other guns kept pounding the Hoosiers, and
Lombardini's gritty *soldados* kept coming on, firing devastating volleys.
Lane ordered two Indiana regiments to move up again. One did, but the
colonel of the 2nd Indiana ordered his regiment to cease fire and retreat,
and the men turned and ran, leaving ninety casualties and a 4-pounder on
the field. Lombardini's assault then fell on the 2nd Illinois and an artillery
section. Two colonels organized a slow, fighting withdrawal in the face of
nearly the entire Mexican division. This widened the gap between the
main North American line and the troops to the east, and Ampudia
stepped up his pressure. The Anglos of the dismounted cavalry retreated to
the mesa, and once the troopers got back to their horses many of them
mounted and galloped in panic north toward Buena Vista. By nine in the
morning Juvera had an opportunity to lead his cavalry around the enemy
left toward the supply dump at the hacienda.

Wool's position was disintegrating, bent back against the road with its
left on Buena Vista. Taylor arrived with his dragoon escort, telling Wool
that Davis' Mississippi Rifles were coming up behind him. Wool advised
Taylor to prepare for a general retreat if necessary, but Old Zach's mere
presence stiffened everyone's spine. Taylor took position near one of the
batteries on the road, leaving Wool in tactical command. He had one great
strength, and that was the several artillery batteries he had deployed along
his position. Major Bliss rode down the line and returned to tell Taylor that
in his opinion the United States troops had been whipped. "I know it," Old
Zach answered, "but the volunteers don't know it. Let them alone, we'll
see what they do."[25]

The Anglos had another advantage. The Mexican *soldados* were as ferocious in the assault as any troops in the world, but they were bad shots.
One soldier wrote a friend about how he and others had retreated into an
arroyo to find cover, but Mexican troops found them. The *soldados* began
firing into the North Americans, but "they are most miserable shots, or
they would have killed every one of us, huddled as we were in the bottom
of that narrow ravine."[26]

When things looked bleakest for Taylor's army the Mississippi Rifles arrived at Buena Vista. "This gallant regiment," said an awed Samuel Chamberlain, "passed by us with the light swinging step peculiar to Indians and hunters." They looked good, too, "their uniforms a red shirt worn outside of their white duck pants, and black slouch hats, armed with Windsor Rifles, and eighteen-inch Bowie Knives." Chamberlain despised volunteer officers, but Jefferson Davis was a West Pointer, "and a brave able officer."[27]

Wool ordered Davis to cover Buena Vista along with an infantry regiment and one gun, with cavalry in front. His position was stronger than it looked. His left, resting on Buena Vista, had just been strengthened with fresh troops. His center was thin but it stubbornly held the high ground, and the right was anchored above the mess of arroyos across the road. Then things went to hell on the left. Juvera's cavalry was aiming for the supply train at the hacienda, and Wool sent his regular dragoons to the threatened area, where they found Yell of the Arkansas cavalry and Colonel Humphrey Marshall of the Kentucky horsemen arguing over seniority. The regular ignored the volunteers, but Marshall's orders to fire and Yell's to hold fire threw everyone into turmoil. When Juvera's lead got to the scene most of the volunteers fled, except for a handful around Yell. An international brawl ensued. Yell went down while the dragoons hit Juvera's column in the flank, splitting it in two. The advance continued past the hacienda into murderous fire from a North American battery guarding the north. The dragoons chased the rear section back into the next section of lancers coming up and scrambled the whole Mexican cavalry, which came under devastating artillery fire. Volleys and a charge from the Mississippi Rifles and other infantry near Buena Vista sent what was left of Juvera's column fleeing into the mountains to the east.

Juvera had been hit from two sides because the remaining *Yanquis* on the east moved up to join the other troops at the hacienda. Anglo fugitives from Lombardini's assault also took up positions on the plateau, the units together forming a long V formation with the open end toward the Mexican cavalry. Juvera charged into the opening, close enough for the Mississippians to empty many saddles. The Mexican survivors retreated into an arroyo where 2,000 men from the divisions of Lombardini, Pacheco, and Ortega huddled. Lieutenant José María Montoya, showing unusual initiative for a Mexican subaltern, was more than equal to this situation. Taking three other officers with him, he galloped to the United States lines bearing a white flag. Firing ceased, and Montoya was taken to see Taylor. In Santa Anna's name he demanded to know "what General Taylor wanted." This confused Old Zach, who sent Wool under a flag to meet with Santa Anna, but Mexican artillery stopped that. Taylor and other officers suddenly realized that Montoya had tricked them: during the lull in shooting, the men in the arroyo had made it back to the main Mexican force.

While the fight for the hacienda continued, Miñón's cavalry showed up at Saltillo, but the commander decided that the town's defenses were too stout to attack. The lancers retired to the southwest followed by a detachment of United States infantry and artillery. The two parties fought a brief skirmish at Molino de Arispa without doing much damage to either side. A yarn spread through Taylor's army that the only reason the Anglo troops caught the Mexican troopers at the mill was because Miñón had stopped to enjoy the charms of a North American teacher living there.[28]

Santa Anna remained convinced that his superior numbers would yet prevail over the devastating artillery and musketry on the other side. He brought up his remaining reserves, advanced his artillery so far as his gunners could do so, and shifted the engineers regiment to the right. He reorganized what was left of Lombardini's, Pacheco's, Ampudia's, and Ortega's corps into a new division under General Francisco Pérez and ordered the attack to resume. The new column stormed onto the mesa at about five in the afternoon, right into a hail of shot and canister from artillery that Wool had shifted to meet the threat. Anglo troops counterattacked with a motley collection of men from three different regiments who crashed into Pérez's main body just as it crested the mesa. The result was a hand-to-hand melee with bodies falling like rain on both sides. The United States artillery blasted bloody holes in the Mexican line, killing half the engineers troops, but the *soldados* persisted grimly, washing over the *Yanquis* like a storm wave. The Anglos retreated, leaving two guns behind. Taylor ordered another battery forward to hold the position before the Mexicans tore the Anglo line open. He told the gunners' commander to fire double loads of canister against the swiftly approaching enemy. The first salvo shocked the Mexican line into stopping. The next two drove it back, and Pérez retreated from the plateau with his survivors. Smoke drifted over the bloody scene, dead and dying men and horses everywhere.

The Division of the North had performed beyond anyone's expectations, but it had given all it had to give. Santa Anna took one last stab at the enemy as night approached, sending Brigadier General Anastasio Torrejón's cavalry brigade against Taylor's right, still protected by a battery on the road. The guns ripped men and horses to shreds. A sudden rain dampened everyone's powder, and the Battle of Angostura (or Buena Vista) was over. The rain ceased and a rainbow came out. The United States regular artillery had won the battle against the ferocious Mexican cavalry and infantry; Santa Anna's army simply could not match the gunnery on the other side. The Mexicans had levied a great butcher's bill on the invaders, however. Taylor's army was exhausted and almost out of ammunition, he had lost 673 killed and wounded, and about 1,500 others had deserted during the day. The victory, if it was one, belonged to Wool rather than to Taylor, who had mostly lent his encouraging presence.

Parties fanned out through the carnage to bring in wounded, while coyotes circled and yipped. As the men shivered in their positions through the frosty night they dreaded the day to come. The Army of Occupation surely faced annihilation when the larger Mexican army stormed into it again.

THE ARMY SEEMED MADE UP OF DEAD MEN

Santa Anna had lost 591 killed in action, 1,048 wounded, and 1,894 missing, of whom about 300 were prisoners of the North Americans. The Soldier of the People ordered his *soldados* to move out quietly after nightfall and retire to Agua Nueva. If Taylor attacked him there, Mexican numbers might tell against the *yanqui* artillery on the open field better than they had at the pass. Allowing for the fierce northern firepower, Santa Anna had contributed to his own defeat. He had had a good opening plan but departed from it when he saw an opportunity on the right. Except for the charge of Lombardini and Pacheco, he had committed troops piecemeal against superior gunnery.

The chief reason Santa Anna lost the battle, however, was a condition that he had helped to bring about since 1821. Mexico had a disorganized government, a corrupt army and civil service, and continual public chaos. Together they kept the country poor. Wars cost money, and although the Soldier of the People tried his hardest, he could never produce enough wherewithal to clothe, equip, or feed his troops. His own corruption and self-focus made it all worse, because he abused his *soldados* to death by the way he conducted the march north. Santa Anna really did not care about those who served under him, but amazingly he made them think that he had their interests at heart. That explains in part their gallant, often ferocious fighting during the battle. Without decent weapons or equipment they made up a far better army than the vainglorious *caudillo* deserved to lead. Now he had betrayed them again with his decision to retire from Angostura. His men were exhausted and hungry, but he had never shown compassion for them before; Santa Anna claimed in his memoirs that he retreated because the government ordered him to twice, in order to put down the Polko Rebellion.[29]

There was no such order, and Santa Anna was nearly to Mexico City before he heard about the *Polkos*. He offered that alibi because his officers declared publicly that his retreat insulted the army. Artillerist Manuel Balbontín believed that the men still had plenty of fight in them. Santa Anna's retreat, he said, "caused general and profound disgust among the troops; they saw with grief that they were going to lose the benefit of all the sacrifices that they had made; that the conquered field would be abandoned, and that the victory would be given to the enemy; and finally, to affirm the idea already general in the army—that it was impossible to conquer the North Americans." This last was a devastating condition, plaguing Mexican conscripts for the rest of the war.[30]

The Division of the North assembled late on February 24 at Agua Nueva. Many of the soldiers had not had any water in two or three days and plunged into a swamp beside the road. "But the water, rather than bring relief," said an officer, "only opened their graves, since as soon as they drank it they died with horrible convulsions." The few wounded who had made it this far died in "that filthy, disgusting and toxic brew." The sights and sounds of the dying destroyed whatever morale remained in the ranks.[31]

Taylor's men gathered all the Anglo and Mexican wounded they could find and sent them to Saltillo on supply wagons. Recalled one officer, "I rode over the whole field. Parties were engaged in burying the dead—but there were still hundreds of bodies lying still and cold with no covering save the scanty remnant of clothing which the robbers of the dead found too valueless to take from them. I saw the human body pierced in every place." The funerary details fought a losing race with coyotes and other scavengers and were visited by grieving *soldaderas* looking for their men among the dead. Even in the cold mountain air of February the blowflies sang.[32]

Santa Anna called a council of war on February 25, and his generals agreed that the retreat, once begun, should continue. Taylor had been stopped. Santa Anna climbed into his fancy carriage, summoned his hussars, loaded his fighting chickens, and hightailed it to Mexico City, leaving his battered army to fend for itself. Major Bliss rode in under a flag of truce on the twenty-sixth to arrange prisoner exchanges and relief for the wounded. Later that day Wool sent a party of dragoons to scout out Agua Nueva, and the next day Taylor himself led his army into the place. The Mexicans were visible retreating in the distance, but the Anglos did not try to catch them. They had left behind wounded by the hundreds, lacking transport or medical services for casualties. A Yankee detail inspected Encarnación on March 1 and found 222 injured Mexicans in the chapel in appalling conditions, the air "so foul and pestiferous that it seemed impossible to breathe it and live." The Anglos did what they could for the sufferers, then returned to Agua Nueva. Spring winds turned the camp there into a dust bowl, so Wool sent his men back to Buena Vista on March 9. Taylor's army had indeed been stopped.[33]

The retreat to San Luis Potosí, through the same harrowing conditions as before, destroyed the remainder of the Division of the North. "The army seemed made up of dead men; the miserable conditions to which the sick were reduced caused the skin of many to stick to their bones, and its shrinking exposed their teeth, giving to the countenance the expression of a forced laugh, which filled one with horror," said a reporter. Without transport, about 800 wounded were abandoned to the cold desert to die, the coyotes and feral dogs closing in. Cold, hunger, dysentery, desertion, and sheer exhaustion claimed at least 3,000 more lives. Among the casualties were uncounted women, probably thousands of them, and hundreds of children. The town of San Luis was devastated by the disappearance of so many of its womenfolk.[34]

Santa Anna raced to Mexico City to proclaim that he had won a great victory. Church bells rang, and for a time most people believed him. As for the rebellious *Polkos,* he claimed in his memoirs, "The terrorists recognized me as their President and obeyed my orders to lay down their arms and retired to their homes."[35]

THE PEOPLE OF THESE STATES HAD A HARD TIME

As Santa Anna rightly guessed, preparing to confront his own army forced Taylor to weaken his rear, so he sent Urrea and his cavalry to join up with Canales' irregulars and prey on the enemy supply lines. The Mexican horse soldiers hit the jackpot on February 22, 1847, when they met a supply train of 110 wagons and 300 pack mules about five miles from the village of Ramos. There were only thirty-four soldiers guarding the train, and they were bunched at its head, where they could not protect it. Most of the teamsters were killed in the first attack, but others were burned in their wagons or run down and killed in the chaparral, the bodies stripped and mutilated. The train was destroyed and the escort taken as prisoners of war. The event sent a shock wave through Taylor's army.[36]

Urrea next moved against Marín. The three-company garrison there held him off until relief arrived from Monterey on February 25. Meanwhile, part of the 2nd Ohio Volunteers assembled at Cerralvo and headed toward Monterey. They reached Marín later on the twenty-fifth, after the relieved troops had left. The Buckeyes resumed their march around midnight and soon skirmished with Urrea's lancers. The skirmishing ended when reinforcements reached the Ohio column. Urrea and Canales had closed the road.[37]

Taylor fanned out mounted patrols that burned villages to the ground on the excuse that they were near the attacks and must have supported them. His worst mistake was to send a company of Texians out under Captain Mabry "Mustang" Gray to investigate the Ramos attack and chase down the culprits. Gray was a veteran bandit and a bloodthirsty savage where Mexicans were concerned. When the Texians rode out Ohio volunteer Luther Giddings said it "seemed to bode evil to the neighboring ranchers." Sure enough, the Texians fell on the nearest *pueblo,* Rancho Guadalupe. They surrounded the place in the middle of the night, rounded up all twenty-four men asleep there, tied them up, and shot them in the head. Thereafter a guerrilla war between Texians and Mexicans went on for months in northeast Mexico and south Texas with appalling butchery on both sides. Other United States troops thought the Texians were nothing but savages, and Taylor himself complained in June that they could not leave camp without killing the first innocent Mexican they saw. He asked that no more troops be sent from Texas and in June sent those still with him home.[38]

Many guerrillas were *vaqueros* by trade and so were skilled with a rope. They used their lassos in battle and to grab North American stragglers and marauders. Wool issued an order that any Mexican found in Saltillo carrying a lasso should be shot, but Taylor countermanded it because it was condemnation without due process. On the other hand, his attempts to fine nearby villages or towns on the assumption that they supported guerrillas also condemned without proof. The road from Camargo to Monterey became the centerline of a miles-wide scorched zone. Raids by irregulars continued anyway.[39]

A soldier from Cincinnati wrote home after Buena Vista that the troops were plagued by "a set of army swindlers," camp followers who preyed on the soldiers. Colonel Yell's body was plundered as soon as he fell, and during the battle the looters stole 300 overcoats and about a thousand blankets from the supply wagons. Even promilitary observers condemned the atrocious parts of Taylor's army for "cowardly, unmanly behavior," as Kendall of the *Picayune* complained of the volunteers. The normally indulgent Taylor finally lost his own temper when he roared at one company of Ohio volunteers, "You are all a G-d d———d set of thieves and cowards; you never came here to fight, but to rob and plunder, and will run at the first sight of the enemy."[40]

Few Mexicans were willing to lodge complaints about Anglo depredations, according to Luther Giddings, "being afraid that they might incur a similar fate." Samuel Chamberlain lamented, "The people of these states had a hard time during the summer of 1847, plundered by both sides, their lives often taken and their wives and daughters outraged and carried off."[41]

Taylor and his Army of Occupation had transformed much of north-east Mexico into a moonscape, the "minds and feelings" of the people forgotten. But they had turned Santa Anna back at Angostura. Never again would a Mexican army, under Santa Anna or anybody else, march on San Antonio. *La Guerra de Tejas,* the Texas War, was at long last over.

PART TWO

LA GUERRA DE 47

(The War of '47)

(1847—1855)

SCENES OF AGONY AND BLOOD
FOLLOW ONE AFTER THE OTHER
(March 1847)

The earth cries out and asks for blood.... Thus is carried out
without cease, from maggot to man, the great law of the violent
destruction of living things. The entire world, continuously saturated
with blood, is nothing but an immense altar where all that lives must be
slaughtered without end ... until the death of death.

—Joseph de Maistre

By the time Winfield Scott was ready to invade Vera Cruz, the
United States had reached its territorial goals—California, New Mexico,
and the Rio Grande boundary. Scott's strategic aim was to force the
Mexican government to agree to the new state of territorial affairs by
appealing to the "minds and feelings" of the Mexican people. Law, not
barbarity, would govern his campaign, and he would provide the law
on his own.[1]

The commanding general turned to the International Law of War for
guidance on control of crime among his troops, occupation government,
the rights of the conquered, and how to deal with resistance. As the Law of
War—as opposed to United States law including its Articles of War, which
were silent—stood in 1847, there was a commonly accepted set of rules

that prescribed the rights and obligations of belligerents. The law defined war and combatants, the status of public property in a conquered area, protection of civilians and private property, treatment of prisoners, purchase of supplies, and the like.[2]

TELL OLD SCOTT HE WAS GOING HOME

Scott issued General Order 20 on February 19, 1847, setting forth rules of conduct for United States soldiers on foreign soil. Scott was as creative a lawgiver as the authors of the Kearny Code, and what he produced was both constitutional and precedent for future military governments.[3]

Rather than try to create a new civil government, as Kearny had done, Scott prescribed military government based on the existing civil authority. Military government must follow careful rules in buying supplies, levying contributions, seizing public property with military value while safeguarding other property, and helping civil authorities maintain order. United States officers could not compel Mexicans to fight nor compel labor. Scott protected freedom of speech and the press, although he had power to suppress hostile publications. He would not subject civilians to military law, but reserved the right to confine those who committed crimes against occupying troops.[4]

Scott's most notable contribution to military and international law was the "military commission," justified as an extension of Congress' power to declare war and raise and regulate armies. He could not use courts-martial to govern crimes against civilians because their jurisdiction did not cover acts outside the United States. Scott called specific war courts "military commissions" to distinguish them from courts-martial. What he did was consistent with the Law of War.[5]

The commissions dealt with crimes committed by his troops against Mexicans or each other. Their jurisdiction included an entire catalog of felonies, along with "the wanton desecration of churches, cemeteries, or other religious edifices and fixtures, the interruption of religious ceremonies," and all property crimes "whether committed by Mexicans or other civilians in Mexico against individuals of the U.S. military forces, or by such individuals against other such individuals or against Mexicans or civilians." Sentences were standard for the day—whipping, confinement at labor, or hanging.

Civilian crime would usually be tried before civil courts, so the chief purpose of Scott's commissions was to regulate the behavior of his soldiers. Military commissions, like courts-martial, ensured due process for defendants and were not a way to dodge the right of the accused to a proper trial. The commissions were repeatedly convened under general order by Scott, Wool, and Taylor, mostly in 1847. Most defendants were Anglo soldiers, and the offenses tried included almost every deed that would be a civil crime in the United States.[6]

The jurisdiction of military commissions did not cover Mexican offenses against the Law of War, so Scott created another novelty, the "council of war," similar to a military commission except for the types of cases it heard. These included violation of the Law of War by guerrillas, and enticing or attempting to entice soldiers to desert the United States service. There were few such trials, and the term "council of war" for a court of any type disappeared after the war in Mexico.[7]

Commissions and councils generally followed the procedures of courts-martial, although they were more summary. Their restraining influence is doubtful, although there were trials and executions for crimes against civilians. Watching one dragoon about to be hanged in January 1848 for "the killing of an inoffensive Mexican," a soldier noted in his diary that "the miserable wretch was intoxicated and . . . said tell old Scott he was going home, that he was one of the b'hoys."[8]

Old Fuss and Feathers declared "martial law" in and around all places occupied by United States troops. This added nothing useful to military government. Martial law, under the Law of War, applied only to military occupation within the army's own country in case of insurrection or other emergency. It was never put to use.[9]

Scott found little guidance from the Law of War on how to deal with *guerrilleros*. International law held that war could be carried on legally only by the recognized soldiery of the state, including regulars, militias, volunteers, and the like so long as officers were equally commissioned and privates equally enlisted and governed by regulations. The Law of War at that time did not recognize as legitimate irregular fighters not part of the organized forces of a belligerent; they could be summarily punished or killed when captured. Mexico's government had already announced the authorization of guerrillas as part of its defensive strategy, meaning patented guerrillas were legitimized in the eyes of their state. The Law of War vaguely granted the opposing side the option of recognizing or not the legality of such irregulars. Scott chose not to and declared guerrillas to be bandits, giving his troops a license to murder. In central Mexico as in the northeast, every dead Mexican became a dead bandit.[10]

Scott got little guidance from the classics. Frederick the Great's much-translated *Instructions to His Generals* did not bother with irregulars or how a regular army should deal with them. Antoine-Henri Jomini was especially popular in North America, his *Art of War* almost a bible. Jomini had seen the original *guerrilla* drive Napoleon out of Spain and watched other partisans ravage the French army in Russia and central Europe. He thought irregulars were beneath contempt.[11]

Treating guerrillas as criminals was counterproductive. Criminalizing an opponent because his appearance and methods were not fit for the parade ground was no substitute for counterguerrilla tactics. Punishing the population for guerrilla raids drove more people to join the resistance. Carl von Clausewitz treated irregulars as a respectable subject, but his works did not gain favor in the United States until after the Civil War. Clausewitz was a Prussian veteran of the Napoleonic wars who devoted a major section of his masterwork, *On War,* to guerrilla warfare. He advised any conquered nation to adopt guerrilla methods to stave off total defeat or submission after its regular armies were dispersed or destroyed. He thought a national resistance by irregular means was almost impossible for an invading regular army to defeat. Neither Scott nor Mexican leaders read Clausewitz, but the Mexicans harkened to his principles if not his words. If Scott had done so, he might have dealt with guerrillas realistically rather than prejudicially, inciting far less bloodshed, especially among civilians.[12]

THIS WAS NO REASON WHY WE SHOULD HAVE RENOUNCED OUR BIRTHRIGHTS

Guerrillas wreaked havoc in northeast Mexico. Tampico was in effect besieged by the occasional shot fired from the forest, unhinging the Anglo commander. He ordered that in the event of fire the entire garrison should turn out under arms, in case it was the signal for an attack. He limited the places on the Pánuco River where Mexican civilians could put in and became so fearful that he fired the whole local police force on the suspicion that they conspired against the occupation.[13]

Guerrillas everywhere produced psychological effects exceeding the physical damage they could do. They flooded Camargo with rumors that Taylor had been whipped at Buena Vista, terrifying the commander there, who asked the governor of Texas to call out 2,000 mounted men. The Matamoros newspaper reported Taylor's defeat on March 3, and New Orleans papers declared that Old Zach had lost 2,000 men and six guns and was cut off from relief. These yarns reached Washington on the twenty-fourth and sent Marcy and Polk into a tizzy. Orders went out to the commander at New Orleans to ask the governors of three southern states for twelve-month volunteers and to advise Scott that he might have to march to the Rio Grande.[14]

Taylor's report of his battle below Buena Vista put an end to the jitters when it reached Washington. He sent it with a civilian volunteer aide on

March 2. The messenger rode with a party of 260 men, mostly Ohio volunteers under Major Luther Giddings, whom Taylor sent to reopen the road from Monterey to Camargo with two guns and 150 wagons. The detail left Monterey on March 5, and on the afternoon of the seventh, scout reports warned of an attack by Canales' irregulars. Giddings parked the wagons, surrounded them with troops, and held off the guerrillas until dark. He lost forty wagons, however, when their teams bolted. The skirmish cost the United States two soldiers and fifteen teamsters dead.[15]

Taylor had more than 9,000 men available to him, all but about a thousand of them volunteers, so he had enough men to reopen his communications with the Rio Grande. After Giddings' rescue, the general sent the Kentucky cavalry down the road to Camargo. Taylor learned after they left that Urrea was near Marín. Gathering up some dragoons, a battery, and Jefferson Davis' Mississippians, he set out after the Kentuckians. Scouts reported Mexicans setting up an ambush on a train coming up from Camargo, so Taylor sent reinforcements to the train and personally led a chase to drive the guerrillas off. He did not catch them. Urrea retired on Montemorelos, and later in March left the region because Taylor's reinforced train escorts became too dangerous to attack.[16]

Putting muscle on the supply trains protected most of them, but the danger to drunks and stragglers persisted. Taylor's orders that neighboring communities must pay for goods lost to attacks on supply trains had little practical effect, especially as the villages burned down or were evacuated one by one. Having Texians in the army also kept the country stirred up.[17]

The other prizes of "Mr. Polk's War" were somewhat quieter. New Mexico was stunned and under Price's heel after the Taos Rebellion, but there were bandits in the hills, and out on the plains they and the Indian tribes preyed on the Santa Fe Trail. The ancient multisided raiding, counterraiding, and slave traffic continued as if the Anglo soldiers had never arrived. The situation in California in March 1847 was both more peaceful and more dubious. The Indians came under increasing pressure from both *Californios*—some southern tribes had sided with the Anglos during the fighting—and from Anglo immigrants. The latter brought in several debilitating diseases, and the native death toll climbed rapidly in the spring of 1847. Only on the Oregon border were the Klamath and affiliated tribes still formidable.[18]

The Californians remained resentful but realistic—with overwhelming *yanqui* military power in the province they would not rise again. Their anger was directed against the Mexican government for not defending the territory. "I admit that the general government of Mexico was like a very mean step-mother to us," Julio Carrillo complained, "but in my estimation this was no reason why we should have renounced our birthrights." The conquest of California by the United States was complete and irreversible. Rumors shook the Anglo command late in March that a Mexican army was marching up from Sonora, but they were false.[19]

Things were not so peaceful among the conquerors as Kearny set about getting his government to work. There were many details, including the absence of a prize court on the Pacific. Kearny established an admiralty court in California to support the navy's blockade. These courts processed ownership and claims of enemy ships and contraband captured in wartime. Kearny's tribunal was challenged and the case went all the way to the Supreme Court. The justices negated the court and its decisions because Kearny had exceeded his authority. This invalidated the whole United States blockade in the Pacific and produced a snarl of follow-up cases.[20]

The navy's campaign was not going well anyway. After the blockade was challenged by the British at Mazatlán in February, USS *Portsmouth* sailed to San José del Cabo and seized the little village on March 30. The ship did the same at San Lucas on April 3. Ten days later her captain hove to off La Paz and demanded the surrender of the province. The governor agreed, with conditions protecting the rights of his citizens and the continuity of his civil government. This collaboration outraged the people, who rose up, declared the governor deposed, and began guerrilla warfare.[21]

Kearny thought himself fully in control with the navy backing him up. Early in March he regularized the California Battalion, Frémont's little army, after Shubrick ordered all navy officers back to their ships. Kearny ordered Cooke of the Mormon Battalion to relieve Gillespie as commander in the south on March 1. This order also directed Gillespie to return to Washington and Frémont to bring his battalion records to Kearny at Monterey. Cooke was to muster out and reenlist the California Battalion as provided for by the laws governing volunteer troops.[22]

Frémont refused to muster his battalion for discharge, so in the middle of March Kearny sent Colonel Richard Mason to Los Angeles to inspect the battalion and give it its orders. He also carried an order for Frémont to report to Monterey prepared to return to Washington. The Pathfinder challenged Mason to a duel. Kearny put a stop to that nonsense and backed Frémont into a corner. As an officer in the army, he must obey orders. His battalion was mustered out in April.[23]

Frémont acknowledged no earthly superior save Senator Benton. He had already prepared a long report to his father-in-law and another to the War Department, presenting his side of the dispute with Kearny. Stockton sent the same kind of self-serving advice to the secretary of the navy, entrusting the message to Lieutenant Edward Beale, still suffering from his ordeal on the trek from San Pasqual to San Diego. He left in a party of ten men commanded by Kit Carson on February 25.

Carson owed his loyalty to Frémont, but he owed obedience to Kearny. If any single man deserved credit for the Anglo conquest of California, it was the talented mountain man. He had led Frémont there, and he had guided Kearny to southern California. Neither expedition would have made it without him. Now he was about to transplant the Kearny-Frémont feud to a new arena and tear a hole in President Polk's political alliance. Carson traveled by a familiar route along the Gila, skirmished with Apaches, and reached Taos in April. There he reunited with Josefa, whom he had not seen in over two years. He did not remain long, however, because he had a duty to fulfill. Besides, he looked forward to the trip east that Kearny had talked him out of earlier.[24]

NOTHING COULD EXCEED THE BEAUTY OF THIS SPECTACLE

While Carson struggled up the Gila River the eyes of two nations focused on Vera Cruz. The walled city covered a space of about a quarter mile by a half mile, the long axis paralleling the coast. Strong forts dominated each end, with several smaller bastions along a stone wall about fifteen feet high. About 19,000 people had lived there early in the 1800s, but warfare combined with yellow fever had reduced the population to only 6,500 by the early 1840s. Vera Cruz's harbor had unreliable and insecure anchorages, exposed to the violent northers. The chief defense was San Juan de Ullúa, standing on a reef about a half mile off the city. Built of red and black fossil coral, it was a large pentagon with corner bastions, covered on the east by a demilune, some redoubts, and a water battery.[25]

San Juan mounted 136 guns. A shipment of fifty tons of cannon powder had arrived in January, so technically there was a good supply of ammunition. Many guns, much of the powder, and large numbers of projectiles were substandard, however. General Juan Morales, the garrison commander, had 113 guns and 3,360 men on the city perimeter and another 1,030 men at San Juan, and they were short on rations. He had already told Mexico City that Vera Cruz was indefensible without reinforcements. Morales' troops included the city's national guard, about 800 men, plus 500 guardsmen from Orizava, 80 artillerists of a national guard artillery company, and 109 other volunteers. He had a few detachments of regulars, light infantry mostly, but the defense of the city really rested in the hands of amateurs.

The wife of the Spanish ambassador was appalled at her first sight of Vera Cruz just before the war. On one side stood the fort, on the other "the miserable, black-looking city, with hordes of large black birds, called *sopilotes* [*zopilotes,* buzzards], hovering over some dead carcass . . . not a tree, or a shrub, or flower, or bird, except the horrid black *sopilote*." The buzzards were protected by law because they kept the streets clean. Said another foreigner, "The galley slaves and the zopilotes constitute a large part of the most useful population of Vera Cruz," the former as laborers, the latter as scavengers.[26]

The walled city sat right on the water. Behind it extended a fairly level sandy plain reaching inland about two miles. Behind the flats a series of sand hills reached another mile or so from the city, the tallest about 300 feet high. Southeast of the city, engineered ponds and marshes drained into a small stream that provided the city's water, supplemented by cisterns. All was surrounded by a jungle, with a thick underbrush of thorny chaparral, towering tropical trees, prickly pear, wild aloes as big as tents, and the occasional palm rising thirty to forty feet. There were a few ranches here and there, but iguanas, colorful birds, and other wildlife dominated the hot, humid woods. And then there were the insects, most notably sand fleas, sand flies, gadflies, "and the chiga of the woods," as one Anglo called chiggers.[27]

Scott could not land at Vera Cruz itself, under the guns of San Juan and in the absence of any place to drive ashore in force. He had to put in somewhere else and make an inland campaign against the city. Vera Cruz faced northeast at the midpoint of a stretch of shore running northwest–southeast. About a mile to the southeast the shoreline made an abrupt turn to the south, and another mile or so farther on turned to run east–west. The gentle shore there, Collado Beach, was protected from weather by Isla de los Sacrificios (Isle of the Sacrifices) and a reef about a half mile offshore. The island and reef confined the space for ships to operate, but the beach was inviting. It was the best landing place, according to Commodore Conner, between Vera Cruz and Antón Lizardo.

Scott was ready to go by March 2, 1847, when most of his shipping was at Isla de los Lobos. His headquarters ship led the procession out, amid much cheering and singing, that afternoon. The landing fleet was nearly all at Lizardo by the fourth. Scott took his division commanders and his staff aboard a little steamer to scout out Vera Cruz harbor and Collado Beach. When the steamer was about a mile off San Juan de Ullúa, the fort fired one shot, the ball going over her, so the captain steered out of range. The fort could have opened with all its guns and decapitated the Yankee campaign.[28]

There was no sign of a defense at Collado. Conner proposed ferrying troops to the area in the larger warships and transport steamers, then rotating the supply ships to permit a buildup on shore without crowding the water. Naval officers would supervise all ship operations to prevent accidents. This altered Scott's original plan to dump everything onshore at once, but the general bowed to Conner's judgment. What resulted was a phased landing similar to the pattern followed later in World War II.[29]

Scott organized his army into three divisions, two of regulars under Worth and Twiggs and one of volunteers under Patterson, about 12,000 men in all. Worth's division would make up the first wave, Patterson's the second, and Twiggs' the third. The troops were distributed among the assault ships and schedules laid out on March 7. Light-draft steamers and gunboats would form a line close to shore to shell any Mexican troops who appeared. Once the beach was clear, the landing barges carrying troops would form a single line abreast, race to the beach, discharge their passengers, and go back for another load. The first wave would secure the beach, then move inland. Conner scheduled the operation for March 8.[30]

He put it off for a day when he was warned that a norther was on its way. The storm did not appear, so the landing fleet reassembled on the ninth. It was a perfect day, the sun blazing in a cloudless blue sky, with a light southeast breeze. Over the lush green jungles beyond the beach, the snowcapped Mount Orizava loomed. The Anglos knew that they followed in the footsteps of Cortés. Raphael Semmes of the navy confessed that his mind "became tinctured with the romance of that remote period, and emulous of the deeds which characterized its actors." He thought himself part of a new wave of history's conquerors, superior people against primitives, a common North American attitude. "Nothing could exceed the beauty of this spectacle."[31]

Sailors began fitting the landing barges and lowering them into the water. The troops readied their muskets, drew ammunition, rations, and water, and paraded on deck. The covering flotilla weighed anchor just before ten in the morning and headed for the landing area. An hour later Conner raised a signal and the landing force proceeded in single file through the narrow entrance to the anchorage. "The shout that now went up from ten thousand anxious soldiers," Private Stephen F. Nunnalee recorded, "almost made the ocean tremble with voices—the echo bounding upon every wave."[32]

A small mounted patrol had appeared on the dunes behind the beach. The *soldados* were awestruck. Great clouds of canvas floated over the sparkling waters, punctuated by rising columns of coal smoke from the larger vessels offshore, laced by the black trails of the smaller steamers showing the angry white teeth of their bow waves. There was not much noise except for the chugging of the little steamers close in or those snorting to draw their tows of barges. The big black hulks of the warships stood off in the distance, every deck covered with men in blue and blue-and-white uniforms. The crews of three European warships anchored off Sacrificios were draped all over the rigging. They looked to one Anglo soldier like "crows on trees watching the dead carcass lying beneath."[33]

The covering force of seven gunboats turned parallel to the beach just after noon. Over the next three hours bigger warships closed in behind them. The tug steamers cut loose the landing barges and the oarsmen glided to the transports to pick up their passengers, climbing down scramble nets. The covering force closed in, and at five in the afternoon a shot from a 24-pounder drove the cavalry off the dunes. There were no shore batteries to fire back. "Why don't they hit us?" a sailor asked. "If we don't have a big butcher's bill, there's no use in coming here."[34]

Worth's division was ready by midafternoon and *Massachusetts* hoisted the signal to go. Unruly currents scrambled the barges, which took two hours to get back in line abreast. Boats from a frigate strung out a pair of hawsers to align the formation, and the surfboat coxswains lined up as well as they could. At five-thirty *Massachusetts* again signaled EXECUTE, and the barges jumped off about 450 yards from shore. A tense stillness fell over the whole fleet, from surfboats to big warships. Just before the barges hit the beach, the gig carrying Worth scooted over to the left flank and the general and his staff jumped into Mexico. The rest of the first wave followed close behind and within minutes the 2,595 men of Worth's division were on the beach without a single casualty. The officers formed their companies and charged the dunes with bayonets. General Morales had recalled his mounted scouts, however, because he did not want to risk battle under the big naval guns. A United States flag arose atop a dune behind the beach and the silence ended as sailors afloat cheered and ships' bands resumed play. The meticulous training that Conner had given his crews paid off handsomely. As soon as they discharged one load of soldiers they returned to the transports for another, and so back to the beach. Over 8,600 men were ashore by eleven that night. Once the men were on land, the barges started transporting supplies and artillery. Horses and mules were carried on other shallow-draft vessels to as close in as possible, then shoved overboard to swim the rest of the way. The army lost a lot of livestock that way.[35]

The volunteers were up to their larcenous tricks as soon as they hit the beach, stealing the company property of regulars as quickly as it landed, then plundering the neighborhood. D. H. Hill complained, "The men have carried off everything that they could lay their hands upon." Hill was appalled that some very high-placed regulars set a bad example. "Genl.

Twiggs captured wine, flour, and beef at a Rancho near here and distributed the former among the men and they are now noisy and turbulent."[36]

THE DEMORALIZING EFFECTS MUST BE VERY GREAT

Morales sallied out of the city with a small party after midnight and fought
an inconclusive skirmish with the Anglos above the beach, then retired.
Conner sent a ship to fire at San Juan early on March 10, trading shots for
twenty minutes. This was a diversion for Patterson's division to start investing the city. As his troops passed through Worth's division, Brigadier
General Gideon Pillow's cavalry brigade drove some Mexican cavalry off
the heights to the north, cutting the Alvarado road and giving the United
States control of the Vera Cruz water supply. Landing of supplies continued but the shortage of wagons and draft animals meant that for the next
few days much of the army's labor went to lugging goods inland.

Scott aimed to establish a line around Vera Cruz, cutting off relief
from Mexico City. The investment met little resistance. There was another
cavalry skirmish on March 11, and Morales attacked a North American
brigade southeast of town with about a thousand men, but was driven
back. Anglo trenches extended northwest, troops leapfrogging each other
as each section was finished. The surround was completed on March 13,
after a delay caused by a norther on the morning of the twelfth and another sharp firefight with the defenders.[37]

Volunteers and irregulars swarmed to the area, skirmishing with the
Yankees while Morales continued to probe for holes in the Anglo lines. The
Alvarado garrison got through during the storm on the twelfth, but not so
successful were the Vera Cruz state militia, who were "dispersed" after trying a frontal assault on the trench line on the nineteenth.

Once he had his trench dug sea to sea, Scott assembled his staff to plan
the next move. According to his own account, he gave a flowery speech
pointing out the need to take the city and San Juan before the *vómito* season
began in April, "if not by head-work, the slow, scientific process, by storming." He preferred a siege to an all-out assault, to keep losses down and to
avoid an "immense slaughter on both sides, including non-combatants."
Scott kept belaboring this point because some of the officers wanted to get
it over with quickly and violently. He predicted United States losses of
2,000 to 3,000 from an assault. "For these reasons, although I know our
countrymen will hardly acknowledge a victory unaccompanied by a long
butcher's bill," he remembered saying, he was "strongly inclined" to favor a
siege.[38]

Vera Cruz's best defense was its surrounding landscape, where the

Anglo troops suffered foul drinking water, scanty and bad rations, howling wolves, dangerous snakes, lizards that crawled into boots overnight, and the whole of creepy-crawly creation. Worst of all were the sand fleas; Vera Cruz seemed to be the ancestral home of the bloodsucking genus. They feasted on the men day and night, so fiercely that they interfered with work and even shooting.[39]

Storms battered the area until March 17, when the navy resumed landing supplies and the troops started digging siege works. Scott had only about a fifth of the siege artillery he had asked for. In his opinion, he had enough to take the city, but not San Juan de Ullúa. The first batteries were emplaced on the sand ridges southeast of the city about a half mile from the walls. The elevated positions multiplied the work involved in wrestling big guns into place, while about 200 to 300 men were at work digging at any one time. The sand kept refilling the ditches, but the loose soil protected the besiegers. The guns of Vera Cruz threw 167 shot and shell into the works on March 19 but hurt nobody.[40]

Another drama played itself out at sea. Perry arrived in USS *Mississippi* on March 20, carrying orders to relieve Conner. The latter had found the landing site, designed the landing procedure, and supervised it all. It was he, not Scott, who had put the army ashore. Secretary Mason told him, "The uncertain duration of the war with Mexico, has induced the President to direct me no longer to suspend the rule" limiting the terms of squadron commands. Grumbling ran through the fleet that Perry had engineered a coup, but on March 5 Conner had asked to be relieved. On the other hand, Perry had plotted his own elevation with the secretary and Polk while his ship was being refitted.

Perry took command during another violent norther on the morning of March 21. After rescuing the crews of two vessels wrecked by the storm, together he and Conner called on Scott. Conner had earlier offered to lend some naval guns to help with the siege. Perry agreed to the deal because the army's guns were not heavy enough to knock the city walls down. He offered a battery of six guns and their crews, provided they fought under their own officers. Their 32-pounder guns and 62-pounder Paixhans shell guns won the favor of Scott and his army.[41]

A forest of cannons and mortars grew up near Vera Cruz. The first guns opened fire on March 22 as construction continued on more batteries. Three siege mortars were ready early on the twenty-third, but high seas prevented much ammunition from getting ashore. Another norther blew in, filling the works with sand as fast as it could be dug out, although a new battery was completed during the night. The storm continued into the twenty-fourth and low ammunition supplies kept the mortar fire slow.

The storm died out that night, and at daylight on March 25 the landing of ammunition resumed. The six naval guns had landed on March 22 while Robert E. Lee supervised construction of the "navy battery," and strong backs and weak minds dragged the pieces across country. They were in place by early on March 24 and began firing at ten that morning. The difference between the navy's big ordnance and that of the army was amazing. Heavy cannonballs smashed the city's coral walls and fragments of shells ripped through casemates and barracks. One shot took out the flagpole at a bastion manned by Mexican sailors and marines. Lieutenants Sebastián Holzinger of the marines and Francisco A. Vélez of the national guard jumped atop the wall to retrieve the flag, and nailed it to what was left of its mast. A cannonball buried them under debris, but they escaped unhurt.

Scott called on Morales to surrender; Morales refused, so Scott and Perry stepped up the pressure. Three newly completed batteries opened fire on March 22 with seven 10-inch mortars, shells exploding in the middle of town. Perry sent two steamers and four schooners to blast away at San Juan, which returned fire without effect. An especially terrifying addition to the bombardment began on March 24 when Lieutenant George H. Talcott's rocket battery launched forty Congreve rockets into the city, followed on the twenty-fifth by Hale rockets. They tore through the sky with a horrible screech that ended in a blast of fragments from their iron warheads. Civilians in the town were already cowering in terror, and this only added to their torment.[42]

THE YANKEES WON'T GIVE UP FIRING

Scott had promised to win the "minds and feelings" of the Mexican people. He told his staff that he wanted to avoid civilian casualties. Yet as soon as the guns opened up he shifted his target from Vera Cruz's defenses to the town itself. The decision to bombard a city of 6,000 innocent civilians contradicted his statements. Such ruthless disregard for the lives of women and children inflamed Mexicans. If this was how Scott treated a provincial city, they wondered, what would he do to the nation's capital? The siege's brutality was also noticed in the United States. Accordingly, Scott later excused the bombardment by asserting that it killed only three civilians—a gross lie. He also suggested that the shelling was justified because he had to leave the area before the fever season. His campaign had started late, but still Scott turned Vera Cruz into hell on earth for civilians in his path.[43]

In the 1840s war had rules, among them that armies should avoid harming noncombatants. Scott's callousness toward the lives of innocents remains inexplicable. He could not claim ignorance, because his own men heard the terror. "It really goes to my heart to be compelled to do my duty when I know that every shot either injures or seriously distresses the poor inoffensive women and children," cried one officer. "Tonight, I was put on picket-guard," a private wrote home, "and I could plainly hear the people cry out for the *rendiren tregar* [*tregua*] *de ciudad* [they should submit to a truce for the city], before they were all killed off. That the Yankees won't give up firing."[44]

Private Stephen F. Nunnalee confided to his journal, "We could thus hear the pieces crashing the buildings and then hear the report of the bomb, and then a heart-rending wail of the inhabitants that was awful, the women and children screaming with terror, running from one part of the city to another." Two days later he exclaimed, "The screams and cries of the Mexicans is most awful."[45]

Conditions were worse than he knew. There was a reporter in Vera Cruz who shortly after the city surrendered published in a Jalapa newspaper a running narrative of what happened. This was republished in English in newspapers around North America, leaving a stain on Scott's reputation. To Mexicans, what he did to the people of Vera Cruz was unforgivable. "How horrible is the scene we are attempting briefly to describe!" the reporter began. "What sympathizing heart can behold it without his eyes filling with the bitterest tears of grief?"

The reporter accused the North Americans of cowardice, because they avoided open battle in favor of "the barbarous manner of assassinating the unoffending and defenceless citizens, by a barbarous bombardment of the city in the most horrible manner." The first victims, he alleged, "were women and children, followed by whole families perishing from the effects of the explosion, or under the ruins of their dwellings." The hospitals filled up quickly. "The bombs entered the walls of the church of Santo Domingo, killing the unfortunate wounded, frightening away the nurses and doctors," who met the "same dismal fate" when they moved to another church. At least two other hospitals were destroyed. "In all quarters perished unfortunate persons, seeking a shelter from this frightful desolation, while the wounded, retaining strength enough to raise themselves, were flying as cripples and sprinkling the streets with their blood." This was all on the first day.

On the second day there was neither bread nor meat. People moved to an area not blasted yet, but on the third day the Anglos shifted their fire "and now every spot was a place of danger. This was the actual condition of the desolate families, suffering so much anguish, without advice, hope, sleep or food, solely engaged in preserving their lives, yet more aggravated by the reflection on the uncertain fate of their sons and brothers, remaining on the fortifications, who in return sympathized with this condition of their parents, known to be subjected to the explosion of every bomb upon their own habitation." By the end of the third day, said the reporter, the people were down to handfuls of beans and rice. Vera Cruz was a "multitude of horrors, desolation, and sorrow," the wrecked houses hiding unburied corpses, the city walls collapsing, and ammunition running out. The people begged Morales to surrender, but he "declared his resolution to defend the post."[46]

When it was all over, North American journalists supported the Mexican reporter's account. Other Mexicans in the city accused Scott of targeting the cathedral and powder magazine, they were hit so often. As one observer summarized, "Scenes of agony and blood follow one after the other."[47]

The bombardment was at full roar by March 25, a greater man-made noise than ever before heard in the Western Hemisphere. The citizens had had all they could take. Even the priests were afraid to leave cellars to tend to the dead and dying. Mexicans outside the city tried to relieve it, so Scott's army had to fight in two directions. One irregular force nearly bagged a United States patrol, and on the twenty-fifth a prisoner said that Santa Anna and 6,000 men were marching down from Mexico City. Scott did not realize that the increased activity in his rear was mostly volunteers trying to do what they could to help the city. He ordered reconnaissances in force, and his commanders too often saw whole armies where there were only scattered irregulars.[48]

Scott could partly justify his bombardment because Morales stubbornly refused to surrender. That was a matter of honor, but the Mexican government had a tradition of shooting generals who surrendered their posts. On March 25 Scott reluctantly began planning an assault on the city, supported by a naval attack on San Juan de Ullúa. A Mexican officer came out of the walls under a white flag late that evening and firing ceased. He carried a proposal from the consuls of Great Britain, Spain, France, and Prussia, asking that the North Americans allow them to evacuate the women and children. Scott refused, although he would allow the consuls themselves to leave. That the foreigners declined to do. The bombardment resumed, and the diplomats approached Morales, who late that night called a council of war. His officers advised surrender. Morales did not have the heart for that and resigned his command to Brigadier General José Juan Landero. As shot and shell fell onto the city another fierce norther struck, knocking down weakened walls, while Perry lost twenty-three ships blown ashore.

Landero sent a party out with a white flag at eight in the morning of March 26. The firing ceased and Scott's inspector Hitchcock escorted the messengers to headquarters. Discussions began with another request from the consuls for a truce to let the civilians out. Scott refused again. Landero had appointed three colonels as his commissioners for surrender negotiations, so Scott appointed two generals and a colonel to work out the terms. The first Anglo offer would release officers and militias on parole, send regular enlisted men to prison in the United States, and take possession of all military materials. Both the city and San Juan would be surrendered. The Mexican commissioners countered with terms that allowed the garrison to withdraw, the Mexican flag flying over Vera Cruz until they were out of sight, while the national guards would be paroled. The city, fort, and all military property would belong to the North Americans. Scott realized that the Mexicans simply wanted to retain some measure of dignity, so he granted parole to the whole garrison and freedom for the civilians to leave. Landero accepted the new terms and the agreement was signed later in the day. Garrisons of both the city and the fort would march out of Vera Cruz with the full honors of war, flags flying, and go on parole. Mexican officers could keep their arms and personal property, including horses and furniture. It was a good bargain on both sides, because Scott's army would not have to face a bloody attack on San Juan de Ullúa.[49]

The ceremony took place on the twenty-ninth, another day of sunshine and blue skies, with a slight breeze. The fortress fired a twenty-one-gun salute and lowered its flag at eight in the morning. At nine-thirty the city guns fired another salute and the Mexican flag came down there also. A half hour later the combined garrisons marched out of the south gate, accompanied by their bands, and stacked their arms, colors, and musical instruments. The United States soldiers watched with admiration for the grit of their opponents. George Furber saw proud, soldierly men with "shouldered muskets and free steps, while the rays of the sun glanced upon their bright arms." The "respect of the conqueror" was something the surrendering troops received gratefully.

Hitchcock accepted the paroles of the *soldados* via their officers. Parole was an old institution by which an army relieved itself of the burden of housing and feeding prisoners. Instead, they were released on condition that they not fight again until "exchanged" for prisoners of equal rank on the other side. Sick and wounded officers and soldiers were allowed to remain in the city, along with medical personnel, and United States surgeons assisted in their care. Civilian persons and property were protected, and "absolute freedom of religious worship and ceremonies is solemnly guaranteed." After the ceremonies, USS *Princeton* sailed away carrying Conner into retirement and Scott's official report of his conquest of Vera Cruz. The news reached Washington on April 10.

VERA CRUZ CALLS FOR VENGEANCE!

Scott's generous treatment of the surrendering Mexicans did not erase the impression his slaughter of innocents left on the rest of Mexico. His guns and mortars had fired nearly 7,000 rounds into the city, with a total weight of 464,000 pounds of metal. The North Americans lost 13 killed and 55 wounded. Against that, at least 350 Mexican soldiers and 400 civilians lay dead, the total wounded uncounted. "The city is much injured and it will be some time before they can repair the damage," reported an Anglo officer. "Our shells were very destructive. Hundreds of poor women and children have been killed or injured." Captain Sydenham Moore wrote his wife that he believed over 600 civilians were dead, "among them, I regret to say, were many women & children." Robert E. Lee told his wife, "My heart bled for the inhabitants."[50]

"The town is a miserable place," Ralph Kirkham wrote home. Many houses were demolished, nearly all damaged. Theodore Laidley told his father that "truly it was a sorry sight to see the desolation that the shells had made among the houses." Shell fragments and corpses were everywhere, the streets were barricaded and sandbagged, and the town was "abominably filthy . . . most offensive odors salute you." Most civilians who survived the battle had left. The *zopilotes,* however, returned.[51]

Scott tried to regain "minds and feelings" by attending mass at the cathedral. He knew that might harm his chances in a future presidential campaign, but he had to do it to win at least the tolerance of the Mexican people. Some civilians returned and opened restaurants to feed the soldiers. Other vendors entered the *yanqui* camps to sell food, and in a gesture of defiance peddled fare such as buzzard eggs passed off as turkey eggs.[52]

A mob of soldiers and sailors invaded a nearby hamlet, Boca del Río, looted a liquor store, robbed their way through the village, raping women as they went, and then burned most of the place down. Nothing, Scott knew, would alienate minds and feelings faster than that kind of behavior. He appointed Worth military governor, closed all liquor shops, and declared General Order 20 in effect. He reiterated the order on April 1, calling on "all who honor their country or respect themselves" to maintain law and order. He identified the Boca del Río culprits, had them whipped in public, and hanged one. On April 10 he hanged a camp follower for the robbery and rape of a Mexican woman.[53]

"It would not surprise me at all if this should lead to a peace very shortly," one of Scott's officers told his wife after the fall of Vera Cruz. "All is however uncertain with the Mexican counsels. They are so changeable and folly abounds with them and their public men." He was wrong about the chances of peace and right about Mexican leadership. News of Vera Cruz's capitulation reached Mexico City on March 31, and Santa Anna issued a bombastic proclamation and began raising a new army. "Mexicans!" he roared. "Your fate is the fate of the nation! Not the Northamericans, but you will decide her destiny! Vera Cruz calls for vengeance!"[54]

Scott prepared to head out for the Halls of the Montezumas but hoped he would not have to go that far to conquer a peace. Any such hopes, however, were made vain by the civilian blood he had spilled. "What the United States army is coming here to do," a Mexico City newspaper declared, was "to burn our cities, loot our temples, rape our wives and daughters, kill our sons, and sacrifice our defenders right in our presence, at the doors of our homes."[55]

The War of '47 had begun.

DEATH CIRCLED HORRIBLY
ABOVE THE CLOUDS OF SMOKE

(April 1847)

Nothing is easy in war. Mistakes are always paid for in casualties and troops are quick to sense any blunder made by their commanders.

—Dwight David Eisenhower

WHEN SCOTT'S MESSENGER REACHED NEW ORLEANS with the news about Vera Cruz, a man in the crowd called out, "How many men has Scott lost?" When he was told, "Less than a hundred," he shouted, "That won't do. Taylor always loses thousands. He's the man for my money." Word of Old Zach's victory at Buena Vista annoyed Polk. The battle would not have been so bloody, he sneered, if Taylor had stayed at Monterey.[1]

Taylor had a common-man image that Whig editors cultivated. Party leaders assumed that his lack of political experience would make him easy to control. He was telling correspondents by April 1847 that he would accept a nomination if it reflected "the spontaneous wishes of his fellow citizens," and he told Jefferson Davis that he believed that he could win the election. Many Democrats agreed.[2]

Taylor had become the president's political nightmare. Polk needed a way to tarnish his shine, perhaps by bogging him down in an endless campaign with rising casualties. Never was the Polk administration's partisan manipulation of the war so crass as when Marcy—reversing again orders to stand at Monterey—urged Taylor to march on San Luis Potosí. Seizing San Luis would put an army on Santa Anna's flank, but getting there would be nearly impossible.

Taylor was disgusted with the political finagling in Washington. He was over his head managing an occupation and was ready to pack it in, except that deserting his post would not look good to the voters. As for marching to San Luis, Scott told Taylor, it "might increase the chances of a peace or an armistice; but many intelligent persons believe that to occupy the capital and fifty other important points would not end the war." Even without an army, Mexicans "would still hold out and operate against our trains, small parties, and stragglers, with rancheros on the guerrilla plan." [3]

Scott had discovered an unpleasant truth: no matter what the North Americans did, the Mexican government could not sue for peace, and the Mexican people would not.

DO NOT THINK THIS IDEA IS ABSURD; IT IS TRUE

As if to illustrate that point, Colonel Atocha returned to Washington on March 20 carrying the Mexican foreign minister's rejection of the latest peace offer. There would be no talks of any kind until the United States evacuated all troops from Mexican territory and ended the blockade. "I at once declared to the cabinet," Polk told his diary, "that no alternative was now left but the most energetic crushing movement of our arms upon Mexico." The president believed that battlefield success must produce diplomatic success. Buchanan knew better and again objected to marching on Mexico City. "I replied that I differed with him in opinion," Polk said. He would not only take the Mexican capital but hunt Santa Anna's army down and destroy it. He would do so, that is, if he "had a proper commander of the army, who would lay aside the technical rules of war to be found in books," a snipe at Scott. Polk ordered that United States officers collect excise duties in areas under their command to squeeze Mexico financially, although the taxes would not affect people in Mexico City. [4]

Scott's success at Vera Cruz did little to lift the mood at the executive mansion. Polk suffered growing criticism from within his own party, and Calhoun heard from southern politicians who said the people were "tired" of the war. "It seems our successes in Mexico," Georgia congressman Robert Toombs charged, "have greatly raised the pretensions of Polk and his cabinet." He feared forcing Mexico to accept "terms which we ought not demand and which will be disgraceful to her and ruinous to us."[5]

In Ohio, a future senator, young John Sherman, told his brother William Tecumseh Sherman, an army officer, that politics had turned into a "hotch potch." He believed that Polk had been coasting along on the series of victories, but when that ended so would any support for the war. "There is no doubt that a large majority of the people consider it an unjust aggression upon a weak republic, excused by false reasons, and continued solely for the acquisition of slave territory," he said.[6]

It had seemed so simple to Polk in the beginning—make enough noise and the Mexicans would sell their territory. That did not work, so threats would, then emissaries, then an army, then battles and invasions. Now the president was sure that Scott's marching into the heart of the country would do the trick, so he wanted a diplomat handy as soon as the Mexicans decided to bargain. Buchanan recommended his chief clerk, Nicholas Trist. The Virginia lawyer and diplomat had the credentials. He was forty-six years old, a West Point dropout, formerly manager of Thomas Jefferson's affairs, and husband of Jefferson's granddaughter. Jefferson had got him his appointment to the military academy, Henry Clay found him a clerkship in the State Department in 1828, and Andrew Jackson hired him as a private secretary, then in 1833 appointed him consul in Havana, where he stayed until 1841. He returned to the State Department as chief clerk in 1845. Trist was a slender, shoulderless man with a big head, very large and wide-spaced eyes, a long nose, a thin mouth, and a sharp chin, all crowned with a mound of brown hair. He was a Virginia aristocrat and acted like it, pompous, bullheaded, and self-righteous, although he was also a man of patriotic ideals, moral principles, and a driving sense of duty. What his duty was he defined for himself.

Polk interviewed the chief clerk and decided he was the man for the job. Trist left Washington on April 16 and Polk gloated that he had kept the envoy's appointment secret outside his cabinet. If news had leaked, he believed, Whigs would have sent agents to Mexico to sabotage the peace talks. "This they would do rather than suffer my administration to have the credit of concluding a just and honourable peace." News of Trist's mission appeared in the *New York Herald* on April 21, and Polk ranted about the traitors all around him. The idea that even some Democrats, in particular Calhoun, were defecting to Taylor drove the president into paranoid gloom.[7]

Mexico's leaders remained fiercely determined to resist the invasion. They paid close attention to newspapers in the United States and were heartened by the growing domestic opposition to the war. Mexican inability to understand the other side was as concrete as that in Washington. Explaining this situation to his wife, Lieutenant George G. Meade said, "Do not think this idea is absurd; it is true."[8]

The Soldier of the People resumed the presidency and hatched a deal with the Church, which offered a loan of 2 million pesos if he annulled the January decree on forced sale of clerical property. Santa Anna stabbed his vice president, Gómez Farías, in the back. He pressed Congress on April 1 to abolish the office of vice president, keeping Gómez Farías from becoming acting president when Santa Anna left for the front. The legislature established the office of interim president and elected Pedro María Anaya to it. Santa Anna once again had firm control of both politics and the army, but the lawmakers pointedly denied him authority to negotiate with the United States. He rode out on April 2 to take charge of the Division of the East, under the temporary command of Major General Valentin Canalizo, headquartered at Jalapa. Once again he had raised an army from nothing, mostly by sending out press gangs. He assembled about 7,000 troops, few with any training, many suffering from various lung and intestinal diseases. Their scant supplies rode in 200 oxcarts.[9]

Santa Anna had been losing confidence in himself since Angostura, however. The day after he left Mexico City, Congressman José Fernando Ramírez told a friend that Santa Anna had said "that in his profession all the generals, including himself, would hardly make good corporals."[10]

One thing that had changed for the better was Santa Anna's determination to fight for his country rather than his own pocketbook. Few other generals felt that way. General Juan Álvarez reported from Acapulco that his army had forty-nine artillery pieces. There is no record of any action involving them, but next he said that he had only fifteen cannons. Álvarez was ordered on May 3 to move 3,000 troops north to the capital, but he objected that he needed them to defend Acapulco. A week later he declared that a change in climates between Acapulco and Mexico City would endanger his men's health. After several direct orders, Álvarez finally marched north, but dallied on the way. There were other generals detached around the country, each saving his troops for future domestic conflicts.[11]

THE MULES WERE WILD,
THE TEAMSTERS COULD NOT SPEAK ENGLISH

As rival *caudillos* maneuvered in his political rear, Santa Anna aimed to confine the *Yanquis* to the coastal lowlands. The place he chose was a mile-long canyon below Jalapa on the National Road, north of the Río del Plan. The village of Plan del Río stood at the lower end of the canyon about three days' march from Vera Cruz. Another village, Cerro Gordo (Fat Hill), sat off the road at the western end. Towering about 500 feet over the road on the north side was a steep hill called el Telégrafo (for an old signal tower on its peak). Just to the northeast of Telégrafo stood another hill, la Atalaya (the Watchtower), while to the southeast across the canyon rose an un-named hill with three points, from each of which artillery could command the road. Canalizo sent his engineer, Lieutenant Colonel Manuel Robles Pezuela, to reconnoiter the area. Robles reported that the canyon would be a good place to harass the invaders on the way to Jalapa but not to make a stand. It could be bypassed and cut off from the rear and there was no water. He advised defending up the road at Corral Falso. Canalizo, how-ever, was under Santa Anna's orders to make a stand at Telégrafo. Santa Anna drafted *peones* from his hacienda, and they prepared fieldworks and dug a canal to channel water to the site.

Canalizo put three batteries totaling nineteen guns on the three-point hill on the south side of the road, supported by 1,800 infantry in three brigades. At the head of the arroyo, uproad on the south side, he planted a six-gun battery supported by 900 men, with 500 grenadiers in reserve. Santa Anna thought Telégrafo was unconquerable, so only 100 men and four 4-pounders defended it, with a few more men and three guns on Atalaya. He posted nothing farther north to defend the flank, declaring that the rough terrain and thick vegetation were impassable. The Napoleon of the West made his stand at a place so confined and broken up that he could not even employ his whole army. Separating his men and guns on hilltops only made his situation worse. His reserves were camped at the village of Cerro Gordo.[12]

A shortage of transport, especially livestock, threatened Scott's plans. He and Perry worked up a joint attack on Alvarado, a ranching center. Brigadier General John A. Quitman and his brigade would march overland to rustle livestock while Perry's mosquito flotilla drove up the river in sup-port. Perry ordered Lieutenant Charles G. Hunter to block the river with his steamer *Scourge*. Hunter for no good reason fired shots at a fort on the river mouth on March 30, then sailed upriver and captured Alvarado, which had been defended by about sixty guns but almost no troops. His ac-tion warned the Mexicans, who burned their stores and retired upriver. The noise caused the ranchers upstream to drive their herds to safety. A second expedition April 8–11 got a few horses, but Scott's hope to get draft animals on the cheap was blown.[13]

Scott wanted to advance his army seventy-five miles to Jalapa, which at 4,700 feet above sea level was out of the fever region. The agricultural area could provide the army with subsistence, and Scott was under the delusion that the people there favored his invasion. The North Americans would cross the Río Antigua on the Puente Nacional (National Bridge) and face possible opposition at Plan del Río, Cerro Gordo, Corral Falso, or above Jalapa.[14]

The logistical challenge was enormous. Quartermaster General Jesup estimated that moving 25,000 men to Mexico City would require 3 million pounds of supplies carried in 9,303 wagons and on 17,413 pack mules. Scott thought that moving his army would not be so big a burden and planned on getting most of his work animals in Mexico. He believed that he needed fewer than 1,000 wagons, 2,000 to 3,000 mules, and 300 to 500 draft animals for the siege train. Scott was wrong, Jesup right.[15]

The quartermasters rounded up wagons and mule teams. "The mules were wild, the teamsters could not speak English, some of them had never harnessed an animal," complained an officer. Mules began breaking down as soon as they left Vera Cruz, and this officer took some men out to get more. "Three Mexicans were given me to lasso the mules," he said, "and five men were required to put them in harness—seasick, wild, little animals."[16]

Scott's supply would become impossible if the Mexican people resisted. He reminded his army on April 1 that requisition of supplies must be orderly. "They must be paid for, or the people will withhold, conceal, or destroy them," he said. "The people, moreover, must be conciliated, soothed, or well treated."[17]

Scott issued another proclamation to the Mexican people on April 11, saying that the North Americans came to liberate them from their oppressors. The general's aim was to ease the acquisition of supplies, but his quartermasters were short of specie (hard money) and merchants accepted government drafts only at a discount. Later, when Scott had access to banks at Puebla and Mexico City, he traded warrants on the United States for specie in the banks' vaults. The behavior of his volunteers was a bigger problem, as when some attacked a man selling beef to commissary officers, breaking into his ranch house, beating him up, robbing him in front of their own officers, and stealing six mules.[18]

Scott's proclamations were so much wind against determined resistance from Mexicans who had many reasons to fight back. He had to provide escorts for all supply trains and details up and down the road, "with a meager cavalry that must from day to day become, from that intolerable service, more and more meager."[19]

Colonel William S. Harney and a small detail forded the Río Antigua near its mouth on April 2, clearing a way inland. Twiggs' division marched up the road on the eighth, followed by Patterson's division and Quitman's brigade the next day. Worth's division remained behind, awaiting more animals and wagons. Dragoons scouting ahead of the army flushed some Mexican lancers out of Plan del Río on April 11 and Twiggs' division closed up there. Scouts reported defenses under construction at the canyon near Cerro Gordo. Lieutenant P. G. T. Beauregard of the engineers discovered that Atalaya offered a way to turn Santa Anna's flank. Twiggs disagreed. When Twiggs reported 4,000 Mexican troops in front of him, Scott rode forward with a dragoon escort, ordering the rest of the army to follow.[20]

IT SEEMED LIKE MURDER TO SEE MEN RUNNING BAYONETS INTO EACH OTHERS' BREASTS

"Old Davy" Twiggs was a big hulk of a man, with mountainous shoulders and a bull neck, standing about six feet tall. He was recklessly aggressive—it was said that the only maneuver he knew was to attack. He learned on the morning of April 12 that the Mexicans held the canyon in strength, so he charged right at them. His advance drew heavy fire, so he retired before being drawn into a slaughter. Twiggs decided to make a frontal attack before dawn on the thirteenth. Patterson's brigades under Pillow and Shields, just arrived, were too worn out for that, so the two brigadiers talked Twiggs into postponing action for another day while Shields sent a frantic message to Patterson. Patterson went forward, took command of both divisions, and suspended what would have been a mass suicide. Scott showed up on the afternoon of the fourteenth and ordered further reconnaissance. Robert E. Lee of the engineers rediscovered the path around the Mexican left to Atalaya, the route Beauregard had found earlier.

Scott ordered Lee's trail widened to pass infantry and artillery. He planned to attack on the morning of April 18, sending Twiggs' division, supported by Shields' brigade, around the Mexican left while Pillow's brigade pinned down the main Mexican line south of the road. Once Twiggs jumped the enemy flank he was to cut across to the Jalapa road behind Santa Anna. Troops worked on the new road all day on the sixteenth, clearing boulders and brush and leveling the surface, undetected by the Mexicans. Twiggs' division moved up on the morning of the seventeenth, the early part of the going screened by the jumbled terrain. The advance ran into Mexican pickets late in the morning, and Twiggs bellowed in a voice heard all over the battlefield, ordering Harney's regulars to charge Atalaya. The men atop that rise were little more than a lookout detail, so Harney's men cleared the summit and pursued the retreating Mexicans down the far side and halfway up Telégrafo until they were pinned down by musketry from the top. A pair of mountain howitzers were dragged to the top of Atalaya to cover Harney's retreat after dark.

The attack, combined with the statement of a Yankee deserter, alerted the Mexican general. But Santa Anna assumed Scott intended to storm Telégrafo rather than cut the road behind him, so he reinforced the infantry on top of the isolated hill and ordered a breastwork and a two-gun battery set up below it. Meanwhile, Scott sent Shields' brigade forward to back up Twiggs, and these volunteers muscled three 24-pounders up Atalaya. Other troops dragged an 8-inch howitzer into a position across the river to where it enfiladed the main Mexican line. Engineers, meanwhile, continued to probe Santa Anna's positions during the night. Lieutenant Gustavus Smith explored Telégrafo and discovered that the fortifications were "very incomplete, offered no effective obstacle, and we could dash over the works without a halt." He returned to the main United States position in the dark, but fell asleep while walking down the hill and stumbled into a hole. He found himself "sprawling on a dead Mexican soldier—his glazed eyes wide open, within a few inches of mine." All he could think was "that, in a short time after daylight . . . I might be as dead as the man upon whom I was lying."[21]

Santa Anna's men were terrified. Most of them were illiterate *Indios* and *Castas,* jerked from their *pueblos.* They feared for their *soldaderas* at the main camp near Cerro Gordo. They were ignorant of what the war was all about, untrained, short of water and food, crawling with insects, footsore, and suffering from dysentery. Many of them had what Anglo soldiers, who could hear them in the night, called the "army cough." Above all, they dreaded the *Gringos bárbaros,* who rumor said were superhuman savages.

Across the space between the two armies, beyond where coyotes could be heard tearing at corpses, Scott revised his battle plan for the eighteenth. Twiggs' division and Shields' brigade would seize Telégrafo and go on to cut the road. The first shots would signal Pillow's brigade to attack the batteries on the three fingers of the hill at the east end of the Mexican line. If Pillow could break through there, he was to turn on the enemy rear. Worth's division, coming up the road, would back up Twiggs and pursue the enemy. Twiggs ordered parts of two brigades to bypass Telégrafo and aim for the Mexican camp while other units drove straight up the towering height, supported by the guns on Atalaya.

The North Americans began to move early in the morning, and an artillery duel broke out between the guns on Atalaya and Telégrafo. A brigade commanded by Harney started up Telégrafo while cannonballs screeched overhead at seven in the morning. The climb was so steep that officers and men literally crawled up the hill, pulling themselves up on boulders and the scrub brush that dotted the slope. The troops made it to about seventy-five yards below the summit, where they ran out of breath. Smoke from muskets and cannons shrouded the scene and the noise was tremendous, but the leather-lunged Harney's order "Charge 'em to Hell!" carried over the racket. The tired Anglos roused themselves and stormed over the incomplete Mexican defenses atop the hill. "Our whole force with a loud shout leaped the breastworks and met [the Mexicans] at the point of the bayonet," said a North American soldier. "Here for just one short minute ensued a kind of fighting I hope never to see again. It seemed like murder to see men running bayonets into each others' breasts." It was a vicious, bloody brawl, the defenders assailed from the front, rear, and above, their own artillery turned around and firing on them.[22]

The *yanqui* cannon fire, said a Mexican who survived this hell, was "like the eruption of a volcano." Solid shot and canister tore men's bodies to pieces. Moreover, "the musket fire was as intense as the ardor of the battle. Beating its wings over a bloodied field set aflame at certain points by enemy projectiles, death circled horribly above the clouds of smoke that covered thousands of men engaged in cruel battle. Our soldiers fell by the dozens in the midst of that confusion, as did the enemy troops, but they were instantly replaced by others."[23]

There was horror on both sides. "You have seen a hail-storm, and witnessed the falling of the hail-stones, accompanied by rain—then you have an idea of our situation," said a North American private of the storming of Telégrafo. The attackers crested the summit and fell into "a short, but bloody, hand to hand struggle, in which bayonets, swords, pistols, and butts of muskets were freely used." Most of the Mexicans retreated, remembered Gustavus Smith, but the Anglos stumbled into a detachment that had taken shelter in a set of old quarry pits. "The struggle here was hand to hand, and sharp for a short time. But they were driven from their quarry holes, back on their main line, which gave way, and their own guns were turned upon them."[24]

The summit of Telégrafo was a ghastly mess, bodies and parts of bodies scattered around, blood standing in pools. Down below, Shields' troops broke through the brush near the Mexican camp only to run into horrendous thunder and grapeshot from five guns Santa Anna had moved there during the night. Shields fell with a ball through the lung, and his second led the surviving troops through the camp and out onto the Jalapa road. Things did not go so well on the Anglo left, where Pillow bungled his assignment. He did not scout his route, so remained ignorant that he had three miles to go on a narrow trail. His men came under heavy fire as they trudged along the trail because the general could not keep his mouth shut, alerting the gunners up ahead. Just one regiment got into action, and it was blasted back by Mexican artillery. The only thing that saved the Anglos from this mess was that the Mexican commanders on the three elevations realized that they had been cut off by *Yanquis* on the road behind them, and voluntarily surrendered.

"Our four thousand untrained militia men defended the fortress valiantly for five hours," Santa Anna claimed later. "However, they were pitted against fourteen thousand trained veterans with heavy armament." In fact, the battle lasted just three hours and Santa Anna's army was routed and scattered, thousands of survivors streaming up the road to Jalapa. Scott had lost 63 killed and 353 wounded. Losses on the other side remain uncertain because the Division of the East went out of existence. About a thousand of its men were killed or wounded, most of them to die later. The North Americans captured at least 3,000 and Scott's inspector general estimated that another thousand got away before they were processed for parole. Santa Anna's defeat was so total that the invaders seized his coach, "peppered with shot," as it headed for Jalapa, along with a wagon carrying 16,000 pesos to pay his troops. United States volunteers later ransacked his lovely mansion at Encero and stole his spare pegleg.[25]

ABSOLUTELY NOTHING WAS SAVED; NOT EVEN HOPE

The scene after the battle was beyond description. Scott paused for a day while his officers processed prisoners and so that the prisoners and Anglo soldiers could fan out to bring in wounded and bury the dead. Mexican army surgeons together with North American doctors saved many wounded from both sides. They could not save those who had fled or crawled off into the brush to die, however. The burial details were made more horrifying by the great numbers of women who had died along with their men.[26]

A North American newspaper correspondent described the roadside as lined with dead humans and horses. Farther along, "they lay thick around, and a more horrible scene it would be difficult to picture. Mexicans lay dead in every direction; some resting up against trees, others with legs and arms extended, and occasionally a lancer lying with his arm upon the charger that received his death wound from the same volley which ended the career of his rider."[27]

The numbers of wounded were beyond the ability of the two armies to handle. Scores of them made it as far as Jalapa, where according to Congressman Ramírez they suffered "the greatest privations and misery."

Many, he said, left the hospitals to "perish in the open country, where the ground is strewn with corpses and cast-off war equipment. Putrefaction has set in." According to another observer, the people of Jalapa were "terrorized by the practically continuous screeching of the saw, the screams of the amputees." The citizens watched uncounted funeral corteges, during which "they could listen to a symphony of tin whistles, which is the saddest thing I have ever heard." [28]

Between Cerro Gordo and Jalapa the stink of gunsmoke gave way to the awful stench of rotting human flesh. The sky filled with buzzards while coyotes and feral dogs tore at the dead and dying. The whine of flies drowned out the calls of the colorful tropical birds. When Scott's troops reached Jalapa they found disabled Mexicans everywhere, "some of whom were wounded, and others wasted to skeletons with diarrhoea," according to one soldier. "Many of them had on shirts which they had evidently worn for weeks, and . . . nearly all of them were infected with vermin." The sight of this pitiful humanity erased any glory from the Anglo victory. [29]

Scott had an enormous problem on his hands in the form of more than 3,000 prisoners of war, including five generals. He could not care for these numbers, so he paroled all the prisoners. He knew that would cause trouble with the Polk administration, but his report would reach Washington too late for the politicians to do anything about it. Some of Scott's officers, however, thought that he had made a big mistake. [30]

As soon as Hitchcock and his officers processed their paroles, the hordes of discharged prisoners trudged up the road toward Jalapa. A news correspondent rode along with some of them and was especially fascinated by the *soldaderas*. They struggled under burdens of bedding and spare clothes for their men, along with food and cooking utensils. He called them "those devoted creatures who follow [the soldiers] through good and evil." It "grieved" him to "see them, worn down with fatigue, moving at a snail's pace, their heavy burthens almost weighing them to the earth." He recognized love when he saw it, however. "These women, like the Indians, are the slaves of the men—a slavery they submit to under the all-powerful influence of affection." [31]

News of the disaster reached Mexico City on April 20, igniting panic. Mexico, wailed one reporter, was "wide open to the iniquity of the invader." Ramírez called the battle "a rout as complete as it was shameful. Everything was lost. Absolutely nothing was saved; not even hope." The soldiers' morale, he continued, also was gone. "As for supplies, the less said the better. No money, no muskets, no artillery." [32]

New yarns sprang up about the invincible *Gringos,* and Ramírez sent a

316   D<small>AVID</small> A. C<small>LARY</small>

sampling to a friend. The enemy soldiers were so huge and strong that they could cut a man in half with a single swipe of their swords. Their horses were "gigantic and very fast" and their muskets fired shots that divided into fifty pieces, "each one fatal and well-aimed." The *yanqui* artillery "inspired fear and terror in all our troops and is undeniable proof of our backwardness in military art." Another writer observed that some of Scott's troops carried the new Walker Colt revolvers. The name *revólver* was said to refer to the bullet it fired, able to "revolve in all directions after its victim, run around trees and turn corners, go into houses and climb up stairs, and hunt up folks generally."[33]

These tales did not temper the defiance of Mexico's disorganized leaders. Congress decreed on the night of April 20 that the "supreme government of the union has power to take the necessary measures to carry on the war" but could not make peace. Anybody who tried to treat with the North Americans was "a traitor to Mexico." The legislature appointed its senior members to act as a council of government, to name a temporary president "in case of vacancy" in that office. Nobody knew where Santa Anna was, and the general assumption was that he was dead.[34]

The Soldier of the People had more lives than a cat. As his army disintegrated Santa Anna rode into the steep valley of the Río del Plan, crossed the stream, and climbed the far side, other fugitives gathering behind him. Ampudia joined him, and together they assembled a small contingent of officers and mounted lancers and headed west toward Jalapa. Enemy troopers spotted them and fired, so the group turned south toward Orizava. The Soldier of the People was despondent because people refused to provide food or fresh horses. One friendly *hacendado* put them up for the night, but the party feared United States patrols and headed out early in the morning. The refugees rode into Orizava two days later, cold, hungry, and worn out. They were greeted by the town officials, but generally the people made their hostility clear. Santa Anna restored his own morale by screaming at another group of fugitive soldiers, flailing at them with his riding crop. Feeling better and more confident, the Savior of His Country set out to form another army, and within a matter of days had 4,000 men around him.[35]

North American soldiers could not understand why the Mexicans refused to give up. Lieutenant E. Kirby Smith told his wife after Cerro Gordo, "What a stupid people they are!" United States troops controlled "the greatest portion of their country and are fast advancing on their Capital which must soon be ours,—yet they refuse to treat!" He sounded very much like British officers in 1776, wondering at the stubbornness of George Washington and his oft-defeated army.[36]

OUR MOUNTAINS REPEAT THE CRY OF WAR AND LIBERTY!

Scott led his troops into Jalapa on April 19. The little city was touchingly neat and clean, set amid emerald hills ablaze in a rainbow of tropical plants, the birds showing every startling color imaginable, the butterflies and dragonflies wondrous. The climate was perfect, the air clear and bracing. It was spring in the tropical uplands.[37]

The troops marched into town flags flying, bands playing. To a Mexican watching them, they appeared "motley," dressed in "the most curious collection of clothing." They lounged around the streets smoking pipes or chewing tobacco, eating the local produce. "They showed much more enthusiasm for cane liquor," he observed. Most of the soldiers were more or less drunk most of the time, and in that condition lost many weapons and some of them their lives to *léperos.* "What was most remarkable about these people was their respect for women," the Mexican declared. He did not think that was reduced by their frequent visits to prostitutes who descended on the town.[38]

Scott sent Worth's division forward to Perote. The advance occupied the grim, infamous fortress San Carlos de Perote, longtime political prison and guesthouse for Texians just outside of town on April 22. Worth's men liberated a large quantity of munitions, several United States prisoners, and Generals José Juan Landero and Juan Morales, whom Santa Anna had tossed into the jug for surrendering Vera Cruz.[39]

Except for Worth at Perote, Scott was stuck at Jalapa. He diverted troops to guard his supply line to Vera Cruz and others ordered to reinforce Taylor. Foul weather and the transportation shortage did not help. Scott claimed that without the need to guard his communications he could take Mexico City with the loss of under a hundred men. He advised Colonel Henry Wilson at Vera Cruz late in April that the connection between that place and Jalapa might soon be cut off. He repeated that prediction to the secretary of war, advising that he wanted to call all his detachments upland before the fever season. It should be possible to do that, he claimed, because he could get enough foodstuffs on his route of march and other supplies already on the way should make his army self-sufficient. The countryside was becoming increasingly dangerous. *Rancheros,* after being pillaged by stragglers from Santa Anna's army, were abused further by North American volunteers. Patterson told his men that their looting, raping, and killing "lessen the confidence of the general in the efficiency of the Division."[40]

Relations between Mexicans and North Americans were about to grow worse. The calamity at Cerro Gordo caused the state and national governments to adopt the traditional tactics of the weak against the strong—guerrilla warfare. This implemented the third strategy proclaimed more than a year before. Congress gave the governor of Vera Cruz state, former interim president José Mariano Salas, power to organize resistance. On April 21 Salas called for a guerrilla army "with which to attack and destroy the invaders, in every manner imaginable," and inviting citizens to sign up for a "warfare of vengeance—war without pity, unto death!" The legislature of México state followed suit. Other states echoed these calls, which within a few days spoke of a "light corps" added to the national guards. "Let the echo of our mountains repeat the cry of War and Liberty!" proclaimed the legislature of Vera Cruz. Santa Anna heard these calls, and from Puebla announced his survival and his support for irregular warfare.[41]

These purple *gritos* (cries) threatened the social order, however. Mexico already had peasant uprisings at every hand, and those in power were afraid to encourage more. Accordingly, with authority from Congress interim president Pedro María Anaya issued a *reglamento* (regulation) on April 28 governing the "light sections" of the state national guards. Units could be raised "by any citizen having sufficient means and influence in the country in which he resides," but only after the government issued a *patente* (license). Each light corps would aid the regular armed forces within its region and apprehend *malhechores* (evildoers). Each patented commander should recruit at least fifty men, appoint officers, keep records of his operations, and confine himself to an assigned area. The commander's rank depended on how many volunteers he raised—800 for a colonel—and the leader could name his corps after himself. Goods captured by the *guerrilleros* would be divided among the troops or sold free of taxes.

Equipping an outfit was expensive, so only the rich could do that. About seventy individuals received patents under the regulations, mostly between Vera Cruz and Mexico City. Some were effective, others left no record of ever doing anything, and a few later rebelled against the national or state governments. Mexico City ordered in August that all people within ninety miles of every place occupied by the enemy should rise en masse, attack with "the arms each may have, fire-arms or cold steel, great or small, long or short—in a word, if there be nothing else, with sticks and stones."[42]

Scott issued an order on April 29 making the nearest *alcalde* liable for irregular attacks in his neighborhood. If he failed to deliver up the guilty raiders, he would be fined $300 for each death they caused, together with the value of property stolen. This just encouraged more guerrilla resistance. Irregulars attacked North Americans everywhere, especially in Vera Cruz, Puebla, and México states. The country was perfect for guerrilla warfare, a landscape of mountains, canyons, forests, and other hiding places. Fugitives from Santa Anna's army took to the woods as *guerrilleros,* joining career *bandidos* already active in the region. The ferocity of North American retaliation for attacks on stragglers and supply trains aroused furious local people to join the fight, and volunteers came from as far as Cuba to kill *Gringos.*

"Groups of soldiers like those of Cortés inflict terrible punishment for the death of any Yankee," Ramírez complained. Ralph W. Kirkham told his wife that "hardly a day passes without someone being wounded or killed traveling alone." The guerrillas were neither equipped nor trained to fight large regular formations, but drunkards and other stragglers were in constant peril. The war between the invaders and Mexican irregulars descended into naked savagery by early summer, with innocent settlers the most frequent victims. By the end of the summer the road from Vera Cruz to Mexico City was a miles-wide swath of ashes and destruction.[43]

The root cause of the chaos in Scott's theater was the same as in Taylor's—the volunteers who ravaged defenseless citizens. When the citizens or guerrillas retaliated, Scott's policies encouraged bestial counterretaliation. Much of the disorder came from drunkenness, but command attempts to stop the liquor trade failed. So did General Order 20, because it applied mostly to regular soldiers. D. H. Hill, a member of several military commissions, was disgusted that regulars typically got thirty lashes for foraging "when the Volunteers commit far worse acts in times of tranquility with perfect impunity."[44]

Scott ordered his army to start marching toward Mexico City on April 30, but he rescinded the command the same day because the enlistments of many twelve-month units were about to expire. Too many of them were also uncontrollable. Several parties from an Illinois regiment fanned out from Jalapa on April 29 to pillage chickens and cows and were attacked by guerrillas, who killed several of them. The regiment lost two more stragglers killed on May 1, along with another from the New York regiment, all just outside the camp. Because the volunteers caused more trouble than good, Scott sent seven regiments down the road early in June, leaving him a little more than 7,000 men to march on Mexico City. The departing units plundered the country like locusts, leaving behind a trail of burned *ranchos* and dead civilians all the way to Vera Cruz.[45]

WHAT IS TO PREVENT YOU FROM SERVING US?

Scott declared guerrilla warfare to be banditry, but he got into the same business when he told Hitchcock to recruit what became the "Mexican Spy Company." The general had permission from Polk and Marcy to recruit career *bandidos,* on the theory that they were outcasts from their own society. Hitchcock chose Manuel Domínguez, in prison in Jalapa and regarded by the people in the area as "a noted and dangerous robber." Hitchcock told the man, "You have been pointed out to me by your enemies in this city as a dangerous man. You are called an enemy by the Mexicans and treated as an enemy and feared as one. What is to prevent you from serving us?" Domínguez agreed, and Hitchcock sprang five of his old gang from jail to join him. Eventually the company totaled about a hundred men, all *ladrones* (robbers), their first uniforms red scarfs on their hats, elaborated later with parrot-green jackets trimmed in red. The company served the United States Army until the last troops left Mexico in 1848. Although Domínguez was the actual leader, the nominal captain was a Virginian named Spooner, who had been one of Domínguez's *bandoleros;* two lieutenants also were foreigners. Domínguez drew most notice, however. "This Captain of robbers is a very fine looking man with a good face and nothing indicating cruelty in it," said Lieutenant Henry Moses. "He can command by a sign, 10,000 men on the road from Mexico to Vera Cruz."

Domínguez and his partners in crime had long terrorized the honest people of the region, so getting into bed with them did not win Scott many minds and feelings. Captain John Kenly of Maryland said the Spy Company was "composed of the worst-looking scoundrels I ever saw. Robbers and banditti before the war, their characters were not improved by it." The bandit-spies crossed enemy lines, penetrated the Mexico City defenses, and carried out a number of special assignments, plundering citizens while they were at it. They received $16,556.50 for their services, and even Polk thought the money well spent.[46]

While Scott consorted with criminals, the war continued on the coast, where the only ports still open were Tuxpán and Tabasco. Perry went after Tuxpán first. It was defended by eight guns in five batteries covering a six-mile approach up the winding Río Tuxpán, manned by 300 to 400 men under Brigadier General Martín Perfecto de Cos. Perry used his mosquito flotilla to land 1,519 men with four guns. The fleet stopped off the bar early on April 17 and on the afternoon of the next day the small vessels, towing thirty barges carrying the landing party, crawled upstream. Cos declined to mount a defense, so the flotilla was off the town's waterfront by about three in the afternoon. The navy took Tuxpán with a loss of two killed and nine wounded. Perry sent a party upriver on the ninth, but the expedition returned with few prizes. The rest of the landing force removed the guns and supplies from the town and leveled the fieldworks. Perry's command evacuated on April 22 and sailed for Antón Lizardo, leaving two small ships behind to blockade the river mouth. Cos led his troops inland to join Santa Anna.[47]

Perry faced shortages of engineers and surgeons, many of his small steamers needed repairs, and some of the bigger ships were scheduled for refit. Perry asked for more marines to garrison captured ports. Instead, he received orders to transfer all his 200 marines to join the fifty already on loan to Scott's army. The commodore protested, and he and Scott compromised. Perry gave the general one officer and twenty-eight men.[48]

While the Home Squadron wound down on the Gulf, the Pacific Squadron was scarcely active. After a frigate seized La Paz on April 14, Kearny received orders on April 23 to take someplace—anyplace—in Baja California to hold as a bargaining chip for peace negotiations. The general asked Commodore James Biddle to ship two companies to Baja, but delayed the movement when he heard rumors that an army was marching out of Mexico to retake Alta California. There was such an expedition, albeit a small one, but political difficulties kept it from going beyond Guanajuato.[49]

The sloop *Cyane* returned to the Gulf of California late in April. She was joined off Mazatlán on April 29 by Shubrick in USS *Independence* and by *Portsmouth*. Shubrick announced that the blockade of Mexico's Pacific coast had been reinstated. People ashore fled to the interior. The two frigates sailed back north, leaving *Cyane* to maintain the blockade alone by shifting between Mazatlán and San José. Every time she left one port she lifted its blockade, but Mazatlán was effectively closed by the summer storm season that began in May. The people of that port returned home, learned about what was going on offshore, and laughed at the *Gringos locos* (crazy Gringos).[50]

So ended the bloody month of April 1847, with Scott stalled at Jalapa, Perry becalmed offshore, and Biddle, Shubrick, and Kearny accomplishing not very much on the other side of the continent. In Washington, Polk was sure that the Mexicans would at long last see the light, while in Mexico City the ever-changing faces of government hoped that the people would rise up against the *Yanquis* instead of their overlords. Always the wild card, Antonio Lopéz de Santa Anna, Soldier of the People, plotted to become once again the Savior of His Country.

THIS WILL ALL BE OVER VERY SOON
(May–July 1847)

If you step to the side you will be safe,
Otherwise you will be caught,
Death is very powerful
When she sweeps with her broom.

—"La Calavera de los Patinadores"

KIT CARSON HEADED UP THE SANTA FE TRAIL, Lieutenant Beale still along for the ride. The first stop was St. Louis, where Carson handed Frémont's account of his dispute with Kearny to Senator Benton. The Thunderer asked Carson to take it to the president. Carson got to the capital the last week of May 1847 but news of the California uproar had preceded him. Polk summoned his cabinet on May 4 to discuss the "unfortunate collision." The president believed that both Stockton and Frémont, "in refusing to recognize the authority of General Kearny, acted insubordinately and in a manner that is censurable." Jessie Frémont twice took Carson to see the president. Carson briefed Polk on affairs in California, but Benton's daughter did most of the talking. She tried, said Polk, to "elicit from me some expression of approbation of her husband's conduct, but I evaded making any." The president sent Carson back to California with dispatches.

Kit Carson crossed the continent for the second time in the same year. On the Santa Fe Trail he and his escort of Missouri cavalry fought a sharp engagement with Comanches. In New Mexico he said hello and goodbye to Josefa and set off with another escort over the Old Spanish Trail, a meandering route more or less west from Santa Fe. This time he skirmished with Paiutes. The scout and his party rode into Los Angeles in October, but Frémont, Stockton, and Kearny were gone, so Carson rode north to Monterey to deliver his messages to Colonel Richard B. Mason, military governor of California. "I well remember the first overland mail," recalled Mason's aide William Tecumseh Sherman. When Carson got there, said Sherman, "we walked together to headquarters, where he delivered his parcel into Colonel Mason's own hands." It was a small event but rich in symbolism. The first transcontinental mail represented the United States' stretching from the Atlantic to the Pacific.[1]

THEY MAKE A WASTELAND AND CALL IT PEACE

While Carson was on the road, Kearny advised the secretary of war on May 13 that he would return overland to the east, taking Frémont with him. Joined by officers of the Mormon Battalion and a dragoon escort, the party set out on May 31. Meanwhile, Biddle had hauled Gillespie aboard his flagship and ordered him to go home. He and Stockton left on June 20. Kearny ordered Lieutenant Colonel Henry S. Burton and two companies of the New York volunteers to occupy a post in Baja California. The troops landed at La Paz on July 21, dug a fieldwork, broiled in the sun, and awaited orders.[2]

Much of the war took a break during the summer of 1847, except in New Mexico and the northeast. Supply lines were under constant assault from Indians, guerrillas, and bandits, and attacks on settlements increased. The raiding Indians felt themselves aggrieved by treaties forced on them. They were cheated in towns and trading posts and beaten, murdered, and robbed in open country, although they gave as good as they got. By taking sides with the whites and Pueblos and against everyone else, the army gave up a chance to occupy a middle ground to bargain for peace.[3]

Affairs within the white community were unsettled. The richer *Hispanos* went into business with the Anglo traders, and the poorer *Nuevomexicanos* remained downtrodden. There would not be another large uprising like the one at Taos, but there were hero-bandits in the mountains and personal retaliation against United States volunteers who robbed, raped, or murdered. Frank P. Blair, a Missouri volunteer officer, told his father that the situation was "horrible. It seems that even respectable men at home, have become so depraved by the license of the region they are in, that they stick at no enormity whatever." *Niles' Weekly Register*'s correspondent in Santa Fe wrote, "All is hubbub and confusion here, discharged volunteers are leaving, drunk, and volunteers not discharged are remaining drunk." Albert Gay, a civilian teamster, told his parents in August, "The Mexicans are not as bad as our own countrymen." In every case when New Mexicans attacked soldiers, the volunteers had provoked it.[4]

Relations between Mexicans and Anglos were, as always, worst in northeast Mexico. The country was so devastated that a United States officer evoked a complaint against the Roman army recorded by Tacitus in the first century: "They make a wasteland and call it peace." The problem was a combination of two factors—the behavior of volunteers and the failure to develop a sensible occupation policy. The volunteers and civilians were locked in a bloody embrace of atrocity and reprisal. Butchery reached so high a level that Taylor corresponded with General Ignacio Mora y Villamil at San Luis Potosí, hoping that cooperation might end the horror. Typically, however, one side complained about atrocities committed by the other, answered with countercharges.[5]

The lapse in policy began with a failure to understand a basic fact: people do not like to be occupied. Some Mexicans did business with the Anglo army, more tolerated the foreigners, and many more resented being subjugated. Irregular resistance was part of the war, but the Anglo generals viewed all resistance as criminal. Irregulars presented a challenge to regular soldiers—there was no visible enemy to fight. Whether the insurgents controlled the people through intimidation or out of sympathy, the rebels lived among the people. Taylor and Scott could think of no better way to fight the insurgency than to intimidate local authorities into giving the rebels up, which did not work. The alternative was massacre and deportation in the Roman style. There was another way, however, and that was to recognize that superior firepower did not guarantee victory. That meant winning the "minds and feelings" of the people. The behavior of the *Gringos bárbaros* made that impossible in northeast Mexico.

Wool tried his best at Saltillo. When two lieutenants shot each other to death in a drunken duel in May he imposed a curfew and set up roadblocks to keep his men out of trouble. To end nightly donnybrooks between drunken volunteers and teamsters he separated the garrison from town. Nevertheless, men continued to sneak into Saltillo, where they acquired venereal diseases en masse from the prostitutes. Soldiers persisted in shooting livestock at random and stealing foodstuffs at gunpoint, so the resistance continued and Wool grew increasingly frustrated. He declared

war to the knife on July 15. "Guerrilla parties," he ordered, "will be executed wherever found." Wool could not see that those fighting him were
not criminals but patriots with real grievances.[6]

I FEAR THAT SCOTT AND TRIST HAVE GOT TO WRITING

As the violence grew, Nicholas Trist landed at Vera Cruz on May 6 carrying a draft of a treaty between the two countries. To make sure that the
Polk administration got credit for any peace settlement, Trist was ordered
to sign the treaty only if the Mexicans accepted it without changes. Any
further negotiations would be handled by Washington. The draft presented
the Rio Grande boundary of Texas as not negotiable. Additional territorial
surrenders by Mexico were New Mexico and one or both Californias, together with a right of transit across the Isthmus of Tehuantepec. There
were Anglo investors interested in building a railroad across Mexico's
southern waist, hence this latter addition. Trist was authorized to pay up
to $30 million for the Mexican territory. Some members of the cabinet
thought the excessive territorial demands would prolong the war.[7]

Trist's package also included letters of credentials, his commission, his
diplomatic passports, and private authority to draw $3 million from the
United States Treasury as a down payment pending ratification of the
treaty. There was also a clumsy letter from Marcy to Scott. Instead of
clearly saying that Scott could implement any armistice Trist negotiated,
Marcy made it look as though Trist had power to handle a purely military
affair. Scott roared at Trist that it was all a plot to "degrade" him because
Marcy's instructions required him to defer to the envoy on whether to dis-
continue hostilities. That was solely Scott's authority as an army commander unless Trist was "clothed with military rank over me." Trist was
stunned. He denied that the orders to Scott contained anything out of the
ordinary, claiming that Perry agreed with him.[8]

Scott was in no mood to hear advice from Perry, because Lieutenant
Raphael Semmes of the navy had showed up in Jalapa with a letter to the
Mexican government protesting the treatment of Midshipman Rogers,
captured at Vera Cruz weeks before. Scott rejected what he saw as a demand that he waste troops to escort pointless messages. Semmes would
not go away, however, and tagged along all the way to Mexico City.[9]

Trist reached Jalapa on May 14, and the hostility between him and
Scott blossomed. Scott said that if Trist sent him a letter, "it is not probable
that I shall find leisure to read, much less give a rejoinder." Trist did send a
note on the twentieth, asking for the return of the secretary of state's note
to the Mexican foreign minister and blistering Scott for not forwarding it.
The general waited until May 29 to blast Trist in return. "My first impulse

was to return the farrago of insolence and arrogance to the author," he sneered at the diplomat, "but on reflection I have determined to preserve the letter as a choice specimen of diplomatic literature." Scott accused Trist of giving him orders. If he did that again, "or indulge yourself in a single discourteous phrase, I shall throw back the communication with the contempt & scorn which you merit at my hands." [10]

Trist stayed with the army, but Scott still refused to talk to him. The situation brought out the worst in the thin-skinned general, who exploded in another obnoxious letter to Marcy on June 4, complaining about "the many cruel disappointments and mortifications I have been made to feel" and about the "total want of support and sympathy" from the War Department. He asked to be "recalled from this army the moment it may be safe for any person to embark at Vera Cruz." Marcy passed this on to the president, saying that Scott seemed to be "in very bad humor." The secretary told a friend, "I fear that Scott and Trist have got to writing. If so, all is lost!" [11]

The United States' chief agents in Mexico were having a childish squabble, a product of their stubborn, pigheaded, and paranoid personalities. The news brought out the worst in the stubborn, pigheaded, and paranoid president. Polk called Scott's complaints "not only insubordinate, but insulting to Mr. Trist and the Government." The president ordered Marcy to reprimand the general. Polk cut loose in his diary. "I have been compelled from the beginning to conduct the war against Mexico through the agency of two generals highest in rank who . . . are hostile to my administration." What really ate at him was the fact that there were now two military heroes who could run for president as Whigs. [12]

Trist sent a note to the British minister in Mexico City, Charles Bankhead, asking that he forward his messages to the government. Bankhead sent his secretary Edward Thornton to pick up the dispatches. Thornton met Trist on June 10 and told him that Foreign Minister Manuel Baranda had resigned under threats from the war party. The British diplomat suggested that others in the Mexican government could be brought around if the $3 million was spread across the right hands. This was Trist's first encounter with *mordida,* and he was shocked. He thought he could get used to the local custom, however, if it could buy a peace. [13]

Bankhead handed the messages to the new foreign minister, Domingo Ibarra, who said that any decision to negotiate must be authorized by Congress. This was diplomatic stalling, but Santa Anna called Congress into special session. Thornton, British consul Edward Mackintosh, and "Mr. Turnbull," an Englishman claiming to be a friend of Santa Anna, visited Trist on June 24. Turnbull declared that the Savior of His Country was ready to deal but needed time to round up support. He suggested that Trist and Scott's army should remain where they were but transfer $10,000 for Santa Anna's benefit immediately, to be followed by $1 million when the treaty was signed. Trist was over his head in this kind of shady transaction, so he asked Generals Pillow and Persifor Smith what they thought about the proposition. Both favored it, although they claimed to be offended by any hint of bribery. The British diplomats, however, had assured Trist that there was no other way to open negotiations. Trist told Scott that he was ready to open talks and for the first time sent the general a copy of his commission. Scott added his agreement with Pillow and Smith. Trist accepted Turnbull's proposal.[14]

In Washington Polk had no idea that Trist and Scott were beginning to pave the way for peace talks. When he saw their whining letters to the secretaries of war and state from mid-June, on July 9 the president complained, "they exhibited a wretched state of things." Instead of talking, the two alleged grown-ups sent "foolish and bitter letters" to each other. "The protraction of the war may properly be attributed to the folly and ridiculous vanity of General Scott," he sneered to his diary.[15]

Polk could never adjust to the fact that delays in communications limited his ability to interfere. Nor was he comfortable with delegating responsibility. It also escaped him that sometimes little things can make a great difference. Trist fell ill early in July, and Scott sent him a box of guava marmalade and sincere wishes for his recovery. From then on they worked hand in glove.[16]

The general and Trist discussed the bribery proposal on July 15 and Scott said that he could make the first payment out of his secret-service fund. Trist asked for the money, as it was the "only way in which the indefinite protraction of this war can possibly be prevented." Scott called his generals to a conference to ask whether they thought the United States ought to pay the bribe. Pillow strongly favored it. Twiggs declared that it was a political matter and refused to comment. Shields, Quitman, and Brigadier General George Cadwalader all objected to being parties to bribery, but not very strongly. Scott therefore sent Trist $10,000 and promised to arrange transfer of the $1 million when a treaty was signed. Most Mexicans and North Americans believed that the ultimate beneficiary of this gravy was Santa Anna, but he kept the record cloudy. In any case, once the money went out of Scott's tent, the senior North Americans in Mexico assumed that peace was at hand.[17]

Then Polk threw a monkey wrench into the works by ordering Buchanan to send Trist new instructions on July 13, drastically revising the proposed boundary between Mexico and the United States by pure geographical fantasy, along impossible alignments. There were no good maps of the borderlands, so the Polk administration had no idea what it was talking about. The instructions also told Trist that the United States wanted Baja California if he could get it, but that it was not an essential part of the North American demands. This and related dispatches were intercepted by *guerrilleros* and reached the Mexican government before Trist ever saw them. Yet another new foreign minister, Francisco Pacheco, forwarded the intercepted mail to Trist on September 9, but the damage had been done. The Mexicans had learned that the United States would not go all out to get the Baja peninsula. By that time the cannons were roaring again.[18]

THIS WAS THE KIND OF FIGHTING THEY LIKED AND THEY WERE GOOD AT IT

While Scott paused and Trist prepared to buy a peace, Perry was again busy on the coast. The biggest headache was Yucatán, a state split between competing planter and commercial elites based at the capital, Mérida, and the port of Campeche. Each side recruited and armed Maya Indians, promising to return lands taken from them. There were two secessionist wars in the decade after 1836, including a brutal and prolonged conflict with the national government from 1839 to 1843 when the Yucatecans drove the federal troops out. Then the upper classes reneged on their promises to the Mayas.

The powers at Campeche declared independence in December 1846, and with Maya soldiers defeated their rivals at Mérida. The Campeche faction formed a government, sent ambassadors to the United States and other countries, and declared neutrality in the war between the Mexicans and the North Americans. Conner had recognized Yucatán's neutrality, then withdrew the courtesy. Perry recognized the neutrality again in May 1847. However, the naval occupation of Carmen, which Perry seized at the same time, was a stress point between Yucatán and the United States. Then the Mayas rose up in July in what became known as the "Caste War." The *Indios* recognized that their real enemy was the dominant white society whose sisal plantations were destroying their subsistence economy. The agrarian uprising—it was more social than racial—was the most severe of the many across Mexico. Besides restoring the lands taken from them since colonial times, the Mayas vowed to drive out the descendants of all colonists. This, in the view of the *criollo* elites, made it a race war. The whites were driven into their last strongholds in Mérida and Campeche by early 1848, while their emissaries begged Washington and Perry for help.[19]

Meanwhile, rumors spread that Santa Anna would try to flee Mexico, and Perry was ordered to grab the *caudillo* if he could. The naval movements alerted authorities in Tabasco and eastern Vera Cruz state that the port still was vulnerable. The commodore had planned to seize Tabasco to cut the trade through the coastal waterways from Carmen, but other demands had postponed an operation. The Home Squadron was ready to strike by June, but Tabasco's defenses had been strengthened since the arrival of Colonel Domingo Echagaray in April. The colonel had been promised reinforcements and built works to accommodate them. He drove piles into the Río Grijalva about four miles below town, supported by three successive breastworks stretching from the winding river to the chaparral on the left. Behind the last of them stood Fort Iturbide, blocking any advance on the town. But Echagaray had only 900 men to spread out across his widened defense; the reinforcements never showed up. There were no cannons in the foremost work on the lower river, and the only real defense was Fort Iturbide.[20]

Perry assembled four small steamers, three brigs, forty ships' boats hauling more than a thousand men, and seven landing barges, each mounting a field gun. It took all day June 14 to get everything in order, cross the bar, and occupy the village of Fronteras at the river's mouth. There was no opposition, but reports of an ambush ahead caused Perry to halt for the night.

The flotilla chugged forty miles upriver on the fifteenth, boiler smoke a great, black cloud advancing on the defenders. There was scattered sniping from the brush, answered by panicky musketry from the sailors. Perry halted for the night at a turn just below the pilings. He sent engineers to inspect the obstructions at sunrise on the sixteenth and they came under fire, so the thousand men and seven guns of the landing party went ashore on the left bank. The defenders of the pilings withdrew upriver. The Anglos plunged into the sweltering jungle, the brush and tall grass tearing at them, until they sighted the middle and main breastwork, Acachapán. It was held by about 600 Mexicans, half of them cavalry, under Colonel Claro Hidalgo, who had two small guns. Perry brought his own guns up and blasted the position. The commodore, waving his cutlass, led the sailors in a frontal charge, disorganized but making enough noise that the defenders ran.

Once the pilings had been blasted out the flotilla chugged on upriver. Fire from Fort Iturbide hit two steamers but did not stop the little fleet from steaming past and taking the fort under fire from the rear. A landing party of about seventy men stormed over the works and drove the Mexican conscripts away. The steamers kept going to Tabasco, which surrendered as soon as they anchored in front of it. The Stars and Stripes rose over the governor's house before noon. Perry's main shore party, mean-while, had continued hacking through the brush. The men were annoyed when they saw a United States flag drooping over Fort Iturbide at about two in the afternoon—they had missed the main show. At a cost to the Mexicans of about thirty killed and wounded and to the Anglos of nine, Perry had closed the last Mexican port on the Gulf.

Echagaray retreated upriver with a few hundred soldiers and civilians and began guerrilla warfare. Perry spent a week destroying military stores, the magazine, and the fort, then left a garrison of marines and three small vessels to hold Tabasco against guerrilla raids. "Mexican troops infiltrated the town every night to pick off Americans," Perry reported. "This was the kind of fighting they liked and they were good at it." Marines marched to Tamulte, Echagaray's base upriver, "but dispersing Mexicans was no more effective than chasing hungry deer out of a vegetable garden. They always drifted back, to take pot shots at 'gringos.' " By July the men were drop-ping from the *vómito,* so Perry ordered an evacuation and all the Anglos were out by the twenty-second. Having given Tabasco back to the Mexicans, the commodore tightened his blockade off the river mouth, sending occasional patrols upstream. This encouraged secession move-ments in Chiapas and Tabasco states. Leaders asked for Perry's support, but he declined to give it, so the movements went nowhere.[21]

Yellow fever spread through the Home Squadron in July and August 1847, leaving most vessels too shorthanded to do anything. On August 4 the secretary of the navy ordered Perry to take no further points on land. The old, boring blockade routine was all the squadron had to look forward to.[22]

HIS VIGILANCE AND ENERGY WERE UNQUESTIONABLE

President Polk, not as bored as the sailors, filled his diary with self-pity all through the spring and summer of 1847, repeatedly complaining about the amount of work the war caused him. Yet he found time to issue nit-picking instructions about the disposition of Scott's prisoners and other interventions into the commander's authority. Taylor's presidential prospects brightened, and Polk reversed earlier orders to transfer some of Scott's troops to the northeast and sent them back to central Mexico.[23]

The prolongation of the war caused other complications for the presi-dent. Most notable was the "All Mexico" movement. The refusal of the Mexicans to negotiate prompted some loud voices to say that the United States should conquer the whole country. Most proponents were in the north or the west of the United States, where there were few strong opin-ions about slavery. They focused on the potential riches to be harvested in the conquered nation, but justified themselves with the claim that Mexico did not have a real government anyway. Some in the northeast, mostly Democrats, saw personal opportunities if Mexico was annexed.[24]

The trouble with calls to expand the war was that the present campaign was about to run short of manpower, owing to the approaching end of twelve-month enlistments. Congress had authorized additional regular regiments for the duration, but they were not enough. Marcy issued calls for new volunteers on April 19, but response was sluggish.[25]

Veterans began returning home, some of them wounded or sick, telling tales of the hard reality of troop life and expressing general disgust at the administration's "inefficient manner" of conducting the war and at the political generals Polk had appointed. An anti-Polk Democrat told Senator Calhoun that the veterans he had met complained "most bitterly of the discomforts and risks to which they have been subjected in the consequence of insufficient supplies, the paucity of men, and . . . a want of decision and energy on the part of the Administration." Polk no longer had much of the public behind him, and the fighting men were also outraged.[26]

Opposition to the war boosted Taylor's prospects for the presidency, and Whig newspapers were full of calls for his nomination. When Democratic newspapers rebuked Old Zach's partisans for talking about that so far in advance, a Kentucky volunteer in his army roared, "National convention be damned! I tell ye, General Taylor is going to be elected by spontaneous combustion!"[27]

Polk's partisan paranoia blinded him to the fact that neither Taylor nor Scott was his enemy. That honor belonged to Santa Anna. Scott certainly thought he was an estimable opponent. "His vigilance and energy were unquestionable," the Anglo general later said of the Mexican, "and his powers of creating and organizing worthy of admiration. He was also great in administrative ability, and although not deficient in personal courage, he, on the field of battle, failed in quickness of perception and rapidity of combination. Hence his defeats." The *caudillo* remained Mexico's best hope.[28]

After assembling a motley army around Orizava, Santa Anna planned to attack the invaders as soon as possible. First he considered setting ambushes in the mountains around Jalapa, but eventually he decided that defending the capital from Mexico's second-largest city, Puebla, with 80,000 people, would be a better idea. There he could gather men and supplies and, not least important, stay close enough to Mexico City to influence the presidential elections scheduled for May 15. Santa Anna arrived at Puebla on May 11, a day after Worth's advance left Perote. The city had been in turmoil since fugitives from Cerro Gordo had come in. Nuns went into constant prayer while priests and monks paraded through the streets urging people to pray and do penance instead of building a defense. Civic leaders declared that they did not want their city to become a battle-ground. Santa Anna moved into the governor's palace and tried to organize a defense anyway. He sent commissaries out to "violently com-mandeer" horses to rebuild his cavalry and seize other requirements. Heavy-handed orders such as that further alienated the citizenry, and the town government declared an open city.

Santa Anna marched east to confront the invasion. His scouts told him that there was a small brigade guarding a large supply train well behind Worth's division, and he thought he had a chance. The Mexican general sent 3,000 cavalry to smash the brigade and train before the two Anglo forces could unite. Worth halted at Amozoc, giving the supplies time to close up. On the morning of May 14 Worth's troops spotted a few lancers, and Worth realized that the target was his supply train, so he sent rein-forcements back down the road. Santa Anna's cavalry found the target strengthened and on the alert and returned to Puebla without attacking. On the morning of the fifteenth Santa Anna led his army off toward Mexico City.[29]

The North Americans were just as happy to get beyond Perote, a dirty, smoky place. The way to Puebla was gorgeous, rich farmlands and color-ful forests with snowcapped mountains looming through the clear air. Midmorning on May 15 Worth's advance reached the crest of a rise over-looking the city, which stood in the middle of a great bowl about 7,000 feet above sea level. There, said South Carolina volunteer H. Judge Moore, "we had a beautiful view of the castles, domes, and spires of that ancient and beautiful city of the angels." Puebla appeared, he said "to sleep in silent but princely grandeur upon the soft velvet bosom of the green valley that lay beneath our feet." The city was famous for cotton mills and beautiful women.[30]

A delegation of city fathers met Worth outside town and practically offered him the keys to the city. The general, a jittery man with a sagging face and an often fearful expression, was relieved at the welcome. He overstepped his authority, however, continuing the civil government with-out imposing military occupation. His terms were so generous that Scott later disapproved them, and a court of inquiry called them "improvident and detrimental to the public service."[31]

Worth's 4,200 men were greeted by crowds so large that they were terrifying, "a shoreless sea of living, moving, animated matter," Moore put it, "composed of thousands of men, women and children, ebbing and flowing like the agitated waves of the ocean." The Anglos thought the friendly reception by the upper classes masked a widespread hatred by the lower orders. "They think us little better than devils and are ready to cut our throats the first opportunity that offers," said Theodore Laidley.[32]

What brought the mobs out was morbid curiosity. Carlos María Bustamante, a prominent Mexican journalist, sniffed that the people were more interested in seeing the enemy than fighting them. He said that "instead of the centaurs we expected," the first Anglos troops he saw were "decrepit in appearance, dressed in uniforms poorly made and ill-fitted." Their horses looked "dull and awkward." Another Mexican also thought the "barbarians from the north" made a poor impression. They wore ragged, dirty uniforms covered with mud and dust. Some of them stopped in the plaza, stacked their muskets, and went to sleep on the pavement. Were these "coarse and clownish men" the "conquerors of our army," the "Messiahs of our civilization"?[33]

The troops were regulars, and there were a lot of generals in town to keep order. The banks handed over hard money in exchange for drafts on the United States Treasury, so the soldiers bought what they wanted with coin, as did the commissaries. Letters to Mexican newspapers reported that the occupying troops were on good behavior, business was brisk, taxes were low, and everyone enjoyed concerts by the regimental bands. The decent treatment of priests and women by the *Gringos* was "almost incredible."[34]

There was much in the clean, beautiful city that was new to the Anglos. *Nieverías* (ice cream and sherbet shops selling treats made from mountain snows), the many *paseos* (public gardens and promenades), and the spectacular cathedral were absolute delights. The elites resumed their evening strolls and horseback rides, and they were courteous without actually welcoming their occupiers. North Americans acquired a taste for *cigarillos* (cigarettes) and *puros* (cigars) and got used to seeing women smoke. For prudish Victorian officers it was startling that Mexican women did not deny that they had legs. "Mexican ladies riding a-straddle on horseback," said one officer, were a shocking sight. It was "quite a common practice" to see "a young lady surrounded by three or four of her beaux, chatting and laughing with them as unconcernedly as if both of her nether limbs had been on the same side of her saddle!" It was all quite innocent, he declared. "Her appearance was in all respects perfectly modest . . . so that the only indecency existed entirely in the imagination of the beholder." That the women in this southern climate did not shroud themselves with the layers of cloth and corsets common in North America was also exciting.[35]

Worth continued issuing panicky false alarms, which the men called "Worth's scarecrows." According to Lieutenant Laidley, Worth inspired "a want of confidence that a General should not, a constant fear of attack which harasses himself and his troops." Hitchcock said Worth behaved with "the powers and airs of a Spanish generalissimo." His frequent alarms wore the troops out and made them drop their guard. The low point was a circular to all officers warning them to watch out for attempts to poison the army's water supply. "Doubtless," Worth declared, "there are among those with whom we are situated many who will not hesitate, as is the habit of cowards, to poison those from whom they habitually fly in battle—a recourse [sic] familiar in Spanish history, legitimately inherited and willingly practised [sic] by Mexicans." Not only was this gratuitous crack bad history, it intimidated the Pueblans, insulted all Mexicans, and took a slap at neutral Spain. Scott arrived at the end of May and put an end to the nonsense. He rescinded the terms of capitulation, imposed military occupation, and squelched the poison-plot order, calling it "highly improper and extremely objectionable." Insulted, Worth demanded a court of inquiry, which reprimanded him. Scott had lost an old friend.[36]

Scott had dropped hints that he might cut himself off from Vera Cruz and live off the land. In June he ordered commanders at Jalapa and Perote to join the main army. He pulled troops up to Puebla because of the guerrilla warfare raging up and down the road from Vera Cruz. The *guerrilleros* could not defeat detachments of any size or break the supply lines altogether, but keeping the road open diverted about a fifth of Scott's army. The steady drain of men killed by irregulars eroded morale, and garrisons at Jalapa and Perote cowered behind their defenses. "The guerrillas were swarming everywhere under vigorous leaders," reported the commander at Perote, "so that for safety the drawbridge was drawn up every night." Scott had warned his men since April that stragglers would "certainly be murdered or captured." Still the blood flowed. Almost as serious were Mexican efforts to get these demoralized men to desert. An estimated 200 to 300 went over the hill at Jalapa alone before the end of May.[37]

Scott would march out of Puebla as soon as the promised reinforcements arrived, but they would have to fight the whole distance from Vera Cruz. He had not, in fact, cut himself off from his base there. The *guerrilleros* had done that for him.

NO ONE IS BRAVE ENOUGH TO PROPOSE PEACE

Mexico City's leaders, including twenty generals and several members of Congress, assembled in April to consider how to defend the capital if the Savior of His Country did not stop Scott. There was a general sentiment against subjecting the capital to bombardment, so few defenses were undertaken.[38]

Then came the calamity at Cerro Gordo. "We are lost, with no way out, if Europe does not soon come to our aid," Lucas Alamán predicted. Mexico's ambassador to Britain, José María Luis Mora, had tried to enlist that country, France, or any other to intervene, with no luck. Lord Palmerston, the foreign minister, told him that Mexico had shown "poor judgment" in not recognizing Texas' independence. "The Mexicans," he further advised, "should put their hands to work and build a solid and last-ing nation."[39]

Mexico was alone, but then she always had been, her prominent men complained. "It is impossible for a nation to go on for any length of time this way without being annihilated," Alamán lamented. "Our situation is truly desperate," wailed Ramírez, "and judging by the way things are going it is doubtful whether we can save our independence, the last refuge and symbol of our honor." To sue for peace was a criminal offense under the law of April 20. "Although the peace party is very large," Ramírez ob-served, "no one is brave enough to propose peace." The loudest opponents of dealing with the United States, he sneered, were the first to oppose every effort to mount a defense.[40]

Santa Anna showed up at the gates of the capital on May 17, 1847. Interim President Anaya declared a state of siege and appointed the Soldier of the People as commandant of the Federal District, preventing Santa Anna from taking over the government at the same time. To make sure, a delegation from Congress visited him outside the capital on the seventeenth and asked him not to resume the presidency; he agreed. Congress restored the constitution of 1824 the next day and Santa Anna entered the city and took military control, then on the twentieth had him-self sworn in as president. This cost Santa Anna political support, and the army's leaders felt that he had abandoned them. He believed that only he could save his country, however, so he drove his opponents out of the city. To the extent Mexico had a government, Santa Anna was it. At least until May 28, that is, when he shifted shape again and renounced the presidency, saying that revolutions were forming against him. When the opposing fac-tions fell apart, the Savior of His Country withdrew his resignation to save Mexico from Scott and anarchy.[41]

Among Santa Anna's talents was an ability to provoke Mexico's tradi-tion of bitter humor. When he withdrew his resignation, *El Monitor Republicano* observed, "What a life of sacrifice is the General's; a sacrifice to take power, to resign, to resume; ultimate sacrifice; ultimate final; ulti-mate more final; ultimate most final; ultimate the very finalest. But let him cheer up. He is not alone in making sacrifices. For twenty-five years the Mexican people have been sacrificing themselves, all of them."[42]

Santa Anna had triumphed, hated by many, disliked by most, distrusted by all, but he appeared to be marching ahead. He could also inspire a fighting spirit. His mere presence energized the leading people of Mexico City, who decided that it would be "more glorious" to go down fighting than to leave the gates open to the *Yanquis bárbaros*. A blizzard of orders flew out of the national palace, calling in church bells and old cannons to be melted and cast into new guns. The government imported muskets from blockade runners and from dealers in Central America. All citizens were ordered to turn in what arms they had. Gunpowder mills went to work and powder came in from Honduras. Arsenals and contractors produced mortars, bayonets, and other hardware.

Santa Anna had about 3,500 men with him. He ordered General Gabriel Valencia to bring the 4,000 remaining veterans of Angostura down from San Luis Potosí. There were about 10,000 national guardsmen and 10,000 regulars in and around Mexico City; 2,500 marched up from Juan Álvarez's Division of the South; a few thousand more came from Canalizo's post near Orizava. Santa Anna hoped to mobilize an army of about 25,000 to 30,000, but the ragtag nature of any force he could assemble meant that he must stand on the defensive.[43]

Santa Anna did not do so well politically. The restoration of the federalist constitution inspired separatist movements in Zacatecas and several northwestern states. The state of Guanajuato stopped raising troops for the federal government, pleading a lack of resources, and there were similar cases in other states. Apathy was a greater obstacle to mobilization, however. The war minister complained about the "indifference noted in all the Republic, particularly in the states of Tamaulipas, Nuevo León, and Coahuila." That was a remarkable statement, because those states had active guerrilla campaigns against Taylor's army. *Pueblos* across the country intensified their uprisings against *hacendados* and governments at all levels.[44]

Politics in the capital did not inspire devotion to the central government. Santa Anna summoned Congress to consider the latest peace overtures from the United States, but it did not meet until July 13 for lack of a quorum. The president asked the lawmakers to repeal the decree of April 20 that made dealing with the other side treasonous. The legislature pointed out that its restoration of the 1824 Constitution gave the executive the power to conduct foreign relations, thus overriding the April 20 law. This equivocal statement left Santa Anna holding the bag if he reopened negotiations, ending any hopes for a deal greased by the bribery scheme, if there had been one. Trist and Scott suspected that Santa Anna had merely chiseled them for pocket money, but he continued his clandestine communications with them. After Congress adjourned in mid-July the president hinted that he would try to negotiate, but needed more money to win over supporters, and had at least to make a show of defending the capital. On July 23 Trist forwarded to the secretary of state the comments of one of his British sources, probably Thornton, who said, "Santa Anna is afraid to make peace now and cannot." The *caudillo* had said in effect that Scott should advance on Mexico City, and then he would "endeavour to make peace." Trist assured Buchanan that the Anglo army would not have to enter the city to end the war because Santa Anna would call for an armistice after the first action.[45]

Santa Anna assembled his generals on July 27 and tried to get them to support his sending a delegation to negotiate with Trist and Scott. His old enemy Valencia declared his opposition; actually, he was looking for a chance to pounce if Santa Anna stumbled. The council of generals postponed any further talk about peace negotiations. Santa Anna lost interest as his self-confidence in being able to defeat Scott rose.[46]

Not everyone in Mexico City shared his optimism. Lucas Alamán thought Scott would be "reckless" to march against a city of 180,000 people and a garrison larger than his own army. "Despite this," he said in dismay, "there is no doubt in my mind that he will take the city, because our army consists mainly of recruits under the command of generals who are renowned for how fast they can flee, and nothing will move the masses, who are watching all this as if it were happening in a foreign country. That is how weary they are after so many revolts. This will all be over very soon."[47]

Mexico was paralyzed again. The next move was up to Scott.

I HAVE NOT HAD THE MEANS OF SENDING A DETACHMENT DOWN TO VERA CRUZ

The secretary of war promised Scott in April that he would have 20,000 additional men by the end of June. He called the general's plan to cut his communications to Vera Cruz "a very strange order," and said that President Polk believed the general was making "a great military error." Nevertheless, Taylor was ordered to send all the troops he could to Scott's theater.[48]

The whole world knew by the middle of the summer that Scott intended to cut his ties to the sea. The decision was greeted with amazement. Scott had no choice—guarding the road and its traffic absorbed too many fighting men. Scott later apologized for his inability to send a major general to the coast, "inasmuch as 1,200 or 1,500 men would have been necessary to escort him, and I have not had the means of sending a detachment down to Vera Cruz." The *guerrilleros,* not the Yankee general, cut his ties to the coast.[49]

Cadwalader's brigade had been diverted from Scott's army to Taylor's during the spring, then was sent back to Vera Cruz. Cadwalader landed with his lead elements on June 1 and watched as Colonel James S. McIntosh led 688 green recruits escorting a train of 128 wagons hauling ammunition and $350,000 in coins out onto the road to Jalapa on June 4. The caravan was attacked twice two days later, losing twenty-four wagons and twenty-five men to ferocious guerrilla strikes. The train was not well managed, the teamsters were incompetent, and the whole thing was strung out so long that it was impossible to defend. It invited attack.

McIntosh's situation introduced the Anglos to one of the most remarkable characters of the war, a Spanish-born Vera Cruz priest named Celestino Domeco de Jarauta, or "Padre Jarauta." A lean, fiery man, he was forty-three years old in 1847, a veteran of the Carlist Wars in Spain during the 1830s and of rebellions in Cuba. He had been a popular priest in Vera Cruz since 1844. He was a born *guerrillero* who raised his first army after Cerro Gordo and fought under a patent to the end of the war. He was an instant Mexican hero because of his effectiveness and because he evoked the memory of the soldier-priests of Spain's *guerrilla* war against Napoleon decades earlier.

After the first two attacks McIntosh sent back to Vera Cruz for reinforcements. Cadwalader reached him with about 500 men on June 11, and the combined force continued the march to Jalapa. Padre Jarauta also sent out for help; with 700 fighters, he attacked furiously at the National Bridge on the thirteenth, costing Cadwalader thirty-two more casualties. Jarauta set an ambush at La Hoya Pass, ten miles past Jalapa, but a cavalry detachment out of Perote, commanded by Sam Walker, struck the guerrillas from the rear. By the time Cadwalader and McIntosh reached Perote, they had lost another twenty-four wagons, 417 mules, and 114 mule carts. Afraid to go on, they waited for another column coming up.[50]

Pillow had left Vera Cruz on June 8 with about 2,000 men but met no opposition. He picked up Cadwalader and McIntosh and the combined force reached Puebla on August 8. About 2,500 men, a mixture of green recruits, new regulars, and the marine battalion, guarding a train of 100 wagons, 700 mules, and a chest of $85,000 worth of treasury warrants, along with another holding $1 million in cash, left the coast on June 19 under Brigadier General Franklin Pierce. The column fought about 1,400 Mexican irregulars at the National Bridge, losing thirty men. Pierce sent back to Vera Cruz for artillery and more troops and fought five more scrapes, losing another sixty men, before he bypassed Pillow and reached

Puebla on August 6. The reinforcements gave Scott a total of 8,061 men present and fit, with another 2,235 on the sick list.[51]

About 550 members of the national militia ambushed a supply column on July 12, forcing it back with a loss of sixty loaded mules and twenty horses. Scott sent two cavalry companies out on July 30 to raid a camp at San Juan de Los Llanos, about twenty-five miles northeast of Puebla. Such strikes had little effect, however, because guerrillas faded into the countryside when facing a stronger force of regulars. Small bands of foragers, drunkards, and stragglers ran the constant danger of capture and execution.[52]

Scott's neighborhood was not the only one under guerrilla assault. Nearly every seaport, especially Tampico, and posts on the Rio Grande, especially Camargo, were under constant, bloody harassment. Raids and sniping threatened to make Tampico untenable during the summer of 1847. Colonel Louis DeRussy led an expedition out of the town in July to free United States prisoners held at Huajutla. His command was ambushed at the Río Calabasa and badly beaten up, and was fortunate to get back to base at all.[53]

Scott had wanted to win the minds and feelings of the Mexican people, in order to conquer a peace. He failed. Polk had thought the government in Mexico City made all the decisions, so with a little more pressure it would give in to his will. He failed also. So did Taylor. Among them they had prolonged rather than ended the war because they had never considered how the other side would react to their actions. All of Mexico, it appeared, had arisen against *los Yanquis malditos.*

CHAPTER

19

THE MESSENGERS OF DEATH FLEW ABOUT ME IN ALL DIRECTIONS

(August 1847)

God of battles, was there ever a battle like this in the world before?

—Alfred, Lord Tennyson

HE SECRETARY OF WAR HAD A NERVOUS BREAKDOWN late in August 1847. Marcy's absence could not have come at a worse time, because the cabinet called out the remaining 6,000 volunteers authorized by prior legislation, if the War Department could find the money to pay and equip them. The search for already appropriated funds turned up some dirty deals. In mid-June the chief clerk of the Treasury Department and Washington banker William W. Corcoran had talked Quartermaster General Jesup into transferring $2 million to Corcoran's New Orleans branch. The quartermasters had spent only $400,000 by late July, while Corcoran's minions had used the rest for stock speculation.

As this thievery came to light, Polk sent Major General William O. Butler to Mexico, on the excuse that a replacement would be needed if

Scott walked off in a huff. That could set off a power struggle between Pillow and Worth. "I have great confidence in Pillow," Polk said, "but he is young in the service & the country do not know his merits as well as I do," so flagrant promotion of his friend would spark outrage. Polk told Butler that "contingencies" might come up "which would in a short time devolve upon you the chief command." Butler was experienced from the War of 1812 and unusually competent among the Democratic major generals. He performed well at Monterey, where he received a wound. Fifty-six years old, he was small and looked frail, but he was a tower of strength and a fountain of common sense. Polk could have done much worse, and often had.[1]

The other war zones were little worry to the president. In New Mexico new volunteers from Missouri and Illinois had replaced those whose enlistments had expired, so Price had an entirely green command. They raised hell and abused the citizenry, while the Indian conflicts continued. California remained quiet, and the Mormons had settled into their new homeland near Salt Lake.

Trouble for the president was approaching from California, however, as Kearny, Frémont, and company neared Fort Leavenworth. Frémont's chief booster, Senator Benton, asked the president on August 17 to head off a court-martial in the Kearny-Frémont controversy. Polk put that off, so Benton threatened to open an investigation in the Senate and belabored Polk through the middle of August. On the twenty-second the Thunderer turned around and demanded a trial to clear his son-in-law's reputation; he even sent a senatorial "order" to that effect to the adjutant general. Kearny placed the Pathfinder under arrest and ordered him to Washington for trial.[2]

If Benton's son-in-law did not come out of the affair smelling like a rose, Polk would find a powerful ally turned into a powerful enemy. The senator had squelched the debate over extending slavery into new territories. Still the furor grew. From June 1847 through the spring of 1850 a barrage of memorials from state legislatures rained down on Congress protesting the spread of slavery or denying Congress' power to stop that spread. Slavery threatened to overwhelm everything else related to the war.[3]

NO QUARTER TO THE DAMNED YANKEES!

"The vile Volunteers and raw levies have been here," D. H. Hill said of an abandoned *pueblo*, "and the inhabitants have fled to escape from these savages." The victims of these atrocities were usually poor *Indios* and *Castas,* already divorced from the national and state governments, and the

volunteers alienated them from the United States as well. The poor farmers saw anyone in any uniform as an enemy.[4]

Taylor was not inclined to crack down on future voters. Wool complained late in August that soldiers were raiding nearby *ranchos,* stealing
and "insulting the families and particularly the women." The volunteer officers were no better than their men. Colonel Robert Treat Paine, a Whig
commanding the North Carolinians at Saltillo, was a sadistic martinet. His
men mutinied and mobbed his tent on the night of August 14. The trouble
spread to the Virginia and Mississippi regiments and became a riot on the
night of the fifteenth. When Paine moved to put it down, his officers refused to back him up. Paine pulled his pistols and fired, killing one soldier
and wounding another. Better-behaved troops restored peace. Wool ordered a court-martial, which sentenced two lieutenants to dismissal, along
with two privates charged as instigators. The officers, both Democrats,
appealed directly to the president. Polk overturned the verdicts, sparking
a long inquiry in the army and two investigations in Congress.[5]

Scott, in central Mexico, had greater problems with guerrillas. Padre
Jarauta and Juan Aburto were especially active, their armies ranging from
a handful of followers to more than a thousand as the situation demanded.
Many of these outfits were colorful. One called themselves "Lancers of
the Poisoned Spear," while another carried a guidon emblazoned "No quarter to the damned Yankees!"

The road out of Vera Cruz was muddy from summer rains by early
August, and the slow going made troops and caravans especially vulnerable. Major Folliot T. Lally left Vera Cruz on August 6 with a thousand men
and sixty-four supply wagons. Rumors spread that the troops escorted a
million dollars, so Jarauta and Aburto gathered about 1,500 *guerrilleros* to
go after the coins. They attacked Lally twice at Paso de Ovejas on August
10, costing the Anglos ten men. Lally halted and sent back for reinforcements. A relief column marched out of Vera Cruz, and the guerrillas
slaughtered all its mules and seized all the ammunition, money, mail, and
baggage in the train. The diversion eased the pressure on Lally, who resumed marching on the twelfth, only to run into another ambush at the
National Bridge, losing a further fifty-one men. On the thirteenth another
column left Vera Cruz to support Lally, who had forced his way past the
bridge. The second relief was struck and forced back to Vera Cruz after
losing all its wagons but one. Lally kept fighting his way up the road, and by
the time he got to Jalapa on August 20 he had lost 105 men in all. His ordeal was not over, because the guerrillas hit him the next day as he left
Jalapa, claiming 100 more casualties. He finally limped into Puebla with
most of his wagons, which carried no money. The irregulars fanned out

and attacked all the fixed posts that Scott still had left behind. A daring band raided a depot at Guadalupe, Puebla state, late in August and stole all the wagon teams from the mule yard there. Anglo troops set out after the rustlers and ran into an ambush by about 300 Mexican lancers, who inflicted a dozen casualties.[6]

The guerrillas and local partisans preyed not just on stragglers but also on scouting or foraging parties if they were small enough. Dragoons were jumped near Chalco on August 14 by 200 lancers, losing several of their number including their commanding officer. A foraging detail rustling sheep was bushwhacked near Santo Domingo and lost four men. As Scott's army advanced toward Mexico City, a scouting party of dragoons and the Mexican Spy Company was attacked on the fifteenth by patented irregulars, leaving several dead and wounded on both sides. The next day Scott's advance stumbled into a large mixed force of Mexicans who hit and ran.[7]

The constant harassment inspired a real dread in North American troops. Major William Booth Taliaferro was part of a convoy that left Vera Cruz early in September. "The last command which left the seaboard was defeated and had to retreat," he told his journal, "and we left with the full expectation of a bloody and severe fight every day until we succeeded in our enterprise, and no day broke over our heads on the march but was looked upon as the last by many of our number." Gunfire was so common after dark that Taliaferro slept through it, "although I may be called to a fierce conflict before morning."[8]

MEXICANS, I CONGRATULATE MYSELF AND YOU

Scott turned his back on the turmoil in his rear and ordered his 10,738 officers and men to advance on Mexico City on August 5. Twiggs led out with his division on the seventh, followed by those of Worth, Quitman, and Pillow at one-day intervals, raising clouds of dust on the highland road. By August 10 only a small garrison remained at Puebla, guarding hospitals and supply stores. "Like Cortez," Scott wrote to the secretary of war, "finding myself isolated and abandoned, and again like him, always afraid that the next ship or messenger might recall or further cripple me, I resolved no longer to depend on Vera Cruz, or home, but to render my little army a self-sustaining machine." Scott always had a flair for the melodramatic, and he was not alone. "Scott is lost," the duke of Wellington, victor at Waterloo, told the *Times* of London.[9]

They both exaggerated, because Scott had plenty of supplies at Puebla and with the army. The North American general was more concerned about the opposition around Mexico City, where Santa Anna had been busy. With Congress in disarray, the Savior of His Country again made himself dictator, ruling with an iron hand. "There was no more law other than his will," Abraham López groused, "but it was said that this was for the good of the fatherland." Once again he created an army of about 25,000, relying on the national guards and his few regulars for backbone, scouring the prisons and drafting laborers to fill out the ranks of *indio* conscripts. Santa Anna knew that the best defense would be forward, in the passes on the road from Puebla. After Cerro Gordo, however, he did not trust his green troops to wage a good fight so far out. They might put up a better scrap with their backs to their homes. "In order to learn the feelings of the leaders of the community," Santa Anna said later, "I called a meeting in the main room of the palace. I begged this delegation for courage, pouring out all the bitterness in my heart. Words straight from the heart always carry more weight, and I moved the hearts of those men." He flattered himself as always, but he did arouse the *Polkos,* while the poor had no choice about being drafted. The rich sat the campaign out.

Santa Anna had natural strengths to work with, because the capital was surrounded by wetlands with limited approaches commanded by well-designed defenses. Scott had only four practical approaches—through Texcoco toward the north and northwest part of the city; along the road on the north shore of Lake Chalco, south of Lake Texcoco past a rise called El Peñón Viejo (the Old Crag); a road through Mexicaltzingo; and south of lakes Chalco and Xochimilco to San Agustín.[10]

The brightest spot of the Mexican army was its small corps of engineers, in particular Lieutenant Colonel Manuel Robles Pezuela, who had advised against making a stand at Cerro Gordo. Santa Anna and his generals agreed that Scott would drive up the main road to the east gate of the city. That road was commanded at the south end of Lake Texcoco by the high, rocky summit of Peñón, about 450 feet tall and a thousand yards long. Robles built formidable fieldworks and batteries for thirty guns there, but pointed out that Peñón could be bypassed south of lakes Chalco and Xochimilco. If the enemy reached San Augustín he could drive north through San Antonio or continue farther west to San Gerónimo, thence toward the southwestern approaches to Mexico City. There were topographical disadvantages to the southward routes, however, and several defensible places along them. Santa Anna ordered other works built at Mexicaltzingo, San Antonio, and Churubusco. To the city's southwest, the hill and "castle" of Chapultepec should defend the city if the North Americans went so far out. Otherwise, a few blockhouses guarded major roads while defenses to the north were not thought necessary. Lieutenant Theodore Laidley was impressed by the Mexicans' efforts. "I had no conception that the city was so well fortified on all sides as it really is," he told his father, "and their field works are beautiful, skillfully and scientifically executed."

Santa Anna assumed that Scott's vulnerability was his supply line to Puebla, which a move to the south would stretch dangerously. While General Gabriel Valencia blocked the invaders at Peñón with about 7,000 men, Major General Juan Álvarez and his cavalry would sweep around Scott and cut his communications. General Nicolás Bravo Rueda would take station at Mexicaltzingo on the southern approach to the city.[11]

On the afternoon of August 9 Scott's approach was announced in Mexico City with a "terrible blast from a 16-pounder artillery piece," according to Abraham López. The working class and the "unfortunate class" (drafted *léperos*) flocked to their assembly points and barracks. The Soldier of the People issued another vainglorious proclamation. "Blinded by pride," he declaimed, "the enemy have set out for the capital. For this, Mexicans, I congratulate myself and you." His government announced "reforms" drafting every citizen between the ages of sixteen and fifty.[12]

The *Polkos* and newly raised national guards marched toward Peñón, where a mixed regiment of national guards and regular draftees was already stationed under General Antonio León. General Pedro María Anaya's regiment led off, trooping past balconies and rooftops crowded with anxious citizens. The Victory Battalion of the *Polkos,* raised from the city's younger merchants, followed with "luxurious uniforms and elegant servants." The Hidalgo Battalion was made up of men usually exempt from military service—the very young, the very old, and the heads of prominent families. The Independence and Bravos battalions brought up the rear, men raised from the working class, ragged but proud of bearing, their dress betraying "a history of privations."

León's men had missed the chance to strut their stuff, so Santa Anna went out to Peñón on the eleventh and reviewed them on parade. The Soldier of the People was greeted with shouts of *"Viva!"* An enormous crowd of civilians followed him and set up eateries and other ramshackle businesses, creating a "portable city that sprouted from the landscape." The defense of Mexico City had taken on the air of a carnival. August 15 was a Sunday, and churchmen raised an altar covered with gold cloth and ornaments. The troops laid down their muskets to take communion. "The canopy of the altar was the diaphanous sky," an observer remembered, "the lighting of that vast temple was the sublime sun." As the *soldados* entrusted their lives to God, the enemy advance was sighted and an alarm given, but not even that interrupted the ceremonies.[13]

Twiggs' advance reached Ayotla, about fifteen miles from Mexico City, on August 11. Over the next two days the other divisions moved into supporting positions at Chalco and Chimalpa. Scott sent his engineers out to find out what he faced. Mexico City stood in the Valley of Mexico, a great bowl about forty-six miles north to south and thirty-two miles wide. Santa Anna relied for its defense on the six lakes and extensive marshes on the valley floor, with farm fields crossed by raised roads and causeways.

Captains Robert E. Lee and James L. Mason and Lieutenant Isaac I. Stevens scouted out Peñón. Lee reported that the position could be taken, but it would be a bloody business. The place could be approached only on a long causeway through a marsh on the south side of Lake Texcoco. Its guns also commanded the village of Mexicaltzingo, which was itself heavily defended. Further scouting revealed that the defenses at Mexicaltzingo were not as strong as they appeared at a distance. Scott thought he might feint toward Peñón, then send his main assault against Mexicaltzingo. If he succeeded there, he would turn the positions at Churubusco and farther south and open the way to the southern gates of the capital. Scott ordered Worth to send one of his own engineers to check out the road south of Lake Chalco. Brevet Colonel James Duncan did so on the fourteenth and described the road "as a whole, excellent" and not easy to block.[14]

Scott decided on August 15 to drive along the south side of lakes Chalco and Xochimilco to the crossroads at San Agustín and weigh his prospects from there. San Agustín was about nine miles south of Mexico City on the road to Cuernavaca and Acapulco and twenty-five miles from Scott's starting point behind Ayotla. Worth's division and the cavalry started out on the afternoon of the fifteenth, followed the next morning by most of the rest of the army. Twiggs' division remained behind at Ayotla most of the sixteenth to mask the move. Duncan had been too optimistic—the road was a wet, muddy mess, covered by water in many places. It was also threatened by cavalry, which had cover in the rough land south of the road. The only skirmish happened on the sixteenth outside Ayotla, however, when Álvarez and a small legion of cavalry and infantry threatened Twiggs' flank. Driven off by artillery, Álvarez withdrew into the city.[15]

Santa Anna realized that Scott was bypassing his main defense. He withdrew all but a covering force from Peñón on the seventeenth, marched the troops back to the city, and put them on the road south. The big rise to the east had seemed impregnable and civilians were sure that the enemy would attack it and lose, so the Anglo shift to the south discouraged soldiers and citizens alike. As the troops marched through town, rich citizens who had not already left fled to the north. Said one who stayed behind, "The sight alone of the deserted city inspired sorrow and a shudder."[16]

Scott's advance reached San Agustín and encountered a road that ran north through San Antonio and Churubusco to the southeast corner of Mexico City. South of Churubusco a secondary road ran westerly to Coyoacán, with a branch northerly to Tacubaya and the southwestern defenses of the city. Scott sent engineers to scout out San Antonio. They ran into artillery fire from Mexican works south of the village, the first round killing the escort commander. The defenses were very strong, the left abutting Lake Xochimilco. The right could not be turned because it was anchored on el Pedregal (the Rocky Place), which one soldier called "a heap of Rocks almost impassable for infantry and totally so for Artillery and Cavalry."

The Pedregal was a lava badlands that ran over five miles southwest from San Antonio, about three and a half miles wide, a jumble of volcanic rocks impenetrable by anything but a goat. Lee and P. G. T. Beauregard checked it out. They topped a hill called Zacatepec at the southwestern corner of the badlands and spotted Mexican troops preparing defenses on a rise at the village of San Gerónimo, across the road from an Indian *pueblo* called Padierna at the lava's edge. These soldiers were from Valencia's army, which had moved into San Ángel to the northeast the day before and extended its position to San Gerónimo. Lee and Beauregard and their escort skirmished with Mexican pickets out of San Ángel, but they had proven that it was possible to get across the Pedregal, though at great risk if the other side realized what was going on.

Scott scheduled a battle for the next day, August 19. Mexican soldiers saw what happened over the next two days as one battle, which they named Padierna for its starting point. The Anglos regarded it as two battles. They called the first one Contreras, after a village to the southwest where none of it took place, and the second Churubusco.[17]

SCREAMING WOMEN RAN BACK AND FORTH LIKE FURIES

Santa Anna had established his defensive line generally along the Río Churubusco, a river that combined a number of creeks just north of San Ángel and ran east to Lake Xochimilco, which it entered just south of Mexicaltzingo. He ordered Valencia with about 5,500 men to San Ángel on the right, forward from the general run of his line on the south side of the river. Francisco Pérez commanded a smaller division two miles east at Coyoacán, and farther east Nicolás Bravo held a *convento* and a tête-de-pont on the south side of the river at Churubusco. The troops holding San Antonio remained in their fieldworks. The positions were strong but isolated. Santa Anna was confident that Scott would attack only one at a time, and good roads along the river made reinforcing any of them possible. Possible, that is, if not for General Valencia, a fat, no-necked man with a loud voice, an obnoxious manner, and striking blue eyes. He was also a drunkard, a dedicated conspirator, and not too bright. He had been Santa Anna's rival for years, and the forty-eight-year-old *caudillo* was not about to take orders from another *caudillo*.[18]

Santa Anna had ordered Valencia to entrench at San Ángel and hold there. Instead, the latter advanced about 4,000 of his men to San Gerónimo and dug in on high ground below the village, overlooking Padierna on the edge of the badlands. He believed he could strike Scott in the flank if the North American advanced due north. He was on poor ground for such a move, however, the terrain craggy and rock-strewn, decorated with puny shrubs and weedy brush. Valencia counted on the Pedregal to defend him. When he was told that the Anglos were active there, he laughed and said, "No! No! You're dreaming, man. The birds couldn't cross that Pedregal!"[19]

Santa Anna ordered Valencia to withdraw to San Ángel on August 18. Valencia "scorned" that, claiming that his "conscience as a military man" prevented him from obeying. What he really thought was that if he beat the *Yanquis* at San Gerónimo, he would be the hero of the day; if he did that at San Ángel, Santa Anna would get the credit. The Soldier of the People left Valencia "to act on his own responsibility."[20]

Scott ordered a road cleared across the badlands to move artillery up and around the flank of the San Antonio position, which Worth would press from the front. Pillow's division would provide the stoop labor while Twiggs' men protected and supported it. A gang of 500 men carved a road beginning on the morning of August 19. The party ran into Mexican pickets around noon, but two companies of riflemen drove them off. An hour or so later some of Valencia's guns opened up on the road crew, who took cover. Pillow ordered the work halted until the Mexican guns could be silenced. He sent a field battery, another of mountain howitzers, and a company of rocketeers to the edge of the lava about a thousand yards from Valencia's position.

The fat general refused to believe reports of that movement until Anglo rounds landed among his men. The North American guns were too light and too few to accomplish much, however, and Mexican counterfire forced them back into the rocks. To the Anglo left, a regiment and battalion of infantry crossed an arroyo to within 200 yards of Valencia's trenches and stayed there. This, it turned out, was the route to victory, but the United States generals failed to follow up. Scott, focused on San Antonio, regarded the action to his left merely as a move around the Mexican position on his north. Events took on a life of their own in the lava bed, however. Early in the afternoon Pillow ordered General Bennett

Riley's brigade from Twiggs' division to seize San Gerónimo behind Valencia, cutting off the latter's avenue of retreat while Persifor Smith's brigade held the Mexicans' attention in front. Valencia sent a small party toward Padierna, whereupon Pillow sent his reserves behind Riley, whose men labored through the rocks, dropped into the arroyo, forded the creek, crossed the road, and slogged up a small valley northwest of Valencia's camp to San Gerónimo.

Santa Anna guessed what was happening and ordered part of his main force to support Valencia, but the troops were stopped by infantry volleys from the edge of the Pedregal. Scott heard the noise and diverted a brigade from the San Antonio area to reinforce Pillow. A major army was now trudging in a long line behind Riley. Smith, meanwhile, told Pillow that he would shift his route to the right, aiming to turn Valencia's left. Leaving his guns and some infantry to pin Valencia down in front, Smith followed Riley and the other corps out of the Pedregal. Without planning to, the Anglos had turned Valencia's position, with three brigades in his rear and another moving up.

Santa Anna realized that Valencia was about to become heavily en-gaged, and sent Pérez and about 3,000 men from Coyoacán to reinforce Valencia, then followed with two regiments and five guns, superseding Pérez in command when he caught up with him. The Soldier of the People deployed his troops on the heights in front of San Ángel at about five o'clock on the nineteenth. He had cut off the three United States brigades around San Gerónimo. If the Mexican army had had a unified command, experienced staff, and tactical flexibility, it could have smashed the *Yanquis* between two strong forces. Lacking those strengths, Santa Anna did not try.

Pérez's advance had given the other side pause, but now the Soldier of the People decided that he should withdraw; Pérez declined. Santa Anna backed up his part of the force, then sat down north of San Ángel. At dark a heavy, cold rain began to fall. Valencia's troops were hungry and so soaked that they could not lie down. Two messengers rode in from Santa Anna with orders to retreat. Valencia asked where Santa Anna was and for the first time learned that his relief had pulled back north. He exploded in a volcano of obscenities. Santa Anna, told that Valencia refused to obey his orders, raged in turn. "Valencia is an ambitious, insubordinate sot," he roared. "He deserves to have his brains blown out, and I will not expose my men to the storm for him." Santa Anna's men spent the night in Indian *pueblos* north of San Ángel. Valencia's greeted the dawn of August 20 shivering from cold and hunger, although the rain had stopped. They looked toward San Ángel for relief but saw none. Some deserted; the rest just sat demoralized and hopeless. Valencia thought that he had scored a great victory on the nineteenth. "After a desperate combat with all the Anglo-American forces," he reported to the war ministry, he had "put them to shameful flight." He wanted only help from Santa Anna to "destroy the miserable remains of the Anglo-Americans."[21]

Santa Anna's last order the night before had told Valencia to spike his guns and sneak his troops past the enemy. Valencia, however, wanted to follow up his "glorious" victory—actually, fire had been limited and casualties few on both sides—and planned to mop up the Anglo survivors at sunrise. Those Anglos were as cold and wet as the Mexicans and, thinking themselves about to be cut off by Santa Anna and Pérez, they were desperate. One of Smith's engineers found an arroyo running southwest from San Gerónimo, a rugged path that came out directly behind Valencia's camp. It was still dark, the rain poured down, and lightning tore the sky. Lee made his way through the jumble of rocks to Scott's headquarters carrying Smith's request for a diversion while he moved against Valencia's rear at three in the morning. Scott ordered Twiggs to round up whatever troops he could and cut across the Pedregal with Lee as a guide. The general ordered Worth to send another brigade to support Twiggs, then sent cavalry to relieve Quitman's brigade at San Antonio. This was not the battle Scott had foreseen, but he adjusted to conditions as they developed.

About 4,000 men following Smith set out through the arroyo. The route was rough and slippery with the rain, and it was after daylight before the corps was ready to attack. A brigade and other troops were left behind to pin Valencia down in front, and Twiggs' units joined them. The plan was for these men to charge down the steep bank at the edge of the lava bed, across a stream, and up the bank opposite into Mexican fire. The distraction worked. Valencia was shifting men to his front to meet this attack when Smith's command hit his troops from behind with a crashing volley followed by a screaming bayonet charge. The shocked *soldados* broke and ran within a quarter hour, Valencia at the head of the stampede. General José Mariano Salas, former president, tried to rally the cavalry, but the troopers rode around him and over some of the infantry in their panic. The frenzy increased when the horse soldiers took fire from their flank, aimed by Anglos at the edge of the Pedregal. Valencia's army simply evaporated from the shock. He lost at least 700 men killed and another 843, including four generals, taken prisoner. The rest scattered over the countryside. When Anglo troops cleaned up the battlefield, they rounded up 700 pack mules, twenty-two cannons, and heaps of muskets and ammunition. United States losses were sixty killed and wounded.[22]

Santa Anna had tried to prevent the calamity by calling up a reserve brigade under Brigadier General Joaquín Rangel to open a way to Valencia. Once the troops advanced south of San Ángel they ran into fugitives from San Gerónimo. Santa Anna flailed at the running men with his riding crop and cursed Valencia for his disobedience. He diverted Rangel's brigade to guard the southwestern approaches to the capital and ordered Bravo at San Antonio and Brigadier General Antonio Gaona at Mexicaltzingo to retire to Churubusco. The position there was strong, and since it sat at the junction of the San Antonio and Mexicaltzingo roads, it was the best place to stop Scott's advance. Santa Anna rode there with the troops accompanying him and sent out orders that if Valencia had survived the catastrophe near Padierna, he should be arrested and shot on the spot.[23]

Manuel Gómez Pedraza blamed the disaster on "the stupidity committed by the disobedient Valencia . . . and the inconceivable conduct of Santa Anna when he stood by as a motionless spectator watching the ruination of his rival." Gómez put his finger on Mexico's fundamental problem when he concluded, "It is not the first time, nor will it be the last, that the criminal desire of generals to surpass one another results in the loss of nations." Mexico, he believed, was already lost.[24]

Salas said bluntly that Valencia "disappeared from among us, at the commencement of the battle." Valencia survived, but played no further part in the war. As for his *soldados*, there was no way to safety, because the Yankees had cut all routes. Those who tried to get through the hills around San Gerónimo and Padierna fell to their deaths "like a torrent from the heights," said a Mexican reporter. Everywhere was chaos and terror as soldiers, mules, horses, and wounded men "peopled the air with their cries, and screaming women ran back and forth like furies." United States cavalry charged through the terrified masses, slaughtering left and right.[25]

The scene was worse than the aftermath of Cerro Gordo. "The battlefield was such a sight as I had never seen before," said one United States soldier, "and which I would have been satisfied never to see again. The ground was covered with gore from the wounds of the dying and dead which lay thick upon the field. The sight was horrible—enough to chill the hardest heart. Some had a leg, a foot, an arm or hand mangled to pieces and were lying upon the cold, muddy ground shivering with cold, begging for a bit of bread or a drink of water." Most distressing of all was the sight of hundreds of dead *soldaderas* scattered among the bodies of their men.[26]

Unfortunately, the day was not over.

IF WE STILL HAD MUNITIONS, YOU WOULD NOT BE HERE

Churubusco was destined to see carnage. The name is a corruption of Huitzilipochco, meaning "place of Huitzilipochtli," after the bloodthirsty

Méxic god, alter ego War Eagle. The village on the south bank of the Río Churubusco was a small collection of whitewashed adobe houses with red tile roofs, surrounded by neat vegetable gardens and bougainvillea vines blooming red and violet. The dominant structure was the walled Convento de San Mateo, an old monastery compound. The river and its radiating canals ran full from the recent rains, and sparkled in the sun. Rows of maguey planted on mounds lined its banks, and the surrounding country was a chessboard of head-high sugarcane and maize fields. The ground everywhere was muddy. This, Santa Anna decided, was a good place to cover the withdrawal of his troops closer to Mexico City. He told three of his best generals to keep the evacuation route open *"a toda costa y hasta el último trance sostuvieron"* ("at all cost and until the last possible moment").

Santa Anna put Pérez and 2,200 men at the tête-de-pont on the south bank of the river, across the road and about 300 yards from the monastery. Rincón and Anaya with 1,500 to 1,800 men would hold the *convento,* while about 1,200 cavalry stood ready to strike the Anglo flank. The *convento* and bridgehead had been partly fortified with earthworks holding seven guns. The approximately 8,000 North Americans bearing down on the place greatly outnumbered the defenders, most of whom were *Polkos,* though two companies of the San Patricio Battalion manned the guns, one company in each position.[27]

The battles of August 20 had so far gone forward without much planning on Scott's part, but he had reacted to events ably enough. He arrived at the west end of the Pedregal just after Valencia's army dissolved, and ordered Pillow and Twiggs to turn east toward Coyoacán to flank San Antonio. Worth sent a brigade and an infantry battalion across the Pedregal by an uncleared route to get behind San Antonio, while another brigade and some field artillery pressed the position from the south. The Mexicans in the trenches received Santa Anna's order to withdraw, so they spiked their guns and pulled out to the north. These were mostly untrained militia unprepared to conduct a fighting retreat. A regiment of Anglo regulars attacked their column and it split into two parts. The forward corps under Bravo reached Churubusco, but the rest scattered. The North Americans south of San Antonio saw what had happened, charged the fortifications, and took four guns, a Mexican general, and a few other prisoners.

Up ahead was chaos and mud. Bravo's disorganized horde of cavalry, infantry, artillery, wagons, livestock, *soldaderas,* officers' servants, camp followers, and civilian refugees churned the road into a sticky soup. Near Churubusco this mob converged with those covering the retreat out of San Ángel. Anglo observers in the tower of the church at Coyoacán reported that Santa Anna's army was thoroughly disorganized, so Scott impulsively ordered everyone forward. His engineers objected; they wanted to scout what was ahead and provide information for a sensible plan of attack. Scott ordinarily favored sound planning, but this time he just bulled ahead, and in the process shed a lot of Anglo blood unnecessarily. Some of the engineers never forgave him.[28]

Rincón and Anaya were as good as Mexican generals came, and ordered their men to hold their fire until the enemy was very close. The first attackers to arrive were Twiggs' men, who made the disorganized charge that Scott believed would do the job. Twiggs sent his units in piecemeal as they reached the scene, and they were blasted back by heavy musketry and artillery fire. A brigade on Twiggs' right fizzled its assault when the men scattered in a cornfield. The defense of the *convento* showed what Mexican troops could do when they were under competent commanders. Rincón knew he was on the defensive in a good position and so would not take any foolish risks. Besides, he had San Patricio gunners with him. The gritty *soldados* in the monastery tossed back every rush by Anglo troops, who were stunned and mauled by what they ran into. Twiggs sent a battery forward to even the odds, but the San Patricios outgunned the North Americans, who withdrew after an hour and a half of cannon duels that cost them twenty-four men and fourteen horses. Thick gunsmoke shrouded the scene, the noise deafening as the mob of refugees struggled to get across the bridge. Worth's division arrived from the south about a half hour after the San Patricios had driven the battery back. He deployed his brigades astride the road and recklessly charged the bridgehead. His best regiment, the 6th Infantry, was driven back twice by heavy and accurate volleys. Blood pooled on the road, and signs of panic spread through the Anglo ranks in the face of this unexpected ferocity and skill on the Mexican side. Worth's troops on the right of the road were spared the worst bloodletting because they bogged down in high corn, ditches, and dikes in the fields, obstacles engineers could have discovered beforehand. The division's artillery did not even get into action before the whole corps reeled back.

United States officers should have known what could happen when even untrained militia stood in protective positions under good leadership—that had been the story of Bunker Hill. Scott had blundered into two uncoordinated attacks, arrogantly assuming that Mexicans would run at the first shot because he misinterpreted what had happened to Valencia's corps in the morning. Those men had run away in panic because they were hit from behind, their position was exposed, and their commander was an idiot.

Scott barged ahead again. After Twiggs had bloodied his men against the *convento,* Scott sent Pierce, followed by Shields, to cross the river on a bridge west of Churubusco, then cut across country northeast to threaten the Mexican rear. Once the Anglos crossed the river they bogged down in cornfields and marshes. By the time they approached the road running north from Churubusco, Santa Anna had sent about 2,200 infantry to meet them on the road and about 1,500 cavalry to threaten their left. The Mexican troops took cover in two ditches and volleyed hell into the North American ranks. Shields' men broke and ran for cover, while Pierce's just hunkered down.

The pressure of numbers and firepower was bound to tell on the out-numbered defenders as Worth kept up his stubborn attacks on the bridge-head. The *soldados* began to lose heart. Worth could not see that, but he did discover that the Mexican left had been shortened by the diversion of men across the river to stop Shields. Worth ordered some units eastward be-yond the Mexican position, across the river, then left to advance on the rear of the tête-de-pont. At the same time he sent parts of two regular in-fantry regiments directly against the twenty-foot-wide ditch in front of the Mexican works. The doughboys, fired with anger at their losses, stormed over the ditch and up the parapet, and took the bridgehead in a hand-to-hand bloodbath. They bagged 192 prisoners, three guns, and the ammunition store, and turned one of the 4-pounders on the *convento.* The position was a mess of bodies and blood.

Rincón was isolated and his ammunition was running low. He had ear-lier sent two aides to Santa Anna to ask for resupply. The Soldier of the People sent the wrong caliber ammunition. Only the San Patricios had a decent supply of the right caliber and they fought like tigers. The action went on for more than three hours, the San Patricios repeatedly tearing down surrender flags. Worth put two guns on the road to bombard the *con-vento,* which they did for about fifteen minutes. The defenders moved a gun that way to return fire, but this thinned the defense at the southern end of the compound. An Anglo infantry regiment saw the weak spot and climbed over the parapet. The defenders backed up but still did not give up. The scene turned into a butcher's yard, the blood streaming until a Yankee cap-tain hoisted a white handkerchief on his sword. The *soldados* threw down their arms, and the San Patricios had no choice but to go along; they were about out of ammunition anyway. Anaya presented his sword to Twiggs, and the North American asked him where the remaining weapons and am-munition were. Anaya replied, "If we still had munitions, you would not be here." The Yankees took seven guns and 1,259 prisoners in the monastery, including three generals. Also in the bag were eighty-five members of the San Patricio battalion.[29]

While the roar from the *convento* continued, Shields regrouped his troops and, with Pierce following, charged the Mexicans in the ditches defending the road. It was a stupid head-on assault into fierce musketry. A third of Shields' brigade went down, including the colonel and lieutenant colonel of the South Carolina regiment and the commander of the New York regiment. Nevertheless, the bloody assault drove the outnumbered Mexicans out of their ditches and captured 380 of them. Shields linked up on the road with Worth's advance. The Mexicans were driven out of Churubusco, but the pursuit was haphazard. Worth halted his infantry after trooping up the road about two miles, but dragoons under Harney continued almost to the Mexico City defenses. Captain Philip Kearny ended this dash with a foolish charge against a battery just outside the San Antonio *garita* (fortified gate). "Oh, what a glorious sight it was to see Phil Kearny riding into them!" wrote an Anglo soldier. Kearny lost an arm.[30]

"Men were shot down on all sides of me, & the messengers of death flew about me in all directions," Lieutenant Edmund Hardcastle, West Point Class of 1846, wrote home after Churubusco. "I have seen fighting enough. I have seen blood enough spilt."[31]

August 20 was the bloodiest day of the whole war. Of his 8,500 men engaged, Scott lost 133 killed and 865 wounded. Santa Anna's army took an even worse beating, over a third of its men, around 10,000 in all. Scott reported the Mexican losses at 4,297 killed and wounded and 2,637 prisoners including eight generals, but that did not allow for the dead, wounded, and refugees who simply disappeared. A roll call in Mexico City a few days later counted 13,828 privates remaining in the Mexican army, about half of what had been available before Scott marched out of Puebla.[32]

The pall of death hung over the Place of Huitzilipochtli, the flies singing and the buzzards and dogs closing in. Bodies and parts of bodies were everywhere, some literally in heaps, and blood coated all. Details fanned out to retrieve the wounded, and other parties went out to plunder and bury the dead. Scott's army could claim victory, but it was in no condition to move on to the Halls of the Montezumas. The Mexican defense had been gallant, stubborn, and deadly, but hopeless against the size and firepower of the North American army. For once in the war, however, Mexican artillery had matched that of the Anglos, thanks especially to the San Patricios. The surviving Mexican troops might be prisoners, but they had nothing to be ashamed of. Nor did the Anglo soldiers, who had charged into hell at the commands of leaders who acted as if they knew nothing about tactics. Chief blame for the ghastly mess rested on Scott's head. Subordinates had seized an opportunity and obliterated Valencia's corps during the morning, and afterward Scott commanded like a bull-headed amateur.

Santa Anna had little to be ashamed of either, but he acted as if he did. He forbade his troops from discussing the day's events, but many of the people in Mexico City had watched the action from the city walls. "Everything, everything has been lost," fumed Congressman Ramírez, "except our honor. That was lost a long time ago." He blamed the catastrophe on "the incompetence and cowardice of our generals and leaders who . . . have given proof of what they have been, are, and will continue to be: cowards, ignoramuses, and men wholly devoid of even one spark of personal honor."[33]

He was not the only demoralized Mexican. Anglo troops intercepted mail pouches in the days after the battle. One letter read by Ralph W. Kirkham said, "We trusted for safety to our numbers, but our enemy sleeps not and knows no fear." D. H. Hill found one that said, "Our enemy has taught us that valor is superior to numbers."[34]

WE ARE IN A STRANGE SITUATION

Santa Anna returned to the capital that night, according to a witness, "possessed of a black despair." He received a note from Scott demanding that he surrender the city. He did not demand surrender of the Mexican army, however, because it was Santa Anna's source of power and Scott thought that keeping him in office would be necessary to getting a final peace. The Savior of His Country bounced back from his dark mood, assembled the members of the cabinet who were still in town, and sent Foreign Minister Francisco Pacheco to ask the British minister, Bankhead, to intervene with Scott and stop a sack of the city. Bankhead refused, but offered to forward a letter to Trist. Pacheco wrote one to Secretary of State Buchanan, answering the North American offer of the previous spring to reopen negotiations. Bankhead sent it along with one of his own to Trist, saying he hoped that peace might finally be at hand.[35]

Scott had no idea what was going on in the Mexican government, so he moved siege guns closer to the city. He, Trist, and the headquarters staff were riding toward Tacubaya early on the morning of August 21 when they met a gorgeously furnished carriage carrying Brigadier General Ignacio Mora y Villamil, crossing the Anglo lines under a flag of truce and carrying the letters from Pacheco and Bankhead. Mora relayed an oral statement from Santa Anna that the latter wanted to negotiate an armistice. He should have requested that formally, but Scott was so eager to end the fighting that he himself offered a truce. "Too much blood has already been shed in this unnatural war between the two great Republics of this

Continent," he wrote Santa Anna. Scott reminded the Mexican leader that Trist was with him as a commissioner "clothed with full powers to negotiate a treaty." To clear the way for that, Scott was "willing to sign, on reasonable terms, a short armistice." He would wait until the twenty-second for an answer, and meanwhile would continue to advance his positions toward the city.[36]

Santa Anna claimed in his memoirs that when Scott proposed an armistice, "I would not have even listened to such a request if it had not been necessary to repair the catastrophe of Padierna." That was true enough, but the *caudillo* had already pointed out to Pacheco that the time it would take for his message to reach Buchanan and for an answer to get back would be enough to rebuild the army and the city's defenses. Doing so would violate the Law of War, which defined an armistice as an agreement to suspend hostilities or preparations for them.[37]

Scott should have known enough about Santa Anna to expect that, but whatever he did would cause trouble back in Washington, so he explained himself to the secretary of war. Scott could have pushed into the city and probably taken it, he claimed, but he ordered a halt because his troops were worn out and needed resupply. There were many dead and wounded to attend to and prisoners to process. He did not think he could keep his volunteers from committing rape, plunder, and murder, and did not want to be responsible for the pillage of a capital city. Mostly, Scott told Marcy, he and Trist had been "admonished by the best friends of peace—intelligent neutrals and some American residents—against precipitation—lest by wantonly driving away the government and others—dishonoured—we might scatter the elements of peace, excite a spirit of national desperation, and thus indefinitely postpone the hope of accommodation." He wanted to leave something to Mexico "on which to rest her pride, and to recover temper."[38]

Mexico's minister of war, Brigadier General Lino José Alcorta, accepted Scott's proposed armistice and appointed commissioners to work out the details. Scott appointed his own agents, and they signed the terms on August 23. Hostilities were suspended within seventy-eight miles of the capital, but fighting could resume on forty-eight hours' notice by either party. Neither side would reinforce its troops or strengthen its fixed positions. The United States would permit supplies to enter Mexico City, and the Mexican government would allow Anglo commissaries into the city to buy provisions. There was also a general exchange of prisoners. Since the North Americans held a surplus, Scott let most loose on parole, except for the San Patricios.[39]

Scott and Trist hoped the armistice would lead to peace talks because

Santa Anna had said earlier that he would negotiate after a battle outside the capital. They did not understand that Mexico had no federal government but merely a flock of contending factions. The first one who showed signs of dealing with the *Yanquis* would be pounced on by many others. Even before the armistice was signed Pacheco asked for a special session of Congress to consider peace talks, but not enough members showed up to make a quorum. The war party still had the peace party cowed.[40]

Santa Anna and his advisers cooked up "points of discussion" for his peace commissioners to give to Trist at the opening of talks. These demanded that the United States drop all claims against Mexico, accept the Nueces River as the border of Texas, lift the naval blockade, abandon California, pay damages caused by the North American invasion, prohibit slavery in any territory ceded by Mexico, accept a guarantee of any peace treaty by a commission of foreign powers, let the San Patricio prisoners go, and return all property seized by the United States. The Savior of His Country knew that this would be rejected out of hand.[41]

The document was for domestic consumption, to satisfy the diehards. Trist got the idea that Santa Anna would enter negotiations once he was safe from internal challenges. This overestimated the *caudillo*'s political strength and underestimated the general hostility to the surrender of any Mexican territory including Texas. Under that misunderstanding, Trist told Santa Anna that he would pay the maximum money authorized in his instructions for agreement to the boundary on North American terms.[42]

Trist told Pacheco on August 25 that he wanted to start negotiations. One nominated commissioner after another turned the honor down, including former president Herrera. Santa Anna went to Herrera personally, saying that two successive Mexican governments had agreed that it was proper to hear any proposals the other side had to offer. Herrera came around, and once he agreed to become a commissioner he provided cover for others. They included José Bernardo Couto, a prominent Mexico City attorney; another lawyer, Miguel Atristáin; and General Mora. But the instructions Santa Anna gave them in his points reflected his own petulance and other prominent Mexicans' ignorance of the reality of the situation.[43]

The first meeting was on neutral ground between the armies at Atzcapuzalco, near Tacubaya, on August 27. The Mexicans said that they were empowered only to relay proposals to their government, and Trist objected, saying that he was authorized to deal only with commissioners possessing full powers to negotiate. Still, he read them a summary of the proposals he would offer. The North American suggested meeting the next day at a more comfortable place, Casa Colorada, closer to Tacubaya. It was behind Mexican lines, so to the fantasy-ridden Mexicans this looked like the United States was suing for peace. Santa Anna presented Trist's summary of the U.S. proposal to his cabinet on the twenty-ninth, and the next day to his generals. All agreed to give the commissioners plenary power to deal with the Anglo diplomat. The commissioners refused to accept this on the grounds that the Mexican terms left no room for negotiation, so Santa Anna let them make any concessions they thought necessary.[44]

Also on August 27, more than a hundred United States Army wagons entered Mexico City to buy supplics. Crowds pelted the drivers with stones and shouts of "Death to the Yankees!" Santa Anna sent lancers to break up the mob, which angered the masses even more. They redirected their stones to the cavalrymen and shouted, "Death to Santa Anna!" One woman threw a rock that knocked an Anglo soldier down, seriously injuring him. A police officer grabbed her and she screamed, "I wanted to kill him, I want to kill all of them! Because of them I have lost my poor son; instead of revenge, we let them come for our food; it is very unjust!" The police let her go.[45]

Revised instructions to the Mexican commissioners on August 30 remained obstinate, telling the delegates to stand firm on the Nueces boundary of Texas, although they could consent to an uninhabited neutral zone between the Río Bravo and the Nueces. The commissioners were not allowed to cede New Mexico or California but could offer the other side a trading factory at San Francisco. Pacheco would not let them grant a transit right across the Isthmus of Tehuantepec, and furthermore they should demand that the United States repay Mexico for lost customs duties. This was not diplomacy, but Trist kept trying until September 6, when the talks ended.[46]

"We are in a strange situation," Kirby Smith complained, "a conquering army on a hill overlooking an enemy's capital, which is perfectly at our mercy, yet not permitted to enter it, and compelled to submit to all manner of insults from its corrupt inhabitants." The "insults" went both ways. Santa Anna refused to allow contacts between North Americans and Mexicans, but Scott permitted "any and all Mexicans to pass freely among us," said D. H. Hill. "I was on the patrol Guard, a Guard for the express purpose of preventing soldiers from committing outrages. Several instances have occurred of depredations by our soldiers."[47]

One diversion for Scott's army during the armistice was the trial of deserters among the San Patricio Battalion. Two lieutenants, four sergeants, six corporals, and twenty-three privates had died fighting at Churubusco. Major Reilly and Captain O'Leary were wounded, along with many enlisted men. Eighty-five in all were taken prisoner out of 200 present at the start of the action, and more than 80 escaped.[48]

Scott charged seventy-two of the prisoners with desertion and had them tried at two courts-martial. One was held August 23 at the village of Tacubaya, the other August 26 at San Ángel. The presidents of both courts were Catholic, albeit nominally, and their names—Bennett Riley and John Garland—were suggestively Irish, although neither was. The chief target of the prosecution was Major John Reilly, formerly a private in the 5th Infantry. He was the ranking turncoat, and Scott's officers believed that he had been the main organizer of the battalion, although the evidence did not support that. One court sentenced thirty-six of its accused to hang, two to be shot, and three to be given fifty lashes and branded with a D (for deserter) on the cheek. The other sentenced all its prisoners to hang. Scott reduced the death sentences of seven to fifty lashes and remitted the judgments against two others entirely. Reilly had deserted before the war started, so he was to be whipped and branded.[49]

The deserters in the San Patricio Battalion had gone over the hill for the reasons that others did—brutal discipline, harassment because they were foreign-born or Catholic, drunkenness, the lure of women, and the inducements of Mexican officials. That put them in company with more than 9,000 other United States deserters, but most of the others were neither apprehended nor prosecuted. Fewer than a hundred in all were executed during and after the war, most for associated crimes. Only fifty-four were executed specifically for desertion, the majority San Patricios. North Americans regarded them as traitors and cowards, but they were definitely not cowards. They fought gallantly and became enduring Mexican heroes, still honored today.

THE HAVOC AMONG THE MEXICANS WAS NOW HORRIBLE IN THE EXTREME

(September 1847)

[The Aztecs] said that by no means would they give themselves up,
for as long as one of them was left he would die fighting,
and that we would get nothing of theirs because they would burn
everything or throw it into the water.

—Hernán Cortés

Scott's MAIN SUPPLY DEPOT AND HOSPITALS were at Puebla,
guarded by about 400 men commanded by Brevet Colonel Thomas Childs.
The people of the city had begun to snipe at the *Yanquis,* and the country-
side swarmed with thousands of *guerrilleros* under Brigadier General
Joaquín Rea. Attacks began with raids on the garrison bakeries and de-
struction of the aqueduct. Mounted irregulars hit the stockyards on
August 25 and drove off 700 horses and mules. Thirty-two North
Americans galloped in pursuit and into a trap that killed ten of them.
Childs divided his command among the old citadel called San José in town,
Fort Loreto on a rise to the northeast, and an old *convento* on a rise east of
Loreto. Rea led about 4,000 irregulars into the city on the night of
September 13 and attacked all the enemy positions. The assaults were

driven back, but the guerrillas made off with most of the cattle and sheep. Rea demanded a surrender on the sixteenth, but Childs refused. Rea then attacked San José but again was driven back. Two days later United States artillery blasted back another assault. Rea settled in for a more traditional siege. The outcome of the standoff depended on who could send help first—Scott to Childs or Santa Anna to Rea.[1]

Santa Anna also had trouble in his rear. Deputy Ramón Gamboa repeatedly accused him before Congress of "treason during this war." The *caudillo*'s collusion with the United States, he charged, had begun during the Texas Revolution. Gamboa's voice was a lone one for a while, but he spoke for many others.[2]

IF I HAD FOLLOWED MY PLANS, ALL WOULD HAVE GONE WELL

Scott's army was spread out in an arc south of the Río Churubusco while Trist and the peace commissioners talked. The latest Mexican offer, presented September 1, sounded much like what Atocha had relayed to Polk early in 1847. It insisted on the Nueces as the boundary of Texas, with an uninhabited buffer between that river and the Río Bravo. Mexico would not cede New Mexico but would sell part of northern California. Rights of transit across Tehuantepec were off the table. Trist replied that the United States would give up on both Baja and Tehuantepec in exchange for all of Alta California. He proposed extending the armistice for a month and a half while he asked for instructions from Washington on the Nueces Strip. The Mexican commissioners declared that they would submit the Alta California proposal to their government.[3]

The delegations got together again on September 6 and the Mexicans offered another counterproposal much like the last. "It would be a new thing," the document declared, "that war should be made upon a people for the simple reason that it refuses to sell a territory which its neighbor wishes to purchase." The chief news was that Mexico had already sold transit rights across the Isthmus of Tehuantepec to a British firm. "Not without sorrow," the document concluded, "ought we to confess that we are giving to humanity the scandalous example of two Christian peoples of two republics" who "mutually do themselves all the injury that is possible, when we have more land than is sufficient to populate and cultivate in the beautiful hemisphere which Providence has cast as our lot." The proposal was Santa Anna's way of ending the talks by making an offer that the other side would regard as obnoxious—the new boundary between the two countries would be the Adams-Onís Line, excepting only Texas across the Nueces.[4]

Trist reported this to Scott, and Old Fuss and Feathers notified Santa Anna that the armistice would terminate in two days. The Soldier of the

People had already decided to resume the fight. Telling his associates that his soldiers were rested enough, on September 3 he banned the sale of foodstuffs to Scott's commissaries, called in all soldiers and militia around the capital, and resumed work on Mexico City's defenses.[5]

Neither Scott nor Trist understood that Santa Anna had no authority to conclude a peace with the United States. Nor were the Mexicans ready to quit fighting. Trist never surrendered his optimism, however. He told the secretary of state on September 27 that he believed Santa Anna, who had suffered more defeats, was ready to make peace, except that the terms the United States was proposing were unacceptable, so the Polk administration should moderate its demands.[6]

Scott summoned his officers to his tent the night of September 6 to discuss what to do next. Much of his army was advanced toward the southwest corner of the city, but to attack the *garitas* (gates) there meant dealing with Chapultepec, which gave everyone shudders. The consensus was to shift against the Niño Perdido and San Antonio *garitas* on the south side of the city. Each *garita* included a wide, paved space surrounded by strong customs and warehouse buildings. Every one was a potential strongpoint.

Scott's planning was again poor. To force a way to the southern *garitas* he needed only to shift Worth's division and his own headquarters eastward out of Tacubaya and concentrate due south of the gates. Scott received a spy report on a massive compound called El Molino del Rey (King's Mill), on the western end of the wall around Chapultepec Park, on the seventh. The spies claimed that troops there had established a foundry to melt church bells and recast them into cannons. Given the absence of smoke at the place, this was ridiculous. Scott ordered a night raid to destroy the foundry, followed by a shift to the east the next morning. Worth instead suggested a daylight assault with a larger force. Scott agreed, abandoning his original plan.[7]

Scott's army was reduced by about 2,000 men by the August battles, and he planned to send it against a strong position that he had failed to scout out. Santa Anna guessed that Scott would go against the southern *garitas* and shifted considerable strength to Molino del Rey, from where he could either strike Scott's flank or sucker the Anglo into attacking there. The massive stone buildings of the mill complex were manned by two brigades under the generals Antonio León and Joaquín Rangel. About 500 yards west of the mill was another massive stone building, la Casa Mata (*casamata,* casemate), which engineers had surrounded with bastioned earthworks manned by 1,500 regulars under Brigadier General Francisco Pérez. There was an arroyo backed by a prickly pear hedge running between the mill and the *casa,* behind which General Simeon Ramírez stood with an infantry brigade and seven cannons. Beyond the Casa Mata was a rough arroyo, and about a mile west General Juan Álvarez was concealed with about 4,000 lancers, under orders from Santa Anna to strike the North American flank if Scott attacked. The position was laid out with interlocking fields of fire, and sat at the bottom of a gentle but rough-surfaced slope. Scott later estimated that there were 12,000 to 14,000 *soldados* in and around the Molino, but the actual figure was about 8,000.

At dawn on September 8 Worth prepared to attack the Molino with his whole division, about 3,250 men in three columns, in a frontal assault. A brigade under Lieutenant Colonel John Garland would storm the east and south sides of the mill, backed by two 24-pounders and two 6-pounders. Major George Wright and 500 men would hit the western side of the complex, while on the left a brigade under Colonel James S. McIntosh and another battery would go after the Casa Mata. Three squadrons of dragoons screened Worth's left, and one of Pillow's brigades feinted toward the southern *garitas*.

Worth sent engineers out before dawn, and they reported that the mill had been abandoned. They were wrong; Ramírez had pulled his guns back to be closer to the buildings. Worth started a short bombardment just before six in the morning, having little idea what his gunners should shoot at. The troops jumped off, aiming to overrun the mill and the Casa Mata in a single rush, until they got close enough for Ramírez's gunners to shatter the North American columns, riddling their ranks with grape and solid shot. Wright alone lost eleven out of fourteen officers. The Anglos reeled back toward their starting point, leaving a trail of dead and wounded. No sooner had they started backing up than Lieutenant Colonel Miguel María Echegaray and a light-infantry regiment counterattacked out of the Chapultepec grounds, smashed into what was left of Wright's column, and nearly obliterated it in a hand-to-hand brawl that made use of bayonets and saw muskets wielded as clubs. False rumors circulated among Anglo troops that the Mexicans slit the throats of the wounded during this melee. Meanwhile, Worth sent up two battalions to retrieve his men from the bloody mess they were in.

In front of the Casa Mata, McIntosh's corps trudged forward under the cover of the supporting battery until they blocked the gunners' line of sight. The Anglo cannons quit shooting and Mexicans in the fieldworks fired a musket volley, followed by a bayonet charge that stopped the Anglos about thirty yards short of their objective. The North Americans beat off the Mexican charge but suffered horrible casualties. The survivors literally crawled back out of range. Once they cleared the line of sight the supporting battery poured solid shot onto the Casa Mata. Pérez had no guns to answer that, and at about six-thirty in the morning he ordered a withdrawal before the walls fell down around his men.

Between them Santa Anna and Álvarez could have destroyed Worth's division entirely at this point. Santa Anna should have sent reinforcements forward but did not. He claimed later that a traitor convinced him that Scott would attack elsewhere. "If I had followed my plans, all would have gone well," he said lamely. When he heard the guns, "I knew then that the attack was exactly as I had previously planned for it." He confusingly claimed that he then ordered all available forces to march to the Molino, but they arrived too late; in fact, there was no such order.[8]

Santa Anna definitely ordered the cavalry to charge the North American left, and if Álvarez had done so, he might have torn Worth's division to pieces. He started in that direction but withdrew. He never explained why he pulled back or why he refused repeated orders to attack. He later claimed that a cavalry charge could have been "launched only when the enemy was breaking up." He said that the Anglo ranks, which were in chaos, had not broken because General Manuel Andrade had failed to attack when Álvarez ordered him to. Andrade denied that Álvarez had any right to give him orders. Álvarez "was on the enemy flank within rifle range, and the enemy was in disorder," Santa Anna complained, "but just as though he had nothing in the world to do, he sat there on his mule, playing the spectator." Álvarez actually was harboring his forces for future domestic struggles.[9]

While the Mexicans lost the battle on the North American left, on the right the action against the Molino turned into a spread-out brawl of small-unit actions, charges, retreats, and rallies. Worth fed infantry into the grinder as units became available, and the pressure told, as the Anglos got to the mill and bashed in two doors. The outnumbered Mexicans resisted ferociously, backing up room to room, losing their artillery. A battalion of sappers counterattacked Yankee regulars holding the cannons, but return fire killed General León and Colonel Lucas Balderas. Anglos kept pouring into the compound until the Mexicans were driven out. Without orders, other Mexican units advanced down from Chapultepec, but infantry to Worth's left drove them back. If the Anglo generals still thought the Mexicans would break and run, they were disabused of their fantasy by *soldados* conducting a stubborn withdrawal that included two strong but unsuccessful counterattacks along the north flank of Chapultepec Park.

The casualties inflicted on the North Americans during the two-hour battle testified to the fierce resistance. Worth lost a quarter of his division, 116 killed, 665 wounded, and 18 missing. One brigade lost half its officers and about a third of its men. Mexican losses are uncertain but probably to-taled around 2,000, including 685 taken prisoner. There was no cannon factory, but Scott ordered the buildings destroyed. The Casa Mata, which housed a powder store, caught fire near the end of the battle and blew up, killing more Anglos. Scott's army was back in its old positions by early afternoon.[10]

The scene was ghastly, blood pooling, bodies and parts of bodies in and around the buildings, smoke rising from the ruins of Casa Mata. "Our troops fought like heroes and were mowed like grass," said Lieutenant John James Peck. Hitchcock called the affair "a sad mistake." Worth was sobered by his losses. He summoned the commander of his engineer com-pany, Gustavus Smith, and asked him to consider how to approach the next objective with the least cost. "There have been too many valuable lives, of officers and men, lost recently in my division, for nothing," he lamented.[11]

Scott had blundered into two ill-conceived actions in a row, and if that continued, he would have no army left. Santa Anna also held on to a dwin-dling army. Many incompetent or cowardly generals had been weeded out, but so had some of the best and bravest. His surviving privates had be-come hard-fighting veterans, but they increasingly dreaded the *Yanquis,* and especially their cannons. Santa Anna might have gone on the offensive against the Anglos in their disarray, but he dared not. His men must fight from cover, and where they would do that was up to Scott.

MEXICANS, THESE ARE THE MEN THAT CALL US BARBARIANS

Scott had other things on his mind, ordering the executions of the San Patricio deserters to go forward. He also ordered all generals and their staffs to attend, along with units from every regiment in the army. Guillermo Prieto said that the San Patricios had "gained great sympathy for their irreproachable conduct and the valor and enthusiasm with which they defended our cause." Delegations of women appealed to Scott for mercy but could not penetrate his "hyena's heart."[12]

The first thirty prisoners were marched into the plaza of the village of San Jacinto, a pretty little town with a lovely church, early on September 10. Twiggs was in charge, and many Mexican priests and civilians were in horrified attendance. Sixteen of the prisoners were halted under a scaffold in the square while the other fourteen were tied to trees in front of the church. Twiggs drafted Mexican teamsters to carry out the lashings. "Why those thus punished did not die under such punishment was a marvel to me," said Captain George T. M. Davis. "Their backs had the appearance of a pounded piece of raw beef, the blood oozing from every stripe as given." It was a "revolting scene."[13]

Twiggs "forgot" the count, so instead of fifty each man received fifty-nine lashes. Branding irons in the shape of a *D* were applied after the whippings to the hips of some, the right cheeks of a few. Reilly's *D* was put on his cheek upside down, so he was branded again on the left side. These prisoners dug the graves of those to be hanged. Their collars connected to chains, they were then lined up and drummed out of camp, headed for prison, while fifes played "The Rogue's March." The others were put in pairs onto the tails of wagons under the long gallows, nooses around their necks, white sacks over their heads. The horses pulling the wagons were whipped into a gallop, leaving the "defenders of the fatherland," said Prieto, hanging in the air with "horrible convulsions" and "clear signs of pain." Mexicans declared themselves appalled at the "savage outrages" and "barbaric tortures." That night the newspaper *Diario del Gobierno* declared, "Mexicans, these are the men that call us barbarians and tell us that they have come to civilize us." The editor continued, "These men have sacked our homes, taken our daughters from their families, camped in our holy burial places, covered themselves in blasphemous uproar. . . . May they be damned by all Christians, as they are by God!" The outrage was not reduced by permitting Catholic priests to retrieve the bodies of the seven out of the sixteen who were Catholics so they could be buried in consecrated ground.[14]

There were more hangings from trees near San Ángel on the eleventh and another mass execution at Mixcoac on the thirteenth, while a battle raged at Chapultepec not far away. Harney, who had a record as a torturer, murderer of prisoners, and rapist during the Seminole War, was in charge. His ceremony was even more grisly than the earlier one, because he beat some prisoners across the face with his sword, and one of the men hanged had lost both legs at Churubusco. Harney barred clergy from the execution area. The whippings were conducted by army corporals with knotted lashes, while the nooses were rigged so that the men strangled to death rather than having their necks broken. Harney's sadistic conduct spread more horror through Mexico City.

I AM CERTAIN THAT TOMORROW WE WILL DIE

The pointless assault on the Molino diverted Scott from going for one of the southern *garitas*. There were three, each connected to a causeway roughly a thousand yards long. From the east, the Acapulco road ran from Churubusco to the San Antonio *garita* on the southeast corner of the city. The San Ángel road led north to the Niño Perdido *garita* just east of the southwest corner. West of it another causeway ran out of the tiny *pueblo* of Piedad to the Belén *garita* off the southwest corner. There were two other gateways available, both on the west side of the city, reached by two causeways running past Chapultepec. The northernmost was a crooked road running northeast from the castle about two miles to a junction at the village of Santo Tomás, then east to the San Cosmé *garita* at the city's northwest corner. The other ran directly from Chapultepec to the Belén *garita*.

Scott sent engineers out on September 8 to check the roads and determine if the terrain could carry infantry. They spotted Mexican troops strengthening the defenses at the San Antonio gate and a line of fieldworks running from there to Niño Perdido. Further scouting the next day concluded that it should be possible to turn the Mexican position at the San Antonio *garita*.[15]

Scott called his generals together on the eleventh. He was still inclined to go to the southern gates, avoiding Chapultepec. Pillow also favored the southern gates, and after they reviewed the engineers' reports, generally so did the other commanders. Twiggs, however, wanted to take Chapultepec and the western gates. When Riley asked which alternative would involve the least time and labor to build batteries, the engineers replied that the western route would do that. "I go in for more fighting and less work," Riley declared. Hitchcock and Trist had been talking to Beauregard, who told them that San Antonio's defenses were growing stronger by the minute. The two dragged him into the conference, and all agreed that the western approach, beginning with an attack on Chapultepec, was the best; Scott went along with the others.[16]

Chapultepec (Grasshopper Hill) was a great park southwest of Mexico City, enclosed on the southern and eastern sides by a stone wall from twelve to fifteen feet high, on the west end by Molino del Rey, and on the north side by an old aqueduct, its arches closed up with masonry, running beside a road. The grounds ran east–west about a mile, and about a third of a mile north–south. There was a narrow fortified gate on the southern flank and another at the southeast. Gardens and cornfields covered the western third of the park, solid ground mostly, ending at a ditch and cypress swamp. There the terrain rose eastward, covered by magnificent trees. Beyond the groves the ground climbed steeply to a narrow rock ridge running east–west and rising about 200 feet.

Atop that ridge sat the "castle." It was really an old summer palace for the Spanish viceroys, dating from the late eighteenth century. Since 1841 it had housed the *colegio militar,* Mexico's military academy, which in 1847 had forty-six cadets. These boys had been ordered to evacuate, but not all of them left. The perimeter of the buildings alone would require more than 2,000 men to defend, but when Santa Anna handed command to

Major General Nicolás Bravo Rueda, an old hero of 1821, he gave him just over 800 infantry and some artillerymen and engineers, along with thirteen guns, mostly small-bore. There were another 4,000 men available, but Santa Anna held them in reserve. Bravo planted two batteries across the Tacubaya road near its junction with the aqueduct and the Belén road, to protect the back of his position from the southeast. He also put two small redoubts along the road that wound up the ridge to the academy, one with a 4-pounder. A fosse (defensive ditch) and a minefield guarded the western end of the castle, while halfway down the slope, near the northern wall, were a redan and breastworks.

Scott planned his battle this time and aimed to go all out, leaving Twiggs' division and Riley's brigade to guard his right flank. Everything else would concentrate on Chapultepec. Quitman demonstrated near Piedad on September 12 to keep Santa Anna pinned down on the southern approaches; Quitman shifted to Tacubaya after dark and joined Pillow there. Assault troops moved up toward the park's west and south sides, and the engineers worked on batteries. One, which included an 8-inch howitzer, was planted next to the Tacubaya–Chapultepec road. The second was on a ridge south of the Molino, mounting a 24-pounder and another 8-inch howitzer. The third stood northeast of the second, boasting a 16-pounder and an 8-inch, and a fourth mounted a 10-inch howitzer near the Molino. A 16-pounder was planted with another 8-inch howitzer north of the Molino.

The first two batteries opened up early on the twelfth and the others joined in as they were completed. They hammered the castle for fourteen hours, a terrible thunder that the defenders lacked any means of answering. The thin walls of the academy were smashed every time a great iron ball hit. The academy was crumbling faster than the engineers could repair the damage with sandbags. Bravo asked for reinforcements, but Santa Anna said he would wait to send any until an attack actually began. "In the corridor, converted into a surgical hospital," said a reporter, "were found mixed up the putrid bodies, the wounded breathing mournful groans, and the young boys of the College." Mexicans never forgave Santa Anna, who, sneered a critic, "in all his conduct of this war never comprehended the enemy's points of vulnerability, nor his own . . . [he] judged that Chapultepec would not be attacked, and sent no reinforcements."[17]

Quitman's demonstration caused Santa Anna to divert guns and troops from the west. He received a spy report that Scott was about to attack the southeast corner of the city, ordered Brigadier General Antonio Vizcaino and his troops there, and followed with his headquarters. He was as far from the real danger as he could be, and did not wise up to what was happening at the other end of the line until the bombardment was well under way. By the time that was over, the best guns were out of action at Chapultepec and the surviving men were too exhausted and terrified to put up a good fight.

Scott had hoped the bombardment would drive the Mexicans out of the academy, but that did not happen. He knew by nightfall that he would have to storm the place. His plan called for Quitman's division to drive down the Tacubaya road toward the battery and crossroads southeast of the castle. Quitman's spearhead—known as a "forlorn hope"—would be a party of 265 men under Captain Silas Casey. Pillow's division, its forlorn hope a corps from Worth's division led by Captain Samuel Mackenzie, would charge through the Molino ruins and the grove straight at the academy. Forlorn hopes deserved their ancient nicknames. Scott wanted sturdy and dependable soldiers for the spearheads and, according to D. H. Hill, offered "strong incentives," including promotions and money. There were plenty of volunteers.[18]

Gallantry was not limited to the North American side. Lieutenant Colonel Juan Cano, veteran of Cerro Gordo and Churubusco, was the senior engineer at Chapultepec. On the night of September 12 he sent his brother Lorenzo with a sealed message to their uncle at Santa Anna's headquarters. It said, "Dear Uncle, I am certain that tomorrow we will die, and because I do not want to give my elderly parents the unbearable bitterness of receiving news of the death of two sons at the same time, I beg you to keep my brother Lorenzo from returning to my side."[19]

The Anglo guns opened up at sunrise on September 13, first throwing solid shot at the buildings and fieldworks, after two hours blasting the grove of trees with grape, canister, and some shell. The bombardment stopped at about eight in the morning and the advance began, infantry and some artillery out of the Molino, others along the southern wall. The *soldados,* according to a Mexican observer, were "dizzy from the bombardment, exhausted, sleepless, and hungry." The Anglos cleared the defenders away from the gate on the south wall and jogged up the zigzag road toward the top of the hill. The other corps crossed the swamp and entered the grove from the west, where the two sides fired from behind trees until the scrap turned into a brawl, driving the exhausted Mexicans out of the woods. The two Anglo parties then joined up.[20]

Santa Anna still believed that the attack on Chapultepec was a feint. When the North Americans cleared the grove and started up the ridge, however, he sent a national guard battalion to the east end of the park, but few men got through. Santa Anna followed that with a light infantry regiment, but by the time it got to the scene the battle was over. The men in the academy, discouraged enough, felt increasingly isolated. Some of the most able leaders, including General Pérez, had fallen.

After clearing the grove, Anglo infantry charged up the western slope of the ridge, but they stopped at the fosse because promised scaling ladders did not show up. Three regiments took cover and sniped at the parapets of the academy. "We found a great many mines about the work," said Ralph Kirkham, "and long leather hoses communicating with them outside, to have blown us sky high after we took possession." The mines were containers of black powder connected by hoses carrying powder trains. Lieutenant Manuel Alemán had volunteered to detonate the mines, but the enemy reached the firing station first.[21]

Pillow panicked when his men stalled below the castle, and he asked for help. Quitman came to his rescue from the south, sending Casey's forlorn hope and a large party of marines, followed by four field pieces. Units became scrambled, officers not knowing the soldiers around them. The men going up the south face of the hill crept up the ditches beside the road until they were blasted to a stop by a five-gun battery. Casey and the marine commander both were wounded and their men backed down the hill. A brigade on Quitman's right moved up, followed by two regiments of volunteers, and flanked the Mexican defense, opening the road, as Shields and two colonels fell wounded. Reinforcements from Worth's division arrived on the western slope at about that time and resumed the attack there, using the now arrived scaling ladders to climb the walls of the academy. The Mexicans on the parapets shoved some of the ladders down, but there were too few of them to hold back the tidal wave of screaming Anglos. "The *Yanquis* climbed like goats," said a Mexican soldier, "clearing all the rocks and the thicket; they came through the main door of the top plaza trampling over everything. There they bumped into Colonel Cano [he of the letter to his uncle], very resolute with gun in hand. . . . Two of them asked for his sword. He shut their mouths with the gun. They fell upon him and destroyed him."[22]

Anglos poured over the parapets while others stormed through the main gate. "The havoc among the Mexicans was now horrible in the extreme," said D. H. Hill. "Our men were shouting 'give no quarter to the treacherous scoundrels' and as far as I could observe none was asked by the Mexicans."[23]

The fight for the castle inspired another legend, that of *los Niños Héroes* (the Boy Heroes). According to the story, six cadets of the military academy refused to evacuate and died in its defense. The story was first celebrated in 1871, when the government of Benito Juárez held up the brave teenagers as paragons of sacrifice, and a monument to the Boy Heroes was unveiled in Chapultepec Park in 1882. The gallant cadets remain among the most celebrated heroes of Mexican history.[24]

The academy campus was littered with dead and wounded, many of them with their throats cut by vengeful *Yanquis.* To stop the slaughter, General Bravo surrendered to a lieutenant of a New York regiment at about nine-thirty in the morning. Scott soon showed up and was mobbed by Anglo troops overjoyed that he had not sent them into a third blunder. It had been bloody enough, Scott losing almost 800 men killed, wounded, or missing, the Mexicans as many as 1,800 in all.[25]

Surgeon Richard McSherry was appalled at what he found in the castle grounds. "Their mangled bodies lay heaped in masses," he remembered, "some among them indeed were not yet dead, but were gasping in the last agonies, with their dark faces upturned to the sun, writhing and struggling in death, like fish thrown on shore by the angler. Crushed heads, shattered limbs, torn up bodies, with brains, hearts, and lungs exposed, and eyes torn from their sockets, were among the horrible visions that first arrested attention." McSherry never outlived that memory.[26]

Santa Anna was shattered when he saw the United States flag rise over the castle. "I believe if we were to plant our batteries in Hell," he cried, "the damned Yankees would take them from us." Another dismayed officer groaned, "God is a Yankee."[27]

TREASON AIDED THEM IN OBTAINING A VICTORY

The Yankees had their blood up. Quitman turned his earlier feint into a real assault on Belén, and without orders proceeded up the causeway with his armed horde. This rash move was stopped by a two-gun Mexican battery about a mile north of Chapultepec, until Anglo artillery came up and then the rifle regiment charged and captured the guns. Mexico City's last defense on the southwest corner was the Belén *garita,* manned by about 180 infantry under Brigadier General Andrés Terrés. Santa Anna sent three small guns and a few extra troops and ordered General Ramírez, veteran of the Molino, to occupy the Paseo, a broad promenade running north from the *garita.* About 300 yards northeast of the gate, within the city walls, was the Ciudadela, an old tobacco factory converted to a strongpoint for the city garrison.

Quitman trudged steadily up the causeway, his guns—an 18-pounder and a 24-pounder—ahead on either side of the road. The Mexicans kept up a heavy fire of muskets and cannons, but Quitman's cannons opened up, blasting chunks out of the buildings, shredding bodies with shell fragments and masonry splinters. About one in the afternoon rumors ran through Mexico City that the North Americans were about to turn Terrés' position at the gate, so the reinforcements Santa Anna had sent turned back without letting Terrés know. He ran out of artillery ammunition and pulled back to the Ciudadela with his seventy surviving men. The Anglo riflemen ran over the few *soldados* remaining at the *garita* and occupied the place, resting among the dead and dying. The North Americans started to turn their guns on the Ciudadela when heavy musketry from that place blasted their ranks, killing or wounding several officers and twenty-seven out of thirty enlisted men. Quitman ran out of artillery ammunition and Terrés launched several fierce counterattacks. Blood was spilled aplenty on both sides, with almost all of Quitman's staff and artillery officers going down.

Scott later rebuked Quitman for his impetuous assault on the *garita,* but it paid off, thanks to Santa Anna. He had assumed Quitman's maneuver was a feint, so he headed off to the San Cosmé *garita* at the northwest corner of the city, arriving too late to keep General Rangel from abandoning Santo Tomás and retreating to the city. Quitman and his remaining ablebodied men were stuck fast in Belén while Terrés conducted his stubborn defense from the Ciudadela. "We resisted the attack," Santa Anna said later, "but treason aided them in obtaining a victory." The Soldier of the People was never responsible for his defeats.[28]

Santa Anna was running from one unthreatened place to another, failing to send help where it was needed or sending too little too late. Rangel had been retreating from Chapultepec when he reached the San Cosmé *garita.* Nobody had believed that the place would be attacked, so it was guarded only by a small parapet that did not even block the road. Rangel extended the parapet and dug trenches, and Santa Anna sent him three battalions of infantry and three guns. Engineers put the extra manpower to work erecting an earthen redoubt, filling in the arches of the nearby aqueduct with sandbags, and posting *soldados* on rooftops. Rangel's abandonment of Santo Tomás opened the way for Worth to advance to San Cosmé. Still shaken by Molino, he told his engineer, Gustavus Smith, "If you find there are two different methods by which the Garita can be carried, one in a shorter time at a sacrifice of men, the other in a longer time, but a saving of men, choose the latter."[29]

Worth's troops ran into no opposition up to the junction at Santo Tomás, where they turned east toward the *garita.* Scott reinforced Worth with two brigades and a battery of siege guns, so he had to deploy, reorganize, and distribute ammunition before he could move on. The troops cleared some small works near the village, beat off an attack by about 1,500 lancers under Torrejón, and about four in the afternoon resumed the advance toward the *garita.* Heavy fire from the Mexicans there stopped the corps almost immediately. This was a battle for resourceful young officers, not generals who thought big. Smith's sappers tunneled through a line of buildings on the north side of the road, clearing the way for infantry. Lieutenant Ulysses Grant led a party carrying a mountain howitzer across some ditches on the right and mounted the piece in the tower of the San Cosmé church. The navy lieutenant Raphael Semmes did something similar on the other side of the road. The two little guns drove the Mexicans out of the redoubt, and an Anglo cannon moved in among the corpses.

Rangel was wounded, and by five o'clock his only big gun was dismounted by Anglo fire. Smith led a party of marines to the top of a three-story house, where they shot down into the Mexicans. "Those who were not killed or disabled by that fire," Smith said, "seemed dazed for an instant; but in a few moments, they precipitately retreated, leaving the San Cosmé Garita without a single defender." The marines charged out of the house, only to run into other Anglos charging down the causeway.[30]

Their horrendous losses devastated the outnumbered Mexicans, who stampeded into the city, running into and driving back Santa Anna and some reinforcements he had led up after belatedly realizing the danger at San Cosmé. Most of the fugitives scattered through the streets, although some joined Terrés at the Ciudadela. Worth's men were inside the city walls by six in the evening, and because it was growing dark the general had his men take shelter for the night in houses around the *garita*. Just to remind Santa Anna that he was there, Worth had one of his mortars drop five 10-inch shells in the neighborhood of the national palace.

The day had been another bloody one. Scott's army lost 130 killed, 703 wounded, and twenty-nine missing. Mexican losses probably were around 3,000 in all, two-thirds at Chapultepec. The United States held 823 prisoners, including six generals. Mexico City's defense had been cracked, but the city had not been taken. The Anglos were exhausted and dreaded the prospect of fighting house to house. Santa Anna still had about 5,000 men and eighteen guns in and near the Ciudadela and maybe as many as 7,000 more men he could round up from around the city.[31]

For the first time in the campaign, the next move was up to Santa Anna rather than Scott.

'TWAS A DAY OF BLOODSHED AND BRUTALITY

D. H. Hill and his men spent the night after the battle in a large, elegant, deserted house in Mexico City's suburbs. "It was badly injured by cannon shot and had been most shamefully pillaged by some of our worthless vagabonds," he said. Worse was to come, because parties of volunteers crept into the city after midnight on September 14 and went on a rampage of looting, raping, and murder. This did not inspire the people of the city to welcome the North Americans with cheers and flowers.[32]

When Santa Anna entered Mexico City late on the thirteenth he noticed the contrast between the sacrifices of his soldiers and the behavior of the city's elite. "I recognized that here passed the *hombres de bien* [the upper class], the cowards and colluders with the invader," he sneered; "sooner or later, their intrigue and their skilled hands would sacrifice me without public use to satisfy political passions." A Mexican historian agreed with him, observing that the wealthiest citizens had hung flags of foreign countries on their palaces. "In these moments, the rich class manifested their cowardice," he charged. "What ought we to hope for the country, with a debased generation, who in the hour of danger were ashamed to be of Mexican birth?"[33]

The better sorts of society would welcome Scott's army; the lower orders had not been heard from. Civic and social leaders, who all along had opposed a defense of the capital, mobbed Santa Anna with appeals to declare México an open city. The Soldier of the People called a council of his remaining generals. "Each general bitterly deplored the lack of enthusiasm the people showed toward the war. The soldiers were the only ones fulfilling their duties," he complained. Further defense of the city would be useless without the support of the people. "They felt that the national honor had been upheld by our defense." The generals fanned out to collect any troops who had not deserted, and by one in the morning of September 14 they had all marched out of the city, heading north for Guadalupe Hidalgo. The city fathers rushed to Scott's camp, asking for "terms of capitulation in favor of the church, the citizens, and the municipal authorities." Scott demanded a peaceful surrender and the payment of $150,000.[34]

The situation was explosive, no matter what the ruling elite promised. The atrocious behavior of the volunteers, if not curbed, could produce disaster. "Our safety is in military discipline," Scott ordered. "Let there be no drunkenness, no disorders, and no straggling. Stragglers will be in great danger of assassination, and marauders shall be punished by courts martial." The "honor of the army, and the honor of our country, call for the best behavior on the part of all."[35]

Worth moved his troops into the Alameda, a great cottonwood-shaded park east of the San Cosmé *garita,* at about six in the morning on the fourteenth, and halted there to await Scott's grand entrance. Quitman sent two officers to receive the surrender of the Ciudadela, which had been offered under a white flag just after Santa Anna left the city. The officer in charge asked Quitman's delegates to sign a receipt for the place, but they told him that North American conquerors gave their receipts "with the points of our swords!" By seven o'clock the United States flag flew over the Ciudadela.

The *hombres de bien* donned their finest apparel to look curiously at the United States troops, who were filthy and tired, with some in bandages. These people waved handkerchiefs as the divisions marched in while above all flew the flags of foreign diplomatic missions. Quitman's division led the parade. Worth's troops followed and took sporadic musket fire from rooftops, one shot wounding a colonel. Worth turned an 8-inch howitzer on the houses where the shots apparently came from.

Regiments entered the *Zócalo,* the grand plaza in front of the national palace, and took formal position around its sides. Old Fuss and Feathers— wearing his fanciest gold-bedecked uniform with a plumed, gold-fringed fore-and-aft chapeau and mounted on a big bay horse—entered the square with his staff behind him. Bands played as he rode along the ranks while the men shouted "Huzzah!" A party of marines entered the palace, chased out *léperos* who had taken over the place, and raised the Stars and Stripes above it. Scott entered the ornate building from which Santa Anna had ruled Mexico. Lucas Alamán pronounced himself sickened when he saw the "detestable" enemy flag.[36]

Before the Battle of Chapultepec, the leading *Santanista* and governor of México state, José María Tornel y Mendivil, had commanded that paving stones be stockpiled on the city's rooftops. He also ordered the jails and prisons to release prisoners who had not been drafted into the army. He thereby assembled the ingredients for chaos. The city's oppressed *léperos,* however, provided most of the manpower for what happened next, along with the working class and stragglers from Santa Anna's army. Some of their betters took up arms also, reacting to the atrocities that had been committed during the night. At least one priest, probably Padre Jarauta, was seen on horseback calling on citizens to fight in the streets, and a militia unit was made up of Mexico City's doctors. Scott's grand ceremony had scarcely concluded when the city exploded. People had armed themselves with stones and bricks along with muskets and even a few artillery pieces. They barricaded streets with sandbags and swarmed to the rooftops. "A perfect torrent of balls and stones rained upon his [Scott's] troops," a Mexican businessman reported to a Spanish trading house in New York. "Many were killed and more wounded." Chaos erupted all over town, with the poorest Mexicans—scorned by the wealthy, who did not seem to care what happened—fighting for their city.[37]

Scott ordered the local authorities to get the situation under control.

The general, the president of the *ayuntamiento* (city council) declared, promised that if the disorder was not curbed within three hours, "he will proceed with all rigor against the guilty, permitting their goods and property to be sacked and razing the block in which are situated the houses from which the American troops are fired upon."[38]

Scott had already unleashed draconian measures. He sent Hitchcock to the cathedral to tell the archbishop to call on the people to stop fighting. Otherwise the general would open the city "& give it over to plunder & further that the Churches and church property would share in the fate of the city."[39]

The rioting continued anyway. D. H. Hill said of the first day's uproar that the Anglos lost about 200 men, "and the Mexicans must have lost far more as we repeatedly fired on the Mob with grape and canister." Scott had set loose an orgy of pillage and murder. Hill called it "unbridled license on the part of our troops." Cannons were turned on any house that Anglos claimed a shot came from, and the soldiers looted hundreds of houses and killed every armed Mexican found in the streets. "This stern course," Hill lamented, "had an undoubted influence in quelling the disturbance but it, alas, corrupted our men most fearfully. Many of them were perfectly frantic with the lust of blood and plunder. In order to sack rich houses many soldiers pretended that they heard firing from them. 'Twas a day of bloodshed and brutality."[40]

The enraged *léperos* could not stand up to Anglo firepower and brutality forever, so the violence wound down on September fifteenth and sputtered out altogether the next day. "Seeing further resistance useless," said the businessman, "our soldiers ceased firing, and on the 16th of September (sad day!) the enemy was in possession of the Mexican capital. Though we inflicted havoc and death upon the Yankees, we suffered greatly ourselves. Many were killed by the blowing up of the houses, many by the bombardment, but more by the confusion which prevailed in the city." He estimated that more than 4,000 Mexicans had been killed or wounded, "among whom are many women and children." Anglo losses, he estimated, exceeded a thousand. "What a calamity!" he despaired.[41]

If Scott had hoped to win minds and feelings by aggravating the differences between the upper and lower classes, he failed. The property of the rich suffered the most loss. Carlos María de Bustamante spent most of the riot hiding at home to keep out of the line of fire. His house was not sacked. He went out late on September 15, and the first thing he came across was five bodies being eaten by dogs. Never had he seen such a horrible sight, he told his diary. No Mexican could go out without being "filled with horror," especially at the sight of "these new North American vandals" swaggering around with their weapons, "entering houses, searching and looting as they pleased, taking whatever they wanted."[42]

On Mexico's Independence Day, the sixteenth, Scott could proclaim possession of the Halls of the Montezumas. "His campaign was unsurpassed in military annals," said the previously skeptical duke of Wellington. "He is the greatest living soldier." Few other generals would have undertaken the campaign at all, but the possibility that he might fail never entered Scott's stubborn mind. He had a sound strategic sense, but his tactical judgment had often been poor. Scott did not so much win as Santa Anna lost. But if the point was to "conquer a peace," that objective remained elusive. Santa Anna was still out there.[43]

The Soldier of the People called another assembly of his officers at Guadalupe Hidalgo on the sixteenth. He had effectively been deprived of the presidency by what remained of the government when he left the capital on the fourteenth. Now he resigned formally, proclaiming that he was leaving an office that he called "as wearisome as it was bitter." He then divided his dwindling army. Herrera, his second in command, went to Querétaro with the infantry and what was left of the heavy artillery. Santa Anna himself led the cavalry and light artillery off to join the siege of Puebla. Both corps, according to Mexican reporters, spun off stragglers and deserters who "left behind them, by their unbridled license, an imprint of horror on the towns through which they passed."[44]

Santa Anna joined Rea outside Puebla on September 22. The next day he sent about 500 men to attack the *convento,* but they were beaten back. Two days later he sent a message to Childs, warning the North American that he was ready to "operate against the points occupied by you." However, "for the sake of humanity" the Mexican general gave Childs a chance to "march out with the honours of war." Otherwise, the Mexican army, which he claimed numbered 8,000 men, would assault all of the North American positions and the men in them would pay for their atrocities. Childs refused the summons bluntly and denied that his troops had abused civilians.

Mexican attacks resumed on the twenty-seventh and went on fitfully until October 1. Santa Anna had received reports of a strong United States column marching up from Vera Cruz under General Joseph Lane, so he withdrew his troops to meet that threat. Rea continued the siege, but his men could not stop a few raids on their forward posts. A detachment sallied out of San José on October 2, attacked a barricade of cotton bales, killed seventeen irregulars, and blew up a nearby building. Another sortie on the fifth cleared Mexican soldiers out of a building from which they had enfiladed the plaza in front of San José. Rea feigned an attack on October 8, then on the excuse of honoring the death of Puebla's archbishop he and Childs agreed to a truce.[45]

EVERY NIGHT OUR PICKETS ARE FIRED ON AND
OUR STRAGGLERS MURDERED

Scott could not relieve Puebla because he had to keep a lid on Mexico City. Rumors plagued him that there were plots to raise another uprising. He issued a series of general orders beginning on September 18, the first distributing his troops across the city, with a guard and two guns at each *garita*. No private house would be used for quarters until all public buildings were full, nor then without the consent of the owners or orders from headquarters. Officers should remain with their troops to maintain discipline. Further orders warned Mexicans of dire consequences if they abetted desertion and reminded the soldiers of what had happened to the San Patricios. A worse danger was the bigotry of his volunteers. An order commanded them to respect Catholic beliefs and avoid inciting trouble. "As any civilized person will never wantonly do any act to hurt the religious feelings of others," he declared, "it is earnestly requested of all Protestant Americans either to keep out of the way or to pay to the Catholic religion and to its ceremonies every decent mark of respect and deference."

He was shouting into the wind. Mexicans complained that their churches were singled out for vandalism. The rapacity of the volunteers caused general outrage because of the widespread looting, the murder of civilians, hundreds of rapes, and nearly universal drunkenness on stolen liquor. Despite his military commissions, Scott did little to punish the malefactors and commuted the sentences of the worst criminals. "You will hear any Mexican in the street," George Gordon Meade complained to his diary, "descanting on the conduct of the 'tropes de linea' as they call us, [and] dread of the 'voluntarios.' And with reason, they have killed five or six innocent persons walking the streets, for no other reason than their own amusement." The volunteers, he said were "always drunk," and liked to "rob and steal the cattle of the poor farmers."[46]

What happened in Mexico City could have been predicted, yet Scott took no security precautions until after the uprising. Besides the *léperos* and *Indios* of the *colonias* on the city's outskirts, along with stragglers from the Mexican army, the city had attracted thousands of refugees. They were *Indios* and *Castas* driven out of their rural homes by the war in general and by the atrocities committed by the volunteers. They transferred their tactics of local retaliation and guerrilla resistance to the city, especially by killing Anglo soldiers found alone or in small groups. "When our troops first entered the city," remembered George Ballentine, "a great number of our men fell by the knives of these miscreants, being stabbed by them when strolling intoxicated and through the low quarters of the city at night." Scott's orders of September 24 cautioned the men not to leave quarters at all except in large groups, or they would be waylaid one by one. That did no good, D. H. Hill complained. "This game has been practiced extensively ever since the battle of Cerro Gordo and has unfortunately succeeded only too well," he observed. "The miserable creatures that we now have in our Army would rush into Hell itself for a bottle of liquor."[47]

Scott's army had turned one of the great cities of the Western Hemisphere into a hellhole. There were fitful efforts to improve the situation. Scott's quartermaster hired a thousand seamstresses to make replacement uniforms, although that was abandoned when the costs got out of hand. Tailors, barbers, storekeepers, innkeepers, restaurateurs, and others thrived. Prostitutes, called "Margaritas," poured into town and did a lively trade. All that, however, aggravated the class tensions inherent in Mexican society. While small merchants prospered, the wealthy hid in their palaces or on their haciendas. Professionals were reduced to begging for charity and government bureaucrats abandoned their duties. The poorest gave up in despair.[48]

Resistance had dropped to a quiet but still deadly level. "We have now been in the city a week," Ralph W. Kirkham told his journal on September 21, "although hardly a day passes without one or more of our soldiers being assassinated. They get intoxicated and wander into by streets and almost invariably are stabbed." Rumors of "the introduction of a large body of armed men into the city" went through the army constantly, he said, but he doubted that would happen. D. H. Hill was more pessimistic. "Should we meet with the slightest reverse at Puebla there will be an insurrection here," he predicted on October 1. "Every night our Pickets are fired on and our stragglers murdered. A little only is wanting towards a general uprising of the inhabitants."[49]

Scott believed he had conquered Mexico City, but that was debatable. He had not conquered Mexico, nor had he conquered a peace. No one from the Mexican government came forward to sue for peace, as Polk had been predicting for a year and a half.

CHAPTER

21

PEOPLE ARE IN ARMS AGAINST US

(October–December 1847)

And what a great charro he was
On the back of his very dark horse;
In the middle of a furious battle
He could light a cigar, of course.

—"El Corrido de Heraclio Bernal"

MARIANO OTERO PUBLISHED A PENETRATING ESSAY on Mexico's humiliation after the fall of the capital. Born in 1817, widely read in political philosophy, his outlook tempered by government service, he was an eloquent liberal. Otero thought that whatever form it took, centralist or federalist, Mexico's government oppressed the majority of the people, who had no reason to fight the *yanqui* invaders. The ruling rich refused to dirty their hands with honest work, while the poor were forbidden to take up trades. "And so it has come about," Otero pointed out, "that while the republic is plagued by hundreds of generals, thousands of superintendents and officials, bureaucrats, clergymen, and doctors, one cannot find a single distinguished Mexican in any art, skill, or trade." Among craftsmen in the cities, every one "will turn out not to be a Mexican but a foreigner." Power concentrated in the hands of a lazy few produced "the most profound disgust between the industrious classes [farmers and laborers] and their governments." Mexico was naturally rich, Otero declared, "but as long as fanaticism, ignorance, and laziness continue being the basis of our education, and as long as we do not have a government which is truly enlightened and energetic," the nation would remain poor and its people would not defend it.

Otero was wrong on one point, because the "industrious classes" did rise up against the invaders.[1]

WELL AND FEARFULLY WAS HIS MANDATE OBEYED

Santa Anna's resignation scrambled what structure the national government had left. He suggested appointing a triumvirate to replace the president, but this required approval by the Council of Government, which could not act because the president of the Supreme Court suddenly died. The surviving senior justice of the Supreme Court, Manuel de la Peña y Peña, former foreign minister, agreed to serve as acting president until the council or the Congress selected an interim one. Peña appointed Herrera to command of the Mexican army on September 30 and a week later ordered Santa Anna to relinquish his command and await a court-martial.[2]

The Soldier of the People was busy at Puebla. The siege continued, musket balls "whizzing through the air where ever you went," said Lieutenant Theodore Laidley. With only short rations of bread, according to Laidley, the few hundred Anglos would have held out forever before they "would surrender to Santa Anna's eight thousand," meaning that the Mexican general's bluff about the size of his force (it was half that) worked.[3]

Relief was on the way: 1,700 men under Brigadier General Joseph Lane had left Vera Cruz on September 19. Santa Anna pulled out of Puebla and set up an ambush, leaving most of his troops near Huamantla. Lane's scouts warned him of the ambush, so he left a strong guard for his wagon train and set out in a blistering heat wave to get around Santa Anna and strike his main force. Major Samuel Walker led four mounted companies who ran into about 2,000 lancers three miles short of Huamantla on October 9. Walker ordered a charge, which drove the Mexicans through the town and out the other side. The lancers counterattacked, devastating the Anglo corps, killing thirteen and wounding eleven. One of the dead was Walker. The survivors of his command forted up in a church until Lane's infantry arrived.

The Mexicans withdrew toward Querétaro, and Lane disgracefully told his soldiers to "avenge the death of the gallant Walker" by sacking the town. "And well and fearfully was his mandate obeyed," reported Lieutenant William Wilkins. When the men were "maddened with liquor every species of outrage was committed. Old women and girls were stripped of their clothing—and many suffered still greater outrages," meaning gang rapes. "Dead horses and men lay about pretty thick, while drunken soldiers, yelling and screeching, were breaking open houses or chasing some poor Mexicans," said Wilkins. "It gave me a lamentable view of human nature, and made [me] for the first time, ashamed of my country." Lane's column staggered into Puebla on October 12.[4]

Most Anglo atrocities in Mexico were acts of individuals or small groups. Huamantla was the only time this medieval savagery was ordered by a general officer. The Mexican casualties were several hundred dead and more injured, the survivors homeless. Mexico was outraged. Santa Anna learned from refugees of the "excesses which the enemy troops were committing" and marched into Huamantla the next morning. "My scouts discovered eleven enemy soldiers who had stayed behind," he said. "We swiftly put them to death with our swords." Several North American newspapers condemned what had happened.[5]

Peña's order to give up his post caught up with Santa Anna on October 16. He later called the order "disgraceful" but at the time offered only a meek protest and handed his troops over to General Manuel Rincón. He also published a farewell to the army. He could have resisted Peña's order, but did not want "to have it said that I avoided presenting myself to answer for my conduct as a public man." Santa Anna left his "companions in misfortune" with the "profoundest regret." The Soldier of the People ended with a hope: "Perhaps the moment is not far distant when conducted by another more fortunate chieftain, fortune will be propitious to you."[6]

Mexico was in a sad state. Rincón's army was down to about 3,000 disorganized and untrained soldiers. Herrera at Querétaro commanded what was left of the Mexico City garrison, also about 3,000 men. Only the *guerrilleros,* the hero-bandits, stood between Mexico and complete subjugation. Peasant revolts had broken out since the national army met its first reverses on the Río Bravo. With that army practically gone and state forces in disarray, in the fall of 1847 the rebellions became more widespread and more revolutionary. General Francisco de Garay reported in November the eruption of "an insurrectional movement of indigenous people in the district of Vera Cruz." Led by Padre Jarauta, these people had taken over three *pueblos* near Tampico, and at the start of 1848 they issued a manifesto demanding "derecognition of all authorities of the government, leaving the people in liberty to choose their employment." The manifesto also declared that the collection of land rents was "absolutely prohibited," and haciendas would thenceforth be "common, to be enjoyed in common without stipend." All taxes would be abolished along with fees paid to the Church. This sentiment echoed those of Hidalgo's *grito* of 1810 and would ring down through Mexico's history to the calls of Emiliano Zapata and other agrarian revolutionaries of 1910. Jarauta's followers offered to help fight the Anglos if Mexico's government restored their rights as they were before the Spanish conquest. The government spurned the call.[7]

Mariano Otero had warned his elite countrymen that the system they imposed on the masses must change. Now the poor had risen against their weakened oppressors. More agrarian revolts broke out all over central Mexico, and the government was helpless even in the state of México. The rebellion there spread into Puebla state, while others erupted in Zacatecas, Durango, Vera Cruz, and several others. Some rebellious *pueblos,* following Jarauta's lead, issued manifestos that combined their calls to restore ownership of land with ones for all Mexicans to resist the *Yanquis.* "Because in the war which we have," said one document, "the United States has as its object the domination and despoliation of our territory . . . it is declared that all of the national territory will be common to all citizens of the republic." This combination of ancient *indio* grievances with appeals to resist the invader popped up in many of the uprisings well into 1848.[8]

HIS COURSE IS MUCH TO BE REGRETTED

Polk had no idea that he had unleashed a revolutionary whirlwind with his decision to invade Mexico. The limited invasion to "conquer a peace" had not worked. The conquest of Mexico City also had failed to drive the other side to the peace table. He blamed Scott and Trist for that.[9]

Looming tall in the president's demonology was Taylor. Old Zach told Jefferson Davis in mid-September 1847 that the Wilmot Proviso was "at best a trifling affair," because he believed no territory would be annexed south of the Missouri Compromise line—a remarkably uninformed statement. By October Taylor was ready to run for president and asked for six months' leave from the army. Marcy approved the request on November 6. Wool took over the Army of Occupation and Taylor caught a ship to New Orleans, which gave him a tumultuous reception. He continued on to his Louisiana plantation, where he awaited the call of history, or at least of the Whig Party.[10]

Polk's iron grip on his cabinet was slipping. He suggested on September 4 that the "obstinacy of Mexico in refusing to negotiate" justified increasing the territory to be ceded by Mexico and lowering the price to be paid. As for what additional territories should be annexed, the cabinet members were all over the map, quarrelling about Tehuantepec, Baja

California, and Tampico. None of them knew that the isthmus and Baja were already out of the picture. Polk learned about Scott's armistice with Santa Anna and exploded—although Scott's authority to conclude an armistice had been part of Trist's instructions. The president snorted that Scott should have demanded an immediate decision by the Mexican government on the North American peace proposals.[11]

Polk would not let go of his fantasy that extracting contributions from Mexican citizens in areas under United States control would encourage wealthy Mexicans to pressure their government to make peace. Scott and Taylor had both resisted that, but Polk repeatedly told the secretary of war to implement his wishes.[12]

Nor would Polk trust his diplomats so far away. With communications taking so long, the president reacted to rumors. "The unofficial information received," he said on October 5, "shows that Mexico has refused to treat for peace upon terms which the United States can accept; and it is now manifest that the war must be prosecuted with increased forces and increased energy." He told his secretary of war to so order Scott, and his secretary of state to recall Trist, because keeping the diplomat in Mexico would make it look as if the United States was eager to end the war on any terms. "Mexico must now first sue for peace," Polk declared, "and when she does we will hear her propositions." He did not know about the fall of Mexico City.[13]

Trist's report about a buffer zone between the Nueces and the Rio Grande arrived, and the furious Polk told the secretary of state again to summon the diplomat home. If he had a draft treaty, he should bring it with him. Otherwise, Trist must suspend negotiations and tell the Mexicans that their proposals would be forwarded to Washington. The key thing, Polk repeated, was that Trist return immediately. Buchanan complied on October 25, adding a private letter blistering the envoy for even thinking about giving up the Rio Grande boundary.[14]

When the administration learned that Scott had taken the Mexican capital, the cabinet agreed on October 12 that the president's annual message to Congress should announce that New Mexico and California "should be retained by the United States as indemnity, and should never be restored to Mexico." Then Trist's message of September 27 arrived. "His course is much to be regretted," Polk fumed. "Mr. Trist has managed the negotiation very bunglingly and with no ability," he snarled.[15]

Other officers and politicians caused the president grief. Kearny, Frémont, and their party reached the east in October and Senator Benton thundered about the approaching court-martial, contradicting his earlier position by demanding that the charges against Frémont be dropped. Polk listened but did not respond. Benton repeated his demand and as much as ordered the president to award army commissions to his son and other relatives. "I may hereafter incur the hostility" of Benton's family, Polk predicted, "because his wishes have not been gratified," but he had no intention of appointing any more officers from the Benton tribe. "I have always been upon good terms with Col. Benton," Polk said, "but he is a man of violent passions and I should not be surprised if he became my enemy . . . especially if I do not grant his wishes in reference to Col. Frémont's trial." This time the president stood up for principle, and Frémont would be tried like any other accused officer.[16]

Polk had Marcy's instructions to the court rule out any discussion of Frémont's actions before the war, meaning there would be no embarrassing questions about why the Pathfinder was in California to begin with. Marcy moved the venue from Washington to Fort Monroe, Virginia, and scheduled trial for November. Benton's voluntary testimony was a violent, high-volume attack on Kearny. The senator continued to disparage the general for most of the next year and in 1848 filibustered in the Senate to block Kearny's confirmation as a brevet major general. The reason for this prolonged hostility was that the court found his son-in-law guilty of mutiny, disobeying a lawful order, and "conduct prejudicial to good order and military discipline." The court sentenced Frémont to dismissal from the service but recommended lenience. Polk vacated the mutiny charge but approved the other two findings. The popinjay Pathfinder resigned his commission in a huff. To Benton's outrage, Polk accepted the resignation on March 15, 1848.[17]

Benton ceased visiting the executive mansion. Polk received a letter from him on November 22 declaring that he would not continue as chairman of the committee on military affairs due to his objection to the way Marcy had handled the court-martial. "I think it probable that Col. Benton intends to break with the administration," Polk concluded, "and will make the quarrel with the Secretary of War the ostensible ground for doing so." Polk's support among the public and in Congress was evaporating, so the loss of his most influential adviser was serious.[18]

Complicating matters further was continued noise from those demanding that the United States absorb "All Mexico." Their propaganda reflected the national urge to bless others with the North American form of government and accorded with Polk's own pronouncements. The *Boston Times* said in October that taking over the country would not be a conquest, but rather would rescue the Mexican people from chaos and corruption. "It is a work worthy of a great people." The *New York Herald* predicted that Mexico would "soon learn to love her ravisher." This non-sense ignored the reality that Mexicans were fighting the invaders every way they could. Polk was not the only ideologue blinded to facts.[19]

Congress convened on December 6 with a Whig majority in the House, and Polk's annual message arrived the next day. The president summarized the attempts to negotiate a peace and outlined Trist's instructions. This set off storms in both houses. Senator Calhoun denounced the annexation of All Mexico. Others objected that nobody wanted to take over the whole of Mexico, and Calhoun countered that the papers talked about little else lately. A resolution appeared in the Senate urging that territorial governments be established in the conquered lands, providing for "the people thereof to form a free sovereign State." All domestic questions—meaning whether to allow slavery—would be handled by the state legislatures. Within a month the resolution acquired two amendments—one prohibiting slavery in the new territories, the other denying anyone's power to prohibit slavery.

Buchanan told a Democratic Party meeting on December 17 that the United States might have to annex all of Mexico if the Mexicans persisted in refusing to negotiate. Democrats in the House of Representatives introduced a resolution supporting the war as just and necessary. Freshman Whig Abraham Lincoln answered that on December 22, saying that the House should require the administration to prove that the first shots had actually been fired on United States soil. John Quincy Adams and forty other northern members introduced a resolution declaring the war unnecessary and unconstitutional, and demanded the immediate evacuation of Mexico. The boundary between the countries would run up the middle of the Nueces Strip, and Mexico was held liable for claims against it. The resolution passed on January 3 by a vote of 85 to 81.[20]

Polk knew he would get little support in Congress unless there was progress in peace talks, but he had choked those off by recalling Trist. Then another of his chickens—the appointment of Pillow as a major general—came home to roost in December. Polk told the cabinet on the eleventh that he had been informed that Scott and Trist had agreed "to pay to Santa Anna a million of dollars as secret money if he would agree to make a treaty of peace." The president condemned this but said he would postpone action until he heard from the generals present at the July council of war. An account of that meeting, which discussed advancing $10,000, leaked to the *Baltimore Sun* and Polk ordered Buchanan and Marcy to demand explanations from Trist and Scott. The president meanwhile wrote Pillow expressing his "unqualified condemnation of the secret negotiations or correspondence, which from your statements I suppose took place at Puebla." Pillow, it is apparent, started the whole controversy.

Shields denied that any bribery scheme had been considered by the generals, Quitman refused to discuss the meeting, Twiggs had no opinion, and Cadwalader denied any knowledge of a bribery plot. Scott said the council of war did not propose to use any of the $3 million advance on a treaty for a bribe. Polk concluded that he just might have an excuse to fire Scott.[21]

This grew out of a larger dispute in Scott's army created by the devious Pillow, who exaggerated his role in his official reports. His claims to glory spread discord among higher ranks who believed that he took credit for their actions. Worth, who since Puebla had had his own axe to grind with Scott, supported Pillow. Scott quietly asked Pillow in October to correct his reports, but the latter answered with an insulting refusal. Then newspapers in Tampico and New Orleans published misleading accounts of operations with Pillow the hero. These reports generated other published stories running down Scott's reputation. He responded on November 12 with a general order to stop the leak of reports to the press, citing a presidential order of January 18, 1847, forbidding private publication of military operations: "The general-in-chief who once submits to an outrage from a junior, must lay his account to suffer the like from all the vicious under him."

Worth decided that this order was aimed at him and appealed directly to Polk, charging Scott with misconduct. Then Brevet Colonel James Duncan confessed that he had written one of the published letters. Scott arrested Duncan on November 28 and ordered him tried for violating the presidential order. Pillow sent a nasty letter to the adjutant general, bypassing the chain of command and appealing directly to the secretary of war for a hearing. Scott brought charges against him also. Soon Worth was under arrest as well. Pillow whined in a violent letter to Polk, laying the whole affair to "the vanity and tyrannical temper of Gen'l Scott."[22]

Marcy handed Polk Scott's letter informing the War Department of the charges lodged against Pillow, Worth, and Duncan at the end of December. "I deplore the unfortunate collisions which have arisen between the general officers in Mexico," the president claimed, quoting Pillow when he blamed the affair on the "vanity and tyrannical temper" of Scott. The commanding general had a "bad temper, dictatorial spirit, and extreme jealousy lest any other general officer should acquire more fame in the army than himself." Polk decided to recall Scott, vindicating his friend Pillow at the expense of the army command. Butler would take charge of the army.[23]

THEY ARE NOT TO BE SO MUCH DESPISED
AS HAS BEEN THOUGHT

Scott's was not the only theater of the war. The bloodbath continued in northeast Mexico. General José Urrea, the regular cavalry commander, had converted his corps into irregulars, although it remained part of the Mexican army. There were patented guerrillas in the region along with freelancers. They raided the Anglo supply lines and towns along the Río Bravo, in one case making off with $30,000 worth of goods belonging to the French consul at Mier. Two actions on the Monterey–Camargo road on November 2 were remarkable. Urrea and 124 mounted irregulars ambushed a patrol of twenty-five dragoons at Agua Fria near Marín, with a loss to the United States of one killed, nine wounded, and one missing. The guerrillas broke off when about 100 Anglo infantry approached the scene, and disappeared into the countryside. While that was going on, irregulars attacked a supply train near Agua Nueva, scattered the guard of 300 soldiers, and captured 121 wagons, 137 mules, and all the cargo. Losses on the United States side included most of the civilian teamsters.[24]

Not a day passed without gunfire heard between Monterey and the river. Taylor granted Wool authority at Saltillo to establish military commissions to try any Mexican accused of crimes against United States personnel or property. The secretary of war gave him power to exact compensation from communities for depredations in their neighborhoods, although instructions did not arrive until December 17. These required local authorities to turn over guerrillas, and held whole villages responsible for raids in their areas. Persons who paid protection money to guerrillas would be treated as guerrillas. Towns also must form police forces. Wool hit the *alcalde* of Salinas with a $500 fine when it was proven that he had cooperated with raiders, and collected $80 from another village to compensate a Mexican citizen who had been robbed in its vicinity.[25]

Threatening and punishing the people only increased resistance. Wool, exasperated, issued Occupation Order 11 in December. Any Mexican, it said, who "countenances or encourages, directly or indirectly, the bandits who infest the country, and who are called guerrillas must be made to feel the evils of war. Individuals will be severely punished and heavy contributions levied upon the inhabitants of all cities, towns, and villages and haciendas, who either harbor them or furnish them with supplies, or who do not give information of their haunts or places of abode." Mexican civilians would lose all they had unless they became informers. Wool claimed at the end of the year that his methods worked, but clashes between guerrillas

and Anglo troops continued. Three days after his order a party of sixty
Indios took revenge on rampaging Texas Rangers with considerable loss
of life on both sides. Supply trains never were wholly safe unless heavily guarded. Sniping, hit-and-run attacks, and killings of stragglers continued.[26]

In New Mexico, newly minted Brigadier General Sterling Price chafed
at fighting Indians and guerrillas. He told the War Department that he proposed to campaign into the "lower provinces of New Mexico," and asked
for authority to enter Chihuahua if he had information that a Mexican
army was forming there to attack New Mexico; the department granted
his request. He moved parts of the 3rd Missouri Mounted Volunteers to El
Paso on November 8, and ordered the rest of the regiment there in
December.[27]

Chihuahua governor Ángel Trías Álvarez guessed rightly that Price
planned to invade his state. He sent a troop of mounted irregulars led by
Captain Manuel Cortés on a raid up the Río Bravo in December. They
went past Socorro and Albuquerque, then set out northeast toward Anton
Chico, about eighty miles southeast of Santa Fe. The raid achieved its purpose by diverting troops from Price's command, a company of the Santa
Fe battalion at Socorro. Price declared these raiders to be "bandits," denying them quarter. The Santa Fe company stopped at Anton Chico, where
many of the men got drunk. The next day those who could ride followed
Cortés over the prairie eastward. The trail led to Santa Rosa Canyon near
the upper Pecos River, which the Anglo company reached around dark.
One private went forward and stumbled into the Mexicans, firing a shot.
They returned fire, but he stood his ground until the others came up behind him and fired a ragged volley. Cortés thought he was outnumbered,
and after three of his men were wounded he abandoned his camp and rode
south. Cortés had left behind his papers, which revealed that he and his
men were not bandits but enrolled troops of the active battalion of
Chihuahua.[28]

The navy also had a war to fight and insurgents to contend with in the
last quarter of 1847. The Home Squadron had taken or closed off all
Mexican ports on the Gulf, so it had little else to do. Perry kept dreaming
up new operations anyway. He proposed in mid-October to remove garrisons from most ports, leaving blockade ships off them. This would free
up enough men, if Scott provided some help, to march across the Isthmus
of Tehuantepec and conquer Tabasco and Chiapas. The war ended before
that happened.

The navy's occupation garrisons suffered the same harassment as army
details. A band of local people broke into a warehouse at Alvarado and

stole cotton and other goods impounded for blockade violations, then ambushed a party of marines sent after them. There were no casualties, but
Perry ordered the *alcalde* and three other community leaders arrested, and
fined the town $1,000. This and similar incidents had about as much effect
as retaliations and fines in the army's zones, meaning not much.[29]

The Pacific Squadron was more active during the fall, after Biddle
turned command over to Shubrick. The squadron's mission was, as always,
to close Mexico's ports on the Pacific and maintain a presence in Baja
California. There was a problem, however. After the governor of Baja cooperated with the North Americans, rebels under Captain Manuel Pineda
rose up and proclaimed Mauricio Castro the legitimate governor. A guerrilla war broke out wherever Anglos could be found. Shubrick sent a sloop
to Mulejé in early October to take the pressure off the army garrison at La
Paz. Pineda's irregulars fought off the landing party in a six-hour battle.
Shubrick sailed into the Gulf of California with most of his squadron in
mid-October, standing off San José. He sent a raiding party ashore on
November 1 to take on a guerrilla force reported to the north, but the
insurgents got away. Three days later the commodore declared that
the United States would seize the whole peninsula and keep it after the
war. This aggravated the divisions between loyalists and collaborators.
Shubrick, however, was focused on the ports farther southeast and satisfied himself with landing a party of marines at San José. There they stayed
while Pineda's *guerrilleros* controlled the dry, rugged countryside.[30]

The turn of the small port of Guaymas on the Mexican mainland
came on October 17, when two frigates under Captain Elie A. F.
LaVallette anchored in the outer roads. LaVallette informally asked for the
port's surrender on the eighteenth and demanded it the next day. The
commandant, Colonel Antonio Campuzano, refused, and retreated inland
with his small garrison. LaVallette bombarded the town on the twentieth.
A delegation went to the beach under a white flag and announced that the
Mexican troops were gone. LaVallette did not have enough men to leave a
garrison, so he blockaded the port by anchoring one ship in the roadstead,
proclaimed the conquest, and sailed away.[31]

LaVallette joined Shubrick, who sailed two frigates and a sloop to
Mazatlán, which they reached on November 10. This was a harder nut to
crack, complicated by the insurgency against the Mexican government led
over the past year by Lieutenant Colonel Rafael Téllez, a pompous little
braggart who commanded a garrison of 560 men. The town was defensible, standing in a rough triangle framed by three hills, but Téllez had not
fortified. The warships leveled their guns on the city, so Téllez marched inland to Palos Prietos and rejected Shubrick's surrender demand with some

shocking insults. LaVallette led a 730-man landing force ashore on the afternoon of November 11, meeting no opposition. The navy left a garrison of 400 sailors and marines, who built defensive fieldworks. Observing the ships' guns offshore, Téllez was not eager to attack.[32]

He was not about to give up, either. He fanned cavalry patrols through the countryside to intercept supplies headed for the Anglo garrison. Téllez sent a raiding party into town, which burned three small vessels in the harbor on November 13. Two days later other Mexicans shoved an Anglo sentry box off a wharf. Shubrick mounted several amphibious raids to pacify the countryside. A patrol tried but failed to take a Mexican post at Urias on November 18. Two days later a larger party attacked Urias, but the defenders got away. Two more skirmishes on the nights of December 12 and 13, and a smaller one on the twenty-fifth, had more effect, and thereafter Mazatlán was peaceful.[33]

Conditions were not quite so calm at Guaymas, where the navy's blockade offshore and Campuzano's inland squeezed the citizens until they left. Guerrillas made a few raids into the town and on November 17 about 250 of them jumped a navy landing party. Other parties struck several Mexican posts in the area between November 1847 and April 1848, and Campuzano's manpower walked away in discouragement.[34]

Baja California, on the other hand, remained in an uproar. Pineda mounted simultaneous attacks against La Paz and San José, on November 18. A party of 180 attacked the outskirts of La Paz, but Anglo gunnery drove it back. Pineda withdrew a few miles to wait for the corps he had sent to San José, which he recalled. The combined force, about 300 guerrillas, attacked the 160 troops at La Paz and conducted a three-day siege before retreating. On the day they left, another party of 150 commanded by Mexican army lieutenant Antonio Mejares hit the garrison at San José with two night assaults. Mejares withdrew in the face of Anglo reinforcements landing on the twenty-first and led his detachment down the coast until he was killed in a skirmish near Mazatlán in mid-December. Pineda tried at La Paz again on November 27, but the troops under Colonel Henry Burton blasted the guerrillas back, causing four North American casualties and a dozen or so for the Mexicans. Burton told Shubrick that the whole peninsula was in a state of "complete insurrection." The attacks on his men on the twenty-seventh, he said, were mounted by "about 400 men, many of them Indians," who used a cannon. "More than 600 people are in arms against us, and they are not to be so much despised as has been thought." Shubrick advised the secretary of the navy in December that unless he got reinforcements he might well lose all of Baja.[35]

It was the same all over Mexico. Wherever there were *yanqui* soldiers, sailors, or marines there were Mexicans prepared to fight them, using whatever means they had.

EARTHQUAKES WILL MAKE THE STERNEST HEARTS
FAIL FROM FEAR

Nowhere was the resistance greater than in the most heavily populated area of the country. Scott told the secretary of war on October 27 that he planned to clear the road from Vera Cruz, then occupy Atlixco, south of Puebla; Toluca, west of Mexico City; and possibly Orizava, on the road between Puebla and Vera Cruz. The War Department had already transferred Joseph Lane's and Caleb Cushing's brigades, almost 3,000 men, from Taylor's to Scott's command, and when they arrived they raised his strength to more than 15,000. Marcy told him to use this manpower to "carry on further aggressive operations; to achieve new conquests; to disperse the remaining army of the enemy in your vicinity; and prevent the organization of another." Everything he did should be designed to pressure the Mexican government into peace talks. And while he was at it, Scott was reminded again, he should levy contributions from occupied areas.[36]

Pacifying Mexico City came first. Scott reissued General Order 20 as General Order 287 on September 17 and followed it with more orders through October. He reaffirmed the jurisdiction of military commissions over soldiers committing crimes against civilians. Mexican criminals, except for collaborators, would be tried by Mexican courts. Scott also established a city police force. "This splendid capital—its churches and religious worship," Scott announced to the people, were "placed under the special safeguard of faith and honor of the American army." Scott also sternly warned the local government to fork over the $150,000 he had levied on the city at its surrender. The money would go to treating the sick and wounded, providing blankets and shoes for the troops, and "other military purposes." The promises of order and stability won over many of Mexico's elite. A small but significant movement arose among prominent Mexicans to annex the whole country to the United States. There were voices calling for Scott to become military dictator of Mexico, a *yanqui caudillo*.[37]

Quitman was Scott's first military governor of Mexico City, but he was not happy about it. He had complained since May that he had not received a command appropriate to his rank of major general. When the first significant wagon train left for Vera Cruz on November 1, Quitman handed his governorship to Persifor Smith and went with it.[38]

Quitman did a creditable job during his short term as governor, in particular setting up the police force. He catered to the Church and to the conservative elite when he prohibited the sale of church property without the approval of the United States Army. This order was probably unnecessary, but it was popular in high places.[39]

Scott made another soothing gesture to the Church when he decided to release the prisoners of war. There were at least 800 of them who had not escaped by early November—the prisons were sieves—and they were a burden to feed. Anglo officers generally objected to letting them go, however, because many of them had violated parole. Juan Manuel Irrizarri y Peralta, archbishop of Mexico City, approached Scott about turning the men free. Most of them had no understanding of what parole meant and had been drafted back into the army by press-gangs. Scott agreed to release the men on the condition that the archbishop himself explain the meaning of parole and personally administer oaths swearing under holy sanction that they would not take up arms again. The last of the prisoners walked out on December 23.[40]

Superficially, the occupation of Mexico City went well, the Anglos and Mexicans getting used to each other. Officers visited the cathedral and the national museum, where they saw the famous "Aztec calendar stone," which Ralph Kirkham declared "one of the wonders of the world." D. H. Hill remembered the "gentlemanly old Mexican who kindly explained everything to me." They even toured the Hospital de Jesús, founded by Cortés and now supervised by Lucas Alamán. They wanted to see a famous portrait of the conquistador, "at which they would gaze with considerable veneration," according to Alamán. Mexico City had its unexpected wonders also, as when a series of strong earthquakes struck in early October. The local people, used to that sort of thing, giggled at *Yanquis bárbaros* cringing in terror. "Ball and bayonet are bad enough," said Hill, "but earthquakes will make the sternest hearts fail from fear."[41]

The Teatro Nacional reopened September 26 with an Italian opera, followed by concerts and vaudeville performances. Bullfights resumed that day, and there was cockfighting on many street corners. Most retail businesses were open by that time, and restaurants catered to every palate. The men had coins in their pockets and bought whatever they wanted—which mostly meant liquor.[42]

There were more serious aspects of the occupation. A Mexican source later claimed that at least 2,000 Anglo soldiers died in Mexico City from wounds, illness, or assassination. There were about twenty military funerals a day. So many died of disease that Mexicans believed "nature herself was helping us reduce the numbers of our enemies." As soon as the roads were dry enough Scott sent the first train to Vera Cruz on November 1, about 400 wagons with a 350-man escort. It carried many wounded from the battles around the city. Departures became more frequent as the road became safer, and shipping wounded out was Scott's highest priority for the moment. The landscape, climate, and guerrillas made it a difficult operation.[43]

December 2, 1847, marked the 300th anniversary of the death of Hernán Cortés. Alamán asked a friend, "In that era, who would ever have imagined that, three centuries after the death of the great Conquistador, the city that he raised from its foundations would be occupied by an army from a nation that had not then even begun to exist?" Given that Mexico's memory of Cortés focused on the atrocious behavior of his soldiers, Alamán's fellow citizens might have drawn a parallel.[44]

Regular officers continued to complain about the volunteers, according to Lieutenant Laidley, "how they rob houses, steal, sack churches, ruin families, plunder and pillage." He groused that the North American press ignored the atrocities, "but the poor sufferers know and hear it." The victims took revenge, killing and mutilating any Anglo caught alone or drunk. "The assassinations of our troops still continue," said D. H. Hill in October, and in November he estimated the deaths had exceeded 100.[45]

The bloodshed increased sharply on both sides on December 6, when, according to Hill, "five hundred cut-throats from Texas under the Command of Col. Hays, entered the City today." These "ragged and dirty" ruffians murdered, raped, and robbed the city's poor. "It is said that the Texians have murdered no less than two hundred Mexicans since their short residence in the City," Hill complained on the twenty-third. Scott's volunteers were generally atrocious, but the Texians were hideous, keeping Mexico City in a constant uproar. The trouble peaked when some *léperos* caught a Texian alone and hacked him to pieces. The next day twenty-five *diablos tejanos* walked into the toughest part of town and slaughtered somewhere between fifty and eighty Mexicans. Scott finally sent them into the countryside—ostensibly to fight guerrillas, but mostly to get them out of the city.[46]

Scott and his military governor, Persifor Smith, decided to interfere in the city government elections set for December 5. Conservatives had generally been shoved aside, and the *ayuntamiento* was in the hands of the *modérado* liberals. The *puro* faction, led by Miguel Lerdo de Tejada, saw a chance to overcome their rivals. The federal government had ordered that no elections be held in occupied areas, so the moderates canceled that of December 5. Lerdo and his group met that day and elected a new government. The moderates responded by scheduling their own election for the nineteenth, but Lerdo persuaded Smith to declare that the vote of the fifth was valid. All members but one of the previous council were ousted and the *puros* controlled the new one. They tried to implement their platform of political, social, and economic reforms but failed because they declined to enlist support from the lower classes. The *puros* earned a reputation as traitors, which conservatives—many of whom also collaborated with the occupation—used against them after the war. This was reflected in their hosting a lavish banquet for Scott and his officers in January, asking the Anglo army to stay in Mexico until the power of the clergy and the military had been destroyed.[47]

YOU CAN PICTURE THE BUZZ THAT WAS ABOUT OUR POST

Scott and his generals failed to appreciate what took place between Vera Cruz and Mexico City after the federal army was destroyed. John R. Kenly asked his readers to picture what happened when a beehive was overturned, then a dozen hives "rudely upset." Instead of bees, "guerrillas were the occupants; then you can picture the buzz that was about our post from the swarms of exasperated Mexicans, who, maddened by the loss of their capital, threw themselves on Scott's communications."[48]

In Scott's theater as in Taylor's, the North Americans saw the insurgency as a criminal problem rather than a military one, and blamed all Mexicans rather than the active culprits. The Anglo tactic was brute force, which made it all worse. Irregular armies between the capital and Vera Cruz followed competent and charismatic hero-bandits including Joaquín Rea, Juan Clímaco Rebolledo, and the flamboyant Padre Jarauta. They remained elites, however, and refused to enlist the rural poor. Exploiting their resentment against Anglo atrocities would have made Scott's problem worse than it was. Instead, the *Indios* and *Castas* devoted their energies to agrarian uprisings.[49]

Scott ordered Colonel Henry Wilson in October to establish posts between Vera Cruz and Jalapa, each with 500 to 750 men, including some cavalry. He also increased the garrisons at Jalapa and Puebla, and together with guards on trains Scott devoted over a quarter of his army to securing the road. Twiggs took over the security operations in December. The road became a long battlefield.[50]

"The guerrilla parties are so thick along the road that it is almost impossible to escape their vigilance," Theodore Laidley complained. Private Jacob J. Oswandel said, "During the skirmish with the infernal guerrillas, we have suffered more frightfully than at the battle of Cerro Gordo with the regular Mexican army. In fact, we would sooner face ten of the regular Mexican army than one of these outlawed guerrillas." The terror went both ways. Lieutenant Colonel George W. Hughes had advised his superiors in mid-September "to destroy all the Ranchos off the road, as they constitute the depots and places of resort." After his corps was attacked by guerrillas, he ordered the nearest ranch to be burned, although there was no connection between that place and the guerrillas. Hughes' heavy-handed approach became policy when the secretary of war told Scott in October that the guerrillas' "haunts and places of rendezvous should be broken up and destroyed." Isolated *jacales* and whole *pueblos* alike were burned to the ground.[51]

The Anglo campaign displaced thousands of peasants without eliminating guerrilla posts. Hordes of hungry and bitter people threatened not just Anglo troops but communities all over central Mexico. Sometimes there was cooperation, as when Childs and Rea met at Puebla to discuss the increasing violence around the city caused by thousands of transients. True banditry exploded along with irregular warfare late in 1847. Sometimes these people operated against the Yankee invaders, and sometimes they preyed on fellow Mexicans. The acting president ordered the general commanding in Nuevo León in October to punish any guerrilla in government service who committed crimes against civilians. The governor of Guanajuato formed a special army unit, drafted from haciendas, to fight criminals and criminal gangs and also "agitators," meaning agrarian dissenters. The governor of Tlaxcala proclaimed that his state was in a condition of "perfect anarchy," overrun with bandits, guerrillas, and agrarian rebels.[52]

The patented guerrillas depended on the sympathy of the people. Depredations by others masquerading as resistance fighters eventually wore out the welcome for all irregulars. Scott, with a rare burst of insight, directed military governors to combine counterguerrilla action with efforts to alienate them from the public. This paid off in Jalapa, where the upper classes rightly feared insurgent excesses would cause indiscriminate retaliation by the *Yanquis*. Jalapa's *ayuntamiento* sent a series of messages to the military governor, one warning of a planned attack on a wagon train, which the city did not want to answer for.[53]

Regular army officers generally reacted to irregulars rather than acting against them. They manned outposts, guarded trains, fended off attacks, and chased raiders usually without catching them. That was how the United States Army had dealt with raiding Indians. Brigadier General Joseph Lane, in contrast, took the war to the enemy. Guerrillas usually avoided open battle, so Lane wanted to corner them. A patrol out of Puebla was fired on by Rea's men near Atlixco, about thirty miles southwest. Lane organized a column of 1,500 cavalry and horse artillery, approached Atlixco late on October 18, and discovered that much of Rea's army was there, lodged among the citizens. He put his artillery atop a rise overlooking the town and at sunrise bombarded the community for nearly an hour. Then he charged into the town and drove Rea's stunned force out. One of the *guerrilleros,* José Eduardo Hernandred, told his father afterward that the assault "appeared to me the day of judgment." Lane captured as many as 300 of Rea's force, most of the captives wounded, but Rea and his principal officers, with their guns and supplies, got away. Lane chose to kill scores, perhaps hundreds, of civilians to limit his own casualties; he lost just two. "So much terror has been impressed upon them," the general said of the townspeople, "at thus having the war brought to their own homes, that I am inclined to believe they will give us no more trouble."[54]

Lane was joined by a band of men who shared his views, Jack Hays and his Texas Rangers, who had used the same tactics against Comanches. They were as ugly as ever, with a "savage appearance," said one of Lane's officers. They were heavily armed, including Colt revolvers. "A hundred of them could discharge a thousand shots in two minutes," said the same officer. They were attacked on November 23 by over 200 lancers south of Puebla; they beat the Mexicans off, retreated, and ran into another 500 mounted men, whom they devastated with their revolvers. Lane and Hays continued leading sweeps across the countryside, keeping the insurgents from getting rest.[55]

Lane exaggerated the number of guerrillas his troops killed, but numbers were less important than constant pressure. He raided Tlaxcala north of Puebla with 500 troopers on the night of November 9–10, looking for loot taken from a merchant train. The United States retrieved twenty-one wagons, found seven others burned, and drove thirteen prisoners and a large herd of cattle and horses back to Puebla. Lane and 135 Texian and Louisiana horsemen attacked a guerrilla band at Izucar de Matamoros on the twenty-third, liberating twenty-three North Americans held prisoner and confiscating two cannons, ammunition, and other goods. Returning to Puebla, Lane's detail was attacked by Rea and about 500 lancers in a pass, but the Texians drove them off.[56]

There were hundreds of skirmishes in central Mexico. Some leaders were killed and a couple captured, but still the insurgency continued. As time passed and the strain told on Mexican supplies and energy, the irregulars became better at avoiding surprises from big units such as Lane's. Almost every small detachment was subject to a bloody surprise, however. Scott was frustrated and on December 12 ordered every command in his army to show no mercy. Any guerrillas captured should be tried by a military commission and put to death with "due solemnity." Scott declared, "No *quarters* will be given to known murderers or robbers whether called guerillos [sic] or rancheros & whether serving under Mexican commission or not. They are equally pests to unguarded Mexicans, foreigners, and small parties of Americans, and ought to be exterminated." Despite the order, executions were few compared to civilians murdered by volunteers.[57]

I WILL MAKE A TREATY, IF IT CAN BE DONE

Bowing at last to the demands that he squeeze Mexico financially, on November 25 Scott forbade shipments of bullion other than coins. The general modified the bullion order on December 2 to permit transfer of gold and silver to a mint, where North American officers would collect a processing tax. Scott ordered local governments on the fifteenth to collect their taxes on schedule but to give the central government's share to United States officers. He also abolished the national lottery in areas under Anglo control, and wiped out interstate customs charges. Collection of stamp and excise taxes on tobacco was farmed out to contractors. At the end of December Scott imposed assessments on the states occupied by his troops, averaging four times what the states had paid to Mexico City before the war.[58]

While the general pushed the Mexicans with financial measures, the diplomat tried a more conventional approach. It appeared at the middle of October that the government was more or less organized at Querétaro. Trist wrote to the new minister of foreign relations, Luis de la Rosa, on the twentieth, answering the last Mexican proposal from September as if there had been no interruption of negotiations. Trist acted at a fortunate time, as there were two movements arising in Mexico—one for peace in general, and another favoring annexation of the whole country to the United States.[59]

The foreign minister answered Trist on October 31, promising to appoint new peace commissioners and resume talks, but Peña canceled the offer. He did not believe his shaky government was in any position to make peace. Trist advised Bancroft that he doubted that the temporary government would be able to get enough support for negotiations for some time. The ice began to break, however. Congress assembled in November to select an interim president, replacing Peña with a moderate, General Pedro María Anaya, who appointed Peña as foreign minister.[60]

The prospects for peace appeared to be improving when Trist received his recall to Washington on November 16. He was stunned. Trist did not have the heart to give the bad news to Peña in person, so he asked British chargé d'affaires Edward Thornton to do it for him. Peña was shocked at the news, according to Thornton. The minister wrote Trist on the twenty-second to say that he hoped Trist would continue negotiations, because the government had appointed new peace commissioners. They were not so new, however, because they were Couto, Cuevas, and Atristáin, Trist's old talking companions from September. Nevertheless, Trist felt himself compelled to notify the foreign minister on November 24 that he must comply with his instructions. He forwarded the Polk government's rejection of the latest Mexican proposals, along with its demands for more territory, and said he would leave early in December.[61]

Thornton, several Mexican liberals, other foreigners, and even Scott urged Trist to defy his recall, because any delay would torpedo all hope of peace. These people knew the situation in Mexico as well as anybody, and were annoyed that the Polk administration had increased its territorial demands. What they did not know, however, was the situation in Washington. Polk's cabinet had split over the demands for additional territory. Nor could they agree on how much to pay for the different parts of Mexico they wanted. Trist, then, could fill a diplomatic vacuum.[62]

Polk and his cabinet had no idea that in recalling Trist they were blowing what could be the last chance to end the war. Trist knew better, and as Scott and the others propped him up he decided to stand fast on principle, for the benefit of his country despite the clumsiness of its government. Trist told Thornton on December 4 that he would hang around Mexico City to see what he could work out. Two days later he told Buchanan the same—he would stay because this might be "the very last chance" for peace. Because of the consequences to the United States that "cannot fail to attend the loss of that chance I will make a treaty, if it can be done."

The blunders of the Polk administration had got the better of Trist's temper. He added sixty-five pages of insults and lectures attacking criticisms of Scott's armistice, the intrigues of Pillow, and the Polk government's failure to understand what was at stake. No matter what the administration thought, there was no way that Mexico could be forced to give up any more territory than it had already lost. If Polk and his hand-maidens did not like the treaty Trist produced, they could disavow it and him. The angry diplomat sent a copy of this tirade to Thornton, who supported him.[63]

While this letter bomb made its way to Washington a new British minister, Percy W. Doyle, arrived in Mexico City, superseding Thornton. The two Britons bluntly told Peña that Her Majesty's Government would not intervene between Mexico and the United States. If there still lingered in Mexico any hope for European intervention, this killed it. The British diplomats advised that commissioners meet with Trist immediately. At the end of December Peña agreed to resume talks.

North Americans and Mexicans watched fireworks celebrating the start of the year 1848, not knowing that a courier was riding into the city with a diplomatic package to be presented to Trist on New Year's Day. Peace, at long last, might be at hand. Then again, it might not. Still, it was a new year, and that was a time to hope.

I *WAS* ASHAMED OF IT, MOST CORDIALLY AND INTENSELY ASHAMED

(1848)

And the monarchy of Rome
Was begun with two thieves' might
Who with their arms and weapons
Took everything in sight.

—Lope de Vega

Tepeyec was a rocky, snake-infested, cactus-studded hill overlooking the *pueblo* of Guadalupe north of Mexico City. In 1531 the Virgin Mary, Mother of God in the Roman Catholic belief, appeared to an Indian called Marcos atop this forbidding place, once the site of the temple of Tonantzin, the Aztec Mother of Gods. He told others about what he had seen, and painted the Virgin's picture. She had dark skin and Indian features and drew widespread devotion from Indians reeling from the Spanish conquest. The Virgin of Guadalupe was rejected by churchmen because she combined *indio* beliefs with an important Catholic totem.

A *criollo* priest, Miguel Sánchez, produced a new version of the Virgin's story in 1648. In this account she appeared before an Indian named Juan Diego and asked that a temple be erected in her honor. Juan took his story to the bishop, who rejected it. He returned to Tepeyec, and the Virgin presented herself five more times, the last time standing on a *nopal* (prickly pear). Roses covered the hill around her. Diego gathered up the roses in his cape and returned to the bishop's palace. He spread his cloak on the floor, and imprinted on it was the image of the Mother of God with radiant Indian features. She got her temple, and her cult spread across New Spain. She became the symbol of a new American identity, one distinctly Mexican, not Spanish.

The Virgin looked Indian, had appeared to an Indian, and was venerated by *los Indios* all over Mexico, but her story justified the rule of the country by white *Criollos* with their Spanish-Catholic heritage and Mexican birth. The *Criollos* who dominated Mexico realized in 1848 that they were in danger of losing control—not just to the Anglo invaders but to the Indians themselves, rebelling everywhere. Where better to reassert *criollo* supremacy than at Guadalupe Hidalgo, by the shrine to the patroness of Mexico?[1]

WE ARE MAKING PEACE AND THIS MUST BE OUR ONLY THOUGHT

Trist received the credentials of the Mexican commissioners on January 1, 1848, and meetings began the next day in Mexico City. Trist accepted a proposed boundary of New Mexico following the Gila River and then on to the line between Alta and Baja California, on the understanding that San Diego would be in United States territory. The diplomats relied on *Mapa de los Estados Unidos de Méjico,* published by John Disturnell in 1846. It included many errors, such as placing El Paso thirty miles too far north and the Rio Grande two degrees too far west.[2]

Negotiations dragged on through January. Anaya's term as president expired on January 8, before Mexico's Congress reassembled, so Peña became acting president again. Atrocities against Mexican civilians continued during the talks, and Scott stepped up the use of military commissions. One notorious case involved a burglary ring including several officers and enlisted men who bungled the looting of a merchant house, leaving three dead and several wounded. Four of the robbers were sentenced to hang, but the end of the war saved their necks. Meanwhile, in the countryside the Texians and the "wretches under that free-booter, General Lane," as D. H. Hill called him, committed "robberies and outrages."[3]

The guerrilla war continued along the Vera Cruz road. A train of wagons and mules, guarded by about 1,300 troops, set out from Vera Cruz on January 3. The procession was more than nine miles long and impossible to protect. Colonel Mariano Cenobio struck on the fifth and Colonel Dixon

H. Miles reported his losses as "one company of mounted riflemen cut up . . . and near 280 pack mules taken." A column under General Twiggs was attacked at about the same time by a few hundred *guerrilleros* who made off with 250 pack mules and property valued around $200,000.[4]

Lane heard on January 18 that Santa Anna was at Tehuacán, about seventy miles southeast of Puebla, and rode out of Mexico City with 350 mounted riflemen, dragoons, and Texas Rangers aiming to bag the *caudillo.* This column marched night and day, and on the twenty-second met a coach traveling under a passport. Its passengers warned Santa Anna, who escaped. From Tehuacán Lane went on to seize Orizava and Cordova, then skirmished with guerrillas under Colonel Manuel Falcón until he reached Mexico City on February 10.[5]

In the last major attack on the Vera Cruz road, on February 18, about 200 *guerrilleros* blocked a wagon train guarded by ninety cavalry and drove the caravan back to the coast with the loss of five men killed. Lane and about 400 dragoons and rangers jumped Padre Jarauta at Zacualtipán on February 25. The Mexicans lost about fifty killed and wounded and forty taken prisoner, but Jarauta got away with most of his band. It was a short, bloody fight, knives out on every side. The Texians went berserk. "Zacualtipan, a rich and luxurious town, was sacked and then burned," according to Hill. It was Huamantla all over again, murders, gang rapes, and the rest, leaving about 150 Mexican bodies on the streets, most civilian. Lane did not order the sack, but he did nothing to stop it. He sent the prisoners to Mexico City, where Hill was judge advocate of the military court and uncovered the truth of what had happened.[6]

Meanwhile, the peace talks dragged on. The Mexican commissioners spent a lot of time arguing issues such as protection of property titles and citizenship for Mexicans in the ceded territories. Trist's patience ran out January 29 and he threatened to break off the talks by February 1 if no more progress had been made. The commissioners accepted a treaty draft on the thirty-first and sent it to the temporary capital at Querétaro for approval. Trist and Scott worried that Peña would be too afraid of domestic opposition to accept the document, so Scott offered to protect the Mexican government after the treaty was signed. The British diplomats bluntly told the president that the terms were as good as Mexico could get. Peña caved in. The signing took place February 2 at Guadalupe Hidalgo within view of the shrine to the Virgin. Bernardo Couto told Trist sadly, "This has to be a moment of great pride for you but humiliating for us." Trist answered, "We are making peace and this must be our only thought." The American later confessed that he thought the war was "a thing for every right-minded American to be ashamed of, and I *was* ashamed of it, most cordially and intensely ashamed of it. . . . My object throughout was . . . to make the treaty as exacting as little as possible from Mexico."[7]

The Treaty of Guadalupe Hidalgo annexed to the United States territories already lost to the invading armies—a third of Mexico, not counting Texas, which made it half. The new boundary ran up the Rio Grande to the southern boundary of New Mexico, then along that to where it was nearest to the Gila River, then north to the Gila and down it to the Colorado River, then downstream to the line between the two Californias, which it followed to the Pacific south of San Diego. The United States paid Mexico $15 million for the transferred territories and absorbed all claims against Mexico predating the war. Mexicans in the annexed territories would enjoy United States citizenship and protection of property titles. There were some other technical measures, including a mechanism for arbitrating future disputes and another to prevent Indians from raiding across the border.

Trist sent the treaty to Washington with New Orleans newspaperman James L. Freaner. The pact called for an end to hostilities, but that was for soldiers to work out. The Mexicans dragged their feet for almost three weeks. Finally, Generals Ignacio Mora y Villamil and Benito Quitano met with Generals Worth and Smith on February 22 and the two parties spent a week haggling over terms. The agreement signed on the twenty-ninth called for a general suspension of hostilities and troop movements. There would be free trade between areas controlled by the two armed forces. The United States would not interfere with local elections in occupied areas, and allowed Mexican police forces and tax collectors to do their duty. The armistice took effect on the Anglo side on March 6, although the Mexicans assumed that it was in force when it was signed.[8]

The war was over, at least in central Mexico. Guerrilla leaders holding patents quit fighting when the federal government told them to. With only two exceptions, the *guerrilleros* complied with the armistice, and those exceptions—an attack on the Vera Cruz road and another near El Paso—happened before March 6.

Also on March 6, the military governor of Mexico City issued a passport for Santa Anna to leave the country. The Soldier of the People enjoyed a banquet at Perote hosted by Colonel George W. Hughes, who ordered both Mexican lancers and Anglo cavalry under Major John R. Kenly to keep Jack Hays' Texas Rangers from lynching their old enemy. The Texians lined the road west of Jalapa on April 29 and debated killing the *caudillo*. Kenly mounted United States flags on the carriage carrying Santa Anna, his wife, and his daughter, and put a full company of troops on either side of the vehicle, with a third bringing up the rear. The Texians watched in glum silence as the procession passed. The Savior of His Country boarded a Spanish ship and sailed for Jamaica on May 5. He diverted to Colombia, however, where he had another great hacienda. There Santa Anna bided his time, sure that his country would summon him to save her yet again.[9]

"*La cucaracha, la cucaracha,*" said another version of the old song, "*ya no quiere caminar.*" That cockroach, it does not want to go away.

HE HAS BECOME THE PERFECT TOOL OF SCOTT

Polk heard a report on January 4 that Trist had resumed negotiations, which he called "most surprising." Trist was "acting, no doubt, upon General Scott's advice. He has become the perfect tool of Scott." This set off a rant to the cabinet that went on for days, because Trist had defied the authority of his government. It also redoubled Polk's determination to fire Scott and replace him with Butler. He also ordered a court of inquiry instead of a court-martial to handle Scott's disputes with Pillow, Worth, and Duncan. Marcy gave Scott the bad news on the thirteenth, saying that he was relieved because of "the present state of things in the Army," and justifying the recall because Scott had asked for it back in June 1847.[10]

Polk spent January and February sputtering in rage. He saw Trist's vitriolic sixty-five-page letter to Buchanan on January 15 and called it "arrogant, impudent, and very insulting." Polk believed he had to assert his authority, but his paranoia got the best of him. "That there is a conspiracy between Scott and himself [Trist] to put the government at defiance and make a treaty of some sort, I have but little doubt," he growled on February 7. Some of Polk's advisers suggested formally notifying the Mexican government that Trist had no authority. The president calmed down, hoping that Trist might really produce a treaty. Colonel Atocha reared his lovely head again, telling the secretary of state on February 8 that if the United States government gave him the money, he could bribe the Mexican Congress to accept a peace. Polk called Atocha "a great scoundrel" and wanted to hear no more from him.[11]

So it continued, Polk fuming in the dark until Freaner reached Washington on February 19. The cabinet spent the next several days arguing. Buchanan and Secretary of the Treasury Walker thought the treaty should be rejected out of hand. Everyone else wanted to accept the document, except for a provision validating Mexican land grants in Texas awarded after that state's independence. Polk thought Trist had "acted very badly," but the president would not reject the treaty on those grounds—after all, it accorded with the diplomat's original instructions. Polk told the cabinet that he would send the treaty to the Senate. If he did not do that, the peace party in Mexico would be overthrown, and the United States Congress would refuse to pay for continuing the war. Buchanan still objected, but Polk chalked that up to the secretary's political ambitions. "No candidate for the presidency ought ever to remain in the Cabinet," he grumbled. "He is an unsafe adviser."[12]

The All-Mexico crowd in Congress had a powerful new leader— Senator Benton. He and others introduced bills to massively increase the army, aiming to enlarge the conquest. Proponents including Commodore Stockton trumpeted the idea that the United States should liberate Mexicans from "the abuses of generations." National will for this was lacking, however, and volunteer enlistments had fallen off; generals on the scene also had predicted that irregular resistance would continue as long as the United States Army was there. Joel Poinsett warned that taking over the whole country would both require a large occupation force and encourage violent opposition. When word got out that there was a treaty at hand, the whole phony debate ended. The House adjourned on March 3, in its last few days giving Polk everything he wanted, including a deficiency appropriation to cover overspending in fiscal 1847.[13]

New York diarist Philip Hone quipped that the Treaty of Guadalupe Hidalgo was "negotiated by an unauthorized agent, with an unacknowledged government, submitted by an accidental president to a dissatisfied Senate." Polk recommended that the Senate reject only the article on Texas land titles and a secret one extending the time for ratification. He wisely advised the senators to consider the treaty on its merits, not its origins. Renegotiation would probably be impossible, he said. The prospect of continuing the war sobered most senators, and the treaty was ratified March 10 by a vote of 38 to 14, the opponents a few All-Mexico diehards and some Whigs.[14]

The United States and Mexico had to exchange ratifications. Polk's first two choices as commissioners fell ill, one so seriously that he was out of the picture, the other—Senator Ambrose Sevier—taking leave. The president appointed Attorney General Nathan Clifford as associate commissioner and sent him to Mexico, empowered to renegotiate if necessary. The $3 million advance had already been released, although Marcy had advised Butler not to pay anything until the Mexican Congress ratified the agreement.[15]

Clifford arrived in Mexico City on April 11. Four days later Sevier joined him, having enjoyed a fast recovery. They presented their credentials at the foreign ministry on the seventeenth, then cooled their heels while the Congress debated the treaty. There was bitter objection to it, but most politicians were sick of the war and worried about the spread of populist rebellions. Both houses approved the treaty in the middle of May, and the ratifications were exchanged on May 30.[16]

This should have been a moment of triumph for President Polk, but instead he thought that the way the treaty had been negotiated was a political embarrassment. He took small-minded revenge by blocking reimbursement of Trist's expenses. The diplomat did not get the money due to him until 1871.[17]

Santa Anna was not the only famous general to leave Mexico that spring. Scott handed his command to Butler on February 19 but had to hang around for the courts of inquiry in the Pillow case. The first one took place in Mexico City from April 13 to 22. The court held that the payment of a bribe to anyone had not been proven. The second inquiry took place at Frederick, Maryland, in June and July. The court found against Pillow on several grounds but cleared him of writing the most contentious letter to the newspapers. He was tried separately by court-martial, accused of stealing two captured howitzers found in his personal baggage, and was acquitted. Marcy advised Scott that Worth could be tried separately, but the commanding general left that decision to the War Department. Polk dropped all the cases.

Scott left Mexico City on April 23, went to Vera Cruz, and caught a navy ship for New York. The man who should have been the war's great hero in the United States received no celebration on his return. His chief difficulties had been caused by Polk's spite and Pillow's plotting, compounded by his own thin skin. He called Pillow "the only person I have ever known who was wholly indifferent in the choice between truth and falsehood, honesty and dishonesty."[18]

WE DO NOT WANT MEXICO

Before Scott left, the war sputtered to a close in several regions as the peace process went forward. Wool claimed that he had broken up all the "bandit" gangs in the northeast, but he had greater trouble with his volunteers. He ordered his commanders in January to round up all persons who had no "pursuit or occupation or who cannot satisfactorily account for themselves, as well as gamblers," and send them across the Rio Grande. Deserters and discharged volunteers committed robberies, murders, and rapes all the way to the river.[19]

Wool received official news of the treaty on March 23, and prepared to evacuate Mexico. He called in his detachments and ordered his quartermasters to sell off property that would not be shipped home. Withdrawals began in June, and on July 6 he reported that all volunteers had been shipped to New Orleans. Two days later Wool asked for leave, and on the twenty-third he transferred command of the Army of Occupation to Colonel William Davenport at Fort Brown opposite Matamoros. Departures were disorderly because many volunteer officers abandoned their troops to rush home early.[20]

Things were also disorderly in New Mexico. Price had moved much of his command to El Paso since November 1847, and by early February the whole force was below Socorro except for an Illinois regiment and some Missourians still upriver. Price himself reached El Paso on February 23 and sent a patrol down the road toward Chihuahua. It captured a courier carrying dispatches that Price claimed showed that a Mexican army was marching on New Mexico. That was not true, but a guerrilla band of about 500 New Mexicans, Apaches, and Comanches—or so the unlikely combination was described—had earlier attacked about 200 United States troops north of El Paso, killing twenty, driving off the horses and mules, and slaughtering the oxen. This gave Price an excuse to invade Chihuahua.[21]

Price marched out of El Paso on March 1 leading six mounted companies. Governor Ángel Trías Álvarez rode to the Sacramento battlefield, where he told Price that a peace treaty had been signed. Price rejected that information. Trías had just been told by the federal government to disband the remaining presidial companies, so he called out the national guard. Price's force marched into the state capital on March 7 as Trías and a growing band of volunteers retreated south to Santa Cruz de Rosales, a hacienda fortified the year before to stop Doniphan. Trías had somewhere between 700 and 900 militia and between eight and eleven guns. Price arrived with about 200 men on March 8, but he had left his guns at El Paso. Trías sent him another message on the tenth asking for a suspension of hostilities because of the peace treaty, and again Price refused. The standoff continued until the morning of March 16, when Price attacked, only to be driven back by undisciplined but ferocious shooting. He tried again in the afternoon, his troopers riding through and around the disorganized Mexicans, capturing Trías and forty-two others before nightfall. Price lost four men killed and nineteen wounded and claimed that he had killed 328 Mexicans—a gross exaggeration.[22]

Butler at Mexico City ordered Price to withdraw from Chihuahua and restore all captured property. The Missouri freebooter received the order on April 15 and sat tight. The secretary of war himself ordered Price back to New Mexico on May 16 and reprimanded him for violating orders. Price led his men back to Santa Fe, where they arrived on August 4. The Missouri volunteers plodded into Brunswick, Missouri, on October 8, where they mustered out.[23]

It was easier to extract the navy from Mexico than it was the army. The secretary told Perry on May 19 to prepare to leave, giving him authority to time the departure and destination of his mosquito flotilla. Perry learned that the Mexicans had ratified the treaty on May 28 and restored customs houses to local control. Vera Cruz was handed back to Mexican authorities on June 11, and four days later the commodore sailed for New York. All vessels in the squadron had sailing orders for Pensacola, except for those going to New Orleans or other ports for sale.[24]

The situation was messier on the other side of Mexico, owing to the persistent insurgency in Baja California. Shubrick could not operate south of Mazatlán because he needed too many craft near the peninsula. He assigned a small tender and a storeship to blockade San Blas and spike the guns in the harbor defenses. When a shore party spiked three small guns at Manzanillo late in January, there were no more Mexican coastal defenses on the Pacific except for a dilapidated fort at Acapulco.[25]

Baja resistance leader Manuel Pineda kept looking for a chance to strike anyplace where there were no ships nearby. San José del Cabo was in that condition early in January, so Pineda concentrated there. Lieutenant Charles Heywood had seventy-two men in his garrison, about a third of them Mexican collaborationist volunteers. Pineda's guerrillas captured a foraging party out of San José on January 22. His men worked their way into the village on February 4 and pinned the garrison down in its mission fort, beating off strong counterattacks on the sixth and seventh. The insurgents drove off a schooner bringing supplies to the Anglos, and on February 11–12 they seized the garrison's water supply. But a sloop sailed into port on the fourteenth and a large landing party broke the siege lines. Pineda withdrew to Santa Anita, about fifteen miles away, and marines and sailors attacked him there on March 24. The guerrillas got away, but the threat to San José was neutralized.[26]

Colonel Burton planned to pacify Baja California with a company of New York volunteers and some recruits from Alta California. Burton attacked a Mexican camp at San Antonio on March 25, freeing five Anglo prisoners. Pineda was seriously wounded in this action and gave up his command. Burton led three companies of infantry against another camp at Todos Santos beside the Pacific Ocean on March 31, killing ten guerrillas and scattering the rest. Survivors of that force, including the rebel governor Mauricio Castro, surrendered when sailors and marines marched against them out of San José. Organized resistance was over in Baja by early April.[27]

It was over everywhere by that point. Shubrick received a copy of Butler's order declaring the armistice and halting all offensive operations on March 30. On May 6 Thomas ap Catesby Jones, once in disgrace for his seizure of Monterey in 1842, arrived to replace him. News of the treaty ratification reached Jones on June 13, and the United States Navy returned ports to local control. Almost 300 Mexican collaborators left La Paz on September 1. New York volunteers who clambered aboard USS *Ohio* at San José were the last United States troops to leave Mexican soil.[28]

The navy and its passengers walked into chaos when they landed in California. Gold had been discovered near Sutter's Fort late in January. Officers of the army and navy watched their units evaporate as men deserted in mobs to head for the gold fields. "The struggle between *right* and six dollars a month," one soldier wrote home, "and *wrong* and seventy-five dollars a day is rather a severe one." Most of them failed in the gold fields, so they turned to crime. The majority of the notorious criminal gangs that terrorized San Francisco in the years after the war were discharged volunteers, especially from New York regiments recruited from street gangs.[29]

The main North American evacuation was from central Mexico, and the men there were impatient. Many officers were frustrated by the time it took for the Mexicans to ratify the peace treaty. "We do not want Mexico," one said. "Its annexation to our country would be productive of far more evil than good, but if we want to close the war, we must commence a new system." His "system" was to loot the country, burn every town that resisted, "blow up their churches and take no prisoners, and they will soon humbly sue for terms."

At last the time came. Butler called in his outposts even before the exchange of ratifications, and by the end of May troops were on the march to the coast. All general court-martial prisoners, including the San Patricios, were released on June 1, and regiments streamed out of Mexico City. Worth's division was the last in the capital on June 12, when it assembled on the *Zócalo* as the Stars and Stripes came down and the Mexican tricolor again rose over the national palace. Worth's men marched out escorting peace commissioner Sevier. He carried the Mexican ratification but had no receipt for the $3 million advance because the Mexicans had not finished counting it. Most units went to New Orleans or Pass Christian, Mississippi, where new hospitals had been built. Butler boarded ship at Vera Cruz on June 20, and Worth's division was afloat by July 15. Among the evacuees were sixty-two men of Dominguez's Mexican Spy Company and thirty of their dependents. The last United States troops left Vera Cruz on August 2.[30]

WE BELIEVE THAT WE HAVE MADE
NO UNREASONABLE REQUESTS

The Anglo volunteers returned home sickly, ragged, and unkempt, so shocking in appearance that they frightened their families. Not returning

with them were about 25,200 fellow soldiers lost to fatal wounds, discharges, desertions, accidents, executions, and especially disease. The
army accounted for the deaths of regulars and volunteers according to categories, but a recent study has revealed about 2,800 dead not in the various groups. Those men were probably lost to murders and other resistance
or retaliation. The figures do not include civilian teamsters, employees, or
camp followers, whose deaths were in the many hundreds.[31]

About 1,700 of the casualties of the United States Army were men
killed in battle with regular Mexican forces, or who died afterward from
wounds. Mexican casualties will never be known, but battle deaths were at
least three times as high as those among Anglos. Total army deaths exceeded 10,000 during the war, owing to exposure, deprivation, and incompetence; Santa Anna's losses on the marches to and from Angostura
alone approached that figure. Guerrilla losses are unknown but were substantial; the same was true of *soldaderas*. Civilian deaths from counterinsurgency campaigns, major battles and bombardments, and atrocities
probably matched or exceeded military figures. Exposure and deprivation
among people driven from their homes raised the total further.

Calculating the total bloodshed of the war of 1846 to 1848 would be
impossible. The war aggravated the pattern of raid and counterraid en-
demic across New Mexico, and caused other fighting in Oregon and on the
Great Plains. Civil wars and irregular resistance in New Mexico, Alta and
Baja California, and other areas produced hundreds or thousands more
deaths. All who died in the Taos Rebellion, for instance, should be counted
as victims of the war. The total butcher's bill for the struggles among
Anglos, Mexicans, and Indians, if it could be added up, would run into the
tens of thousands. And that would not include the carnage from agrarian
rebellions and political coups in Mexico set off by the North American invasion.

The United States spent $147 million to take its big piece of Mexico.
The war itself cost $73 million, including the $15 million to end it by
treaty. Deferred costs included $10 million in interest on war loans and
$64 million in veterans' pensions and benefits awarded by Congress in
1887. The treaty transferred 529,017 square miles of land at under fifty
cents an acre.[32]

This territory was roamed over by about a quarter million migratory
Indians, whom the war made residents of the United States—about
25,000 in Texas, 150,000 or more in the Mexican Cession, and 25,000 in
Oregon, to which should be added others who crossed back and forth over
the northern and southern boundaries of the United States. Indian lives
were already disrupted and became more so with swelling Anglo migra-

tions to California and Oregon and spreading agricultural settlement. Many of the tribes were dependent on game for survival, but Anglo pressure reduced wildlife habitat. Deadly diseases struck many tribes as a result of increasing contact with whites, and the white man's liquor took its own toll. It is estimated that in the period before the Civil War, Indians killed 200 whites and took or destroyed $1 million worth of property in New Mexico alone, only partly counting losses among the 60,000 or so people who passed through the area on their way to California. How many Indians were killed by whites or by other Indians is not known.[33]

The United States had made a big mistake in its territorial demands in the treaty. Trist's instructions had emphasized setting the border west of El Paso along the thirty-second parallel. Kearny's topographical engineer, William H. Emory, returned to Washington near the end of 1847 and advised that the boundary should include territory south of the Gila River if the government wanted to build a railroad. The experience of the Mormon Battalion confirmed this judgment. The Polk administration knew even before the treaty was concluded that the United States would want to get more territory from Mexico, one way or another. A second war, however, was politically impossible.[34]

What had already been acquired was a doubtful bargain. The claim that Texas extended to the Rio Grande had been a principal North American excuse for the war. The Nueces Strip was in fact a no-man's-land bordered on either side by scattered settlements, crossed over by roving bands of Indians, attracting the dregs of society from two nations. The United States and Mexican armies were powerless to impose order. Everyone went armed in this lawless land, complained a French missionary. "The Americans of the Texian frontiers are, for the most part, the very scum of society," he snorted, "bankrupts, escaped criminals, old volunteers, who after the Treaty of Guadalupe Hidalgo, came into the country protected by nothing that could be called judicial authority, to seek adventure and illicit gains." Things were no better on the Mexican side. The war had merely traded the quarrel over who owned the Nueces Strip for an extended trouble zone from the Gulf of Mexico to the Pacific shore.[35]

Declaring that the border of Texas was on the Rio Grande was dubious. Saying that the capital of New Mexico, Santa Fe, was in Texas was absurd. Polk was stuck with that, however, because if he denied the Texian claims, what would that say about the justification for the war? Texas governor Pinckney Henderson wrote to the secretary of state in January 1847 to ask if Kearny had organized a government in New Mexico and whether the federal government would claim any land east of the Rio Grande. If this was true, he registered a strong protest. However, the government of

Texas would not object to a territorial government in New Mexico so long as the national government recognized that New Mexico was part of Texas. Buchanan reassured the governor that the federal government had no desire to offend Texas. "Nothing, therefore, can be more certain," he answered in February, "than that this temporary government [in New Mexico], resulting from necessity, can never injuriously affect the right which the President believes to be justly asserted by Texas to the whole territory on this side of the Rio Grande."[36]

Polk mentioned the Texas–New Mexico issue in his annual message for 1847. He noted the limits of Texas as defined by her statutes, which encompassed "all that portion of New Mexico lying east of the Rio Grande." Mexico still claimed that territory. The president consequently advised Congress that the "adjustment of this question of boundary is important." He meant the international boundary, but the Texas–New Mexico border would become a question for the United States after the war.[37]

Many bands of Comanches, Kiowas, Apaches, and others hunted in the vast spaces between the Texas and New Mexico settlements, passed through on their way to and from Mexico, and staged raids to both east and west. Commissioner of Indian Affairs William Medill described relations with the Indians in western Texas in May 1848 as "precarious." The United States and Texas were in a special situation regarding Indian affairs because the authority of each had not been defined. Medill had told the Indian agent in western Texas in March 1847 that the Indian Bureau would "assume the exercise of no doubtful powers." Important questions about Indian relations were deferred until geographical jurisdictions were sorted out.[38]

The Treaty of Guadalupe Hidalgo required the United States to provide governments and protection for the inhabitants of the ceded provinces. It was obvious early on that the slavery debate would interfere with any attempt to organize the lands taken from Mexico. "An Act to Establish the Territorial Governments of Oregon, California, and New Mexico" passed the Senate on July 26, 1848, and two days later went to its death in the House.[39]

Every effort to establish territorial governments and boundaries sparked a slavery debate, so Congress dodged its duty through most of 1848. The business of living and governing proceeded, however, and congressional inaction caused problems. One of them involved land claims. The commissioner of the general land office reminded Congress in December of its responsibility to provide for the examination and adjudication of titles and claims in New Mexico and California. He proposed establishing tribunals to settle claims in Spanish and Mexican land grants.

The Senate Committee on Public Lands had reported a bill to do just that on July 31, 1848. It went back to the committee at Senator Benton's urging on January 12, 1849, for modification in light of the discovery of gold in California.[40]

The people of New Mexico grew impatient. Price had been succeeded by Colonel John M. Washington, a regular officer who continued the military dictatorship. Resistance to that led to a convention in Santa Fe in October 1848. Representatives of both the anti–United States *Hispanos* and the Anglo traders petitioned Congress to establish a territorial government. Stipulating that that government be civil rather than military, the delegates remarked that continuation of the Kearny Code would be "acceptable." The convention concluded that since "New Mexico contains from 75,000 to 100,000 souls, we believe that we have made no unreasonable requests, and we confidently rely upon Congress to provide for us laws as liberal as enjoyed by any of her Territories." The petition dragged New Mexico into the sectional debate when it protested both the introduction of slavery to the province and "the dismemberment of our Territory in favor of Texas." The United States government had ignored its responsibilities to thousands of new citizens, subjecting them to the will of one man.[41]

Colonel Washington was a reluctant dictator, however. He told the secretary of war that it was "very advisable, for many reasons, that the territorial laws which are designed to be permanent should go into effect as soon as possible." In February 1849 he pleaded, "To avoid embarrassment in regard to recognizing the jurisdiction of the authorities of Texas over a large portion of this territory, it is desirable that Congress should act in the matter before the demand is made."[42]

Senator Benton aimed to defuse the Wilmot Proviso by suggesting in January 1848 that slavery already existed in New Mexico. He asked that the travel journal of F. A. Wislizenus, M.D., be printed "for the use of the Senate." In his *Memoir of a Tour to Northern Mexico, Connected with Colonel Doniphan's Expedition, in 1846 and 1847,* the German tourist offered, besides an excellent description of the country and its people, a strong denunciation of peonage. "This actual slavery," he called it, "exists throughout Mexico." That comforted senators from slave states, but what he said about the border with Texas did not. He tried to fix the eastern and southern boundaries of the Mexican Department of New Mexico, but could give only an approximation. "They have never been clearly defined," he said.[43]

As long as Congress dithered over slavery in the new territories and Texas lawmakers and their southern friends dragged that state's western border into the dispute, Polk could not meet his obligations under the

Treaty of Guadalupe Hidalgo to provide governments to the new citizens. He tried to get Congress to extend the Missouri Compromise line to the Pacific, but the abolitionists would not hear of it. Some New York Democrats proposed that Polk follow his annexation of Mexican territory by buying Cuba from Spain. Sounding as he had earlier about California, Polk said that taking Cuba would keep a European power from getting it. He told his minister to Spain to offer $100 million, but the Spanish did not like the idea.[44]

Polk was one of the hardest-working presidents ever, and also the most ill-tempered. He was worn out late in 1848, and he looked it, as if he had aged twenty years over the last four. It was no comfort to him that one of the winners of the war was the officer corps of the army, particularly the military academy at West Point. He, like others, had condemned that institution as the seedbed of a new military aristocracy. "The Military Academy had hosts of enemies," one of its graduates recalled. "But for the demonstrations of the Mexican War, it would have been abandoned." Scott gave credit for victory to West Point officers, and anyone who read a newspaper could see the contrast between their performance and that of political appointees. Graduates of West Point adopted a caveat they had been taught at the academy—that political activity was incompatible with military service. Inhibiting military partisanship in turn helped Polk's successors curb their own partisanship when acting as commander in chief. Future presidents who did not learn the error of Polk's ways did so at their peril.[45]

Polk himself paid the ultimate political price for his partisanship on November 8, 1848, when he learned that Zachary Taylor had been elected president, taking the office from the Democratic Party. "Should this be so, it is deeply to be regretted," the president lamented. "The country will be the loser by his election." This was not what Polk had expected for his many achievements—the thanks of a grateful nation.[46]

THE HOSTILE INDIANS HAVE SET UP A CLAIM TO THE LAND

There was no gratitude for Mexico's leaders, either. The peace commissioners put the best face on the situation when they said the treaty was unavoidable in the face of the "great disgrace suffered by our arms in the war." The other side had not dictated a punitive peace, and although Mexico had lost much territory it retained its independence; the territorial loss was "necessary and inevitable." The peacemakers claimed credit for avoiding a greater territorial loss, getting back by diplomatic means what the military had found impossible.[47]

The most optimistic interpretation was that losing half the country's territory should be compared to an amputation, surgery to preserve what was left of the national body. The amputation did not seem to help much, with secession a fact in Yucatán and likely in the northern states, bandits overrunning the countryside, French and *yanqui* filibusters invading over the borders, and agrarian revolutions everywhere. Still the *criollo* factions contended for control, while a rising *mestizo* class wondered if it could do better.[48]

Some diehards called for renewing the war with the United States. Most leaders, however, were relieved that the *Yanquis* were off their backs, leaving them free to fight domestic challenges to their dominance. The worst problem, and the most complicated, was Yucatán. The *criollo* junta that had taken over the province and declared independence in 1847 was on the ropes by early 1848. The Maya *Indios* they had abused for so long and betrayed so often had driven the whites into a few strongholds.

The struggle was portrayed to outsiders as a "caste" or "race" war, but race was incidental to the agrarian land-reform rebellion. Perry kept an eye on the situation through the first half of 1848, and with the Polk administration's approval provided transportation for white refugees and arms and other supplies to the state government. The *Criollos* described the rebel army in terms that caused North American whites to think of legendary Indian massacres during their own colonial period. "The white race," Governor Justo Sierra O'Reilly told Buchanan in March, "the civilized class of this State, is now attacked in an atrocious and barbarous manner by the aboriginal caste, which . . . is making a savage and exterminating war upon us." Polk ordered Perry to provide more arms and ammunition "for the use of the whites in protecting themselves from the Indians." The rebellious Mayas were not howling scalp takers, however. They were not out for blood so much as to get their land back. Polk and his advisers did not understand that, so they interfered.[49]

The *criollo* government was desperate by April. It had hoped to attract help from Anglo troops. The governor appealed to the United States, Britain, and France, offering to surrender his country "to any government which would protect & save them from extermination." After rebels killed 200 to 300 state troops in a great battle, the central government in Mexico City sent an envoy to Washington to ask for a few thousand Anglo soldiers to fight Indians in Yucatán and elsewhere. Polk objected that he could not employ the army outside the United States without the Senate's permission.[50]

The Yucatán government placed ads in newspapers looking for Anglo soldiers to help the white side in the Caste War. Some took their discharges in Mexico so they could fight in Yucatán, and other freebooters drifted in from the southern United States. They were not effective in jungle warfare, however, so the Mayas won most skirmishes and the *Gringos* went home. The civil war continued into the 1850s, when the Mexican national government suppressed it savagely.[51]

Yucatán drew the most international attention, but similar events were going on all over Mexico in 1848. By January the country had become a swirl of struggles that thoroughly confused the North Americans— Mexican guerrillas fighting the Anglo invaders, Mexican peasants fighting the state and federal governments, and the central government confronted by too many domestic and foreign challenges to handle at once. The Anglos could recognize a revolt against government, and under the peace treaty the North American army had authority to help the Mexican government fight rebels. This was especially the case when hero-bandits including Jarauta and Rea objected to the treaty as a sellout of "our moribund patria," as Rea put it. Former president Paredes raised a revolution in Guanajuato. Jarauta and other *guerrilleros* joined him but local support was lacking. The United States provided arms and ammunition to the Mexican government, which raised an army to go after the rebels. This included a reconstituted Batallón de San Patricio, among its members men who had been whipped and branded months earlier. The rebellion was finished by July 1848, with Paredes in exile and Jarauta in front of a firing squad.[52]

The greater threat to Mexico's established order was not uprisings by *caudillos* but local rebellions by villagers against the *hacendados* and the state forces. Fear of a countrywide race war spread through the ruling elite. This fear was worsened by the way the army and national guards were recruited, with press-gangs drafting peasants from the same classes who were in rebellion, making them undependable if the disorder was really racial.[53]

So desperate was the leadership to keep the social structure as it always had been that it turned to the hated *Yanquis* for help. One United States commander, after fighting a skirmish with *indio* rebels, gave an excellent description of these uprisings. "The hostile Indians have set up a claim to the land in that section of the country based upon the right of being the original owners prior to the invasion of Cortés," he said, "but do not design to war with the United States." The ruling *Criollos* thought it was a race war, but this officer was correct—it was about land.[54]

Other officers echoed him, but they emphasized the racial identity of the rebels or dismissed them as "bandits." The agrarian rebels avoided fights with Anglo troops, but officers failed to distinguish events around them from the kind of Indian wars they had known in the United States. The authorities in Mexico gained the balance of power when the North

American army returned captured military property and sold the Mexican and state armies guns and ammunition at fire-sale prices. The United States thereby established a pattern that it would pursue in Latin America for the next century and a half—supporting the existing order against even democratic rebellions, in the interest of stability. Mexico's minister of war reported at the end of 1848 that his government had more than 21,000 troops in the field fighting its own people. Thanks to the material help from the invaders, gradually Mexican armies suppressed the rebellions with customary savagery. At the same time, attacks by the "barbarous" tribes increased in the north.[55]

The Mexican government considered its own people a greater threat than the Anglo invasion had been. A widening range of critics charged that the real reason the government had made peace with the United States was so that it could turn on its own. Peña claimed that the only alternatives to the peace treaty were surrender or anarchy. *Puro* spokesman Manuel Crescencio Rejón told the chamber of deputies that the treaty would spell "the political death of the Republic," because *Gringos* would again filter across the border and repeat the loss of Texas. Neither, however, was willing to face up to why so many of their own people rebelled.

The growing numbers of educated *Mestizos* thought they knew what had really happened. Rather than give up the top of the heap, the *Criollos* gave up half the country's territory, betraying the republic to serve their own selfish interests. Mexico, these new voices maintained, should become a *mestizo* nation, part Indian and part white, run by those who combined the two bloods. The Virgin of Guadalupe was not *criolla*. She was *mexicana*.

NATIONS, LIKE INDIVIDUALS, ARE PUNISHED FOR THEIR TRANSGRESSIONS
(1849–1855)

Do you want Mexicans? Mexicans you shall have:
with leather chaps and decorated charro's sombrero;
passionate about women, horses, and weapons; jealous of their
independence and liberties; defenders of their home territory;
a threat to invaders, who are amazed at their stoicism in the face of death.

—Federico Gamboa

PRESIDENT-ELECT TAYLOR PAID A COURTESY CALL on outgoing President Polk. The weather was good for the inauguration, March 5, 1849, and the two presidents exchanged small talk. Polk was eager to get home, so he and his wife left on March 6 and followed a winding itinerary that took them by carriage and boat through six southeastern states. He was not up to that trip. His face was hollow and a mass of lines, his eyes dull, his hair colorless. He was sick most of the way.

The last stage of the journey was by boat up the Mississippi River from New Orleans, then up the Cumberland to Nashville, where the whole city turned out to welcome him on April 2. The Polks had called at Mobile and New Orleans just as yellow fever broke out in both places, and the epidemic followed him home, where he died on June 15. He had never been a happy man, but he had looked forward to an active retirement, casting off the resentments that had consumed him for so long. Even that was denied him.[1]

DID YOU SEE THOSE TRAITORS?

"The United States will conquer Mexico," Ralph Waldo Emerson predicted in 1846; "but it will be as the man swallows the arsenic which brings him down in turn. Mexico will poison us." Four decades later, looking back on the devastation of the Civil War that followed the conquest of Mexico, Ulysses S. Grant said, "Nations, like individuals, are punished for their transgressions."[2]

The first signs that the United States would tear itself apart appeared with the Wilmot Proviso of 1846. The extension of southern slavery into territories taken from Mexico remained the issue over the next several years, but debate was sidetracked at the end of 1848 when the petition of the Santa Fe Convention arrived in Washington. The petitioners told Congress, "We do not desire to have domestic slavery within our borders" and protested Texian designs on New Mexico's territory.[3]

Extending Texas into the Mexican Cession meant extending slavery without the inhabitants having a say. The legislature of Rhode Island sent Congress a set of resolutions on March 1, 1849, declaring that the territory east of the Rio Grande was the "common property of the United States" and asking Congress to "protect it from the claims of the State of Texas, and prohibit the extension over it of the laws of Texas, or the institution of domestic slavery." New York's lawmakers chimed in.[4]

Taylor and Secretary of War George W. Crawford told officers in New Mexico, California, and Oregon to advise the people to hold constitutional conventions and petition Congress for admission to the Union. Both believed that state formation would hand the slavery question to the people affected and prevent a brawl in Washington. California, filling up with Anglos on account of the gold rush, sent Congress a state constitution that forbade slavery early in 1849.

New Mexico was a more complicated story. Colonel Edward F. Beall became military governor in the summer of 1849 and discovered a "territorial machine" dominated by the Anglo merchants. An early version of the notorious "Santa Fe Ring," this group favored territorial status over statehood in the belief that it could exert more control over appointed territorial officers than over those elected in a state. The machine held a convention in September 1849 and sent a delegate to Congress to lobby for a territorial government. This plot ran into a complication, however, when James S. Calhoun arrived as superintendent of Indian affairs and as Taylor's agent to guide a statehood movement.[5]

The secretary of the interior recommended that Congress extend the land laws of the United States over New Mexico, California, and Oregon; that an office of surveyor general and land offices be established in each territory; that treaties be made with the Indian tribes; and that a judicial commission be established to handle Spanish and Mexican land titles in New Mexico. Taylor echoed him on December 24, urging Congress to accept California's statehood petition and announcing that he expected the people of New Mexico to submit a similar petition soon. "By awaiting their action," the president advised Congress, "all causes of uneasiness may be avoided, and confidence and kind feeling prevail." Let the people of the new provinces decide the slavery question, in other words.[6]

The Senate generally objected to statehood for the new territories. Senator Henry S. Foote of Mississippi moved on December 27 that Congress "establish suitable Territorial governments for California, for Deseret [Utah], and for New Mexico." The southerner's resolution soon acquired an amendment offered by John P. Hale of New Hampshire, requiring new territorial governments to protect "all the privileges and liberties secured to the inhabitants of the Northwest Territory by the ordinance of July 13, 1787." The Northwest Ordinance had outlawed slavery north of the Ohio River.[7]

Colonel John Munroe, new commander in New Mexico, ordered Major Jefferson Van Horne at El Paso to extend the Kearny Code over his district on December 18, 1849. Sectional tempers were so high that he had to rescind the order as soon as the news reached Washington. If that area was part of Texas, Texas law should govern it.[8]

The military command at Santa Fe was under orders to refrain from offending Texian sensibilities. But some of the people of New Mexico lived under military dictatorship and the rest were allowed no government at all. Many situations cried out for resolution—whether land claims, Indian affairs, or basic governance.[9]

Senator Sam Houston of Texas suggested on January 14, 1850, that the people of the territories should decide whether they wanted slavery. Henry Clay of Kentucky introduced a set of compromise resolutions on the twenty-ninth. Because slavery did not exist and was not likely to exist in any of the new territories, it was "inexpedient for Congress to provide by law either for its introduction into, or exclusion from, any part of the said territory." Territorial governments should be established with no mention of slavery; California should be granted statehood; the questions of the Texas–New Mexico boundary and the unpaid national debt of the Republic of Texas should be settled; slavery should be allowed to continue in the District of Columbia; a fugitive slave law should be passed; and Congress had no power to obstruct the slave trade among the states.

The chief difference between Clay's proposals and the earlier ones of Foote was the border between New Mexico and Texas. Clay urged that the Texas border be fixed along the Rio Grande to the southern border of New Mexico, then east and north to the Adams-Onís Treaty line, "excluding any portion of New Mexico." In return for surrendering her claim to New Mexico, Texas would have her old republican debts assumed by the United States. Foote, in contrast, demanded that the boundaries of Texas be honored as she claimed them, but that, in return for a payment, Texas should cede her claims north of the thirty-fourth parallel. Foote attacked Clay's proposals with three debilitating resolutions, insisting that Congress could establish a territory or not at its own discretion, that Congress had no power over slavery in the West, and that California was not yet entitled to statehood.[10]

The Senate, meanwhile, had asked the president to submit "all the official information in the possession of the Executive" concerning California and New Mexico. What he sent was mostly related to California; the scant information about New Mexico was about Indian fights. Taylor for the first time told Congress that he had advised the peoples of the territories to form state governments to avoid a showdown over slavery, because each state had power over its own laws. Taylor favored statehood for New Mexico to let the Supreme Court resolve the interstate border dispute.[11]

The Senate had also asked Taylor to deliver all correspondence with the military authorities at Santa Fe and with the government of Texas relating to the boundary. The president provided accounts of Indian battles and the 1847 exchange between Buchanan and Henderson about the Kearny government. Taylor said that he had not heard from the Texas governor and knew of no "acts of interference" against the alleged authority of Texas in New Mexico. Taylor did not think Texas would push its claim on the ground.[12]

Congress had thrown itself into the sectional fight in earnest by February, with the Texas–New Mexico border as a proxy for slavery. Southerners supported Texas' claim to New Mexico, while northerners backed Clay's suggested border. The political dogfight diverted attention from the government's immediate challenge: how to integrate the conquered provinces into the United States in obedience to the Treaty of Guadalupe Hidalgo. Getting them, after all, was what the war had been about.

424

Senator John Bell of Tennessee introduced a resolution on February 28 that Texas be divided into five states with the consent of its people. All its territory north of the thirty-fourth parallel would be incorporated into New Mexico, which would be admitted as a state without restrictions on slavery. All territory west of New Mexico and east of California would become a territory, without slavery. Northerners noticed that Bell's proposal would produce eight new slave-state senators in Congress.[13]

Bell's resolution brought all elements of the sectional controversy together. The storm in Congress passed through its most critical phase during March and April, after which a compromise sentiment arose. The Senate appointed a special committee to resolve the crisis, and it reported on May 8. Its recommendations resembled Clay's. The committee rejected the division of Texas unless the people asked for it. The panel advised admitting California as a state, but establishing territorial governments for New Mexico and Utah, which were not ready for statehood. The committee also proposed a boundary for Texas and New Mexico; it was geographically impossible, but a step in the right direction. For giving up New Mexico, Texas would receive a "large pecuniary equivalent." Finally, the group proposed a fugitive slave law and the abolition of the slave trade in the District of Columbia.[14]

Just when it appeared that Congress would sort everything out, the governor of Texas threatened to start a civil war. The Senate asked the president to divulge what orders had been given to the army at Santa Fe to thwart official Texas activities in New Mexico. Taylor replied curtly: "No such orders have been given." However, the president was outraged that "a certain Robert S. Neighbors, styling himself commissioner of the State of Texas, has proceeded to Santa Fe, with a view of organizing counties in that district, under the authority of Texas." As far as Taylor was concerned, New Mexico belonged to the United States, and Texas had no legal standing to interfere with federal possession. Robert S. Neighbors had been Texas' "commissioner" to New Mexico during the Santa Fe expedition of 1841. Now he was at it again. In November 1849, the Texas legislature protested the election of a delegate from New Mexico to lobby Congress for a territorial government, and Governor P. Hansbrough Bell fiercely demanded authority to invade New Mexico. Failing to get the legislature to support that, he appointed Neighbors as state commissioner to organize New Mexico into four Texas counties. Neighbors was also supposed to gain Munroe's cooperation to suppress local movements toward forming any kind of government. The commissioner arrived in Santa Fe on April 15, 1850.

Soon after Neighbors got there, the territorial party heard from its delegate in Washington, who said that its cause was hopeless. New Mexico's only chance, he advised, lay in independent action—formation of a state government and application for admission to the Union. That combined with Neighbors' presence to unite the statehood and territorial parties. Munroe called for a general election to be held on May 6 to choose delegates to a constitutional convention on May 15. Munroe was in cahoots with the Anglo merchants' machine and did not really favor statehood, but he despised Texians and ran Neighbors out of town. Munroe released the commissioner's letters protesting the statehood movement against "the will of the State of Texas." But the Texian also stirred up an anti-slavery statehood campaign on the sly, to give Governor Bell an excuse to invade New Mexico.[15]

The New Mexico constitution provided for officers and a legislature, all elected. The eastern border was set at the 100th meridian and black slavery was forbidden. The constitution was approved by the voters on June 20, 1850, by a lopsided margin of 6,771 to 39. In the general elections of state officers, the Anglo and native factions again opposed each other. For the first time in their history *Nuevomexicanos* picked their own rulers, because the native side won decisively. The statehood party, although a majority was *hispano,* actually represented interethnic cooperation. The new governor, Manuel Álvarez, confirmed Richard H. Weightman on July 15 as "a senator of the United States," to deliver the legislature's petition for statehood.[16]

Events proceeded in Washington in ignorance of what happened in Santa Fe. Taylor's message had satisfied southern senators that he was not trying to thwart Texian ambitions. The Senate again asked about the formation of a state government in New Mexico on June 27, but the executive had no information. The New Mexicans were forming a state, however, and the Texians knew it. Taylor soon received news that the government of Texas would send an army to enforce its claims to New Mexico. Governors of southern states offered troops to support the Texians, and Taylor vowed to fight any such action. Two southern senators visited him to protest, he blew up, and they ran from the presidential mansion in fright. Two Whig supporters came into the president's office and Taylor roared, "Did you see those traitors? I told them that if it becomes necessary I will take command of the army myself to enforce the laws. And I said that if you men are taken in rebellion against the Union, I will hang you with less reluctance than I hanged spies and deserters in Mexico!"[17]

The country faced a threat of civil war in the summer of 1850, and only Old Zach's ferocious temper kept the peace. Then Taylor died on July 9, succeeded by Vice President Millard Fillmore, a genial political hack from upstate New York, a pudgy man who thought of himself as a compromiser. He handed Congress a letter that Governor Bell had written to Taylor in June, complaining that the military had joined with the populace to stop his commissioner from organizing counties in New Mexico. Fillmore told Congress that Bell had threatened to establish Texian jurisdiction over New Mexico by force. If southerners thought that the new president had a banana spine, they were shocked by what Fillmore had to say. Any unlawful actions by the state of Texas or its citizens would be "prevented or resisted by the authority of the United States," the president declared. Reaffirming his government's obligations under the treaty to protect the citizens of the Mexican Cession, he promised to do just that until Congress acted. Fillmore advised the lawmakers to produce "an immediate decision or arrangement or settlement" and figure what Texas should be paid to surrender its claim.[18]

The threat of a shooting war was just what was needed to put Congress to work. Despite the fact that it had recently defeated an "omnibus bill" incorporating the recommendations of the select committee in May, Congress ended the sectional crisis within a month after Fillmore's message. A border was established between Texas and New Mexico, on the 103rd meridian instead of the 100th. The national debt of the Republic of Texas was assumed, New Mexico and Utah received territorial governments without mention of slavery, California was admitted as a free state, a fugitive slave law passed, and the slave trade was abolished in the District of Columbia. The United States had absorbed its conquest at last.[19]

California gold had changed the dynamics of the situation. Southerners in Congress wanted to claim it as a slave state, but they had argued that the people of the territories should decide on slavery. California's free-state constitution could not, therefore, be denied. The Compromise of 1850 temporarily muted the sectional quarrel, but California—the chief object of "Mr. Polk's War"—continued to strain north-south tensions. Pro-slavery forces spent the next decade trying to extend slavery to the Pacific by such misbegotten measures as the Kansas-Nebraska Act, which repealed the Missouri Compromise. Of all the avenues that led from the war of 1846–48 to the Civil War of 1861–65, California was one of the most traveled.[20]

New Mexico haunted the government of the United States like a ghost. Fillmore sent the Senate the state constitution on September 9 but declined to offer a recommendation. The accompanying memorial described the insufferable situation that had grown up in the territory since 1846. The New Mexico legislature reminded Congress of its obligations under the Treaty of Guadalupe Hidalgo. New Mexicans, it pointed out,

were citizens of the United States, but their government had not protected them "in their lives, their liberties, their property, nor in the free
exercise of their religion," nor had the people "been in the enjoyment of
any political privileges whatsoever." Instead of protecting New Mexicans,
the army subjected them to a military government, taxed them without
consent, and infringed their religion. The people of New Mexico believed
that what they had done "simply takes the place . . . of an unacknowledged
government, which has utterly failed . . . to preserve the plighted faith of
the government of the United States."[21]

Weightman went back to Santa Fe without receiving an audience. New
Mexicans had been neglected by Spain and by Mexico, and conquered by a
country that promised to do better; instead, the old neglect became future
neglect.

IT HAS CEASED TO BE REGARDED AS A WRONG

The War Department sent Colonel George McCall to inspect New
Mexico, but he did not see the seething resentment among *Nuevomexicanos*
toward *los Yanquis malditos.* Even well-intentioned measures backfired. The
people were insulted by Taylor's readiness to send troops to repel a Texian
invasion, while he appeared unwilling to assign enough soldiers to deal
with the Indians. Actually, Taylor was hampered in sending troops for either purpose in 1850 by the slavery hysteria.[22]

Taylor and others were deluded by their belief that New Mexico's
people enjoyed continuation of the former laws and the protection of the
army. In reality, the province's government under Mexico had been sup-
planted by the Kearny Code, which had in turn been abolished, so the
army filled a vacuum with a military dictatorship. Troops who should have
been guarding against Indian raids, people complained, stayed in towns
protecting their rule from the threat of rebellion. Local sentiments were
inflamed further by admitting California as a state while denying the same
to New Mexico.[23]

The Compromise of 1850 changed little at first. Munroe suppressed
news of the compromise laws as long as he could, and willfully disobeyed
orders to "abstain from all further interference in civil as well as political
affairs." When the popular Indian superintendent James S. Calhoun was
appointed first governor of the Territory of New Mexico, the colonel was
shoved aside. Calhoun's inauguration on March 3, 1851, it was hoped, signaled the end of the reign of about a thousand Anglo traders over more
than fifty times that many *Hispanos.*[24]

It did not, and the corruption of the Santa Fe Ring became legendary.
Moreover, the *Nuevomexicanos* had been conquered and suppressed, but

Anglo officials seemed surprised that they resented the situation. They answered resentment with insults. Governor William Carr Lane told the people in 1852 that their territory was "a burden to the United States." Congressman John S. Phelps of Missouri told New Mexicans in 1859 that their only importance was to his state's economy. Statements such as these, after four years of neglect by Congress, caused enduring bitterness. It was small wonder that Lane described the resistance to everything Anglo as "uncompromising" and New Mexico's government as "chaotic." Offices were mostly held by Anglos sent by Washington, so the opposition of the natives to anything they regarded as *gringo* continued for decades. *Hispanos* believed, for example, that the attempts of successive governors to provide for public education were really disguised efforts to subvert their religion. An effective education law did not pass the legislature until 1891.[25]

The hostility of a conquered people challenged everything the United States did in New Mexico. By 1852 a three-way feud had developed among the people via the legislature and the press, Governor Calhoun, and Colonel Edwin V. Sumner, commanding the military department of New Mexico. Sumner despised all parties, especially the Anglo merchants he claimed were feathering their nests with military supply contracts. He declared, "The New Mexicans are thoroughly debased and totally incapable of self-government, and there is no latent quality about them that can ever make them respectable." He suggested that the army be withdrawn so the residents could reap the fruit of the seeds they had sown among the Indians.[26]

Governors and army commanders tried to reform the army into an Indian-fighting service, establish Indian agencies, improve mail service, and leave the legislature free to enact its own laws. When they advised establishing a separate territory to govern the huge western part of New Mexico, however, creation of a Territory of Arizona was prevented until the 1860s by sectional disputes in Congress. Anglo negligence and incompetence, therefore, continued to rankle native New Mexicans. Governor Lane noted in 1852 that nine-tenths of the Anglos in Santa Fe, himself included, went armed by day and slept armed at night. "Us versus them" was the prevalent attitude between the United States government and *Nuevomexicanos* for decades.[27]

The continuing war among the several Indian tribes, New Mexicans, and the Anglo army received the most notice from federal officials. It would be many years, however, before the army reduced the level of Indian raiding. Military policy was haphazard and constantly changing, and it catered as much to vested interests as to real needs. Tactics ranging from annihilation and deportation to bribing the Indians into peace were tried, and all failed. The government spent $12 million on defense in New Mexico from 1848 to 1853, most of it reparations to settlers harmed by Indian raids because there were only 885 troops to spend it on. The disgusted Sumner told a Santa Fe newspaper in 1853 that the only solution was to abandon the territory, "which hardly seems fit for the inhabitations of civilized man."[28]

The "wild" Indians saw no reason to change their ways because of the Treaty of Guadalupe Hidalgo, although the treaty required the government to prevent raiding across the border. The Mexican government lodged diplomatic protests reminding the North American government of its treaty obligations. One such note late in 1850 concluded, "The government of Mexico can give no greater proof of the confidence which it entertains in the honor and good faith of the government of the United States, than by its desire that a military force may be kept on the frontier, which it is well assured will not be employed in any other way than in repressing the wild Indians."[29]

Some of the disorder could have been quelled if the government had stamped out the slave trade. That, however, would incite more battles over other slavery issues. New Mexicans themselves were divided over both slavery and peonage. In his inaugural address, Manuel Álvarez, the only governor under the 1850 constitution, recommended protection of peonage by law. Governor Lane arrived in Santa Fe with two black slaves in 1852. Black slavery remained insignificant, but the legislature passed a law protecting it in 1859.[30]

Calhoun advised Congress in 1850, "The trading in captives has been so long tolerated in this Territory, that it has ceased to be regarded as a wrong." The governor vetoed a bill authorizing the enslavement of all captured Indians in 1860, but both slavery and peonage continued. The Indian slave trade ended with the Indian wars. Peonage was finally abolished in 1867 under the Thirteenth Amendment to the Constitution.[31]

To poor *Nuevomexicanos* who held one or two slaves in their households or on their farms, and to rich ones who commanded the services of many *peones,* this was yet another case of Anglo interference in their lives. California had become an Anglo province as a result of the gold rush, the few *Californios* reduced to a powerless minority. New Mexico, the greatest patch of land taken from Mexico, remained essentially Mexican, the minds and feelings of its people unconquered and resentful. This would not begin to change until after 1912, when New Mexico was admitted to the Union as a state and *Hispanos* could feel themselves full citizens of the United States.

LET THE EARTH TREMBLE TO ITS CORE

New Mexico's motherland, Mexico, was devastated. Lucas Alamán lamented the loss of territory to the *Yanquis,* the mountain of internal as well as foreign debt, and the destruction of the army. Dominating all the country's troubles, he complained, was the "complete extinction of public spirit, which has swept away every idea with a national content; not finding any Mexicans in Mexico and contemplating a nation which has moved from infancy to decrepitude" without an intervening youth. Who was to blame? José María Luís Mora, wartime ambassador to Britain, blamed Mexico's misfortunes on the whims of one *caudillo*—Santa Anna, the "Attila of Mexican Civilization."[32]

Alamán was afraid that the war with the North Americans was not really over and Mexico faced more invasions if it did not reform itself. He predicted that the slavery controversy in the United States would worsen until the slave states seceded and set about conquering Mexico, Panama, and the Spanish and English colonies in the Caribbean. This new empire would "subject Indians and Castes of the countries it occupied into more or less harsh servitude." He had reason to fear that: several North American adventurers set out, mostly from California, to conquer northwestern Mexico and Central America during the years after the war. All of them failed, but they added to the grief in the northern states inflicted by *Indios bárbaros* from the United States.[33]

The Treaty of Guadalupe Hidalgo and the United States' failure to meet its obligations provided safe havens in Texas and New Mexico for Indians raiding into the country. Apaches and Comanches especially cut swaths of destruction as far from the border as Durango, San Luis Potosí, and Zacatecas. They crossed the paths of bandit gangs that controlled all roads and roamed freely across countryside that was up in arms with agrarian rebellions. Mexico's population was not enough to settle the vast areas left to the country after the war. There was almost no immigration and infant mortality was extremely high. The hacienda remained the basic unit of rural society and peonage the rule, except where the indigenous rebellions held out. Aside from the mines and a few textile factories in Puebla, there was little industrial development. Basic means of transportation remained mules and horses over wretched roads. The first railroad did not open until 1857. The old fiscal burdens persisted—the country owed foreigners 52 million pesos.[34]

There was reason to hope for improvement, however. The *moderados* had made peace at great political and even physical peril. Yet the nation was too stunned to jump immediately into another factional struggle for power. José Joaquín de Herrera became president again in June 1848 and served out his full term. In 1852 he peacefully turned the office over to his successor, Mariano Arista, another general once disgraced but rehabilitated by the more spectacular defeats of others. The moderate government of Herrera and Arista was notably honest and intelligent. They cut the military budget by two-thirds, and the other generals were too ashamed of their failures to fight back. European bondholders were pacified by being assigned three-fourths of future customs receipts. The money transferred by the United States under the peace treaty went to consolidating the internal debt.

Not all problems were solved, however. The treasury was too empty to meet the debts left by earlier governments, so the current one lived beyond its means. Soldiers, bureaucrats, and churchmen grew increasingly resentful about attempts to discipline them. Customs officers wrecked financial planning by reducing or stealing duties. The countryside was in an uproar with revolts and banditry, and foreigners were in peril wherever they traveled. Under the restored Constitution of 1824, some states developed honest, effective governments, while others were in anarchy or in the clutches of thieves. Mexico developed an international reputation as a land of banditry and barbarism.

The situation could not last. The army deposed Arista in January 1853 and he left the country. The conservative-centralist-monarchist block was back in the saddle, but it had no outstanding leaders. It had some thinkers, however, led by Alamán, still holding on to visions of a monarchy. The next best thing to a king was Santa Anna, the only Mexican with the potential to lead the country out of chaos, or so Alamán and others believed. They invited the Savior of His Country to return on the excuse that he was needed to defend the Catholic religion from its liberal enemies. "We are opposed to the federal form of government; against the representative system through election," Alamán told him. "We are convinced that nothing can be accomplished by a Congress and desire you to govern aided by councils few in number." Santa Anna returned home on April 1, 1853, and on April 20 became president of Mexico for the eleventh time. Alamán was expected to keep the *caudillo* in line, but he died on June 1. In mid-December Santa Anna became "Dictator in Perpetuity."[35]

The *caudillo* surpassed his worst self of years past. Years of alcohol and opium had taken their toll, but he remained crafty. He courted the Church, inviting the Jesuits to return to Mexico for the first time since they were expelled in 1767. He revived the old Spanish Order of Guadalupe and sold memberships in it. He wooed the army by raising its strength to 100,000 men and selling generalships left and right.

There were more questionable actions. Santa Anna raided the treasury shamelessly, saying it should repay what he had advanced out of his own pocket to fight Taylor. He revived his old habit of giving himself dozens of new, grand titles, most notably requiring that he be addressed as "His Most Serene Highness." He surrounded himself with a bodyguard in expensive Swiss uniforms and raised outlandish new taxes, including one on house-hold dogs. He replaced his old love of cockfighting with ever grander pub-lic spectacles. The dictator patronized the opera at the Gran Teatro Santa Anna, each performance prefaced by an elaborate tribute to himself. His Most Serene Highness persecuted Indians who had rebelled against him in the 1840s and officers who had surrendered to the North Americans. He created a spy network and exiled any who spoke against him. Among the banished were such rising stars of Mexican politics as governors Melchor Ocampo of Michoacán and Benito Juárez of Oaxaca, along with intellec-tuals including Mariano Riva Palacio and Guillermo Prieto. They fled to New Orleans and marshaled opinion against the Savior of His Country.[36]

Santa Anna commissioned scores of operas, operettas, plays, and or-chestral works, all of them quickly forgotten. Only one that premiered during his last presidency has survived, and that is the Mexican national anthem, which incorporated lines from his proclamations. It was a blood-thirsty ode to war in ten stanzas, each followed by the chorus:

> Mexicans! When you hear the cry of war!
> Ready your swords and your horses!
> And let the earth tremble to its core
> At the sonorous roar of the cannon!

El himno nacional has sometimes been compared to "La Marseillaise," but that song reflected the triumph of a "nation at arms" during the French Revolution. This anthem had no basis in history and was really a vainglori-ous attempt to mask Mexico's despair, its political and economic chaos, its social disorder, and its record of defeat on the battlefield. It was the swan song of the *criollo* nation.[37]

Santa Anna's official behavior became steadily more bizarre. Filibus-tering expeditions into northwest Mexico by Anglo adventurers in the early 1850s gave him the loony idea of recruiting foreigners in California to settle the northwest frontier and defend it against such attacks. This led to a deal with Gaston, comte de Raousset, who had plans unknown to

Santa Anna to resettle 3,000 Frenchmen in Sonora and declare independence. The comte rounded up 350 Frenchmen in San Francisco and landed
them in Guaymas at the end of June 1854. They attacked the Mexican barracks and customs house but were soundly whipped. The *comandante* put
Raousset in front of a firing squad and sent some of the survivors back to
San Francisco, the others to Perote.[38]

Santa Anna saw the northern border as a means to extract more
money from the North Americans. Both countries had a strong interest in
completing a joint survey of the line, as required under the Treaty of
Guadalupe Hidalgo. The United States had an equal interest in exploring
its new territories. Three explorations early in 1849 searched for a route
from San Antonio to El Paso and two from Fort Smith, Arkansas, to Santa
Fe. Also in 1849, four explorations set out to find routes from the
Mississippi River to New Mexico and beyond, one was planned within
New Mexico, and one was to go from Fort Hall in the northern Rockies to
Santa Fe via Salt Lake.[39]

When Trist and his Mexican colleagues fixed the boundary using the
Disturnell map they knew they worked with an inaccurate depiction of
the country, but they did not know just what the errors were. Both sides
appointed boundary commissioners to sort it all out on the ground, supported by surveyors, astronomers, and topographers. The first North
American commissioner was a midnight appointment by Polk, his sole
qualification being that he was a Democratic politician out of a job. He was
replaced in 1850 by John Russell Bartlett, a travel-book seller from Rhode
Island and New York, qualified on account of his Whig connections. Major
William H. Emory replaced him in 1851, and finally the North American
side had competent leadership. Surveyors and other technicians were a
mixed bag, although the commission used the army's topographical engineers for geodesy and surveying. Talent ruled from the outset on the
Mexican side, beginning with the commissioner, a highly competent and
experienced military engineer and surveyor, General Pedro García
Condé, veteran of the Sacramento.

The commissions reached San Diego in July 1849. Running the line
from the Pacific to the Colorado River involved several technical difficulties. Hordes of gold seekers crossing the desert were also a problem because many of them needed relief and their presence drove up local
prices. The international party nevertheless completed the California
stretch of the line before the end of 1849.

Work resumed from the east at El Paso in the summer of 1850. Both
commissions had fought Indians on the way there, and the American laborers were a lot of drunken bums who committed three murders en route.

A battle between Bartlett and García Condé began over the border of New Mexico because the Disturnell map conflicted with geography and local tradition. The commissioners compromised on alignments and began their surveys while fighting off Apaches and Comanches. About 2,000 settlers from New Mexico and El Paso moved into the area and founded the town of Mesilla, thinking they were in Chihuahua. Bartlett's surveyor, A. B. Gray, showed up and rejected the compromise because it would put the Mesilla Valley into Mexico rather than the United States. That was not all that was at stake, because the treaty boundary excluded from the United States a suitable route for a transcontinental railroad. Gray was soon dismissed by the Whig secretary of the interior because he was a Democrat, which at least let Emory and other army experts rise to the top of the program. Before they could make much progress on the compromise border, García Condé died late in 1851, and the United States Congress stopped the whole business late in 1852 pending a readjustment of the border by treaty.

President Franklin Pierce, who had been a political general during the war and had since led the Democrats back to the executive mansion, wanted a new treaty, and so did Santa Anna. There were several disputes to settle. The Mexican government had taken up the claims of its former citizens who had been deprived of their property and political rights. Migratory Indians still raided into Mexico from the United States. There were disagreements over transit rights across the Isthmus of Tehuantepec. Finally, the border between Mexico and New Mexico was declared a matter of international contention.

Railroad developer James Gadsden became minister to Mexico with instructions to resolve all issues between the countries. He was also told to make a new bid for Baja California, although he did not follow through on that. He approached Foreign Minister Manuel Díez de Bonilla in the summer of 1853 and the two negotiated in a friendly spirit. Santa Anna really called the shots, however, and he desperately wanted money to buy support from the army. He had mostly put down the rebellion in Yucatán, selling captured Mayas into slavery in Cuba, but that did not bring in enough to meet his needs. Santa Anna later claimed that the United States had taken "knife in hand" to "cut another piece from the body which she had just horribly mutilated. We were threatened with yet another invasion." Since resistance would be futile, he "decided to take the alternative which patriotism and prudence decreed—a peaceful settlement." That was self-serving baloney. He was eager to sell another chunk of his country to the *Yanquis,* and pocketed half the money they paid him.[40]

The Tratado de la Mesilla (Treaty of Mesilla) was signed in Mexico

City on December 30, 1853. The United States Senate amended the Gadsden Purchase, as it was known in the north, and Santa Anna's government accepted the minor revisions in June 1854. Mexico—mostly Santa Anna—received $10 million for a comparatively small patch of Sonoran desert that included the towns of Mesilla and Tuscon, and for rights of transit across Tehuantepec. The Mexican government also agreed to give up provisions in the Treaty of Guadalupe Hidalgo that required the United States to compensate Mexican citizens harmed by Indian raids across the border. Former Mexicans in the ceded territories were set adrift.

Emory and Mexican commissioner José Salazar Ilarregui began working westward from El Paso to Nogales in January 1855, and in March Captain Francisco Jiménez and Lieutenant Nathaniel Michler started east from the Colorado River. The new border was fixed by October. It had been a diplomatic mess, but a splendid scientific and geographical achievement. There was a story in Mexico that, soon after the Mesilla Treaty was signed, a cartographer presented Santa Anna a revised map of Mexico and for the first time the Savior of His Country saw how much territory his fatherland had lost to the United States. He broke into tears, so it was said, over the humiliation of the generation of *Criollos* who had been so optimistic in 1821 but had turned Mexico into a wreck of a nation.[41]

The end came fairly swiftly for this most persistent *caudillo.* Liberals from Acapulco proclaimed the Plan de Ayutla at a little *pueblo* in the mountains on March 1, 1854. Their leaders were the *mestizo* Juan Álvarez, who had failed to mount a cavalry charge at Molino del Rey and now was a leather-faced old *guerrillero,* and General Ignacio Comonfort, *criollo* collector of customs at Acapulco. The plan called only for a new president and a new constitutional convention, but Santa Anna had made his country ripe for revolution. Selling out to the *Yanquis* in the latest treaty aggravated what had become widespread hatred of His Most Serene Highness.

Santa Anna marched out of Mexico City at the head of 5,000 men to put the uprising down, but the rebels beat him off outside Acapulco on April 20. The Soldier of the People burned some Indian villages, shot a few liberals, and declared the rebellion crushed. He returned to the capital, where his remaining followers built a triumphal arch with a statue of Santa Anna on top. He saw the handwriting on the wall, however, and secretly began transferring money out of the country. The rebellion spread until all the northern states and many in other parts of the country declared for Ayutla. Twice Santa Anna marched out of Mexico City and twice he returned in a hurry. He had not kept enough money to pay his soldiers, so desertions vaporized his army. Santa Anna slipped out of Mexico City on August 9, 1855, and reached Vera Cruz before anybody knew he was gone. He took ship for Cuba, then moved on to his hacienda in Colombia. There the Savior of His Country once again awaited its call for him to save it again.[42]

Santa Anna had ruined Mexico for the conservatives, so the liberals again had a turn at power. There was something different about the factions this time, however. There were some *Criollos* among the new leaders, but mostly they were *Mestizos*. Some were *Indios,* Juárez the outstanding example. Moreover, they were educated and thoughtful and had worked their way up through government and the professions. They wanted power to serve their country, not themselves, or at least they said so. The *criollo* nation was finished after thirty-four years, and gone with it was the last remnant of New Spain. Mexico had become Mexican at last.

PART THREE

REFORMAS Y INTERVENCIONES

(Reforms and Interventions)

(1855—2008)

24

LET THERE BE A DESERT BETWEEN STRENGTH AND WEAKNESS

(1855–2008)

Methinks I see in my mind a noble and puissant nation rousing herself
like a strong man after sleep, and shaking her invincible locks.
Methinks I see her as an eagle mewing her mighty youth,
and kindling her undazzled eyes at the full midday beam.

—John Milton

Antonio López de Santa Anna was sixty-one years old when he
went into exile in 1855. His odor was sweeter to the north than it was at
home. Santa Anna was Uncle Sam's man, minister to Mexico John Forsyth
told the secretary of state in March 1858. "Santa Anna *will* have money, &
he is not afraid to sell Territory if that be necessary to obtain it."[1]

The Napoleon of the West moved to St. Thomas in the Caribbean in
1858 and began a fruitless correspondence with the conservatives, who
were willing to have him back in Mexico but not in power. After the
French invaded his country, Santa Anna landed at Vera Cruz in 1864 promising to stay out of politics. The first thing he did when he stepped ashore,
however, was to issue a proclamation favoring a constitutional monarchy.
His enemies tossed him out of the country again. Santa Anna returned to

St. Thomas, where he enjoyed a pension granted by Emperor Maximilian. The end of the U.S. Civil War in 1865 meant the emperor's days in Mexico were numbered, so the Savior of His Country courted the liberals but lost both his pension and Manga de Clavo when Maximilian got wind of that. Maximilian was out of the picture by 1867 and the liberals returned to power under Benito Juárez. The next year Santa Anna met with the North American secretary of state, William Seward, who wondered whether the exile would serve United States interests if he returned to Mexico. The Juárez government made sure that did not happen.

His Most Serene Highness spent some time in New York, where swindlers made off with most of his fortune. He tried to return to Mexico but was arrested by Mexican authorities. A court-martial exiled him once more and he went to Havana. He stayed there a year until the Spanish government threw him out and he moved to the Bahamas. When the liberal government in Mexico excluded Santa Anna from a general amnesty in 1870, he declared Juárez to be a traitor and organized plots to overthrow him. Juárez's successor granted amnesty, and the Savior of His Country returned to Mexico City early in 1874. Broke, senile, depressed, supported by a few sympathizers, he died on June 21, 1876. "I believe that I have merited the title of a good patriot," he said before his death.[2]

The Age of Santa Anna was over, and that came as a shock. "The last hours of his life inspire the saddest of reflections: the man who controlled millions, who acquired fortune and honors, who exercised an unrestricted dictatorship, has died in the midst of the greatest want, abandoned by all except a few of his friends," mourned *El Siglo Diez y Nueve*. "A relic of another epoch, our generation remembered him for the misfortunes he brought upon the republic, forgetting the really eminent services he rendered to the nation." Said *Dos Repúblicas*: "However he may have been condemned by parties, his career formed a brilliant and important portion of the History of Mexico. . . . Peace to his ashes."[3]

Santa Anna was one of the world's greatest political opportunists. He was also one of his country's greatest generals, bold and brave. He could not deal with adversity, however. He never admitted error, and blamed defeats on traitors he saw all around him. He more than anyone else made Mexico what it was in the nineteenth century, a faction-torn charade of a country that lost half its territory and much of its natural wealth to an aggressive neighbor. Santa Anna deserved most of the blame for that catastrophe.

His passing was noted in the United States, but without much regret, although he left an enduring mark on that country. His secretary and interpreter in New York, James Adams, noticed that Santa Anna would occasionally cut a piece of something he carried in a pouch, pop it into his mouth, and chew it. When Adams asked what it was, the old *caudillo* said it was chicle—the sap of the tropical sapodilla tree—and gave him some. Adams imported more of the latex, added sweeteners, and founded the Adams Chewing Gum Company, introducing a new habit to the United States.[4]

WE SHALL TEACH THEM

The origins of the chewing gum industry say something about the differences between Mexico and the United States at that point. Indians had chewed chicle since time immemorial, and their conquerors adopted the habit. When the Yankee saw the stuff, he made some improvements and put it on the market. One country was dominated by people at the top of the social scale who wanted to keep things as they were. The other was energized by people at the bottom who looked for something new to exploit.

Few Anglo-Americans know and even fewer Mexicans can forget that the histories of the two countries have been intertwined since before either existed. The United States is a famously inward-looking society—few of its people know much about Canada, either. Living next to a rambunctious nation such the United States meant that neither Canadians nor Mexicans escaped its influence. Both were invaded by the Yankees, and Mexico especially still lives with the effects of *la Intervención Norteamericana*, the North American Intervention, as the war of the 1840s is known there. Yet the parallels between the two countries and their interactions go beyond military and diplomatic events. The United States and Mexico both were bent on self-destruction by 1848. The war sped them on their course.

The ouster of Santa Anna in 1855 propelled liberal reformers to the top of the Mexican government under the leadership of Juan Álvarez, a moderate who stocked his cabinet with *puros,* radical reformers. Most of them were *Mestizos,* but they included a few *Indios* such as Benito Juárez, who became justice minister. Miguel Lerdo de Tejada took over the treasury and Melchor Ocampo took charge of bright young men in the middle offices of government. Feeling outclassed amid all this brainpower, Álvarez resigned in favor of Ignacio Comonfort, the last *criollo* president of Mexico.

This group governed by decree, issuing a series of reformist *leyes.* The first measure abolished military and clerical *fueros.* The second terminated the right of corporate entities to hold land, which was sold off while the government profited from sales taxes. This broke the power of the

Church, but it also abolished the *ejidos*, the communal landholdings of rural Indians. This was a prescription for trouble, because not only would the Church fight back but so would the *Indios* and *Castas*. The idealists at the head of the government had no sympathy with prehistoric methods of agriculture and naively wanted to create a nation of small landholders. They failed because the lands forced onto the market depressed prices and were grabbed by rich speculators in large tracts. Wiping out the Church corporations ended what little educational and charitable work had gone on in rural areas.

These and other reforms were embodied in the Constitution of 1857, which governed the country until 1917. The document was a negative constitution, outlining what the government could not do, to prevent a revival of centralist authoritarianism. The Constitution was no sooner in place than the Church, the army, and other conservative forces counterattacked. Comonfort toppled his own government in favor of General Félix María Zoloaga, although under the Constitution Juárez was next in line. Liberals denied Zoloaga's legitimacy and the country plunged into *la Guerra de la Reforma,* the War of the Reform. It was utter, bloody chaos, the campaigns on both sides mostly in the hands of guerrillas and bandits, fighters slaughtering each other and civilians, agrarian rebels waging their own campaigns. The liberals under Juárez were victorious by early 1861 and he assumed the presidency in June. His country was as broke as it ever had been, the foreign debt over 80 million pesos. British bankers held most of the foreign debt, but the conservatives had also borrowed heavily from France and Spain. Juárez repudiated the conservative debt and suspended payments to creditors.

The United States, meanwhile, had torn itself apart over slavery. The usual issue was its extension to western territories, but there was growing sentiment in northern states for abolishing the "peculiar institution" altogether. Defenders of slavery feared losing their domination of Congress. An opportunistic Illinois Democrat, Senator Stephen A. Douglas, joined with southerners to repeal the Missouri Compromise of 1820, opening the way to extend slavery into the west and increasing enforcement of the fugitive slave law. This ignited a bloody guerrilla war in Kansas Territory and mob action against slave catchers in northern cities. James Buchanan became president in 1857, one of the least effective occupants of that office ever. The crisis boiled over in the fall of 1860 when Abraham Lincoln won a four-way contest for the presidency. Lincoln's position on slavery was not abolitionist, merely opposed to its territorial extension. Even before Lincoln took office in March 1861 southern states seceded from the

Union and formed their own government. Buchanan dithered while the Confederate States of America formed armies, seized federal properties, and threatened war. A month after Lincoln became president, southern guns fired on Fort Sumter at Charleston, South Carolina, and forced its surrender. There followed four years of mostly regular warfare that killed two-thirds of a million North Americans. This also was a war of reform, in the aftermath abolishing slavery and guaranteeing all citizens equal protection of the laws.

Mexico's chief creditors—France, Britain, and Spain—seized the customs house and port at Vera Cruz late in 1861; when the other two realized that France's Emperor Napoleon III had greater ambitions, they pulled out. Napoleon wanted an American empire, and during its civil war Washington could not enforce the Monroe Doctrine. Mexican conservatives wanted French troops to support their struggle against Juárez and the liberals. A French expedition landed at Vera Cruz in 1862, only to be tossed back into the ocean on May 5 (Cinco de Mayo) by a combination of Mexican troops, militia, and volunteers. The invaders returned in greater strength in 1863 and proceeded to conquer the country and install an Austrian archduke as Emperor Maximilian. The War of the Reform thus slid into the War of the French Intervention. The French presence raised the countrywide savagery to new heights. The transfer of United States troops to the border in April 1865 at the end of the northern civil war pressured Napoleon into withdrawing his country's troops in 1867. The last two years had seen the French defeated with heavy loss, the conservatives killed or scattered, about 300,000 Mexicans dead, villages and haciendas burned to the ground.

Mexico became known by the 1870s as a "bandit nation," while a similar tradition emerged in the United States. The problem persisted in both countries into the twentieth century. Bandits were at odds with the government or other centers of power such as banks and railroads, so they were celebrated as hero-bandits, from Billy the Kid to Heraclio Bernal. Mexicans sang ballads about their hero-bandits, while North Americans read dime novels about theirs. Indian wars, meanwhile, continued until the early 1880s in the north and into the 1900s in Sonora and Chihuahua.[5]

Banditry spilled across the national border in both directions. United States troops or law enforcement posses crossed the Mexican border at least twenty-three times between 1874 and 1882—a fact not familiar to most Anglo-Americans but still recalled in Mexico. This disregard for national sovereignty raised continual alarms about another *yanqui* invasion. Lerdo de Tejada succeeded Juárez as president in 1872 and refused to allow the construction of railroads toward the northern parts of the country, or to connect those already existing to tracks on the other side of the line. "Let there be a desert between strength and weakness," he said.[6]

Porfirio Díaz, Juarista liberal and hero of the war against the French, gained the presidency in 1876 and except for four years in the 1880s stayed there until 1910, violating the Constitution's one-term limit. He wanted to lead his country into the modern world under a regime of "liberal authoritarianism." Mexico continued to be ruled by an entrenched elite, *Mestizos* replacing *Criollos*. The difference this time was that Díaz wanted change, and for the better. He catered to the Church and the *hacendado* class, but mostly he catered to foreigners.

The dictator told the world that Mexico's bandit problem had been solved, that the country was under a stable government, and that it was safe for investment. This was the height of the industrial revolution and there was money to burn in foreign markets. Díaz surrounded himself with highly educated *científicos* (scientific ones), engineers, planners, economists, and other experts to guide the country into the modern world. Laws promoted railroading, utilities, and other industries, and money and foreigners poured in, especially from the United States and Britain. As far as poor Mexicans were concerned, however, Don Porfirio sold his country out to *Gringos*. Farm and ranch lands in the millions of hectares were taken from Indians and handed to outsiders. Mines reopened and factories sprang up. The Díaz government sent troops to put down strikes or rural protests. Resentment grew, and by the early twentieth century rebellions and banditry again spread over the country.[7]

The United States did not send in troops, but private detectives and even territorial law officers crossed the border to help put down strikes or terrorize rebellious farmers. Meanwhile, Theodore Roosevelt became president of the United States in 1901. Three years later, following threatened attacks against Venezuela and the Dominican Republic by Britain and Germany, he declared the Roosevelt Corollary to the Monroe Doctrine. It exchanged a policy of forbidding intervention in American nations by Europeans into one of intervention by the United States to correct conditions that invited trouble, especially defaulting on foreign debts. Over the next three decades the United States invaded and occupied—for years at a stretch in some cases—countries around the Caribbean and in Central America. It saddled Cuba with provisions guaranteeing a Yankee invasion in case of misbehavior before granting that country's independence years after a war to "free" the island from Spain. Roosevelt also engineered an independence movement in Panama so that his country could gain transit rights that Colombia would not hand over.

This behavior earned the United States a reputation all over Latin America as the "Colossus of the North," an international bully. A pattern that had started informally in Mexico in 1848 gradually became national policy. The United States used its muscle to prop up dictators who kept order by suppressing democratic movements. Thus the North Americans sponsored such beastly tyrannies as those of the Somoza family in Nicaragua, Rafael Trujillo in the Dominican Republic, and Gerardo Machado and Fulgencio Batista in Cuba.[8]

Mexico felt its neighbor's sting especially sharply. Díaz again sought reelection in 1910, and a lawyer named Francisco Madero ran against him. The honest vote gave Madero the presidency, but Díaz rigged the results and declared himself the victor, then arrested Madero. The whole country rose up, beginning the Revolution of 1910, bloodiest of them all. Díaz went into exile, and Madero took office promising a wide range of social and political reforms. He owed his victory to many forces around the country, but especially to two hero-bandits, Francisco "Pancho" Villa (who was a bandit) in the north, and Emiliano Zapata (who was not, but dressed like one) in the south. Both represented land-reform movements, Zapata's a continuation of the Indian farmer rebellions that had flared throughout the country's history, Villa's a more general one against foreign expropriations and oligarchic rule. Madero, however, had to keep peace with the oligarchs, the foreign interests, and the regular army, so he declared that achieving true reform would take time. Small rebellions broke out here and there. President William Howard Taft was under tremendous pressure from North American business interests to intervene. He offered mediation, without success.

Madero and his vice president were overthrown and murdered in a coup led by General Victoriano Huerta in February 1913, two weeks before Woodrow Wilson became president of the United States. Huerta was a sadistic, weak-eyed drunkard. Wilson was an intellectual snob and bigot who believed that his class of Anglo-Saxons was superior to all darker peoples and also to most other whites. North American business interests believed that Huerta's military dictatorship offered stability. Wilson, however, was personally offended by the bloody way Huerta gained power, demanded the general's abdication, and in November 1913 openly declared his support for the opposition. Villa, Zapata, and others had reassembled their rebel armies, so Wilson incited a civil war. The North American stepped up the pressure on Huerta, famously saying, "We shall teach them to elect good men." A minor incident at Tampico turned into an affair of international honor, and Wilson ordered the fleet to close the port. In April 1914 United States forces seized the customs house at Vera

Cruz and marines occupied the city. Diplomatic relations between the two countries broke off, other nations offered mediation, and by November Huerta was out of office and the United States Navy was out of Vera Cruz. A world war, meanwhile, had broken out in Europe.

The civil war in Mexico continued, the three main forces led by Zapata, Villa, and General Venustiano Carranza, a *caudillo* with a professorial beard. Wilson called an international conference in 1915 to determine how to restore order. Failing in that, he took sides. His government formally recognized Carranza as president in October and embargoed all arms going to Mexico except areas controlled by Carranza. The United States even gave Carranza's troops a lift by railroad to reinforce his corps fighting Villa south of the Arizona line. This interference outraged Carranza's opponents. About 1,500 men of Villa's army crossed the New Mexico border in March 1916 and shot up an army outpost and the town of Columbus. Wilson sent a "punitive expedition" into Mexico to find and kill Villa, which it failed to do over many months. Other Anglo army units crossed into northeastern Mexico until Carranza's patience wore thin. He threatened military action, the Wilson administration agreed to international arbitration, and the Anglo soldiers withdrew. A month after that happened, in February 1917 the British government released an intercepted note from the German foreign office, promising Mexico the return of territories lost in 1848 if it declared war on the United States. Carranza's government spurned the offer, but it ignited anti-Mexico agitation in the United States.

The North Americans had turned their attention from Mexico to Germany by the spring of 1917. They declared war against that nation in April and left their southern neighbor alone, except for troops camped along the border who occasionally crossed the line chasing raiders. The constitution of 1917 was adopted in Mexico, and Carranza formed a government. The Constitution declared the natural resources of Mexico to be the property of the nation, not that of foreign concerns who had acquired rights to minerals and oil during the Díaz regime. The civil war tapered off over the next several years, after claiming between 2 million and 3 million lives and driving a quarter million refugees into the United States.

One Mexican leader after another was overthrown or killed into the 1920s, but disorders ebbed. The United States Army abandoned many of its border posts in 1924, although patrols by cavalry and aircraft continued. There was another brief civil war from 1927 to 1929, after which the Mexican tradition of *caudillismo* gave way to one-party rule to the end of the century. Mexican relations with the United States continued under a strain. This was owing particularly to the vow of successive presidents to implement the constitutional provision reserving subsurface resources to the Mexican people. The administrations of Warren Harding, Calvin Coolidge, and Herbert Hoover threatened each time that the United States would invade Mexico to prevent nationalization of the affected industries.

Hoover quietly dropped the Roosevelt Corollary after he assumed office in 1929. Franklin Roosevelt formally renounced it in 1933 and declared that his government's policy toward Latin American would be that of a "good neighbor." The United States tried to heal relations with all its southern neighbors, but people in Latin America remained suspicious. Many countries were run by *caudillos* who found granting concessions to foreign investors personally rewarding. Good relations with the south were bought by North American businessmen, not earned by diplomats.

The real test came in 1938 when Mexico nationalized its oil reserves, driving alien companies out. The Roosevelt administration protested but did not send in the army and navy. There was a bigger war ahead. During World War I the Wilson administration had failed to get the countries of Latin America to declare war against Germany. During World War II all but one broke relations, the holdout being Argentina, which did that after Germany was defeated. Mexico and Brazil actually declared war and sent armed forces into the conflict.

Things changed for the worse during the Cold War as the United States became obsessed with the idea that communists were trying to take over the world. Military dictators claimed that any domestic opposition was the work of communists and so received help from the United States. That country renewed its reputation for backing the forces of order against those of democracy, and the oldest revolutionary power in the world became downright counterrevolutionary. It intervened to overthrow democratically elected regimes—most notably in Guatemala in the 1950s and Chile in the 1970s—and conducted other interventions in the region through the 1980s. The lingering effect of these policies remained almost universal distrust of the United States in Latin America, even as dictatorships gave way to more democratic governments. Demagogues earned applause by condemning the *Yanquis malditos,* and even in Mexico presidents must show their willingness to stand up to the northern giant. Opposition to popular and agrarian revolutions often backfired, giving Cuba and Venezuela, as examples, governments especially obnoxious to the United States.

The most persistent problems remained between Mexico and the United States. Mexican farm laborers were invited into the north during the boom years of the 1920s and driven back across the border during the

Depression of the 1930s. They were recruited again during World War II, to be sent home some years later. Efforts to resolve fundamental economic problems often produced unintended consequences. The United States re-formed its immigration laws in the 1980s, allowing undocumented resi-dents to apply for citizenship. The North American Free Trade Agreement of 1995, involving Canada, Mexico, and the United States, was intended to encourage new industries in Mexico. Factories and assembly plants sprouted along the border, attracting hordes of people from Mexico's in-terior. But the United States also preached a gospel of free trade—or glob-alization, as it became known—and many of the factories moved to Asia, where costs were lower, leaving the hordes no sources of income. There were jobs for them in the United States, so many crossed the border without visas.

"Illegal immigration" became the demagogue's handiwork early in the twenty-first century, as easy a way to please a crowd in North America as condemning the United States was in Latin America. Attempts in Congress to "reform" the immigration laws yet again failed in 2006 and 2007. The is-sue became so noisy that the Mexican government denied repeated charges by Anglo politicians that it promoted illegal immigration as a way to retake the territories lost in the 1840s. Those *Yanquis* sounded very much like Mexicans of the 1830s and 1840s who warned that illegal Anglo immigration could cost Mexico part of its territory. There were about 12 million unauthorized aliens in the United States in 2007. Many of them were people from Europe, Asia, and Africa who entered the country legally and overstayed their visas. Border jumpers from Mexico and Central America were the ones shown on television, however. Tightening of border enforcement actually made the situation worse, because many Mexicans who crossed the line stayed part of the year, then returned home. Now they were trapped in the north for fear of being arrested try-ing to leave.

Thus leaders in the United States aggravated relations with Mexico to no good end. The fault was not all one-way, however, as Mexico refused to acknowledge its own contributions to this issue. The corruption and inef-ficiency that had plagued the country and retarded its economy since colo-nial days persisted. Wealth and power were concentrated in the hands of too few, and too many remained poor, uneducated, and dispossessed. Too much of the country's income made the rich richer, and not enough cre-ated work for the exploding population, while efforts to control popula-tion growth were dismal. Any suggestion by North Americans that such problems ought to be addressed was greeted in Mexico with howls of anger and wounded national pride.

Perhaps neither the United States nor Mexico learned enough from their bloody conflict during the 1840s; they still talk past each other. The war formally ended 160 years ago, but just as it did not begin in 1846, it did not stop in 1848. The struggle for the continent continued in 2008, an enduring legacy of the War of Texas and the War of '47.

THEY GAVE THEIR BODIES TO THE COMMONWEALTH

Doth the eagle mount up at thy command,
and make her nest on high? She dwelleth and abideth on the rock,
upon the crag of the rock, and the strong place. From thence she seeketh
the prey, and her eyes behold afar off. Her young ones also suck up blood:
and where the slain are, there is she.

—*Job* 39:27–30

MANY NORTH AMERICANS called the conflict "Mr. Polk's War." They opposed the affair from the beginning or grew disillusioned with its cost and slow progress. It was a fair characterization, because the president started the war and controlled its course as tightly as he could. James K. Polk owned the war from beginning to end.

It could as easily be called "*Señor* Santa Anna's war." Many Mexicans blamed the Napoleon of the West for the disaster that befell their country. He had been in exile when the fighting started, but he returned and was the nation's most important general. He assembled armies, faced the invaders, and lost every battle, but it seems to be going too far to hand him sole responsibility for the way things turned out. No other Mexican leader could have done better.

Mexican intellectuals from 1848 to the present have attributed the outbreak of the war to two phenomena—North American "expansionism" and Mexico's weakness, with the former taking advantage of the latter. Certainly Mexican factionalism prevented a unified response to the *yanqui* invasions. The country was outnumbered three to one, and more greatly outweighed in material goods. Santa Anna did not cause all of Mexico's problems after 1821, but he epitomized the ruling *criollo* class that did. No one showed up on the national stage more often or wielded greater influence over a longer time. He was no more self-serving than any other *caudillo,* but he enjoyed more opportunities for self-service. If anyone had the influence to push Mexico to become the liberal republic envisioned in 1824, it was Santa Anna.

The Napoleon of the West did much to set the stage for war. His suppression of the federalist uprisings in 1835 and 1836 was horribly savage, turning a federalist rebellion into a war for independence. The atrocities at the Alamo and Goliad inflamed the rebellion, and by his blunders the Savior of His Country lost the campaign, and Mexico lost Texas.

Mexican historians long described the conflict with the United States as two wars—the Texas War and the War of '47. Some have combined them into one—the War of the North American Intervention. The division into two wars makes sense, while the intervention idea suggests national self-pity. "Poor Mexico!" Porfirio Díaz is said to have wailed. "So far from God, so close to the United States!" Mexicans have recast their entire history as a series of interventions, beginning with Cortés and continuing through later ones by Spain, the United States, and France. This grows out of a national identity founded on the Aztec Empire, but the México dominated only a fraction of the present area of Mexico, and their Mexico was not an eternal paradise. The Aztecs were latecomers, invading and conquering and spilling more blood than Cortés ever did. Their arrival was an "intervention," and not the first in that region.

If the Spaniards usurped the lands they invaded, then how valid were the claims Mexico inherited from Spain at independence? Neither Spain nor Mexico ever had enough power in the northern territories to enforce a claim to ownership, because most native inhabitants—descendants themselves of invaders—refused to submit. When the North Americans marched in they established their claim by right of conquest, but subduing the inhabitants took decades.

The conflict between the United States and Mexico has tended, more than most wars, to be wrapped up in questions of guilt or injustice. That is the present imposing its values onto the past. Landscapes all over the world have been conquered by one invader after another, and that is as

452 DAVID A. CLARY

true of North America as of any other patch of dirt. Western civilization in the nineteenth century accepted that. The United States forcibly took lands from Mexico, another chapter in an old story. No North American now proposes to return the cession to Mexico, nor does any Mexican demand that.

Calling the war's cause North American "expansionism" is to summon up an abstraction. The word describes a phenomenon, not a policy. The British colonies, unlike those of Spain, were populated by adventurers and nonconformists. They were ungovernable, as the king of Britain learned in 1763 when he forbade settlement west of the Appalachians. The settlers who crossed the mountains were willing to fight the peoples already there just to reach their goals. Governors of New Spain saw that, and feared it.

The population of the United States grew rapidly and spread over the continent. The government could not have stopped the process if it had wanted to. When the phrase "manifest destiny" was coined in the 1840s the Anglo tidal wave was already flooding Texas and rushing into New Mexico and California, and it was probably inevitable that those provinces would become part of the United States. A war to force that transfer was avoidable. So why did it happen?

It happened because Polk was an impatient man. He wanted California in the United States during his term in office, so he pressured Mexico to sell its title to the Pacific dreamland. First he used the claims issue, then the Texas border; then he started troops marching; then he invaded across the Rio Grande and out to the western provinces. He had decided, in his ignorance of conditions on the other side, that the Mexicans must see the logic of the situation, bow before the might of the United States, and hand over part of their country in return for a nice wad of cash. The Mexicans defied him at every step, but they played into his hands. Standing up to the *Yanquis* was almost the only thing their leaders could agree on, but they did not act decisively or cohesively. If they had fortified the right bank of the Nueces before Taylor got there, they would have called Polk's bluff. The president would not have invaded over the defended river because that would have been naked aggression, and there was little political support for that. The Mexicans, however, refused to admit that Texas was lost and claimed that their country was invaded as soon as Anglos crossed the Sabine River, something they could not stop.

The war's lingering image of a bully nation beating up on a weaker neighbor has some validity to it, but Polk did not start a fight because he was consumed by visions of conquest. He wanted to meet his territorial goals without war and actually thought that each additional provocation would force the Mexican side to the bargaining table. He was wrong. Polk started the war not because he was evil but because he was ignorant and pigheaded. Failure to understand the other side characterized the whole Anglo conduct of the conflict. The North Americans refused even to learn from their own history. They were surprised that the Mexicans did not surrender after losing every battle. George Washington and his Continentals went through the same thing in 1776 and did not quit. Taking the Mexican capital was also supposed to make the other side see the light. It had not worked for the British in 1814. All across the continent Indian tribes and nations refused to accept Anglo invasion of their homelands.

The biggest mistake on the northern side was the failure to understand that people do not like to be invaded. Ill-prepared *soldados* fought like tigers even where their commanders made their situation impossible, as at Cerro Gordo. When the Mexican army was destroyed, its soldiers and civilians turned to guerrilla war. Insurgencies broke out in all occupied areas. The sorriest case of failing to expect the predictable came when Scott's army marched into Mexico City assuming there would be no resistance because the Mexican army was defeated. The common people—who had no love for their government but did for their liberty—bombarded the *Yanquis* with rocks and musketry until superior firepower overwhelmed them. As in later wars, Anglo generals were surprised by popular resistance. They did not know how to deal with it other than by brute force, which only made the situation worse. Scott's appeal to "minds and feelings" brings to mind the "hearts and minds" of Vietnam.

Polk did not do a good job on the home front. The way he asked for a declaration of war—sending troops into danger, then wrapping the declaration in the need to support them—alienated a good part of the Congress. The Whigs felt abused and were outraged that the president equated criticism or opposition with treason. He achieved his territorial ambitions, but he lost his party's hold on the presidency. His partisanship, especially his manipulation of the army, was too extreme to be stomached for long.

North American victories were achieved by privates led by younger regular officers—and a few capable volunteers—despite rather than because of their commanders. The superior Yankee artillery carried the day in most engagements. The pattern was similar on the Mexican side, although the tactics were different. The generals led their armies to destruction, yet the war continued because the common people carried it on as irregulars.

The behavior of the United States Army in Mexico matched that of the mercenary armies of the late Middle Ages more than what was expected of a modern army in the 1840s. Anglo historians have tended to downplay the overwhelming record. Atrocities occur because either the troops are undisciplined or disaffected (as in Vietnam, with its draftee army under poor leadership) or the command adopts tactics that cause civilians to fight back (as happened in Iraq, with ransacking of homes and humiliation of fathers). Both problems arose in Mexico, the first mostly with the volunteers, the second with command decisions to target civilians as a way to put down insurgency.

Both Mexican and United States historians have periodically reexamined the war between their countries. Mexicans began immediately after the peace treaty with critical examination of their own nation's failures. As the "intervention" outlook grew during the twentieth century they shifted the blame to the Anglos for starting it all, making Mexico a victim rather than a participant, despite the fact that Mexico's stubbornness over Texas played a real part in setting the stage for war.

Anglo historians rediscovered the war in Mexico when their own country got into other conflicts. The major work, Justin Smith's *The War with Mexico* (1919), prepared during World War I, glorified the rightness of the North American cause and vilified the Mexicans. Bernard DeVoto's *The Year of Decision: 1846* (1942) performed a similar service early in World War II, celebrating the triumph of the United States, right taking the world away from wrong. It was a magnificent piece of writing, but now it comes across as jingoistic and racist. More recent wars caused domestic political conflict similar to what happened in the 1840s, so Anglo historians looked at the war in Mexico in light of what was going on around them. During the Vietnam War Glenn Price's *Origins of the War with Mexico: The Polk-Stockton Intrigue* (1967) reflected the anti-government conspiracy theorizing then coming into vogue. The author claimed that Polk and Stockton cooked up a plot to justify invading Mexico by creating a pretext, much as President Lyndon Johnson allegedly conspired with the navy to create the Tonkin Gulf "incident" to justify invading Vietnam. K. Jack Bauer's *The Mexican War, 1846–1848* (1974) focused on Polk's "application of graduated force," which he equated to the "escalation" in Vietnam. The 2003 invasion of Iraq and prolonged violence there inspired Joseph Wheelan's *Invading Mexico: America's Continental Dream and the Mexican War, 1846–1848* (2007). In his account everything that President George W. Bush had been charged with could also be laid at Polk's feet, including dubious justifications for the war, political interference in its conduct, and demonizing of critics and opponents.

One glaring weakness in the war's historiography was its lopsidedness. Mexicans focused on the Mexican side and North Americans on their own. A typical case was John S. D. Eisenhower's *So Far from God: The U.S. War with*

Mexico, 1846–1848 (1989), which focused on the United States Army. Another prevalent weakness in the histories was a tendency to truncate their accounts in time and space. Only the Mexican writers recognized that the origins of the war lay in the eighteenth century. Historians from neither side realized that the war continued until the Gadsden Purchase in 1855 and in New Mexico until 1912. Nor did the roles of the *Indios bárbaros* or the multiparty raiding and slave trading get much notice.

I have tried here to fill these gaps and several more. Above all, I have tried to deal equally and objectively with both major parties to the conflict and with the other parties, the migratory Indians and the various peoples of Mexico and its outlying provinces, and of course the hero-bandits. Their roles were not minor.

The eagles, the golden one of Mexico and the bald one of the United States, are still in the air. As predators, they remind us that war is a bloody business, that of the 1840s included. Tens of thousands of people died in that conflict, which set off others in both countries that claimed millions more. "So they gave their bodies to the commonwealth and received, each for his own memory, praise that will never die," Pericles of Athens said during another war long ago, "and with it the grandest of all sepulchers . . . a home in the minds of men, where their glory remains fresh."

Let us remember the soldiers and the *soldados,* the *soldaderas* and the mountain men, the whores and the gamblers, the Taoseños and the *Indios bárbaros,* the mule skinners and the hero-bandits, the engineers and the lancers, the boy heroes and the scalp hunters, the volunteers and the conscripts, the deserters and the *guerrilleros,* the villagers and the *léperos,* the Great Western and the Angel of Monterey, and all the other "common" people who played out the uncommon events of so long ago. They are gone now, but they gave us our world.

NOTES

Complete data on works cited in the chapter notes are presented in the Bibliography. Names of months are given standard three-letter abbreviations (English) in the notes. Annual reports of cabinet members and subordinate officers of the U.S. government are appended to the Annual Message of the President (AMP) for the given year.

ABBREVIATIONS USED IN NOTES

A	Appendix (with page numbers)
adc	Aide-de-camp
AG	Adjutant General
ALSA	Antonio López de Santa Anna
Alcaraz	Alcaraz y otros, *Apuntes para la historia de la guerra*
AMP	Annual Message of the President (U.S.)
AR	Annual Report (U.S.)
ARAG:	Annual Report of the Adjutant General
ARCE:	Annual Report of the Chief of Engineers
ARCG:	Annual Report of the Commanding General
ARCIA:	Annual Report of the Commissioner of Indian Affairs
ARCLO:	Annual Report of the Commissioner of the Land Office
ARIG:	Annual Report of the Inspector General
ARQMG:	Annual Report of the Quartermaster General
ARSG:	Annual Report of the Surgeon General
ARSI:	Annual Report of the Secretary of the Interior
ARSN:	Annual Report of the Secretary of the Navy
ARSS:	Annual Report of the Secretary of State
ARST:	Annual Report of the Secretary of the Treasury
ARSW:	Annual Report of the Secretary of War
BMW	Bauer, *Mexican War*
Callahan	Callahan, *List of Officers*
Cd.	*Ciudad* (city)
CD	Consular Dispatches

CG	Commanding General (General in Chief, U.S.)
Ch.	Chapter (of a book)
CIA	Commissioner of Indian Affairs (U.S.)
Cong	Congress, *Congreso*
CLO	Commissioner of the Land Office (U.S.)
CSW	*Correspondence Between the Secretary of War and Generals Scott and Taylor*
DF	*Distrito Federal* (Federal District)
Doc	Document
Ecos	Libura y otros, *Ecos de la Guerra*
Ex	Executive
Frazier	Frazier, *United States and Mexico*
H	House of Representatives (U.S.)
Heitman	Heitman, *Historical Register*
IG	Inspector General (U.S.)
JB	James Buchanan
JBF	Jessie Benton Frémont
JCC	John C. Calhoun
JCF	John Charles Frémont
JKP	James Knox Polk
JT	John Tyler
LR	Letters received
LS	Letters sent
MDC	Manning, *Diplomatic Correspondence*
Mex	*México, mexicano* (Mexico, Mexican)
MF	Millard Fillmore
Misc	Miscellaneous
MWC	*Mexican War Correspondence* (H Ex Doc 60)
n	Note
nd	No date given
NL	Nuevo León
np	No place given
NPD	Nevins, *Polk Diary*
npub	No publisher given
PM	*Presidente de México* (President of Mexico)
PUS	*President of the United States*
QDP	Quaife, *Diary of Polk*
QMG	Quartermaster General (U.S.)
Ramsey	Ramsey, *The Other Side*
Rep	Report
RFS	Robert F. Stockton
RG	Record Group (U.S. National Archives files and microfilm)
RG 45:	Office of Naval Records and Library
RG 59:	Department of State
RG 80:	Department of the Navy

RG 94:	Adjutant General's Office, Department of War
RG 98:	United States Army Commands
RG 107:	Secretary of War's Office
RG 127:	United States Marine Corps
RG 153:	Office of the Judge Advocate General, Department of War
RMP	Richardson, *Compilation of Messages and Papers of the Presidents*
Sen	Senate (U.S.)
Sess	Session
SG	Surgeon General (U.S.)
SI	Secretary of the Interior (U.S.)
SN	Secretary of the Navy (U.S.)
SS	Secretary of State (U.S.)
ST	Secretary of the Treasury (U.S.)
SW	Secretary of War (U.S.)
SWK	Stephen Watts Kearny
SWM	Smith, *War with Mexico*
THB	Thomas Hart Benton
USA	United States of America
USN	United States Navy
VC	Vera Cruz
WLM	William L. Marcy
WS	Winfield Scott
ZT	Zachary Taylor

PROLOGUE

1. This summary of pre-Columbian Mexico and New Spain follows several standard histories of Mexico, including Ruiz, *Triumphs and Tragedy*, 15–26; Meyer, Sherman, and Deeds, *Course of Mexican History*, 3–90; Krauze, *Mexico*, 25–29; Fehrenbach, *Fire and Blood*, 3–101; Susan Schroeder, "The Mexico That Spain Encountered," in Meyer and Beezley, *Oxford History*, 47–77; and primary and secondary accounts in Joseph and Henderson, *Mexico Reader*, 55–94.

2. The North American golden eagle (*Aquila chrysaetos*) is one of the largest of all hunting eagles. They typically measure 24–40 inches in length with wingspans of 59–95 inches, and a weight ranging from 5.5 to 15.4 pounds; females are larger than the males. They are very amenable to falconry. The eagle on the cactus is sometimes misidentified as the Mexican brown eagle, now usually called the harpy eagle *(Harpia harpyja)*, a large forest eagle.

3. The American bald eagle, *Haliaeetus leucocephalus*, is one of the largest of the fish eagles, nearly as large as the golden eagle.

CHAPTER 1

1. Quoted ALSA, *Eagle*, 257 n. 10.

2. Weber, *Mexican Frontier*; Horgan, *Great River* 1:83–442.

3. Ruiz, *Triumphs*, 206; Goetzmann, *When Eagle*, 8–11.

4. Goetzmann, *When Eagle,* 5–6; Horgan, *Great River* 1:395–402.

5. Quoted Horgan, *Great River,* 1:404; Hollon, *Lost Pathfinder;* Weigley, *History,* 107, 113–14, 122–23.

6. Horgan, *Great River,* 1:395–402, 2:403–22; Goetzmann, *When Eagle,* 13–16; Fehrenbach, *Fire and Blood,* 375–76; Josefina Zoraida Vázquez, "War and Peace with the United States," in Meyer and Beezley, *Oxford History,* 339–70.

7. Horgan, *Great River,* 2:981, offers a list of the river's names.

8. Bemis, *John Quincy Adams Foundation,* 317–40; Goetzmann, *When Eagle,* 13–16; Vázquez, "War and Peace," 324–33.

9. Vázquez, "War and Peace," 324–33; Weber, *Mexican Frontier,* 122–39, 160–62.

10. Quoted Fehrenbach, *Fire and Blood,* 281.

11. Anna, *Fall of Royal Government,* 10.

12. Archer, *Army in Bourbon Mexico;* Scheina, *Santa Anna,* 4–5, 10; Fehrenbach, *Fire and Blood,* 315–16.

13. Fehrenbach, *Fire and Blood,* 310–11.

14. Levinson, *Wars Within,* 4–5; Virginia Guedea, "The Old Colonialism Ends, the New Colonialism Begins," in Meyer and Beezley, *Oxford History,* 277–300, at 284–85. The summary of the War of Independence follows Ruiz, *Triumphs,* 144–65; Krauze, *Mexico,* 91–118; and Meyer and others, *Course,* 270–83; Woodward, "Spanish Army"; Fehrenbach, *Fire and Blood,* 319–52.

15. Lieutenant General Don Félix María Calleja, quoted Fehrenbach, *Fire and Blood,* 319, see also 331–32, 339; Guedea, "Old Colonialism," 292; Levinson, *War Within,* 5–7.

16. Meyer and others, *Course,* 338–39.

17. Zavala and Alamán quoted Krauze, *Mexico,* 121–22, see also 119–35; Fehrenbach, *Fire and Blood,* 348–52; Robertson, *Iturbide;* Bravo Ugarte, "Un nuevo Iturbide."

18. Christon I. Archer, "Fashioning a New Nation," in Meyer and Beezley, *Oxford History,* 301–38; Guedea, "Old Colonialism," 284–85.

19. Quoted Ruiz, *Triumphs,* 66.

20. Alamán, *Historia de México* (1844), quoted Krauze, *Mexico,* 15–16.

21. Iturbide quoted Fehrenbach, *Fire and Blood,* 352; Poinsett, *Notes,* 68–69.

22. Robertson, *Iturbide;* Ruiz, *Triumphs,* 166–69; Archer, "Fashioning a New Nation"; Meyer and others, *Course,* 292–93; Anna, *Forging Mexico;* Anna, *Mexican Empire;* Beezley, "Caudillismo"; Horace Harrison, "The Republican Conspiracy Against Agustín de Iturbide," and Joseph McElhannon, "Relations between Imperial Mexico and the United States," in Cotner and Castañeda, *Essays,* 127–41, 142–65.

23. Quoted somewhat differently in Fehrenbach, *Fire and Blood,* 379, and Weber, *Mexican Frontier,* 12. See also Meyer and others, *Course,* 188–89.

24. Weber, *Mexican Frontier,* ch. 6; Weber, "Unforgettable Day."

25. Archer, "Fashioning a New Nation"; Ruiz, *Triumphs,* 316.

26. Ruiz, *Triumphs,* 168; Levinson, *War Within,* 7.

27. Alamán and Paz quoted Krauze, *Mexico,* xiv, 129; Archer, "Fashioning a New Nation"; and other sources cited in n. 22 above.

28. Archer, "Fashioning a New Nation"; Scheina, *Santa Anna,* 11–14; ALSA, *Eagle,* 16–18; Krauze, *Mexico,* 128–29.

29. Quotes in Archer, "Fashioning a New Nation," and Krauze, *Mexico,* 127–28, 130,

135–38. Biographies include Muñoz, *Santa Anna;* Hanighen, *Santa Anna;* Callcott, *Santa Anna;* Pasquel, *Antonio López de Santa Anna;* Scheina, *Santa Anna;* Fowler, *Tornel and Santa Anna;* ALSA, *Eagle.*

30. ALSA, *Eagle,* 3.

31. ALSA to Pedro de Landero, January 17, 1830, quoted Krauze, *Mexico,* 135.

32. Quoted Krauze, *Mexico,* 137.

33. Quoted Ruiz, *Triumphs,* 175.

34. Quoted Krauze, *Mexico,* 137.

35. This adventure and the impression it made on others is summarized ibid., 135.

36. Quoted Robinson, *View,* xvii.

37. Fowler, *Tornel and Santa Anna;* Sordo Cedeño, "El General Tornel"; Frazier, 431–32.

CHAPTER 2

1. Fehrenbach, *Fire and Blood,* 179–80, 290–93; Hobsbawm, *Bandits;* Caro Baroja, *Ensayo;* Bernardo de Quirós, *El bandolerismo en España ye México;* Frazer, *Bandit Nation;* Simmons, *Corrido.*

2. Virginia Guedea, "The Old Colonialism Ends, the New Colonialism Begins," and Christon I. Archer, "Fashioning a New Nation," in Meyer and Beezley, *Oxford History,* 277– 300, 301–38; Meyer and others, *Course,* 281–82.

3. Gilmore, "Condition"; Meyer and others, *Course,* 281–82, 342–43.

4. Archer, "Fashioning a New Nation," 319–20.

5. Sierra, *Political Evolution,* 175; Meyer and others, *Course,* 300–3, 723–24; Krauze, *Mexico,* 137.

6. Krauze, *Mexico,* 133; Archer, "Fashioning a New Nation," 314.

7. Fehrenbach, *Fire and Blood,* 309–11.

8. Ibid., 354–55; Martin, "Lucas Alamán"; Ruiz, *Triumphs,* 159–71; Meyer and others, *Course,* 297–307; Gutiérrez, *Nationalist Myths;* Lomnitz-Adler, *Deep Mexico;* and Paz, *Other Mexico.*

9. Meyer and others, *Course,* 297–98; Archer, "Fashioning a New Nation," 316–17.

10. Quoted Krauze, *Mexico,* 5.

11. Quoted Meyer and others, *Course,* 298.

12. Ibid., 298–300; see also Ruiz, *Triumphs,* 159–71; Labastida, *Documentos,* 131–53; Frazier, 108–10. The franchise in the early national period was rigorously limited by socio-economic class, and 95 percent of the citizens had no say. Levinson, *Wars Within,* 10–12.

13. General Manuel Mier y Terán to José Luis Mora, Nov nd, 1831, quoted Krauze, *Mexico,* 138. On the republican period in general, see Meyer and others, *Course,* 297–307; Flores Caballero, *Role of the Spaniards;* Fowler, *Mexico in the Age;* Sims, *Expulsion;* Tenenbaum, *Politics of Penury;* Stevens, *Origins of Instability;* Weber, *Mexican Frontier;* Di Tella, *National Popular Politics;* Guardino, *Peasant Politics;* and Green, *Mexican Republic.* On U.S. interference, see Rippy, *Joel R. Poinsett.*

14. Archer, "Fashioning a New Nation," 320–21; Meyer and others, *Course,* 304–6.

15. Krauze, *Mexico,* 132.

16. Archer, "Fashioning a New Nation," 329–30; Fehrenbach, *Fire and Blood,* 165–66, 357; Krauze, *Mexico,* 130–32. See also DePalo, *Mexican National Army;* Kahle, *El ejército;* Neve, *Historia gráfica.*

17. Fehrenbach, *Fire and Blood*, 364–65.

18. Archer, "Fashioning a New Nation," 324–25; Ruiz, *Triumphs*, 171–72; Meyer and others, *Course*, 300–3; Krauze, *Mexico*, 129–30.

19. Archer, "Fashioning a New Nation," 328–29; Levinson, *Wars Within*, 1–14; Reina, *Las rebeliones campesinas*.

20. Quoted Krauze, *Mexico*, 119.

21. Meyer and others, *Course*, 342–48. On Mexico City, see Arnold, *Bureaucracy*, and Kendall, *La Capital*.

22. Poinsett, *Notes*, 73.

23. Tayloe, *Mexico*, 50–51. See also Cue Cánovas, *Historia social*; Wasserman and Johnson, *Everyday Life*; Callcott, *Church and State*; Costeloe, *Church and State*; Costeloe, *Primera república*; Ruiz, *Triumphs*, 169–204; Olivera and Crété, *Life*; and Gilmore, "Condition."

24. Meyer and others, *Course*, 341–42; Poinsett, *Notes*, 23–24. In the cane country, *aguardiente de caña* (sugarcane brandy) was also available if there was a still in the neighborhood. Ruiz, *Triumphs*, 196–97.

25. Meyer and others, *Course*, 341–43; Poinsett, *Notes*, 23–24.

26. Meyer and others, *Course*, 339–40; Ruiz, *Triumphs*, 196–97.

27. Thompson, *Recollections*, 12, 150.

28. Poinsett to SS, Mar 1, 1829, in Joseph and Henderson, *Mexico Reader*, 13, and *Ecos*, 169–76.

29. On the northern territories see Weber, *Mexican Frontier*, and Medina Castro, *El gran despojo*. See also Spicer, *Cycles*, and Sides, *Blood and Thunder*.

30. Bemis, *John Quincy Adams Founding*, 363–408; Goetzmann, *When Eagle*, 24–32; Josefina Zoraida Vázquez, "War and Peace with the United States," in Meyer and Beezley, *Oxford History*, 339–70; Arteta, *Destino manifiesto*, passim.

31. Vázquez, "War and Peace with the United States," 346–47; Goetzmann, *When Eagle*, 21–22.

32. On Poinsett's life and career, see Rippy, *Joel R. Poinsett*, and the sketches in Frazier, 322–23, and (from the Mexican viewpoint) *Ecos*, 169, and Joseph and Henderson, *Mexico Reader*, 11. See also Poinsett, *Notes*, and Tayloe, *Mexico*.

33. Martin, "Lucas Alamán." See also Alamán, *Historia de Méjico* and *Obras*.

34. Weber, *Mexican Frontier*, 12–13; Goetzmann, *When Eagle*, 21–22; SWM 1:58–60.

35. SWM 1:58–60, quotation at 417 n. 3; Vázquez, "War and Peace with the United States."

36. Zavala, *Viaje*, excerpted *Ecos*, 13–18. See also Frazier, 489–90.

37. Vázquez, "War and Peace with the United States." On Texas and the Comanches and other *Indios bárbaros*, see Utley, *Lone Star Justice*, 3–36.

38. Vázquez, "War and Peace with the United States," 347.

39. On Jackson and Texas, see Brands, *Andrew Jackson*, 508–22; Goetzmann, *When Eagle*, 22–24; and SWM 1:62–63.

40. Brands, *Andrew Jackson*, 508–22; SWM 1:62–63; Vázquez, "War and Peace with the United States," 347. On Butler, see also Frazier, 64.

41. Brands, *Andrew Jackson*, 508–13 (quotation); Goetzmann, *When Eagle*, 22–24; Schlesinger, *Age of Jackson*, 428–33.

42. Vázquez, "War and Peace with the United States," 348–49; Goetzmann, *When Eagle*, 24–32; Frazier, 261; Morton, "Life of General Mier y Terán."

43. A complete list of claims from 1821 to 1837 accompanies SS John Forsyth to Francisco Pizarro Martínez, Mexican minister to USA, Dec 11, 1837, *United States and Mexico.* See also Curtis R. Reynolds, "The Deterioration of Diplomatic Relations, 1833–1845," in Faulk and Stout, *Mexican War,* 33–44; and Kohl, *Claims.* The U.S. assumed the claims in the Treaty of Guadalupe Hidalgo in 1848, and established a commission that reduced or eliminated most of them.

44. Zavala, *Viaje,* excerpted in *Ecos,* 21. How the Anglo denizens of Texas became "Texians" is addressed below.

45. Brands, *Andrew Jackson,* 513–18; Frazier, 64. Not everything between the two countries was a flop. When Comanches and Kiowas stepped up their raids on the Santa Fe Trail in 1828, the two armies cooperated on patrols and escorts. Prucha, *Sword,* 237–38.

46. Ruiz, *Triumphs,* 176; Meyer and others, *Course,* 316–17.

47. Archer, "Fashioning a New Nation"; Sims, *Expulsion.*

48. Hanighen, *Santa Anna,* 43–44 (quotation); Callcott, *Santa Anna,* 54–56; Pasquel, *Antonio López de Santa Anna,* 53; Scheina, *Santa Anna,* 14–15.

49. Archer, "Fashioning a New Nation"; Scheina, *Santa Anna,* 18–20; Mier quoted Krauze, *Mexico,* 135; see also Morton, "Life of General Mier y Terán," and Muñoz, *Santa Anna,* 107–22.

50. Jones, *Santa Anna,* 125 (the 1853 signature); Muñoz, *Santa Anna,* 107–22; Scheina, *Santa Anna,* 18–20; Meyer and others, *Course,* 304.

51. Krauze, *Mexico,* 130; Scheina, *Santa Anna,* 15–18.

52. Quoted Krauze, *Mexico,* 130.

53. Ibid., 131.

54. Meyer and Beezley, *Oxford History,* 330–32; Ruiz, *Triumphs,* 175–78; Frazier, 180; see also Santoni, *Mexicans at Arms,* passim.

55. ALSA, *Manifesto del presidente de los Estados Unidos Mexicanos a sus conciudadanos,* June 18, 1833, in Krauze, *Mexico,* 137. See also Archer, "Fashioning a New Nation."

56. Archer, "Fashioning a New Nation"; Meyer and others, *Course,* 308–15; Fehrenbach, *Fire and Blood,* 373. On ALSA's centralism in general, see also Callcott, *Santa Anna;* Callcott, *Church and State;* Jones, *Santa Anna;* DePalo, *Mexican National Army;* Costeloe, *Central Republic;* Mayo, "Consuls and Silver"; Robertson, "French Intervention"; Samponaro, "Santa Anna and Abortive Revolt." See also Stevens, *Origins of Instability,* and Tenenbaum, *Politics of Penury.* See also ALSA, *Eagle,* 27–64.

57. Meyer and others, *Course,* 308–14; Fehrenbach, *Fire and Blood,* 373; Archer, "Fashioning a New Nation."

CHAPTER 3

1. Documentation is in *The Taking Possession of Monterey.* See also SWM 1:69; Howarth, *Shining,* 149–52; Beach, *United States Navy,* 146–47; Smith, "The War That Wasn't"; High, "Jones at Monterey"; Brooke, "Vest Pocket War"; Frank A. Knapp Jr., "The Mexican Fear of Manifest Destiny in California," in Cotner and Castañeda, *Essays.* On Jones' career, see Bradley, "Contentious Commodore," and his entry in Callahan. See also Johnson, "United States Naval Forces on Pacific Station."

2. Josefina Zoraida Vázquez, "War and Peace with the United States," in Meyer and Beezley, *Oxford History,* 339–70; Meyer and others, *Course,* 311–12; Ruiz, *Triumphs,* 178–79; Frazier, 109.

3. Roa Bárcena, *Recuerdos,* excerpted *Ecos,* 30.

4. Ruiz, *Triumphs,* 178–79; Frazier, 489; Vasconcelos, *Breve Historia,* 433–35.

5. Mier's and Almonte's reports are excerpted in *Ecos,* 23–26. See also Meyer and others, *Course,* 319–24, and Weber, *Mexican Frontier,* ch. 9.

6. Quoted Vasconcelos, *Breve Historia,* 434. See also ALSA, *Eagle,* 49–50.

7. ALSA, *Eagle,* 49–50. See also his *Manifiesto que de sus operaciones en la campaña de Tejas y en su cautiverio dirige a sus conciudadanos del general Antonio López de Santa Anna,* May 1837, excerpted Krauze, *Mexico,* 139.

8. Quoted Ruiz, *Triumphs,* 209.

9. Sordo Cedeño, "El General Tornel"; Frazier, 432, 505. See also Fowler, *Tornel and Santa Anna.* The decree was published in the *Telegraph and Texas Register,* Mar 12, 1836.

10. Brands, *Andrew Jackson,* 518–22; SWM 1:63–64; Bauer, "U.S. Navy."

11. Meyer and others, *Course,* 321–23; ALSA, *Eagle,* 51–52, 263–64; Krauze, *Mexico,* 138–40; Vázquez, "War and Peace with the United States"; Alonzo, *Tejano Legacy;* Bacariss, "Union of Coahuila and Texas"; Jones, *Santa Anna;* Lack, *Texas Revolutionary;* Matovina, *Alamo Remembered;* Miller, "Stephen F. Austin"; Pletcher, *Diplomacy of Annexation;* ALSA, *Eagle;* Tijerina, *Tejanos and Texas;* Vázquez, "Texas Question."

12. ALSA to Portilla, Mar 23, 1836, quoted Callcott, *Santa Anna,* 132–33; Portilla diary quoted Meyer and others, *Course,* 323.

13. Vázquez, "War and Peace with the United States"; Meyer and others, *Course,* 324.

14. Brands, *Andrew Jackson,* 522–26; Vázquez, "War and Peace with the United States."

15. ALSA, *Eagle,* 54–58; ALSA, *Manifiesto . . . ,* May 1837, excerpted Krauze, *Mexico,* 140 (see n. 7 above). The alibis of the various generals are collected in Castañeda, *Mexican Side.*

16. Vázquez, "Causes of the War with the United States," 47–49.

17. Pizarro Martínez to SS, Dec 11, 1837, *United States and Mexico,* 6. Pizarro Martínez's family, incidentally, lived in New Orleans.

18. For an overview, mostly from the U.S. perspective, see Kohl, *Claims as a Cause.* Documentation is in Moore, *History and Digest* 2:1209–59, and in *United States and Mexico.*

19. *New Orleans Picayune,* Apr 6, 1842, and Foreign Office statement, Dec 31, 1844, quoted SWM 1:120, 425 n. 24.

20. Vázquez, "Causes of the War with the United States," 47–49; SWM 1:74–81, 425 n. 24; Goetzmann, *When Eagle,* 57.

21. The chief history of the Pastry War is Peña y Reyes, *Primera guerra.* ALSA's actions are covered in Callcott, *Santa Anna,* 154–60, and Scheina, *Santa Anna,* 36–40. His own self-serving account is ALSA, *Eagle,* 58–64. See also Robertson, "French Intervention"; Ruiz, *Triumphs,* 179–80; and Christon I. Archer, "Fashioning a New Nation," in Meyer and Beezley, *Oxford History,* 301–38 (at 332–33).

22. ALSA to Ministro de Guerra y la Marina, published in *El Cosmopolito,* Dec 8, 1838, quoted Krauze, *Mexico,* 140.

23. Both quoted Krauze, *Mexico,* 140–41.

24. Meyer and others, *Course,* 314–15; Stevens, *Origins,* passim; Prieto in Joseph and

Henderson, *Mexico Reader,* 210; Sierra quoted Ruiz, *Triumphs,* 196; Scheina, *Santa Anna,* 46 (commissions); Brantz Mayer quoted Olivera and Crété, *Life in Mexico,* 28.

25. Meyer and others, *Course,* 312–14; Archer, "Fashioning a New Nation," 334–35; Vázquez, "War and Peace with the United States," 355–56; Levinson, *Wars Within,* 12–14.

26. Olivera and Crété, *Life,* 84–86.

27. Calderón de la Barca, *Life in Mexico,* 32–33; second foreigner quoted ibid., 29–30; see also Ann Fears Crawford, "Preface," in ALSA, *Eagle.*

28. Meyer and others, *Course,* 315–16; Fehrenbach, *Fire and Blood,* 390–91; Scheina, *Santa Anna,* 44–46.

29. Prieto quoted Krauze, *Mexico,* 141. See also Olivera and Crété, *Life in Mexico,* 113–17. See also Prieto, *Guillermo Prieto;* Prieto, *Memorias.*

30. Scheina, *Santa Anna,* 44; Callcott, *Santa Anna,* 200–4.

31. Prieto in Joseph and Henderson, *Mexico Reader,* 211.

32. The original statements are frequently quoted, as in Pratt, "John L. O'Sullivan."

33. Merk, *Monroe Doctrine;* Weinberg, *Manifest Destiny;* Merk, *Manifest Destiny.*

34. Examples include García Cantú, *Las Invasiones* (Jamestown); Vázquez de Knauth, *Mexicanos y Norteamericanos* (Louisiana Purchase). See also Brack, *Mexico Views;* DiTella, *National Popular Politics.*

35. Alcaraz, excerpted *Ecos,* 29.

36. Goetzmann, *When Eagle,* 32–33; Richard V. Francaviglia, "The Geographic and Cartographic Legacy of the U.S.-Mexican War," in Francaviglia and Richmond, *Dueling Eagles,* 1–18; British minister quoted SWM 1:67. On the sectional issue in the U.S., see Sydnor, *Development;* Van Deusen, *Jacksonian Era,* especially ch. 7–10; and Nichols, *Stakes,* especially the early chapters.

37. Meyer and others, *Course,* 326–27; Utley, *Lone Star,* 39; Charles O'Gorman to Palmerston, Jun 21, 1836, quoted Vázquez, "Causes of the War with the United States," 62 n. 19.

38. Goetzmann, *When Eagle,* 33–36. On the wars between Texas and Mexico, see Nance, *After San Jacinto,* and Nance, *Attack and Counterattack.* See also Adams, *British Activities,* ch. 4.

39. The navies of both sides are summarized in Frazier, 285–87.

40. Utley, *Lone Star,* 37–39.

41. Alamán, "Dictamen sobre la independencia de Tejas," May 29, 1840, in Alamán, *Obras* 10:545–52; Vázquez, "Causes of the War with the United States," 49–50.

42. Mariano Arista, General en Jefe del Cuerpo del Ejército del Norte, Jan 3, 1841, proclamation to the inhabitants of the Departments of Tamaulipas, Coahuila, and Nuevo León, quoted Olivera and Crété, *Life in Mexico,* 159.

43. Loomis, *Texan-Santa Fe;* Kendall, *Narrative;* Utley, *Lone Star,* 39–41; Neighbours, *Robert Neighbors,* 12–15; Copeland, *Kendall,* 42–107; Horgan, *Great River,* 2:569–85. The reaction of New Mexicans to these events is covered in McClure, "Texan–Santa Fe Expedition." Álvarez's difficulties are outlined in Chavez, "Trouble with Texans."

44. Nance, *Attack,* ch. 1–5; Utley, *Lone Star,* 41–42; Cutrer, *Ben McCulloch,* 66–67.

45. Bocanegra to SS, May 12 and 31, 1842, and to Diplomatic Corps at México, Jul 30, 1842, quoted SWM 1:67–68.

46. SS to Waddy Thompson, dispatches 9 and 11, 1842, quoted ibid., 1:68.

47. SWM 1:68–69; British consular report of Aug 15, 1842, quoted Sam W. Haynes, "'But What Will England Say?': Great Britain, the United States, and the War with Mexico," in Francaviglia and Richmond, *Dueling Eagles,* 19–40 (at 20–21).

48. SS to Thompson, dispatches numbered 9 and 11, 1842, and Jan 31, 1843, and *El Provisional,* Oct 4, 1842, all quoted SWM 1:69–70, and 423 n. 14.

49. Vázquez, "Causes of the War with the United States," 50–51; Haynes, "'But What Will England Say?'" 19–40.

50. Charles Elliot to Lord Aberdeen, Sep 15, 1842, quoted Vázquez, "Causes of the War with the United States," 62 n. 19.

51. Nance, "Brigadier General Adrián Woll's Report"; Nance, *Attack,* ch. 14–24; Haynes, *Soldiers of Misfortune;* Neighbours, *Robert Neighbors,* 15–23; Utley, *Lone Star,* 43–55; Nance and McDonald, *Dare-Devils;* Wooster, "Texas Military Operations."

52. Doyle to Minister of Relations, and Baron Alleye de Cyprey to Minister of Relations, both Apr 20, 1843, quoted SWM 1:432 n. 1.

53. Vázquez, "War and Peace with the United States," 356–57; SS quoted SWM 1:70.

54. Bocanegra to Minister of the United States, Aug 23, 1843, in *Ecos,* 41.

55. Both quoted SWM 1:84.

56. Dana, *Two Years.*

57. Wilkes, *Narrative.* See also Howarth, *Shining,* 142–45, 149.

58. Utley, *Life,* 91–92 and passim.

59. Goetzmann, *When Eagle,* 42–45.

60. Thomas O. Larkin, "Description of California Prior to the Year 1846," nd 1846, CD, RG 59; Rives, *United States and Mexico,* 2:22–52; Graebner, *Empire,* 83–102; Coughlin, "California Ports," Weber, *Mexican Frontier,* 135–39.

61. See reports in *Ecos,* 95; Bauer, *War,* 13; and Consul Thomas O. Larkin's reports in CD, RG 59.

62. Crapol, *John Tyler,* 130–73.

63. Both quoted Weber, *Mexican Frontier,* 40, see also ch. 12; Olivera and Crété, *Life,* 41.

64. Weber, *Mexican Frontier,* ch. 10.

65. Reports on these events appeared in the *New York Herald,* Nov 11, 1843, and the *Boston Atlas,* Jan 26, 1844, cited SWM 1:72–73.

66. Prescott, *History of the Conquest.* Even the Mexicans were fascinated by this phenomenon, after the war publishing a translation with extensive notes by historians Alamán, José Fernando Ramírez, and Juan Ortega y Medina. Prescott, *Historia de la Conquista.*

67. Quoted Crapol, *John Tyler,* 5. This is the chief source for what follows.

68. SWM 1:84–85. On JCC's activities in the cabinet, see Wiltse, *John C. Calhoun,* 199–216.

69. JCC to Isaac Van Zandt and J. P. Henderson, Apr 11, and to William J. Murphy, Apr 13, 1844, MDC 12:71–72; AG to SW, Oct 7, 1845, LS, RG 94; SN to Conner, Apr 15, and to ZT, Apr 27, 1844, *Proceedings of the Senate on the Annexation of Texas,* 76, 78–79; Conner to SN, May 27, 1844, Home Squadron Letters, RG 45; Howarth, *Shining,* 155; Bauer, *Zachary Taylor,* 111–12.

70. SWM 1:85; Bocanegra to Green, May 30, 1844, in *Ecos,* 42.

71. Vázquez, "War and Peace with the United States," 356–57.

72. Crapol, *John Tyler,* 214–19.

73. Almonte quoted SWM 1:105; Alcaraz excerpted *Ecos,* 42–43.

74. Woll to Houston, Jun 19, Jack C. Hays to G. W. Hill, Jun 21, and Anson Jones to T. A. Howard, Aug 6, 1844, cited BMW, 6–7.

75. PUS to House of Representatives, Jun 10, 1844, RMP 5:2176–80; Wilentz, *Andrew Jackson,* 162; Brands, *Andrew Jackson,* 544–47; Crapol, *John Tyler,* 218–19.

76. Vázquez, "Santa Anna y el reconocimiento"; Vázquez, "War and Peace with the United States," 358; Alcaraz excerpted *Ecos,* 43–44; Ruiz, *Triumphs,* 180–81.

77. AMP 1844, RMP 5:2194; Crapol, *John Tyler,* 219–22.

78. Adams, *British Interests,* 168–218; Rives, *United States and Mexico* 1:705–10; Rivers, "Mexican Diplomacy"; Ramsey, *Other Side,* 27; F. M. Dimond (U.S. consul Vera Cruz) to SS, Apr 12 and May 8, 1845, CD, RG 59.

79. Utley, *Lone Star,* 57–58.

80. Emerson quoted BMW, 10; Teófilo Romero to General Mariano Paredes, nd 1845, quoted Christensen, *U.S.-Mexican,* 45.

CHAPTER 4

1. JKP, Inaugural Address, Mar 4, 1845, RMP 5:2223–32, and in Farrell, *James K. Polk,* 25–34. JKP biographies include McCormac, *James K. Polk;* Sellers, *James K. Polk;* McCoy, *Polk and the Presidency;* Haynes, *James K. Polk;* Leonard, *James K. Polk;* Seigenthaler, *James K. Polk;* and for young readers, Severn, *Frontier President.* Documents from his presidency are in Farrell, *James K. Polk.*

2. Seigenthaler, *James K. Polk,* 18–20.

3. Quoted NPD, xix.

4. Quoted Wheelan, *Invading,* 9.

5. Webster to his son, Mar 11, 1845, quoted SWM 1:130.

6. Andrew, *For President's Eyes,* 13–14; Franklin Chase (consul Tampico) to SS, Sep 26, and John Black (Mexico City) to SS, June 21, 1845, CD, RG 59.

7. Cotner, *Career of Herrera,* 130–35; *Ecos,* 43; Ruiz, *Triumphs,* 181; Josefina Zoraida Vázquez, "War and Peace with the United States," in Meyer and Beezley, *Oxford History,* 359.

8. Almonte to SS, Mar 6, and SS to Almonte, Mar 10, 1845, MDC 8:163, 699–700.

9. Preliminary to a Treaty Between the Republic of Texas and the Republic of Mexico, May 19, 1845, in Butler, *Documentary History,* 4.

10. Sam W. Haynes, " 'But What Will England Say?': Great Britain, the United States, and the War with Mexico," in Francaviglia and Richmond, *Dueling Eagles,* 21–22; SN to Conner, Mar 20 and Apr 20, and to RFS, Apr 22, 1845, Confidential Letters, RG 80; Morison, *Old Bruin,* 182–85; Howarth, *Shining,* 157.

11. Morison, *Old Bruin,* 182–85; Conner's entry in Callahan; Frazier, 107; Beach, *United States Navy,* 159–60; Howarth, *Shining,* 159–61.

12. Beach, *United States Navy,* 196–222; Howarth, *Shining,* 154–55; Sprout, *Rise,* 125; BMW, 174; Stockton's entry in Callahan; Frazier, 393–94.

13. Jones Proclamations, Apr 15 and May 5, 1845, in AMP 1845, 54–55, 63–64; Donelson to SS, May 6, 1845, ARSS 1845, 56–57.

14. Jones quoted Howarth, *Shining,* 157; Merk, *Monroe Doctrine,* 150–51; BMW, 15 n. 17.

15. SS to Donelson, May 23 and Jun 15, 1845, MDC 12:92–96; SW to ZT, May 28, and SN to ZT, Jun 15, 1845, MWC, 79–82; SN to RFS, Jun 15, 1845, Confidential Letters, RG 80; JKP to Donelson, Jun 15, 1845, in Sioussat, "Polk-Donelson Letters," 67–68.

16. BMW, 10. On Dec 22, 1845, the U.S. Congress admitted Texas as a state.

17. Tornel to Woll, Jul 7, 1843, *Proceedings of the Senate on the Annexation of Texas,* 84; Fulmore, "Annexation"; SWM 1:138–39; BMW, 10–11; Connor and Faulk, *North America Divided,* 26.

18. Bancroft to Henry Wikoff, May 12, 1845, quoted BMW, 11–12; Sears, "Slidell's Mission"; DeConde, *History of American Foreign Policy,* 194–95.

19. SS to Parrott, Mar 28, and Parrott to SS, Apr 26, 1845, MDC 8:164–65, 712–20.

20. Cotner, *Career of Herrera,* 130–35; Herrera, *Decreto de 4* Jun 1845, forwarded by U.S. consul Vera Cruz and John Black (consul Mexico City) to SS, Jun 10 and 21, 1845, CD, RG 59. Herrera's *Decreto,* published in *Niles' National Register* Jul 19, 1845, Butler, *Documentary History,* 5.

21. London *Times,* Apr 15, 1845, quoted SWM 1:105; see also 108–16; Richard V. Francaviglia, "The Geographic and Cartographic Legacy of the U.S.-Mexican War," in Francaviglia and Richmond, *Dueling Eagles,* 1–18.

22. All quoted SWM 1:106–7.

23. Alcaraz, excerpted *Ecos,* 55.

24. Donelson to ZT, Jun 28, 1845, MWC, 804–6.

25. Biographies of ZT include Hamilton, *Zachary Taylor Soldier;* Bauer, *Zachary Taylor;* Hoyt, *Zachary Taylor.* See also his entry in Heitman; SWM 1:140–41; and Frazier, 405–7.

26. ZT's costumes summarized in Henry, *Story,* 42.

27. Bauer, *Zachary Taylor,* passim; Hamilton, *Zachary Taylor Soldier,* passim; Bliss entry in Heitman; Frazier, 46–47; SWM 1:140–41.

28. Donelson to ZT, Jun 28, ZT to AG, Jun 30, and SN to Conner, Jul 11, 1845, MWC, 232–33, 801, 804–6; SW to ZT, Jul 8, 1845, LS, RG 107; Hamilton, *Zachary Taylor Soldier,* 159–62; Bauer, *Zachary Taylor,* 115–16.

29. Black to SS, Jul 19 and 24, 1845, MDC 8:33–39.

30. *La Voz,* Mar 26 and Jul 17, 1845, and other papers quoted SWM 1:434 n. 8.

31. SWM 1:87–88, and Luis Gonzaga Cuevas to ministers, Jul 30, 1845, quoted 1:434 n. 9.

32. ARSW 1845, 193. On the pre-war army, see Prucha, *Sword.*

33. ZT to AG, Jul 25, 1845, MWC, 97; Hamilton, *Zachary Taylor Soldier,* 163; Henry, *Campaign Sketches,* 12–16; Hitchcock, *Fifty Years,* 194; BMW, 18–19.

34. SW to ZT, Jul 30, 1845, MWC, 82–83.

35. ZT to AG, Aug 15, 1845, MWC, 99–100; Henry, *Campaign Sketches,* 17–19.

36. Henry, *Story,* 22–23; Foos, *Short Offhand,* 18; Grant, *Memoirs,* 31; Bauer, *Zachary Taylor,* 117–18.

37. Bauer, *Zachary Taylor,* 117–18; Hitchcock, *Fifty Years,* 198–99; John P. Hatch to sister, Oct 28, 1845, quoted BMW, 34.

38. ARSW 1845, 193; AG to ZT, Nov 14, 1845, LS, RG 94; Sylvester Churchill to CG, Mar 2, 1846, LR, RG 107; SW Regulation, Mar 12, Childs to AG, Feb 2, Worth to ZT, Feb 24, 1846, LR, RG 94; BMW, 33–36; SWM1:144; Eisenhower, *Agent,* 221–22; Bauer, *Zachary Taylor,* 122–23.

39. Risch, *Quartermaster Support,* 241–43.

40. ZT to AG, Sep 6, Oct 4, and Nov 7, and SW to ZT, Oct 16, 1845, MWC, 89–90, 107–9, 111; J. D. Marks to ZT, Sep 23, 1845, LR, RG 94; Hitchcock, *Fifty Years,* 199; Henry, *Campaign Sketches,* 35–39; ibid., 244–45; Bauer, *Zachary Taylor,* 120–21; BMW, 21.

41. Risch, *Quartermaster Support,* 244–45; Henry, *Campaign Sketches,* 45–47; Hitchcock, *Fifty Years,* 207; Duncan, "Medical History"; SWM 1:143–44; BMW, 34–36; Bauer, *Zachary Taylor,* 123; Army of Occupation Orders 1, Jan 2, 1846, quoted BMW, 34; Spell, "Anglo-Saxon Press."

42. Clary and Whitehorne, *Inspectors General,* 177–81; Spencer, *Victor and Spoils.*

43. SS to JCC, Aug 22, 1845, quoted BMW, 20; SW to ZT, Aug 23 and 30, 1845, MWC, 84–85, 88–89; SW to governors, Aug 25 and 28, LS, RG 107; SN to Conner, Aug 30, 1845, Confidential Letters, RG 80; QDP 1:5–6, 9–12. The states were Louisiana, Alabama, Mississippi, Tennessee, and Kentucky.

44. NPD, 7; Parrott to SS, Aug 16 and 24, 1845, MDC 8:746–47, also quoted Bemis, *Diplomatic History,* 235n; C. Palmer to Caleb Cushing, Aug 14, 1845, quoted John Belohlavek, "Race, Progress, and Destiny: Caleb Cushing and the Quest for American Empire," in Haynes and Morris, *Manifest Destiny,* 39; Haynes, " 'But What Will England Say?' ", 19; newspapers quoted SWM 1:118–26.

45. *The Calling of Volunteers Without Authority;* Silver, *Edmund Pendleton Gaines,* 259–60.

46. *New York Herald,* Sep 2, 1845, quoted Haynes, "But What Will England Say?", 22; SS to U.S. minister London, Sep 13, 1845, quoted SWM 1:131.

47. Aberdeen quoted SWM 1:434 n. 10; NPD, 36; Millis, *Arms and Men,* 92.

48. *Siglo XIX,* Jul 27, 1845, quoted *New Orleans Picayune,* Sep, 1845; SWM 1:104.

49. QDP, 1:33–36; SS to Black, Sep 17, 1845, MDC 8:167–69; Rivers, *United States and Mexico* 2:53–80; Callahan, *American Foreign Policy,* 45–73; BMW, 17–29; Reeves, *American Diplomacy,* 268–88; Sears, *John Slidell,* 56–73; Sears, "Slidell's Mission."

50. Sears, *John Slidell.*

51. Larkin to SS, Jul 10, 1845, MDC 8:735–36; Hussey, "Origin of Gillespie Mission"; Adams, "English Interest."

52. SS to Larkin, Oct 17, 1845, quoted BMW, 23; Gillespie Testimony, *California Claims,* 30; NPD, 22; QDP 1:83–84; Hussey, "Origins of Gillespie Mission." On Gillespie, see Marti, *Messenger of Destiny,* and Frazier, 177.

53. Black to Peña, Oct 13, and to SS, Oct 17, and Peña to Black, Oct 15, 1845, MDC 8:761–65; Alcaraz, excerpted *Ecos,* 51–53.

54. Dimond to SS, Oct 21, 1845, CD, RG 59; Conner to Dimond, Oct 23, 1845, MDC 8:769n; NPD 25–26.

55. QDP 1:92–97; JKP, Letter of Credence (Slidell's credentials), Nov 10, 1845, MWC 27–28; SS to Slidell, Nov 10, 1845 (his instructions), and enclosures, MDC 8:172–82; Vázquez, "War and Peace with the United States," in Meyer and Beezley, *Oxford History,* 339–70 (at 359).

56. All quoted SWM 1:436 n. 25.

57. Black to SS, Dec 18, 1845, MDC 8:783–84; Cotner, *Career of Herrera,* 143–45.

58. Slidell to Peña, Dec 8, 14, and 20, Peña to Slidell, Dec 16 and 20, Black to Slidell, Dec 15, and Slidell to SS, Dec 17, 1845, all in MWC 27–40; Peña to Consejo de Gobierno, Dec 11, and Consejo de Gobierno, Dictamen, Dec 16, 1845, both in Cabrero,

Diario 2:70–81; Slidell to JKP, Dec 29, 1845, BMW, 25; Peña to SS, Dec 20, 1845, Butler, *Documentary History,* 19; *Ecos,* 53–54.

59. Newspapers quoted SWM 1:120–21; SS to Slidell, Jan 20, 1846, MDC 8:185–86.

60. Slidell to Castillo y Lanzas, Mar 1 and 17, and SS to Slidell, Mar 12, 1846, MDC 8:189–92, 814–15, 818–19; Consejo de Gobierno, Dictamen, Mar 6, 1846, in Cabrera, *Diario* 2:11–15.

61. *Ecos,* 45.

62. Josefina Zoraida Vázquez, "Causes of the War with the United States," translated by Douglas W. Richmond, in Francaviglia and Richmond, *Dueling Eagles,* 41–67; Ramírez, *Mexico During War,* 11–39; Cotner, *Career of Herrera,* 145–49; Bravo Ugarte, *Historia de México* 3 pt. 2:191–97; Henderson, *Glorious Defeat,* 152–53. On the Spanish plot, see Soto, *Conspiración,* and Delgado, *La Monarquía.*

63. Ruiz, *Triumphs,* 180; Alcaraz, excerpted *Ecos,* 55; Frazier, 310–11; sources cited n. 65 below.

64. Pletcher, *Diplomacy of Annexation,* 370; Tymitz, "British Influence," 147; Haynes, " 'But What Will England Say?' ", 29–31.

65. AMP, Dec 2, 1845, RMP 5:2235–66, and Farrell, *James K. Polk,* 35–48; DeConde, *History of American Foreign Policy,* 194–98.

66. DeConde, *History of American Foreign Policy,* 162–74.

67. Vázquez, "Causes of the War with the United States," 59–60; Ruiz, *Triumphs,* 181–82; SWM 1:438 n. 31.

68. Rives, *United States and Mexico* 2:119–22; QDP 1:223, 225–27, 233; BMW, 27–28; C. Alan Hutchinson, "Valentín Gómez Farías and the Movement for the Return of General Santa Anna to Mexico in 1846," in Cotner and Castañeda, *Essays,* 186–87; Jones, *Santa Anna,* 100. Atocha left little record beyond a Supreme Court decision related to his claim against Mexico. *Ex parte Atocha.* 84 US 439 (1873).

69. Paredes, Manifesto of Mar 21, 1846, and Alcaraz, both in *Ecos,* 59–60; Castillo to Slidell, Mar 21, and Slidell to SS, Mar 27, 1846, MWC, 77–79.

70. Ramsey, *Other Side,* 36.

71. Frazier, 239.

72. Ibid., 17–19, 242–43.

73. Ibid., 13; *Ecos,* 57–59, 70; Ramsey, *Other Side,* 39.

74. SW to ZT, Jan 13, 1846, MWC, 90; SN to Commodore Home Squadron, Jan 17, 1846, Letters to Officers, RG 80; BMW, 26–27.

75. Canales to ZT, Jan 29, Carbajal to ZT, Feb 6 and Mar 4, ZT to AG, Feb 7, 1846, LR, RG 94; SW to ZT, Mar 2, 1846, MWC, 92; Connor and Faulk, *North America,* 138–40; Smith, "Republica."

76. Sibley to ZT, Feb 23, 1846, LR, RG 94; Risch, *Quartermaster Support,* 245, 265–67; Hamilton, *Zachary Taylor Soldier,* 171; BMW, 37.

77. Thomas R. Irey, "Soldiering, Suffering, and Dying," in Faulk and Stout, *Mexican War,* 111–12; Army of Occupation Orders 26, Mar 4, and 30, Mar 8, 1846, quoted BMW, 37–38; scrounger quoted Risch, *Quartermaster Support,* 249.

78. ZT to AG, Mar 11, 1846, in *Message from the President, Existing Relations* (Sen Doc 337), 110; Henry, *Story,* 41; SWM 1:146–48; BMW, 38; Grant, *Memoirs,* 34–35.

79. Quoted Horgan, *Great River,* 610.

80. Castillo Negrete, *Invasión* 1:114; Twiggs to Bliss, Mar 15, 1846, cited BMW, 38; Henry, *Campaign Sketches,* 58.

81. ZT to AG, Mar 21, and Mejía proclamation, Mar 18, 1846, MWC, 123–29; Butler, *Documentary History,* 25; Henry, *Campaign Sketches,* 59–60.

82. Army of Occupation Orders, Mar 22 and 26, RG 94; Jenés Cardenas to ZT, Mar 23, and ZT to AG, Mar 25, 2846, MWC, 129–30; Henry, *Campaign Sketches,* 61–62. Cardenas' protest is also in Butler, *Documentary History,* 28.

83. Henry, *Campaign Sketches,* 63; Alcaraz, excerpted *Ecos,* 56–57; Ramsey, *Other Side,* 37.

84. ZT to Mejía, Mar 28, 1846, CSW, 393; Minutes of Interview Between Generals Worth and Díaz, MWC, 134–38; Henry, *Campaign Sketches,* 55–57; Butler, *Documentary History,* 30–32.

85. Winders, *Mr. Polk's Army,* 173–74.

86. *Regulations 1841,* 15. I have dealt with the bathing issue more extensively in Clary, *These Relics,* passim. The United States Army did not require regular bathing until late in the century.

87. For example, Kirby Smith to his wife, Mar 29, 1846, quoted Eisenhower, *So Far,* 55–56.

88. Ibid., 61–62; Prucha, *Sword,* 324–26.

89. Hitchcock, *Fifty Years,* 213.

CHAPTER 5

1. Nevins, *Frémont;* Rolle, *John Charles Frémont;* and JCF, *Memoirs.* The 1851 reissues of his official reports are JCF, *Report on an Exploration,* and *Report of the Exploring Expedition.* On his wife, see Herr, *Jessie Benton Frémont.* On explorations of the west generally, see Goetzmann, *Exploration and Empire,* and Goetzmann, *Army Exploration.* See also Utley, *Life,* 189–91.

2. Sherman, *Memoirs,* 46–47; Brewerton quoted Dunlay, *Kit Carson,* 13. Other biographies include Sides, *Blood and Thunder;* Guild and Carter, *Kit Carson;* Estergreen, *Kit Carson;* and Utley, *Life.*

3. SN to Commodore Pacific Squadron, Mar 21 and May 5, 1845, Confidential Letters, RG 45; SN to Commodore Pacific Squadron, Jun 24, 1845, MWC, 231.

4. Sherman, *Life of Sloat;* Frazier, 389; Sloat entry in Callahan. See also Oakah L. Jones Jr., "The Pacific Squadron off California," in Faulk and Stout, *Mexican War,* 144–45.

5. Sloat to SN, Nov 19, and Dec 3 and 25, 1845, Pacific Squadron Letters, RG 45.

6. SN to Commodore Pacific Squadron, Dec 5, 1845, and Feb 23, 1846, Letters to Officers, RG 45; BMW, 166; Gillespie to SN, Feb 11 and 18, and Apr 15, 1846, in Ames, "Gillespie"; Simms, *United States Marines,* 40–41.

7. Wood to Sloat and to SN, Jun 4, 1846, Pacific Squadron Letters, RG 45; Parrott to SS, Jun 4, 1846, CD, RG 59; BMW, 67.

8. Sloat to SN, May 31 and Jun 6, 1846, *California Claims,* 70; Sloat to SN, Jul 31, 1846, MWC, 258–60; Sherman, *Life of Sloat,* 65–66; SWM 1:333; Bancroft, *History of California* 5:204; Larkin to SS, Jun 1, 1846, CD, RG 59.

9. Quoted Utley, *Life,* 247–48.

10. J. J. Abert to JCF (his orders), Feb 12, 1845, in Goetzmann, *Army Exploration,* 117; Goetzmann, *Exploration and Empire,* 251–52; Josiah Royce to H. L. Oaks, Aug 8, 1885 (family plot), quoted BMW, 165.

11. Ames, "Gillespie"; Hussey, "Commander Montgomery"; Utley, *Life,* 231–34; JCF, *Memoirs* 1:503–9, including JCF to THB, Jul 25, 1846, at 546; BMW, 168.

12. Larkin to SS, Mar 27 and Apr 2, 1846, MDC 8:834–36, 839–41; Larkin to John Parrott, Consul Mazatlán, Mar 9, 1846, CD, RG 59; JCF to Larkin, Mar 10, 1846, Butler, *Documentary History,* 141–42; Utley, *Life,* 234–35; JCF quoted JCF, *Memoirs* 1:459, see also 439–64, 491; Nevins, *Frémont,* 226–30; Bancroft, *History of California* 5:3–18; JCF testimony in *Proceedings of the Court-Martial of Colonel Frémont;* JCF, "Conquest."

13. Gillespie and JCF depositions, *California Claims,* 12, 33–34; Frémont, *Memoirs* 1:488–90; Nevins, *Frémont,* 239–50; Roa Bárcena, *Recuerdos* 1:240; Ames, "Gillespie"; Benton, *Thirty Years* 2:689–90; BMW, 165–67; Royce, "Montgomery and Frémont"; Utley, *Life,* 235–39, JCF quotation at 238; Gillespie to SN, July 25, 1846, in Ames, "Gillespie"; Stenberg, "Polk and Frémont"; Tays, "Frémont Had No Secret"; Utley, *Life,* 362 n. 30; Marti, *Messenger of Destiny,* ch. 2; Hussey, "Origin."

14. Ames, "Gillespie"; Hussey, "Commander Montgomery"; JCF to THB, Jul 25, 1846, in JCF *Memoirs* 1:546, see also 503–9; BMW, 168; Utley, *Life,* 243–44, Jacob Dye quoted 244.

15. Richman, *California,* 307–9; Bancroft, *History of California* 5:105–12; Utley, *Life,* 245; Bryant, *What I Saw,* 187–88; Davis, *Seventy-Five Years,* 142–43; JCF, *Memoirs* 1:509.

16. Both proclamations are in Butler, *Documentary History,* 144.

17. Quoted DeVoto, *Year,* 226.

18. Ide proclamation in Butler, *Documentary History,* 145; Utley, *Life,* 245–47; JCF to THB, Jul 15, 1846, in JCF, *Memoirs* 1:546, see also 515–16; Bancroft, *History of California,* 5:134–36, 165–79; Richman, *California,* 31; Marti, *Messenger of Destiny,* 61.

19. BMW, 169–70; Utley, *Life,* 247.

20. Frazier, 408–9.

21. Levinson, *Wars Within,* 119; Josefina Zoraida Vázquez, "War and Peace with the United States," in Meyer and Beezley, *Oxford History,* 339–70 (at 359–60); Brack, "Mexican Opinion." See also Santoni, *Mexicans at Arms;* Vázquez, *México al tiempo;* Berge, "Mexican Dilemma"; Costelo, "Church-State Financial"; Robinson, *View from Chapultepec;* Ruiz, *Mexican War;* Santoni, "Failure of Mobilization"; C. Alan Hutchinson, "Valentín Gómez Farías and the Movement for the Return of General Santa Anna to Mexico in 1846," in Cotner and Castañeda, *Essays in Mexican History,* 161–91.

22. *London Times,* Feb 10, 1846, quoted SWM 1:216; Manuel Gómez Cosío quoted Scheina, *Santa Anna,* 48.

23. Quoted SWM 1:485 n. 22.

24. Levinson, *Wars Within,* 49–50; Castillo Lanras, Mar 26, 1846, quoted at 49.

25. NPD, 58–59, 65–67.

26. Ibid., 67–72, 79–86; QDP 1:319–27, 337–38, 375, 383–86.

27. Goetzmann, *When Eagle,* 46–48; DeConde, *History of American Foreign Policy,* 162–74.

28. Lyman B. Kirkpatrick Jr., "Intelligence and Counterintelligence," in DeConde, *Encyclopedia* 2:418–19; Andrew, *For President's Eyes,* 14; ZT to Henderson, Apr 3, 1846,

quoted BMW, 42; ZT to AG, Mar 29 and Apr 6, and AG to ZT, Apr 20, 1846, MWC, 96–97, 132–33.

29. ZT to Mejía, Mar 30, and Mejía to ZT, Mar 31, 1846, CSW, 393–95; ZT orders quoted BMW, 41; Hitchcock, *Fifty Years,* 218; Henry, *Campaign Sketches,* 68.

30. Horgan, *Great River,* 664; Hamilton, *Zachary Taylor Soldier,* 175; ZT quoted BMW, 40–41.

31. Roa Bárcena, *Recuerdos* 1:61; Bravo Ugarte, *Historia* 3:198.

32. Tornel to Arista, Apr 4, 1846, in BMW, 42; Arista to Ampudia, Apr 10, 1846, in Ampudia, *Ciudadano,* 15–16; Carreño, *Jefes del ejército,* 44–57; Robinson, *Mexico and Her Military,* 255; Vázquez, "War and Peace with the United States," 360.

33. Roa Bárcena, *Recuerdos* 1:148; Valades, *Breve Historia,* 115.

34. Proclamations of Ampudia, Apr 2, and Arista, Apr 20, Arista to Ampudia, Apr 30, and Mejía to Arista, May 4, 1846, LR, RG 94, also in Butler, *Documentary History,* 41–42, and Henry, *Campaign Sketches,* 74.

35. ZT to AG, May 30, enclosing Description of Deserters Supposed to Have Been Shot in Attempting to Cross Rio Grande, May 31, 1846, MWC, 302–3, and in Butler, *Documentary History,* 85.

36. Miller, *Shamrock and Sword;* Wynn, *San Patricio Soldiers;* Hogan, *Irish Soldiers;* Stevens, *Rogue's March.*

37. Ampudia to ZT, Apr 12 and 22, ZT to Ampudia, Apr 12 and 22, and ZT to AG, Apr 15, 1846, MWC, 138–40, 144–47; Ramsey, *Other Side,* 39–40; Castillo Negrete, *Invasión* 2:112; Robinson, *Mexico and Her Military,* 259.

38. Ampudia to ZT, Apr 16, 1846, MWC, 147–48; Report of Board of Officers, Apr 23, 1846, LR, RG 94; Henry, *Campaign Sketches,* 77–78.

39. Arista to ZT, Apr 24, and ZT to Arista, Apr 25, 1846, CSW, 395–96, and in Butler, *Documentary History,* 47–48; Roa Bárcena, *Recuerdos* 1:62; Ramsey, *Other Side,* 42.

40. Paredes Manifesto, Apr 23, 1846, in Rives, *United States and Mexico* 2:141–42; Black to SS, Apr 25, 1846, CD, RG 59.

41. Hardee to ZT, Apr 26, Thornton to Bliss, Apr 27, and Army of Occupation Orders 74, Jun 8, 1846, all in MWC, 490–92; Torrejón to ZT, Apr 25, 1846, LR, RG 94; Henry, *Campaign Sketches,* 82–85; Torrejón to Arista, Apr 26, 1846, cited BMW, 63 n. 7; Butler, *Documentary History,* 53–55; Bauer, *Zachary Taylor,* 149–50.

42. Broadside and brag quoted SWM 1:155, 160; Arista to Torrejón, Apr 26, 1846, in Butler, *Documentary History,* 52.

43. ZT to AG, Apr 26, 1846, MWC, 288; Grant, *Memoirs,* 33.

44. QDP 1:287–89; Coit, *John C. Calhoun,* 440.

45. Besides THB's memoirs, *Thirty Years,* biographies include Chambers, *Old Bullion;* Meigs, *Life of Benton;* Rogers, *Thomas Hart Benton;* and Smith, *Magnificent Missourian.*

46. NPD, 86–89.

47. RMP 5:2287–93; 9 Stat. 9–10. Initial appropriations were $7.25 million to the army, $2.75 million to the navy. BMW, 79 n. 10.

48. Bemis, *John Quincy Adams and Union,* 496–99; John R. Collins, "Sectionalism and Political Fragmentation," in Faulk and Stout, *Mexican War,* 70–71; Wiltse, *John C. Calhoun,* 283–84; BMW, 68–69.

49. The additional measures are summarized SWM 1:190–91. The proclamation is in RMP 5:2320.

50. Giddings to W. G. Howell, Jun 8, and McHenry to John Hardin, May 12, 1846, both quoted BMW, 69.

51. QDP 1:395–400; NPD, 91–92.

52. THB, *Thirty Years*, 2:680.

53. Congress Decreto, Jul 2, 1846, *Ecos*, 60; Paredes Decreto, Jul 6, 1846, and Conner report of Black's message on this, SWM 1:212–17.

54. Peña quoted Levinson, *Wars Within*, 16; Pletcher, *Diplomacy*, 441.

55. Alcaraz, *Apuntes*, 40; Meyer and Beezley, *Oxford History*, 3.

56. Quoted Sonnichsen, *Pass of North*, 110.

CHAPTER 6

1. WS, *Memoirs;* Eisenhower, *Agent;* Elliott, *Winfield Scott;* Johnson, *Winfield Scott;* WS' entry in Heitman; Clary and Whitehorne, *Inspectors General,* 109–14, 172–88, 198–205.

2. NPD, 90, 93–94; Eisenhower, *Agent,* 223–25.

3. Ampudia to Arista, Apr 27, 1846, in Ampudia, *El Ciudadano,* 16–17; Arista to Ministro de Guerra y Marina, Apr 29, 1846, in Castillo Negrete, *Invasión* 1:167; Walker to ZT, May 2, 1846, LR, RG 94; Ramsey, *Other Side,* 44; Buchanan, "George Washington Trahern."

4. Jenkins, *History,* 99; Utley, *Lone Star,* 59–61; quotation in Haynes, *Soldiers of Misfortune,* 20; Walker entry in Heitman.

5. Oficial, *Campaña,* 5; Ramsey, *Other Side,* 43–44; ZT to AG, May 3, 1846, MWC, 486–88; Henry, *Campaign Sketches,* 86.

6. Sources on the account of the siege of Fort Texas include Arista to Ministro de Guerra y Marina, May 7, 1846, in Brooks, *Complete History,* 135–36; Ramsey, *Other Side,* 44; Requeña to Ampudia, May 31, 1846, in Ampudia, *El Ciudadano,* 18; Roa Bárcena, *Recuerdos* 1:63; Oficial, *Campaña,* 7; Jenkins, *History,* 101–6; Singletary, *Mexican War,* 32; Edgar S. Hawkins to W. W. S. Bliss, May 10, 1846, *Operations and Recent Engagements,* 31–37, and in Butler, *Documentary History,* 63–66.

7. Jenkins, *History,* 103–4.

8. Arista to Officer Commanding U.S. Forces Opposite Matamoros, May 6, Hawkins to Arista, May 6, Hawkins to Bliss, May 10, Mansfield to ZT, May 12, 1846, all in *Operations and Recent Engagements,* 312–37; Arista to Ministro de Guerra y Marina, May 7, 1846, in Brooks, *Complete History,* 135–36; Brown to Bliss, May 4, 1846, MWC, 193–94. Fort Brown (originally Texas) continued in service off and on until 1944. Fort Polk was abandoned in 1850. Frazer, *Forts,* 144–45, 157.

9. She followed the army to Monterey and to Buena Vista/Angostura. After the war she became a saloon keeper in Arizona. She died at Fort Yuma in 1866, and was buried with full military honors. Johannsen, *To Halls,* 140–41; Wallace, "The Great Western"; account by Lewis Leonidas Allen in Smith and Judah, *Chronicles,* 305–7.

10. ZT to AG, May 5, and Army of Occupation Orders 58, May 7, 1846, MWC, 292–93, 487.

11. Robert Hazlitt to sister, May 14, 1846, quoted BMW, 52; SWM 1:163–64.

12. Alcaraz, 30. Sources on Palo Alto include Alcaraz, 29–51; ZT to AG, May 16 and

17, 1846, and enclosures, *Operations and Recent Engagements,* 6–30; Arista to Ministro de Guerra y Marina, May 8, 1846, in Robinson, *Mexico and Her Military,* 318–21; Ampudia, *El Ciudadano,* 90–94; Ramsey, *Other* Side, 45–50; Oficial, *Campaña,* 8–14; Brooks, *Complete History,* 125–33; Roa Bárcena, *Recuerdos* 1:67; *Report of the Secretary of War Showing the Number of Troops in Service,* 15; *Military Forces Employed in the Mexican War;* Bauer, *Zachary Taylor,* 150–63; Henry, *Story,* 54–63. ZT to AG, May 16, and Arista to Ministro, May 8, are also in Butler, *Documentary History,* 67, 77–78.

13. Arista to Ministro de Guerra y Marina, May 8, 1846, in Robinson, *Mexico and Her Military,* 318–21.

14. Alcaraz, excerpted *Ecos,* 63–64.

15. Grant, *Memoirs,* 49.

16. Alcaraz, excerpted *Ecos,* 64.

17. BMW, 59. Sources on the Battle of Resaca include Ampudia, *El Ciudadano,* 18–23; Oficial, *Campaña,* 15–20; Roa Bárcena, *Recuerdos* 1:84–85; Ramsey, *Other Side,* 50–55; ZT to AG and enclosures, May 17, 1846, *Operations and Recent Engagements,* 6–21; McIntosh to Bliss, Dec 2, 1846, MWC, 1102–4; George Deas to Brooke, Jul 22, and Childs to SW, May 12, 1846, LR, RG 94; Lavender, *Climax,* 73–77; Hamilton, *Zachary Taylor Soldier,* 186–90; SWM 1:170–76; Ripley, *War* 1:125–31; Brooks, *Complete History,* 137–47; *Report of the Secretary of War Showing the Number of Troops in the Service,* 16; Eisenhower, *So Far,* 71–85; *Ecos,* 66–69; Frazier, 354–57; BMW, 59–62. ZT's report, ZT to AG, May 17, 1846, is also in Butler, *Documentary History,* 79–81.

18. Quoted Ramsey, *Other Side,* 53. See also *Ecos,* 68, and Jackson, "General Taylor's 'Astonishing' Map."

19. BMW, 62–63, including Díaz quotation.

20. Smith, *To Mexico,* 53; Ramsey, *Other Side,* 57; Roa Bárcena, *Recuerdos* 1:85; Oficial, *Campaña,* 22–26; Castillo Negrete, *Invasión* 1:193; Henry, *Campaign Sketches,* 104; Arista to ZT and endorsements, May 10, 1846, LR, RG 94.

21. Smith, *To Mexico,* 53; Horgan, *Great River,* 691; ranger quoted Eisenhower, *So Far,* 104.

22. Horgan, *Great River,* 690.

23. Smith, *To Mexico,* 51.

24. Tilden, *Notes on the Upper Rio Grande.*

25. Army of Occupation Orders 61 and 64, May 14 and 15, 1846, MWC, 488–89, 522; BMW, 81–82.

26. Arista to ZT, May 17, 1846, CSW, 396–97; ZT to AG, May 18, 1846, MWC, 297–98; Henry, *Campaign Sketches,* 107–8; Hamilton, *Zachary Taylor Soldier,* 192–93. ZT to AG, May 18, 1846, is also in Butler, *Documentary History,* 83.

27. Alcaraz, excerpted *Ecos,* 68–69; Ramsey, *Other Side,* 58–61; Roa Bárcena, *Recuerdos,* 1:89–90; Vigil y Robles, *Invasión,* 19; Oficial, *Campaña,* 29–36; Valades, *Breve Historia,* 120; Hogan, *Irish Soldiers,* 41; Miller, *Shamrock and Sword,* 43. Arista became a reformist minister of war and president during the 1850s. In 1880 he was proclaimed *Benemérito de la Patria.* Frazier, 17–18.

28. All quoted SWM 1:179; JKP to ZT, May 30, 1846, Butler, *Documentary History,* 86.

29. Smith and Judah, *Chronicles,* 71.

30. These remarks are sampled mostly from Johannsen, *To Halls,* 21–23. See also Brooks, *Complete History,* 354; and Semmes, *Service Afloat,* 71.

31. Quoted SWM 1:179–80.

32. *Ecos,* 69; Ramírez, *Mexico During War,* 135; superhuman stories in *New York Herald,* Jul 18, 1846, quoted Johannsen, *To Halls,* 21.

33. Quoted Christensen, *U. S.-Mexican,* 67.

34. General Anastasio Parrodi, Commandant Department of Tamaulipas, to troops under his command, May 13, 1846, Butler, *Documentary History,* 76.

35. Don Sebastian Bermúdez, Jun 22, 1846, quoted Sonnichsen, *Pass of the North,* 110.

36. Henry, *Story,* 73.

37. Winders, *Mr. Polk's Army,* 121.

38. Proclamation quoted SWM 2:210–11.

39. Army of Occupation Orders 62, May 17, 1846, Butler, *Documentary History,* 82.

40. Eisenhower, *So Far,* 101–3; Smith and Judah, *Chronicles,* 19; officer quoted SWM 2:211.

41. Hughes and Johnson, *Fighter,* 3; Colonel Balie Peyton to ZT, Jun 27, 1846, in Smith and Judah, *Chronicles,* 286–87.

42. Moore Journal, Jul 19, 1846, in Butler, *Eutaw Rangers,* 16; ZT and enlisted man quoted SWM 2:212; Charleston, South Carolina, *Mercury,* Mar 2, 1847, quoted Foos, *Short Offhand,* 116; press and correspondent quoted Johannsen, *To Halls,* 31–33. WS offered an appalling account of atrocities near the Rio Grande, and concluded, "As far as I can learn, not one of the felons has been punished." WS to SW, Jan 16, 1847, quoted SWM 2:450 n. 6.

43. Sanislaus Lasselle to Malenie Lasselle, Feb 10, 1847, quoted Foos, *Short Offhand,* 99.

44. Quoted SWM 2:216.

45. Utley, *Lone Star,* 60–61; Smith, "La Republica"; Johannsen, *To Halls,* 23–24; Levinson, *Wars Within,* passim; quotations from Ramsey, *Other Side,* 442, and Frost, *History,* 626.

46. From the selection of contemporary comments in Johannsen, *To Halls,* 23–24.

CHAPTER 7

1. Cardenas de la Peña, *Semblanza marítimo* 2:27; *Memoria del Ministro de Guerra y Marina, 9 de Diciembre de 1846;* Roa Bárcenas, *Recuerdos* 1:249; Scheina, "Forgotten Fleet"; Scheina, "Seapower Misused"; Frazier, 285–86, 498–99.

2. Black to SS, Jul 29, 1846, conveying Paredes Manifesto of Jul 26, 1846, CD, RG 59; *Reglamentos para el corso de particulares;* Commodore Home Squadron to SN, Jun 30, 1846, Home Squadron Letters, RG 45; BMW, 112.

3. Beach, *United States Navy,* 159–76; Howarth, *To Shining,* 153–61; Bauer, *Surfboats.*

4. ARSN 1847, 945; Paullin, *Paullin's History,* 228; Bauer, *Surfboats,* 25–26, 253–63; Beach, *United States Navy,* 159–76; Howarth, *To Shining,* 153–61; SWM 2:189–91; BMW, 398, 399 nn. 8 and 9.

5. SN to Commander Home Squadron, May 13, 1846, MWC, 233–35; Commander Home Squadron to SN, Jun 10, 1846, Home Squadron Letters, RG 45.

6. Conner to wife, May 29, 1846, quoted BMW, 109; Semmes, *Service Afloat,* 78; Valadés, *México, Santa Anna,* 148.

7. SN to Commodore Home Squadron, May 30, 1846, Confidential Letters, and Commander Home Squadron to SN, Jun 11 and 12, 1846, Home Squadron Letters, RG 45; Morris to Conner, Jun 10 and 24, cited BMW, 111.

8. Morison, *Old Bruin,* 186; Conner to SN, May 8 and 13, cited BMW, 109, see also 110, 123 n. 14; Trens, *Historia* 4:361–62; Rivera Cambas, *Historia* 3:765–66.

9. Manno, "Yucatán en la guerra."

10. Saunders to English and French Consuls Tampico, May 20, to SN, Jun 5, and to Conner, Jun 20, 1846, Home Squadron Letters, RG 45; U.S. Consul Tampico to SS, Jun 28, 1846, CD, RG 59; Trens, *Historia* 4:334; Ramsey, *Other Side,* 100; BMW, 110; Parrodi, *Memoria,* 4.

11. Home Squadron Blockade Instructions, May 14 (and revision Jun 28), Conner to Fitzhugh, May 14, and to Saunders and to Gregory, May 17, 1846, Home Squadron Letters, RG 45; SN to Thomas ap Catesby Jones, Oct 28, 1847, ARSN 1847, 1304.

12. Semmes, *Service Afloat,* 76; Commodore Home Squadron to SN, Jun 5, 1846, Home Squadron Letters, RG 45; BMW, 112.

13. Daniel Noble Johnson quoted Howarth, *To Shining,* 169–70.

14. Howarth, *To Shining,* 171; BMW, 114–15.

15. Quoted Howarth, *To Shining,* 170.

16. Weigley, *History,* 175–83; Marcy quoted White, *Jacksonians,* 56–57; Callan, *Military Laws,* 379–82; Ganoe, *History,* 217; Spaulding, *United States Army,* 211–12.

17. Christon I. Arthur, "Fashioning a New Nation," and Josefina Zoraida Vázquez, "War and Peace with the United States," in Meyer and Beezley, *Oxford History,* 301–38, 339–70; Sordo Cedeño, "El General Tornel"; Fowler, *Tornel and Santa Anna;* Frazier, 314–15, 431; Meyer and others, *Course,* 329.

18. *Regulations 1847,* 8–9; SWM 1:198–200, 183, 350–54; Elliott, *Winfield Scott,* 523–24; Bauer, "Vera Cruz Expedition"; Weigley, *History,* 178–219; Risch, *Quartermaster Support,* 237–39; Jesup in ARQMG 1847, 549.

19. Chartrand, *Santa Anna's Mexican Army,* 10–12; foreigner quoted Olivera and Crété, *Life in Mexico,* 28–29; DePalo, *Mexican National Army,* passim.

20. Weigley, *History,* 172; Mills, *Arms and Men,* 95; Chartrand, *Santa Anna's Mexican Army,* 50–51; Fehrenbach, *Fire and Blood,* 286; SWM 1:156.

21. Kreidberg and Henry, *Military Mobilization,* 70–78; Callan, *Military Laws,* 367–87; Weigley, *History,* 182–83; DeWeerd, "Federalization," 147; Winders, *Mr. Polk's Army,* 9; Hill, *Minute Man,* 22–25; Millis, *Arms and Men,* 93–94.

22. Winders, *Mr. Polk's Army,* ch. 8; Kreidberg and Henry, *Military Mobilization,* 70–77; Tapson, "Sutler and Soldier."

23. Johannsen, *To Halls,* 52–53; May, "Invisible Men."

24. Winders, *Mr. Polk's Army,* ch. 3; Weigley, *History,* 181–82 and notes; WS quoted Cullum, *Biographical Register,* 1:11.

25. Johannsen, *To Halls,* 24–25; Vázquez, "War and Peace with the United States," 362; Chartrand, *Santa Anna's Mexican Army,* 7.

26. Chartrand, *Santa Anna's Mexican Army,* 6–7, 51–53; Ruiz, *Triumphs,* 200–1.

27. Perry quoted Morison, *Old Bruin,* 201; Gilmore, "Condition"; Mariano Otero, "Considerations Relating to the Political and Social Situation of the Mexican Republic in the Year 1847," in Joseph and Henderson, *Mexico Reader,* 232; Ruiz, *Triumphs,* 200; Olivera and Crété, *Life,* 160–61; Chartrand, *Santa Anna's Mexican Army,* 3–8; Balbontín, *Invasión,* excerpted *Ecos,* 80; DePalo, *Mexican National Army;* Hefter, "Cronica"; Thompson, *Recollections,* 169–73.

28. Juan Weber quoted SWM 1:408 n. 5.

29. General Luis Garfías, quoted Christensen, *U.S. Mexican,* 153; Salas, *Soldaderas.*

30. Vázquez, "War and Peace with the United States," 362; Olivera and Crété, *Life,* 167–70.

31. Thompson, *Recollections,* 169, 170–71.

32. Edwards, *Campaign in New Mexico,* 18–19.

33. Risch, *Quartermaster Support,* 237–99; Winders, *Mr. Polk's Army,* 117–26; Kreidberg and Henry, *Military Mobilization,* 77–80; Spencer, "Overseas War"; White, *Jacksonians,* 57–59; *Regulations 1847,* 85–87, 179–85.

34. Winders, *Mr. Polk's Army,* 101–12.

35. Traas, *From Golden Gate;* Ashburn, *History of Medical Department,* 40–60; Thomas R. Irey, "Soldiering, Suffering, and Dying," in Faulk and Stout, *Mexican War,* 110–19; Private Stephen F. Nunnalee journal, Jan 19, 1847, in Butler, *Eutaw Rangers,* 100.

36. Winders, *Mr. Polk's Army,* 129–35; Johannsen, *To Halls,* 53–54; Reilly, "American Reporters"; Mitchel Roth, "Journalism and the U. S.-Mexican War," in Francaviglia and Richmond, *Dueling Eagles,* 103–26.

37. Chartrand, *Santa Anna's Mexican Army,* 3, 3n, 13–14, 27–32; SWM 1:462 n. 1.

38. Chartrand, *Santa Anna's Mexican Army,* 44–57; SWM 1:156, 461–62 n. 1, Thompson quoted 1:11.

39. Winder, *Mr. Polk's Army,* 92–101; Weigley, *History,* 172; SWM 1:450–51 n. 6.

40. Birkhimer, *Historical Sketch,* 50–51; Donald E. Houston, "The Superiority of American Artillery," in Faulk and Stout, *Mexican War,* 101–9; Winders, *Mr. Polk's Army,* 89–92; Nichols, *Zach Taylor's,* 84; Dillon, *American Artillery; Instructions for Field Artillery.*

41. Olejar, "Rockets in Early American Wars"; Clary, *Rocket Man,* 28–33.

42. Simmons, *Mexican Corrido;* SN to Commodore Home Squadron, May 13, 1846, Confidential Letters, RG 45. Published in *Niles' National Register,* Jan 22, 1848, reproduced in Butler, *Documentary History,* 187.

CHAPTER 8

1. Eisenhower, *Agent,* 216; NPD, 47.

2. John R. Collins, "Sectionalism and Political Fragmentation," in Faulk and Stout, *Mexican War,* 71; Hinckley, "Anti-Catholicism." See also Germain, *Catholic Military,* 36–39; and McEniry, *American Catholics,* 34–35, 54–66.

3. QDP 2:104; NPD, 97–98; SW to ZT, May 20, to Vorhagen [sic], to McElroy, and to Rey, May 21, and to Kendrick, May 29, 1846, LS, RG 107; Germain, *Catholic Military,* 36–39; McEniry, *American Catholics,* 34–35, 54–66. Fathers John McElroy and Antony Rey traveled to Mexico immediately. McElroy stayed until mid-1847. Rey was killed by bandits Jan 15, 1847.

4. SW to ZT, Jun 16, 1846, and proclamation, MWC, 284–87.

5. *Cincinnati Truth Teller,* Apr 16, 1846, quoted Foos, *Short Offhand,* 26–27.

6. Hinckley, "Anti-Catholicism"; Fuentes Días, *Intervención,* 216; Foos, *Short Offhand,* 127–32.

7. ZT to AG, May 21 and Jun 3, SW to ZT, May 28 and Jun 8, WS to ZT, Jun 12 and 15, and AG to ZT, Jun 16, 1846, MWC, 281–82, 300, 305–6, 323–27, 454–55, 1328–29.

8. ZT to Governor (Texas) J. Pinckney Henderson, Apr 26, 1846, quoted Utley, *Lone Star,* 313 n. 5; Gaines to SW, May 3, 11, and 15, and to various governors through May, AG to Gaines, May 18 and 22, Jun 20, SW to Gaines, May 8, SW Order, Jun 2, 1846, and scores of other documents, *The Calling of Volunteers;* ZT to AG, May 20, 1846, in Butler, *Documentary History,* 84; SW to ZT, May 23, 1846, MWC, 263; SW to AG, LR, and AG to various commanders, May 9 and 10, 1846, LS, RG 94; Silver, *Gaines,* 263–67; Kreidberg and Henry, *History of Military Mobilization,* 74–78; Weigley, *History,* 183; Hill, *Minute Man,* 22–25.

9. Moore's journal and letters in Butler, *Eutaw Rangers,* 9–22; Johannsen, *To Halls,* 56; Risch, *Quartermaster Support,* 263; ZT to AG, Jun 3, 1846, MWC, 306.

10. Ballentine quoted Johannsen, *To Halls,* 30–31; Joseph Jefferson quoted Hamilton, *Zachary Taylor Soldier,* 194–95.

11. Henderson to ZT, May 3, 1846, quoted Utley, *Lone Star,* 61, see also 61–63.

12. Utley, *Lone Star,* 63; Kendall, *Dispatches;* Reid, *Scouting Expeditions;* Wilkins, *Highly Irregular;* Spurlin, *Texas Volunteers.*

13. Chamberlain, *My Confession,* 39; Smith, *Chile,* 294–95; Nackman, "Making of Texan"; Johannsen, *To Halls,* 37–38.

14. Rankin Dillworth diary, nd, and ZT to R. C. Wood, Jul 7, 1846, both quoted Utley, *Lone Star,* 63; Johanssen, *To Halls,* 37–38.

15. Furber, *Twelve Months,* 419.

16. Thomas to Bliss, Jun 1 and 11, 1846, LR, RG 94; ZT to AG, Sep 9, and Jesup memorandum, nd, 1846, MWC, 549–60, 557–58; QDP 2:117–19; Risch, *Quartermaster Support,* 257–58, 267–70.

17. Weigley, *American Way,* 72–73.

18. Mullins, "British Press"; Black to SS, May 21, 1846, CD, RG 59; SWM 1:183–84; Kreidberg and Henry, *History of Mobilization,* 70–71; McCoy, *Polk,* 119–20.

19. The financing of the war is summarized in SWM 2:255–67.

20. John Blount Robertson in Smith and Judah, *Chronicles,* 5–6; recruiter quoted Leckie, *Wars* 1:337; editorials quoted McDonald, *Mexican War,* 47; Miguel A. González Quiroga, "The War Between the United States and Mexico," in Francaviglia and Richmond, *Dueling Eagles,* 91–102; Johannsen, *To Halls,* 10.

21. Sumner quoted Curti, *American Peace,* 5; Melville in Cunliff, *Soldiers,* 69–70; Millis, *Arms and Men,* 91; Filler, *Crusade,* 183–84; Habenstreit, *Men Against War,* ch. 2; DeWitt, "Crusading for Peace."

22. Merk, *Manifest Destiny,* 94–96; Merk, "Dissent in the Mexican War," in Morison and others, *Dissent,* part 1; Haun, "Whig Abolitionists."

23. John R. Collins, "Sectionalism and Political Fragmentation," in Faulk and Stout, *Mexican War,* 67–76.

24. Smith and Judah, *Chronicles,* 9–10.

25. Eisenhower, *Agent,* 223–25.

26. QDP 1:400–1.

27. SW to governors, May 15–29, 1846, LS, RG 107; WS to heads of staff departments, May 15, 1846, MWC, 546–47; SW Memoranda, May 18 and Jun 3, 1846, LS, RG 94; Kreidberg and Henry, *History of Mobilization,* 75–76.

28. NPD, 95–97.

29. WS' plans include WS to ZT, May 18, 1846, MWC, 446, asking for ZT's advice, and revised in WS to SW, May 25, 1846, *The Calling of Volunteers,* 10–12; Clary and Whitehorne, *Inspectors General,* 49n, 94–96, 108–10, 150; Weigley, *History,* 129–30.

30. WS to SW, May 21 and 25, and SW to WS, May 25, 1846, *The Calling of Volunteers,* 5–9; QDP 1:408–9, 412–16, 419–21, 425; WS, *Memoirs* 2:384–85; NPD, 99–105; SWM 1:198–99; BMW, 73–74.

31. NPD, 105; SW to Wool, May 13, 1846, quoted BMW, 160 n. 1; WS to SW, May 27, 1846, *The Calling of Volunteers,* 14–17; AG to Wool, Jun 11, 1846, Butler, *Documentary History,* 87; Baylies, *Narrative;* Hughes, *Memoir Descriptive.*

32. BMW, 74–75; 9 Stat. 17–18.

33. NPD, 98–99.

34. NPD, 106–9; QDP 1:495–96; SN to Commodore Pacific Squadron, May 13 and 15, Jun 8, and Jul 12, 1846, MWC, 233–39.

35. Moorhead, *New Mexico's Royal Road,* 156; AG to Major Richard B. Lee, Aug 31, 1845, LS, and SWK to SW, Mar 4, 1846, LR, RG 94; Clarke, *Stephen Watts Kearny.*

36. Grant, *Memoirs,* 21; Magoffin, *Down Santa Fe Trail,* 106–7, 132–33; *Matamoros American Flag,* Jul 27, 1846, quoted Henry, *Story,* 123–24; corn liquor dialogue quoted DeVoto, *Year,* 236–37; SWK, Report of a Summer Campaign to the Rocky Mountains . . . in 1845, ARSW 1846, 211ff; Goetzmann, *Exploration,* 250–51; Frazier, 234–35; BMW, 130–31.

37. QDP 1:396; SW to Edwards and to Howard, both May 13, 1846, LS, RG 107; SW to SWK, May 14, 1846, *Correspondence with General Taylor,* 235; AG to SWK, May 13 and 14, 1846, LS, RG 94; Oliva, *Soldiers,* 57.

38. Oliva, *Soldiers,* 58; SWM 1:289; Bieber, *Journal of a Soldier,* 28–29.

39. NPD, 10, 66; QDP 1:439, 443, 473; SW to SWK, Jun 3, 1846, *California and New Mexico,* 236–39; WS to C. Q. Tompkins, Jun 20, 1846, MWC, 245–46; Bloom, "New Mexico Viewed"; Goetzmann, *Exploration,* 52; SWM 1:341; BMW, 169.

40. NPD, 106–7; QDP 1:429, 438–39; WS to SWK, May 31, 1846, MWC, 241–42; Clarke, *Stephen Watts Kearny,* 101–15.

41. SW to Edwards, Jun 2 and 3, and to Price, Jun 3, 1846, *Report of the Secretary of War as to the Employment of Any Individual,* 2–4; QDP 1:429–39, 443–46, 473; NPD, 108–9 (JKP quotation); Edwards to SW, Aug 11, 1846, in Golder, *March,* 97–99, see also 75–88; Tyler, *Concise History,* 111–12; Roberts, *Mormon Battalion,* 8–11; Cooke, *Journal of the March.*

42. SW to SWK, Jun 3 and 4, 1846, *Correspondence with General Taylor,* 239–42.

43. SW to SWK and to Wool, both Jun 18, 1846, *Correspondence with General Taylor,* 240–41; SW to PUS, Apr 1, and Magoffin to SW, Apr 4, 1849, in Twitchell, *Conquest of Santa Fe,* 52–66; DeVoto, *Year,* 256–59; Benton, *Thirty Years* 2:683; SWM 1:289. SW to SWK, Jun 18, 1846, is also in Magoffin, *Down Santa Fe Trail,* 263–64.

44. Magoffin family history summarized in introduction to Magoffin, *Down Santa Fe Trail.*

45. Ibid., 2–3, 11–12.

46. SWK to AG, May 28, and to SW, Jun 15, 1846, LR, RG 94; SW to SWK, May 27, 1846, *Correspondence with General Taylor,* 236.

47. SWK to G. T. Thomas, Jun 4, to AG, Jun 5, and to Captain Benjamin D. Moore

(commanding the dragoons), Jun 5 and 6, 1846, LR, RG 94; Journal of Abraham R. Johnston in Bieber, *Marching,* 73.

48. Army of the West Orders 4, Jun 27, and SWK to AG, Jun 29, 1846, LR, RG 94; SWM 1:286; SWK to Allen, Jun 19, 1846, *Correspondence with General Taylor,* 236; Risch, *Quartermaster Support,* 249, 277–83; ARQMG 1847, 545; Bancroft, *History of Arizona and New Mexico,* 409; Clarke, *Stephen Watts Kearny,* 108–9; Robinson, *Journal,* 1; Hughes, *Doniphan's Expedition,* 27, 81–82 (quotation).

49. Clarke, *Stephen Watts Kearny,* 110, 114; quotation in Edwards, *Campaign in New Mexico,* 6.

50. Clarke, *Original Journals,* 67–72; Bieber, *Journal,* 170–95; Edwards, *Campaign in New Mexico,* 36–45; Hughes, *Doniphan's Expedition,* 19–21 (quotations), 58–79; Traas, *From Golden Gate.*

51. Hughes, *Doniphan's Expedition,* 23.

CHAPTER 9

1. QDP 2:119, 181, 250, 393–94; Halleck quoted Millis, *American Military Thought,* 136n; Weed, *Autobiography,* 571–73; Hamilton, *Zachary Taylor Soldier,* 198–99.

2. Callcott, *Santa Anna,* 231–34; Rives, *United States and Mexico* 2:233–36; QDP 2:290.

3. SS to Minister of Foreign Relations, Jul 17, 1846, MDC 8:193; PUS to President of the Senate, Aug 4, 1846, RMP 5:2307; QDP 2:75–77; Sellers, *Polk,* 431–32.

4. SWM 1:486 n. 27; Commodore Home Squadron to SN, Aug 16, 1846, in *Niles' National Register,* Jan 22, 1848, and in Butler, *Documentary History,* 188.

5. Ramírez, *México During War,* 71; *Mexico City Monitor Republicano,* Aug 25, 1846, quoted SWM 1:488 n. 38.

6. Callcott, *Santa Anna,* 237–38; ALSA, *Pronunciamiento,* MWC, 776–85; coverage of the day's events in *Vera Cruz El Indicador,* Aug 16, 1846, quoted SWM 1:219.

7. SWM 1:487 n. 33; ALSA, *Las Guerras,* 218; Semmes, *Service Afloat,* 117–20; Rives, *United States and Mexico* 2:242–46; Manuel Crecencio Rejón to SS, Aug 31, 1846, ARSS 1846, 43.

8. QDP 2:104–5.

9. PUS to House and Senate, Aug 8, 1846, RMP 5:2309–10; BMW, 77–78; Hamilton, *Prologue,* ch. 1–5.

10. Merk, *Manifest Destiny,* 94–96; Merk, "Dissent in the Mexican War," in Morison and others, *Dissent,* part 1; Haun, "Whig Abolitionists"; John R. Collins, "Sectionalism and Political Fragmentation," in Faulk and Stout, *Mexican War,* 67–76; *National Intelligencer,* Nov 7, 1846, quoted SWM 2:269.

11. Josefina Zoraida Vázquez, "Causes of the War with the United States," translated by Douglas W. Richmond, in Francaviglia and Richmond, *Dueling Eagles,* 41–65; SWM 1:438 n. 31; Ruiz, *Triumphs,* 205–19.

12. Josefina Zoraida Vázquez, "War and Peace with the United States," in Meyer and Beezley, *Oxford History,* 339–70; Hanighen, *Santa Anna,* 203–4; Scheina, *Santa Anna,* 49; Vigil y Robles, *Invasión,* 19; Callcott, *Santa Anna,* 237–47; Callcott, *Church and State,* 182–91; SWM 1:213–19, 485 n. 25, 2:3–14.

13. Levinson, *Wars Within,* 50–54; *Ecos,* 61.

14. Semmes quoted Morison, *Old Bruin,* 182; Commodore Home Squadron to SN, Jul 28, 1846, Home Squadron Letters, RG 45; Scheina, "Seapower"; Bancroft, *History of Mexico,* 5:490n.

15. Parker, *Recollections,* 65–66; Cardenas de la Peña, *Semblanza* 1:125–26; Roa Bárcena, *Recuerdos* 1:249–52; Toro, *Compendia,* 449–50; Commodore Home Squadron to SN, Jul 30 and Aug 10, 1846, Home Squadron Letters, RG 45; Bauer, *Surfboats,* 34–35; SWM 2:197–99; Conner to wife, Jun 26, Jul 3, and Sep 4, 1846, cited BMW, 113–14.

16. BMW, 114.

17. ZT to Editor, New Lisbon, Ohio, *Palladium,* Jul 21, 1846, Butler, *Documentary History,* 89.

18. ZT to AG (two letters), Jul 2, 1846, MWC 155–58, 331.

19. QDP 3:5, 16–17; SW to ZT, Jul 9, 1846, MWC, 329–32; Sellers, *Polk,* 430.

20. ZT to SW, Aug 1, 1846, MWC, 336–38.

21. Whiting to QMG, Aug 28, 1846, quoted Risch, *Quartermaster Support,* 271–72, see also 253–73; ZT to AG, Jul 22, Army of Occupation Orders 93, Jul 30, ZT to SW, Sep 1, and Whiting to QMG, Nov 30, 1846, all MWC, 398–401, 558, 686; ZT to AG, Sep 1, 1846, Butler, *Documentary History,* 91; Hamilton, *Zachary Taylor Soldier,* 199–201; Nichols, *Zach Taylor's,* 183–84; Foos, *Short Offhand,* 99–100.

22. ZT to AG, Aug 8, 1846, MWC, 408; Henry, *Campaign Sketches,* 120; Brooks, *Complete History,* 163–64; Lewis, *Captain Sam Grant,* 162; Leckie, *Wars* 1:341; Henry, *Story,* 86–90, 139; Smith, *Company A,* 5–6; McCaffrey, *Army,* 50–51 and ch. 4; Butler, *Eutaw Rangers,* 86; Thomas R. Irey, "Soldiering, Suffering, and Dying," in Faulk and Stout, *Mexican War,* 113; SWM 1:211–12; BMW, 88–89.

23. Reid, *Scouting Expeditions,* 78–82, 96–102; Utley, *Lone Star,* 64–65; Webb, *Texas Rangers.* 95–99.

24. ZT to AG, Sep 3 and 12, Whiting to QMG, Sep 3, Army of Occupation Orders 98, 102, 108, 109, 112, 113, Aug 17–Sep 4, Special Order 124, Aug 19, 1846, all MWC, 417–22, 500–4, 608–18; Henry, *Campaign Sketches,* 152; Webb, *Texas Rangers,* 101–2; Utley, *Lone Star,* 65–68; BMW, 89.

25. Balbontín, *Invasión,* 10–11, 24; Ramsey, *Other Side,* 64; Roa Bárcena, *Recuerdos* 1:90–91; ALSA to Ministro de Guerra y Marina, Sep 26, 1846, in Smith, "Letters of Santa Anna," 364–65.

26. NPD, 106; AG to Wool, Jun 11, 1846, MWC, 328; Wool to Bliss, Jul 24, 1846, LR, RG 94; Eisenhower, *So Far,* 155–57; Thomas, *Robert E. Lee,* 113–18; Chamberlain, *My Confession,* 35; Brown, "Mexican War Experience"; Wallace, *Life and Letters,* 14–19.

27. Harney to Bliss, Jul 27, Aug 12 and 15, ZT to AG, Jul 29, and Wool to ZT, Sep 15, 1846, all LR, RG 94; Reavis, *Life and Military Services,* 154–55.

28. Wool to AG, Sep 2 and 3, and to ZT, Aug 18 and Sep 15, 1846, LR, RG 94, and MWC, 426; Chamberlain, *My Confession,* 38–43; Brown, "Mexican War Experiences"; Hughes, *Memoir Descriptive,* 6; SWM 1:267–70; Wool quoted BMW, 146.

29. Lewis, *Captain Sam Grant,* 161, 168; Leckie, *Wars* 1:340–41.

30. Army of Occupation Orders 62, May 17, 1846, MWC, 489; Kurtz, "First Regiment of Georgia Volunteers"; *Niles' Weekly Register,* Jul 25, 1846, quoted BMW, 83.

31. Johannsen, *To Halls,* 65–67, WS quoted 42; McClellan quoted DeVoto, *Year,* 236; Irey, "Soldiering, Suffering, and Dying."

32. ZT to AG, Jun 18, 1846, LR, RG 94; ZT to AG, Jul 1 and 16, Army of Occupation Orders 92, Jul 21, and Special Order 126, Aug 22, 1846, MWC, 315–18, 495–96, 524–25; Henry, *Campaign Sketches,* 152; Clary and Whitehorne, *Inspectors General,* 177–80; Johnston, *Life of Johnston,* 135–36; Foos, *Short Offhand,* 87–89; Utley, *Lone Star,* 64; Roland, *Albert Sidney Johnston,* ch. 8.

33. Henry, *Story,* 88–91; Winders, *Mr. Polk's Army,* 136–38, 174–76.

34. Henry, *Campaign Sketches,* 157–58.

35. Ruxton, *Adventures,* 144; Smith and Judah, *Chronicles,* 403; Johannsen, *To Halls,* 34.

36. SW to ZT, Jul 9, 1846, MWC, 157; see also Levinson, *Wars Within,* 68–69.

37. Quoted DeVoto, *Year,* 235–36.

38. Quoted McCaffrey, *Army,* 126. See also Oates, *Vision of Glory,* ch. 2, reprinted as "*Los Diablos Tejanos:* The Texas Rangers," in Faulk and Stout, *Mexican War,* 120–36.

39. Hogan, *Irish Soldiers,* 140–49; WS quoted Elliott, *Winfield Scott,* 448.

40. Foos, *Short Offhand,* 83–84; McCaffrey, *Army,* 126–28; Johannsen, *To Halls,* 34–39; quotation in Hughes, *Memoir Descriptive,* 44.

CHAPTER 10

1. Beck, *New Mexico,* 120–21; Richards, "From Traders to Traitors?"; LeCompte, "Armijo's Family"; Tyler, "Gringo Views"; Tyler, "Governor Armijo's Moment of Truth"; Ruxton, *Adventures,* 118; Horgan, *Great River,* 572–73.

2. Álvarez quoted SWM 1:289–90; Lavender, *Bent's Fort,* 269–73; Tyler, "Governor Armijo's Moment of Truth."

3. Edwards, *Campaign in New Mexico,* 8–9.

4. Quoted Henry, *Story,* 126–27.

5. Hughes, *Doniphan's Expedition,* 27.

6. All quoted Henry, *Story,* 125–26.

7. Hughes, *Doniphan's Expedition,* 30, 34–35.

8. SW to Governor Edwards, Jul 18, 1846, LS, RG 107; AG to James Shields, Jul 18, 1846, LS, RG 94; QDP 2:31; Clarke, *Stephen Watts Kearny,* 121.

9. Cooke, *Conquest,* 2–4.

10. Lavender, *Bent's Fort,* passim, especially 275–78.

11. Hughes, *Doniphan's Expedition,* 33; Henry, *Story,* 129.

12. SWK, A Proclamation to the Citizens of New Mexico, Jul 31, 1846, MWC, 168.

13. Hughes, *Doniphan's Expedition,* 32.

14. Sloat to Montgomery, Jul 6 and 7, 1846, ARSN 1847, 1014–15; Sloat to SN, Jul 31, 1846, and enclosures including proclamation, MWC, 258–63; Neasham, "Raising Flag"; Sherman, *Life of Sloat,* 74–78; Bancroft, *History of California* 5:230–35; Bauer, *Surfboats,* 149–54; Ames, "Horse Marines." Sources on the conquest of California include D. E. Livingston-Little, "U.S. Military Forces in California," in Faulk and Stout, *Mexican War,* 156–62; Alcaraz, 353–61; Ramsey, *Other Side,* 405–14; Howarth, *To Shining,* 161–63; and Grivas, *Military Governments;* Moyano Pahissa, *La Resistencia.*

15. Grivas, *Military Governments,* 83; Bancroft, *History of California* 5:231–33; Ames, "Horse Marines."

16. Montgomery to Commodore Pacific Squadron, Jul 9 and 11, Proclamation to the Inhabitants of Yerba Buena, Jul 9, Lieutenant J. S. Misroon to Montgomery, Jul 9, and

Lieutenant J. W. Rever to Montgomery, Jul 11, 1846, ARSN 1847, 1015–22; Cutts, *Conquest,* 118; BMW, 171–72.

17. Montgomery to Commodore Pacific Squadron, Jul 11 and 20, 1846, ARSN 1847, 1019–20; Adams, "English Interest"; Cutts, *Conquest,* 119; Sherman, *Life of Sloat,* 81.

18. Bancroft, *History of California* 5:252–53; BMW, 172.

19. JCF, *Memoirs* 1:530–32; Gillespie to SN, Jul 25, 1846, and Feb 16, 1847, in Ames, "Gillespie"; Bancroft, *History of California* 5:247–48; Utley, *Life,* 248–49; Reverend Walter Colton and Purser Rodman M. Price quoted Estergreen, *Kit Carson,* 146–47.

20. Sloat to SN, Jul 31, 1846, MWC, 258–60; RFS to SN, Feb 18, 1848, ARSN 1848, 1037–38; Bauer, *Surfboats,* 160–61; Sherman, *Life of Sloat,* 85.

21. RFS to JCF, Jul 22, 1846, with officer commissions, RFS Letter Book, RG 45; RFS to JCF, Jul 13, 1846, *Proceedings of the Court Martial,* 17; BMW, 173; Utley, *Life,* 248.

22. RFS proclamation, Jul 31, 1846, ARSN 1849, 31–33; Bauer, *Surfboats,* 277; Bancroft, *History of California* 5:257–59; BMW, 174; DeVoto, *Year,* 174.

23. RFS to JCF, Jul 23, 1846, *Proceedings of Court Martial,* 175; Bancroft, *History of California* 5:262–63, 272–73; exchanges between Sloat and Castro and RFS and Castro, MWC, 1010–20; SWM 1:337; Richman, *California,* 319; BMW, 175–76; Frémont, *Memoirs,* 1:563–66; Utley, *Life,* 248–49.

24. RFS proclamations, Aug 15–22, 1846, *Occupation of Mexican Territory,* 107–10; RFS to SN, Feb 18, 1848, ARSN 1848, 1037–54; RFS to PUS, Aug 26 and Nov 30, 1846, RFS Letter Book, RG 45; RFS testimony, *Proceedings of Court Martial,* 109–10.

25. RFS proclamation, Aug 19, 1846, ARSN 1846, 670–71; SN to Commodore Pacific Squadron, Dec 24, 1846, ARSN 1847, 1304.

26. RFS to Hull and to DuPont, both Aug 20, 1846, ARSN 1846, 670–71; Gerhard, "Baja California"; Bancroft, *History of North Mexican States* 2:665; BMW, 344.

27. RFS circular, Sep 1, General Order, Sep 2, and RFS to Gillespie, Aug 31, 1846, *Commodore Stockton's Dispatches,* 7–18; RFS to JCF, Aug 24, and JCF's commission, Sep 2, 1846, *Proceedings of Court Martial,* 109–10; SWM 1:338; Bancroft, *History of California* 5:290.

28. RFS to PUS, Aug 26, 1846, RFS Letter Book, RG 45, quoted Utley, *Life,* 249–50.

29. Ricketts, *Mormon Battalion,* 1–9, 11–63; Tyler, *Concise History,* 138–44; Bliss, "Journal"; Golder, *March;* 147–71; Bigler, "Extracts"; Steele, "Extracts"; Cooke, *Journal of the March,* preface.

30. Bieber, *Journal of a Soldier,* 244–45; Richardson, *Journal,* 9–22. Biographies of Price include Shalhope, *Sterling Price,* and Castel, *General Sterling Price.*

31. SWK to AG, and to Armijo, both Aug 1, 1846, LR, RG 94; Keleher, *Turmoil,* 6, 11–13; Magoffin, *Down Santa Fe Trail,* 84.

32. Boundless solitude quoted Henry, *Story,* 129–30; Henry Turner to Wife, Aug 5, 1846, in Clarke, *Original Journals,* 137 (sick and tired), see also 67–72; Bieber, *Journal of a Soldier,* 170–95; Emory, *Notes,* 15–32; Edwards, *Campaign,* 36–45; Magoffin, *Down Santa Fe Trail,* 78–79; Cooke, *Conquest,* 13–14.

33. Armijo Proclamation, Aug 8, 1846, in Butler, *Documentary History,* 123; Keleher, *Turmoil,* 10–11; Bancroft, *History of Arizona and New Mexico,* 413; Twitchell, *History of Military Occupation,* 60–63; Cooke, *Conquest,* 7–34; Tyler, "Governor Armijo's Moment."

34. Bancroft, *History of Arizona and New Mexico*, 413; Twitchell, *History of Military Occupation*, 60–63; Clarke, *Stephen Watts Kearny*, 133; Cooke, *Conquest*, 7–34, quote at 32; Keleher, *Turmoil*, Lamar, *Far Southwest*, 60–62; Tyler, "Governor Armijo's Moment."

35. On whether Armijo sold out his province, see Tyler, "Governor Armijo's Moment"; Lavender, *Bent's Fort*, 281–83; SWM 1:516 n. 13; and sources in previous note.

36. Edwards, *Campaign in New Mexico*, 20; soldier quoted Henry, *Story*, 130.

37. Sides, *Blood and Thunder*, 1–2.

38. SWK's proclamation is in Clarke, *Stephen Watts Kearny*, 135, and Emory, *Notes*, 27.

39. Edwards, *Campaign in New Mexico*, 23; Armijo to SWK, Aug 16, 1846, quoted Lamar, *Far Southwest*, 62. Armijo was tried for cowardice and desertion, but was acquitted. He died in Limitar, New Mexico, in 1853. Magoffin, *Down Santa Fe Trail*, 96n.

40. Vigil quoted Bloom, "New Mexico as Viewed"; soldiers quoted McCaffrey, *Army*, 151; Keleher, *Turmoil*, 12–13.

41. SWK proclamations and Vigil replies, MWC, 120–21; Twitchell, *Military Occupation*, 73–75; SWM 1:295–96; Keleher, *Turmoil*, 13–16; Horgan, *Centuries*, 195–226; Butler, *Documentary History*, 124; Twitchell, *Old Santa Fe*, 245–74; Clarke, *Original Journals*, 74.

42. Edwards, *Campaign in New Mexico*, 24–26; Winders, *Mr. Polk's Army*, 121, 173.

43. SWK to AG, Aug 25, 1846, MWC, 121–22; Butler, *Documentary History*, 125.

44. Quoted Weber, *Mexican Frontier*, 275.

45. Ibid., 24–25.

46. *Petition of the People of New Mexico* (1848); *Communication of R. H. Weightman* (1850); Bent quoted Lamar, *Far Southwest*, 54–56, 64–66; Lane quoted Bieber, "Letters of Lane," 198.

47. Quoted Lamar, *Far Southwest*, 54–55.

48. Ibid., 279–82; ARSW 1847, 520–26.

49. Amar, *America's Constitution*, 359–63; Weber, *Mexican Frontier*, 141–42; Kraemer, "Origins and Early Development"; González, *Refusing the Favor*.

50. Quoted McCaffrey, *Army*, 67.

51. Emory, *Notes*, 98–99; Goetzmann, *Army Exploration*, 109–52.

52. ARSW 1847, 30, 54, 70; Lamar, *Far Southwest*, 66; Bancroft, *History of Arizona and New Mexico*, 418; Utley, *Frontiersmen*, 78–80; Bender, "Frontier Defense."

53. Charles Bent to CIA, Nov 10, 1846, and related documents in *California and New Mexico*; ARSW 1849 pt. 1, 91–94 (quotation), pt. 2, 999–1000; Bender, *March of Empire*, 21; Utley, *Frontiersmen*, 81–83; Bender, "Frontier Defense."

54. On the Navajos, see Bailey and Bailey, *History of Navajos*, in particular 11–21.

55. Wallace and Hoebel, *Comanches*, 8, 39, 288–90; Fehrenbach, *Comanches*, 221–26.

56. Weber, *Mexican Frontier*, 94–98, 212–13; Utley, *Frontiersmen*, 83–84.

57. Worcester, *Apaches*, 46–47.

CHAPTER 11

1. ALSA to Ministro de Guerra y Marina, Sep 26, 1846, Smith, "Letters," 366; Jones, *Santa Anna*, 109; Callcott, *Santa Anna*, 243; SWM 1:223, 274–77; Ripley, *War* 1:363.

2. NPD, 144–45; WS to SW, Sep 12, and SW to WS, Sep 14, 1846, MWC, 372–73.

3. QDP 2:147–49; SW to ZT, and to Patterson, Sep 22, AG to Patterson, Sep 28, and

SN to Conner, Sep 22, 1846, MWC, 341–43, 373–74, 472–73; SS to Minister of Foreign Relations of Mexico, Sep 26, 1846, BMW, 254 n. 3; Conner to SN, Oct 7, 1846, Home Squadron Letters, RG 45; Patterson entry in Heitman; Clary, *Fortress America,* 45–46; ARSW 1846, 56–57; ARSW 1847, 67; ARCE 1847, 594–96; Prucha, "Distribution."

4. Patterson entry in Heitman; Frazier, 321; Waugh, *Class of 1846,* 80.

5. Miguel A. González Quiroga, "The War Between the United States and Mexico," in Francaviglia and Richmond, *Dueling Eagles,* 91–102, Manuel Flores letter, Sep 6, 1846, in state archives, quoted 98–99; Cossío, *Historia de Nuevo León,* ch. 6. Sources on the Monterey campaign include the reports of ZT and his officers with ZT to AG, Sep 25, 1846, MWC, 345–50; ZT to AG and enclosures, Oct 9, 1846, ARSW 1846, 83–102; Ampudia, *Manifesto* and *El ciudadano;* Balbontín, *Invasión,* 24–25; Brooks, *Complete History,* 174–89; Henry, *Story,* 138–55; BWM, 81–105; SWM 1:237–60, 497–506; Duncan, "Medical History"; Ramsey, *Other Side,* 62–80; Alcaraz, 52–66; *Ecos,* 70–75; Grant, *Memoirs,* 55–61; Hamilton, *Zachary Taylor Soldier,* 204–16; Henry, *Campaign Sketches,* 189–216; Lavender, *Climax,* 102–20; Valades, *Breve Historia,* 131–35; Vigil, *Invasión,* 21–22; Webb, *Texas Rangers,* 105–7; Utley, *Lone Star,* 65–74; Eisenhower, *So Far,* 117–43; Bauer, *Zachary Taylor,* 177–85; Wheelan, *Invading Mexico,* 179–203; Balbontín, "Siege of Monterey." ZT to AG, Sep 22, 23, and 25, 1846, are also in Butler, *Documentary History,* 93–96.

6. Ramsey, *Other Side,* 63–64; Roa Bárcena, *Recuerdos,* 1:90–92; Ampudia Proclamations, Aug 31 and Sep 15, 1846, MWC, 420–26; Proclamations of Aug 4, Sep 14 and 15, 1846, BMW, 104 n. 31; citizen quoted *Ecos,* 70.

7. The units of the Mexican army there are listed in Chartrand, *Santa Anna's Mexican Army,* 55, and Frazier, 274. On the San Patricios, see Hogan, *Irish Soldiers,* 43, 57–59, and Finke, "Organization and Uniforms." U.S. deserters made up less than a third of the corps at this time.

8. ZT to AG, Sep 1, 3, and 12, 1846, Army of Occupation General Orders 115, 119, 120, Sep 11–18, 1846, and QMG to SW, Dec 5, 1846, MWC, 417–21, 504–5, 557–60; Brooks, *Complete History,* 169–70; Valades, *Breve Historia,* 131; Balbontín, *Invasión,* 25; Ramsey, *Other Side,* 67; Webb, *Texas Rangers,* 102; Utley, *Lone Star,* 64–67; Holland, "Diary of a Texas Volunteer."

9. Johannsen, *To Halls,* 80; Holland, "Diary of a Texas Volunteer," 23–25; Utley, *Lone Star,* 67–68, including Ohioan quotation; BMW, 93.

10. Hill in Hughes and Johnson, *Fighter,* 23; Worth entry in Heitman; Frazier, 484–85.

11. Mexican account in *Ecos,* 71; Worth quoted BMW, 94; Utley, *Lone Star,* 68–69.

12. Johannsen, *To Halls,* 137, an account drawn entirely from U.S. sources. This story circulated in ZT's army even during the Monterey battles. Henry, *Campaign Sketches,* 233–41.

13. BMW, Twiggs quoted 105 n. 34, ZT quoted 95.

14. Davis' role is covered in Strode, *Jefferson Davis,* 164–67.

15. Balbontín, "Siege of Monterey," 339; ibid., 166; Winders, *Mr. Polk's Army,* 121.

16. Balbontin, "Siege of Monterey," 348.

17. BMW, 96–97.

18. Booster quoted BMW, 99; a summary of explanations for this decision is at 105 n. 6.

19. Quoted SWM 1:258.

20. Alcaraz, excerpted *Ecos,* 71.

21. Smith and Judah, *Chronicles,* 90, from *Niles' National Register,* Dec 19, 1846.

22. Lyns, "Heroine Martyr." See also Johanssen, *To Halls,* 138; Ramsey, *Other Side,* 76–77.

23. The ZT–Ampudia correspondence and text of the capitulation accompany ZT to AG, Nov 8, 1846, MWC, 348–60. See also Hamilton, *Zachary Taylor Soldier,* 214–15; Rives, *United States and Mexico* 2:272–75.

24. ZT to Robert Wood, Sep 28, 1846, quoted BMW, 100.

25. SWM 1:494, 496; BMW, 100–1; Frazier, 272.

26. Grant, *Memoirs,* 61; Mississippi volunteer quoted Strode, *Jefferson Davis,* 169.

27. Alcaraz, excerpted *Ecos,* 75.

28. Cossio, *Historia de Nuevo León* 6:282–83; González Quiroga, "The War Between the United States and Mexico," 96; Ampudia, *El ciudadano.*

29. Nunnalee journal, Sep 28, 1846, in Butler, *Eutaw Rangers,* 89; Reid and Giddings quoted Utley, *Lone Star,* 73.

30. González Quiroga, "The War Between the United States and Mexico," 96; Henry, *Campaign Sketches,* 231–34; Ferrell, *Monterey Is Ours!,* passim.

31. Hughes and Johnson, *Fighter,* 28; Foos, *Short Offhand,* 121.

32. ZT to AG, Oct 6, and Ramírez to United States Commander, Nov 15, 1846, MWC, 430, 508; Giddings quoted Utley, *Lone Star,* 73.

33. ZT to AG, Oct 11, and SW to ZT, Nov 25, 1846, MWC, 408, 431; Smith, "American Rule."

34. Henry, *Campaign Sketches,* 233–41; private quoted SWM 2:230.

35. Henry, *Campaign Sketches,* 233–41.

36. Hughes, *Memoir Descriptive,* 31–35; González Quiroga, "The War Between the United States and Mexico," 97; Miguel A. González Quiroga, "Nuevo León ante la invasión norteamericana," in Herrera Serna, *México en guerra,* 425–71.

37. AMP 1847, 9–12.

38. Sonnichsen, *Pass of the North,* 110–12.

39. Army of the West Orders 16 and 20, Aug 25 and 30, 1846, LR, RG 94; SWK to AG, Sep 16, 1846, MWC, 175–76; Hughes, *Doniphan's Expedition,* 99–117; Clarke, *Stephen Watts Kearny,* 151–54; Cooke, *Conquest,* 49.

40. Frank Edwards quoted Clarke, *Stephen Watts Kearny,* 158.

41. Hughes, *Doniphan's Expedition,* 51; Worcester, *Apaches,* 44; Worcester, "Apaches in History."

42. Army of the West Orders 23 and Special Orders 7, both Aug 16, and SWK Proclamation, Oct 18, 1846, LR, RG 94; Hughes, *Doniphan's Expedition,* 128–30; Keleher, *Turmoil,* 23.

43. SWK Proclamation Aug 27, and SWK to AG, Sep 22, 1846, with Organic Law of the Territory of New Mexico, Laws for the Government of the Territory of New Mexico, and Appointment of Civil Officials, all MWC, 172–73, 195–229; Lamar, *Far Southwest,* 63–65; Thomas, *History of Military Government,* 101–5; Crane, *Desert Drums,* 293.

44. PUS to Speaker of the House, Dec 22, 1846, RMP 5:2356–57; QDP 2:281–82; SW to Price, Jun 11, 1847, *New Mexico and California,* 31–33; Thomas, *Military Government,* 106–12. The Kearny Code courts continued to function after the Code was abrogated. The Supreme Court declared them legitimate because they were ratified by the Congress when

it established the territorial government. *Leitensdorfer v. Webb,* 61 US (20 Howard) 176 (1857). See also Winthrop, *Military Law* 2:802–3.

45. ARSW 1847, 520; Lamar, *Far Southwest,* 63–68; Bender, *March of Empire,* 45; Frazier, "Purveyors."

46. SWK to AG, Aug 24 and Sep 16, 1846, MWC, 169, 175–76; Army of the West Orders 30, Sep 23, 1846, LR, RG 94; Hughes, *Doniphan's Expedition,* 126.

47. SWK to AG, Dec 12, 1846, ARSW 1847, 513–14; Emory, *Notes,* 30–31; Clarke, *Original Journals,* 76–124; Clarke, *Stephen Watts Kearny,* 163–94; Cooke, *Conquest,* 74.

48. RFS to SN, Sep 18 and Oct 1, 1846, *Commodore Stockton's Despatches,* 1–2, 13; RFS to SN, Feb 18, 1848, ARSN 1848, 1037–54; Bancroft, *History of California* 5:290.

49. RFS to Mervine, Sep 30, and to SN, Oct 1, 1846, *Commodore Stockton's Depatches,* 12–13; RFS to JCF, Sep 28, 1846, in Frémont, *Memoirs* 1:572–73.

50. Ramsey, *Other Side,* 40–8; SWK quoted Henry, *Story,* 210.

51. Alcaraz, excerpted *Ecos,* 102–3. Accounts of the California rebellion include *Ecos,* 102–5; Antonio Ríos Bustamante, "La resistencia popular en Alta California durante la guerra de 1846–1848," in Herrera Serna, *México en Guerra,* 117–30; Bancroft, *History of California* 5:306–9; JCF, *Memoirs* 1:570, 596–97 (critical of RFS); Bayard, *Sketch* (favorable to RFS); Colton, *Three Years,* 89–91 (the cautious view of a naval officer); Utley, *Life,* 254–55; Gillespie to SN, Feb 16, 1847, in Ames, "Gillespie"; Marti, *Messenger,* 77–83; Guinn, *History* 1:127; BMW, 183–84; SWM 1:338–39; Guinn, "Siege"; Romer, "Lean John"; Woodward, "Juan Flaco's Ride"; Carmen Lugo, "Life of a Rancher."

52. Flores Proclamation, Oct 1, 1846, *Commodore Stockton's Despatches,* 13–14, and in Butler, *Documentary History,* 153.

CHAPTER 12

1. Morison, *Old Bruin,* quotation at 187; Bauer, *Surfboats,* 44–45; Perry entry in Callahan.

2. QDP 2:60–61, 66, 125; BMW, 116.

3. SWM 2:280; Spencer, *Victor and Spoils,* 215–19; Wallace, "First Regiment"; Wallace, "Raising a Volunteer Regiment"; Campbell in Smith and Judah, *Chronicles,* 10.

4. Merk, "Dissent in the Mexican War," in Morison and others, *Dissent,* pt. 1; pamphlet quoted Habenstreit, *Men Against War,* 39; Adams to Albert Gallatin, Dec 26, 1846, quoted Bemis, *John Quincy Adams and Union,* 499–500.

5. THB, *Thirty Years* 2:693; Smith, *Magnificent Missourian,* 216; McCormac, *James K. Polk* 2:560.

6. QDP 2:181; NPD, 155–56; SW to ZT, Oct 13, 1846, MWC, 355–57.

7. ZT to Robert Wood, Dec 10, 1846, cited BMW, 375 n. 5; Bauer, *Zachary Taylor,* 217–19.

8. SW to Patterson, Oct 13, 1846, MWC, 358; JKP to Patterson, Oct 22, 1846, BMW, 254 n. 7.

9. WS, "Vera Cruz and Its Castle," MWC 1268–69; QDP 2:179–80, 195–97; SW to Dimond, Oct 27, 1846, LS, RG 107; McCormac, *James K. Polk* 2:451–52.

10. QDP 2:198–204; SW to ZT, Oct 22, 1846 (2 letters), MWC, 362–67; McCormac, *James K. Polk* 2:451–52.

11. QDP 2:204, 221–28; NPD, 163–65; SW to Patterson, Oct 28, 1846, MWC,

367–69; Spencer, *Victor and Spoils,* 160–61; Smith, *Magnificent Missourian,* 216; Chambers, *Old Bullion,* 309–10; Meigs, *Life of Benton,* 363–65; Rogers, *Thomas Hart Benton,* 238–40; MacPherson, "Controversy"; Eisenhower, *Agent,* 229–30.

12. ZT to AG, Oct 15 and Dec 14, 1846, MWC, 351–54, 381–82.

13. THB, *Thirty Years* 2:694–95; Eisenhower, *So Far,* 161–62; NPD, 167.

14. WS, "Vera Cruz and Its Castle—New Line of Operations, Thence Upon the Capital," Nov 12, and WS, Memorandum, Nov 16, 1846, MWC, 1271–74; QPD 2:232.

15. QDP 2:239–45; NPD, 168–71; WS, *Memoirs* 2:399–400.

16. QDP 2:243–46; WS to SW, Nov 19, 1846, MWC, 836; WS to SW, Feb 25, 1848, CSW, 3; WS, *Memoirs* 2:399.

17. AMP 1846, RMP 5:2321–56; McCormac, *James K. Polk* 2:456–59.

18. Debates are recorded in the *Journal* each of the House and Senate, and in *Congressional Globe,* 29 Cong 2 Sess (Dec 1846–Mar 1847). JKP's ruminations are in QDP 2:169–70, 362–71. The outstanding overview of the debates leading to the Compromise of 1850 is Hamilton, *Prologue.* See also Fuller, "Slavery Question," and Fuller, "Slavery Propaganda."

19. Both quoted SWM 2:4.

20. Ramsey, *Other Side,* 83–84, 88–89; Inocencio Noyola, "La Ciudad sitiada: San Luis Potosí ante la intervención norteamericana," in Herrera Serna, *México en guerra,* 543–64; Alessio Robles, *Saltillo,* 209.

21. Balbontín, *Invasión,* quoted Scheina, *Santa Anna,* 51; Ramsey, *Other Side,* 81–98; Olivera and Crété, *Life,* 162; Roa Bárcena, *Recuerdos* 1:126–27.

22. Callcott, *Santa Anna,* 248–49, 249n; Leckie, *Wars* 1:350; ALSA quoted SWM 2:9.

23. All quoted SWM 1:379.

24. Ramsey, *Other Side,* 86–92, 149–54; Rives, *United States and Mexico* 2:308–20.

25. ALSA quoted Scheina, *Santa Anna,* 53.

26. Callcott, *Santa Anna,* 249; organizational data in Ramsey, *Other Side,* 94.

27. Lieutenant William E. Hunt to Conner, Sep 7, and Conner to SN, Sep 12, 1846, Home Squadron Letters, RG 45; Neeser, *Statistical and Chronological History* 2:66, 312.

28. Quotations BMW, 116–17; Conner to SN, Oct 17, 1846, ARSN 1847, 630–31; Semmes, *Service Afloat,* 88; Parker, *Recollections,* 71–72; Riva Palacio, *México a través* 4:645; Trens, *Historia* 4:371–73; Roa Bárcena, *Recuerdos* 1:252–54; Hurtado y Nuño, "Ataque y defensa"; Cardenas, *Semblanza* 1:127–29; Bauer, *Surfboats,* 45–47.

29. Perry to Conner, Nov 3, 5, and 11, 1846, and enclosed reports, ARSN 1847, 632–39; Semmes, *Service Afloat,* 88–90; Parker, *Recollections,* 74; Roa Bárcena, *Recuerdos* 1:149–560; Mestre Ghigliazza, *Invasión,* 23–46; Ramsey, *Other Side,* 433–34; Morison, *Old Bruin,* 193–98; Bauer, *Surfboats,* 49–52; Dios Bonilla, *Historia marítima,* 284–85.

30. Morison, *Old Bruin,* 97–98; Bauer, *Surfboats,* 51–53; Neeser, *Statistical and Chronological History* 2:314–15.

31. QDP 2:147; SW to ZT, Sep 22, and ZT to AG, Oct 15, 1846, MWC, 341–43, 351–54; SN to Conner, Sep 27, 1847, Confidential Letters, RG 45; ALSA to Anastasio Parrodi, Oct 12, 1846, Smith, "Letters of Santa Anna," 371; Ramsey, *Other Side,* 99–113; Ripley, *War* 1:313.

32. Conner to SN, Nov 5, 11, and 24, and Dec 1, with enclosures, and Conner

Proclamation, Nov 15, 1846, ARSN 1846, 632–35; Bauer, *Surfboats,* 54–56; SWM 1:276–80; Ramsey, *Other Side* 103–5; Parrodi, *Memoria,* 4, 32–33; Morison, *Old Bruin,* 198–201.

33. Quoted McCaffrey, *Army,* 166.

34. Semmes, *Service Afloat,* 91; Parker, *Recollections,* 59–60.

35. Tattnall to Conner, Nov 22, 1846, ARSN 1847, 1174–75; Ramsey, *Other Side,* 105.

36. SN to Perry, Mar 27, 1847, MWC, 977–78; Semmes, *Service Afloat,* 91–92, 158; Parker, *Recollections,* 60.

37. Semmes to Commodore Home Squadron, Dec 10, and Commodore Home Squadron to SN, Dec 12, 1846, *Message from the Secretary of the Navy in Relation to the Loss of the United States Brig Somers,* 1–5; Semmes, *Service Afloat,* 94–95. On *Somers'* history, see Melton, *Hanging Offense.*

38. Perry to Conner, Dec 27, and Conner to SN, Dec 28, 1846, ARSN 1847, 1176–77; Morison, *Old Bruin,* 202–3.

39. Morison, *Old Bruin,* 202–6.

40. ZT to AG, Nov 26 and Dec 8, 1846, May to Bliss, Jan 2, Patterson to H. L. Scott, Jan 24, 1847, MWC 879–80; Smith, *Company A,* 19–20; Henry, *Campaign Sketches,* 262; Furber, *Twelve Months,* 383; Hamilton, *Zachary Taylor Soldier,* 229; Frazier, 462–63; *New York Herald,* Feb 6, 1847, quoted SWM 1:360.

41. Captain Sydenham Moore journal, Dec 20, 1846, Butler, *Eutaw Rangers,* 56.

42. Accounts of atrocities include Henry, *Story,* 174–75; Leckie, *Wars* 1:349; DeVoto, *Year,* 236; Foos, *Short Offhand,* 123–24, 142–43; Butler, *Eutaw Rangers,* 90–96; Hughes and Johnson, *Fighter,* 46; Smith and Judah, *Chronicles,* passim; Fulton, *Diary of Gregg,* 327–29; Levinson, *Wars Within,* 48.

43. Hughes, *Memoir Descriptive,* 43–44.

44. Utley, *Lone Star,* 74–75; Haven and Belden, *History of the Colt Revolver,* 272–96.

45. ZT to AG, Oct 15, MWC, 353; ZT to Edmund Gaines, Nov 5, 1846, quoted Eisenhower, *So Far,* 167n.

46. ZT to AG, Nov 3, and to ALSA, Nov 5, and ALSA to ZT, Nov 10, 1846, MWC, 358–59, 437–38; Henry, *Campaign Sketches,* 239; Hughes and Johnson, *Fighter,* 33.

47. ZT to AG, Nov 9 and 10, and SW to ZT, Oct 22, 1846, MWC, 361, 364, 374–75; Jenkins, *War,* 189–90.

48. WS to ZT, Sep 26, and ZT to Robert Wood, Nov 10, 1846, both quoted Eisenhower, *So Far,* 160; see also Eisenhower, *Agent,* 228.

49. ZT to AG, Nov 16 and 24, and Aguirre to ZT, Nov 16, 1846, MWC, 377–78, 436, 511; Henry, *Campaign Sketches,* 245–46.

50. Army of Occupation Orders 146 and 149, Nov 27 and Dec 2, 1846, MWC, 512–13; Henry, *Campaign Sketches,* 245–47, 254; Hughes and Johnson, *Fighter,* 47, 58.

51. Engelmann to Mama and Papa, Jan 2, 1847, Engelmann, "Second Illinois," 423–24.

52. Worth to daughter, Nov 17, 1846, quoted SWM 2:213.

53. SW to ZT, and WS to ZT, both Nov 25, 1846, MWC, 369–71, 373–74.

54. Jesup to Stanton, Nov 8, and to SW, Dec 3, 1846, quoted Risch, *Quartermaster Support,* 276.

55. Wool to AG, Sep 28, 1846, LR, RG 94; Risch, *Quartermaster Support,* 273–77. Sources on Wool's campaign include Buhoup, *Narrative;* Baylies, *Narrative;* Hughes, *Memoir*

Descriptive; Chamberlain, *My Confession;* Freeman, *R. E. Lee,* vol 1; Carleton, *Battle;* BMW, 145–51, SWM 1:298–314.

56. Wool order, Oct 9, 1846, BMW, 161 n. 11; Engelmann to Mama and Papa, Oct 13, 1846, Engelmann, "Second Illinois."

57. Chamberlain, *My Confession,* 68.

58. Wool to Castañeda, Oct 12, 1846, Wool Letter Book, RG 94; ibid., 51; Jenkins, *History of the War,* 186; Wallace, *Life and Letters,* 21; Buhoup, *Narrative,* 22–23, 31–32; Hughes, *Memoir Descriptive,* 6–7; Colonel John J. Hardin quoted BMW, 148.

59. Carleton, *Battle,* 166–69; Wallace, *Life and Letters,* 22; SWM 1:272.

60. Hughes, *Memoir Descriptive,* 18–26; Fulton, *Diary and Letters* 1:256–60; Carleton, *Battle,* 164; Baylies, *Campaign,* 13–16; Buhoup, *Narrative,* 30–102.

61. Buhoup, *Narrative,* 67–72; Wallace, *Life and Letters,* 25; Engelmann to Mama and Papa, Nov 7, 1846, Englemann, "Second Illinois," 407–8.

62. Chamberlain, *My Confession,* 73–74.

63. Ibid., 58.

64. Henry, *Campaign Sketches,* 241; quotations from Kenly, *Memoirs,* 167.

65. Wool to ZT, Nov 1 and 12, 1846, Baylies, *Campaign,* 16–17; Wool to AG, Nov 16, 1846, LR, RG 94; Buhoup, *Narrative,* 60; Chamberlain, *My Confession,* 61–63; BMW, 150, 161 n. 21.

66. Wool to Bliss, Nov 19, 1846, in Baylies, *Campaign,* 18–19; BMW, 150.

67. BMW, 150, citing officers to Wool, Nov 22, and Wool's gambling order, Nov 23, 1846; Hughes, *Memoir Descriptive,* 27–33; Baylies, *Campaign,* 19; Fulton, *Diary and Letters* 1:278–329; Wallace, *Life and Letters,* 29.

68. Wool to People of Parras, Dec 5, to ZT, Dec 16, 1846, and to AG, Jan 3 and 17, 1847, LR, RG 94; Fulton, *Diary and Letters* 1:298–99; Hughes, *Memoir Descriptive,* 41.

69. MWC, 385–90, 515; Baylies, *Narrative,* 23–24.

70. Jesup to SW, Jan 2, 1847, quoted BMW, 205.

CHAPTER 13

1. Quoted Ricketts, *Mormon Battalion,* 323 n. 1.

2. Description from Hughes, *Doniphan's Expedition,* 13, biographical sketch by Joseph G. Dawson III, vii–ix; Dawson, "Zealous for Annexation"; Dawson, "American Xenophon"; Johannsen, *To Halls,* 43; ibid.; Doniphan entry in Heitman; Frazier, 133.

3. Biographical summary in Ricketts, *Mormon Battalion,* 323 n. 2; Tyler, *Concise History,* 164; Cooke entry in Heitman; Cooke, *Conquest.*

4. Clarke, *Stephen Watts Kearny,* 166–75; Utley, *Life,* 251–52; Ruhlen, "Kearny's Route"; quotations in Sides, *Blood and Thunder,* 133.

5. Quoted Clarke, *Stephen Watts Kearny,* 184–85.

6. Ibid., 183–84; Captain A. R. Johnson quoted Worcester, *Apaches,* 43.

7. Turner quoted Clarke, *Stephen Watts Kearny,* 184–85.

8. SWK quoted ibid., 185.

9. Utley, *Life,* 254; Sides, *Blood and Thunder,* 144–47.

10. Ricketts, *Mormon Battalion,* 65; Hughes, *Doniphan's Expedition,* 143–44; Tyler, *Concise History,* 164; Golder, *March,* 171.

11. Cooke, *Conquest,* 91–93.

12. Adjutant quoted Ricketts, *Mormon Battalion,* 67–69; Cooke, *Conquest,* 90–92; Tyler, *Concise History,* 166–67; Bancroft, *History of Arizona and New Mexico,* 421; Roberts, *Mormon Battalion.*

13. Cooke, *Conquest,* 90–110; Ricketts, *Mormon Battalion,* 70–76, Guy M. Keysor quoted 78.

14. Cooke, *Conquest,* 103–4; Ricketts, *Mormon Battalion,* 85–90.

15. Cooke, *Conquest,* 131.

16. Ibid., 137; William Coray quoted Ricketts, *Mormon Battalion,* 90, Samuel H. Rogers quoted 91.

17. Ricketts, *Mormon Battalion,* 91–95, Boyle quoted 91; Roberts, *Mormon Battalion,* 46–48; Cooke, *Conquest,* 143–44, 145–46.

18. Ricketts, *Mormon Battalion,* 94–95.

19. Cooke, *Conquest,* 148; Coray quoted ibid., 96.

20. Ricketts, *Mormon Battalion,* 97–101, 324 n. 3; Sonnichsen, *Tucson,* 32–34.

21. Ricketts, *Mormon Battalion,* 103–29; Cooke, *Conquest,* 125–97; Cooke, "Journal of the March of the Mormon Battalion," in Bieber, *Exploring Southwestern Trails,* 67–240. The battalion was assigned mostly to civic construction duties in San Diego, then moved to Los Angeles, where the remaining 317 men were mustered out on July 16. Most went on to Salt Lake. Ricketts, *Mormon Battalion,* 131–60, 169–83.

22. Bailey and Bailey, *History of Navajos,* 18; Hughes, *Doniphan's Expedition,* 143–90; Richardson, *Journal,* 23–28; Bancroft, *History of Arizona and New Mexico,* 421–22; Sides, *Blood and Thunder,* 152–54.

23. Sonnichsen, *Mescaleros,* 65.

24. Magoffin, *Down Santa Fe Trail,* 152.

25. Boye, *Tales from the Journey;* ibid., entries for Sep–Dec, 1846; Hughes, *Doniphan's Expedition,* 129–30.

26. Sonnichsen, *Pass of North,* 112–13; Doniphan to AG, Mar 4, 1847, ARSW 1847, 497–98.

27. Vidal to Ponce, Dec 25, and Ponce to Vidal, Dec 26, 1846, in Gallaher, "Official Report"; Sonnichsen, *Pass of North,* 113.

28. Doniphan quoted Hughes, *Doniphan's Expedition,* 131. Sources for the Battle of Brazito include Doniphan to AG, Mar 4, 1847, ARSW 1847, 497–98; Gallaher, "Official Report"; Ramsey, *Other Side,* 169–71; Hughes, *Memoir Descriptive,* 259–69; Richardson, *Journal,* 46–48; Robinson, *Journal,* 65–67; Edwards, *Campaign in New Mexico,* 83–87; Cutts, *Conquest,* 77–78; Jenkins, *History,* 309–10; Hughes, *Doniphan's Expedition,* 132–34; Alcaraz, excerpted in *Ecos,* 91; Cooke, *Conquest,* 87–88; DeVoto, *Year,* 396; Lieutenant Christian H. Kribben to family, Dec 26, 1846, Butler, *Documentary History,* 127–28; Sonnichsen, *Pass of North,* 113–17; Mangum, "Battle of Brazito"; Haecker, "Brazito Battlefield."

29. Hughes, *Doniphan's Expedition,* 132.

30. Ibid.; Sonnichsen, *Pass of the North,* 115.

31. Gallaher, "Official Report"; Sonnichsen, *Pass of North,* 116–17.

32. Edwards, *Campaign in New Mexico,* 53–58.

33. Richardson, *Journal,* 48; Sonnichsen, *Pass of North,* 177–222; ibid., 65; Hughes, *Doniphan's Expedition,* 65. A "stand" is a complete set of arms for one soldier—musket, flint, strap, bayonet, rod, etc.

34. RFS to SN, Nov 23, 1846, *Commodore Stockton's Despatches,* 10; Utley, *Life,* 254–55; BMW, ch. 11.

35. Mervine to RFS, Oct 9 and 25, 1846, Pacific Squadron Letters, and Adjutant's Report, Oct 7 and 8, 1846, Area File, RG 45; Bancroft, *History of California* 5:304–5; Marti, *Messenger,* 87–90; Driver, "Carrillo's Flying Artillery."

36. Commodore Pacific Squadron to SN, Nov 23, 1846, and Pacific Squadron General Order, Oct 26, 1846, *Commodore Stockton's Despatches,* 10, 16–17; Commodore Pacific Squadron to SN, Feb 18, 1847, ARSN 1847, 1037–54; Colton, *Three Years,* 73–83, 98; Bryant, *What I Saw,* 332–33; Bancroft, *History of California* 5:304–5, 322, 358n, 367; Nevins, *Frémont,* 295; Captain Henry S. Turner to RFS, Dec 23, 1846, *Proceedings of the Court-Martial,* 190.

37. Roa Bárcena, *Recuerdos* 1:231; Bancroft, *History of California* 5:32021; Richmond, *California,* 329; Guinn, *History of California* 1:133; SWM 1:340–41; BMW, 198 n. 8.

38. Commodore Pacific Squadron to SN, Nov 23, 1846, *Commodore Stockton's Despatches,* 16–17; copy in Butler, *Documentary History,* 154–56.

39. SWK to RFS, Dec 2, and RFS to SWK, Dec 3, 1846, *Commodore Stockton's Despatches,* 26–27; RFS Testimony, *Proceedings of the Court-Martial,* 18; Clarke, *Stephen Watts Kearny,* 190–92; Woodward, "Lances"; Ames, "Doctor."

40. SWK to AG, Dec 12 and 13, 1846, ARSW 1847, 513–16; Turner to Stockton, Dec 6, 1846, *Commodore Stockton's Despatches,* 27–28; Gillespie to SN, Feb 16, 1847, in Ames, "Gillespie," 281–84; Roa Bárcena, *Recuerdos* 1:131–36; Emory, *Notes,* 105–9; Alcaraz, excerpted *Ecos,* 104; SWK Testimony, *Proceedings of the Court-Martial,* 47; Marti, *Messenger,* 95–100; Clarke, *Stephen Watts Kearny,* 195–220; Ames, "Doctor," Woodward, "Lances"; Bancroft, *History of California* 5:343–45; Utley, *Life,* 256–58; Simmons, *United States Marines,* 41–42.

41. Utley, *Life,* 256–59, Emory quoted 258; Sides, *Blood and Thunder,* 161–63. During the 1850s Beale supervised an experiment to introduce camels to the United States southwest. Faulk, *U.S. Camel Corps;* Lesley, *Uncle Sam's Camels.*

42. Commodore Pacific Squadron to SN, Feb 18, 1847, and Gillespie to SN, Feb 18, 1847, ARSN 1847, 1037–54, 1049; RFS Testimony, *Proceedings of the Court-Martial,* 188–89; SWK to AG, Dec 13, 1846, ARSW 1847, 513–16; RFS to Turner (two letters), Dec 7, 1846, RFS Letter Book, RG 45; Emory, *Notes,* 109–12; Bayard, *Sketch,* 109–12; Sides, *Blood and Thunder,* 163; Emory also quoted Utley, *Life,* 259.

43. BMW, 194.

44. Frémont, *Memoirs* 1:598–601; Colton, *Three Years,* 125; Bryant, *What I Saw,* 375–91; Bancroft, *History of California* 5:375–404.

45. SWK to RFS, Dec 22, 23, and 24, and RFS to SWK, Dec 23 and 24, 1846, LR, RG 94; RFS to SN, Feb 18, 1847, ARSN 1847, 1037–54; Gillespie to SN, Feb 16, 1847, in Ames, "Gillespie"; Hensley Statement, *California Claims,* 190.

46. Both quoted SWM 2:216–17; Utley, *Frontiersmen,* 84–85; Twitchell, *Military Occupation.*

47. All in Smith and Judah, *Chronicles,* 133–34.

48. Quoted Twitchell, *Old Santa Fe,* 275–76.

49. Worcester, *Apaches,* quotations at 44–45; Bailey and Bailey, *History of Navajos,* 18.

50. Bender, "Government Explorations"; Jackson, *Wagon Roads West,* 107–20;

Goetzmann, *Exploration and Empire,* 231–354; Goetzmann, *Army Exploration;* ARSW 1847, 496.

51. Price to AG, Feb 15, 1847, ARSW 1847, 520–26; Bent to SS, Dec 26, 1846, and Bent, Proclamation to the People of New Mexico, Jan 5, 1847, *New Mexico and California,* 17–25; Rea, *Sterling Price,* 19; Price report excerpted Smith and Judah, *Chronicles,* 128–33.

52. Roa Bárcena, *Recuerdos,* excerpted *Ecos,* 94.

53. Anonymous letter dated Santa Fe, December 4, 1846, *St. Louis Missouri Republican,* reprinted *Niles' National Register,* Mar 6, 1847, Smith and Judah, *Chronicles,* 127–28

CHAPTER 14

1. *El Monitor Republicano,* Jul 9, 1848, quoted Olivera and Crété, *Life,* 174; AMP 1847, 10.

2. Price to AG, Jul 20, 1847, and enclosures, ARSW 1847, 534–37; McNitt, "Navajo Campaigns"; Utley, *Frontiersmen,* 66–68; Oliva, *Soldiers,* 82–85.

3. Levinson, *Wars Within,* 48–51; John H. Coatsworth, "Measuring Influence," in Nugent, *Rural Revolt,* 68, see also passim; Reina, *Rebeliones;* López y Rivas, *Guerra.*

4. Ramsey, *Other Side,* 149–54; Rives, *U.S. and Mexico* 2:308–20; Levinson, *Wars Within,* 53; Henry, *Mexican War,* 254; Hogan, *Irish Soldiers,* 64–66; quotations SWM 2:110–11.

5. Ramsey, *Other Side,* 154–66 (quotation); Carlos Rodríguez Vinegas, "Las Finanzas públicas," in Vázquez, *México al tiempo,* 124–25; *Ecos,* 109–11; SWM 2:12–16; Balbontín, *Invasión,* 103–5; Roa Bárcena, *Recuerdos* 1:24–48; Levinson, *Wars Within,* 69–70; Rives, *U.S. and Mexico* 2:314–23; Beach, "Secret Mission."

6. Livermore, *War with Mexico.* See also BMW, 365.

7. Hitchcock to Reverend Theodore Parker, Feb 27, 1847, Smith and Judah, *Chronicles,* 27.

8. Walton, "Election of Thirtieth," and for one region, Dodd, "West and War"; NPD 182–83.

9. NPD, 180–81.

10. QDP 2:323–33; SS to Minister of Foreign Relations, Jan 18, 1847, MDC 8:197–98.

11. Risch, *Quartermaster Support,* 287–88.

12. Ibid., 287–90; WS to SW, Feb 24, and QMG to SW, Apr 17, 1847, CSW, 38–39; AG to WS, Jan 23, 1847, LS, RG 94; WS to SW, Jan 26, MWC, 845–46.

13. Bill, *Rehearsal,* 186; BMW, 236–37 (quotation); QDP 2:146–47, 388.

14. SW to WS, Nov 2, 1846, MWC, 372; Elliott, *Winfield Scott,* 445; Eisenhower, *Agent,* 233–36.

15. BMW, 237; Thomas, *Robert E. Lee,* 118–24; Hitchcock entry in Heitman; Hitchcock, *Fifty Years,* 179–80, 236, 254; Clary and Whitehorne; *Inspectors General,* 179–80; Robinson, *Account of the Organization* 1:39–40.

16. WS to ZT, Nov 25 and Dec 20, and to Conner, Dec 26, 1846, MWC, 373–74, 839–40, 846–47; BMW, 225 n. 21; Elliott, *Winfield Scott,* 445.

17. Elliott, *Winfield Scott,* 446; Leckie, *Wars* 1:347–48; WS to SW, Jan 12, 1847, MWC, 844–46; Eisenhower, *Agent,* 235–36.

18. ZT to WS, Dec 26, 1846, and Jan 15, 1847, to H. L. Scott, Jan 15, and to AG, Jan

26, 1847, MWC, 848, 862–63, 1100–2; ZT to J. P. Taylor, Jan 14, 1847, in McWhinney, *To Mexico,* 77; Hamilton, *Zachary Taylor Soldier,* 228; SWM 1:362.

19. NPD, 198.

20. Bliss to Patterson, Nov 28, 1846, WS to ZT, Jan 3 and 26, and to Butler, Jan 3, 1847, General Order 23, Jan 8, 1847, and ZT to AG, Jan 26, 1847, MWC 383–84, 851–60, 864–65, 1097–98; Furber, *Twelve Months,* 278–81; Kearny, *General Philip Kearny,* 77.

21. WS to SW, to Brigadier General George M. Brooke, and to Conner, all Dec 23, 1846, and to SW, Jan 26, 1847, MWC, 840–43, 865–66; Moore, *Scott's Campaign,* 1; BMW, 28–39.

22. WS to SW, Jan 26, 1847, MWC, 866–67; Risch, *Quartermaster Support,* 284–87.

23. WS to SW, Feb 12 and 28, to Worth, Feb 14, and to Patterson, Feb 19, 1847, MWC, 891–92, 896–901; WS, *Memoirs* 2:413; SWM 1:358; Moore, *Scott's Campaign,* 3; Furber, *Twelve Months,* 432.

24. Lieutenant Theodore Laidley to his father, Feb 12, 1847, Laidley, *Surrounded,* 32; diary of H. Judge Moore, Feb 19, 1847, quoted Foos, *Short Offhand,* 139.

25. Flores to RFS, Jan 1, 1847, and Commodore Pacific Squadron to SN, Jan 11 and 15, 1847, *Commodore Stockton's Despatches,* 19–22.

26. Sources on San Gabriel include RFS General Order, Dec 23, 1846, *Proceedings of the Court-Martial,* 113; Commodore Pacific Squadron to SN, Jan 11 and 15, and RFS Proclamation, Jan 5, 1847, *Commodore Stockton's Despatches,* 19–22, 30–36; Emory, *Notes,* 115–19; Clarke, *Stephen Watts Kearny,* 233–45; Bancroft, *History of California* 5:288–90, 356, 385–86; Chartrand, *Santa Anna's Mexican Army,* 55.

27. Commodore Pacific Squadron to SN, Feb 5, 1847, *Commodore Stockton's Despatches,* 30–36; Emory, *Notes,* 119; SWM 1:343–44; Bayard, *Sketch,* 144–46; Bancroft, *History of California* 5:391–95; Marti, *Messenger,* 103–6; Bauer, *Surfboats,* 193–96; Tanner, "Campaigns."

28. Griffin to Emory, Jan 11, and Commodore Home Squadron to SN, Feb 5, 1847, *Commodore Stockton's Despatches,* 30–36; SWK to AG, Jan 12, 1847, ARSW 1847, 516–17; Emory, *Notes,* 120–21; Bancroft, *History of California* 5:369, 395, 406–7; Bauer, *Surfboats,* 196–99; Tanner, "Campaigns"; Clarke, *Stephen Watts Kearny,* 249–53; Bayard, *Sketch,* 147–48.

29. JCF to RFS, Jan 2 and 3, 1847, LR, RG 94; SWK to JCF, Jan 10, and JCF Proclamation, Jan 12, 1847, *Proceedings of the Court-Martial,* 217–23; Articles of Capitulation (Treaty of Cahuenga), Jan 13, 1847, ARSW 1847, 1067–68; JCF, *Memoirs* 1:598–601; Bryant, *What I Saw,* 375–91; Colton, *Three Years,* 125; Ellison, "San Juan"; Bancroft, *History of California* 5:375–404.

30. Commodore Pacific Squadron to SN, Jan 15, 1847, *Commodore Stockton's Despatches,* 20–21; SWK to JCF, Jan 12 and 13, to RFS, Jan 13, and to AG, Jan 14, and JCF to SWK, Jan 13, 1847, *Proceedings of the Court-Martial,* 6–7, 73–74, 80, 109; Utley, *Life,* 259–60.

31. SWK to RFS, Jan 16, 1847, *Commodore Stockton's Despatches,* 28.

32. JCF to SWK, Jan 17, 1847, *Proceedings of the Court-Martial,* 190.

33. JCF commission, Jan 16, JCF to SWK, Jan 17, and SWK to RFS, Jan 17, 1847, *Proceedings of the Court-Martial,* 190–96; SWK to RFS, and RFS to SWK, both Jan 16, and Commodore Home Squadron to SN (demanding SWK's recall), Feb 4, 1847, *Commodore Stockton's Despatches,* 20, 28–29.

34. Clarke, *Stephen Watts Kearny,* 256–87; Grivas, *Military Governments,* 63–78; Kearny, "Mexican War." JKP ultimately sided with SWK. QDP 3:10–11.

35. Hirshson, *White Tecumseh,* 27–28; Ames, "Doctor Comes," part 3:41.

36. Howarth, *To Shining,* 162; BMW, 195, 200 n. 2; SWK to AG, Mar 15, 1847, *California and New Mexico,* 283–84; Colton, *Three Years,* 172–75; Clarke, *Stephen Watts Kearny,* 246; Bancroft, *History of California* 5:428–29.

37. Shubrick and SWK, Declaration, Mar 1, and SW to SWK, Jan 11, 1847, *California and New Mexico,* 244–45, 288–89; RFS to SN, Jan 22, 1847, *Commodore Stockton's Despatches,* 23.

38. SWK Proclamation, Mar 1, 1847, *California and New Mexico,* 289.

39. Valléjo journal quoted Christensen, *U. S.-Mexican,* 6.

40. Hughes, *Memoir Descriptive,* 286–301; Richardson, *Journal,* 53–61; Edwards, *Campaign in New Mexico,* 102–11; SWM 1:303.

41. "La Resistencia del Pueblo de Chihuahua ante la invasión norteamericana," in Herrero Serna, *México en guerra,* 157–84; Bustamante, *Nuevo Bernal* 1:224–25; Ramsey, *Other Side,* 173–78; Lister, *Chihuahua,* 117; Alcaraz, 139–50; *Ecos,* 92–93.

42. Hughes, *Doniphan's Expedition,* 148–51; Edwards, *Campaign,* 112; SWM 1:304.

43. Hughes, *Doniphan's Expedition,* 152n; other original accounts give slightly different versions, but all report the eagle. Sources on the Battle of the Sacramento include "La Resistencia del Pueblo de Chihuahua," 157–84; Jaurrieta, "Batalla"; Bustamante, *Nuevo Bernal* 1:224–25; Lister, *Chihuahua,* 117–20; *Ecos,* 92–93; Hughes, *Doniphan's Expedition,* 152–57; Alcaraz, 139–50; Ramsey, *Other Side,* 172–78; Hughes, *Memoir Descriptive,* 301–24; Edwards, *Campaign in New Mexico,* 111–20; Richardson, *Journal,* 61–64; Robinson, *Journal,* 74–76; Brooks, *Complete History* 174–79; Wilcox, *History,* 156–59; and Doniphan's report, Doniphan to AG, with enclosures, Mar 4, 1847, ARSW 1847, 497–513.

44. Edwards, *Campaign in New Mexico,* 81–82.

45. *Ecos,* 93; Richardson, *Journal,* 63; Olivera and Crété, *Life,* 106; Hughes, *Doniphan's Expedition,* 164 (bathhouses).

46. Doniphan to Wool, Mar 20, 1847, ARSW 1847, 247–49, and in Hughes, *Doniphan's Expedition,* 167–68.

47. Magoffin, *Down Santa Fe Trail,* 228–29.

48. Wislizenus, *Memoir,* 62; BMW, 157; Edwards, *Campaign in New Mexico*, 92 (lizards).

49. Edwards, *Campaign in New Mexico,* 90.

50. Captain John Reid to Wool, May 21, 1847, CSW, 334–35; Hughes, *Doniphan's Expedition,* 173–91.

51. Roa Bárcena, *Recuerdos,* excerpted *Ecos,* 94. Sources on the Taos Rebellion include Price to AG, with enclosed reports, Feb 15, 1847, ARSW 1847, 520–26; *Insurrection Against the Military Government in New Mexico and California, 1847 and 1848* (1900); Bancroft, *History of Arizona and New Mexico,* 433–34; Lamar, *Far Southwest,* 68–70; Twitchell, *Old Santa Fe,* 275–320; McNierney, *Taos 1847;* Lavender, *Bent's Fort,* 291–318; Sides, *Blood and Thunder,* 173–84; Horgan, *Great River* 2:762–68; Goodrich, "Revolt at Mora"; Murphy, "United States Army in Taos."

52. Unpublished testimony of Teresina Bent Scheurich, quoted Eisenhower, *So Far,* 236–37.

53. SW to Price, Jun 26, 1847, *California and New Mexico,* 252–53.

54. Price to AG, Feb 15, 1847, ARSW 1847, 520; Lamar, *Far Southwest,* 70–82; Horgan, *Centuries,* 221; Utley, *Frontiersmen,* 84–85; see also Twitchell, *Military Occupation.*

CHAPTER 15

1. ZT to AG, Jun 4, 1847, and enclosures, LR, RG 94; Chamberlain, *My Confession,* 86–88; Engelmann, "Second Illinois," 439; Buhoup, *Narrative,* 106–8; Johannsen, *To Halls,* 37; Foos, *Short Offhand,* 124.

2. WS to ZT, Jan 3 and 26, to Butler, Jan 3, General Order 23, Jan 8, Worth to WS, Jan 9, and ZT to AG, Jan 26, 1847, MWC, 851–61, 864–65, 1097–98; ZT to Wood, Jan 3, and to R. F. Allen, Feb 12, 1847, cited BMW, 226 n. 11; Kearny, *General Philip Kearny,* 77.

3. Quoted Levinson, *Wars Within,* 22–23.

4. Utley, *Lone Star,* 75–76; Wool to Bliss, Jan 27, 1847, MWC, 1106–8.

5. Gaines to WS, May 3, 1847, LR, RG 94; Lavender, *Climax,* 155–57; Chamberlain, *My Confession,* 94–96; Scott, *Encarnación Prisoners,* 35–36.

6. McDowell to Yell and Wool to Yell, both Jan 25, 1847, LR, RG 94; Wool to Bliss, Jan 27, 1847, MWC 1106–8; Chamberlain, *My Confession,* 93.

7. ZT to AG, Jan 30, 1847, MWC, 1106; BMW, 207.

8. ZT to AG, Feb 4 and 7, MWC, 1109–11; SWM 1:373–74.

9. Webb, *Texas Rangers,* 112; Utley, *Lone Star,* 76–77; Lavender, *Climax,* 168–69; Carleton, *Battle,* 12–19.

10. Chamberlain, *My Confession,* 110–11. This was ZT's only retreat during the war.

11. Quoted BMW, 209.

12. *New York Tribune,* Mar 29, 1847, quoted SWM 1:374.

13. ALSA to Ministro de Guerra y Marina, Oct 10, 1846, Smith, "Letters," 369; ALSA, *Las Guerras de México,* 220; ALSA, *Eagle,* 88–91.

14. Balbontín, "Battle of Angostura," 126–27; Balbontín, *Invasión,* 60–62. Other sources on the march to Saltillo include Alcaraz, 91–104; Ramsey, *Other Side,* 114–29; Inocencio Noyola, "La Ciudad sitiada: San Luis Potosí ante la intervención norteamericana," in Herrera Serna, *México en guerra,* 543–64; Krauze, *Mexico,* 143; Roa Bárcena, *Recuerdos* 1:150–65; Alessio Robles, *Saltillo,* 210; Alessio Robles, *Coahuila y Tejas,* 2:353.

15. ALSA, *Las Guerras de México,* 220; Callcott, *Santa Anna,* 244–49; SWM 1:375–79; Scheina, *Santa Anna,* 53–54.

16. ALSA Proclamation, Jan 28, 1847, in ARSW 1847, 153–56, and in Ramsey, *Other Side,* 114–15.

17. ALSA to Ministro de Guerra y Marina, Feb 2, 1847, Smith, "Letters," 411; Ordenes Generales del Ejército del Norte, Jan 26, 1847, copy in ARSW 1847, 153–54; Ramsey, *Other Side,* 94–96; Alessio Robles, *Coahuila y Tejas* 2:353; Balbontín, *Invasión,* 60–62; Alessio Robles, *Saltillo,* 210; Rives, *U.S. and Mexico* 2:339.

18. Roa Bárcena, *Recuerdos* 1:150–65; Ramsey, *Other Side,* 115–17.

19. ALSA, *Eagle,* 91–93; Balbontín, *Invasión,* 68; Olivera and Crété, *Life in Mexico,* 163–64; Ruiz, *Triumphs,* 215–16; *Ecos,* 82; Webb, *Texas Rangers,* 112.

20. ALSA to ZT, and ZT to ALSA, both Feb 22, 1847, MWC, 98, and in Brooks, *Complete History,* 205–8, and Butler, *Documentary History,* 103–4.

21. Ramsey, *Other Side,* 121–22; officer on scenery quoted Johannsen, *To Halls,* 92; Alessio Robles, *Saltillo,* 221; octopus quotation, *Ecos,* 81; volunteers both quoted McCaffrey, *Army,* 143.

22. Mexicans called the battle Angostura, North Americans Buena Vista. Sources include Alcaraz, 91–104; *Ecos,* 78–86; Balbontín, "Battle of Angostura"; ALSA, *Las Guerras de México,* 237–50; Alessio Robles, *Coahuila y Tejas* 2:357–70; Ramsey, *Other Side,* 121–28; Roa Bárcena, *Recuerdos* 1:158–209; Rea, *Apuntes,* 18; Vigil y Robles, *Invasión,* 23; Balbontín, *Invasión,* 53–101; Olivera and Crété, *Life in Mexico,* 163–65; ZT to AG, Feb 24 and Mar 8, 1847, and enclosures, and to SW, Mar 3, 1847, ARSW 1847, 97–98, 132–40; ZT to AG, Mar 6, 1847, MWC, 134–35; Carleton, *Battle;* Chamberlain, *My Confession,* 111–31; Benham, *Recollections;* Buhoup, *Narrative,* 111–27; Fulton, *Diaries of Gregg* 2:46–54; Henry, *Campaign Sketches,* 307–27; Baylies, *Campaign,* 27–41; SWM 1:381–400, 555–62; BMW, 209–18; Hamilton, *Zachary Taylor Soldier,* 232–41; Eisenhower, *So Far,* 166–91; Bauer, *Zachary Taylor,* 195–206; Henry, *Story,* 238–57; Jenkins, *History,* 217–39; Lavender, *Climax,* 174–212; Ripley, *War* 1:393–423; Rives, *U.S. and Mexico* 2:360–61; Duncan, "Medical History"; Chartrand, *Santa Anna's Mexican Army,* 55–56.

23. Chamberlain, *My Confession,* 118–19; see also Wilcox, *History,* 217; SWM 1: 388–89.

24. "Extract from Report of a Mexican Engineer on Santa Anna's Staff," quoted BMW, 228 n. 30.

25. Quoted BMW, 214.

26. Will Wallace, Illinois volunteer, to George, Mar 1, 1847, quoted McCaffrey, *Army,* 146.

27. Chamberlain, *My Confession,* 122–23.

28. Ibid., 132–33. Chamberlain admitted that the romantic tale was unfounded.

29. ALSA, *Eagle,* 93–94; Scheina, *Santa Anna,* 53–60.

30. Balbontín, "Battle of Angostura," 148.

31. Roa Bárcena, *Recuerdos,* excerpted *Ecos,* 84.

32. Smith and Judah, *Chronicles,* 104–5.

33. ALSA, *Las Guerras de México,* 243–47; ZT to AG, Feb 25, Mar 1 and 14, 1847, MWC, 1118–19; Chamberlain, *My Confession,* 43–47; Carleton, *Buena Vista,* 146–47; officer quoted BMW, 218.

34. Quotation Ramsey, *Other Side,* 137. Accounts of the retreat include Roa Bárcena, *Recuerdos,* excerpted *Ecos,* 84; Alessio Robles, *Saltillo,* 225–26; Ruiz, *Triumphs,* 215–16; Noyola, "La Ciudad sitiada: San Luis Potosí ante la intervención norteamericana"; Alcaraz, 105–22; Frías, *Guerra,* 67.

35. ALSA, *Eagle,* 94.

36. Chamberlain, *My Confession,* 175–76; Giddings, *Sketches,* 303–5; Smith, *Chile,* 160–62; Johannsen, *To Halls,* 37; Carpenter, *Travels,* 49–54; Furber, *Twelve Months,* 485–87.

37. Reports of these actions in ARSW 1847, 210–13; Giddings, *Sketches,* 293–94; Smith, *Chile,* 152–59; Furber, *Twelve Months,* 487–88.

38. Giddings, *Sketches,* 324; *Niles' National Register,* May 22, 1847, quoted Foos, *Short Offhand,* 192 n. 13; Utley, *Lone Star,* 77–79; ZT to AG, Jun 16, 1847, MWC, 141–45.

39. Smith and Judah, *Chronicles,* 269–71; Johannsen, *To Halls,* 36; *Ecos,* 85; Bauer, *Zachary Taylor,* 208–10.

40. *Daily Cincinnati Gazette,* Jun 3, 1847, quoted Foos, *Short Offhand,* 100, ZT quoted 122–23, see also 125.

41. Chamberlain, *My Confession,* 176; Giddings, *Sketches,* 326.

CHAPTER 16

1. Weigley, *American Way,* 71–72, 74–75; Elliott, *Winfield Scott,* 553–56, 563–65; Spaulding, *United States Army,* 223–24; Weigley, *History,* 188–89; SWM 2:163–68, 220–21, 226–30, 252, 459–61; Wallace, "United States Army."

2. The first attempt to formalize a Law of War was that of Hugo Grotius in 1625, which remained influential more than two centuries later. Attempts to develop a modern international code began with a convention in Paris in 1856. Additional conventions (at The Hague, Geneva, and other places) imposed more rules, mostly piecemeal, over the next century. The modern Law of War derives from the United Nations Charter, the record of the Nuremburg and Tokyo war crimes trials, and subsequent conventions and treaties. Grotius, *Law of War and Peace;* Neff, *War and the Law;* Byers, *War Law.* On U.S. domestic military law as it stood in 1847, see O'Brien, *Treatise.* See also Halleck, *Elements of International Law and Laws of War.* On WS' innovations, I rely on the most scholarly legal treatment, Winthrop, *Military Law,* 2:773–900, and as cited. For the definitions above, see 2:773, 778–98.

3. General Order 20, Feb 19, 1847, MWC, 873–74; WS, *Memoirs* 2:392–95; SWM 2:455–56 n. 22; Winthrop, *Military Law* 2:798–817.

4. Winthrop, *Military Law* 2:799, 808–12, 815–16.

5. Ibid., 2:831–33. Military commissions were next created in 1861 and authorized by statute in 1863.

6. Ibid., 2:832. General Orders authorizing the convening of military commissions include, from WS, Numbers 81, 82, 121, 145, 147, 171, 194, 215, 239, 267, 270, 273, 292, 334, 335, 380, and 392 of 1847, and 9 of 1848; from ZT, Numbers 66, 106, 112, and 121 of 1847; and from Wool, Numbers 140, 179, 216, 463, 476, and 514 of 1847. Ibid., 2:832n.

7. Ibid., 2:832–33. General Order 372 of 1847 set forth the composition, powers, and so forth of the councils as courts. Councils were convened under order Numbers 181, 184, 187, 195, and 291 of 1847, and Numbers 22, 35, and 41 of 1848, all in WS' command. Ibid., 2:833n.

8. Ibid., 2:841–42; soldier quoted Foos, *Short Offhand,* 117.

9. Ibid., 2:822–23. Winthrop calls this a "superfluous and unnecessary proceeding."

10. Ibid., 2:782–84.

11. Luvaas, *Frederick the Great on the Art of War;* Jomini, *Art of War;* Johnson, *Winfield Scott,* 167; Pohl, "Influence of Jomini."

12. Clausewitz's text on guerrilla warfare in a modern translation is Clausewitz, *Short Guide,* 223–28, and Clausewitz, *On War* 3:Book VI (Defence), ch. XXVI (Arming the Nation).

13. Levinson, *Wars Within,* 47–48.

14. QDP 2:428, 435; SW to General George M. Brooke, Mar 22 and 23 and Apr 2, to governors of Alabama, Mississippi, and Alabama, Mar 23, and to WS, Mar 22, 1847, Military Affairs, RG 107; AG to General George Cadwalader, Mar 20 and 26, 1847, LS, RG 94.

15. Giddings to Mitchell, Mar 16, 1847, ARSW 1847, 213–14; Smith, *Chile,* 256–64; Giddings, *Sketches,* 307–20.

16. ZT to AG, Mar 20 and 28, 1847, MWC, 1119–20, 1125; Henry, *Campaign Sketches,* 329.

17. Smith, *Chile,* 294–95; Giddings, *Sketches,* 325; BMW, 229 n. 43; Utley, *Lone Star,* 77.

18. Utley, *Frontiersmen,* ch. 6; Dunlay, *Kit Carson,* 144–45.

19. Carrillo quoted Weber, *Mexican Frontier,* 275; D. E. Livingston-Little, "U.S. Military Forces in California," in Faulk and Stout, *Mexican War,* 160–61.

20. Shubrick and SWK Circular, and SWK Proclamation, both Mar 1, and SWK, Notice, Mar 14, 1847, *California and New Mexico,* 288–89, 291–92; Scott, *Prize Cases* 2:1393.

21. Montgomery to Alcalde of San José, Mar 29, to Governor at La Paz, Apr 13, to Missroon, Apr 13, Montgomery Proclamations, Mar 30 and Apr 3, Missroon to Montgomery Mar 30 and Apr 13, Council of San José to Montgomery, Mar 30, Governor Miranda to Montgomery, Apr 13, 1847, all ARSN 1847, 1057–62; Martínez, *Historia de Baja,* 365–73; Cardenas de la Peña, *Semblanza* 1:146; Chamberlain, "Nicholas Trist and Baja California."

22. Shubrick to JCF, Feb 23, and SWK to Cooke, Mar 1, 1847, LR, RG 94; SWK to JCF, Mar 1, 1847, *Proceedings of the Court-Martial,* 33; BMW, 195–96.

23. Turner to SWK, Mar 25, W. H. Russell to Cooke, Mar 1, SWK to Mason, Mar 27, and to JCF, Mar 28, and Mason to Turner, Apr 10, 1847, LR, RG 94; Clarke, *Stephen Watts Kearny,* 309; Grivas, *Military Governments,* 77–78.

24. Utley, *Life,* 260–62; Sides, *Blood and Thunder,* 185–87; Dunlay, *Kit Carson,* 125–27.

25. Olivera and Crété, *Life,* 92; Clary, *Fortress,* 4, 59. Sources on Vera Cruz and its defenses include Roa Bárcena, *Recuerdos* 1:268–70; *Memoria del Ministerio de Guerra y Marina, 9 de Diciembre de 1846,* chart 11; Ramsey, *Other Side,* 182–83; SWM 2:182, 333–34; Lerdo de Tejada, *Apuntes históricos* 2:508–10; Riva Palacio, *México a través* 4:647; Rivera, *Historia antigua* 3:864–66; Chartrand, *Santa Anna's Mexican Army,* 53–56, 53n; WS to SW, Mar 19, 1847, ARSW 1847, 229–30.

26. Both quoted Oliver and Crété, *Life,* 92.

27. Reid, *Sketches,* 13.

28. WS to SW, Mar 1, 1847, CSW, 92; Commodore Home Squadron to SN, Mar 10, 1848, ARSN 1847, 1177–79; Parker, *Recollections,* 82; Hitchcock, *Fifty Years,* 237; Blackwood, *To Mexico,* 112; Smith quoted Eisenhower, *Agent,* 238–39.

29. Commodore Home Squadron to SN, Mar 10, 1847, ARSN 1847, 1177–79; Semmes, *Service Afloat,* 125; Lott, "Landing."

30. BMW, 257 n. 8, see also 240–44; Eisenhower, *Agent,* 422 n. 2, see also 233–44. Other sources on the landings include Risch, *Quartermaster Support,* 283–96; Semmes, *Service Afloat,* 126–27; Henry, *Story,* 258–71; *Ecos,* 109–13; Morison, *Old Bruin,* 206–11; Ramsey, *Other Side,* 180–97; Alcaraz, 151–67; Bauer, *Surfboats,* 79–82; Simmons, *United States Marines,* 42–47; Bauer, "Vera Cruz Expedition"; Parker, *Recollections,* 83–85; Ripley, *War* 2:23–26; WS, *Memoirs* 2:413–21; Semmes, *Service Afloat,* 25–27; SWM 2:66–68. The reports of U.S. commanders are WS to SW, Mar 12, 1847, ARSW 1847, 216–17, and Commodore Home Squadron to SN, Mar 10, 1847, ARSN 1847, 1177–79; Beach, *United States Navy,* 59; Weigley, *American Way,* 75–76; Morison, *Old Bruin,* 206.

31. Semmes, *Service Afloat,* 126–27.

32. Nunnalee journal, Mar 9, 1847, Butler, *Eutaw Rangers,* 102.

33. Jacob J. Oswandel, Pennsylvania Volunteers, quoted Wheelan, *Invading,* xiv.

34. Quoted Leckie, *Wars* 1:355.

35. Risch, *Quartermaster Support,* 290–91.

36. Hughes and Johnson, *Fighter,* 80, 83.

37. Smith, *Company A,* 19–27; BMW, 246, see also 246–49. Other sources on the siege of Vera Cruz include *Military Forces Employed in the Mexican War;* Bauer, *Surfboats,* 83–96; Frías, *Guerra,* 100–2; Bonilla, *Historia marítima,* 286–88; Bustamante, *El nuevo Bernal,* 265; Cardenas de la Peña, *Semblanza* 1:131–36; Simmons, *United States Marines,* 42–47; Freeman, *R. E. Lee* 1:228–32; Lerdo de Tejada, *Apuntes históricos* 2:540–46; Ramsey, *Other Side,* 183–84; Rivera, *Historia antigua* 3:860–73; Roa Bárcena, *Recuerdos* 1:267–325; WS, *Memoirs* 2:423–30; Hitchcock, *Fifty Years,* 233–48; Jenkins, *History,* 254–62; Morison, *Old Bruin,* 215–20; Ripley, *War* 2:27–30; Risch, *Quartermaster Support,* 290–91; Semmes, *Service Afloat,* 127–42; SWM 2:27–33, 339–43; Trens, *Historia de Vera Cruz* 4:417–43; Henry, *Story,* 258–71; Eisenhower, *So Far,* 353–65; Eisenhower, *Agent,* 233–44.

38. WS, *Memoirs* 2:423–24.

39. Complaints about varmints are universal in original accounts. Examples include Henry, *Story,* 266; Winders, *Mr. Polk's Army,* 172–73; Waugh, *Class of 1846,* 87; Captain Sydenham Moore to wife, Apr 13, 1847, Butler, *Eutaw Rangers,* 70. Chiggers are now widespread in the U.S. Most original accounts suggest that the Anglos had never encountered them before.

40. Lieutenant Edmund Bradford, Smith and Judah, *Chronicles,* 189.

41. SN to Conner, Mar 3, 1847, in Griffis, *Matthew Calbraith Perry,* 221; BMW, 258 n. 43; Morison, *Old Bruin,* 211–14; Eisenhower, *Agent,* 241–42.

42. On the origins and technical details of these missiles, see Clary, *Rocket Man,* 29–31; on their employment by the U.S. Army from the 1840s through the 1860s, see Olejar, "Rockets."

43. Levinson, *Wars Within,* 30–31; WS, *Memoirs* 2:427–49. WS contradicted what he said at 2:421, which was that ALSA was raising an army to attack him, so he had to end the siege quickly.

44. Both quoted Levinson, *Wars Within,* 29–30.

45. Nunnalee journal, Mar 23 and 25, 1847, Butler, *Eutaw Rangers,* 107–8.

46. "Mexican Narrative of Events at the Heroic City of Vera Cruz, While Besieged by the North-American Army," Smith and Judah, *Chronicles,* 192.

47. Ramsey, *Other Side,* 184; quotation Alcaraz, excerpted *Ecos,* 112–13.

48. Colonel William S. Harney to H. L. Scott, Aug 5, 1847, ARSW 1847, A2–3; QDP 2:314–16; MWC, 853–54.

49. Sources for the surrender negotiations and ceremony include Hitchcock, *Fifty Years,* 246–48; WS to SW, Mar 27 and 29, with Terms of Capitulation, Mar 27, 1847, ARSW 1847, 229–30, 235–36; QDP 2:465; BMW, 252–53; Ramsey, *Other Side,* 196–97; Lerdo, *Apuntes históricos* 2:566–68; Private Hagner to M. M. Hagner, Mar 30, 1847, Smith and Judah, *Chronicles,* 195–96; Semmes, *Service Afloat,* 145–46; Chartrand, *Santa Anna's Mexican Army,* 53; Furber, *Twelve Months,* 557–59.

50. Casualty reports vary but generally resemble the figures given. BMW, 252;

Levinson, *Wars Within,* 28–29, officer quoted 29–30; Roa Bárcena, *Recuerdos* 1:301–2; Captain Sydenham Moore to wife, Mar 28, 1847, Butler, *Eutaw Rangers,* 66; Lee to wife, nd, quoted Thomas, *Robert E. Lee,* 123.

51. Ralph W. Kirkham to wife, Apr 19, 1847, Kirkham, *Mexican War Journal,* 4; Theodore Laidley to father, Apr 2, 1847, Laidley, *Surrounded,* 56.

52. Eisenhower, *Agent,* 245–46; Winders, *Mr. Polk's Army,* 121–23.

53. Foos, *Short Offhand,* 125; WS to SW, Apr 5, and orders issued Mar 28 and 29, and Apr 1, 3, 4, and 9, 1847, MWC, 908–14, 930–36; BMW, 258 n. 49.

54. Sydenham Moore to wife, Mar 28, 1847, Butler, *Eutaw Rangers,* 66; ALSA, Proclamation, Mar 31, 1847, in Butler, *Documentary History,* 203; Ramsey, *Other Side,* 130–48.

55. *El Republicano,* Apr 1, 1847, quoted Christensen, *U.S.-Mexican,* 163.

CHAPTER 17

1. New Orleans quoted Leckie, *Wars* 1:359; NPD, 206–9.

2. Dodd, "Election of Thirtieth"; Weed, *Autobiography,* 573–74; ZT to [Davis], Aug 16, 1847, cited BMW, 366.

3. Utley, *Lone Star,* 78; ZT to AG, Apr 21, 1847, LR, RG 94; ZT to H. L. Scott, Apr 16, WS to ZT, Apr 24, and SW to ZT, May 6, 1847, CSW, 139, 360–61, 411–12; BMW, 130 n. 44.

4. Ministro de Relaciones to SS, Feb 22, 1847, MDC 8:896–97; NPD, 205–6; PUS to ST, Mar 23, and to SN and SW, Mar 31, ST to PUS, Mar 30, 1847, RMP 5:2372–80; AMP 1847, 567–75.

5. Wilson Lumpkin to JCC, Mar 11, and Toombs to JCC, Apr 30, 1847, quoted BMW, 365.

6. John Sherman to William Sherman, May 2, 1847, Thorndike, *Sherman Letters,* 38–39.

7. NPD, 211–14, 218. Biographies and studies of Trist include Drexler, *Guilty;* Sobarzo, *Deber y conciencia;* Griswold del Castillo, *Treaty;* Reeves, *American Diplomacy;* Sars, "Nicholas Trist"; Chamberlain, "Nicholas Trist"; Graebner, "Party Politics"; Northrup, "Nicholas Trist's Mission."

8. Ramírez, *Mexico During War,* 107; Meade quoted Henry, *Story,* 239–40.

9. ALSA to Canalizo, Mar 21, 1847, Smith, "Letters," 415; Ramsey, *Other Side,* 142–55; Valadés, *Historia del pueblo* 2:395; Roa Bárcena, *Recuerdos* 2:10–12; Bravo Ugarte, *Historia* 3:200–1; Callcott, *Santa Anna,* 255–57; DePalo, *Mexican National Army,* 115–16; Hanighen, *Santa Anna,* 216–18; Scheina, *Santa Anna,* 62; Josefina Zoraida Vázquez, "War and Peace with the United States," in Meyer and Beezley, *Oxford History,* 339–70 (at 365–66).

10. Quoted DePalo, *Mexican National Army,* 114.

11. Levinson, *Wars Within,* 52–53; Bushnell, "Political and Military Career of Álvarez."

12. Ramsey, *Other Side,* 205; ALSA, *Eagle,* 95–96; Alcaraz, excerpted *Ecos,* 114; BMW, 263–64; Frazier, 89–91.

13. Commodore Home Squadron to SN, Apr 4, 1847, ARSN 1847, 1200–2; WS to SW, Apr 5, and Quitman to H. L. Scott, Apr 7, 1847, MWC, 909–11, 917–18; Morison, *Old Bruin,* 222–23; Risch, *Quartermaster Support,* 292; Bauer, *Surfboats,* 100–2; Frazier, 11; Hunter entry in Callahan.

14. WS to SW, Apr 8, 1847, CSW, 126; WS, *Memoirs* 2:430–31; Callcott, *Santa Anna,* 257–59; Jones, *Santa Anna,* 113.

15. Risch, *Quartermaster Support,* 291–94; QMG to Colonel Henry Stanton, Feb 12, 1847, cited BMW, 274 n. 1; WS to QMG, Mar 19, 1847, MWC, 913.

16. Smith, *Company A,* 29.

17. General Orders 87, Apr 1, 1847, quoted Levinson, *Wars Within,* 24.

18. WS, Proclamation, Apr 11, 1847, CSW, 937; WS to SW, Apr 11, 1847, and enclosed orders and proclamations, including complaint of Nicholas Dorich, Apr nd, 1847, MWC, 928–39.

19. WS to Colonel Henry Wilson, Apr 13, 1847, CSW, 136.

20. Harney to H. I.. Scott, Apr 4, and WS orders for march, Apr 6, WS to Patterson, Apr 9, Twiggs to H. L. Scott, and Pillow to H. L. Scott, both Apr 11, 1847, MWC, 914–22, 936–40; Jenkins, *History,* 273; Williams, *With Beauregard,* 12–13; Selby, *Eagle and Serpent.* Sources on the Battle of Cerro Gordo include WS to SW, Apr 19 and 23, 1847, with enclosures, ARSW 1847, 255–300; Hitchcock to H. L. Scott, Apr 24, 1847, CSW, 279–80; Callcott, *Santa Anna,* 259–60; Alcaraz, 168–88; Ramsey, *Other Side,* 198–219; Elliott, *Winfield Scott,* 464–68; Freeman, *R. E. Lee* 1:238–41; Furber, *Twelve Months,* 600–1; Grant, *Memoirs,* 67–70; Henry, *Story,* 272–90; Hitchcock, *Fifty Years,* 250–53; Jenkins, *History,* 273–87; Ramírez, *México,* 128; Ripley, *War,* 2:63–77; Rivera, *Historia de Jalapa* 3:880–93; Roa Bárcena, *Recuerdos* 2:90–150; WS, *Memoirs* 2:431–32; ALSA, *Eagle,* 96; ALSA, *Las Guerras,* 250–57; Semmes, *Service Afloat,* 175–83; SWM 2:44–58, 350–55; Smith and Judah, *Chronicles,* 207–12; Wilcox, *History,* 178–97; Williams, *With Beauregard,* 12–13, 32–38; BMW, 261–68; Eisenhower, *Agent,* 254–58; Eisenhower, *So Far,* 266–83; Chartrand, *Santa Anna's Mexican Army,* 56; Thomas, *Robert E. Lee,* 125–28; Wheelan, *Invading Mexico,* 309–32.

21. Smith, *Company A,* 32–33.

22. Soldier quoted Christensen, *U.S.-Mexican,* 182.

23. *Ecos,* 114.

24. Private in Smith and Judah, *Chronicles,* 212; Smith, *Company A,* 34.

25. ALSA, *Eagle,* 96; BMW, 267–68; Laidley, *Surrounded,* 75–77; Frazier, 91; *Ecos,* 116. ALSA's artificial leg was on display at the Illinois state capitol for decades.

26. Ballentine, *English Soldier,* 199–200. Ballentine was on a burial detail.

27. Smith and Judah, *Chronicles,* 216.

28. Ramírez, *Mexico During the War,* 134; Roa Bárcena, *Recuerdos,* excerpted *Ecos,* 119.

29. Ballentine, *English Soldier,* 207.

30. Eisenhower, *Agent,* 257.

31. Smith and Judah, *Chronicles,* 216.

32. Ramsey, *Other Side,* 214; Ramírez, *Mexico during the War,* 120–21.

33. Ramírez, *Mexico during the War,* 135; revolver quote McCaffrey, *Army,* 173–74.

34. These documents are in MWC, 951–52, 1051–52; see also Riva Palacio, *México a través* 4:656; Rives, *U.S. and Mexico* 2:434.

35. Ramsey, *Other Side,* 214–21.

36. Quoted Eisenhower, *So Far,* 295.

37. Semmes, *Service Afloat,* 189–93; Captain Sydenham Moore journal, Apr 22, 1847, Butler, *Eutaw Rangers,* 73; Kirby Smith quoted ibid., 294; Smith and Judah, *Chronicles,* 217–22.

38. Roa Bárcena, *Recuerdos,* excerpted *Ecos,* 120–21.

39. Worth to H. L. Scott, Apr 22, 1847, ARSW 1847, 300–1; Inventory of Artillery in Fort San Carlos de Perote, nd 1847, LR, RG 94.

40. WS to Wilson, Apr 23 and 28, 1847, LR, RG 94; WS to SW, Apr 28, 1847, MWC, 944–46; Patterson order, Apr 24, 1847, quoted BMW, 268–69.

41. Gobernador Mariano Salas, Proclamation, Apr 21, 1847; La Legistura del Estado de México a los Habitantes, Apr nd, 1847, and other proclamations, MWC, 945–52.

42. Reglamento para el servicio de secciones ligera de la guardia nacional de los estados y territorios de la republica, Apr 28, 1847, in Levinson, *Wars Within,* 34–35, see 36–39 for a complete listing of all patented commanders and their units; proclamation of Aug 16, 1847, quoted SWM 2:421 n. 3; Roa Bárcena, *Recuerdos,* excerpted *Ecos,* 121; Ramsey, *Other Side,* 439–42.

43. General Order 127, Apr 29, 1847, BMW, 269; SWM 2:171–72; Roa Bárcena, *Recuerdos,* excerpted *Ecos,* 121; Ramírez, *Mexico During the War,* 134; Ralph W. Kirkham to wife, Apr 22, 1847, Kirkham, *Mexican War Journal,* 6.

44. Hughes and Johnson, *Fighter,* 107.

45. H. L. Scott to Wilson, May 3, 1847, MWC, 955; Volunteer Division Order 17, May 5, 1847, in Furber, *Twelve Months,* 613; SWM 2:64; Levinson, *Wars Within,* 46.

46. Caruso, *Mexican Spy Company;* Hitchcock, *Fifty Years,* 259–64, 330–45; Levinson, *Wars Within,* 32; Kenly, *Memoirs,* 370; Moses journal, Smith and Judah, *Chronicles,* 231.

47. Commodore Home Squadron to SN, Apr 24, 1847, and enclosures, ARSN 1847, 1192–2004; Semmes, *Service Afloat,* 150–56; Bauer, *Surfboats,* 103–5; Morison, *Old Bruin,* 224–27; Jenkins, *History,* 445–46. Perry's report to SN, Apr 24, 1847, is also in Butler, *Documentary History,* 209.

48. QDP 3:23–24; SN to Commodore Home Squadron, May 13 and 22, and Commodore Home Squadron to SN, May 19, and Jul 1 and 23, 1847, Home Squadron Letters, RG 45; Perry's negotiations with General Franklin Pierce, acting for WS, in documents with Commodore Home Squadron to SN, Jul 4, 1847, ARSN 1847, 1224–26; Morison, *Old Bruin,* 221.

49. Lieutenant John S. Misroon to Commander John B. Montgomery, Apr 14, 1847, ARSN 1847, 1228; SWK to SW, Apr 28, 1847, *California and New Mexico,* 286–87; BMW, 345.

50. Wise, *Los Gringos,* 85–86; BMW, 345.

CHAPTER 18

1. NPD, 226–27, 240–42, 244; Utley, *Life,* 260–62, Sherman quoted 261–62.

2. SWK to Burton, May 30, 1847, *California and New Mexico,* 310; BMW, 196, 345; Ricketts, *Mormon Battalion,* 161–68; Nunis, *Mexican War in Baja;* Moyana Pahissa, *La Resistencia.*

3. Spicer, *Cycles,* 210–43; Bender, *March of Empire,* 48–49; ARCIA 1850, pt. 2, 997; AMP 1847, 9–12, 30; ARSW 1847, 70; Bender, "Frontier Defense"; *Communication from the Commissioner of Indian Affairs* (1848); *Documents in Relation to a Treaty* (1850).

4. Newspapers quoted SWM 2:453 n. 16; Myers, "Illinois Volunteers"; Gay to his parents, Aug 5, 1847, Meketa, "A Soldier in New Mexico," 16–17.

5. ZT to AG, Jun 16, 1847, MWC, 1178; Mora to ZT, May 10, ZT to Mora, May 19, and ZT to AG, May 23, 1847, CSW, 238–331; Wislizenus, *Memoir,* 80.

6. Luttwak, "Dead End"; SWM 2:170; BMW, 221–22; Wool, Circular, Jul 25, 1847, LR, RG 94.

7. QDP 2:466–75; SS to Trist, with treaty draft, Apr 15, 1847, MDC 8:201–7; *Treaty Between the United States and Mexico,* 38–40, 81–86, 108.

8. WS to Trist, May 7, 1847, MDC 8:902n; Trist to SS, May 6 and 7, 1847, CSW, 3, 153; Trist to WS, May 9 and 20, and to SS, May 21, WS to SW, May 20, and to Trist, May 29, 1847, *Treaty Between the United States and Mexico,* 153–68, 172–73. The WS–Trist relationship is summarized in Eisenhower, *Agent,* 261–65.

9. Perry to Semmes and to WS, both Apr 28, Semmes to WS, May 8, and WS to Semmes, May 9, 1847, all in Semmes, *Service Afloat,* 159–61, 198–202.

10. Trist to WS, May 9 and 20, and to SS, May 21, WS to SW, May 20, and to Trist, May 29, *Treaty Between the United States and Mexico,* 153–73.

11. WS to SW, Jun 4, 1847, MWC, 993–94; Elliott, *Winfield Scott,* 471; Scammon, "Chapter"; BMW, 302 n. 16; Marcy to friend quoted SWM 2:129.

12. NPD, 242–44.

13. Trist to Bankhead, Jun 6, and to SS, Jun 13, 1847, MDC 8:908–14.

14. Ibarra to SS, Jun 22, 1847, MDC 8:914; BMW, 284–85.

15. NPD, 247–48, 251.

16. WS to SW, Jul 25, 1847, MWC, 1011–14; SWM 2:391; Rives, *United States and Mexico* 2:443–44; Elliott, *Winfield Scott,* 495–99.

17. WS' disbursements, especially this one, later came under close scrutiny in the Congress. See *Pay and Emoluments of Lieutenant-General Scott* for a roundup of pertinent documents and figures, and testimony of witnesses. See also SWM 2:130–32, 391; Rives, *United States and Mexico* 2:443–44; Roa Bárcena, *Recuerdos* 2:156–62; Elliott, *Winfield Scott,* 495–99; Hitchcock, *Fifty Years,* 266–69; Jones, *Santa Anna,* 165; Cuevas, *Historia,* 663–67; Krauze, *Mexico,* 142–44; Castañeda, "Relations."

18. SS to Trist, Jul 13 and 19, 1847, MDC 8:909–13, 915–17; Chamberlain, "Nicholas Trist and Baja"; Johnson, "Baja California." The 32nd parallel runs north of present El Paso, Texas, along the present southern border of New Mexico. The southwest corner of New Mexico had never been fixed.

19. Gilbert M. Joseph, "The United States, Feuding Elites, and Rural Revolt in Yucatán, 1836–1915," in Nugent, *Rural Revolt,* 167–97; Reed, *Caste War;* Levinson, *Wars Within,* 79–80; BMW, 338–39.

20. Sources on the Tabasco campaign include Commodore Home Squadron to SN, May 24, Jun 8, 24, and 16, 1847, and enclosures, ARSN 1847, 1204–21; Bauer, *Surfboats,* 111–20; Griffis, *Matthew Calbraith Perry,* 242–48; Jenkins, *History,* 448–51; Mestre Ghigliazza, *Invasión norteamericana,* 229–47; Morison, *Old Bruin,* 230–37; *Relación historica,* 3–10; Roa Bárcena, *Recuerdos* 3:171.

21. Commodore Home Squadron to SN, Jun 26 and 28, 1847, with enclosures, ARSN 1847, 1221–23, 1230–32; Perry quoted Morison, *Old Bruin,* 238; Griffis, *Matthew Calbraith Perry,* 252–53; Johnson, "Yellow Jack."

22. Johnson, "Yellow Jack," BMW, 242–43.

23. NPD, 230–31, 234, 251; QDP 2:430–31, 3:79–82.

24. Fuller, *Movement,* 40–43; Merk, *Manifest Destiny,* 107–43; Weinberg, *Manifest Destiny,* 165; Lambert, "Movement"; Fuller, "Slavery Question."

25. QDP 2:475–80; BMW, 269–70, 276 n. 23.

26. Prescott to JCC, Aug 20, 1847, quoted BMW, 367. JKP had also been steadily losing friends in Congress. Sam Houston told his wife in Feb that the president was "not a great favorite with Congress." Sam Houston to Margaret Houston, Feb 12, 1847, Roberts, *Houston Correspondence* 2:213.

27. Bauer, *Zachary Taylor,* 215–28; volunteer quoted Leckie, *Wars* 1:353.

28. WS, *Memoirs* 2:466.

29. Ramsey, *Other Side,* 214–19; Rea, *Apuntes históricos,* 25; ALSA, *Eagle,* 97; Callcott, *Santa Anna,* 260; *Ecos,* 122–23; ALSA, *Mi historia,* 69–70; Worth to H. L. Scott, May 15, 1847, MWC, 944–95; Wilcox, *History,* 308–9; SWM 2:69–70.

30. Moore in Smith and Judah, *Chronicles,* 227; Semmes, *Service Afloat,* 237–38.

31. Worth to H. L. Scott, May 15, 1847, MWC, 994–95; Hitchcock, *Fifty Years,* 258; Eisenhower, *Agent,* 265–66.

32. Moore in Smith and Judah, *Chronicles,* 227–28; Laidley to his father, May 19, 1847, Laidley, *Surrounded,* 88.

33. Bustamante, *El nuevo Bernal,* excerpted *Ecos,* 123; Johannsen, *To Halls,* 31.

34. Cristina Gómez Álvarez y Francisco Téllez Guerrero, "Las finances municipales y la guerra: el impacto de la intervención estadunidense en la ciudad de Puebla," in Herrera Serna, *México en guerra,* 523–42; *El Republicano,* Jun 14, and *El Nacional,* Jun 24, 1847, both quoted SWM 2:225.

35. Quoted Henry, *Story,* 304.

36. Laidley to his father, Jun 3, 1847, Laidley, *Surrounded,* 92; Hitchcock, *Fifty Years,* 258; Eisenhower, *Agent,* 165–66; poison circular also quoted SWM 2:72.

37. WS to Quitman, May 31, and to Thomas Childs, Jun 3, 1847, MWC, 997–98, 1002–3; Jenkins, *History,* 295; Ramírez, *Mexico During War,* 127; Levinson, *Wars Within,* 45–48, Perote quoted 47, WS order on stragglers Apr 30, 1847, quoted 45–46.

38. Vigil y Robles, *Invasión,* 41–42; SWM 2:79–80; Jenkins, *War,* 289.

39. Alamán (quoted 243), and Mora to the Gobierno de México, Jun nd, 1847, (quoted 144), Krauze, *Mexico.*

40. Alamán to the Duque de Terranova y Monteleone, May 28, 1847, quoted Krauze, *Mexico,* 143; Ramírez, *Mexico During War,* 139.

41. Ramsey, *Other Side,* 236–37; SWM 2:82–85.

42. Quoted SWM 2:84–85.

43. Ramsey, *Other Side,* 238; SWM 2:87–88.

44. Levinson, *Wars Within,* 53–54, 76–77.

45. Trist to SS, Jul 23 and 31, and Aug 14, and Thornton to Trist, Jul 29, 1847, MDC 8:915–21; Rives, *U.S. and Mexico* 2:436–37; Ripley, *War* 2:148–63.

46. Thornton to Trist, Jul 29, 1847, MDC 8:918n.

47. Alamán to the Duque de Terranova y Monteleone, Jun 28, 1847, quoted Krauze, *Mexico,* 143.

48. SW to WS, Apr 30 and Jul 19, 1847, MWC, 922–23, 1002–4; SW to ZT, Jul 15, 1847, CSW, 192–94; QDP 3:84, 89.

49. WS to SW, Oct 27, 1847, CSW, 216–17.

50. Ibid.; McIntosh to H. L. Scott, Jul 9, and enclosures, and Cadwalader to H. L. Scott, Jul 12, 1847, and enclosures, ARSW 1847, A4–14; Molino Álvarez, *La pasión del*

Padre Jarauta; Jenkins, *History,* 299–32; Roa Bárcena, *Recuerdos,* 107–8; Castillo Negrete, *Invasión* 3:450–54; Frazier, 210–11; Levinson, *Wars Within,* 42.

51. Hitchcock, *Fifty Years,* 265; SWM 2:77; Jenkins, *History,* 302; Pierce to WS, Aug 1, 1847, ARSW 1847, A25; McWhinney, *To Mexico,* 184; Lieutenant Colonel José María Mata to Governor Juan Soto, Jul 25 and 30, 1847, cited Levinson, *Wars Within,* 42–43; Ramsey, *Other Side,* 437–38.

52. Persifor F. Smith to H. L. Scott, Aug 2, 1847, ARSW 1847, A25–26; SWM 2:427; Levinson, *Wars Within,* 43.

53. Scott, *Encarnación Prisoners,* 70; BMW, 278 n. 40; Levinson, *Wars Within,* 48.

CHAPTER 19

1. QDP 3:113, 123–35, 137–399, 140–41, 158–59; Spencer, *Victor and Spoils,* passim; White, *Jacksonians,* 61–62; JKP to Butler, Aug 7, 1847, quoted BMW, 272.

2. NPD, 254–56; QDP 3:120–21; THB to AG, Aug 22, SWK to AG, Aug 22 and Sep 11, and JCF to AG, Sep 17, 1847, *Proceedings of the Court-Martial;* Jessie Benton Frémont to JKP, Sep 21, 1847, BMW, 376 n. 22. JCF, Jessie, and THB released much of their correspondence to the newspapers.

3. On the debates leading to the Compromise of 1850, see Hamilton, *Prologue.* See also the *Resolutions* of the state legislatures listed in the Bibliography. Representative congressional resolutions are *Senate Miscellaneous Documents* 35, 37, and 44, 30 Cong 1 Sess (1848).

4. Hughes and Johnson, *Fighter,* 110.

5. Wool quoted BMW, 222; Richard Bruce Winders, "'Will the Regiment Stand It?': The 1st North Carolina Mutinies at Buena Vista," in Francaviglia and Richmond, *Dueling Eagles,* 67–90; Wallace, "First Regiment"; Smith and Judah, *Chronicles,* 424–31; Foos, *Short Offhand,* 91–92; *Alleged Mutiny at Buena Vista;* SW to ZT, Oct 18 and 25, 1847, and to Wool, Jan 17, 1848, CSW, 398–400; records of the other congressional inquiry in *Dismissal from the Public Service of J. S. Pender and G. E. B. Singletary.*

6. Hughes and Johnson, *Fighter,* 109; ARSW 1847, 482–91; Brooks, *Complete History,* 453–54; Levinson, *Wars Within,* 43–44; Jenkins, *History,* 349–52; Wilcox, *History,* 410–14.

7. Levinson, *Wars Within,* 46–47; Hughes and Johnson, *Fighter,* 108–9.

8. Taliaferro journal, Sep 10, 1847, quoted Levinson, *Wars Within,* 44–45.

9. Twiggs quoted BMW, 274; WS quoted Leckie, *Wars* 1:364; *London Times,* May 10, 1847, quoted Weigley, *American Way,* 75, and SWM 2:89.

10. López quoted *Ecos,* 126; Callcott, *Santa Anna,* 265; DePalo, *Mexican National Army,* 126–27; Scheina, *Santa Anna,* 66; ALSA, *Eagle,* 97–98; Ramsey, *Other Side,* 246–54.

11. Alcaraz, excerpted *Ecos,* 124–25; Bravo Ugarte, *Historia* 3:2, 221; Ramírez to D. F. Elorriaga, Aug 11, 1847, Ramírez, *Mexico During War,* 150; SWM 2:89–90; Laidley to his father, Jan 11, 1848, Laidley, *Surrounded,* 135.

12. López quoted *Ecos,* 126; ALSA and *El Diario,* Aug 10, 1847, quoted SWM 2:92.

13. Alcaraz, excerpted *Ecos,* 126–28; ALSA to the Troops Engaged in the Army of the United States of America, Aug 15, 1847, Smith and Judah, *Chronicles,* 433.

14. The engineers' reports and maps are in *Map of the Valley of Mexico.* See also Lee to J. L. Smith, Aug 12, 1847, Smith and Judah, *Chronicles,* 236; Lee to Mrs. J. G. Totten, Aug 22, 1847, in Freeman, *R. E. Lee* 1:252–53; WS to SW, Aug 19, 1847, ARSW 1847,

303–15; Ramsey, *Other Side,* 246–54; Hitchcock, *Fifty Years,* 274; Semmes, *Service Afloat,* 351–55; Williams, *With Beauregard,* 41–44.

15. Twiggs to H. L. Scott, Aug 16, and WS to SW, Aug 19, 1847, ARSW 1847, 303–15, A28.

16. Alcaraz, excerpted *Ecos,* 128; quotation Ramsey, *Other Side,* 256.

17. Soldier quoted BMW, 291. Sources on Padierna/Contreras/Churubusco and the armistice include WS to SW, Aug 19 and 28, 1847, and subordinate reports, ARSW 1847, 303–46, A38–134, and MWC, 10–18; testimony in *Proceedings of Two Courts of Inquiry;* Alcaraz, 231–58; Ramsey, *Other Side,* 268–99; Callcott, *Santa Anna,* 267–70; Elliott, *Winfield Scott,* 506–18; Thomas, *Robert E. Lee,* 128–36; Eisenhower, *Agent,* 270–84; Freeman, *R. E. Lee* 1:258–64; Grant, *Memoirs,* 73–84; Hitchcock, *Fifty Years,* 275–82; Ripley, *War* 2:216–80; Rives, *U.S. and Mexico* 2:462–74; *Ecos,* 127–37; Chartrand, *Santa Anna's Mexican Army,* 56; Eisenhower, *So Far,* 316–25; Roa Bárcena, *Recuerdos* 2:213–305; ALSA, *Detalles,* 12–16; ALSA, *Las Guerras,* 273–86; ALSA, *Mi historia,* 72–74; ALSA, *Eagle,* 98–100; Scheina, *Santa Anna,* 65–76; WS, *Memoirs* 2:477–502; Semmes, *Service Afloat,* 379–402; SWM 2:100–9; Smith and Judah, *Chronicles,* 239–44; Valencia, *Detalle,* 558; Vigil y Robles, *Invasión,* 43–51; Wilcox, *History,* 358–404; Williams, *With Beauregard,* 48–55; Smith, *Company A,* 39–45; Museo, *Churubusco en la acción;* Ramírez, *Mexico During War,* 151–52; Blackwood, *To Mexico,* 197–204; *La Batalla de Churubusco,* especially Alejandra Rodriguez Diez, "Reseña Histórica del Ex-convento de Santa María de los Ángeles de Churubusco," pp. 167–68; Stevens, *Rogue's March,* 236–44; Hogan, *Irish Soldiers,* 75–81; BMW, 290–301; Wheelan, *Invading Mexico,* 347–61; Henry, *Story,* 329–45.

18. ALSA, *Eagle,* 99.

19. Alcaraz, excerpted *Ecos,* 129; Valencia quoted Hogan, *Irish Soldiers,* 72.

20. Quoted Ripley, *War* 2:208, citing ALSA's report to the war ministry.

21. ALSA quoted Christensen, *U.S.-Mexican,* 201; Valencia quoted Rives, *U.S. and Mexico* 2:473–74; ALSA reaction in Ripley, *War* 2:212–13, 239.

22. The figures are from BMW, 295, and are as reasonable as any.

23. Frías, *Guerra,* 133; ALSA, *Eagle,* 99–100.

24. Quoted Christensen, *U.S.-Mexican,* 202.

25. Salas quoted Henry, *Story,* 336–37; Alcaraz, excerpted *Ecos,* 131. Valencia escaped ALSA's wrath. In Jan 1848 he surrendered to U.S. forces, and died later that year.

26. J. Rufus Smith to William M. Stakely, Oct 23, 1847, quoted McCaffrey, *Army,* 187.

27. ALSA, *Detalles,* 16–17; Frías, *Guerra,* 133–37.

28. Smith, *Company A,* 45–53, complains about WS' impulsiveness and its costs at great length.

29. Anaya quoted *Ecos,* 134.

30. Quoted SWM 2:118.

31. Quoted Waugh, *Class of 1846,* 114–15.

32. Figures are from BMW, 305 n. 38, and Frazier, 113.

33. Ramírez, *Mexico During War,* 152–53.

34. Kirkham, *Mexican War Journal,* 53; Hughes and Johnson, *Fighter,* 119.

35. Witness quoted Ramsey, *Other Side,* 301; Pacheco to SS, Aug 20, and Bankhead to Trist, Aug 21, 1847, MDC 8:921–22, 926n; Rives, *U.S. and Mexico* 2:500–7.

36. Hitchcock, *Fifty Years,* 279–80; WS to Commander Army of Mexico, Aug 21, 1847, MDC 8:922–23; WS to SW, Aug 28, 1847, ARSW 1847, 314.

37. ALSA, *Eagle,* 100; Winthrop, *Military Law* 2:787; WS, *Memoirs* 2:504; on the armistice and peace talks in general, sources include Ramsey, *Other Side,* 300–31; Alcaraz, 259–88; Sears, "Nicholas P. Trist"; Northrup, "Nicholas Trist's Mission"; Graebner, "Party Politics."

38. WS to SW, Aug 28, 1847, ARSW 1847, 303–15; Hughes and Johnson, *Fighter,* 111.

39. Alcorta to WS, Aug 21, and Terms and Ratifications of an Armistice Between the Forces of the United States and Mexico, with Appendixes, Aug 23, 1847, *Treaty Between the United States and Mexico,* 308–13, 350–58; Hitchcock, *Fifty Years,* 285.

40. Minister of relations to president of Congress, and A. M. Salonio to minister of relations, both Aug 21, 1847, *Treaty Between the United States and Mexico,* 309–10.

41. ALSA and others, Points for Discussion in the Conferences with the Commissioners of the United States, Aug 24, 1847, *Treaty Between the United States and Mexico,* 314–15.

42. Trist to SS, Aug 24 and Sep 4, 1847, MDC 8:927–29.

43. Herrera to Pacheco, Antonio Fernández Monjardín to Pacheco, Pacheco, Instructions to Commissioners, all Aug 25, Pacheco to Herrera, Antonio Garay to Pacheco, both Aug 26, 1847, *Treaty Between the United States and Mexico,* 314–25; Cabrero, *Diario del Polk* 3:377n; Ramsey, *Other Side,* 309–15; SWM 2:135; Henry, *Story,* 348–49.

44. Pacheco to Trist, and Trist to Pacheco, both Aug 26, and Trist to SS, Aug 29, 1847, MDC 8:9, 30–33; Pacheco, Revised Instructions, Aug 30, Pacheco to Herrera and other commissioners, Aug 31, 1847, *Treaty Between the United States and Mexico,* 330–35.

45. Alcaraz, excerpted *Ecos,* 138–39.

46. Pacheco, Instructions to commissioners, Aug 30, 1847, *Treaty Between the United States and Mexico,* 330–35; SWM 2:396.

47. Smith quoted Eisenhower, *So Far,* 331; Hill diary, Hughes and Johnson, *Fighter,* 119.

48. ARSW 1847, 319; Miller, *Shamrock and Sword,* 89; Frías, *Guerra,* 141–42; Hogan, *Irish Soldiers,* 159–60.

49. Hogan, *Irish Soldiers,* 90–93, 160–61; McEniry, *American Catholics,* 86; SWM 2:318–19, 511–12; BMW, 304 n. 37; Miller, *Shamrock and Sword,* 176. The executions are discussed below.

CHAPTER 20

1. ARSW 1847, 471–75, A28–35; Jenkins, *History,* 456–65; Wilcox, *History,* 493–96; Brooks, *Complete History,* 489–97; SWM 2:174–78; Winders, "Puebla's Forgotten Military Heroes."

2. García and Pereyra, *México durante su guerra* 29:6.

3. Trist to SS, Sep 4, 1847, MDC 8:928–29.

4. Pacheco, Revised Instructions, and Commissioners of Mexico, *Contraproyecto,* both Sep 5, Mexican Commissioners (Herrera, Couta, Mora, and Atristáin) to Trist, and WS to ALSA, both Sep 6, and WS to SW, Sep 11, 1847, *Treaty Between the United States and Mexico,* 335–46, 354–61. The commissioners' letter to Trist was published in *Niles' National*

Register, Oct 16, 1847, and in Butler, *Documentary History,* 226–27; Josefina Zoraida Vázquez, "War and Peace with the United States," in Meyer and Beezley, *Oxford History,* 339–70.

5. WS to ALSA, and ALSA to WS, both Sep 6, 1847, *Treaty Between the United States and Mexico,* 346, 360–61.

6. Trist to SS, Sep 27, 1847, MDC 8:953–56; Hughes and Johnson, *Fighter,* 121.

7. Sources for the Battle of Molino del Rey include WS to SW and enclosures, Sep 11, 1847, ARSW 1847, 354–75, 425–31, A134–37, A192–98; Balbontín, *Invasión,* 125–29; Alcaraz, 289–301; Ramsey, *Other Side,* 332–48; Ramírez, *Mexico During War,* 155–56; Rea, *Apuntes Históricos,* 39; Roa Bárcena, *Recuerdos* 3:9–55; ALSA, *Detalles,* 23–25; ALSA, *Mi historia,* 75–78; ALSA, *Eagle,* 102–4; Blackwood, *To Mexico,* 216–17; Brooks, *Complete History,* 405–9; Castillo Nájera, *Invasión,* 20–27; Elliott, *Winfield Scott,* 531–35; Eisenhower, *So Far,* 334–37; Eisenhower, *Agent,* 285–99; Butler, *Documentary History,* 228–37; Chartrand, *Santa Anna's Mexican Army,* 56; Grant, *Memoirs,* 80–82; Hitchcock, *Fifty Years,* 293–99; Jenkins, *History,* 385–97; SWM 2:140–47; BMW, 308–12; Wheelan, *Invading Mexico,* 366–71; Henry, *Story,* 351–56.

8. ALSA, *Eagle,* 102–4.

9. Ibid., 101–2; Álvarez and Andrade quoted Levinson, *Wars Within,* 132 n. 56; Bushnell, "Political and Military Career of Álvarez," 203.

10. Figures are from BMW, 310–11, and Frazier, 268.

11. Peck quoted Christensen, *U.S.-Mexican,* 266; Hitchcock, *Fifty Years,* 303; Worth quoted Smith, *Company A,* 56.

12. Prieto in *Ecos,* 135–37. Unless otherwise indicated descriptions of the executions and quotations are from Hogan, *Irish Soldiers,* 175–89.

13. Smith and Judah, *Chronicles,* 436.

14. *Diario del Gobierno,* Sep 10, 1847, quoted Hogan, *Irish Soldiers,* 177.

15. Reconnaissance reports are with J. L. Smith to H. L. Scott, Sep 26, 1847, ARSW 1847, 425–30.

16. Riley quoted BMW, 312; Elliott, *Winfield Scott,* 536–39; Williams, *Beauregard,* 68–72; Eisenhower, *Agent,* 291–94. Other sources on the Battle of Chapultepec and the taking of the *garitas* include WS to SW and enclosures, Sep 18, 1847; ARSW 1847, 375–425, A169–231; testimony in *Proceedings of Two Courts of Inquiry;* Alvear Acevedo, *La guerra,* 59–62; Balbontín, *Invasión,* 130–31; ALSA, *Eagle,* 102–4; Hitchcock, *Fifty Years,* 302–3; Molino, "El Assalto"; Ripley, *War* 2:396–402; Riva Palacio, *México a través* 4:690–95; Roa Bárcena, *Recuerdos* 3:5–112; Sanchez Lamego, *El Colegio militar;* ALSA, *Detalles,* 26–29, 38–52; ALSA, *Mi historia,* 81–82; Semmes, *Service Afloat,* 453–61; SWM 2:208–10; Chartrand, *Santa Anna's Mexican Army,* 54–56; Lewis, *Captain Sam Grant,* 249–54; Rea, *Apuntes históricos,* 46–47; Smith and Judah, *Chronicles* 264–66; Wessels, *Born,* 18–20; Eisenhower, *So Far,* 338–42; Ramsey, *Other Side,* 349–73; Alcaraz, 302–24; Henry, *Story,* 357–65; Wheelan, *Invading Mexico,* 371–79; Smith, *Company A,* 54–60; Grant, *Memoirs,* 79–85.

17. Reporter quoted Ramsey, *Other Side,* 359–60; critic in *Ecos,* 142–43.

18. J. L. Smith to H. L. Scott, Sep 26, 1847, ARSW 1847, 425–30; Williams, *With Beauregard,* 76–77; Hill Diary, Sep 14, 1847, in Smith and Judah, *Chronicles,* 262.

19. Quoted Christensen, *U.S.-Mexican,* 208.

20. Quoted *Ecos,* 143.

21. Kirkham journal Sep 13, 1847, Kirkham, *Mexican War Journal,* 62.

22. Quoted Christensen, *U.S.-Mexican,* 209.

23. Hughes and Johnson, *Fighter,* 126.

24. The story behind the legend is recounted in *Ecos,* 143.

25. Scheina, *Santa Anna,* 73; Balbontín, *Invasión,* 130–32; DePalo, *Mexican National Army,* 135–37; Hitchman, "Rush to Glory."

26. Quoted McCaffrey, *Army,* 187.

27. Alcaraz, excerpted *Ecos,* 144; ALSA and officer quoted BMW, 318.

28. Alcaraz, excerpted *Ecos,* 145; ALSA, *Eagle,* 104–6.

29. Smith, *Company A,* 56.

30. Grant, *Memoirs,* 83–84; ibid.

31. BMW, 321.

32. Hughes and Johnson, *Fighter,* 128; Foos, *Short Offhand,* 126. On the fall of Mexico City generally, see Alcaraz, 325–33, and Ramsey, *Other Side,* 374–93.

33. ALSA, "La Atalaya de Xalapa," and B. J. Y. M. Bocanegra, "Diario de la entrada de los Norteamericanos a la Capital," both quoted Levinson, *Wars Within,* 74.

34. ALSA, *Eagle,* 108–9; Manuel R. Veramendi and others to WS, Sep 13, 1847, cited BMW, 325 n. 18; WS to SW, Sep 18, 1847, ARSW 1847, 375–425; Eisenhower, *Agent,* 298–99; Ramsey, *Other Side,* 371–84.

35. General Order 284, Sep 14, 1847, ARSW 1847, 381, and in Butler, *Documentary History,* 230.

36. Worth to H. L. Scott, Sep 16, Huger (commander of the gun that shot up the houses) to H. L. Scott, Sep 20, Quitman to H. L. Scott, Sep 29, 1847, and other reports, ARSW 1847, 381–86, 409–25; SWM 2:167; WS, *Memoirs,* 2:535; Elliott, *Winfield Scott,* 551–52; BMW, 321–22; Alamán quoted Krauze, *Mexico,* 143–44.

37. López y Rivas, *Guerra de 47,* 135–36; Levinson, *Wars Within,* 59–60; Reina, *Rebeliones campesinas,* 342–46; Wasserman, *Capitalists, Caciques,* 9–10; Guardino, *Peasants, Politics,* 137–58; Robinson, *View,* 17; Bodson, "Description," 180–81; businessman, *New York Sun,* Oct 5, 1847, Smith and Judah, *Chronicles,* 268–69; Alcaraz, excerpted *Ecos,* 146; Hughes and Johnson, *Fighter,* 134.

38. Quoted SWM 2:240 n. 2.

39. Quoted Levinson, *Wars Within,* 72.

40. Hughes and Johnson, *Fighter,* 128–29.

41. *New York Sun,* Oct 5, 1847, Smith and Judah, *Chronicles,* 268–69.

42. Bustamante diary, Sep 15, 1847, excerpted *Ecos,* 149.

43. Wellington is quoted in virtually every history of the campaign, including BMW, 322.

44. ALSA a sus compatriotas, Sep 16, 1847, quoted Krauze, *Mexico,* 144; Ramsey, *Other Side,* 385–93.

45. ALSA to Childs, and Childs to ALSA, both Sep 25, 1847, Brooks, *Complete History,* 489–97, and Butler, *Documentary History,* 238–39; ARSW 1847, 471–75, A28–35; Jenkins, *History,* 156–65; Wilcox, *History,* 293–96.

46. General Orders 189, Sep 18, 196, Sep 22, 297, Sep 23, and 198, Sep 24, 1847, General Orders, RG 94; Ramsey, *Other Side,* 399–403; SWM 2:226–28, 459–61; Meade

quoted Levinson, *Wars Within,* 26; María Gayón Córdova, "Los invasores yanquis en la Ciudad de México," in Herrera Serna, *México en guerra,* 195–232.

47. Ballentine, *English Soldier,* 272; Hughes and Johnson, *Fighter,* 131–32.

48. James R. Irwin, quartermaster report, Sep 17, 1847, Risch, *Quartermaster Support,* 255, 255n; Alcaraz, excerpted *Ecos,* 150–51; Ramsey, *Other Side,* 416.

49. Kirkham, *Mexican War Journal,* 68; Hughes and Johnson, *Fighter,* 134–35.

CHAPTER 21

1. Mariano Otero, "Considerations Relating to the Political and Social Situation of the Mexican Republic in the Year 1847," Robinson, *View,* 5–31, and Joseph and Henderson, *Mexico Reader,* 226–38.

2. ALSA, *Discurso;* Brooks, *Complete History,* 477–79; ALSA, *Eagle,* 112–15; SWM 2:179–81; Cotner, *Military and Political Career,* 163; Luis de la Rosa to ALSA, Oct 7, and ALSA to His Companions in Arms, Oct 16, 1847, cited BMW, 352 n. 14.

3. Laidley to his father, Oct 16, 1847, Laidley, *Surrounded,* 108–9.

4. Lane to H. L. Scott, MWC, 1030–31, and to AG, Oct 18, 1847, ARSW 1847, 477–79; W. D. Wilkins to R. Wilkins, Oct 22, 1847, Smith and Judah, *Chronicles,* 270–71; Ramsey, *Other Side,* 399–403; Jenkins, *History,* 462–65; Alcaraz, 344–52. Three other large forces followed Lane's.

5. Laidley to his father, Oct 16 and 18, 1847, Laidley, *Surrounded,* 109, 114; Hill diary, Hughes and Johnson, *Fighter,* 140; ALSA, *Eagle,* 110–11.

6. The General-in-Chief of the Army to His Companions in Arms, Oct 16, 1847, *Niles' National Register,* Dec 4, 1847, and Butler, *Documentary History,* 240; ALSA, *Eagle,* 112–15; Ramsey, *Other Side,* 403.

7. Garay, Nov 14 and Dec 4, 1847, quoted Levinson, *Wars Within,* 77; manifesto quoted Molina Álvarez, *Pasión,* 108–9.

8. Quoted Levinson, *Wars Within,* 78–79.

9. White, *Jacksonians,* 51; BMW, 394.

10. ZT to Davis, Sep 18, 1847, quoted BMW, 366; AT to AG, Oct 6 and 23, and AG to ZT, Nov 6, 1847, CSW, 397, 400–4; Baylies, *Campaign,* 52; Hamilton, *Zachary Taylor Soldier,* 248–49; Bauer, *Zachary Taylor,* 215–38.

11. QDP 3:160–65, 167–72.

12. Ibid. 3:156; SW to WS, Sep 1, 1847, CSW, 195–96; ST to PUS, Nov 5 and 16, 1847, RMP 5:2381–82; SW to WS, Nov 8, 1847, MWC, 1014; SW to WS, Nov 17, 1847, ARSW 1847, 588.

13. NPD, 267; QDP 3:185–87; SS to Trist, Oct 6, 1847, MDC 8:214–16; SW to WS, Oct 6, 1847, MWC, 1006–9.

14. QDP 3:196; SS to Trist, Oct 25, 1847, MDC 8:217–18; SS to Trist, Oct 25, 1847 (private), BMW, 389 n. 10.

15. NPD, 268, 270–71, 272.

16. Ibid., 271–75.

17. *Proceedings of the Court-Martial;* Clarke, *Stephen Watts Kearny,* 347–73; Nevins, *Frémont,* 327–29; McCormac, *James K. Polk,* 477; *Congressional Globe,* 30 Cong 1 Sess (1848), A977–80.

18. NPD, 282; THB, *Thirty Years* 2:715–19.

19. *Boston Times,* Oct 22, and *New York Herald,* Oct 8, 1847, both quoted Hogan, *Irish Soldiers,* 109.

20. AMP 1847, also in RMP 5:2382–2414; *Senate Miscellaneous Document 6,* 30 Cong 1 Sess (1847); Basler, *Works of Lincoln* 1:420–22; debates in *Congressional Globe,* 30 Cong 1 Sess, passim; Merk, *Manifest Destiny,* 119–20, 149–50; Weinberg, *Manifest Destiny,* 174–77; Donald, *Lincoln,* 122–32, 140–41; Carwardine, *Lincoln,* 11, 22–26.

21. NPD, 284–85, 287; QPD 3:245–46, 262–63; SS to Trist, Dec 21, 1847, MDC 8:218–19; SW to WS, Dec 24, 1847, Letters to Generals, RG 107; correspondence and exhibits in *Proceedings of Two Courts of Inquiry;* JKP to Pillow, Dec 19, 1847, BMW, 372, which summarizes the controversy 372–73.

22. *Proceedings of Two Courts of Inquiry;* CSW, 205–10; Semmes, *Service Afloat,* 361–66; BMW, 376 n. 31. WS' order quoted SWM 2:187–88. See also QDP 3:266, and SWM 2:434–35.

23. NPD, 288–91.

24. Ramsey, *Other Side,* 442; Levinson, *Wars Within,* 65, 135 n. 33; Tibbatts to Bliss, Sep 1, and John Butler to E. G. W. Butler, Sep 9, 1847, LR, RG 94; Belknap to Bliss, Sep 9, Campbell to Bliss, Nov 3, ZT to AG, Nov 14, 1847, CSW, 488–89; Wallace, "First Regiment."

25. SW to ZT, Oct 11, 1847, CSW, 377–78; Baylies, *Campaign,* 54; BMW, 223.

26. Wool, Order Number 11, Dec 17, Wool to AG, Dec 20, 1847, and to Bragg, Jan 1, 1848, LR, RG 94; Fulton, *Diary and Letters* 2:206; BMW, 223–24; Levinson, *Wars Within,* 65–68.

27. AG to Price, Jul 23, Oct 1, and Nov 20, 1847, LS, RG 94; Price to AG, and many orders to subordinates, fall 1847, LR, RG 94, and others in ARSW 1848, 113; Rea, *Price,* 23; Bieber, *Marching,* 339–53; BMW, 159.

28. Captured Mexican documents and Robert Walker to W. E. Prince, Dec 29, 1847, enclosed with Price to AG, Jan 21, 1848, LR, RG 94; McNitt, "Navajo Campaigns."

29. Commodore Home Squadron to SN, Oct 17 and 22, 1847, Home Squadron Letters, RG 45; BMW, 342–43.

30. Commodore Pacific Squadron to SN, Jun 15, Nov 1, 4, and 5, and Dec 5, 1847, and enclosed reports and proclamation, ARSN 1848, 1058, 1073–75, 1083–88, 2222; Kemble, "Amphibious Operations"; Cardenas de la Peña, *Semblanza* 1:148; Martínez, *Historia,* 368–71; Bauer, *Surfboats,* 211–13; Kemble, "Naval Conquest"; Gerhard, "Baja California"; Wise, *Los Gringos,* 136–40; Meadows, *American Occupation,* 20.

31. LaVallette to Shubrick, and enclosures including proclamation, Oct 28, 1847, ARSN 1848, 1076–83; Bauer, *Surfboats,* 214–17; Ripley, *War* 2:603–4; Cardenas de la Peña, *Semblanza* 1:1488–89.

32. Commodore Pacific Squadron to SN, and enclosed reports including "Memoranda of American Defenses at Mazatlán (Sinaloa)" and Shubrick proclamation of Nov 15, Nov 12 and 27, 1847, ARSN 1848, 1089–120; Wise, *Los Gringos,* 142–45; Ramsey, *Other Side,* 425; Gaxiola, *Invasión* 2:149, 161–84; Bauer, *Surfboats,* 224–25; Chartrand, *Santa Anna's Mexican Army,* 56.

33. Commodore Pacific Squadron to SN, Nov 26 and Dec 13, LaVallette to Commodore Home Squadron, Nov 20 and Dec 14, 1847, and enclosed reports, ARSN 1848, 1104–10, 1117–22; Shubrick to WS, Nov 16, and WS to Shubrick, Dec 2, 1847,

MWC, 1035–36; Ramsey, *Other Side,* 431; Gaxiola, *Invasión* 2:186–88; Wise, *Los Gringos,* 155–56.

34. Pacific Squadron reports and correspondence, Nov 21, 1847, to Apr 10, 1848, ARSN 1848, 1102–4, 1135–36, 1158–61; Bauer, *Surfboats,* 218–19; Kemble, "Amphibious Operations."

35. Commodore Home Squadron to SN, Dec 17, 1847, MWC, 1083–84; Pacific Squadron reports and correspondence Nov 15, 1847, to Apr 29, 1848, ARSN 1848, 1095–96, 1111–16, 1122–26; ARSW 1848, 103–12; Commodore Home Squadron to SN, Dec 18, 1847, citing Burton's report, CSW, 273–74; Gerhard, "Baja California"; Martínez, *Historia,* 374–80; Meadows, *Occupation,* 21–22; Frost, *History,* 161, 622–25.

36. AG to WS, Sep 25 and Oct 6, 1847, LS, RG 94; SW to WS, Oct 6, and WS to SW, Oct 27, Nov 27, Dec 14 and 17, 1847, and Jan 8, 1848, and General Order 373, Dec 13, 1847, MWC, 1006–9, 1027–28, 1031–51, 1061–63.

37. General Order 287, Sep 17, 1847, ARSW, 386–87; subsequent orders in MWC, 56, and Claiborne, *Life and Correspondence,* 395n; Davies, "Assessments"; Wallace, "United States Army in Mexico City"; Gabriel, "American Experience."

38. Quitman to H. L. Scott, May 29 and 30, Jun 3, and Oct 25, 1847, CSW, 211–17; BMW, 351 n. 1; Claiborne, *Life and Correspondence.*

39. Quitman proclamations, Oct 6 and Nov 13, 1847, quoted Levinson, *Wars Within,* 73, 136 n. 45; Carlos Rodríguez Vinegas, "Las fianzas publicas," in Vázquez, *México al tiempo,* 124–25.

40. Archbishop to WS, Nov 5, Dec 16 and 23, and WS to Archbishop, Dec 16 and 23, 1847, MWC, 1054–57, and in CSW, 244–49. Not surprisingly, WS' decision in this matter caused some grumbling in the JKP administration.

41. Kirkham journal, Sep 25 and Oct 2, 1847, Kirkham, *Mexican War Journal,* 68–69, 70; Hughes and Johnson, *Fighter,* 130–31, 135; Alamán to Duque de Terranova y Monteleone, Oct 28 and Nov 28, 1847, quoted Krauze, *Mexico,* 144.

42. Henry, *Story,* 369, 380–81; Wallace, "United States Army in Mexico City"; Wilcox, *History,* 511; Wallace, *Destiny,* 15–30; Johannsen, *To Halls,* 54; Winders, *Mr. Polk's Army,* 121–23; Risch, *Quartermaster Support,* 295–96; WS to SW, Dec 15, 1847, MWC, 1047.

43. *Ecos,* 147; WS to Patterson or Lane, Oct 28, 1847, LR, RG 94; BMW, 352 n. 15.

44. Alamán to Duque de Terranova y Monteleone, Nov 28, 1847, quoted Krauze, *Mexico,* 144; Alcaraz, excerpted *Ecos,* 152.

45. Laidley, *Surrounded,* 121; Hughes and Johnson, *Fighter,* 135–42.

46. Hughes and Johnson, *Fighter,* 146–52; Utley, *Lone Star,* 81; Stephen B. Oates, "*Los Diablos Tejanos;* The Texas Rangers," in Faulk and Stout, *Mexican War,* 130–32.

47. Baker, "Mexico City," 179; Levinson, *Wars Within,* 74–75; Olliff, *Reforma Mexico,* 12.

48. Kenly, *Memoirs,* 323.

49. Levinson, *Wars Within,* 57–58, 68–69.

50. WS to Wilson, Oct 13, 1847, MWC, 1028–29; AG to Bankhead, Nov 8, and to WS, Nov 9, 1847, LS, RG 94; Roa Bárcena, *Recuerdos* 3:168.

51. Laidley to his father, Oct 16, 1847, Laidley, *Surrounded,* 107; Hughes to AG, Sep 13, 1847, and Oswandel both quoted Levinson, *Wars Within,* 63–65; SWM 2:156; SW to WS, Oct 6, 1847, in Kenly, *Memoirs,* 309.

52. Childs to AG, Sep 4, 1847, LR, RG 94; Levinson, *Wars Within,* 80–83.

53. Ayuntamiento de Jalapa to Gefe [*sic*] Politico de Este Departmento, Oct 12 and 13, Angel to Ayuntamiento, Oct 14, 24, and 27, and Ayuntamiento to Governador Militar, Nov 11, 1847, Jalapa Papers, Yale University, cited BMW, 352 n. 17.

54. Lane to AG, Oct 22, 1847, ARSW 1847, 479–82, quote at 481; José Eduardo Hernandred to his father, Oct 20, 1847, *Niles' National Register,* Dec 4, 1847, Butler, *Documentary History,* 242; SWM 2:178–79; Brooks, *Complete History,* 508–10; Levinson, *Wars Within,* 62–63, 134 n. 14.

55. Albert Bracket, and Lane to AG, Dec 1, 1847, quoted Utley, *Lone Star,* 80–81; BMW, 330.

56. Lane to AG, Dec 12, 1847, ARSW 1848, 87–88.

57. Commodore Home Squadron to SN, Nov 2, 1847, Home Squadron Letters, RG 45; Wynkoop to Patterson, Nov 22, 1847, LR, RG 94; Roa Bárcena, *Recuerdos* 2:118–20; SWM 2:423; BMW, 334; General Order 372, Dec 12, 1847, General Orders, RG 94, also quoted Levinson, *Wars Within,* 67; see also 65–68, 114.

58. CSW, 142–43, 240–41, 253–57. BMW, 353 n. 29 lists the assessments on each state.

59. Trist to SS, Oct 25, 1847, MDC 8:217–18; and an edited version of this sent to Congress, in *Treaty Between the United States and Mexico,* 205–12; Magner, *Men of Mexico,* 342–43.

60. Rosa to Trist, and Trist to SS, both Oct 31, 1847, MDC 8:969–71; Peña to Trist, Nov 22, 1847, *Treaty Between the United States and Mexico,* 98–99; Brooks, *Complete History,* 576.

61. Peña y Peña to Trist, Nov 22, 1847, *Treaty Between the United States and Mexico,* 98–99; Thornton to Trist, Nov 22, Trist to Peña y Peña, Nov 24, and Trist to SS, Nov 27, 1847, MDC 8:973n, 978–84; Trist to Thornton, Nov 24, 1847, BMW, 389 n. 14; McCormac, *James K. Polk* 2:520.

62. QDP 3:215–18, 269–93; BMW, 382, 389 n. 15.

63. Trist to Thornton, Dec 4, and to SS, Dec 6, 1847, MDC 8:984–1020; *Treaty Between the United States and Mexico,* 100–2, wherein SS deleted Thornton's name as an addressee when passing this on to Congress; Thornton to Trist, Dec 11, 1847, BMW, 390 n. 17.

CHAPTER 22

1. There are many versions of the two stories of the Virgin. This summary combines those presented in Ruiz, *Triumphs,* 69, 101–2, and Fehrenbach, *Fire and Blood,* 208–9.

2. The official United States copy of the final Treaty of Guadalupe Hidalgo is in *Treaty Between the United States and Mexico.* Sources for the final peace talks include Trist to SS, Jan 12 and 25, 1848, MDC 8:1032–39; Rives, *U.S. and Mexico* 2:602–13; Graebner, *Empire,* 206–8; SWM 2:238–40; McCormac, *James K. Polk* 2:536–37; Ramsey, *Other Side,* 445–50. Sources on the treaty's aftermath include Griswold del Castillo, *Treaty;* Cutter, "Legacy of Treaty"; Meyer and Brescia, "Treaty of Guadalupe Hidalgo." Errors in the Disturnell map are summarized in Frazier, 78–80.

3. Foos, *Short Offhand,* 127, on the burglary ring; Laidley, *Surrounded,* 150; Hughes and Johnson, *Fighter,* 163, 171–74, 179; Utley, *Lone Star,* 81–85; Grant, *Memoirs,* 94–100.

4. Miles to Marshall, Jan 5, and Marshall to H. L. Scott, Jan 6, 1848, MWC, 1068–69; Miles to AG, Jan 5, 1848, CSW, 259; Minister Percy Doyle to Butler, and Twiggs to AG, both Jan 5, and Butler to Doyle, Apr 13 and 16, 1848, LR, RG 94; Baker, "Mexico City"; Levinson, *Wars Within,* 64.

5. Lane to WS, Feb 10, 1848, ARSW 1848, 93–95; Callcott, *Santa Anna,* 273–74; Brooks, *Complete History,* 517–19.

6. Lieutenant Walter Bisco to AG, Mar 1, 1848, LR, RG 94; reports of Lane and other officers, ARSW 1848, 95–103; Stephen B. Oates, "*Los Diablos Tejanos:* The Texas Rangers," in Faulk and Stout, *Mexican War,* 133–34; Hughes and Johnson, *Fighter,* 172.

7. Both quoted Drexler, *Guilty of Making Peace,* 129, and Sobarzo, *Deber y conciencia,* 233.

8. Trist to SS, Feb 2, 1848, MDC 8:1059–60; BMW, 384–85.

9. Kenly, *Memoirs,* 394–97; Callcott, *Santa Anna,* 274–76; Utley, *Lone Star,* 85–86.

10. NPD, 293ff; QDP 3:245–46, 262–63; SW to W. O. Butler, and SW General Order 2, both Jan 13, 1848, MWC, 1043–44; SW to WS, Jan 13, 1848 (two letters), CSW, 230–35; SW to AG, Jan 13 and Mar 17, 1848, LR, RG 94.

11. QDP 3:283, 300–1, 311–14, 329; NPD, 301.

12. QDP 3:345–50.

13. Merk, *Manifest Destiny,* 119–20, 149–50; Weinberg, *Manifest Destiny,* 174–77; Foos, *Short Offhand,* 149–54; Ripley, *Joel R. Poinsett,* 229; BMW, 364, 370; 9 Stat. 149–52, 169–75, 188; debates in *Congressional Globe* during this period.

14. Hone quoted BMW, 399; QDP 3:335; PUS to Senate, Feb 23, 1848, RMP 5:2423–24; *Treaty Between the United States and Mexico,* 4–36; Rives, *U.S. and Mexico* 2:614–27; SWM 2:246–48.

15. QDP 3:375–80; PUS to Senate, Mar 18, 1848, RMP 5:2427; SS to commissioners, Mar 18 and 22, 1848, MDC 8:228–35; SW to Butler, Feb 24 and Mar 15, Letters to Generals, RG 107; SS to ST, and ST to Butler, both Feb 23, 1848; *Treaty Between the United States and Mexico,* 108–9.

16. Sevier and Clifford to foreign minister, Apr 17, and to SS, Apr 18 and May 25 and 30, 1848, MDC 8:1079–87; Rives, *U.S. and Mexico* 2:641–55; Rejón, "Observaciones sobre los Tratados de Guadalupe," Moreno, *Manuel Crescencia Rejón,* 93–145.

17. BMW, 387; Frazier, 439–40. President Grant supported Trist's claim for compensation. He died in 1874. Drexler, *Guilty of Making Peace;* Sears, "Nicholas P. Trist."

18. *Proceedings of Two Courts of Inquiry;* Hitchcock, *Fifty Years,* 328; Memorandum on Pillow Court-Martial, Apr 26, 1848, LR, RG 94; Smith and Judah, *Chronicles,* 437–42; Eisenhower, *Agent,* 309–20; WS, *Memoirs* 2:416.

19. Paine to G. A. Porterfield, Jan 17, Hamtramck to McDowell, Jan 20, McDowell to H. C. Webb, Jan 24, and to Hamtramck, Feb 22, 1848, LR, RG 94; Wool to SW, Feb 26, 1848, cited BMW, 230 n. 58.

20. Baylies, *Campaign,* 55; BMW, 225, 231 n. 61 and 62; McDowell to Davenport, Butler, and Webb, Mar 24, Wool to Hamtramck, Mar 27, to D. H. Vinton, Apr 17, to AG, May 9 and Jul 6, to SW, Jul 8, and to Davenport, Jul 23, 1848, LR, RG 94.

21. AG to Price, Nov 20, 1847, LS, RG 94; Price to AG and many orders to subordinates, Fall 1847, LR, RG 94, and others ARSW 1847, 113; Bieber, *Marching,* 339–53; BMW, 159; report of guerrilla attack in *Mexico City American Star,* Feb 9, 1848, following an account from a Chihuahua newspaper, cited Levinson, *Wars Within,* 86.

22. Ramsey, *Other Side,* 451–55; Price to AG and enclosures, including Trías' reports, Apr 5, 1848, LR, RG 94; Smith and Judah, *Chronicles,* 143; SWM 2:419; Roa Bárcena, *Recuerdos* 2:187–90, 3:535–37; Lister, *Chihuahua,* 132; Levinson, *Wars Within,* 103–4; Wilcox, *History,* 538–44.

23. BMW, 159; Rea, *Sterling Price,* 24; McNitt, "Navajo Campaign."

24. Commodore Home Squadron to SN, Jan 10, and SN to Commodore Home Squadron, Feb 24, Jul 3, and May 19, 1848, Home Squadron Letters, RG 45; Griffis, *Matthew Calbraith Perry,* 258; BMW, 343.

25. Commodore Pacific Squadron to SN, Jan 24 and 31 and enclosures, 1848, ARSN 1848, 1127–29; SWM 2:448.

26. Heywood to Shubrick, Feb 21 and 22, DuPont to Shubrick, Feb 16, Mar 25, and Apr 29, 1848, ARSN 1848, 1138–50, 1155–57; Heywood to Burton, Feb 20, 1848, *California and New Mexico,* 513–15.

27. Burton to Sherman, Mar 10 and 20, Apr 13, Steele to Sherman, Mar 20, Burton to H. M. Naglee, Mar 31, 1848, *California and New Mexico,* 21–24; Burton to Shubrick, Mar 20, Commodore Pacific Squadron to SN, Apr 8 and 15, DuPont to Shubrick, Apr 6, 1848, ARSN 1848, 1149–52.

28. Gaxiola, *Invasión* 2:215–17; Meadows, *Occupation,* 28–29; Gerhard, "Baja California."

29. Richards, *California Gold Rush; Pittsburgh Daily Dispatch,* Dec 16, 1848, quoted Bieber, "California Gold Fever," 12; Foos, *Short Offhand,* 163–66.

30. Lieutenant William D. Wilkins to Ross Wilkins, Apr 22, 1848, Smith and Judah, *Chronicles,* 442; see more sensible views at 442–44; ARSW 1848, 170–73; BMW, 387–88.

31. Foos, *Short Offhand,* 166–70; BMW, 397; Levinson, *Wars Within,* 123–24 (the recent study).

32. *Statistical History of the United States,* 1140. BMW, 397–98, using the Census Historical Statistics for 1960, gives similar figures.

33. Utley, *Frontiersmen,* 4–5; Bender, *March of Empire,* 50; Hollon, *Southwest,* 186.

34. Goetzmann, *Exploration,* 257.

35. Quoted Clendenen, *Blood,* 5; see also ch. 1 and 2.

36. Henderson to SS, Jan 4, and SS to Henderson, Feb 12, 1847, *Message from the President . . . in Relation to the Boundary of Texas,* 2–3.

37. AMP 1847, 10–11.

38. Medill to D. R. Atchison, May 6, 1848, and to Robert S. Neighbors, Mar 19, 1847, *Communication from the Commissioner of Indian Affairs* (1848), 1, 5.

39. *Journal of the Senate,* 30 Cong 1 Sess (1848), 477, 499–500, 503; *Journal of the House,* 30 Cong 1 Sess (1848), 1122, 1124.

40. *Report of the Secretary of the Treasury Communicating the Annual Report of the Commissioner of the General Land Office* (1848–49), 15–16; *Journal of the Senate,* 30 Cong 1 Sess (1848), 514; *Senate Miscellaneous Document 14* (1849).

41. *Petition of the People of New Mexico* (1849).

42. These messages are in ARSW 1849, 94, 105.

43. *Senate Miscellaneous Document 22* (1848); Wislizenus, *Memoir of a Tour* (1848).

44. NPD, 321–28, 340.

45. Weigley, *History,* 178; Kemble, *Image,* 57, 66, quote at 38.

46. NPD, 352.

47. "Exposición dirigida al superemo gobierno por los comisionados que firmaron el tratado de paz con los Estados Unidos," *Ecos,* 155–57.

48. Meyer and Beezley, *Oxford History,* 3; Ruiz, *Triumphs,* 218; "Frutos de la guerra," *El Monitor Republicano,* Jul 7, 1848, *Ecos,* 161–62; Carrion, "Effectos psicológicos"; Hale, "War with the United States."

49. Justo Sierra O'Reilly to SS, Mar 7, and Santiago Mendez to SS, Mar 26, 1847, MDC 8:1071–74. Sources on the Caste War of Yucatán include Reed, *Caste War;* Wallace, *Destiny and Glory;* Williams, "Secessionist Diplomacy"; QDP 2:394–95, 425; 3:374, 765; Manno, "Yucatán"; McCormac, *James K. Polk* 2:697; PUS to House and Senate, Apr 29, 1848, RMP 5:2431–32; Levinson, *Wars Within,* 88–91; Krauze, *Mexico,* 145–47; Ruiz, *Triumphs,* 216–17; Olivera and Crété, *Life,* 178–80.

50. Yucatán government quoted Levinson, *Wars Within,* 91; SS to Nathan Clifford (U.S. minister to Mexico), Aug 7, 1848, MDC 9:4.

51. Wallace, *Destiny and Glory,* 31–52; Ruiz, *Triumphs,* 216–17.

52. Riva Palacio, *México a través* 4:712; Hogan, *Irish Soldiers,* 202; Levinson, *Wars Within,* 83–87.

53. Krauze, *Mexico,* 145–47; Levinson, *Wars Within,* 85–86, 92–93.

54. Major Folliot T. Lally at Tampico to Major Lorenzo Thomas, Apr 8, 1848, quoted Levinson, *Wars Within,* 94.

55. Ibid., 96–99, 109–10; *Memoria del Secretario del Estado y del Despache de Guerra y Marina* (1849), 6–9.

CHAPTER 23

1. Leonard, *James K. Polk,* 195–96; Seigenthaler, *James K. Polk,* 154–53.

2. Emerson quoted DeVoto, *Year,* 492; Grant, *Memoirs,* 27.

3. *Petition of the People of New Mexico* (1849). Other New Mexico petitions include *California and New Mexico; Organization of a State Government in the Territory of New Mexico; Constitution Adopted by the Inhabitants of New Mexico; Communication of R. H. Weightman;* and *Memorial of Enrique Sanchez and Others,* published by Congress in 1850, cited more fully in the Bibliography.

4. *Resolutions of the Legislature of Rhode Island* (1849); *Resolutions of the Legislature of New York* (1850).

5. Washington to AG, Feb 3, 1849, ARSW 1849, 105; Lamar, *Far Southwest,* 73–81; *Organization of a State Government in the Territory of New Mexico; Constitution Adopted by the Inhabitants of New Mexico; Communication of R. H. Weightman.*

6. AMP 1849, pt. 1, 11–12; ARSI 1849, pt. 2, 8–9; statements of the secretaries of state and war, in *California and New Mexico,* 10, and *Boundary of Texas,* 6.

7. *Senate Miscellaneous Documents 14* and *15* (1850).

8. Van Horne to Assistant AG Ninth Military Department, and Munroe endorsement, Sep 23, Munroe to Van Horne, Dec 18, 1849, and AG to Munroe, Mar 8, 1850, *Claims of Texas,* 3–6. Van Horne reported to the Ninth Department (New Mexico), but his station was in the Eighth (Texas), and El Paso, his assigned post, was in Chihuahua.

9. *Claims of Texas,* 5–6; *Boundary of Texas,* 4; ARSW 1849, 135; *California and New Mexico,* 113–16.

10. *Senate Miscellaneous Documents 27* and *36* (1850).

11. *California and New Mexico,* 1–3.

12. *Boundary of Texas,* 1–37, referring to SS to Henderson, Feb 12, 1847, reprinted p. 3; also SW to Commanding Officer, Santa Fe, Mar 26, 1849, 2–4. On this issue in general, see also Stegmaier, *Texas, New Mexico;* Larson, *New Mexico's Quest,* 13–40; Nevins, *Ordeal* 1:219–315.

13. *Senate Miscellaneous Document 62* (1850).

14. *Senate Report 123* (1850).

15. Neighbors to Munroe, Apr 7 and 15, and Public Notice, Apr 20, 1850, *Claims of Texas,* 7–9, 14–15, see also 1–2; Neighbours, *Robert Simpson Neighbors,* 81–101; Lamar, *Far Southwest,* 75–79; Hamilton, *Prologue,* 103–4; Nevins, *Ordeal* 1:327–32.

16. *Constitution Adopted by the Inhabitants of New Mexico,* 2–18; Lamar, *Far Southwest,* 79–80; *Communication of R. H. Weightman,* 9.

17. *Organization of a State Government in the Territory of New Mexico;* ZT quoted Nevins, *Ordeal* 1:331, following Thurlow Weed's account of the meeting.

18. *Claim of Texas to Jurisdiction,* 1–13.

19. Hamilton, *Prologue,* appendix; Peterson, *Great Triumvirate,* ch. 8.

20. For a fuller exploration of this argument, see Richards, *California Gold Rush.*

21. *Constitution Adopted by the Inhabitants of New Mexico; Communication of R. H. Weightman.*

22. McCall, *New Mexico;* Hamilton, *Prologue,* 105–6.

23. *Communication of R. H. Weightman,* 2.

24. Bancroft, *History of Arizona and New Mexico,* 630; Lamar, *Far Southwest,* 82.

25. Bieber, "Letters," 184, 186, 189, 198; Lamar, *Far Southwest,* 108, 189.

26. Sumner quoted Bender, "Frontier Defense," 270; Lamar, *Far Southwest,* 94–95.

27. Bancroft, *History of Arizona and New Mexico,* 503–4, 506; Bieber, "Letters," 185–87.

28. ARSW 1847, 70; ARSW 1848, 28–29, 42–43, 125–29, 131–35, 137–40; ARSW 1849, pt. 1, 184; Bender, *March of Empire,* passim; Bender, "Frontier Defense," 249–72; *Santa Fe Gazette,* Feb 19, 1853, quoted Lamar, *Far Southwest,* 96.

29. AMP 1849, 13; ARSW 1849, 91, 105, 107–8, 110, 182; AMP 185, 11–12, 29; Bender, "Frontier Defense," 265; *Translation of a Note from the Mexican Minister.*

30. ARCIA 1850, pt. 2, 137; *Communication of R. H. Weightman,* 7; Hamilton, *Prologue,* 175–76; Lamar, *Far Southwest,* 105.

31. Calhoun to CIA, Mar 31, 1850, ARCIA 1850, pt. 2, 137; Lamar, *Far Southwest,* 89; Murphy, "Reconstruction in New Mexico."

32. Alamán, *Historia* 5:903; Mora quoted Krauze, *Mexico,* 148.

33. Alamán, *Historia* 5:927; Joseph A. Stout Jr., "Post-War Filibustering, 1850–1865," in Faulk and Stout, *Mexican War,* 192–202.

34. Krauze, *Mexico,* 147–48; Olivera and Crété, *Life,* 174–77.

35. Alamán quoted Scheina, *Santa Anna,* 78; Olivera and Crété, *Life,* 15–16; Callcott, *Santa Anna,* 281–88; Krauze, *Mexico,* 148–49.

36. Krauze, *Mexico,* 148–50; Scheina, *Santa Anna,* 78–79; Callcott, *Santa Anna,* 186–94; Hanighen, *Santa Anna,* 269–82.

37. Krauze, *Mexico,* 150–51, citing Jesús C. Romero's *La verdadera historia del himno nacional* (1961).

38. Bancroft, *History of North Mexican States* 2:684–86; Rives, *U.S. and Mexico* 2:169; Hanighen, *Santa Anna,* 269–70; Scheina, *Santa Anna,* 79–80. The prisoners were released in 1854.

39. *Report from the Secretary of War Communicating the Report Made by Lieutenant Simpson;* Simpson, *Journal;* Sitgreaves, *Report; Reports of the Secretary of War, with Reconnaissances,* 4–7, 13–26, 55–283; ARSW 1849, 154–55, 194–99; *Report of the Secretary of the Interior . . . Boundary Between the United States and Mexico;* Bender, "Frontier Defense," 262. The summary of the boundary surveys that follows relies on Rebert, "Mapping the United States-Mexico Boundary"; Richard V. Francaviglia, "The Geographic and Cartographic Legacy of the U.S.-Mexican War," in Francaviglia and Richmond, *Dueling Eagles,* 1–18; Emory, "Running the Line"; Rebert, *La Gran Línea;* Hine, *Bartlett's West;* Utley, *Changing Course;* Goetzmann, *Army Exploration,* 153–208; Goetzmann, *Exploration and Empire,* 257–64. John Russell Bartlett (1805–86) should not be confused with John Bartlett (1820–1905), collector of quotations.

40. ALSA, *Eagle,* 144; Vasconcelos, *Breve historia,* 468–70; Bravo Ugarte, *Historia* 3:216; Hanighen, *Santa Anna,* 280; Scheina, *Santa Anna,* 80–81.

41. Krauze, *Mexico,* 149.

42. Callcott, *Santa Anna,* 307–10; Scheina, *Santa Anna,* 81–86; Fehrenbach, *Fire and Blood,* 411–12.

CHAPTER 24

1. Forsyth to SS, Mar 18, 1858, quoted Scheina, *Santa Anna,* 82. This account of ALSA's last years follows Scheina, 82–86; Hanighen, *Santa Anna,* 282–98; Callcott, *Santa Anna,* 312–55; ALSA, *Eagle,* 137–252. The remainder of the chapter is a summary of the combined histories of Mexico and the United States, citing events covered in standard histories of both. Citations will be limited. See in general Vázquez, *United States and Mexico.*

2. ALSA, *Eagle,* 241.

3. Both quoted ibid., 251–52.

4. Scheina, *Santa Anna,* 83; Callcott, *Santa Anna,* 298.

5. See Frazer, *Bandit Nation;* Bernardo de Quirós, *Bandolerismo.*

6. Fehrenbach, *Fire and Blood,* 451–53.

7. The extent to which the wealth of the country passed into foreign hands, and abuse of Mexicans by the outsiders, are documented in Hanrahan, *Bad Yankee.*

8. Studies of these policies and actions include Szulc, *United States and Caribbean;* Schoutz, *Beneath the United States;* Perkins, *Constraint of Empire.*

CHRONOLOGY of MEXICO
and the UNITED STATES

1783	Treaties of Paris and Versailles; United States gains independence, and Spain gains Florida
1795	Pinckney Treaty, Spain grants United States rights of navigation on Mississippi River
1800	Louisiana transferred from Spain to France
1803	The "great betrayal," France sells Louisiana to the United States
1804–7	Lewis and Clark and Pike expeditions
1810	Mexican Insurgency (War of Independence) begins
1811–13	Insurgency spreads to Texas, attracts Anglo filibusters; bloody suppression
1819	February 22: Adams-Onís (Transcontinental) Treaty signed
1820	Suppression of last agrarian revolutions; Mexican Insurgency becomes counterrevolutionary War of Independence
	March 3: Missouri Compromise
1821	January 17: Spain grants Moses Austin permission to colonize Texas
	March 29: Santa Anna goes over to rebel forces under Iturbide
	September 28: Mexico declares independence from Spain
1822	May: Iturbide becomes emperor of Mexico
	December 12: U.S. recognizes independence of Mexico
1823	March: Iturbide abdicates, after affirming Spain's agreement with Austin on Texas
	December 2: U.S. proclaims Monroe Doctrine
1824	Mexican Constitution of 1824 adopted
	May 7: Mexican law makes Texas part of the state of Coahuila y Tejas
1825	March 24: Mexican Congress opens Texas to colonization by foreigners
	Efforts by successive U.S. presidents to purchase Texas resume
1829	Final defeat of Spanish, at Tampico, by Mexican forces under Santa Anna
1830	April 8: Mexican Congress prohibits slavery and further settlement of Texas by U.S. citizens; Texian resistance to Mexican rule begins
1833	May 16: Santa Anna elected president for first time; relinquishes and resumes office several times over next two years

1835   Texian resistance becomes violent
                December 15: Santa Anna establishes centralist government, abolishes all
                      local rights, raises army, and marches against Zacatecas and Texas
                December 31: Tornel Decree
1836   February 23–March 6: Siege of the Alamo
                March 2–3: Texas declares independence, establishes government, claims
                      the Rio Grande as its western boundary
                March 27: Goliad Massacre
                April 21: Texans defeat and capture Santa Anna at Battle of San Jacinto
                May 14: Santa Anna signs treaty, later repudiated by Mexican Congress,
                      pledging to secure recognition of Texian independence
                July: Both houses of U.S. Congress resolve to recognize Republic of Texas,
                      but President Jackson resists, maintaining American neutrality
1837   March 3: Jackson relents, appoints chargé d'affaires to Texas
                August 4: Texas petitions for annexation to U.S. for first time
                August 25: Texian petition rejected in Washington
                Fall: Slavery controversy boils over in U.S. Congress with "gag rule" debate
1838   Pastry War between France and Mexico
                October 12: Texas withdraws request for annexation
                December 5: Santa Anna becomes hero again with repulse of French at Vera
                      Cruz, losing left leg below the knee
1839   March 18–July 10: Santa Anna's fifth presidency
1841   Texas expedition to Santa Fe
                October 10: Santa Anna begins sixth presidency (relinquished October 26,
                      1842)
1842   March: Mexico invades Texas; troops plunder San Antonio, then withdraw
                September: Mexican troops invade again, seize San Antonio
                October 19: Commodore Jones seizes Monterey, California
                December: Texian troops raid Mier, are defeated and captured
1843   British and French ministers arrange truce between Mexico and Texas
                March 5: Santa Anna begins seventh presidency (relinquished October 4)
                August 23: Santa Anna warns U.S. that any attempt to annex Texas would
                      be equivalent to a declaration of war against Mexico
                October 16: Negotiations begin for annexation treaty between U.S. and
                      Texas
1844   Santa Anna as provisional president introduces forced loans on the church,
                      establishes conscription, imposes new taxes, then claims illness and
                      retires to his hacienda
                April 12: U.S. and Texas sign Texas Annexation Treaty
                April 27: U.S. President Tyler sends troops to Texas border and navy to
                      Gulf of Mexico
                June 4: Santa Anna begins eighth presidency (relinquished September 12)
                June 8: Annexation treaty fails in U.S. Senate
                December: Herrera leads a coup, becomes "temporary president" of
                      Mexico, then (June 1845) exiles Santa Anna for life

Fall: U.S. presidential campaign, Democrat Polk defeats Whig Clay

Tyler recommends that Congress annex Texas by joint resolution

1845   March 1: Tyler signs resolution annexing Texas

March 4: Polk becomes president of U.S.

March 28: Mexico breaks diplomatic relations with U.S.

May: British minister persuades Mexico to recognize Texas independence

May 28: Taylor ordered to prepare for advance across Sabine River into
         Texas

June 23: Texas congress accepts annexation

July 26: Taylor enters Texas with about 3,500 troops

July 31: Taylor establishes camp on south bank of Nueces River near
         Corpus Christi

December 6: Slidell arrives in Mexico City; not received

December 29: Texas becomes a state of U.S.

December 31: Herrera overthrown by Paredes

1846   January 2: Paredes enters Mexico City, becomes interim president two days
         later

January 7–10: Frémont at Sutter's Fort, California

January 12: Polk administration learns of Slidell's rejection by Mexico

January 13: Taylor ordered to advance to the Rio Grande (Río Bravo)

January 24–27: Frémont moves to Monterey, California

February 3: Taylor receives orders to advance

February 13: Polk and Atocha meet

February 22: Frémont starts for the coast; Gillespie embarks at Mazatlán

March 1846–January 1848: Téllez Rebellion, Sinaloa

March 8–11: Taylor starts for Rio Grande

March 20: Slidell formally told Mexico refuses to negotiate

March 21: Frémont back at Sutter's Fort

March 24: Taylor reaches Point Isabel

March 28: Taylor arrives on the Rio Grande

March 30: Frémont at Lassen's ranch

April 5–11: Frémont to Mt. Shasta and return

April 7: Polk learns of Slidell's formal rejection

April 12: Ampudia orders Taylor to retire beyond the Nueces; Taylor
         refuses, and requests naval blockade of the lower Rio Grande, which
         begins April 19

April 17: Gillespie arrives at Monterey, California

April 23: U.S. Congress terminates "joint occupation" of Oregon

April 24: Arista succeeds Ampudia, informs Taylor that hostilities have
         already begun, sends troops across Rio Grande; Frémont sets out for
         Oregon

April 25: Thornton Incident, first U.S. casualties

April 26: Taylor informs Washington that hostilities "may now be
         considered as commenced," calls for volunteers from Texas and
         Louisiana

524

April 30: Mexican army crosses Rio Grande in force, besieges Fort Texas
    beginning May 3

May 8: Battle of Palo Alto

May 9: Battle of Resaca del Guerrero/Resaca de la Palma; news of
    hostilities reaches Washington; Gillespie overtakes Frémont

May 11: Polk asks Congress to declare war on Mexico, which happens
    May 13

May 18: U.S. troops occupy Matamoros

May 24: Frémont reaches Lassen's ranch on way south

June 10–July 5: Frémont organizes "Bear Flag" revolt; skirmishing begins
    in California

June 11: Magoffin wagon train leaves Independence, Missouri

June 15: Polk agrees (and the Senate concurs) to accept an extension of
    U.S.-Canadian boundary on the 49th parallel to the Pacific Ocean

June 16–29: Army of the West marches out of Fort Leavenworth

June 25: Frémont at Sonoma

July 2: Sloat arrives off Monterey, California

July 6: Taylor starts marching upriver

July 7: U.S. naval forces occupy Monterey, California; vía Atocha, Santa
    Anna agrees to return to Mexico and negotiate with U.S.

July 9: Sonoma, California, falls to U.S. forces

July 14: U.S. troops occupy Camargo

July 19: Frémont enters Monterey

July 21: Taylor orders discharge of three- and six-month volunteers

July 21–22: Mormon Battalion starts out for Fort Leavenworth

July 26: Frémont sent to San Diego; Magoffin party reaches Bent's Fort

July 28–30: Army of the West reaches Bent's Fort

July 30: Anglo atrocities and Mexican guerrilla resistance increase in
    northeast Mexico

August 1: Mormon Battalion reaches Fort Leavenworth

August 1–2: Army of the West leaves Bent's Fort

August 3–6: Paredes deposed, Salas becomes acting president

August 8: Wilmot Proviso introduced in U.S. House of Representatives;
    Frémont starts north from San Diego

August 12: Cooke and Magoffin reach Santa Fe, meet Armijo

August 13: Stockton and Frémont occupy Santa Barbara, Mormon
    Battalion marches out of Fort Leavenworth

August 14: Stockton and Frémont occupy Los Angeles

August 16: Santa Anna passes through U.S. blockade, lands in Vera Cruz

August 17: Stockton issues proclamation declaring annexation of California
    by U.S. and establishing a new regime with himself as governor

August 18: Kearny occupies Santa Fe, New Mexico

August 19: Taylor marches out of Camargo toward Monterey, Nuevo León

September 5: Carson starts east with Stockton's report

September 19: Santa Anna rejects American peace feeler

September 20–24: Battle of Monterey, Nuevo León
September 22–30: Mexican revolt retakes most of southern California
September 23–25: Wool leaves San Antonio for Chihuahua
September 25: Monterey surrenders, armistice begins
September 25–28: Kearny marches out of Santa Fe, bound for California
September 28: Salas appoints Santa Anna to command of the army
October 4: Gillespie evacuates Los Angeles
October 6: Kearny meets Carson
October 7: Battle of Dominguez Rancho, southern California
October 9–12: Mormon Battalion reaches Santa Fe; Magoffin party leaves
     for Chihuahua
October 19: Mormon Battalion leaves Santa Fe
October 27: Stockton reaches San Pedro, California
November 13: Mormon Battalion turns west from Rio Grande
November 14–15: U.S. Navy seizes Tampico
November 16: Taylor occupies Saltillo; Battle of Natividad, northern
     California
November 18: Decision to invade at Vera Cruz affirmed, Scott given
     command
November 20–22: Doniphan meets with Navajos at Bear Spring
November 22: Kearny reaches junction of Gila and Colorado rivers
November 25: Kearny crosses Colorado River into California
December 2: Kearny reaches Warner's ranch
December 5: Wool occupies Parras
December 6: Battle of San Pasqual, southern California
December 9: Mormon Battalion reaches San Pedro River
December 11: Battle of the Bulls, Sonora
December 12: Kearny reaches San Diego
December 12–23: Doniphan's command assembles at Doña Ana, New
     Mexico
December 16: Mormon Battalion reaches Tucson, Sonora
December 24: Santa Anna elected provisional president (relinquished April
     12, 1847), while assembling army at San Luis Potosí
December 25: Battle of El Brazito/Temascalitos, New Mexico
December 27: Doniphan occupies El Paso del Norte, Chihuahua
December 29: Kearny and Stockton leave San Diego for Los Angeles
1847   January 1847–October 1849: Sierra Gorda agrarian revolt, north-central
     Mexico
January 2: Battle of Santa Clara, California
January 8: Battle of Río San Gabriel, California
January 9: Battle of La Mesa, California
January 10: Los Angeles retaken by U.S. forces
January 10–11: Mormon Battalion crosses Colorado River into California
January 13: Treaty of Cahuenga, ending last Mexican resistance in
     California

January 19: Taos Rebellion erupts, New Mexico

January 24: Battles of Cañada and Mora, New Mexico

January 29: Battle of Embudo Pass, New Mexico

January 29–30: Mormon Battalion reaches San Diego

February 3–4: Battle of Pueblo de Taos, New Mexico

February 5: Doniphan leaves El Paso del Norte for Cd. Chihuahua

February 10: Arkansas troops massacre villagers near Catana,
    Nuevo León

February 18: Scott arrives at Tampico

February 19: Scott issues General Order No. 20

February 22: Mexican irregulars destroy supply train near Ramos,
    northeast Mexico

February 22–23: Battle of Buena Vista/Angostura

February 24: Texians massacre villagers at Rancho Guadalupe, northeast
    Mexico

February 28: Battle of the Sacramento, Chihuahua; Polko Rebellion,
    Mexico City

March 1–2: Doniphan occupies Cd. Chihuahua

March 9: Troops under Scott land on beaches near Vera Cruz

March 9–29: Siege and bombardment of Vera Cruz

March 27: Surrender of Vera Cruz, occupied by U.S. forces March 29

March 31: Alvarado falls to U.S. army-navy expedition

April 8: Scott begins marching out of Vera Cruz

April 18: Battle of Cerro Gordo; Battle of Tuxpan

April 19: Jalapa occupied

April 22: Perote occupied

April 25–28: Doniphan marches out of Cd. Chihuahua

May 6: Trist arrives at Vera Cruz

May 15: Scott occupies Puebla

May 20: Santa Anna becomes president for tenth time (relinquished
    September 16)

May 23: Doniphan's Expedition marches out of Monterey, headed home

May 31: Kearny and Frémont start east; Carson reaches Washington

June 15: Carson leaves Washington for California

August 7: Scott marches out of Puebla for Valley of Mexico

August 14–15: Paine mutiny

August 19–20: Battle of Contreras/Padierna

August 20: Battle of Churubusco; Santa Anna withdraws to Mexico City

August 24: Armistice of Tacubaya takes effect

August 27–September 6: Trist negotiates with Mexican commission

September 7: Armistice terminated, Scott resumes advance

September 8: Battle of Molino del Rey

September 13: Battle of Chapultepec

September 13–14: Battle for Mexico City

September 14–October 12: Siege of Puebla

September 15: American occupation of Mexico City begins, puts down rebellion

September 16: Scott reissues General Order No. 20; Santa Anna relinquishes presidency

October 2: Battle of Mulejé, Baja California

October 7: Santa Anna deposed as head of army

October 9: Skirmish and sacking of Huamantla

October 19: Battle of Atlixco

October 25: Carson delivers first transcontinental mail at Monterey, California

November 8–22: Siege of San José del Cabo, Baja California

November 11: Anaya elected interim president of Mexico

November 16: Trist receives order for his recall

November 22: Anaya government informs Trist that it has appointed a commission to negotiate peace

December 4: Trist decides to remain and negotiate a treaty

December 24: Skirmish at Cañon Santa Rosa, near Anton Chico, New Mexico

1848   All year: Agrarian revolts by displaced *Indios* spread all over Mexico; raids by migratory Indian tribes from the North increase; Caste War in Yucatán becomes ever more bloody

January 2: Treaty negotiations begin at Guadalupe Hidalgo

January 22–February 14: Second siege of San José del Cabo, Baja California

January 24: Gold discovered near Sutter's Fort, California

February 2: Treaty of Guadalupe Hidalgo signed

February 18: Scott leaves Mexico City for Washington

February 19: Treaty text arrives in Washington

February 23: Polk sends treaty to Senate for ratification

February 25: Battle and sacking of Zacualtipán

February 29: Armistice declared

March: Price invades Chihuahua and occupies Cd. Chihuahua

March 10: U.S. Senate ratifies treaty

March 16: Battle of Santa Cruz de Rosales, Chihuahua

March 31: Last action of the war, Todos Santos, Baja California; U.S. troops evacuate Mexico City

April 15: Santa Anna exiled

May 25: Mexican Congress ratifies treaty

May 30: The two governments exchange ratifications

July 4: Polk declares treaty in effect

August 2: Last U.S. troops leave Mexico via Vera Cruz

1849   March 5: Taylor inaugurated as president of the U.S.; sectional divisions erupt in U.S. Congress

June 15: Polk dies at home in Tennessee

November 13: California state constitution forbids slavery

1850   January 19–September 20: Debates leading to the Compromise of 1850

March 12: California petitions Congress to enter the union as free state

July 9: Taylor dies; Fillmore becomes president

1853   April 1: Santa Anna becomes president eleventh time

December 30: Gadsden Purchase signed; ratified June 29, 1854

1854   March 1: Plan de Ayutla; liberal uprising starts

1855   August 9: Santa Anna overthrown, exiled

1857   War of the Reform breaks out in Mexico

1861   Civil war in Mexico ends with triumph of liberals under Juárez.

April: Civil war begins in U.S.

June: Juárez becomes president of Mexico; country bankrupt

July 17: Juárez government suspends payment on foreign debts for two years

1862   April: French forces invade Mexico at Vera Cruz; War of the Reform resumes

May 5 (Cinco de Mayo): Mexicans defeat the French invaders

1863   French reinvade with greater forces, begin gradual conquest of Mexico with support from conservative Mexicans; guerrilla warfare and fratricidal fighting continue for next several years

July: In U.S., Union victories at Gettysburg and Vicksburg

1864   Maximilian assumes throne in Mexico City

1865   April–June: U.S. civil war ends; U.S. army of 42,000 sent to Brownsville, Texas, to intimidate French; Mexican bloodbath deepens

1866   Reconstruction and occupation of defeated South begins in U.S.; Ku Klux Klan founded

January 15: French emperor announces he will withdraw French troops from Mexico between October 1866 and October 1867, later accelerated to March 1867

1867   Díaz rises as Mexican national hero with victories over conservative forces

February 5: French troops leave Mexico City

March 16: Last French troops leave Mexico via Vera Cruz

June 19: Maximilian executed near Querétaro

June 21: Díaz captures Mexico City

July 15: Juárez returns to Mexico City; War of the Reform resumes

1871   Juárez reelected president for second term, dies within a year

1875   Last military occupation of South ends in U.S.; Reconstruction ends

1876   Díaz seizes presidency, establishes authoritarian rule that will last, with minor interruptions, until the revolution of 1910; favors foreign investment in Mexico, producing increasing resentment of U.S. and Britain

June 21: Santa Anna dies in Mexico City

1901   September 14: Theodore Roosevelt becomes U.S. president

1904   Roosevelt Corollary proclaimed, policy continued until 1933

1910   Revolution and civil war erupt in Mexico

June 20: U.S. Congress passes act enabling New Mexico and Arizona to petition for statehood; statehood granted 1912

1913   February 22: Mexican president Madero assassinated; Huerta seizes
                power
            March 4: Woodrow Wilson becomes U.S. president
            August: Wilson announces policy of "watchful waiting" regarding events in
                Mexico; later calls for Huerta's abdication
            November: Wilson announces support for Huerta's opponents,
                encouraging a wider civil war in Mexico; famously says, "We shall teach
                them to elect good men."
1914   April 9: Tampico Incident starts; U.S. admiral demands salute to U.S. flag
                by Mexican troops
            April 11: Huerta refuses the demanded salute at Tampico
            April 14: Wilson orders U.S. fleet to Tampico
            April 19: Wilson asks U.S. Congress for authority to use force in Mexico;
                granted April 22
            April 21: U.S. forces seize Vera Cruz
            April 22: Mexico severs diplomatic relations with the U.S.
            April 25: Argentina, Brazil, and Chile offer to mediate between U.S. and
                Mexico; both governments accept
            July 15: Huerta forced out of office
            August: World War I breaks out in Europe
            November 23: U.S. forces withdraw from Vera Cruz
1915   Bandit activity across the U.S.–Mexico border increases steadily
            August 5: Conference convenes in Washington to consider how to end
                disorder in Mexico
            October 19: Wilson administration recognizes Carranza as president of
                Mexico
            October 20: Wilson administration declares an embargo on shipment of
                arms to Mexico except to territories controlled by Carranza
1916   March 9: About 1,500 irregulars loyal to Villa attack Columbus, New Mexico
            March 15: Pershing leads a "punitive expedition" into Mexico to capture
                Villa
            June 16: Carrancista General Trevino warns Pershing against further
                movement of U.S. troops into Mexico
            June 17: Other U.S. troops cross into northeast Mexico
            June 20: U.S. Secretary of State notifies Mexico that U.S. troops will not
                withdraw until order is restored on the border
            June 21: Battle of Carrizal, Chihuahua
            July 28: U.S. accepts proposal by Carranza government to submit
                differences between the nations to an international commission
1917   January 28: U.S. forces recalled from Mexico
            February 24: British government hands over to the American ambassador
                to Mexico the "Zimmerman Telegram"; note made public March 1
            April 2: U.S. declares war against Germany and its allies; U.S. interference
                in Mexican affairs begins to taper off
            Summer: Mexico adopts the Constitution of 1917

1919–45   Zapata assassinated by Carrancistas 1919; Carranza loses influence, is
            overthrown by Obregón; Villa reduced to insignificance, then
            assassinated by Obregónistas in 1923; violence tapers off in Mexico;
            reconstruction of nation begins under Constitution of 1917,
            interrupted by another civil war 1927–29; final repudiation of
            caudillismo, 1929; after tentative attempts during the 1920s to
            implement constitutional provision reserving subsurface resources to
            the Mexican people were thwarted by threats of military intervention
            from the U.S., in 1938 the government expropriates oil reserves,
            driving U.S. and British petroleum companies out of the country;
            during World War II, Mexico allies with the U.S. and sends forces into
            the war effort

1995   North American Free Trade Agreement; "illegal immigration" increasingly
            becomes political issue in U.S.

ACKNOWLEDGMENTS

No historian works alone. The work depends absolutely on the dedicated staffs and volunteers who run the institutions that guard our documentary, material, and published heritage—in this case, in two nations. I offer my profound thanks to the people of the following organizations who have been so helpful in this and relevant earlier projects. And I tip my hat in particular to the technical wizards in most of them who make more and more material available every year over the Internet.

Libraries, archives, and other historical organizations: Horgan Library, New Mexico Military Institute, Roswell; Golden Library, Eastern New Mexico University, Portales; Center for Southwest Research, Division of Iberian and Latin American Resources, and Spanish Colonial Research Center, Zimmerman Library, University of New Mexico, Albuquerque; Library of Congress, Washington, DC; Biblioteca Nacional de México, México, DF; National Archives, Washington, DC; Archivo General de la Nación, México, DF; Federal Records Center, Fort Worth, Texas; Latin American Collection, University of Texas Library, Austin; Center for Greater Southwestern Studies and Special Collections Division, University of Texas Library, Arlington; Indiana University Library, Bloomington; Library of Eastern New Mexico University at Roswell; Roswell Public Library; Center of Military History, Department of the Army, Washington, DC; U.S. Army Military History Institute, Carlisle Barracks, Pennsylvania; Naval Historical Center, Department of the Navy, Washington, DC; Mexican War Media Collection, University of Vermont; Descendants of Mexican War Veterans, Richardson, Texas.

Museums and managed historic sites: Museo Nacional de las Intervenciones (Museo Histórico de Churubusco), Templo y Ex-Convento de Churubusco, Coyoacán, DF; Chapultepec Parque y Castillo, Museo Nacional de Historia, México, DF; Museo del Ejército, México, DF; U.S. National Cemetery, México, DF; Museo Carrillo Gil, San Ángel, DF; Casa Mata, Matamoros, Tamaulipas; Museo Regional de Nuevo León, Obispado, Monterrey, Nuevo León; Museo de la Historia de Nuevo León, Palacio Municipal, Monterrey, Nuevo León; Museo en el Baluarte de Santiago, Cd. Veracruz, Veracruz; El Encero, Hacienda de Antonio López de Santa Anna, Veracruz; Fortaleza Loreto, Cd. Puebla, Puebla; Palo Alto Battlefield National Historic Site, Texas; Bent's Old

Fort National Historic Site, Colorado; Chamizal National Memorial, Texas; El Camino Real International Heritage Center, New Mexico.

A number of individuals also contributed advice, information, or other assistance. Bea Clary, Jim Donovan, John Elsegood, John Flicker, the late Roger Hernández, Jay Miller, Ernesto Ortega, and Joseph Sánchez gracefully agreed to read part or all of an early draft of the manuscript, and offered comments that kept me from putting my foot where it would interfere with eating. Dave Ferguson of the Rio Grande Botanic Garden, Albuquerque, patiently answered my questions about the flora and fauna of Mexico and the southwestern United States, although not even he could explain the sea of yellow lizards south of Cd. Chihuahua. Thanks to Jim Donovan, my agent, for making the project happen, and to my editor, John Flicker, who with his assistant Jessica Waters turned it into what you hold in your hands.

Unless otherwise indicated, illustrations are from the author's collection.

As always, my fondest thanks to my long-suffering but eternally patient quartermaster general, my wife, Beatriz Clary. This army of one could not begin to march without her, nor slog on through the struggle without her continuing support. She is really the one who keeps the guns in action.

Credit belongs to all of these good people for whatever is worthy of merit in this book. Blame for whatever falls short rests entirely on my doorstep.

BIBLIOGRAPHY

Note: Libraries, archives, museums, historic sites, and other institutions important to the subject of this book are cited in the Acknowledgments. Newspaper and newsletter articles are cited in the chapter Notes only; the same is true of articles included in books listed in the Bibliography. Record Groups consulted in files and microfilm publications of the National Archives of the United States are listed in the Abbreviations under "RG." Annual Reports of the officers of the United States government, appended to the Annual Messages of the President, are listed in the Abbreviations under "AR."

PRINTED DOCUMENTS: UNITED STATES CONGRESS

Abert, J. W. *Report of Lieutenant J. W. Abert of His Examination of New Mexico in theYears 1846–1847*. Senate Executive Document 23, 30th Congress, 1st Session (1848).

Alleged Mutiny at BuenaVista, about 15th August 1847. Senate Executive Document 62, 30th Congress, 1st Session (1848).

Annual Message of the President 1844. Senate Executive Document 1, 28th Congress, 2nd Session (1844).

Annual Message of the President 1845. Senate Executive Document 1, 29th Congress, 1st Session (1845).

Annual Message of the President 1846. Senate Executive Document 1, 29th Congress, 2nd Session (1846).

Annual Message of the President 1847. Senate Executive Document 1, 30th Congress, 1st Session (1847).

Annual Message of the President 1848. Senate Executive Document 1, 30th Congress, 2nd Session (1848).

Annual Message of the President 1849. Senate Executive Document 1, 31st Congress, 1st Session (1849).

Annual Message of the President 1850. Senate Executive Document 1, 31st Congress, 2nd Session (1850).

Boundary of Texas. Senate Executive Document 24, 31st Congress, 2nd Session (1850).

California and New Mexico. Senate Executive Document 17, 31st Congress, 1st Session (1850).

California Claims. Senate Report 75, 30th Congress, 1st Session (1848).

The Calling of Volunteers . . . Without Legal Authority. Senate Document 378, 29th Congress, 1st Session (1846).

The Claim of Texas to Jurisdiction over Part of New Mexico. Senate Executive Document 67, 31st Congress, 1st Session (1850).

Claims of Texas. Senate Executive Document 56, 31st Congress, 1st Session (1850).

Commodore Stockton's Despatches. Senate Executive Document 31, 30th Congress, 2nd Session (1849).

Communication from the Commissioner of Indian Affairs, and Other Documents in Relation to the Indians in Texas. Senate Report 171, 30th Congress, 1st Session (1848).

Communication of R. H. Weightman, and Accompanying Memorial of the Legislature of New Mexico, Setting Forth Sundry Grievances, and Calling upon Congress for Their Correction. Senate Executive Document 76, 31st Congress, 1st Session (1850).

Congressional Globe. 29th Congress, 1st Session through 31st Congress, 2nd Session (1845–1851).

Constitution Adopted by the Inhabitants of New Mexico. Senate Executive Document 74, 31st Congress, 1st Session (1850).

Cooke, Philip St. George. *Journal of the March of the Mormon Battalion of Infantry Volunteers under the Command of Lieutenant Colonel P. St. George Cooke (also Captain of Dragoons), from Santa Fe, New Mexico, to San Diego, California, Kept by Himself by Direction of the Commanding General of the Army of the West.* Senate Document 2, 31st Congress, Special Session (1849).

Correspondence Between the Secretary of War and Generals Scott and Taylor and Between General Scott and Mr. Trist. House Executive Document 56, 30th Congress, 1st Session (1848).

Correspondence in Relation to the Boundary of Texas, Called for by a Resolution of the Senate. Senate Executive Document 24, 31st Congress, 1st Session (1850).

Correspondence with General Taylor. House Executive Document 17, 30th Congress, 1st Session (1848).

Dismissal from the Public Service of J. S. Pender and G. E. B. Singletary. Senate Executive Document 78, 30th Congress, 1st Session (1848).

Documents in Relation to a Treaty Proposed to be Negotiated with the Indians of the Prairie South and West of the Missouri River, to the Northern Line of Texas, Embracing the Indians of the Mountains, and Including Those of New Mexico. Senate Miscellaneous Document 70, 31st Congress, 1st Session (1850).

Emory, William H. *Notes of a Military Reconnaissance from Fort Leavenworth, in Missouri, to San Diego, in California, Including Part of the Arkansas, Del Norte, and Gila Rivers.* Senate Executive Document 7, 30th Congress, 1st Session (1848).

Hughes, George W. *Memoir Descriptive of the March of a Division of the United States Army, Under the Command of Brigadier General John E. Wool, from San Antonio de Bexar, in Texas, to Saltillo, in Mexico.* Senate Executive Document 32, 31st Congress, 1st Session (1850).

Information Called for by a Resolution of the Senate of the 17th Instant, in Relation to California and New Mexico. Senate Executive Document 18, 31st Congress, 1st Session (1850).

Information Relating to Military Orders Issued to the United States Officers at Santa Fe, and Correspondence Between Those Officers and the War Department in Relation to the Claims of Texas over That Country. Senate Executive Document 56, 31st Congress, 1st Session (1850).

Insurrection Against the Military Government in New Mexico and California, 1847 and 1848. Senate Document 442, 56th Congress, 1st Session (1900).

Journal of the House of Representatives of the United States. 29th Congress, 1st Session, through 31st Congress, 2nd Session (1845–1851).

Journal of the Senate of the United States. 29th Congress, 1st Session, through 31st Congress, 2nd Session (1845–1851).

Map of the Valley of Mexico, by Lieutenants Smith and Hardcastle. Senate Executive Document 19, 30th Congress, 2nd Session (1849).

Memorial of Enrique Sanchez and Others, Citizens and Residents of the Territory of the Rio Grande, Praying the Establishment of a Territorial Government. Senate Miscellaneous Document 61, 31st Congress, 1st Session (1850).

Message from the President of the United States Communicating Information of the Existing Relations Between the United States and Mexico, and Recommending the Adoption of Measures for Repelling the Invasion Committed by the Mexican Forces upon the Territory of the United States. Senate Document 337, 29th Congress, 1st Session (1846).

Message from the Secretary of the Navy . . . in Relation to the Loss of the United States Brig Somers. Senate Document 43, 29th Congress, 2nd Session (1847).

Mexican War Correspondence. House Executive Document 60, 30th Congress, 1st Session (1848).

Military Forces Employed in the Mexican War. House Executive Document 24, 31st Congress, 1st Session (1850).

New Mexico and California. House Executive Document 70, 30th Congress, 1st Session (1848).

Occupation of Mexican Territory. House Executive Document 19, 29th Congress, 2nd Session (1847).

Operations and Recent Engagements on the Mexican Frontier. Senate Document 388, 29th Congress, 1st Session (1846).

Organization of a State Government in the Territory of New Mexico. Senate Executive Document 60, 31st Congress, 1st Session (1850).

Pay and Emoluments of Lieutenant-General Scott. Senate Executive Document 34, 34th Congress, 3rd Session (1857).

Petition of the People of New Mexico, Assembled in Convention, Praying the Organization of a Territorial Government. Senate Miscellaneous Document 5, 30th Congress, 2nd Session (1849).

Proceedings of the Court-Martial of Colonel Frémont. Senate Executive Document 33, 30th Congress, 1st Session (1848).

Proceedings of the Senate on the Annexation of Texas. Senate Document 341, 28th Congress, 1st Session (1844).

Proceedings of the Two Courts of Inquiry in the Case of Major-General Pillow. Senate Executive Document 65, 30th Congress, 1st Session (1848).

Report from the Secretary of War Communicating . . . the Report and Map of the Route from Fort Smith, Arkansas, to Santa Fe, New Mexico, Made by Lieutenant Simpson. Senate Executive Document 12, 31st Congress, 1st Session (1850).

Report of the Secretary of the Interior in Answer to a Resolution of the Senate Calling for Information in Relation to the Operations of the Joint Commission Appointed to Run and Mark the Boundary

Between the United States and Mexico. Senate Executive Document 34, 31st Congress, 1st Session (1850).

Report of the Secretary of the Treasury Communicating the Annual Report of the Commissioner of the General Land Office. Senate Executive Document 2, 30th Congress, 2nd Session (1848–1849).

Report of the Secretary of War . . . as to the Employment of Any Individual [Authorized] to Raise Volunteers. Senate Document 439, 29th Congress, 1st Session (1846).

Report of the Secretary of War Showing the Number of Troops in the Service. Senate Executive Document 36, 30th Congress, 1st Session (1848).

Report of the Senate Committee on Military Affairs. Senate Report 171, 30th Congress, 2nd Session (1849).

Report of the Senate Committee on Post Offices and Post Roads. Senate Report 310, 30th Congress, 2nd Session (1849).

Reports of the Committees of the Senate, 123. 31st Congress, 1st Session (1850).

Reports of the Secretary of War, with Reconnaissances of the Routes from San Antonio to El Paso . . . Also, the . . . Route from Fort Smith to Santa Fe; and the Report of . . . an Expedition into the Navajo Country; and the Report of . . . Reconnaissances of the Western Frontier of Texas. Senate Executive Document 64, 31st Congress, 1st Session (1850).

Resolutions of the Legislature of Connecticut, in Relation to Slavery. Senate Miscellaneous Document 15, 30th Congress, 1st Session (1847).

Resolutions of the Legislature of Florida, on the Subject of Slavery. Senate Miscellaneous Document 58, 30th Congress, 2nd Session (1849).

Resolutions of the Legislature of Illinois, in Favor of the Exclusion of Slavery from the Territories Acquired from Mexico. Senate Miscellaneous Document 38, 30th Congress, 2nd Session (1849).

Resolutions of the Legislature of Michigan, in Favor of the Prohibition of Slavery within Any Territory of the United States Now or Hereafter to be Acquired. Senate Miscellaneous Document 41, 30th Congress, 2nd Session (1849).

Resolutions of the Legislature of Missouri, on the Subject of Slavery. Senate Miscellaneous Document 24, 31st Congress, 1st Session (1850).

Resolutions of the Legislature of New Hampshire, in Relation to Slavery. Senate Miscellaneous Document 17, 30th Congress, 1st Session (1848).

Resolutions of the Legislature of New York for the Abolition of the Slave Trade in the District of Columbia; Against an Extension of Slavery into the Territory Acquired from Mexico; Against the Extension of Slavery or the Jurisdiction of Texas over Any Part of New Mexico; for the Admission of California, and in Favor of the Preservation of the Union. Senate Miscellaneous Document 52, 31st Congress, 1st Session (1850).

Resolutions of the Legislature of Rhode Island, in Relation to Slavery. Senate Miscellaneous Document 62, 30th Congress, 2nd Session (1849).

Resolutions of the Legislature of South Carolina, in Relation to the "Wilmot Proviso." Senate Miscellaneous Document 51, 30th Congress, 2nd Session (1849).

Resolutions of the Legislature of Virginia, in Relation to Slavery. Senate Miscellaneous Document 48, 30th Congress, 2nd Session (1849).

Resolutions of the Legislature of Wisconsin, in Relation to Slavery. Senate Miscellaneous Document 61, 30th Congress, 2nd Session (1849).

Senate Miscellaneous Document 6, 30th Congress, 1st Session (1848).

Senate Miscellaneous Document 8, 30th Congress, 1st Session (1848).

Senate Miscellaneous Document 12, 30th Congress, 2nd Session (1849).

Senate Miscellaneous Document 14, 30th Congress, 2nd Session (1849).

Senate Miscellaneous Document 14, 31st Congress, 1st Session (1850).

Senate Miscellaneous Document 15, 31st Congress, 1st Session (1850).

Senate Miscellaneous Document 22, 30th Congress, 1st Session (1848).

Senate Miscellaneous Document 27, 31st Congress, 1st Session (1850).

Senate Miscellaneous Document 35, 30th Congress, 1st Session (1848).

Senate Miscellaneous Document 36, 31st Congress, 1st Session (1850).

Senate Miscellaneous Document 37, 30th Congress, 1st Session (1848).

Senate Miscellaneous Document 44, 30th Congress, 1st Session (1848).

Senate Miscellaneous Document 62, 31st Congress, 1st Session (1850).

Simpson, James Harvey. *Journal of a Military Reconnaissance from Santa Fe, New Mexico, to the Navajo Country, Made with Troops under Command of Brevet Lieutenant Colonel John M. Washington, Chief of the Ninth Military Department and Governor of New Mexico in 1849.* Senate Executive Document 64, 31st Congress, 1st Session (1850).

Sitgreaves, Charles L. *Report of an Expedition Down the Zuni and Colorado Rivers.* Senate Executive Document 64, 31st Congress, 1st Session (1850).

Thian, Raphael P. *Legislative History of the General Staff of the Army of the United States (Its Organization, Duties, Pay, and Allowances), from 1775 to 1901.* Senate Document 229, 56th Congress, 2nd Session (1901).

The Taking Possession of Monterey by Commodore Thomas ap Catesby Jones. House Document 166, 27th Congress, 3rd Session (1843).

Translation of a Note from the Mexican Minister in Relation to the Wild Indians of the United States on the Frontier of Mexico. Senate Executive Document 44, 31st Congress, 1st Session (1850).

Treaty Between the United States and Mexico. Senate Executive Document 52, 30th Congress, 1st Session (1848).

United States and Mexico. House Document 351, 25th Congress, 2nd Session (1838).

Wislizenus, F. Adolphus. *Memoir of a Tour to Northern Mexico, Connected with Colonel Doniphan's Expedition, in 1846 and 1847.* Senate Miscellaneous Document 26, 30th Congress, 1st Session (1848).

PRINTED DOCUMENTS: UNITED STATES WAR DEPARTMENT

General Regulations for the Army of the United States. Washington: Globe, 1835.

General Regulations for the Army of the United States, 1841. Washington: Gideon, 1841.

General Regulations for the Army of the United States, 1847. Washington: Gideon, 1847.

Instruction for Field Artillery, Horse and Foot. Baltimore: Robinson, 1845.

PRINTED DOCUMENTS: MEXICO

Dublán, Manuel, y José María Lozanos, editores. *Legislación mexicana: colección completa de las disposiciónes legislativas desde la independencia de la República.* 6 tomos. Cd. México: Imprenta del Commercio, 1876–1877.

México, Gobierno de. *Contestaciones habides entre el supremo gobierno mexicano ye el general en jefe del ejército norteamericano y el comissionado de los Estados Unidos.* Cd. México: Imprenta de Vicente García Torres, 1847.

———. Ministerio de Guerra y Marina. *Memoria del ministro de guerra y marina, 11 de septiembre 1845.* Cd. México: Ministerio de Guerra y Marina, 1845.

———. ———. *Memoria del ministro de guerra y marina, 9 de diciembre de 1846.* Cd. México: Torres, 1846.

———. ———. *Memoria del ministro de guerra y marina, 1–2 de mayo de 1849.* Cd. México: Ministerio de Guerra y Marina, 1849.

———. ———. *Reglamentos para el corso de particulares contra los enemigos de la nación.* Cd. México: Aguila, 1846.

———. ———. *Reglamentos sobre la organización del cuerpo de artillería.* Cd. México: Aguila, 1846.

México, Legislatura del Estado de. *La legislatura del estado libre y soberano de México a los habitantes del mismo.* Toluca, DF: Quijána y Gallo, 1847.

Memoria del secretario del estado y del despacho de guerra y marina leide en la Camera de Diputados el dia 9 y en la de Senadores el 11 de enero de 1849. Cd. México: Imprenta de Vicenta García Torres, 1849.

PUBLISHED ORIGINAL SOURCES: BOOKS

Alamán, Lucas. *Historia de Méjico: desde los primeros movimientos que preparan su independencia en el año de 1808 hasta la epoca presente.* 5 tomos. Cd. México: J. M. Lara, 1849–1852.

———. *Obras: documentos diversos.* 10 tomos. Cd. México: Editorial Jus, 1945.

Alcaraz, Ramón, Alejo Barreiro, José Maréa Castillo, Félix María Escalente, José María Iglesias, Manuel Muñoz, Ramón Ortiz, Manuel Payno, Guillermo Prieto, Ignacio Ramírez, Napoleón Saborío, Francisco Schiafino, Francisco Segura, Pablo María Torrescano, y Francisco Urquidi. *Apuntes para la historia de la guerra entre México y los Estados-Unidos.* Cd. México: Tipografia de Manuel Payno (Hijo), 1848. Republicado Cd. México: Consejo para la Cultura y los Artes, 1991.

Allen, G. N. *Mexican Treacheries and Cruelties: Incidents and Sufferings in the Mexican War.* Boston: Hull, 1847.

Ampudia, Pedro de. *Manifesto del General Ampudia a sus conciudadamos.* Cd. México: Ignacio Cumplido, 1847.

———. *El ciudadamo General Pedro de Ampudia ante el tribunal respectable de la opinión publica, por los primeros sucesos ocurrides en la guerra a que nos provaca, decreta y sostiene del gobierno de los Estados Unidos de América.* San Luis Potosí: Imprenta del Gobierno, 1846.

Balbontín, Manuel. *La invasión americana, 1846 a 1848: apuntes del subteniente de la artillería Manuel Balbontín.* Cd. México: G. A. Esteva, 1883.

Ballentine, George. *An English Soldier in the U.S. Army.* New York: Stringer and Townsend, 1853.

Basler, Roy P., editor. *The Collected Works of Abraham Lincoln.* 11 volumes. New Brunswick, New Jersey: Rutgers University Press, 1953.

Bayard, Samuel J. *A Sketch of the Life of Com. Robert F. Stockton.* New York: Derby and Jackson, 1856.

Baylies, Francis. *A Narrative of Major General Wool's Campaign in Mexico in the Years 1846, 1847, and 1848.* Albany, New York: Little, 1851.

Benham, Henry. *Recollections of Mexico and the Battle of Buena Vista, February 22 and 23, 1847.* Boston: Privately printed, 1871.

Benton, Thomas Hart. *Thirty Years' View, or, A History of the Working of the American Government for Thirty Years, from 1820 to 1850.* 2 volumes. New York: Appleton, 1856.

Bieber, Ralph P., editor. *Journal of a Soldier under Kearny and Doniphan, 1846–1847: George Rutledge Gibson.* Glendale, California: Arthur H. Clark, 1935.

———, editor. *Marching with the Army of the West, 1846–1848.* Glendale, California: Arthur H. Clark, 1936.

Blackwood, Emma, editor. *To Mexico with Scott: Letters of Captain E. Kirby Smith to His Wife.* Cambridge: Harvard University Press, 1917.

Bosh García, Carlos. *Material para la historia diplomática de México (México y los Estados Unidos, 1820–1848).* Cd. México: Escuela Nacional de Ciencias Políticas y Sociales, 1957.

Brooks, Nathan C. *A Complete History of the Mexican War, Its Causes, Conduct, and Consequences: Comprising an Account of the Various Military and Naval Operations, from Its Commencement to the Treaty of Peace.* Philadelphia: Lippincott, 1849. Reprinted Chicago: Rio Grande Press, 1965.

Bryant, Edwin. *What I Saw in California: Journal of a Tour . . . in the Years 1846 and 1847.* New York: Appleton, 1848.

Buhoup, Jonathan W. *Narrative of the Central Division, or, Army of Chihuahua, Commanded by Brigadier General Wool.* Pittsburgh: Morse, 1847.

Bustamante, Carlos María. *Campaña sin gloria teneda en el recinto de México, causada por habes persistido Don Valentín Gómez Farías, vice-presidente de la República Mexicana en llevan adelante las leyes de 11 de enero y 4 de febrero de 1847, llamades de mano-muertas, que depojan al clero de sui propriedades, con oposición caci general de la nación.* Cd. México: Ignacio Cumplido, 1847.

———. *El nuevo Bernal Díaz del Castillo o sea: historia de la invasión de los anglo-americanos en México.* 2 tomos. Cd. México: Secretaría de Educación Pública, 1949.

Butler, Steven R., editor. *A Documentary History of the Mexican War.* Richardson, Texas: Descendants of Mexican War Veterans, 1995.

———, editor. *The Eutaw Rangers in the War with Mexico: The Mexican War Journal and Letters of Capt. Sydenham Moore and the Mexican War Journal of Pvt. Stephen F. Nunnalee, Company D, First Regiment of Alabama Volunteers.* Richardson, Texas: Descendants of Mexican War Veterans, 1998.

Cabrero, Luís, editor. *Diario del Presidente Polk (1845–1847): reproducción de todos los asientos relativos a México, tomados de la edición completa de M. M. Quaife con numerosos documentos anexados relacionados con la guerra entre México y los Estados Unidos.* 2 tomos. Cd. México: Antigua Labrería Robredo, 1948.

Calderón de la Barca, Frances Erskine Inglis. *Life in Mexico During a Residence of Two Years in That Country.* 1843. Reprinted New York: Dutton, 1931.

Callan, J. F. *The Military Laws of the United States.* Philadelphia: Childs, 1863.

Carleton, James Henry. *The Battle of Buena Vista: With the Operations of the Army of Occupation for One Month.* New York: Harper, 1848.

Carpenter, William C. *Travels and Adventures in Mexico.* New York: Harper, 1848.

Carreño, Alberto María. *Jefes del ejército mexicano en 1847: biografías de generales de división y de brigada y de coroneles del ejército méxicano por fines del año de 1847*. Cd. México: Secretaría de Formento, 1914.

Castañeda, Carlos E., translator and editor. *The Mexican Side of the Texas Revolution*. Dallas: Turner, 1928.

Castillo Negrete, Emilio del. *Invasión de los norte-americanos en México*. 2 tomos. Cd. México: Imprenta del Editor, 1890.

Chamberlain, Samuel E. *My Confession: Recollections of a Rogue*. New York: Harper and Brothers, 1956. Reprinted, unexpurgated edition. Edited by William H. Goetzmann. Austin: Texas State Historical Association, 1997.

Clarke, Dwight L., editor. *The Original Journals of Henry Smith Turner with Stephen Watts Kearny to New Mexico and California, 1846–1847*. Norman: University of Oklahoma Press, 1966.

Clausewitz, Carl Maria von. *Vom Krieg (On War)*. 1831. Translated by J. J. Graham, edited by F. N. Maude. 3 volumes. London, UK: Routledge and Kegan Paul, 1962. One-volume edition. Edited by Roger Ashley Leonard. New York: Putnam, 1967.

Colton, Walter. *Three Years in California*. New York: Barnes, 1850.

Cooke, Philip St. George. *The Conquest of New Mexico and California: An Historical and Personal Narrative*. New York: Putnam, 1878. Reprinted New York: Arno Press, 1976.

Coolidge, Richard H. *Statistical Report of the Sickness and Mortality in the Army of the United States: Compiled from the Records of the Surgeon General's Office, Embracing a Period of Sixteen Years, from January, 1839, to January, 1855*. Washington: Nicholson, 1856.

Crescencio Rejón, Manuel. *Manuel Crescencio Rejón: pensamiento politico*. Preparado por Daniel Moreno. Cd. México: Universidad Nacional Autónoma, 1968.

Cutts, James M. *The Conquest of California and New Mexico by the Forces of the United States in the Years 1846 and 1847*. Philadelphia: Carey and Hart, 1847.

Dana, Richard Henry, Jr. *Two Years Before the Mast*. Boston: Houghton Mifflin, 1840. Reprinted with addendum as *Two Years Before the Mast, and Twenty-four Years After*. Boston: Houghton Mifflin, 1869. Harvard Classics reprint of the 1869 edition. New York: Collier, 1909, 1937.

Davis, William Heath. *Seventy-Five Years in California*. San Francisco: Howell, 1929.

Edwards, Frank S. *A Campaign in New Mexico with Colonel Doniphan*. Philadelphia: Carey and Hart, 1847. Reprinted Albuquerque: University of New Mexico Press, 1996.

Exposición de una persona residente en la República Mexicana sobre la guerra que actualmente sostiene con los Estados-Unidos del Norte. Cd. México: Topografia de R. Rafael, 1847.

Farrell, John J., editor. *James K. Polk, 1795–1849: Chronology—Documents—Bibliographical Aids*. Dobbs Ferry, New York: Oceana, 1970.

Farrell, Robert H., editor. *Monterrey Is Ours! The Mexican War Letters of Lieutenant Dana, 1845–1847*. Lexington: University of Kentucky Press, 1990.

Ferry, Gabriel. *Vagabond Life in Mexico*. New York: Harper and Brothers, 1856.

Frederick II ("the Great") of Prussia. *Frederick the Great on the Art of War*. Edited and translated by Jay Luvaas. New York: Free Press, 1966.

Frémont, John Charles. *Memoirs of My Life*. 2 volumes. Chicago: Belford and Clarke, 1887.

―――. *Report on an Exploration of the Country Lying Between the Missouri River and the Rocky Mountains on the Line of the Kansas and Great Platte Rivers*. Buffalo, New York: Derby, 1851.

————. *Report of the Exploration Expedition to the Rocky Mountains in the Year 1842, and to Oregon and Northern California in the Years 1843–44*. Buffalo, New York: Derby, 1851.

Frost, John. *The History of Mexico and Its Wars*. New Orleans: Hawkins, 1882.

Fry, J. Reese. *A Life of Gen. Zachary Taylor; Comprising a Narrative of Events Connected with His Professional Career, Derived from Public Documents and Private Correspondence*. Philadelphia: Grigg, Elliot, 1848.

Fulton, Maurice Garland, editor. *Diary and Letters of Josiah Gregg*. 2 volumes. Norman: University of Oklahoma Press, 1941, 1944.

Furber, George C. *The Twelve Months Volunteer: Journal of a Private in the Tennessee Regiment of Cavalry in the Campaign in Mexico, 1846–7*. Cincinnati: Jones, 1857.

García, Genero, y Carlos Pereyra, editores. *México durante su guerra con los Estados Unidos en documentos inéditos or muy raros para la historia de México*. Cd. México: Editorial Bouret, 1906.

Garrard, Lewis H. *Wah-To-Yah and the Taos Trail*. 1856. Reprinted Palo Alto, California: American West Publishing, 1968.

Gayón Córdova, María, compiladora. *La ocupación yanqui de la ciudad de México, 1847–1848*. Cd. México: Instituto de Antropología e Historia, 1997.

Giddings, Luther. *Sketches of the Campaign in Northern Mexico by an Officer of the First Regiment of Ohio Volunteers*. New York: Putnam, 1853.

Golder, Frank A., editor. *The March of the Mormon Battalion from Council Bluffs to California, Taken from the Journal of Henry Standage*. New York: Century, 1928.

Grant, Ulysses S. *Personal Memoirs of U. S. Grant*. 2 volumes. 1884, 1885. Penguin Classics Edition, 2 volumes in 1. New York: Penguin, 1999.

Grotius, Hugo (Huig van Groot). *The Law of War and Peace (De Jure Belli ac Pacis)*. 1625. Translated by Louise R. Loomis. Roslyn, New York: Walter J. Black, 1949.

Halleck, Henry Wager. *Elements of International Law and Laws of War*. Philadelphia: Lippincott, 1872.

Hanrahan, Gene Z. *The Bad Yankee (El Peligro Yankee): American Entrepreneurs and Financiers in Mexico*. 2 volumes. Chapel Hill, North Carolina: Documentary Publications, 1985.

Henry, William S. *Campaign Sketches of the War with Mexico*. New York: Harper and Brothers, 1847.

Hitchcock, Ethan Allen. *Fifty Years in Camp and Field: Diary of Ethan Allen Hitchcock*. Edited by W. A. Croffut. New York: Putnam, 1909.

Hughes, John T. *Doniphan's Expedition, Containing an Account of the Conquest of New Mexico*. Cincinnati, Ohio: U. P. James, 1847. Reformatted edition. Washington: Government Printing Office, 1914. Reprinted New York: Arno, 1973. Reprinted College Station: Texas A&M University Press, 1977.

Hughes, Nathaniel Cheairs, Jr., and Timothy D. Johnson, editors. *A Fighter from Way Back: The Mexican War Diary of Lt. Daniel Harvey Hill, 4th Artillery, USA*. Kent, Ohio: Kent State University Press, 2002.

Jay, William A. *A Review of the Causes and Consequences of the Mexican War*. Boston: Mussey, 1849.

Jenkins, John S. *History of the War Between the United States and Mexico, from the Commencement of Hostilities to the Ratification of the Treaty of Peace*. Auburn, Massachusetts: Derby and Miller, 1851.

Jomini, Antoine-Henri, Baron de. *The Art of War.* 1838. First edition in English, translated by G. H. Mendell and W. P. Craighill. Philadelphia: Lippincott, 1862. Reprinted Westport, Connecticut: Greenwood, nd.

Joseph, Gilbert M., and Timothy J. Henderson, editors. *The Mexico Reader: History, Culture, Politics.* Durham, North Carolina: Duke University Press, 2002.

Kendall, George Wilkins. *Dispatches from the Mexican War.* Edited by Lawrence Delbert Criss. Norman: University of Oklahoma Press, 1999.

————. *Narrative of the Texan Santa Fe Expedition.* 2 volumes. New York: Harpers, 1844.

Kenly, John R. *Memoirs of a Maryland Volunteer, War with Mexico, in the Years 1846–7–8.* Philadelphia: Lippincott, 1873.

Kirkham, Ralph W. *The Mexican War Journal and Letters of Ralph W. Kirkham.* Edited by Robert Ryal Miller. College Station: Texas A&M University Press, 1991.

Labastida, Horacio. *Documentos para la historia del México independiente: reforma y república restaurada, 1823–1877, estudio histórico y selección.* Cd. México: Miguel Ángel Porrúa, 1988.

Laidley, Theodore. *"Surrounded by Dangers of All Kinds": The Mexican War Letters of Lieutenant Theodore Laidley.* Edited by James M. McCaffrey. Denton: University of North Texas Press, 1997.

Lerdo de Tejada, Miguel Mená. *Apuntes históricos de la heróica ciudad de Vera Cruz.* 3 tomos. Cd. México: García Torres, 1850–1858.

Lesley, Lewis Burt, editor. *Uncle Sam's Camels: The Journal of May Humphreys Stacy, Supplemented by the Report of Edward Fitzgerald Beale.* Los Angeles: Huntington Library Press, 2006.

Lewis, Oscar. *The Autobiography of the West: Personal Narratives of the Discovery and Settlement of the American West.* New York: Holt, 1958.

Libura, Krystyna, Luis Gerardo Morales Moreno, and Jesús Velasco Márquez, compiladores. *Ecos de la guerra entre México y los Estados Unidos.* Cd. México: Ediciones Tecolote, 2004.

Livermore, Abiel Abbott. *The War with Mexico Reviewed.* Boston: American Peace Society, 1850.

Magoffin, Susan Shelby. *Down the Santa Fe Trail and into Mexico: The Diary of Susan Shelby Magoffin, 1846–1847.* Edited by Stella M. Drumm. New Haven: Yale University Press, 1926, 1962. Reprinted Lincoln: University of Nebraska Press, 1982.

Manning, William R., editor. *The Diplomatic Correspondence of the United States: Latin American Affairs.* 21 volumes. Washington: Carnegie Endowment for International Peace, 1932–1939.

Maury, Dabney H. *Recollections of a Virginian in the Mexican, Indian, and Civil Wars.* New York: Scribner, 1894.

McCall, George Archibald. *New Mexico in 1850: A Military View.* Edited by Robert W. Frazer. Norman: University of Oklahoma Press, 1968.

McNierney, Michael, editor. *Taos 1847: The Revolt in Contemporary Accounts.* Boulder, Colorado: Johnson, 1980.

McWhinney, Grady, and Sue McWhinney, editors. *To Mexico with Taylor and Scott, 1845–1847.* Waltham, Massachusetts: Blaisdell, 1969.

Mestre Ghigliazza, Manuel. *Invasión norteamericana en Tabasco (1846–1847): Documentos*. Cd. México: Imprenta Universitaria, 1948.

Meyer, Brantz. *History of the War Between the United States and Mexico*. New York: Wiley and Putnam, 1848.

Moore, H. Judge. *Scott's Campaign in Mexico, from the Rendezvous on the Island of Lobos to the Taking of the City*. Charleston, South Carolina: Nixon, 1849.

Moore, John Bassett. *History and Digest of the International Arbitrations to Which the United States Has Been a Party*. 6 volumes. Washington: Government Printing Office, 1898.

———, editor. *The Works of James Buchanan*. 12 volumes. Philadelphia: Lippincott, 1908–11.

Nevins, Allan, editor. *Polk: The Diary of a President, 1845–1849, Covering the Mexican War, the Acquisition of Oregon, and the Conquest of California and the Southwest*. New York: Longmans, Green, 1929.

Nunis, Doyce B. Jr., editor. *The Mexican War in Baja California: The Memorandum of Captain Henry W. Halleck Concerning His Expedition in Lower California, 1846–1848*. Los Angeles: Dawson's Bookshop, 1977.

O'Brien, John. *A Treatise on American Military Laws, and the Practice of Courts Martial, with Suggestions for Their Improvement*. Philadelphia: Lea and Blanchard, 1846.

Oficial de Infantería, un (an Infantry Officer). *Campaña contra los americanos del norte, primera parte: relación histórica de las cuarenta días que mandó en jefe el ejército del norte Excelentísimo Señor General de División Don Mariano Arista*. Cd. México: Ignacio Complido, 1846.

Parker, William Harwar. *Recollections of a Naval Officer, 1841–1865*. New York: Scribner, 1883.

Parrodi, Anastasio. *Memoria sobre la evacuación militar del puerto de Tampico en Tamaulipas*. San Luis Potosí: npub, 1848

Parsons, John E., editor. *Samuel Colt's Own Record*. Hartford: Connecticut Historical Society, 1949.

Poinsett, Joel R. *Notes on Mexico Made in the Autumn of 1822, Accompanied by an Historical Sketch of the Revolution*. 1824. Reprinted New York: Praeger, 1969.

Prescott, William H. *History of the Conquest of Mexico*. Philadelphia: Lippincott, 1843. Reprinted Chicago: University of Chicago Press, 1966, 1985.

———. *Historia de la conquista de México*. Traducio al Castellano por Don José Maria González de la Vega. Anotada por Don Lucas Alamán, con notas criticas y esclarecimientos de Don José Fernando Ramírez, y prólogo, notas y apendices por Juan A. Ortega y Medina. 1850. Republicado Cd. México: Editorial Porrúa, 1976.

Prieto, Guillermo. *Guillermo Prieto*. Compilado por Carlos J. Sierra. Cd. México: Club de Periodistas de México, 1962.

———. *Memorias de mis tiempos*. 1906. Republicado Cd. México: Editorial Patria, 1958.

Prucha, Francis Paul, editor. *Army Life on the Western Frontier: Selections from the Official Reports Made Between 1826 and 1845 by Colonel George Croghan*. Norman: University of Oklahoma Press, 1958.

Quaife, Milo M., editor. *The Diary of James K. Polk During His Presidency, 1845 to 1849*. 4 volumes. Chicago: A. C. McClurg, 1910.

Ramírez, José Fernando. *Mexico During the War with the United States*. Edited by Walter V.

Scholes. Translated by Elliott B. Scherr. Columbia: University of Missouri Press, 1950.

Ramsey, Albert C., translator and editor. *The Other Side: Or, Notes for the History of the War Between Mexico and the United States, Written in Mexico.* New York: John Wiley, 1850.

Reid, Mayne. *Sketches by a Skirmisher: The Mexican War Writings of Capt. Mayne Reid, Co. B, 2nd Regiment of New York Volunteers.* Edited by Steven R. Butler. Richardson, Texas: Descendants of Mexican War Veterans, 1998.

Reid, Samuel C., Jr. *The Scouting Expeditions of McCulloch's Texas Rangers.* Philadelphia: Zieber, 1847. Reprinted Austin: Steck, 1935.

Relación histórica de la segunda invasión que hicieron los Norteamericanos en Tabasco, y de la conducto que observó en ella el comandante general de aquel estado Don Domingo Echagaray, escrita por un testigo imparcial y verídico. Vera Cruz: Blanco, 1847.

Richardson, James D., editor. *A Compilation of the Messages and Papers of the Presidents.* 20 volumes. New York: Bureau of National Literature, 1897–1922.

Richardson, William H. *The Journal of William H. Richardson, a Private Soldier in the Campaign of New and Old Mexico.* New York: Richardson, 1848.

Ridge, John Rollins (pseudonym Yellow Bird). *Life and Adventures of Joaquín Murieta: The Celebrated California Bandit.* 1854. English edition. Norman: University of Oklahoma Press, 1977.

———. *Vida de Joaquín Murieta.* 1854. Republicado Cd. México: Libros de Umbral, 2001.

Rivera Cambas, Manuel. *Historia antigua y moderna de Jalapa y de las revoluciones del estado de Veracruz.* 5 tomos. Cd. México: Ignacio Cumplido, 1869–1871.

Roa Bárcena, José María. *Recuerdos de la invasión norte-americana (1846–1848).* 3 tomos. 1883. Republicado Cd. México: Editorial Porrúa, 1947.

Roberts, Madge Thornall, editor. *The Personal Correspondence of Sam Houston, Volume II: 1846–1848.* Denton: University of North Texas Press, 1998.

Robinson, Cecil, translator and editor. *The View from Chapultepec: Mexican Writers on the Mexican-American War.* Tucson: University of Arizona Press, 1989.

Robinson, Fayette. *An Account of the Organization of the Army of the United States.* 2 volumes. Philadelphia: Butler, 1848.

———. *Mexico and Her Military Chieftains, From the Revolution of Hidalgo to the Present Time.* Hartford, Connecticut: Andrus, 1848.

Robinson, Jacob S. *A Journal of the Santa Fe Expedition under Colonel Doniphan.* Princeton, New Jersey: Princeton University Press, 1932.

Ruxton, George Frederick Augustus. *Adventures in Mexico and the Rocky Mountains.* New York: Harper, 1848.

Santa Anna, Antonio López de. *Detalles de las operaciones ocurridas en la defensa de la capital de la república, atacada por el ejército de los Estados-Unidos del Norte en la año de 1847.* Cd. México: Ignacio Cumplido, 1848.

———. *The Eagle: The Autobiography of Santa Anna.* Edited by Ann Fears Crawford. Austin, Texas: State House Press, 1988.

———. *Las guerras de México con Tejas y los Estados Unidos.* Cd. México: Bouret, 1910.

———. *Mi historia militar y política, 1810–1874.* Cd. México: Bouret, 1905.

———. *Parte oficial del Excelentísimo Señor General de División Benemérita de la Patria Don*

Antonio López de Santa Anna, al supremo gobierno, sobre la sorpesa, que el General Lane intentó darle en Techuoacan la madregada del dia 23 de enero próximo pasado, y el documento que mismo parte menciona. Orizava, VC: Imprenta de la Amistad, 1848.

Sartorius, Carl. *Mexico About 1850.* 1855. Reprinted Stuttgart: Brockhaus Komm, 1961.

Scott, John A. *Encarnación Prisoners: Comprising an Account of the March of the Kentucky Cavalry from Louisville to the Rio Grande.* Louisville: Prentice and Weissanger, 1848.

Scott, Winfield. *Memoirs of Lieut.-General Scott, LL.D.* 2 volumes. New York: Sheldon, 1864.

Semmes, Raphael. *The Campaign of General Scott in the Valley of Mexico.* Cincinnati: Moore and Anderson, 1852.

————. *Service Afloat and Ashore During the Mexican War.* Cincinnati: Moore, 1851.

Shepard, Elihu H. *The Autobiography of Elihu H. Shepard.* St. Louis: George Knapp, 1869.

Sherman, William Tecumseh. *Memoirs of William T. Sherman.* Bloomington: Indiana University Press, 1957.

Smith, E. Kirby. *To Mexico with Scott: Letters of Ephraim Kirby Smith to His Wife.* Cambridge: Harvard University Press, 1917.

Smith, George Winston, and Charles Judah, editors. *Chronicles of the Gringos: The U.S. Army in the Mexican War, 1846–1848, Accounts of Eyewitnesses and Combatants.* Albuquerque: University of New Mexico Press, 1968.

Smith, Gustavus Woodson. *Company "A" Corps of Engineers, U.S.A., 1846–1848, in the Mexican War.* New York: Battalion Press, 1896. Modern edition, edited by Leonne M. Hudson. Kent, Ohio: Kent State University Press, 2001.

Smith, S. C. *Chile con Carne, or, The Camp and the Field.* New York: Curtis and Miller, 1857.

Tayloe, Edward Thornton. *Mexico, 1825–1828: The Journal and Correspondence of Edward Thornton Tayloe.* Edited by C. Harvey Gardiner. Chapel Hill: University of North Carolina Press, 1959.

Thompson, Waddy. *Recollections of Mexico.* New York: Wiley and Putnam, 1846.

Thorndike, Rachel Sherman, editor. *The Sherman Letters: Correspondence Between General and Senator Sherman from 1837 to 1891.* New York: Scribner, 1894.

Tilden, Brant Parrot. *Notes on the Upper Río Grande, Explored in the Months of October and November, 1846, on Board the U.S. Steamer Major Brown, Commanded by Capt. Mark Sterling, of Pittsburgh, by Order of Major-General Patterson, USA, Commanding the Second Division, Army of Occupation, Mexico.* Philadelphia: Lindsay and Blakiston, 1847.

Valencia, Gabriel. *Detalle de las acciones de los días 19 y 20 en los campos de Padierna, y otros pormenores recientemente comunicados por personas fidedignos.* Morelia, DF: Ignacio Arango, 1847.

Weed, Thurlow. *Autobiography of Thurlow Weed.* Edited by Harriet A. Weed. Boston: Houghton Mifflin, 1883.

Wilkes, Charles. *Narrative of the United States Exploring Expedition, During the Years 1838, 1839, 1840, 1841, 1842.* 5 volumes. Philadelphia: Lea and Blanchard, 1845.

Williams, T. Harry, editor. *With Beauregard in Mexico: The Mexican War Reminiscences of P. G. T. Beauregard.* New York: DaCapo, 1969.

Wise, Henry A. *Los Gringos, or, an Inside View of Mexico and California, with Wanderings in Peru, Chile, and Polynesia.* New York: Baker and Scribner, 1849.

Zavala, Lorenzo de. *Viaje a los Estados Unidos del Norte de América.* 1833. Republicado Cd. México: Porrúa, 1976.

PUBLISHED ORIGINAL SOURCES: PERIODICALS

Ames, George W. Jr., editor. "A Doctor Comes to California: The Diary of John F. Griffin, Assistant Surgeon with Kearny's Dragoons, 1846–47." *California Historical Society Quarterly* 21 (September and December 1942): 193–224, 323–30, and 22 (March 1943): 41–66.

Balbontín, Manuel. "The Battle of Angostura (Buena Vista)." Translated by F. H. Hardie. *Journal of the United States Cavalry Association* 2: (June 1894): 125–54.

———. "The Siege of Monterey." Translated by John Strother. *Journal of the Military Services Institution of the United States* 8 (1887): 325–54.

Beach, Moses Y. "A Secret Mission to Mexico." *Scribner's* 18 (May 1879): 136–40.

Bieber, Ralph P., editor. "Letters of William Carr Lane." *New Mexico Historical Review* 3 (April 1928): 179–203.

Bigler, Henry W. "Extracts from the Journal of Henry W. Bigler." *Utah Historical Quarterly* 5 (April–October 1932): 35–64, 87–112, 134–60.

Bliss, Robert S. "The Journal of Robert S. Bliss with the Mormon Battalion." *Utah Historical Quarterly* 4 (July–October 1931): 67–96, 110–28.

Bloom, John Porter. "New Mexico as Viewed by Americans, 1846–1849." *New Mexico Historical Review* 34 (July 1959): 165–98.

Brack, Gene. "Mexican Opinion and the Texas Revolution." *Southwestern Historical Quarterly* 72 (October 1968): 170–82.

Carmen Lugo, José del. "Life of a Rancher." *Publications of the Historical Society of Southern California* 32 (September 1950): 185–236.

Engelmann, Otto B., translator and editor. "The Second Illinois in the Mexican War: The Mexican War Letters of Adolph Engelmann, 1846–1847." *Journal of the Illinois State Historical Society* 26 (January 1934): 357–452.

Frémont, John Charles. "The Conquest of California." *Century Magazine* 41 (April 1891): 917–27.

Gallaher, F. M., editor. "Official Report of the Battle of Temascalitos (Brazito)." *New Mexico Historical Review* 3 (October 1928): 381–89.

Holland, James K. "Diary of a Texan Volunteer in the Mexican War." *Southwestern Historical Quarterly* 30 (July 1926): 1–33.

Lyons, James Gilborne. "The Heroine Martyr of Monterey." *American Quarterly Register* 2 (June 1849): 483–84.

MacPherson, John D. "A Controversy of the Mexican War." *Century Magazine* 56 (July 1898): 467–68.

Mahon, John K. "A Board of Officers Considers the Condition of the Militia in 1826." *Military Affairs* 15 (Summer 1951): 85–94.

Meketa, Jacqueline Dorgan, editor. "A Soldier in New Mexico, 1847–1848." *New Mexico Historical Review* 66 (January 1991): 15–32.

Nance, Joseph M., editor. "Brigadier General Adrián Woll's Report of His Expedition into Texas in 1842." *Southwestern Historical Quarterly* 58 (April 1955): 523–52.

Royce, Josiah. "Montgomery and Frémont: New Documents on the Bear Flag Affair." *Century Magazine* 41 (March 1891): 780–83.

Sioussat, St. George L., editor. "Polk-Donelson Letters: Letters of James K. Polk and Andrew J. Donelson, 1843–1848." *Tennessee Historical Magazine* 3 (March 1917): 51–74.

Smith, Gustavus W. "Company A, Engineers, in Mexico, 1846–1847." *Military Engineer* 56 (September–October 1964): 336–40.

Smith, Justin H., editor. "Letters of General Antonio López de Santa Anna Relating to the War Between the United States and Mexico, 1846–1848." *Annual Report of the American Historical Association for the Year 1917.* Washington: Government Printing Office, 1920.

Steele, John. "Extracts from the Journal of John Steele." *Utah Historical Quarterly* 6 (January 1933): 3–28.

Tyler, Daniel. "Gringo Views of Governor Manuel Armijo." *New Mexico Historical Review* 45 (January 1970): 23–36.

Tyler, Ronnie C. "The Mexican War: A Lithographic Record." *Southwestern Historical Quarterly* 89 (1986): 309–44.

Warren, Vida Lockwood. "Dr. John F. Griffin's Mail, 1846–53." *California Historical Society Quarterly* 33 (June 1954): 97–123.

Weber, David J., editor. "An Unforgettable Day: Facundo Melgares on Independence." *New Mexico Historical Review* 48 (January 1973): 27–44.

SECONDARY SOURCES: BOOKS

Acuña, Rodolfo. *Occupied America: A History of Chicanos.* Second edition. New York: Harper and Row, 1981.

Adams, Ephraim D. *British Interests and Activities in Texas, 1838–1846.* Baltimore: Johns Hopkins University Press, 1910.

Alessio Robles, Vito. *Coahuila y Tejas desde la consumación de la independencia hasta el tratado de paz de Guadalupe Hidalgo.* 2 tomes. Cd. México: Talles Grafios de la Nación, 1945, 1976.

————. *Saltillo en la historia y la leyenda.* Cd. México: Del Bosque, 1934.

Alonzo, Armando C. *Tejano Legacy: Rancheros and Settlers in South Texas, 1734–1900.* Albuquerque: University of New Mexico Press, 1998.

Alvear Acevedo, Carlos. *La guerra del '47.* Cd. México: Editorial Jus, 1957.

Amar, Akhil Reed. *America's Constitution: A Biography.* New York: Random House, 2005.

Andrew, Christopher. *For the President's Eyes Only: Secret Intelligence and the American Presidency from Washington to Bush.* New York: HarperCollins, 1995.

Anna, Timothy E. *The Fall of the Royal Government in Mexico City.* Lincoln: University of Nebraska Press, 1978.

————. *Forging Mexico.* Lincoln: University of Nebraska Press, 1998.

————. *The Mexican Empire of Iturbide.* Lincoln: University of Nebraska Press, 1990.

Archer, Christon I. *The Army in Bourbon Mexico, 1760–1810.* Albuquerque: University of New Mexico Press, 1977.

Arnold, Linda. *Bureaucracy and Bureaucrats in Mexico City, 1742–1835.* Tucson: University of Arizona Press, 1988.

Arteta, Begoña. *Destino manifiesto: viajeros anglosajones en México, 1830–1840.* Cd. México: Ediciones Gernika, 1989.

Ashburn, Percy N. *A History of the Medical Department of the United States Army*. Boston: Houghton-Mifflin, 1929.

Asprey, Robert B. *War in the Shadows: The Guerrilla in History*. 2 volumes. Garden City, New York: Doubleday, 1975.

Astié-Burgos, Walter. *Europa y la guerra de Estados Unidos contra México*. Cd. México: el autor, 2001.

Athearn, Robert G. *War with Mexico*. New York: American Heritage, 1963.

Bailey, Garrick, and Roberta Glenn Bailey. *A History of the Navajos: The Reservation Years*. Santa Fe: School of American Research Press, 1986.

Bancroft, Hubert Howe. *History of Arizona and New Mexico*. San Francisco: Bancroft, 1889.

————. *History of Mexico*. 6 volumes. San Francisco: Bancroft, 1883–1888.

————. *History of California*. 7 volumes. San Francisco: Bancroft, 1884–1890.

————. *History of the North Mexican States and Texas*. 2 volumes. San Francisco: Bancroft, 1884–1889.

La batalla de Churubusco, el 20 de agosto de 1847. Cd. México: Departamento del Distrito Federal, 1983.

Bauer, K. Jack. *The Mexican War, 1846–1848*. New York: Macmillan, 1974.

————. *Surfboats and Horse Marines: U.S. Naval Operations in the Mexican War*. Annapolis: Naval Institute Press, 1969.

————. *Zachary Taylor: Soldier, Planter, Statesman of the Old Southwest*. Baton Rouge: Louisiana State University Press, 1985.

Bazant, Jan. *A Concise History of México from Hidalgo to Cardenas, 1805–1940*. London, UK: Cambridge University Press, 1977.

Beach, Edward L. *The United States Navy: 200 Years*. New York: Holt, 1986.

Beck, Warren A. *New Mexico: A History of Four Centuries*. Norman: University of Oklahoma Press, 1962.

Beers, Henry P. *The Western Military Frontier, 1815–1846*. Philadelphia: Lippincott, 1975.

Bemis, Samuel Flagg. *A Diplomatic History of the United States*. New York: Holt, Rinehart and Winston, 1965.

————. *John Quincy Adams and the Foundations of American Foreign Policy*. New York: Knopf, 1965.

————. *John Quincy Adams and the Union*. New York: Knopf, 1965.

————. *The Latin American Policy of the United States: An Historical Interpretation*. New York: Harcourt, Brace, 1943.

Bender, Averam Burton. *The March of Empire: Frontier Defense in the Southwest, 1848–1860*. Lawrence: University of Kansas Press, 1952.

Bergquist, Charles. *Labor and the Course of American Democracy: US History in Latin American Perspective*. London, UK: Verso, 1996.

Bernardo de Quirós, Constancio. *El bandolerismo en España y en México*. Cd. México: Editorial Jurídica Mexicana, 1959.

Bieber, Ralph P., editor. *Exploring Southwestern Trails, 1846–1854*. Glendale, California: Arthur H. Clark, 1938.

Bill, Alfred Hoyt. *Rehearsal for Conflict*. New York: Knopf, 1947.

Birkhimer, William E. *Historical Sketch of the Organization, Administration, Matériel, and Tactics of the Artillery, United States Army*. Washington: Chapman, 1884.

Boye, Alan. *Tales from the Journey of the Dead: Ten Thousand Years of an American Desert.* Lincoln: University of Nebraska Press, 2006.

Brack, Gene M. *Mexico Views Manifest Destiny, 1821–1846.* Albuquerque: University of New Mexico Press, 1975.

Brands, H. W. *Andrew Jackson: His Life and Times.* New York: Doubleday Anchor, 2005.

Bravo Ugarte, José. *Historia de México.* 3 tomos. Cd. México: Editorial Jus, 1959.

Byers, Michael. *War Law: Understanding International Law and Armed Conflict.* New York: Grove, 2005.

Callahan, Edward W. *List of Officers of the Navy of the United States and of the Marine Corps from 1775 to 1900.* New York: Hamersly, 1901. Published on line by the Naval Historical Center, Department of the Navy, at history.navy.mil.books/callahan/

Callahan, James M. *American Foreign Policy in Mexican Relations.* New York: Macmillan, 1932.

Callcott, Wilfrid H. *Church and State in Mexico, 1822–1857.* Durham, North Carolina: Duke University Press, 1926.

————. *Santa Anna: The Story of an Enigma Who Once Was Mexico.* Norman: University of Oklahoma Press, 1936.

Cardenas de la Peña, Enrique. *Semblanza marítima del México independiente y revolucionario.* 2 tomos. Cd. México: Secretaría de la Marina, 1970.

Caro Baroja, Julio. *Ensayo sobre la literatura de cordel.* Madrid: Revista de Occidente, 1969.

Carwardine, Richard. *Lincoln: A Life of Purpose and Power.* New York: Knopf, 2006.

Caruso, A. Brooke. *The Mexican Spy Company: United States Covert Operations in Mexico, 1845–1848.* Jefferson, North Carolina: McFarland, 1991.

Castel, Albert. *General Sterling Price and the Civil War in the West.* Baton Rouge: Louisiana State University Press, 1968, 1993.

Castillo Fernández, Francisco del. *Apuntes para la historia de San Ángel.* Cd. México: Museo Nacional de Arqueología, Historia, e Etnología, 1913.

Castillo Nájera, Francisco. *Invasión norte-americana: efectivos y estado de los ejércitos beligerentes y consideraciones sobre la campaña.* Cd. México: npub, 1947.

Chambers, William N. *Old Bullion Benton, Senator from the New West.* Boston: Little, Brown, 1956.

Chartrand, René. *Santa Anna's Mexican Army, 1821–48.* Botley, Oxford, U.K.: Osprey, 2004.

Christensen, Carol and Thomas. *The U. S.-Mexican War.* San Francisco: Bay Books, 1998.

Churchill, Franklin Hunter. *Sketch of the Life of Bvt. Brig. Gen. Sylvester Churchill, Inspector General U.S. Army, with Notes and Appendices.* New York: Willis McDonald, 1888.

Claiborne, J. F. H. *Life and Correspondence of John A. Quitman, Major-General, U.S.A., and Governor of the State of Mississippi.* New York: Harper, 1860.

Clarke, Dwight L. *Stephen Watts Kearny: Soldier of the West.* Norman: University of Oklahoma Press, 1961.

Clary, David A. *Fortress America: The Corps of Engineers, Hampton Roads, and United States Coastal Defense.* Charlottesville: University Press of Virginia, 1990.

————. *Rocket Man: Robert H. Goddard and the Birth of the Space Age.* New York: Hyperion, 2003.

————. *These Relics of Barbarism: A History of Barracks and Guardhouses of the United States Army to 1880.* Washington: Government Printing Office, 1985.

————, and Joseph W. A. Whitehorne. *The Inspectors General of the United States Army, 1877–1903.* Washington: Department of the Army, 1987.

Clendenen, Clarence G. *Blood on the Border: The United States Army and the Mexican Irregulars.* New York: Macmillan, 1969.

Cline, Howard F. *The United States and Mexico.* Third Edition. Cambridge: Harvard University Press, 1967.

Coffman, Edward M. *The Old Army: A Portrait of the American Army in Peacetime, 1784–1898.* New York: Oxford University Press, 1986.

Coit, Margaret L. *John C. Calhoun, American Portrait.* Boston: Houghton Mifflin, 1950.

Collier, Christopher, and James Lincoln Collier. *Hispanic America, Texas, and the Mexican War, 1835–1850.* New York: Benchmark, 1999.

Connor, Seymour V., and Odie B. Faulk. *North America Divided: The Mexican War, 1846–1848.* New York: Oxford University Press, 1971.

Copeland, Fayette. *Kendall of the Picayune: Being His Adventures in New Orleans, on the Texan Santa Fe Expedition, in the Mexican War, and in the Colonization of the Texas Frontier.* Norman: University of Oklahoma Press, 1943, 1997.

Corder, Jim W. *Hunting Lieutenant Chadbourne.* Athens: University of Georgia Press, 1993.

Cordova, María Gayon, editora. *La ocupación yanqui de la ciudad de México, 1847–1848.* Cd. México: Consejo Nacional para la Cultura y las Artes, 1997.

Corona del Rosal, Alfonso. *La guerra, el imperialismo, el ejército mexicano.* Cd. México: Grijalbo, 1989.

Cossío, David Alberto. *Historia de Nuevo León, Tomo 6.* Monterrey, NL: Editorial J. Cantú Leal, 1936.

Cossío, José Lorenzo. *Coyoacán, capital de la Nueva España.* Cd. México: Editorial Vargas Rea, 1946.

Costeloe, Michael P. *The Central Republic in Mexico, 1835–1846: Hombres de Bien in the Age of Santa Anna.* Cambridge, UK: Cambridge University Press, 1993.

————. *Church and State in Independent Mexico: A Study of the Patronage Debate, 1821–1857.* London, UK: Royal Historical Society, 1978.

————. *La primera república federal en México (1824–1835).* Cd. México: Fonda de la Cultura Económica, 1975.

Cotner, Thomas E. *The Military and Political Career of José Joaquín de Herrera, 1792–1854.* Austin: University of Texas Press, 1949.

————, and Carlos E. Castañeda, editors. *Essays in Mexican History.* Austin, Texas: Institute of Latin American Studies, 1958.

Cox, Patricia. *Batallón de San Patricio.* Cd. México: Editorial Stylo, 1954.

Crane, Leo. *Desert Drums: The Pueblo Indians of New Mexico, 1540–1928.* Boston: Little, Brown, 1928. Reprinted Glorieta, New Mexico: Rio Grande Press, 1972.

Crapol, Edward P. *John Tyler: The Accidental President.* Chapel Hill: University of North Carolina Press, 2006.

Crawford, Mark. *Encyclopedia of the Mexican-American War.* Santa Barbara, California: ABC-Clio, 1999.

Cue Cánovas, Agustín. *Historia social y económica de México, 1821–1854.* Cd. México: Editorial F. Trillas, 1963.

Cuevas, Mariano. *Historia de la nación mexicana.* Cd. México: Editorial Porrua, 1967.

Cullum, George W. *Biographical Register of the Officers and Graduates of the United States Military Academy.* 3 volumes. Boston: Houghton Mifflin, 1891.

Cunliffe, Marcus. *Soldiers and Civilians: The Martial Spirit in America, 1775–1865.* Boston: Little, Brown, 1968.

Curti, Merle E. *The American Peace Crusade, 1815–1860.* New York: Octagon, 1965.

Cutrer, Thomas W. *Ben McCulloch and the Frontier Military Tradition.* Chapel Hill: University of North Carolina Press, 1993.

Dary, David. *The Santa Fe Trail: Its History, Legends, and Lore.* New York: Knopf, 2000.

DeConde, Alexander. *A History of American Foreign Policy.* New York: Scribner, 1963.

———, editor. *Encyclopedia of American Foreign Policy.* 2 volumes. Jefferson, North Carolina: McFarland, 1991.

Delgado, Jaime. *La monarquía en México, 1845–1847.* Cd. México: Editorial Porrua, 1990.

DePalo, William A. *The Mexican National Army, 1822–1852.* College Station: Texas A&M University Press, 1997.

DeVoto, Bernard. *The Year of Decision: 1846.* Boston: Little, Brown, 1943. Reprint. New York: St. Martin's, 2000.

Díaz Díaz, Fernando. *Caudillos y caciques: Antonio López de Santa Anna y Juan Álvarez.* Cd. México: El Colegio de México, 1972.

Dillon, Lester R. *American Artillery in the Mexican War, 1846–1848.* Austin, Texas: Presidial Press, 1975.

Dios Bonilla, Juan de. *Historia marítima de México.* Cd. México: Editorial Litorales, 1962.

Di Tella, Torcuato S. *National Popular Politics in Early Independent Mexico, 1820–1847.* Albuquerque: University of New Mexico Press, 1996.

Dodd, William. *Jefferson Davis.* New York: Russell and Russell, 1966.

Donald, David Herbert. *Lincoln.* New York: Simon and Schuster, 1995.

Drexler, Robert W. *Guilty of Making Peace: A Biography of Nicholas P. Trist.* Lanham, Maryland: University Press of America, 1991.

Dunlay, Tom. *Kit Carson and the Indians.* Lincoln: University of Nebraska Press, 2000.

Eisenhower, John S. D. *Agent of Destiny: The Life and Times of General Winfield Scott.* New York: Free Press, 1997.

———. *So Far from God: The U.S. War with Mexico, 1846–1848.* New York: Random House, 1989. New York: Doubleday Anchor, 1990.

Ekirch, Arthur A. *The Civilian and the Military.* New York: Oxford University Press, 1959.

Elliott, Charles W. *Winfield Scott: The Soldier and the Man.* New York: Macmillan, 1937.

Estergreen, M. Morgan. *Kit Carson: A Portrait in Courage.* Norman: University of Oklahoma Press, 1962.

Estrada, Genaro, y Carlos Peregra. *México durante la guerra con los Estados Unidos.* Cd. México: Librería Bouret, 1905.

Faulk, Odie B. *The U.S. Camel Corps: An Army Experiment.* New York: Oxford University Press, 1976.

———, and Joseph A. Stout, Jr., editors. *The Mexican War: Changing Interpretations.* Chicago: Swallow Press, 1973.

Fehrenbach, T. R. *Comanches: The Destruction of a People.* New York: Knopf, 1974.

———. *Fire and Blood: A History of Mexico.* Updated edition. New York: Da Capo, 1995.

Filler, Louis. *The Crusade Against Slavery, 1830–1860.* New York: Harper and Row, 1960.

Fincher, E. B. *Mexico and the United States: Their Linked Destinies.* New York: Crowell, 1983.

Flores Caballero, Romeo. *The Role of the Spaniards in the Independence of Mexico.* Lincoln: University of Nebraska Press, 1974.

Foos, Paul. *A Short, Offhand, Killing Affair: Soldiers and Social Conflict During the Mexican-American War.* Chapel Hill: University of North Carolina Press, 2002.

Fowler, Will. *Mexico in the Age of Proposals, 1821–1853.* Westport, Connecticut: Greenwood, 1998.

————. *Tornel and Santa Anna: The Writer and the Caudillo, Mexico, 1795–1853.* Westport, Connecticut: Greenwood, 2000.

Francaviglia, Richard V., and Douglas W. Richmond, editors. *Dueling Eagles: Reinterpreting the U.S.-Mexican War, 1846–1848.* Fort Worth: Texas Christian University Press, 2000.

Frank, Patrick. *Posada's Broadsheets: Mexican Popular Imagery, 1890–1910.* Albuquerque: University of New Mexico Press, 1998.

Frazer, Chris. *Bandit Nation: A History of Outlaws and Cultural Struggle in Mexico, 1810–1920.* Lincoln: University of Nebraska Press, 2006.

Frazer, Robert W. *Forts of the West: Military Forts and Presidios and Posts Commonly Called Forts West of the Mississippi River to 1898.* Norman: University of Oklahoma Press, 1965.

Frazier, Donald S., editor. *The United States and Mexico at War: Nineteenth-Century Expansionism and Conflict.* New York: Macmillan, 1998.

Freeman, Douglas Southall. *R. E. Lee.* 4 volumes. New York: Scribner, 1934.

Frías, Heriberto. *Episodios militares mexicanos.* Cd. México: Secretaría de la Defensa Nacional, 1983.

————. *La guerra contra los gringos.* Cd. México: Ediciones Leega-Juear, 1984.

Fuentes Días, Vicente. *La intervención norteamericana en México.* Cd. México: Nuevo Mundo, 1947.

Fuller, John D. P. *The Movement for the Acquisition of All Mexico.* New York: Da Capo, 1969.

Ganoe, William A. *History of the United States Army.* New York: Appleton-Century, 1936.

García Cantu, Gaston. *La intervención norteamericana en México, 1846–1848.* Cd. México: Ediciones Era, 1971.

Gaxiola, F. Javier. *La invasión norte-americana en Sinaloa: revista histórica del estado de 1845 a 1849.* 2 tomos. Cd. México: Rosas, 1891.

Germain, Dom Aidan Henry. *Catholic Military and Naval Chaplains, 1776–1917.* Washington: Catholic University of America Press, 1929.

Goetzmann, William H. *Army Exploration in the American West, 1803–1863.* New Haven: Yale University Press, 1959.

————. *Exploration and Empire: The Explorer and the Scientist in the Winning of the American West.* New York: Knopf, 1967. Reprinted Austin: Texas State Historical Association, 2000.

————. *When the Eagle Screamed: The Romantic Horizon in American Expansionism, 1800–1860.* Norman: University of Oklahoma Press, 2000.

González, Deena. *Refusing the Favor: The Spanish-Mexican Women of Santa Fe, 1820–1880.* New York: Oxford University Press, 1999.

Graber, D. A. *Crisis Diplomacy: A History of U.S. Intervention Policies and Practices.* Washington: Public Affairs Press, 1959.

Graebner, Norman A. *Empire on the Pacific: A Study in American Continental Expansion.* New York: Ronald, 1955.

Green, Stanley C. *The Mexican Republic: The First Decade, 1823–1832.* Pittsburgh: University of Pittsburgh Press, 1987.

Griffis, William E. *Matthew Calbraith Perry: A Typical American Naval Officer.* Boston: Houghton Mifflin, 1890.

Griswold del Castillo, Richard. *The Treaty of Guadalupe Hidalgo: A Legacy of Conflict.* Norman: University of Oklahoma Press, 1990.

Grivas, Theodore. *Military Governments in California; With a Chapter on Their Prior Use in Louisiana, Florida, and New Mexico.* Glendale, California: Arthur H. Clark, 1963.

Guardino, Peter F. *Peasants, Politics, and the Formation of Mexico's National State: Guerrero, 1800–1857.* Stanford, California: Stanford University Press, 1996.

Guild, Thelma S., and Harvey L. Carter. *Kit Carson: A Pattern for Heroes.* Lincoln: University of Nebraska Press, 1984.

Guinn, James M. *A History of California and an Extended History of Los Angeles and Environs.* 3 volumes. Los Angeles: Historic Record, 1915.

Gutiérrez, Natividad. *Nationalist Myths and Ethnic Identities: Indigenous Intellectuals and the Mexican State.* Lincoln: University of Nebraska Press, 1999.

Habenstreit, Barbara. *Men Against War.* Garden City, New York: Doubleday, 1973.

Hamilton, Holman. *Prologue to Conflict: The Crisis and Compromise of 1850.* Lexington: University of Kentucky Press, 1964.

————. *Zachary Taylor: Soldier of the Republic.* Indianapolis: Bobbs-Merrill, 1941. Reprinted Hamden, Connecticut: Archon Books, 1966.

Hanighen, Frank C. *Santa Anna: The Napoleon of the West.* New York: Coward-McCann, 1934.

Harris, Charles H. *A Mexican Family Empire: The Latifundio of the Sánchez Navarros, 1765–1867.* Austin: University of Texas Press, 1975.

Haven, Charles T., and Frank E. Belden. *A History of the Colt Revolver and the Other Arms Made by Colt's Patent Fire Arms Manufacturing Company from 1836 to 1940.* New York: Bonanza, 1978.

Haynes, Sam W. *James K. Polk and the Expansionist Impulse.* Third edition. New York: Longman, 2006.

————. *Soldiers of Misfortune: The Somervell and Mier Expeditions.* Austin: University of Texas Press, 1990.

————, and Christopher Morris, editors. *Manifest Destiny and Empire: American Antebellum Expansionism.* College Station: Texas A&M University Press, 1997.

Heering, Patricia Roche. *General José Cosme Urrea: His Life and Times.* Spokane, Washington: Arthur H. Clark, 1995.

Heitman, Francis B. *Historical Register and Dictionary of the United States Army, From Its Organization, September 19, 1789, to March 2, 1903.* 2 volumes. Washington: Government Printing Office, 1903. Reprinted Urbana: University of Illinois Press, 1965.

Henderson, G. F. R. *Stonewall Jackson and the American Civil War.* New York: Longmans, Green, 1936.

Henderson, Timothy J. *A Glorious Defeat: Mexico and Its War with the United States.* New York: Hill and Wang, 2007.

Henry, Robert Selph. *The Story of the Mexican War.* Indianapolis: Bobbs-Merrill, 1950.

Herr, Pamela. *Jessie Benton Frémont: A Biography.* New York: Franklin Watts, 1987.

Herrera Serna, Laura, coordinadora. *México en guerra (1846–1848): perspectivas regionales.* Cd. México: Dirección General de Publicaciones del Instituto Nacional de Antropología e Historia, 1997.

Hill, Jim Dan. *The Minute Man in Peace and War: A History of the National Guard.* Harrisburg, Pennsylvania: Stackpole, 1963.

Hine, Robert V. *Bartlett's West: Drawing the Mexican Boundary.* New Haven: Yale University Press, 1968.

Hirshson, Stanley P. *The White Tecumseh: A Biography of General William T. Sherman.* New York: Wiley, 1997.

Hobsbawm, Eric. *Bandits.* Revised edition. New York: Pantheon, 1981.

Hogan, Michael. *The Irish Soldiers of Mexico.* Guadalajara, Jalisco: Fondo Editorial Universitario, 1999.

Hollon, W. Eugene. *The Lost Pathfinder: Zebulon Montgomery Pike.* Norman: University of Oklahoma Press, 1949.

———. *The Southwest: Old and New.* New York: Knopf, 1961.

Horgan, Paul. *The Centuries of Santa Fe.* New York: Dutton, 1956.

———. *Great River: The Rio Grande in North American History.* 2 volumes. Fourth edition. Hanover, Connecticut: Wesleyan University Press, 1984.

Howarth, Stephen. *To Shining Sea: A History of the United States Navy, 1775–1998.* Norman: University of Oklahoma Press, 1999.

Hoyt, Edwin P. *Zachary Taylor.* Chicago: Reilly and Lee, 1966.

Jackson, W. Turrentine. *Wagon Roads West.* New Haven: Yale University Press, 1965.

Johannsen, Robert W. *To the Halls of the Montezumas: The Mexican War in the American Imagination.* New York: Oxford University Press, 1985.

Johnson, Timothy D. *Winfield Scott: The Quest for Military Glory.* Lawrence: University Press of Kansas, 1998.

Johnston, William Preston. *The Life of Gen. Albert Sidney Johnston.* New York: Appleton, 1878.

Jones, Okah L., Jr. *Santa Anna.* New York: Twain, 1968.

Kahle, Gunter. *El ejército y la formación del estado en los comienzos de la independencia de México.* Cd. México: Fondo de Cultura Económica, 1997.

Kendell, Jonathan. *La Capital: The Biography of Mexico City.* New York: Random House, 1988.

Katz, Friedrich, editor. *Rebellion and Revolution: Rural and Social Conflict in México.* Princeton, New Jersey: Princeton University Press, 1988.

Kearny, Thomas. *General Philip Kearny: Battle Soldier of Five Wars.* New York: Putnam, 1937.

Keleher, William A. *Turmoil in New Mexico, 1846–1848.* Santa Fe: Rydal, 1952. Reprinted Albuquerque: University of New Mexico Press, 1982.

Kemble, C. Robert. *The Image of the Army Officer in America: Background for Current Views.* Westport, Connecticut: Greenwood, 1973.

Kohl, Clayton C. *Claims as a Cause of the Mexican War.* New York: New York University Graduate School, 1914.

Krauze, Enrique. *Mexico, Biography of Power: A History of Modern Mexico, 1810–1996.* Translated by Hank Heifetz. New York: HarperCollins, 1997.

Kreidberg, Marvin A., and Merton G. Henry. *History of Military Mobilization in the United States Army, 1775–1945.* Washington: Department of the Army, 1955.

Lack, Paul D. *The Texas Revolutionary Experience: A Political and Social History, 1835–1836.* College Station: Texas A&M University Press, 1992.

Lamar, Howard R. *The Far Southwest.* New Haven: Yale University Press, 1966.

Larson, Robert W. *New Mexico's Quest for Statehood, 1846–1912.* Albuquerque: University of New Mexico Press, 1968.

Lavender, David. *Bent's Fort.* Lincoln: University of Nebraska Press, 1954.

————. *Climax at Buena Vista: The Decisive Battle of the Mexican-American War.* Philadelphia: Lippincott, 1966. Reprinted Philadelphia: University of Pennsylvania Press, 2003.

Lawson, Don. *The United States in the Mexican War.* New York: Crowell, 1976.

Leckie, Robert. *The Wars of America.* 2 volumes. New York: Harper and Row, 1968.

Leonard, Thomas M. *James K. Polk: A Clear and Unquestionable Destiny.* Wilmington, Delaware: Scholarly Resources, 2001.

Levinson, Irving W. *Wars Within War: Mexican Guerrillas, Domestic Elites, and the United States of America, 1846–1848.* Ft. Worth: Texas Christian University Press, 2005.

Lewis, Lloyd. *Captain Sam Grant.* Boston: Little, Brown, 1950.

————. *Sherman: Fighting Prophet.* New York: Harcourt, Brace, 1958.

Lister, Florence C., and Robert H. Lister. *Chihuahua: Storehouse of Storms.* Albuquerque: University of New Mexico Press, 1966.

Lomnitz-Adler, Claudio. *Deep Mexico, Silent Mexico: An Anthropology of Nationalism.* Minneapolis: University of Minnesota Press, 2001.

Longacre, Edward G. *General Ulysses S. Grant: The Soldier and the Man.* New York: Da Capo, 2006.

Loomis, Noel M. *The Texan–Santa Fe Pioneers.* Norman: University of Oklahoma Press, 1958.

López y Rivas, Gilberto. *La guerra de 47 y la resistencia popular a la ocupación.* Cd. México: Editorial Nuestro Tiempo, 1976.

Magner, James A. *Men of Mexico.* Milwaukee: Bruce, 1942.

Marti, Werner H. *Messenger of Destiny: The California Adventures, 1846–1847, of Archibald H. Gillespie, U.S. Marine Corps.* San Francisco: Howell, 1960.

Martínez, Pablo. *Historia de Baja-California.* Cd. México: Editorial Baja-California, 1956.

Martínez Carazo, Leopoldo. *La intervención norteamericana en México, 1846–1848.* Cd. México: Editorial Panama, 1981.

Matovina, Timothy M. *The Alamo Remembered: Tejano Accounts and Perspectives.* Austin: University of Texas Press, 1995.

McCaffrey, James M. *Army of Manifest Destiny: The American Soldier in the Mexican War, 1846–1848.* New York: New York University Press, 1992.

McCormac, Eugene I. *James K. Polk: A Political Biography.* 2 volumes. Berkeley: University of California Press, 1922. Reprinted Newton, Connecticut: American Political Biography Press, 1995, 2000.

McCoy, Charles A. *Polk and the Presidency.* Austin: University of Texas Press, 1960.

McDonald, Archie P., editor. *The Mexican War: Crisis for American Democracy.* Lexington, Massachusetts: Heath, 1965.

McEniry, Sister Blanche Marie. *American Catholics in the War with Mexico*. Washington: Catholic University of America Press, 1932.

Meadows, Don. *The American Occupation of La Paz*. Los Angeles: Dawson, 1955.

Medina Castro, Miguel. *El gran despojo: Téjas, Nuevo México, y California*. Cd. México: Editorial Diogenes, 1974.

Melton, Buckner F., Sr. *A Hanging Offense: The Strange Affair of the Warship Somers*. New York: Free Press, 2003.

Meigs, William M. *The Life of Thomas Hart Benton*. Philadelphia: Lippincott, 1904.

Merk, Frederick. *Manifest Destiny and Mission in American History: A Reinterpretation*. New York: Knopf, 1963.

————. *The Monroe Doctrine and American Expansion, 1843–1846*. New York: Knopf, 1966.

Mestre Ghigliazza, Manuel. *Invasión norteamericana en Tabasco, 1846–1847*. Cd. México: Imprenta Universitaria, 1948.

Meyer, Michael C., William L. Sherman, and Susan M. Deeds. *The Course of Mexican History*. Seventh Edition. New York: Oxford University Press, 2003.

Meyer, Michael C., and William H. Beezley, editors. *The Oxford History of Mexico*. New York: Oxford University Press, 2000.

Miller, Robert Ryal. *Shamrock and Sword: The Saint Patrick's Battalion in the U.S.-Mexican War*. Norman: University of Oklahoma Press, 1989.

Millis, Walter. *Arms and Men: A Study in American Military History*. New York: Putnam, 1956. Reprint edition. New York: New American Library, nd.

————, editor. *American Military Thought*. Indianapolis: Bobbs-Merrill, 1966.

Mills, Bronwyn. *America at War: The Mexican War*. New York: Facts on File, 1992.

Molina Álvarez, Daniel. *La pasión del Padre Jarauta*. Cd. México: Gobierno de la Ciudad de México, 1999.

Moorhead, Max. *New Mexico's Royal Road: Trade and Travel on the Chihuahua Trail*. Norman: University of Oklahoma Press, 1958.

Morison, Samuel Eliot. *"Old Bruin": Commodore Matthew C. Perry, 1794–1858*. Boston: Little, Brown, 1967.

————. *The Oxford History of the American People*. New York: Oxford University Press, 1965.

————, Frederick Merk, and Frank Freidel. *Dissent in Three American Wars*. Cambridge: Harvard University Press, 1970.

Moyano Pahissa, Angela. *La resistencia de las Californias a la invasión norteamericana (1846–1848)*. Cd. México: Consejo Nacional Para la Cultura y las Artes, 1992.

Muñoz, Rafael F. *Santa Anna: el dictador resplandeciente*. Cd. México: Fondo de Cultura Económica, 1983.

Museo Histórico de Churubusco. *Churubusco en la acción militar del 20 de agosto de 1847*. Cd. México: Museo Histórico de Churubusco, 1947.

Nagel, Paul C. *John Quincy Adams: A Public Life, a Private Life*. New York: Knopf, 1997.

Nance, Joseph Milton. *After San Jacinto: The Texas-Mexican Frontier, 1836–1841*. Austin: University of Texas Press, 1963.

————. *Attack and Counter-Attack: The Texas-Mexican Frontier, 1842*. Austin: University of Texas Press, 1963.

————, and Archie McDonald. *Dare-Devils All: The Texan Mier Expedition, 1842–44*. Austin: Eakin, 1998.

Neeser, Robert W. *Statistical and Chronological History of the United States Navy, 1775–1907*. 2 volumes. New York: Macmillan, 1909.

Neff, Stephen C. *War and the Law of Nations: A General History*. New York: Cambridge University Press, 2005.

Neighbours, Kenneth Franklin. *Robert Simpson Neighbors and the Texas Frontier, 1836–1869*. Waco: Texian Press, 1975.

Neve, Carlos D. *Historia gráfica del ejército mexicano*. Cuernavaca: Quesada Brandi, 1967.

Nevins, Allan. *Frémont: Pathmaker of the West*. New York: Longmans, Green, 1955.

————. *Ordeal of the Union, Volume I: Fruits of Manifest Destiny, 1847–1852*. New York: Scribner, 1947.

Nichols, Edward J. *Zach Taylor's Little Army*. Garden City, New York: Doubleday, 1963.

Nichols, Roy F. *The Stakes of Power, 1845–1877*. New York: Hill and Wang, 1961.

Nugent, Daniel, editor. *Rural Revolt in México: U.S. Intervention and the Domain of Subaltern Politics*. Durham, North Carolina: Duke University Press, 1988.

Oates, Stephen B. *Visions of Glory: Texans on the Southwestern Frontier*. Norman: University of Oklahoma Press, 1970.

Oliva, Leo E. *Soldiers on the Santa Fe Trail*. Norman: University of Oklahoma Press, 1967.

Olivera, Ruth R., and Liliane Crété. *Life in Mexico under Santa Anna, 1822–1855*. Norman: University of Oklahoma Press, 1991.

Olliff, Donathan C. *Reforma Mexico and the United States: A Search for Alternatives to Annexation, 1845–1861*. Tuscaloosa: University of Alabama Press, 1981.

Pace, Robert F., and Donald S. Frazier. *Frontier Texas: History of a Borderland to 1880*. Austin: State House Press, 2004.

Pasquel, Leonardo. *Antonio López de Santa Anna*. Cd. México: Instituto de Mexicología, 1990.

Paullin, Charles O. *Paullin's History of Naval Administration, 1775–1911*. Annapolis: Naval Institute Press, 1968.

Paz, Eduardo. *La invasión norteamericana en 1846: ensayo de historia patria-militar por el mayor de caballeros*. Cd. México: Imprenta Moderna de Carlos Paz, 1889.

Paz, Ireneo. *Vida y aventuras del más célebre bandido sonorense, Joaquín Murrieta: sus grandes proezas en California*. 1904. Reprinted Houston: Arte Público, 1999.

Paz, Octavio. *The Other Mexico: Critique of the Pyramid*. New York: Grove, 1972.

Peña y Reyes, Antonio de la. *La primera guerra entre México y Francia*. Cd. México: Secretería de Relaciones Exteriores, 1927.

Perkins, Whitney T. *Constraint of Empire: The United States and Caribbean Interventions*. Westport, Connecticut: Greenwood, 1981.

Peterson, Merrill D. *The Great Triumvirate: Webster, Clay, and Calhoun*. New York: Oxford University Press, 1987.

Pletcher, David M. *The Diplomacy of Annexation: Texas, Oregon, and the Mexican War*. Columbia: University of Missouri Press, 1973.

Price, Glenn W. *Origins of the War with Mexico: The Polk-Stockton Intrigue*. Austin: University of Texas Press, 1967.

Prucha, Francis Paul. *The Sword of the Republic:The United States Army on the Frontier, 1783–1846*. New York: Macmillan, 1969.

Ramírez, José Fernando. *México During the War with the United States*. Edited by Walter V. Scholes. Translated by Elliott B. Scheer. Columbia: University of Missouri Press, 1950.

————. *México durante su guerra con los Estados Unidos*. Cd. México: Bouret, 1905.

Rea, Robert R. *Sterling Price:The Lee of the West*. Little Rock, Arkansas: Pioneer Press, 1959.

Rea,Vargas, editor. *Apuntes históricos sobre los acontecimientos notables de la guerra entre México y los Estados Unidos del Norte*. Cd. México: Biblioteca Aportación Histórica, 1965.

Reavis, L. U. *The Life and Military Services of Gen.William Selby Harney*. St. Louis: Bryan and Brand, 1878.

Read, Benjamin M. *Guerra México-Americana*. Santa Fe, New Mexico: Compañía Impresora del Nuevo Mexicano, 1910.

Rebert, Paula. *La Gran Línea: Mapping the United States–Mexico Boundary, 1849–1857*. Austin: University of Texas Press, 2001.

Reed, Nelson. *The Caste War of Yucatán*. Stanford, California: Stanford University Press, 1964.

Reeves, Jesse S. *American Diplomacy under Tyler and Polk*. Baltimore: Johns Hopkins University Press, 1907.

Reina, Leticia. *Las rebeliones campesinas en México, 1819–1906*. Cd. México: Siglo Vientiuno, 1980.

Richards, Leonard L. *The California Gold Rush and the Coming of the Civil War*. New York: Knopf, 2007.

Richman, Irving B. *California Under Spain and Mexico, 1535–1847*. Boston: Houghton Mifflin, 1911.

Richmond, Douglas, editor. *Essays on the Mexican War*. College Station: Texas A&M University Press, 1986.

Ricketts, Norma Baldwin. *The Mormon Battalion, U.S. Army of the West, 1846–1848*. Logan: Utah State University Press, 1996.

Ripley, Roswell S. *War with Mexico*. 2 volumes. New York: Harper, 1899.

Rippy, J. Fred. *Joel R. Poinsett:Versatile American*. New York: Greenwood, 1968.

————. *The United States and Mexico*. New York: Knopf, 1962.

Risch, Erna. *Quartermaster Support of the Army: A History of the Corps*. Washington: Department of the Army, 1962.

Riva Palacio, Vicente, editor. *México a través de los siglos*. 6 tomos. Cd. México: Editorial Cumbre, 1940.

Rives, George L. *The United States and Mexico, 1821–1848*. 2 volumes. New York: Scribner, 1913.

Roberts, Brigham Henry. *The Mormon Battalion: Its History and Achievements*. Salt Lake City, Utah: Deseret News, 1919. Reprinted Provo, Utah: Maasai, 2001.

Robertson,William Spence. *Iturbide of Mexico*. Durham, North Carolina: Duke University Press, 1952.

Robinson, Cecil, editor. *The View From Chapultepec: Mexican Writers on the Mexican-American War*. Tucson: University of Arizona Press, 1979.

Rogers, Joseph M. *Thomas Hart Benton*. Philadelphia: Jacobs, 1905.

Roland, Charles P. *Albert Sidney Johnston: Soldier of Three Republics*. Austin: University of Texas Press, 1964.

Rolle, Andrew. *John Charles Frémont: Character as Destiny*. Norman: University of Oklahoma Press, 1991.

Ruiz, Ramón Eduardo. *Triumphs and Tragedy: A History of the Mexican People*. New York: Norton, 1992.

————, editor. *The Mexican War: Was It Manifest Destiny?* New York: Holt, Rinehart and Winston, 1963.

Salas, Elizabeth. *Soldaderas in the Mexican Military: Myth and History*. Austin: University of Texas Press, 1990.

Sánchez Lamego, Miguel A. *El colegio militar y la defensa de Chapultepec en septiembre de 1847*. Cd. México: Departamento del Distrito Federal, 1947.

Santoni, Pedro. *Mexicans at Arms: Puro Federalists and the Politics of War, 1845–1848*. Ft. Worth: Texas Christian University Press, 1996.

Scheina, Robert L. *Santa Anna: A Curse Upon Mexico*. Washington, DC: Brassey's, 2002.

Schlesinger, Arthur M., Jr. *The Age of Jackson*. Boston: Little, Brown, 1945.

Schoutz, Lars. *Beneath the United States: A History of U.S. Policy Toward Latin America*. Cambridge: Harvard University Press, 1998.

Schroeder, John H. *Mr. Polk's War: American Opposition and Dissent, 1846–1848*. Madison: University of Wisconsin Press, 1973.

Scott, James B., editor. *Prize Cases Decided in the United States Supreme Court, 1789–1918*. 3 volumes. Oxford, UK: Oxford University Press, 1923.

Sears, Louis M. *John Slidell*. Durham, North Carolina: Duke University Press, 1925.

Seigenthaler, John. *James K. Polk*. New York: Times Books, 2003.

Selby, John. *The Eagle and the Serpent: The Spanish and American Invasions of Mexico, 1519 and 1846*. London, UK: Hamish Hamilton, 1978.

Sellers, Charles. *James K. Polk, Continentalist, 1843–1846*. Princeton, New Jersey: Princeton University Press, 1966.

Severn, Bill. *Frontier President: The Life of James K. Polk*. New York: Ives Washburn, 1965.

Shalhope, Robert E. *Sterling Price: Portrait of a Southerner*. Columbia: University of Missouri Press, 1971.

Sherman, Edwin A. *The Life of the Late Rear Admiral John Drake Sloat*. Oakland, California: Carruth, 1902.

Shorris, Earl. *The Life and Times of Mexico*. New York: Norton, 2004.

Sides, Hampton. *Blood and Thunder: An Epic of the American West*. New York: Doubleday, 2006.

Sierra, Justo. *Evolución política del pueblo mexicano*. Cd. México: Fondo de Cultura Económica, 1940.

————. *The Political Evolution of the Mexican People*. Translated by Charles Ramsdell. Austin: University of Texas Press, 1969.

Silver, James W. *Edmund Pendleton Gaines, Frontier General*. Baton Rouge: Louisiana State University Press, 1949.

Simmons, Edwin Howard. *The United States Marines: A History*. Fourth Edition. Annapolis: Naval Institute Press, 2003.

Simmons, Merle E. *The Mexican Corrido as a Source for the Interpretive Study of Modern Mexico, 1870–1950*. Bloomington: Indiana University Press, 1957.

Sims, Harold D. *The Expulsion of Mexico's Spaniards, 1821–1836.* Pittsburgh: University of Pittsburgh Press, 1990.

Singletary, Otis A. *The Mexican War.* Chicago: University of Chicago Press, 1960.

Smith, Elbert B. *Magnificent Missourian: The Life of Thomas Hart Benton.* Philadelphia: Lippincott, 1958.

Smith, Justin H. *The War with Mexico.* 2 volumes. New York: Macmillan, 1919.

Sobarzo, Alejandro. *Deber y conciencia: Nicolás Trist, el negociador norteamericano en la guerra del 1847.* Cd. México: Diana, 1990.

Sonnichsen, C. L. *The Mescalero Apaches.* Second edition. Norman: University of Oklahoma Press, 1973.

————. *Pass of the North: Four Centuries on the Rio Grande.* El Paso: Texas Western University Press, 1968.

————. *Tucson: The Life and Times of an American City.* Norman: University of Oklahoma Press, 1982.

Soto, Miguel. *La conspiración monárquica en México, 1845–1846.* Cd. México: EOSA, 1988.

Spaulding, Oliver Lyman. *The United States Army in War and Peace.* New York: Putnam, 1937.

Spencer, Ivor D. *The Victor and the Spoils: A Life of William L. Marcy.* Providence, Rhode Island: Brown University Press, 1959.

Spicer, Edward H. *Cycles of Conquest: The Impact of Spain, Mexico, and the United States on the Indians of the Southwest, 1533–1960.* Tucson: University of Arizona Press, 1962.

Sprout, Harold, and Margaret Sprout. *The Rise of American Naval Power, 1775–1918.* Princeton, New Jersey: Princeton University Press, 1942.

Spurlin, Charles D. *Texas Volunteers in the Mexican War.* Austin: Eakin, 1998.

The Statistical History of the United States, Colonial Times to the Present (Historical Statistics of the United States, Colonial Times to 1970, Prepared by the United States Bureau of the Census). New York: Basic Books, 1976.

Stegmaier, Mark J. *Texas, New Mexico, and the Compromise of 1850: Boundary Dispute and Sectional Crisis.* Kent, Ohio: Kent State University Press, 1996.

Stevens, Donald F. *Origins of Instability in Early Republican Mexico.* Durham, North Carolina: Duke University Press, 1991.

Stevens, Peter F. *The Rogue's March: John Riley and the St. Patrick's Battalion, 1846–48.* Washington: Potomac Books, 1999.

Strode, Hudson. *Jefferson Davis: American Patriot, 1808–1861.* New York: Harcourt, Brace and World, 1955.

Sydnor, Charles S. *The Development of Southern Sectionalism, 1819–1848.* Baton Rouge: Louisiana State University Press, 1948.

Szulc, Tad, editor. *The United States and the Caribbean.* Englewood Cliffs, New Jersey: Prentice-Hall, 1971.

Tenenbaum, Barbara. *The Politics of Penury: Debts and Taxes in Mexico, 1821–1856.* Albuquerque: University of New Mexico Press, 1986.

Tijerina, Andrés. *Tejanos and Texas under the Mexican Flag, 1821–1836.* College Station: Texas A&M University Press, 1994.

Thomas, David Y. *A History of Military Government in Newly Acquired Territory of the United States.* New York: Columbia University Press, 1904.

Thomas, Emory M. *Robert E. Lee.* New York: Norton, 1995.

Thornton, Bruce. *Searching for Joaquín: Myth, Murieta, and History in California.* Los Angeles: Encounter, 2003.

Tornel y Mendívil, José María. *Breve resena historia de los acontecimientos mas notable de la nación mexicana.* Cd. México: Instituto Nacional de Estudios Históricos de la Revolución Mexicana, 1985.

Toro, Alfonso. *Compendia de la historia de México.* Cd. México: Editorial Patria, 1943.

Traas, Adrian George. *From the Golden Gate to Mexico City: The U.S. Army Topographical Engineers in the Mexican War, 1846–1848.* Washington: Department of the Army, 1992.

Trens, Manuel B. *Historia de Veracruz.* 4 tomos. Cd. México: npub, 1947–1950.

Turner, Frederick C. *The Dynamics of Mexican Nationalism.* Chapel Hill: University of North Carolina Press, 1968.

Twitchell, Ralph Emerson. *The Conquest of Santa Fe, 1846.* Truchas, New Mexico: Tate Gallery, 1967.

———. *The History of the Military Occupation of the Territory of New Mexico from 1846 to 1851 by the Government of the United States, Together with Biographical Sketches of Men Prominent in the Conduct of the Government During That Period.* Denver: Smith-Brooks, 1909.

———. *Old Santa Fe: The Story of New Mexico's Ancient Capital.* 1925. Reprinted Chicago: Rio Grande Press, 1963.

Tyler, Daniel. *A Concise History of the Mormon Battalion in the Mexican War, 1846–1847.* 1881. Reprinted Glorieta, New Mexico: Rio Grande Press, 1988.

Tyler, Ron, editor. *Posada's Mexico.* Washington: Library of Congress, 1979.

Upton, Emory. *The Military Policy of the United States.* Washington: Government Printing Office, 1904.

Utley, Robert M. *Changing Course: The International Boundary, United States and Mexico, 1848–1963.* Tucson: Southwest Parks and Monuments Association, 1996.

———. *A Life Wild and Perilous: Mountain Men and the Paths to the Pacific.* New York: Holt, 1997.

———. *Frontiersmen in Blue: The United States Army and the Indian, 1848–1865.* New York: Macmillan, 1967.

———. *Lone Star Justice: The First Century of the Texas Rangers.* New York: Oxford University Press, 2002.

Valadés, José C. *Breve historia de la guerra con los Estados Unidos.* Cd. México: Editorial Patria, 1947.

———. *Historia del pueblo de México.* 2 tomos. Cd. México: Editores Mexicanos Unidos, 1967.

———. *México, Santa Anna, y la guerra de Tejas.* 1936. Reprinted Cd. México: Editorial Diana, 1979.

Van Deusen, Glyndon G. *The Jacksonian Era, 1828–1848.* New York: Harper, 1966.

Vandiver, Frank E. *Mighty Stonewall.* New York: McGraw-Hill, 1957.

Vasconcelos, José. *Breve historia de México.* Cd. México: Editorial Polis, 1944.

Vázquez, Josefina Zoraida. *La intervención norteamericana, 1846–1848.* Cd. México: Secretaría de Relaciones Exteriores, 1997.

———, editora. *México al tiempo de su guerra con los Estados Unidos, 1846–48.* Cd. México: Fondo de Cultura Económica, 1997.

———, y Lorenzo Meyer, editores. *México frente a los Estados Unidos.* Cd. México: Secretaría de Relaciones Exteriores y el Fondo de Cultura Económica, 1982.

————, editors. *The United States and Mexico.* Chicago: University of Chicago Press, 1985, 1995.

Vázquez de Knauth, Josefina. *Mexicanos y norteamericanos ante la guerra del 47.* Cd. México: Secretaría de Educación Pública, 1972.

Vigil y Robles, Guillermo. *La invasión de México por los Estados Unidos en los años de 1846, 1847, y 1848.* Cd. México: Tipografía Editorial Correccional, 1923.

Villalpondo Cesar, José Manuel. *Las balas del invasor: la expansión territorial de los Estados Unidos a costa de México.* Cd. México: Amargur, 1998.

Wallace, Edward S. *Destiny and Glory.* New York: Coward-McCann, 1957.

Wallace, Ernest, and E. Adamson Hoebel. *The Comanches: Lords of the South Plains.* Norman: University of Oklahoma Press, 1952.

Wallace, Isabel. *Life and Letters of General W. H. L. Wallace.* Chicago: Donnelly, 1909.

Wasserman, Mark. *Capitalists, Caciques, and Revolution: The Native Elite and Foreign Enterprise in Chihuahua, Mexico, 1854–1911.* Chapel Hill: University of North Carolina Press, 1984.

————, and Lyman L. Johnson. *Everyday Life and Politics in Nineteenth Century Mexico: Men, Women, and War.* Albuquerque: University of New Mexico Press, 2000.

Waugh, John C. *The Class of 1846 from West Point to Appomattox: Stonewall Jackson, George McClellan, and Their Brothers.* New York: Warner, 1994.

————. *On the Brink of Civil War: The Compromise of 1850 and How It Changed the Course of American History.* Wilmington, Delaware: Scholarly Resource Books, 2003.

Webb, Walter Prescott. *The Texas Rangers.* Boston: Houghton Mifflin, 1935.

Weber, David J. *The Mexican Frontier, 1821–1846: The American Southwest under Mexico.* Albuquerque: University of New Mexico Press, 1982.

Weems, John Edward. *To Conquer a Peace: The War Between the United States and Mexico.* College Station: Texas A&M Press, 1974.

Weigley, Russell F. *The American Way of War: A History of United States Military Strategy and Policy.* New York: Macmillan, 1973.

————. *History of the United States Army.* New York: Macmillan, 1967.

Weinberg, Albert K. *Manifest Destiny: A Study of Nationalist Expansion in American History.* Chicago: Quadrangle, 1963.

Wessels, William L. *Born to Be a Soldier: The Military Career of William Wing Loring of St. Augustine, Florida.* Ft. Worth: Texas Christian University Press, 1971.

Wheelan, Joseph. *Invading Mexico: America's Continental Dream and the Mexican War, 1846–1848.* New York: Carroll and Graf, 2007.

White, Leonard D. *The Jacksonians: A Study in Administrative History.* New York: Macmillan, 1954.

Wilcox, Cadmus M. *History of the Mexican War.* Washington: Church News, 1892.

Wilkins, Frederick. *The Highly Irregular Irregulars: Texas Rangers in the Mexican War.* Austin: Eakin, 1990.

Wilentz, Sean. *Andrew Jackson.* New York: Times Books, 2005.

Williams, John Hoyt. *Sam Houston: A Biography of the Father of Texas.* New York: Simon and Schuster, 1993.

Wilson, Beckles. *John Slidell.* New York: Minto, Balch, 1932.

Wiltse, Charles M. *John C. Calhoun, Sectionalist, 1840–1850.* Indianapolis: Bobbs-Merrill, 1951.

Winders, Richard Bruce. *Mr. Polk's Army: The American Military Experience in the Mexican War.* College Station: Texas A&M University Press, 1997.

Winthrop, William. *Military Law and Precedents.* Second edition. 2 volumes. Washington: Government Printing Office, 1920.

Woodward, Arthur. *Lances at San Pascual.* San Francisco: California Historical Society, 1948.

Worcester, Donald E. *The Apaches: Eagles of the Southwest.* Norman: University of Oklahoma Press, 1979.

Wynn, Dennis J. *The San Patricio Soldiers: Mexico's Foreign Legion.* El Paso: Texas Western University Press, 1984.

Zorrilla, Luis. *Historia de las relaciones entre México y los Estados Unidos de América, 1800– 1858.* 2 tomos. Cd. México: Editorial Porrúa, 1965.

SECONDARY SOURCES: PERIODICALS

Adams, Ephraim D. "English Interest in Annexation of California." *American Historical Review* 14 (July 1909): 744–63.

Ames, George Walcott, Jr. "Gillespie and the Conquest of California." *California Historical Society Quarterly* 17 (September 1938): 271–81.

———. "Horse Marines, California, 1846." *California Historical Society Quarterly* 18 (March 1939): 72–84.

Armstrong, Andrew. "The Brazito Battlefield." *New Mexico Historical Review* 35 (January 1960): 63–74.

Arnáiz y Freg, J. "El Dr. Mora, teórico de la reforma liberal." *Historia Mexicana* 5 (abril-junio 1956): 18–40.

Bacarisse, Charles A. "The Union of Coahuila and Texas." *Southwestern Historical Quarterly* 61 (1958): 341–49.

Bauer, K. Jack. "The U.S. Navy and Texas Independence: A Study in Jacksonian Integrity." *Military Affairs* 34 (April 1970): 44–48.

———. "The Vera Cruz Expedition of 1847." *Military Affairs* 20 (October 1956): 162–69.

Beezley, William H. "Caudillismo: An Interpretive Note." *Journal of Inter-American Studies* 11 (1969): 345–52.

Benjamin, Thomas. "Recent Historiography on the Origins of the Mexican War." *New Mexico Historical Review* 54 (July 1979): 169–82.

Bender, Averam Burton. "Frontier Defense in the Territory of New Mexico, 1846–1853." *New Mexico Historical Review* 9 (July and October 1934): 249–72, 345–73.

———. "Government Explorations in the Territory of New Mexico, 1846–1859." *New Mexico Historical Review* 9 (January 1934): 1–32.

———. "Military Posts in the Southwest, 1848–1860." *New Mexico Historical Review* 16 (April 1941): 125–47.

Berge, Dennis E. "A Mexican Dilemma: The Mexico City Ayuntamiento and the Question of Loyalty, 1846–1848." *Hispanic American Historical Review* 50 (1970): 229–56.

Bieber, Ralph P. "California Gold Mania." *Mississippi Valley Historical Review* 35 (June 1948): 3–28.

———. "The Southwestern Trails to California in 1849." *Mississippi Valley Historical Review* 12 (December 1925): 342–75.

Blaisdell, Lowell L. "The Santangelo Case: A Claim Preceding the Mexican War." *Journal of the West* 11 (April 1972): 248–59.

Bravo Ugarte, José. "Un nuevo Iturbide." *Historia Mexicana* 2 (octubre-diciembre 1952): 267–76.

Brooke, George M., Jr. "The Vest Pocket War of Commodore Jones." *Pacific Historical Review* 31 (August 1962): 217–34.

Brown, Walter Lee. "The Mexican War Experiences of Albert Pike and the 'Mounted Devils' of Arkansas." *Arkansas Historical Quarterly* 12 (Winter 1953): 301–15.

Buchanan, A. Russell, editor. "George Washington Trahern: Texas Cowboy Soldier from Mier to Buena Vista." *Southwestern Historical Quarterly* 78 (July 1954): 60–90.

Carrion, Jorge. "Effectos psicológicos de la guerra de 1847 en el hombre de México." *Cuadernos Americanos* 7 (enero-febrero 1948): 116–32.

Castañeda, Carlos E. "Relations of General Scott with Santa Anna." *Hispanic American Historical Review* 24 (November 1949): 455–73.

Chamberlain, Eugene K. "Nicholas Trist and Baja California." *Pacific Historical Review* 32 (February 1963): 49–64.

Chavez, Thomas Esteban. "The Trouble with Texans: Manuel Álvarez and the 1841 'Invasion.' " *New Mexico Historical Review* 53 (April 1978): 133–44.

Costeloe, Michael P. "Church-State Financial Negotiations in Mexico During the American War, 1846–1847." *Revista de Historia de América* 60 (1965): 91–124.

Coughlin, Sister Magdalen. "California Ports: A Key to West Coast Diplomacy, 1820–1845." *Journal of the West* 5 (April 1966): 153–72.

Curti, Merle E. "Pacifist Propaganda and the Treaty of Guadalupe Hidalgo." *American Historical Review* 23 (April 1928): 596–98.

Cutter, Donald C. "The Legacy of the Treaty of Guadalupe Hidalgo." *New Mexico Historical Review* 53 (October 1978): 305–16.

Davies, Thomas M., Jr. "Assessments During the Mexican War." *New Mexico Historical Review* 41 (July 1966): 197–216.

Dawson, Joseph G. III. "American Xenophon, American Hero: Alexander Doniphan's Homecoming from the Mexican-American War as a Hallmark of Patriotic Fervor." *Military History of the West* 27 (Spring 1997): 1–31.

———. "Zealous for Annexation: Volunteer Soldiering, Military Government, and the Service of Colonel Alexander Doniphan in the Mexican-American War." *Journal of Strategic Studies* 19 (December 1996): 11–13.

De Armond, Louis. "Justo Sierra O'Reilly and Yucatán–United States Relations, 1847–1848." *Hispanic American Historical Review* 31 (August 1951): 420–36.

De Weerd, H. A. "The Federalization of Our Army." *Military Affairs* 6 (July 1942): 143–52.

De Witt, Charles J. "Crusading for Peace in Syracuse During the War with Mexico." *New York History* 14 (April 1933): 100–12.

Dodd, William E. "The West and the War with Mexico." *Illinois State Historical Society Journal* 5 (July 1912): 159–72.

Donnelly, Ralph W. "Rocket Batteries of the Civil War." *Military Affairs* 25 (Summer 1961): 69–93.

Driver, Leo. "Carrillo's Flying Artillery: The Battle of San Pedro." *California Historical Society Quarterly* 48 (December 1969): 335–49.

Duncan, Louis C. "A Medical History of General Zachary Taylor's Army of Occupation in Texas and Mexico, 1845–1847." *Military Surgeon* 48 (1921): 76–104.

Ellsworth, Charles S. "American Churches and the Mexican War." *American Historical Review* 45 (January 1940): 301–26.

Emory, Deborah Carley. "Running the Line: Men, Maps, Science, and Art of the United States and Mexico Boundary Survey, 1849–1856." *New Mexico Historical Review* 75 (April 2000): 221–66.

Finke, Detmar H. "The Organization and Uniforms of the San Patricios Unit of the Mexican Army, 1846–1848." *Military Collector and Historian* 9 (1957): 36–38.

Frazer, Robert W. "Purveyors of Flour to the Army: Department of New Mexico, 1849–1861." *New Mexico Historical Review* 47 (July 1972): 213–38.

Fuller, John D. P. "Slavery Propaganda During the Mexican War." *Southwestern Historical Quarterly* 38 (April 1935): 235–45.

———. "The Slavery Question and the Movement to Acquire Mexico, 1846–1848." *Mississippi Valley Historical Review* 21 (June 1934): 31–48.

Fulmore, Z. T. "The Annexation of Texas and the Mexican War." *Texas State Historical Association Quarterly* 5 (July 1901): 28–48.

Gabriel, Ralph H. "American Experience with Military Government." *American Historical Review* 49 (July 1944): 630–43.

Gerhard, Peter. "Baja California in the Mexican War." *Pacific Historical Review* 14 (November 1945): 418–24.

Gilmore, N. Ray. "The Condition of the Poor in Mexico, 1834." *Hispanic American Historical Review* 37 (1957): 213–26.

Goodrich, James W. "Revolt at Mora, 1847." *New Mexico Historical Review* 47 (January 1972): 49–60.

Graebner, Norman A. "The Mexican War: A Study in Causation." *Pacific Historical Review* 49 (1980): 405–26.

———. "Party Politics and the Trist Mission." *Journal of Southern History* 19 (1953): 137–56.

Guinn, James M. "Siege and Capture of Los Angeles, September 1846." *Publications of the Historical Society of Southern California* 3 (1893): 47–53.

Haecker, Charles M. "Brazito Battlefield: Once Lost, Now Found." *New Mexico Historical Review* 72 (July 1997): 229–38.

Hale, Charles A. "The War with the United States and the Crisis in Mexican Thought." *The Americas* 14 (October 1957): 153–74.

Harstad, Peter T., and Richard W. Rush. "The Causes of the Mexican War: A Note on Changing Interpretations." *Arizona and the West* 6 (1964): 289–302.

Haun, Cheryl. "The Whig Abolitionists' Attitude Toward the Mexican War." *Journal of the West* 11 (April 1972): 260–72.

Hefter, Joseph. "Crónica del traje militar en México del Siglo XVI al XX." *Artes de México* 15 (No. 102, 1968).

High, James. "Jones at Monterey." *Journal of the West* 5 (April 1966): 173–86.

Hinckley, Ted C. "Anti-Catholicism During the Mexican War." *Pacific Historical Review* 31 (May 1962): 121–38.

Hitchman, Richard. "Rush to Glory." *Strategy and Tactics* 127 (June–July 1989): 14–26, 60–62.

Hurtado y Nuño, Enrique. "Ataque y defensa del puerto de Alvarado." *Revista General de la Armada de México* 3 (agosto-octubre 1963): 11–18, 37–41.

Hussey, John A. "Bear Flag Revolt." *American Heritage* 1 (Spring 1950): 24–27.

————. "Commander John B. Montgomery and the Bear Flag Revolt." *U.S. Naval Institute Proceedings* 75 (July 1939): 973–80.

————. "The Origin of the Gillespie Mission." *California Historical Society Quarterly* 19 (March 1940): 43–58.

Jackson, Jack. "General Taylor's 'Astonishing' Map of Northeastern Mexico." *Southwestern Historical Quarterly* 101 (October 1997): 142–73.

Jaurrieta, Rómulo. "Battalla de Sacramento 28 de Febrero de 1847." *Boletín de la sociedad chihuahuense de estudios historicos* 7 (julio-agosto 1950): 413–20.

Johnson, Kenneth M. "Baja California and the Treaty of Guadalupe Hidalgo." *Journal of the West* 11 (April 1972): 328–47.

Johnson, Lucius W. "Yellow Jack: Master of Strategy." *U.S. Naval Institute Proceedings* 86 (July 1950): 175–83.

Kearny, Thomas. "Kearny and 'Kit' Carson as Interpreted by Stanley Vestal." *New Mexico Historical Review* 5 (January 1930): 1–16.

————. "The Mexican War and the Conquest of California." *California Historical Society Quarterly* 8 (September 1929): 251–61.

Kemble, John H., editor. "Amphibious Operations in the Gulf of California, 1847–1848." *American Neptune* 5 (April 1945): 121–36.

————. editor. "Naval Conquest in the Pacific." *California Historical Society Quarterly* 20 (June 1941): 193–234.

Kraemer, Paul. "Origins and Early Development of New Mexico's Wine Industry." *La Crónica de Nuevo México* No. 64 (March 2005): 4–8.

Lambert, Paul F. "The Movement for the Acquisition of All Mexico." *Journal of the West* 11 (April 1972): 317–27.

LeCompte, Janet. "Manuel Armijo's Family History." *New Mexico Historical Review* 48 (July 1973): 251–58.

Lott, W. S. "The Landing of the Expedition Against Vera Cruz in 1847." *Journal of the Military Services Institution of the United States* 24 (May 1895): 422–28.

Luttwak, Edward N. "Dead End: Counterinsurgency Warfare as Military Malpractice." *Harper's Magazine* 314 (February 2007): 33–42.

Mangum, Neil C. "The Battle of Brazito: Reappraising a Lost and Forgotten Episode in the Mexican-American War." *New Mexico Historical Review* 72 (July 1997): 217–28.

Manno, Francis J. "Yucatán en la guerra entre México y los Estados Unidos." *Revista de la Universidad de Yucatán* 5 (julio-agosto 1963): 51–64.

Martín, Luis. "Lucas Alamán: Pioneer of Mexican Historiography." *The Americas* 32 (1975): 239–56.

May, Robert E. "Invisible Men: Blacks and the U.S. Army in the Mexican War." *The Historian* 49 (August 1987): 25–50.

Mayo, John. "Consuls and Silver Contraband on Mexico's West Coast in the Era of Santa Anna." *Journal of Latin American Studies* 19 (1987): 389–411.

McClure, Charles B. "The Texan–Santa Fe Expedition of 1841." *New Mexico Historical Review* 48 (January 1973): 45–56.

McNitt, Frank. "Navajo Campaigns and the Occupation of New Mexico, 1847–1848." *New Mexico Historical Review* 43 (July 1968): 173–94.

Meyer, Michael C., and Michael M. Brescia. "The Treaty of Guadalupe Hidalgo as a Living Document: Water and Land Use Issues in Northern New Mexico." *New Mexico Historical Review* 73 (October 1998): 321–46.

Miller, Howard. "Stephen F. Austin and the Anglo-Texan Response to the Religious Establishment in Mexico, 1821–1836." *Southwestern Historical Quarterly* 91 (July 1988): 283–316.

Molina, Ignacio. "El asalto al castillo de Chapultepec el día 13 de septiembre de 1847." *Revista Positiva* 2 (octubre 1902): 444–64.

Morton, Ohland. "Life of General Don Manuel de Mier y Terán, as It Affected Texas-Mexican Relations." *Southwestern Historical Quarterly* 46 (July 1942): 262–89.

Mullins, William H. "The British Press and the Mexican War: Justin Smith Revised." *New Mexico Historical Review* 52 (July 1977): 207–28.

Murphy, Lawrence R. "Reconstruction in New Mexico." *New Mexico Historical Review* 43 (April 1968): 99–115.

————. "The United States Army in Taos, 1847–1852." *New Mexico Historical Review* 47 (January 1972): 33–48.

Myers, Lee. "Illinois Volunteers in New Mexico, 1847–1848." *New Mexico Historical Review* 47 (January 1972): 5–32.

Nackman, Mark E. "The Making of the Texan Citizen Soldier, 1835–1860." *Southwestern Historical Quarterly* 78 (January 1975): 235–52.

Neasham, Aubrey. "The Raising of the Flag at Monterey, California, July 1846." *California State Historical Society Quarterly* 25 (June 1946): 193–203.

Northrup, Jack. "Nicholas Trist's Mission into Mexico: A Reinterpretation." *Southern Historical Quarterly* 71 (1968): 321–46.

Olejar, Paul D. "Rockets in Early American Wars." *Military Affairs* 10 (Winter 1946): 16–34.

Pohl, James W. "The Influence of Antoine Henri Jomini on Winfield Scott's Campaign in the Mexican War." *Southwestern Historical Quarterly* 67 (1973–1974): 85–110.

Paredes, Raymund A. "The Mexican Image in American Travel Literature." *New Mexico Historical Review* 52 (January 1977): 5–30.

Pratt, Julius W. "John L. O'Sullivan and Manifest Destiny." *New York History* 14 (July 1933): 223–24.

Prucha, Francis Paul. "Distribution of Regular Army Troops Before the Civil War." *Military Affairs* 16 (Winter 1952): 169–73.

Rebert, Paula. "Mapping the United States–Mexico Boundary: Cooperation and Controversy." *Terrae Incognitae—The Journal for the History of Discoveries* 28 (1996): 58–71.

Richards, Susan V. "From Traders to Traitors? The Armijo Brothers Through the Nineteenth Century." *New Mexico Historical Review* 69 (July 1994): 215–19.

Rives, George L. "Mexican Diplomacy on the Eve of War with the United States." *American Historical Review* 18 (January 1913): 275–94.

Robertson, William S. "French Intervention in Mexico in 1838." *Hispanic American Historical Review* 24 (1944): 222–52.

Romer, Margaret. " 'Lean John' Rides for Help." *Journal of the West* 5 (April 1966): 203–6.

Ruhlen, George. "Kearny's Route from the Rio Grande to the Gila." *New Mexico Historical Review* 32 (July 1957): 213–30.

Scammon, Parker. "A Chapter in the Mexican War." *Magazine of American History* 14 (December 1885): 567.

Samponaro, Frank N. "Santa Anna and the Abortive Anti-Federalist Revolt of 1833 in Mexico." *The Americas* 40 (1983): 95–108.

Santoni, Pedro. "The Failure of Mobilization: The Civic Militia of Mexico in 1846." *Mexican Studies* 12 (No.2, 1996): 169–94.

Scheina, Robert L. "The Forgotten Fleet: The Mexican Navy on the Eve of War, 1845." *American Neptune* 30 (January 1978): 46–55.

———. "Seapower Misused: Mexico at War, 1846–48." *Mariner's Mirror* 57 (1971): 203–14.

Sears, Louis Martin. "Nicholas P. Trist: A Diplomat with Ideals." *Mississippi Valley Historical Review* 11 (1926): 85–92.

———. "Slidell's Mission to Mexico." *South Atlantic Quarterly* 12 (January 1913): 12–26.

Smith, Gene A. "The War That Wasn't: Thomas ap Catesby Jones's Seizure of Monterey." *California History* 66 (1987): 104–13, 155–57.

Smith, Justin H. "American Rule in Mexico." *American Historical Review* 23 (January 1918): 287–302.

———. "La República de Río Grande." *American Historical Review* 25 (July 1920): 660–75.

Sordo Cedeño, Reynaldo. "El General Tornel y la guerra de Tejas." *Historia Mexicana* 42 (abril-junio 1993): 919–53.

Spell, Lola M. "The Anglo-Saxon Press in Mexico, 1846–1848." *American Historical Review* 38 (October 1932): 20–31.

Spencer, Ivor. "Overseas War—in 1846!" *Military Affairs* 9 (1945): 306–13.

Stenberg, Richard R. "The Failure of Polk's Mexican War Intrigue of 1845." *Pacific Historical Review* 4 (March 1935): 36–68.

———. "Polk and Frémont, 1845–1846." *Pacific Historical Review* 7 (September 1938): 211–27.

Tanner, John D. "Campaigns for Los Angeles, December 29, 1846, to January 10, 1847." *California Historical Society Quarterly* 48 (September 1969): 219–41.

Tapson, Alfred J. "The Sutler and the Soldier." *Military Affairs* 21 (Winter 1957): 175–81.

Tays, George. "Frémont Had No Secret Instructions." *Pacific Historical Review* 9 (May 1940): 157–71.

Tyler, Daniel. "Governor Armijo's Moment of Truth." *Journal of the West* 11 (April 1972): 307–16.

Vázquez, Josefina Zoraida. "The Texas Question in Mexican Politics." *Southwestern Historical Quarterly* 89 (1986): 309–44.

———. "Santa Anna y el reconocimiento de Tejas." *Historia Mexicana* 36 (1987): 553–62.

Wallace, Edward S. "The Great Western." *Brand Book of the New York Posse of the Westerners* 5 (1958): 58–66.

———. "The United States Army in Mexico City." *Military Affairs* 13 (1949): 158–66.

Wallace, Lee A., Jr. "The First Regiment of Virginia Volunteers, 1846–1848." *Virginia Magazine of History and Biography* 87 (January 1969): 46–77.

————. "Raising a Volunteer Regiment for Mexico, 1846–1847." *North Carolina Historical Review* 35 (January 1958): 25–35.

Walton, Brian G. "The Elections for the Thirtieth Congress and the Presidential Candidacy of Zachary Taylor." *Journal of Southern History* 25 (May 1969): 186–202.

Williams, Mary W. "Secessionist Diplomacy of Yucatán." *Hispanic American Historical Review* 9 (May 1929): 132–43.

Winders, Richard Bruce. "Puebla's Forgotten Military Heroes." *Military History of the West* 24 (Spring 1994): 1–23.

Woodward, Arthur. "Juan Flaco's Ride." *Historical Society of Southern California Quarterly* 19 (January 1937): 22–39.

Woodward, Margaret L. "The Spanish Army and the Loss of America, 1810–1824." *Hispanic American Historical Review* 48 (November 1968): 586–606.

Wooster, Ralph A. "Texas Military Operations Against Mexico, 1842–1843." *Southwestern Historical Quarterly* 67 (April 1964): 465–84.

Worcester, Donald E. "Apaches in the History of the Southwest." *New Mexico Historical Review* 50 (January 1975): 25–44.

SECONDARY SOURCES: OTHER

Baker, George Towne III. "Mexico City and the War with the United States: A Study in the Politics of Military Occupation." Ph.D. dissertation, Duke University, 1970.

Berge, Dennis E. "Mexican Response to United States Expansionism, 1841–1848." Ph.D. dissertation, University of California at Berkeley, 1965.

Bloom, John Porter. "With the American Army into Mexico, 1846–1848." Ph.D. dissertation, Emory University, 1956.

Bodson, Robert L. "A Description of the United States Occupation of Mexico as Reported by American Newspapers Published in Veracruz, Puebla, and Mexico City, September 14, 1847, to July 31, 1848." Ed.D. dissertation, Ball State University, 1971.

Bradley, Udolpho Theodore. "The Contentious Commodore: Thomas ap Catesby Jones of the Old Navy, 1788–1858." Ph.D. dissertation, Cornell University, 1933.

Bushnell, Clyde G. "The Political and Military Career of Juan Álvarez, 1790–1867." Ph.D. dissertation, University of Texas, 1958.

Chaney, Homer Campbell, Jr. "The Mexican–United States War as Seen by Mexican Intellectuals, 1846–1956." Ph.D. dissertation, Stanford University, 1959.

Clary, David A. *The Inspectors General of the United States Army: A History, 1777–1903.* Report DAC-11. 3 volumes. Bloomington, Indiana: David A. Clary and Associates, 1983.

Johnson, Robert Erwin. "United States Naval Forces on Pacific Station, 1818–1923." Ph.D. dissertation, Claremont Graduate School, 1956.

Reilly, Thomas. "American Reporters and the Mexican War, 1846–1848." Ph.D. dissertation, University of Minnesota, 1984.

Tymitz, John Paul. "British Influence in Mexico, 1840–1848." Ph.D. dissertation, Oklahoma State University, 1973.

INDEX